Growing up
COMMUNIST and JEWISH
in Bondi

JOHN DOCKER is a writer and cultural historian who lives in Sydney with his wife the historian Ann Curthoys. He researches and writes in a number of fields, including Australian literature in international contexts, Jewish identity and diaspora, genocide and massacre studies. In exploring cultural theory, he has written on Edward Said, Gandhi, Derrida, Mikhail Bakhtin and Walter Benjamin. He contributes essays to the *Journal of Holy Land and Palestine Studies*. With Ann Curthoys he published *Is History Fiction?* (2005, 2010) as well as essays in genocide studies and cultural studies, for example, 'Stuart Hall and Cultural Studies, circa 1983' (2017). He is currently writing a book entitled *Sheer Folly and Derangement: Disorienting Europe and the West, from the Enlightenment to Modernity*.

VOLUMES IN THIS WORK:
  Volume 1: My Father, Ted Docker
  Volume 2: My Mother, Elsie Levy
  Volume 3: I am Born

ALSO BY JOHN DOCKER
  Australian Cultural Elites: Intellectual Traditions in Sydney and Melbourne, Angus and Robertson, 1974
  In a Critical Condition, Penguin Books, 1984
  The Nervous Nineties, Oxford University Press, 1991
  Postmodernism and Popular Culture: A Cultural History, Cambridge University Press, 1994
  1492: The Poetics of Diaspora, Continuum, 2001
  The Origins of Violence: Religion, History and Genocide, UNSW Press, 2008
  Race, Colour and Identity in Australia and New Zealand, edited with Gerhard Fischer, UNSW Press, 2000
  Rethinking Gandhi and Nonviolent Relationality: Global Perspectives, edited with Debjani Ganguly, Routledge, 2007

Growing up
COMMUNIST and JEWISH
in Bondi

*An Ego Histoire, a Dictionary of Modernity,
an Autobiography, a Romance*

My Mother, Elsie Levy ^{Volume 2}

JOHN DOCKER

KERR
Melbourne, Victoria

First published 2020
Kerr Publishing Pty Ltd
Melbourne, Victoria
ABN 64 124 219 638

© 2020 John Docker

This book is copyright. Apart from fair dealing for the purpose of private study, research, criticism or review, or under Copyright Agency Ltd rules of recording, no part may be reproduced by any means.
The moral right of the author has been asserted.

ISBN (volume 2)   978-1-875703-34-0 (Print on Demand, PoD)
ISBN (set)   978-1-875703-32-6 (Print on Demand, PoD)
ISBN (volume 2)   978-1-875703-38-8 (eBook)
ISBN (set)   978-1-875703-36-4 (eBook)

BIC Category:	Biography & Autobiography
BISAC Category 1:	BIO006000 BIOGRAPHY & AUTOBIOGRAPHY/ Cultural, Ethnic & Regional/General
BISAC Category 2:	BIO006000/Historical; BIO037000/Jewish; BIO10000/ Political
BISAC Category 3:	HIS004000/Australia & New Zealand
Cover photograph:	Ted, Elsie and John Docker

Cover and book design: Paul Taylder of Xigrafix Media & Design
Typeset in Verdigris MVB Pro Text 10.5/14pt

Print-on-Demand and eBook distribution: ebookalchemy.com.au

National Library of Australia PrePublication Data Service:

 A catalogue record for this book is available from the National Library of Australia

For Ann, Ned, Shino and Leo

Contents

9	An English Jew: thoughts on my mother, Elsie Levy	1
10	East End Jews, Anti-Semitism, Bloomsbury	21
11	'One's inner tears of bitterness'	41
12	A Parvenu in Ceylon: Leonard Woolf as Executioner, with thoughts on Periclean Athens and the Enlightenment	79
13	Conscious Pariahs	121
14	Cultural Genocide: T S Eliot, vicious Anti-Semite	165
15	T S Eliot, an Architect of the Holocaust: Reflections on *After Strange Gods*	191
16	T S Eliot, an Architect of the Holocaust: Further reflections on *After Strange Gods*	215
17	Jewish Culture as co-creator of Modernism and Modernity: A Journey from London to Odessa	243
18	A Radical Jewish Intelligentsia in the 1930s	309
19	Dostoevsky's *Notes from Underground*	343
20	Undutiful Daughters	377
21	Israel Zangwill's *The Melting Pot*: An Undutiful Daughter, Marrying Out, a Troubled Utopia	421

22	Sephardi slave trading and slave plantations in Suriname	447
23	Complicating world history: Continuities between Sephardi settler colonialism in Suriname, Zangwill's support for Exodus-colonialism, and Zionist Israel	485
24	My Mother Elsie Levy in the 1930s: A Diaspora Consciousness encounters William Zukerman	503
25	1938–9: In the Shadow of the Holocaust: G E R Gedye's *Fallen Bastions*, Veza Canetti's *The Tortoises* and Virginia Woolf's *Three Guineas*	521
26	The Holocaust and Jewish Communists in Australia 1943	567
27	The Holocaust in Australia: fallout in 1979 of the Kastner-Eichmann association in Hungary in World War II	597
28	How I came to see Zionist Israel	621

My Mother, Elsie Levy Volume 2

9

An English Jew: thoughts on my mother, Elsie Levy

Elsie Levy was an English Jew. More specifically, she was an East End London Jew, and like other East End Jews I've met or read about, was proud of being so. In my 2001 book *1492: The Poetics of Diaspora*, my uncle Lew wrote: 'My parents were born and bred in London's East End, within the sound of Bow Bells, and they took a cockney pride in their origins.' Lew adds: 'I don't know precisely' why my father 'decided to uproot himself and take his wife and three children to Australia'.[1] My mother in later life also once said to me that she never really knew why the family left London in 1926 to travel for weeks in the old and rusty ss *Herminius* to far-away Sydney. The father, Philip Levy, it would appear, had assumed the historical role and power of the patriarch making absolute decisions for his family to follow. The only explanation my mother could recall for my grandfather, a tall powerful man even in his old age when I knew him, deciding that the family should migrate to Sydney was that, because as a young man he had lived in Johannesburg for many years, he couldn't stand the cold of London winters. He had returned to London from South Africa when his mother died, working as a taxi driver, and in 1911 married Rose Simmons, a cousin, who was then working in a cigar making factory. In 1926, my mother Elsie Levy was 14, the eldest child; she had two younger brothers, Lewis who was 12, and Jerome Abraham (who in Australia would become known as Jock), who was 10.

My grandmother Rose, known to us children as Nan, was a small woman, beloved in the family, in my childhood memory a wonderful cook; I feel sure she would have continued East End food and cooking traditions, which was possible in Bondi where *Mitteleuropa* delicatessens served its large Jewish community. My grandparents lived in a semi-detached house in Bondi, in O'Brien Street, which was a little west of Six Ways, from which Hall Street led to Campbell Parade and the beach. We visited pretty well every day after school, as, I like to think, would occur with an East End family in London. I would often accompany my mother when she went shopping in Six Ways, and I particularly recall that on one corner there was a Jewish cake shop, with large trays of uncut cheese cake. Across from the cake shop was a Jewish delicatessen, owned by a family who lived in a house opposite our block of flats in Edward Street, several streets southward and uphill from Six Ways. At my grandparents I have a memory of my grandmother rolling flour on a board to make pastry, bringing out of the oven large round apple tarts, or buttering matzo for us children. In the Concluding Mosaic to *1492: The Poetics of Diaspora*, I recall that 'when Nan buttered the matzos, we kids would say more, more on that corner, that bit, Nan'.[2] In this chapter I will be drawing on *1492: The Poetics of Diaspora*, which mixes intellectual and cultural histories with autobiography and family history reminiscences and genealogy. I'm pleased to think of *1492: The Poetics of Diaspora* as an ego histoire before I knew of and engaged with ego histoire.

Mikhail Bakhtin notes that through the ages authoritarian figures such as fathers are mocked during carnival times or in joking outside carnival times.[3] I think that the family could never quite accept my grandfather's explanation for leaving England, that it was because of the cold. Why, they would ask, did he not want to take us to South Africa where he said he had friends, some of them perhaps his cousins, gone there to make their fortune. My uncle Jock recalls that when the family stopped over in South Africa it was clear my grandfather certainly had friends there: 'when we came over in the boat and stopped at Cape Town, I remember that he took us up to Johannesburg to meet certain people'.[4]

My grandfather's stay in South Africa, which apparently lasted many years, is worth a little pondering, a little contextualising, if we wonder about the situation of Jews as migrants to settler colonial societies in the British Empire. From family stories, it is clear that my grandfather and other Jews from England and Europe were accepted as citizens of a British-controlled settler colonial society, with an appalling history over many centuries of European racism and dispossession and attempted destruction of African societies; there were centuries of slavery conducted by the Dutch of people from elsewhere in Africa and across the Indian Ocean from South East Asia.[5] In recent years there has also been increasing attention to South Africa's terrible history of genocide in relation to the San.[6] In becoming part of a settler colonial society, English and European Jews joined the *herrenvolk*, to use a term of the sociologist Pierre van den Berghe in his 1967 book *Race and Racism*. In Johannesburg my grandfather would have belonged to a Jewish community which was very successful commercially and politically, perhaps best known now for producing famous radicals like Helen Suzman, Joe Slovo, Ruth First, Albie Sachs, and Ronnie Kasrils.[7] Nothing in the family stories I heard suggested that my grandfather was in the least bit radical, or for that matter political in any way.

It very much appears that my grandfather and his friends and the Jewish community as a whole were, despite considerable anti-Semitism in the late nineteenth and first half of the twentieth century, accepted as whites with civic and property rights, unlike black South Africans and immigrant Indians. In their introduction to their collection *Memories, Realities and Dreams: Aspects of the South African Jewish Experience*, Milton Shain and Richard Mendelsohn observe that Jews, in an ironic reversal of fortune, having been victims of discrimination and oppression, arrived in South Africa to 'find themselves, simply by virtue of their skin colour, beneficiaries of a system built on racial exploitation'.[8]

Jeremy Krikler, in *Revolution from Above, Rebellion from Below* (1993), concerning agrarian Transvaal at the time of the South African War, refers to the betrayal after the war by the British of the African peoples of the Transvaal, who had been violently dispossessed of their ancestral lands throughout the nineteenth century by the Boers. Krikler argues that during the war the colonised, the African rural working people, actively sought to reclaim their land and restore their distinctive communal world. Africans, Krikler says, not only provided intelligence to and scouted for the British army, they also engaged in armed combat, cutting off hundreds of square miles of territory and its resources from the Boer forces, making it difficult for Boer commandos to obtain food by seizing Boer livestock and crops. In turn, Boer forces engaged in widespread massacres of black people. Yet after victory, Krikler observes, the British harshly returned Africans, who had played a central role in the Boer defeat, to a deprived state of colonisation.[9]

Indians were disadvantaged and discriminated against in South Africa, if we recall Gandhi's experiences there from 1893, when as a young lawyer from India he arrived in Durban and met his employer, Abdulla Sheth, one of the most affluent Indian businessmen in Natal. Gandhi soon left for Pretoria, capital of the Transvaal, where he had work to do in relation to a lawsuit. A first-class ticket was booked for him, but he was forced from the train by railway officials alerted by a fellow passenger irate that there was a 'coloured' man in first class. Gandhi details more humiliations and violence directed against him as he struggled to get to his destination, including being refused a room in a hotel, the Grand National Hotel, in Johannesburg, the manager telling him the hotel was full.[10] Gandhi of course would lead famous struggles in South Africa against discrimination towards Indians. He also was friends with two Jewish men who assisted him in establishing ashrams in South Africa: fellow Tolstoyans Henry Polak and Hermann Kallenbach. Polak inspired Gandhi to found the self-sufficient rural community Phoenix Settlement, while with Kallenbach he founded Tolstoy Farm, with its communal living arrangements, Kallenbach offering financial support and also being the owner of the property.[11] Outsiders are drawn to outsiders: perhaps we can see Jewish radicals in South Africa in terms of Isaac Deutscher's notion of the stranger who comes today and stays tomorrow, disturbing the society they are uneasily part of by a critical detachment.[12]

Despite having friends in Johannesburg, my grandfather, then, insisted on moving the family on to Australia. The family would jokingly speculate that he probably had another family in South Africa. I was recently telling this story to our friend, the historian Desley Deacon, who laughed and said, 'Remember the British TV genealogy show *Who Do You Think You Are?* How many of the fathers turn out to be bigamists?' My mother once said to me that they had had a good life in London, they were not poor, they 'even had servants'. 'Why did we have to leave', she asked.

My mother late in life, in melancholy mood, looking over her life, felt torn from a world she didn't want to leave and had no say in leaving. She would keep that British world alive, part of her being, in diasporic memory, in layered consciousness.

There may be a historical reason that influenced why my grandfather chose emigration in the mid-1920s. Gerhard Fischer points out in his book *Enemy Aliens* how the Australian prime minister William Morris Hughes had used World War I to destroy the German community in Australia as part of an overall attempt to make Australia somehow purely British. In the 1920s, Gerhard records, migration from Britain was intensely encouraged, migration from anywhere else vigorously discouraged.[13] My family were part of waves of subsidised British migrants, probably part of the Assisted Passage Scheme in the 1920s, jointly arranged by the Australian and British governments as part of general Empire settlement of populations. Between 1921 and 1929 Australia received 323,000 British migrants, mostly young family groups from English cities and provincial and industrial centres, of whom 212,000 were assisted.[14]

There may be – I'm wildly speculating – another possible aspect to think about for why my grandfather insisted on going to Sydney: perhaps there was something of the *Luftmensch* about him. I think of Lew remarking of his father in *1492: The Poetics of Diaspora*, that 'my memory of him was that he lived in a kind of fantasy land. I think maybe staying in Johannesburg led him to believe that the streets were paved with gold.'[15]

I recall reading with great enjoyment Sholom Aleichem's epistolary novel *The Adventures of Menahem-Mendl*, evoking the figure of the *Luftmensch* as an incurable optimist whose every venture ends in disaster and who never ceases to build yet another castle in the air. In his final letter to his long-suffering wife Sheineh-Sheindl, Menahem-Mendl tells her he has just escaped a new round of misfortunes and calamities. However he has a new infallible plan, he tells her in a postscript:

> Just remembered! I forgot to tell you where I am going. My dearest wife, I am going to America! I am not alone. I am traveling with a whole group. That is to say, for the time being, we are going only to Hamburg. But from Hamburg we shall sail for America. Why America all of a sudden? Because they say that in America life is good for Jews. They say that gold is rolling in the streets, yours for the picking. Their money is reckoned in dollars, and people

– people are held above rubies! As for Jews – they are considered the cream of the lot in America! Everybody assures me that in America I'll make good, please God – and they mean, *good*.[16]

Menahem-Mendl assures his wife that he 'shall not forget' her nor his 'dear little children' when he is 'successful, please God': 'I *will* be successful is as sure as the sun shines'; he will 'send steamship tickets for you and the children, and I'll bring you to America, and you'll live with me in comfort and in honor like a princess, wanting for nothing and having everything your heart desires, and I'll watch over you…'[17]

In these terms, we might think of my grandfather as a fantasist *Luftmensch*. Unlike Menahem-Mendl, however, he did not leave his wife and children behind. My grandfather assured his family that when they got to the wharf at Sydney they would be met by one of his brothers, Godfrey (I think the name was Godfrey), who would bountifully look after them.

But Godfrey the fabled brother was not at the Quay in Sydney's harbour when they arrived in 1926 on the ss *Herminius*. The family waited and waited, and then was taken in by the Salvation Army, and later would move to the then working-class Sydney suburb of Paddington, to begin their life in Australia.

Perhaps, I think now, Godfrey's non-appearance was a fatal blow to my grandfather's assumed authority in the family, along with my mother being the first in the family to secure paid employment. When I was a child, it was my grandmother Nan who provided the warmth and hospitality when we visited; my grandfather known as Pop seemed a distant figure.

My Uncles Recall Early Twentieth-Century London's East End

Writing *1492: The Poetics of Diaspora* in the late 1990s became something of a collaborative family affair, deliberately so, because I was following a postmodern idea of decentring and dispersing the narrative among different narrators. Curious about my Jewish genealogy for a frankly fantastical reason I will later discuss, I asked Ann's mother Barbara Curthoys, who had become an expert genealogist for her own family, to prepare a genealogy of my mother's East End lineage for me. It then happily occurred to me to send the genealogy to my uncles Lew and Jock Levy, who got together and taped a discussion on their pre-migration childhood experiences in London, which they then sent to me. Ann and I transcribed the tape, which, along with an essay Lew had written reflecting on his mother's life and his early migration experiences in Sydney and Melbourne during the 1930s Depression, became the centre piece of Chapter 8, 'More family stories: London, Sydney, Melbourne'. The brothers obviously got on extremely well all their lives, and had great fun, along with prompting by their wives, my aunts Anne and Jeannette, in recalling details of being children roaming the streets of the East End. Their stories were fascinating, funny, intriguing and touching.[18] At the beginning of what turns out to be an extraordinarily rich ethnography of their childhood, Jock says they hope they are making a 'contribution to oral history à la Studs Terkel'.[19] As so often in diasporic memory and why it's so valuable as oral history, these memories are remarkably detailed about a particular time in their lives; they are not overlaid with later memories of the same place. (I owe this point to Ann Curthoys.)

In their taped conversation, Jock says that the family wasn't 'exactly poverty-stricken in England, I mean on a Day of Atonement, that is Yom Kippur, they were able to pay a servant to come in and lay the fire and do certain manual things Jewish people weren't supposed to do that day'. Jock recalls that there were 'levels, social levels, of Jewish people in London' that favoured their family. In this hierarchy, the 'Anglicised Jews were top of the ladder and then down below that there were possibly the Russians, the Poles, and… kind of a Spanish… Portuguese, that's the word I'm looking for. The Portuguese were possibly the lowest on the ladder.'[20] Jock and Lew also remembered the variety of foods the family enjoyed. On special days, for example a Friday night, there were no candles lit and no prayers spoken. However, in Jock's memory:

> Rose would always have fried fish on the table, possibly plaice which is a kind of a fish somewhat larger than a sole, and on very special occasions we might have chicken but these were special occasions. Plus the fact that the old man at times would bring home fruit of the season, wonderful whiteheart cherries I remember very vividly. I loved them, plus the fact that he would go sometimes down to the fish market and bring home a box. This was a box that would be about three times bigger than a cigar box, it was made of wood and inside it would be chitlings. Now chitlings are the soft liver of the cod and Rose would cook that up and we would have it cold with vinegar, just a little vinegar, and pepper. I still remember it…'[21]

Jock recalled occasions when Rose would exchange her fried fish for some 'wonderful Dutch pastry – Monicadams – that is absolutely right, Lew', made by a neighbourhood friend of hers, pastry that was 'absolutely delicious'. Lew confirmed that Rose was an 'artist with the frying of fish'. Jock also recalls that 'one of our greatest pleasures was that Rose would take us, I remember she took me once or twice, to Woolfs, in Whitechapel, who specialised in beef, that is, salt beef on a sandwich with a pickled cucumber. It was absolute heaven…'[22]

Lew remembers Rose as a 'caring, loving tender woman'. Jock recalled that Rose came from a large family. Her sisters Sarah, Abby and Prissy, would visit and chat. Jock adds that his older brother Lew could be mischievous on such occasions: 'Lew was getting into trouble with Sarah, when she used to come to the place and sit down there and they would converse and Lew would get a pin and stick it in Sarah's arse and this of course created all sorts of problems.' Rose also once said that one of her brothers 'had died of TB and another had been killed in the Great War', the name of the one who had been killed possibly being Harry.[23]

Lew said their father was 'more distant from us', but they also felt that he may have been influential on their later lives in Australia:

> JOCK: Now from a cultural point of view and possibly this could have influenced us in some way or another the old man, that is Phil, that is Father, was very fond of the theatre and I remember him taking Lew and I to see a… a Rhinegold? no, Reinhardt, a Max Reinhardt production of a German mime play, no words, some music, but everything was mimed. Wonderful play, wonderful production. Also, I remember taking us I think it was to the Palace, I'm not quite sure on that one or the Palladium, to see *Chu Chin Chow*… had a wonderful effect on us. So the old man was quite good about that and I remember him taking us to Wembley stadium where they had an exhibition of a sea battle. I think it was at Zeebrugge and all the models were there and it showed you the warships, how they manoeuvred, and the consequence, how of course Great Britain, that the British Navy was triumphant. I remember that very vividly.'[24]

Jock's anecdote here about the reenactment of a British Navy exploit at Zeebrugge in Belgium in April 1918 (supposedly a triumph, actually a fiasco) might indicate a conventional British patriotism on my grandfather's part, along with enjoyment of the theatricality of the display.

Lew also noted that he and Jock enjoyed music hall and vaudeville songs 'that went back to Victorian England'.[25]

For me, these are very interesting recollections, since Jock,

Lew and my mother would in the later 1930s in Sydney help create a Jewish Youth Theatre and become involved in radical theatre more broadly like the New Theatre: their interest in theatre in Australia was continuous with their pre-migration family experience and enjoyments, a powerful inheritance. Perhaps, the interest in the family in popular theatre going back to early twentieth-century London influenced my own decision to become a literary critic and cultural historian interested not so much in theatre (which has never excited me) but theatricality, in film and popular TV, and more generally what Walter Benjamin said of Kafka in his essay in *Illuminations*, 'Franz Kafka: On the Tenth Anniversary of His Death', that Kafka saw the world as a *theatrum mundi*: 'Kafka's world is a world theater. For him, man is on the stage from the very beginning.'[26]

Near the end of their reminiscences Lew underlines the differences between boys and girls in upbringing in relation to the public world. Lew says that I will have 'noted that we haven't made any reference to Elsie. But that is not because of any particular reason except this: that she was several years older than Jock and I and being a woman or rather shall I say being a girl she was more or less put to the back of our minds, because Jock and I specifically sought refuge in our own company'.[27] As boys, it's clear Lew and Jock were allowed to wander the streets of the East End; my mother, as a girl, would have led a much more confined life. What they perceived as their London worlds would have been different, and we can see inklings here of how boys and girls, men and women, could see each other as different beings, with boys enjoying the privilege of entering the public world from a very young age.

My Mother Elsie Levy Recalls Growing Up in the East End

In *1492: The Poetics of Diaspora*, I record that when I was growing up, my mother would quite frequently talk of her London life as a child, and of being called at school 'Jaw-me-dead' because she talked so much.[28] In my mother's stories told over the years referring to family life in London there was, I think, fear and regret mixed with happier memories. A story I particularly recall involved a hint of the violence, or possible violence, of the family patriarch. She would say that Father was very bad-tempered, not least around the dinner table, especially 'with the boys', her brothers, and if he got too bad-tempered she would escape and stay overnight or for a few days with her grandmother, who lived nearby. Like Jock, my mother also recalled how mischievous Lew could be. Once, she said, Lew farted at the dinner table, but looked unblinkingly at his brother and said reproachfully, 'Jock!'

My mother could be nostalgic for the family's London life. Like Lew and Jock, she remembered that their father would take her to the theatre, and she got used to sitting 'in the gods'. She said how sad it was that her mother never saw her mother Esther again, and that Rose 'never wrote to her once she got to Australia'. This chimes in with a comment of Lew's in the taped conversation with Jock, that his mother and father 'were just barely literate': 'Words seemed to overwhelm them...'[29] My mother recalled how hard were their lives when they first migrated to Sydney, of the rag-trade factories she worked at, where you were under constant surveillance and were lucky to have time off to go to the toilet; and the number of places they had to leave because they couldn't pay the rent, before they settled in the semi-detached house in Bondi.[30]

(I will talk more later about my grandparents' home, when – or if – I ever find myself, like Tristram Shandy, actually born. I remain hopeful.)

Like Lew and Jock, my mother also had memories of the importance of food to her pre-1926 London life. Such became clear in one of the fragments that close *1492: The Poetics of Diaspora*, where I record stories and happenings when my mother in April

1974 came to stay with us in London. Ann and I were living in Stoke Newington at the time, in north-east London (on the bus 73 route). My mother had flown from Sydney to London to see where she had grown up. To us, Stoke Newington was rather dismal and rundown, with boarded-up houses and closed-down shops. My mother, however, was almost over-excited by being in a Jewish area, with Orthodox Jews in black strolling purposefully in the street and local delicatessens where there were jars and jars of different kinds of pickled cucumbers. Soon she wanted to explore other parts of London, tracking down her memories of being in the East End 47 years before. Over several days Ann, a flawless map reader, navigated from the London street directory our journeys to the East End. 'Eyes of diamonds and sides of silver! Eyes of diamonds and sides of silver!' my mother kept repeating joyfully, as we strolled about and negotiated the crowd and stalls and spruikers of the East End's famous Petticoat Lane. 'That's what one of my aunts used always to say about the smoked salmon we could get at Petticoat Lane.' My mother insisted on buying some on the spot, choosing carefully, rejecting some, staring hard, and then pointing to an enormous piece, to be eaten later with lemon juice and black pepper when we got back to our Stoke Newington flat.[31]

Ann navigated the way to Blooms to taste Jewish food, and my mother told her story to the waiter, that she'd left London 47 years ago. We found Malmsbury Road School, which Jock and Lew describe in their reminiscences.[32] My mother shouted '47 years! 47 years ago I was here!' and rushed inside, to emerge some time later beaming, telling us, who had waited somewhat embarrassed in the school grounds, that a teacher had invited her to tell the class of her childhood experiences at the school. We tried to locate the family house in 23 Alfred Street, Bow, where she had lived as a child, only to find that neither the house nor the street had survived the bombing of London in World War II. 'Where's the

Roman Road? There's a library there I used to go to.' Ann found the Roman Road in the street directory and we walked along it and found the library. Then we found the pedestrian tunnel under the railway line, the same one, I think, that Lew remembers as Tom Thumb's Arch. Bow Street Station seemed to have a special significance for her, and we spent some time going down onto its darkened platform and talking of war and how East Londoners sheltered from the bombing.[33] Ann remembers my mother pointing to a dark corner where my mother thought she and her family may have sat. My mother must only have been about five years old.

I think now this refers to the Zeppelin bombing by the Germans towards the end of World War I, bombing I will soon talk about in relation to the Bloomsbury circle: how diverse histories entwine.

There is one more connection with South African racial history. We went with my mother to see a play by Athol Fugard, I can't now remember its name, from memory a protest at the harsh treatment of Africans by the apartheid regime; at one point, alluding to Shylock's great speech, the main character disrobes, revealing his penis, asking wasn't he a man like any other man. Sitting next to one's mother while this was happening on stage was undoubtedly unnerving. I think my mother loved the whole experience.

An English Jewish Genealogy

One of Jock's comments in his conversation with Lew strikes me as a little strange, when he thinks of Portuguese-descended Jews in London as the 'lowest on the ladder' of the internal hierarchy that helped shape the grain of London Jewish life. I'm sure it's not a view my mother held. I recall her once saying admiringly that Lew had olive skin and this may be because the family had Portuguese ancestry; there was a family legend as well that in the eighteenth century they had come from Holland. Coupling a possible Portuguese ancestry with Holland could mean – though my mother did not say this – that the family may have been of Sephardi Spanish ancestry, given that quite a few Sephardi Jews, expelled from Spain in 1492, had moved to Portugal and had become New Christians during the Inquisition, then some (as with Spinoza's family) had moved northwards to the more liberal and open society of Holland.[34] In the mid-seventeenth century, Sephardi community leaders in Holland requested of Cromwell that Jews be permitted to again live in Britain; in medieval times, Jews across Christian Europe had suffered expulsion from various countries; in 1290 they were totally expelled from England and not re-admitted until the latter half of the seventeenth century, in 1656, Cromwell having agreed to a quiet re-entry.

As I explain in *1492: The Poetics of Diaspora*, while working on my mother's genealogy, Ann's mother Barbara had got in contact with Aubrey Jacobus, an English genealogist interested in the history of the Dutch Jewry who had come from Holland to England and settled in certain streets in Spitalfields, Whitechapel. I began emailing with Jacobus, who told me that from his research ex-Dutch Jews in the East End in the nineteenth century were overwhelmingly Ashkenazi in origin, coming from northern and eastern Europe rather than being Sephardim of Spanish descent. Jacobus felt that there was a long history of bad relations existing between the Ashkenazi and Sephardic communities in England stretching back before the nineteenth century; there was bitterness against wealthy Sephardim who appeared reluctant to help their poorer brethren; and marriages between Sephardim and Ashkenazim were rare. Nonetheless, Jacobus says that he is aware that many Jews in contemporary England forlornly hope that because their families came from, or may have come from, Holland that they must be Sephardi, the word 'Sephardi' still retaining an elitist cachet.[35]

I was one of these deluded souls. Because of the family legend of coming from Holland and also my mother's comment about

Lew as of possible Portuguese ancestry, I nursed the utopian wish that my mother's genealogy would show that the family was of Sephardi origin, which to me meant a bodily connection to an historical world I admired, the medieval pre-1492 Judeo-Islamic trading and social world of plurality and *convivencia* that stretched from Moorish Spain to India and China. Indeed, the desire to connect with this historical world, in idea and story and fantasy, structures the narrative of *1492: The Poetics of Diaspora*. When she had completed the genealogy, however, composed of converging lines from the late eighteenth century of the Levy, Simmons, Marks, Jacobs and Lazarus families, Barbara concludes that Elsie Levy is a 'descendant of the Ashkenazi Jews who were well established in London before the middle of the nineteenth century': 'it seems that Elsie's lineage on the Levy side dates back to the Jews who migrated to England in the mid-eighteenth century or even earlier, and that they are most likely either of German or East European stock'. 'Dutch origin', she adds, 'cannot be ruled out but it appears unlikely'. It is true, Barbara writes, that the Simmons family included cigar-makers (both Rose and her father Lewis and mother Esther were cigar-makers), a prevalent occupation among Dutch Jews; but there is still not enough evidence to show that my mother's family came from Holland. There were, however, Barbara notes, occasional marriages to Sephardic Jews. For example, the genealogy indicates that by 1891, Elsie's grandfather Abraham Levy, living in Houndsditch Street, Central London, would appear to have been a well-to-do merchant, whose daughter in that year married Isaac Anidjar Romain in the Sephardic Synagogue, Bevis Marks.[36]

When Barbara had finished her excellent genealogy presented in a professional format, I asked her to write about the experience of being approached by her son-in-law to do the family tree. Clearly, Barbara had quickly worked me out. She comments: 'If any of John's ancestors came from Holland I suspect that John would prefer that their origins were Sephardi, but, pragmatically, I say to myself "Sephardi or Ashkenazi? Facts are facts and I will follow where the genealogical path takes me"'.[37] And indeed Barbara did so, quite beautifully.[38]

Given my almost completely Ashkenazi genealogy, I set about in *1492: The Poetics of Diaspora* trying to connect to the medieval pre-1492 Judeo-Islam world of plurality and *convivencia* through a fragmented, perhaps demented, jumble of narratives, going back and forwards from 1492 when, as I explain in the Preface, 'three key happenings occurred within a very short time... Columbus sailed for the Americas; eight centuries of Moorish Spain finally ended in the surrender by the sultan Boabdil of Granada, with its legendary fortress-palace the Alhambra; and the Jews of Spain... were subject to one of history's recurring crimes against humanity, mass expulsion'.[39]

I wasn't too disappointed that my family tree showed up solidly Ashkenazi. I thought it would be so from the family's names, but, as I emailed Aubrey Jacobus, 'it is the genealogical journey itself which I find exciting and enchanting'.[40]

1   John Docker, *1492: The Poetics of Diaspora* (Continuum, London and New York, 2001), p.159.
2   John Docker, *1492: The Poetics of Diaspora*, p.264.
3   John Docker, *Postmodernism and Popular Culture: A Cultural History* (Cambridge University Press, Melbourne, 1994), p.179.
4   Docker, *1492: The Poetics of Diaspora*, p.153.
5   See Nigel Worden, *Slavery in Dutch South Africa* (Cambridge University Press, Cambridge, 1985, reprinted 2010).
6   See Mohamed Adhikari, *The Anatomy of a South African Genocide: The Extermination of the Cape San Peoples* (Ohio University Press, Athens, Ohio, 2011), and Mohamed Adhikari (ed.), *Genocide on Settler Frontiers: When hunter-gatherers and commercial stock farmers clash* (UCT Press, Cape Town, 2014).

7   For the story of a remarkable family, see Gillian Slovo, *Every Secret Thing: My Family, My Country* (Little, Brown and Company, London, 1997); also Robin Renwick, *Helen Suzman: Bright Star in a Dark Chamber* (Biteback Publishing, London, 2014), pp.9–10; Albie Sachs, *The Strange Alchemy of Life and Law* (Oxford University Press, Oxford, 2009).

8   See Milton Shain and Richard Mendelsohn (eds), *Memories, Realities and Dreams: Aspects of the South African Jewish Experience* (Jonathan Ball Publishers, Johannesburg and Cape Town, 2002), Introduction, p.13, and review by Saul Dubow in *The Journal of African History*, Vol.45, no.1, 2004, pp.141–2.

9   Jeremy Krikler, *Revolution from Above, Rebellion from Below: The Agrarian Transvaal at the Turn of the Century* (Clarendon, Oxford, 1993), and John Docker, 'Storm Troopers of empire? Historical representation in *Breaker Morant*, Naguib Mahfouz's *Palace Walk* and other war histories', *History Australia*, Vol.8, no.1, 2011, pp.68, 72–3.

10 M.K. Gandhi, 'On the Way to Pretoria', in Homer A. Jack (ed.), *The Gandhi Reader: A sourcebook of his life and writings* (Grove Press, New York, 1956), pp.29–34.

11 See Thomas Weber, 'Gandhi moves: Intentional communities and friendship', in Debjani Ganguly and John Docker (eds), *Rethinking Gandhi and Nonviolent Relationality* (Routledge, London and New York, 2007), pp.86–91.

12 Georg Simmel, *The Sociology of George Simmel*, edited and translated Kurt H. Wolff (The Free Press, Glencoe, Ill., 1950), essay on 'The stranger', pp.402–8; Docker, *1492: The Poetics of Diaspora*, pp.86–7.

13 Gerhard Fischer, *Enemy Aliens* (University of Queensland Press, St. Lucia, 1989). See also John Docker, *Dilemmas of Identity: The Desire for the Other in Colonial and Post Colonial Cultural History* (Working Papers in Australian Studies no.74, Sir Robert Menzies Centre for Australian Studies, University of London, 1992), pp.12–17.

14 Docker, *1492: The Poetics of Diaspora*, p.151.

15 Docker, *1492: The Poetics of Diaspora*, p.153.

16 Sholom Aleichem, *The Adventures of Menahem-Mendl*, translated from the Yiddish by Tamara Kahana (Sholom Aleichem Family Publications, New York, 1969), p.221.

17 Sholom Aleichem, *The Adventures of Menahem-Mendl*, pp.221–2.

18 Docker, *1492: The Poetics of Diaspora*, pp.151–2.

19 Docker, *1492: The Poetics of Diaspora*, p.152.

20 Docker, *1492: The Poetics of Diaspora*, p.153.

21 Docker, *1492: The Poetics of Diaspora*, p.154.

22 Docker, *1492: The Poetics of Diaspora*, pp.154–5.

23 Docker, *1492: The Poetics of Diaspora*, p.157.

24 Docker, *1492: The Poetics of Diaspora*, p.156.

25 Docker, *1492: The Poetics of Diaspora*, p.156.

An English Jew: thoughts on my mother, Elsie Levy

26 Walter Benjamin, *Illuminations*, edited with an introduction by Hannah Arendt (Schocken, New York, 2007), p.124.
27 Docker, *1492: The Poetics of Diaspora*, p.158.
28 Docker, *1492: The Poetics of Diaspora*, p.252.
29 Docker, *1492: The Poetics of Diaspora*, pp.153, 252.
30 Docker, *1492: The Poetics of Diaspora*, pp.153, 252.
31 Docker, *1492: The Poetics of Diaspora*, p.250.
32 Docker, *1492: The Poetics of Diaspora*, p.155.
33 Docker, *1492: The Poetics of Diaspora*, pp.154, 251.
34 Docker, *1492: The Poetics of Diaspora*, pp.88–89.
35 Docker, *1492: The Poetics of Diaspora*, pp.30–31.
36 Docker, *1492: The Poetics of Diaspora*, pp.26, 27, 29–30.
37 Docker, *1492: The Poetics of Diaspora*, pp.21–4.
38 Barbara Curthoys also figures importantly in my essay, 'Troubled reflections on my father', in Ann Curthoys and Joy Damousi (eds), *What Did You Do in the Cold War, Daddy? Personal stories from a troubled time* (NewSouth Publishing, Sydney, 2014) pp.87–113.
39 Docker, *1492: The Poetics of Diaspora*, Preface, p.vii.
40 Docker, *1492: The Poetics of Diaspora*, p.32.

10

East End Jews, Anti-Semitism, Bloomsbury

> No people is saintly. No people is intrinsically good or bad eternally and by their essence. No people is destined always to be victims. All peoples have been victims and executioners by turns, and all peoples count among their number both victims and executioners.
>
> Maxime Rodinson, *Cult, Ghetto, and State*, 1983[1]

Thinking about these remarkable sentences from the great French scholar of the Middle East reflecting on world history makes me wonder about the long history, if interrupted for many centuries, of the Jews in England: did they 'count among their number both victims and executioners'? Were they sometimes victims of othering, exclusion, expulsion, prejudice, intense dislike, violence, cruelty, and sometimes – or at the same time – participants in the oppression of others? Zionist historiography in particular wishes us to see Jews as eternal victims, as history's chosen people of suffering. Is this discourse of victimology borne out by my own family history, or the wider history of Jews in Britain it relates to? My own feeling is that modern English Jewish history is testament to Rodinson's insight in diverse, multiple and contradictory ways, which extend into the history of the British Empire.

In this and the following chapters I'd like to braid together what I perceive to be connecting threads between the reminiscences of their East End childhood of my mother and uncles, and general English histories of Jewishness and anti-Semitism. These histories extend to Bloomsbury and involve Virginia Woolf and Leonard Woolf: Virginia Stephen, who became the wife of a Jewish man Leonard Woolf and took a Jewish name and yet was not beyond being anti-Semitic herself in ways hurtful to think about. Virginia Woolf is also important for me – and this is very much not to my credit, the more I unhappily brood on it – as an absence in my reading and critical life, and that relates to my being a Leavisite: that is to say, a kind of teenage follower of the Cambridge critics F R Leavis and Q D Leavis who had been prominent in the world of academic literary criticism in and from the 1930s, and influential in Australia in the 1960s. More to say about these matters soon, for it is only recently that I learnt something about Q D Leavis's family background that I never knew before, indeed, had no inkling of. I certainly didn't know about it when in my *Postmodernism and Popular Culture: A Cultural History* (1994), I devoted a chapter to her 1932 book *Fiction and the Reading Public*.[2]

I will also tell how my recent interest in Leonard Woolf in relation to this ego histoire came about.

My Family and English Anti-Semitism

Perhaps, in the previous chapter, I was a little gratuitously harsh on my grandfather as an authoritarian patriarch making absolutist decisions for his family, albeit a decision that took them most of the way around the world. Perhaps I underplayed how important an issue feeling cold is. I think humanity is roughly divided between those who never seem to feel the cold, and those like myself who feel cold at the first tremor of a breeze even in summer. In his childhood reminiscences in my *1492: The Poetics of Diaspora*, Jock reports of his father: 'The old man was a taxi driver as I remember it and during our period in England he had two taxis, one was a Unic and the other was a Fiat. The old man used to go out in the winter weather wrapped up in a rather large blanket that he would put round his middle, and I think he suffered quite a lot with the weather over there. One of the reasons I think that possibly we came to Australia was the fact that he had been in South Africa for a number of years and got the sunshine into his bones in Johannesburg.' Lew recalled the cold of London's winter: 'What comes to mind, John, is my response, I would imagine it would also correspond to Jock's memory, to winter in working-class London. What used to rile me was that people would talk quite lyrically about the soft snow falling. To both of us what it meant was bitter cold and inadequate clothing and to this day I can never look at snow with any kind of benign appreciation.'[3]

Now I think as well that there could have been a good historical reason – even if he didn't feel the need to explain it to his children – for my grandfather wishing to migrate in the middle 1920s to Australia. This is the anti-Semitism that East End and other Jews in England experienced in the early twentieth century, during and following on from World War I. The thought occurs to me: what if Godfrey – the brother who said he would be at the wharf in Sydney to greet my grandfather and his family and mysteriously never appeared – had written to my grandfather saying come to Sydney where I am, Australia is much less anti-Semitic than Britain and South Africa. While my uncle Lew considered that his father and mother were barely literate, there must have been some sort of correspondence between my grandfather and this Godfrey.

At night, my grandfather Phil and my grandmother Rose, thinking their three young children were out of earshot or asleep, could have talked about things in a way the children didn't know about (even if children, when parents are talking quietly to each other, can somehow hear through walls).

The parents might have discussed between themselves

worrying incidents involving the children. For example, when I was growing up my mother mentioned more than once that she felt a teacher at her East End school was being anti-Semitic towards her in the way she would pronounce her name, Miss Levy, and perhaps this was visibly affecting her enjoyment of school. My mother also, perhaps drawing on a collective memory about medieval times before English Jews were expelled (in 1290) for some three and a half centuries, would sometimes say that in England people would accuse 'us' at Easter time of drinking the blood of Christian children. Saying these things her voice still retained a slight bitterness after all the years that had gone by. Jock relates of their East End childhood that he and older brother Lew were 'pretty street-wise in those days, Lew couldn't have been any more than eight or nine, I couldn't have been any more than five or six and yet we wandered around I should imagine the Clapham area and Stepney area so we were always on our own'.[4] Trouble, nonetheless, could suddenly occur, even outside their own home, for the two boys.

> JOCK: There's also a grim side of it. I remember Lew and myself playing in the street outside our home and along the avenue were horse chestnut trees and these had what we called conkers on them and if you could get four or five of these conkers, hold them on the stem, they were a pretty decent sort of a weapon and I remember some louts coming along and hitting Lew on the head and drawing blood and calling out bloody Jews, Jew bastards, and Rose came out, of course when Lew told her what happened, and she sprinted up that road and if she had caught them she'd have killed them. This is just a little grimmer side of what our childhood was.[5]

Perhaps, too, when my grandparents and the children, in my mother's memory, would shelter from German bombing down below in Bow station, my grandfather and grandmother registered things being said by others there that the children didn't understand.

It would be surprising if my grandparents did not anxiously discuss such incidents and possible experiences. Jock's remembering his mother Rose sprinting up the street after the anti-Semitic louts is interesting, perhaps foreshadowing the later active resistance in the East End to Mosely's fascists in the 1930s, as in the famous struggle for Cable Street.

Perhaps, she might have suggested to my grandfather, we can fight back against anti-Semitism. My grandfather, however, who had moved elsewhere once in his life, could have said it would be safer to move far away and to another, warmer, hemisphere. I recall here a wise remark of a friend of ours, Christine Winter, who had migrated from Germany to Australia where she became the historian of German missions in Papua New Guinea, that if you have moved once in life you can always move again.

I'm wildly speculating of course, but who among us would doubt the pervasiveness of anti-Semitism in English history, and how difficult it would be to know how on a personal and family level to respond to it?

As for my mother's memory of an anti-Semitic teacher, it's interesting that neither my mother nor Jock nor Lew reflected on their being sent by my grandparents to Malmsbury Road School, a state school, rather than being enrolled in a school for Jewish children, such as the Jews' Free School located in the East End. Gerry Black, in his book *J.F.S. The History of the Jews' Free School, London since 1732* (1998), suggests that the Jews' Free School was one of the great achievements of Anglo-Jewry. Black notes that when Jews were readmitted to Britain in 1656, the Jewish population of London was little more than 400 though it steadily grew so that by 1800 there were 20,000 Jews in the East End. The Jewish population continued to grow in the nineteenth century, its numbers boosted by the surge of immigration that followed the assassination of Tsar Alexander II in 1881, so that by 1888 the East End Jewish population had risen to 60,000, and by 1900 to 115,000, its peak year. The Jews' Free School was founded in 1732 in Spitalfields, in the Jewish quarter of the East End, near Duke's Place, Petticoat Lane and Brick Lane, and by 1900, when it had 4250 pupils, was the largest school in Europe, teaching both secular and religious studies.[6]

Black's book offers a clue as to why my mother and her brothers went to Malmsbury rather than a Jewish school. Black tells us that the Jewish population of the East End declined in the early twentieth century as Jews moved away to other areas of London. Enrolment at the Jews' Free School dropped to less than 1000, a consequence being that during the 1920s the London County Council considered closing it down, though it survived; furthermore, Black relates, the Education Act of 1870 ushered in the introduction of rate-maintained Board schools, which increasingly attracted Jewish pupils.[7] For Lew, Jock and my mother, then, there would have been nothing surprising in going to a state school.

Attending a state school perhaps reflects how secular many Anglo Jews became as part of a strong desire to integrate into British society, even while retaining a distinctive culture, in my family's case centred on food with religious elements muted. From Jock and Lew's reminiscences, it's apparent that while on Friday nights there were no candles lit and no prayers spoken, Jock does recall that the children 'were taken to synagogue on certain holidays, not regularly on a Friday night or Saturday, but mainly on the holidays'.[8] My grandparents also must have sought out a Hebrew teacher for the boys, perhaps to prepare them for a bar mitzvah, leading to a kind of minor revolt:

JOCK: Now we used to go, Lew and I, to a Chader, that is, a religious school where they taught you Hebrew and Lew even remembers some. I certainly do... *baruch ato adinoy alo heinu melech h'olam* (blessed art thou, O lord our God, king of the world), which is the first part of the blessing for cutting the bread, drinking the wine, something like that. And at this particular Chader, a very dingy morbid sort of joint, the teacher was shall I say a typical Jewish Russian who had come out into England, couldn't speak English very well, black coat, black hat, pince-nez and food stains all over his waistcoat, and he was a bearded man and if you didn't get the alphabet right (*alaf, bet, gimmal*) you got a rap over the knuckles and Lew and I decided, I think Lew did more than I did, I just followed, we decided rather than go along to the Chader we would experiment and go along and see where the barges went, and if we could get a lift on the barges. Lew, you take over from there.

> LEW: My memories centre around this Dickensian teacher, as Jock described him, Jewish teacher, who... really his inability to transmit knowledge in a civilised way led us to becoming what I think could be called religious fringe dwellers. We... he drove us crazy and our retaliation of course was to totally desert the Chader.[9]

(Lest it be thought my uncles Lew and Jock conceived a lifelong dislike of Russian Jews, it can be noted here that in the 1930s, in the Jewish Youth Theatre in Sydney, Lew and Jock met and married two Russian Jewish young women, my aunts Anne and Jeannette.)[10]

My mother, Lew and Jock, then, were sent to a state school, though my grandparents would have known there was some danger of anti-Semitism. Lew and Jock make no mention of any anti-Semitism in relation to themselves at Malmsbury Road School, Lew even recalling that 'what particularly endears it to my memory was the fact that at the age I think of 11 before we left

I'd won a prize at that school'. My mother's anecdote, however, of an anti-Semitic teacher was etched in her memory, though when Ann and I in 1974 were walking around with her in the East End, trying to keep up with her as she eagerly tracked her childhood memories, she rushed with joy into her old school to talk to a teacher and children.[11]

Fish, we will now see, so beautifully cooked by my grandmother as her children remembered, Lew saying 'she was an artist with the frying of fish' (my mother also memorably cooked fish in an 'English Jewish' way), figure in these stories of resonances between my grandparental family life and wider histories. So too does the apparently distinctive ways Jews talked to each other in the East End, perhaps how my family talked together at 23 Alfred Street, Bow.

English Anti-Semitism in World War I and Beyond

The First World War, among all its manifold disasters, imposed particular strains and stresses on English Jewish communities. My uncle Lew writes of his father: 'My father had soldiered through the 1914–18 war unscathed…. The only skill he acquired from his army service was driving (he was in Army Transport), and in civvy street he eked out a precarious living driving a London taxi.'[12] Did serving in the British army during the war protect one from anti-Semitism?

Tony Kushner and Kenneth Lunn, in the introduction to their collection *The Politics of Marginality: Race, the Radical Right and Minorities in Twentieth Century Britain* (1990), suggest that the marginality of ethnic and racial groups is particularly evident in times of conflict,[13] a thought explored by David Cesarini in his essay in the volume, 'An Embattled Minority: The Jews in Britain during the First World War'. Cesarini observes that it is 'now widely accepted that the First World War engendered a serious deterioration in the position of Jews in British society', a society which, he feels, historically finds it difficult to accept or welcome the distinctiveness of minority cultures. Part of the distinctiveness of the Jewish community was, Cesarini argues, that Jews felt they belonged both to Britain yet were also part of the international life of Jewry, potentially putting into question during war time their loyalty, patriotism, and commitment to the war, and placing English-born Jews under considerable pressure because of the threat, and increasing actuality, of anti-Semitic dislike and violence. World War I drove a 'wedge into relations between Jews and the majority population', provoking a crisis for Anglo-Jewish identity.[14]

Cesarini highlights what occurred with the entry into Britain of Russian Jews, who were met with hostility in the wider society including in wartime, even though the Tsarist regime was allied with Britain. There was resentment against the Russian Jews, especially the young men, around 25,000 or 30,000, who as refugees and not citizens were not required to do military service, and such resentment flowed into suspicion of British-born Jews.[15]

I can add a personal note here. My mother would occasionally say that when she was a young girl in London, her mother Rose would warn her 'not to play with the Polish Jewish children', a comment which perhaps relates to the fear British-born Jews had that they would be identified with foreign-born Jews and draw a harsh anti-Semitism down on them. As a child in Bondi, I recall that my mother said firmly – this must have been 1956 or a little later – that I must play with some Hungarian boys, they've just come to Australia; she said that she always regretted her mother not being nice to the Polish Jews when they came to London's East End when she was a child and forbidding her to play with their children.[16]

Cesarini observes that as 'jingoism and xenophobia' intensified as the war wore on, 'Jews and Germans were regularly conflated in the press'. During 1914 and 1915 physical violence was directed at Jews in towns and cities. While there were Jewish volunteers from the war's beginning, there were 'reports of discrimination and abuse against Jews' from a number of recruiting depots, and 'word spread that Jews were unwelcome in certain units'. To counter charges that Jews were not doing enough to assist the war effort, that they were war shirkers, the *Jewish Chronicle* regularly published the names of Jewish volunteers, and, later in the war, listed 'casualties as well as Jews earning medals and promotions'. Nonetheless, in British cities there was 'growing antagonism towards Jews', with 'major anti-Jewish riots in Leeds in June, and Bethnal Green in September, 1917'.[17] (Bethnal Green, I exclaim to myself; looking again at my mother's genealogy, I see that my grandmother Rose's father Lewis Simmons married Esther Jacobs in Bethnal Green, 28 August 1878.)[18]

Relations between Jews and non-Jews were also, Cesarini suggests, aggravated by heavy German bombing raids in the summer of 1917, east London being one of the Germans' target areas. Jews who stayed in the East End were criticised for crowding the air-raid shelters and tube stations, and of 'spreading panic'. When large numbers of Jews sought safety in towns along the south coast from Brighton to Cardiff, as well as in the Home Counties and Birmingham and Manchester, there were grumbles in the local and national press that the influx of Jews was causing a shortage of housing, pushing up rents, and bringing 'disease and dirt'. Also, Jews were held 'responsible for the overcrowding on trains carrying commuters to and from London and at weekends'. Letters to the press and editorials complained that on the trains Jews 'played cards and ate fried fish'; they also gave offence by talking 'in an animated fashion'.[19]

In this context, I think of my East End family, both during the war and into the 1920s, fond of the fried fish so expertly cooked by Rose, talking in an animated way that I find myself now guilty of in conversation, and expert at cards as I recall them being.

Perhaps, my grandfather felt that the pleasures of their London life among themselves were outweighed by the surrounding anti-Semitism. He may also have heard from old acquaintances in Johannesburg of the intensifying of anti-Semitism in South Africa during the war.[20]

Come, he might have said, I've heard of a government scheme to assist British migrants to go to Australia, let's take ship and cross the seas and be met by my brother, Godfrey. All will be well.

Becoming interested in Bloomsbury

David Cesarini concludes that the 'war years savagely eroded the status of Jews in Britain'.[21] Yet I wonder: did the status of Jews deteriorate for all British Jews, in Britain as well as in the Empire? What of differentiations of class, and the associated opportunities for careers opened up by education for boys and young men, including Jews? Maxime Rodinson's haunting leitmotif on world history comes to mind again: 'No people is destined always to be victims' and 'all peoples count among their number both victims and executioners'.[22] Here I'm thinking of Leonard Woolf in his early twentieth-century years at Cambridge and then career as a functionary of Empire when a colonial administrator in Ceylon from 1904 to 1911, for which being at Cambridge was a conduit, if we accept that in the nineteenth century and early twentieth century Cambridge was integral to the workings of Empire, a thought that only occurred to me while thinking about his early life. Was Leonard Woolf a victim or an executioner? Was he both a victim and an executioner?

First, however, I should explain how my interest in writing about Leonard Woolf for this ego histoire came about, pretty well accidentally. I've just looked at my tattered, falling apart, 2014 pocket diary. On 12 June 2014, Ann and I went to Victoria Station and caught the train to Lewes and were greeted by our friend Anna Cole there; I gratefully mentioned in the Introduction that

Anna had, with her friends Vanessa Castejon and Oliver Haag, introduced us to the notion of ego histoire. We drove with Anna to Charleston Farmhouse, long a heritage house open to the public, which is not far away, where some of the Bloomsbury people stayed, not Virginia Woolf and Leonard Woolf who had a house in the same area, but her sister Vanessa and Vanessa's ménage of Roger Bell and Donald Grant and visitors such as Maynard Keynes.

It was a warm, even hot sunny day, and after eating lunch in the little café we went on a tour of the rooms with a guide. From memory, all the rooms had various art work done to various surfaces by Bloomsbury artists living or staying there. After the guided tour, we went outside and found a seat in the shade looking at the garden and pond, while confiding to each other that we didn't think much of the art, how mediocre it was, but the garden and pond were lovely to look at. It was idyllic sitting there, and an idea for my ego histoire's section on my mother began to form from something that either the guide had said, or from information panels on the walls where we ate lunch, though perhaps my memory is wrong here. Disturbing the tranquillity, I suddenly said to Ann and Anna, I think I've got an idea. Their eyes glazed, but commendably they heard me out, though quite rightly intimating, don't be too long John, we want to appreciate how nice the house's surrounds are, we'll probably never come here again.

There was a sort of connection, I said, that wasn't an actual connection, during the First World War between East End Jews escaping German bombing by seeking refuge in the south of England, and Bloomsbury people, who were pacifists and, very admirably in my view – I thought as well of the IWW in Australia or Bertrand Russell in Britain – opponents of the war, also escaping London and coming down south to Lewes or near Lewes and the river Ouse. I said, I suddenly feel very interested in Leonard Woolf. What if I try to recover my mother's pre-1926 Jewish life in working-class parts of the East End, and also explore Leonard Woolf's kind of Jewishness, then the East End can be seen as part of a range of ways of being Jewish in Britain in the early twentieth century, I can fit them into a broader picture, what do you think? Ann said that when she and I first met in the late 1960s she was very interested in Virginia Woolf and read a lot of her work, and also that she was sure she once owned an autobiographical volume by Leonard Woolf, though I had never shown any interest in him then, or, for that matter, in Virginia Woolf. Here I was, said Ann smiling, getting together with a literary critic, and he hadn't read a word of Virginia Woolf!

Happily, Ann added that the Leonard Woolf interest was a great idea, and to follow it up when we got back to London, which I did. In the British Library I got out Victoria Glendinning's 2006 *Leonard Woolf: a biography*, and, sitting there in the Rare Books and Music Room reading it, started taking notes to use when I got back to Sydney in early July. I hadn't got far when we returned to Sydney, and then I bought Glendinning's biography at Gleebooks and kept reading, writing all over it. From Sydney University's Fisher Library I borrowed all the volumes of Leonard Woolf's autobiography except *Down Hill All the Way* on the years 1919 to 1939, which we could buy online. I then proceeded to read all of them, which led me to become – oh so belatedly in my life! – interested in Virginia Woolf, so that I've started reading Hermione Lee's biography and also to read with great enjoyment and fascination the Penguin Classics edition of *A Room of One's Own* with its helpful introduction and notes by Michèle Barrett. I thought about it being based on talks she had given at Newnham and Girton colleges in 1928 and its publication in 1929, not too long after my mother had left England in 1926.

How can I explain such culpable ignorance, and that at the age of 69 I'm finally getting around to reading Virginia Woolf and Leonard Woolf?

I'll say more later about being a Leavisite when, after being born in the 1940s, I make a dash for the 1960s. I'll just note here that as an undergraduate student from 1963 to 1966 aspiring to be a Leavisite devotee, you learned to think, as one might expect in a messianic movement, within certain preferred frameworks. In terms of 'high' modernist literature, you were to take a very positive interest in the poetry of T S Eliot, especially the earlier poems like *Prufrock* and *Gerontion* up to *The Waste Land*, and also the novels of D H Lawrence, focusing on *The Rainbow* and *Women in Love*. You absorbed also certain negative intimations, for example, I can't remember any interest being urged concerning Joyce, even though S L Goldberg our chief Leavisite on the spot in the Sydney English department had written a book on Joyce. You also learned to despise Bloomsbury and all its works, for you absorbed that whereas learning to be a Leavisite meant believing one day one could become a fully professional academic literary critic in the distant image of Leavis and 'Cambridge', 'Bloomsbury' represented the opposite of Cambridge, a kind of superficial journalistic belletristic meretricious amateurism characteristic of metropolitan centres like London, not to be taken seriously as proper criticism. Indeed, to be regarded, if thought about at all, with disdain and superiority. I also can't remember any interest in the Leavisite courses I took in Virginia Woolf. In any case, what I can say is when Ann and I met I still unthinkingly retained an inherited Leavisite aloofness towards 'Bloomsbury' though I had read nothing by them, including Virginia Woolf's novels.

So it was, then, that when Ann and I began relating to each other in late 1968 when I escaped 'Leavisite' Melbourne to Sydney and proclaimed my new anti-Leavisite proclivities, she met a rather strange young man, with large blackframed glasses, often drunk as part of de-Leavising, always late, with certain unfortunate limitations in his intellectual capital, not least his ignorance of brilliant essays like *A Room of One's Own* and novels like *Mrs Dalloway* and *To the Lighthouse*, while 'Leonard Woolf' was someone he had distantly heard of as somehow related to Virginia Woolf but hadn't read a word of.

A curious result of my interest in questions of Jewishness, however, is that some of this mental damage is being repaired, leading me in *1492: The Poetics of Diaspora* to read Joyce because of the presence of Leopold Bloom in *Ulysses*, and, now, for this ego histoire, to begin reading Virginia Woolf and Leonard Woolf. Not before time.

Yet now I think: I let Ann down when we first met, not knowing anything about a great modernist like Virginia Woolf, let alone not revealing any interest in Leonard Woolf, nor for that matter knowing anything at all about Bloomsbury.[23]

Conclusion

Were my Jewish family 'victims or executioners' in terms of world history? English working-class Jews in the East End were indeed victims of anti-Semitism, as we can see in David Cesarini's account of the war years, and my uncles' evocation of their childhood experiences in the East End in the early 1920s. In more general terms, the anti-Semitism that Cesarini evokes sounds very like the racism and associated violence that was directed by British settlers in British Empire history towards groups they didn't feel had the same right to be in – to invade – a land as they did. In Australian colonial history in the mid nineteenth century, British and British-descended (and other European) settlers expressed their hostility to Chinese gold miners in terms of aspersions, accompanied by violence, concerning their strange food, their different way of speaking, and allegations about hygiene.

My mother and her family experienced poverty and hardship when they first migrated to Australia, evoked by my uncle Lew in his contribution 'Lew Levy: his story' to my *1492: The Poetics of Diaspora*. Yet, and here I certainly include myself in this history,

Jews like my East End family who migrated to Australia were, like all migrants and descendants of migrants, advantaged by the destructive settler colonisation of Australia launched by the British from 1788, a settler colonisation I regard as genocidal.[24]

Postscript: Virginia Woolf on German Air Raids

I ponder what my mother said in Chapter 8, that she and her family and other East Enders sheltered in Bow Street Station from German air-raids during World War I. Given that my mother must then have been a little child, I sometimes wondered if she was misremembering. And I associated German bombing raids on London with the Second World War, not the first; later, I thought there could have been Zeppelin raids by the Germans. When I became interested in Bloomsbury, I read through Hermione Lee's biography of Virginia Woolf and saw with interest that in her chapter 'War' Lee talks of the German air-raids during World War I, zeppelin raids on London beginning in January 1915 and from 1917 German plane bombing. Hermione Lee also alerted me to look out for Virginia Woolf's 1937 novel *The Years* for its section on '1917'.[25]

When I was alerted by Gleebooks that *The Years* had arrived and was ready to be picked up, I felt excited, got it, and immediately looked up the '1917' section.[26] As everyone else knows except ignorant me, in '1917' Eleanor is visiting, in the black-out darkness of a cold winter's night, some friends living near Westminster Abbey. Interesting things go on in this story, including Eleanor meeting Nicholas, a gay man, a European, who intrigues her and to whom she feels drawn, but I'll home in on the German air-raid that occurs while Eleanor is there, as the group she is with eat dinner in the basement. They hear the wailing of a siren, and the rush of feet on the pavement outside as people seek shelter. They hear the dull boom of anti-aircraft guns in the distance trying to defend the city, and they move down into the cellar.

From the sound of the guns, they can estimate where the zeppelin is. They sit in profound silence, sensing that the zeppelin was over Hampstead, then the Embankment, then 'overhead' where they are.

> 'On top of us,' said Nicholas, looking up. They all looked up. At any moment a bomb might fall. There was dead silence… Then a gun boomed again. It was fainter – farther away.

After the raid, Eleanor asks, what were we talking about, for she 'felt that they had been in the middle of saying something very interesting when they were interrupted. But there had been a complete break; none of them could remember what they had been saying.'[27]

In her biography, Hermione Lee quotes this sentence about the air-raid as a complete break for the characters in *The Years* in 1917, suggesting that the war was the catastrophic event in the twentieth century that haunts Virginia Woolf's work: 'Her books are full of images of war: armies, battles, guns, bombs, air-raids, battleships, shell-shock victims, war reports, photographs of war-victims, voices of dictators'.[28]

Perhaps, too, the air-raids in London in the First World War, sitting in Bow Street Station, as German zeppelins and planes moved overhead, were traumatic events for that little child who was my mother, that her life, and the lives of those she held dear, would always be shadowed by a sense of history as danger and destruction.[29]

38 Growing Up Communist and Jewish in Bondi

1. Maxime Rodinson, *Cult, Ghetto, and State: The Persistence of the Jewish Question*, trans. Jon Rothschild (Al Saqi Books, London, 1983), p.182.

2. John Docker, *Postmodernism and Popular Culture: A Cultural History* (Cambridge University Press, Melbourne, 1994), chapter three, 'Modernism versus Popular Literature', pp.24–35.

3. John Docker, *1492: The Poetics of Diaspora* (Continuum, London and New York, 2001), pp.152–3, 157.

4. Docker, *1492: The Poetics of Diaspora*, pp.154, 252.

5. Docker, *1492: The Poetics of Diaspora*, p.155.

6. Gerry Black, *J.F.S. The History of the Jews' Free School, London since 1732* (Tymsder Publishing, London, 1998), Introduction, pp.1–4. Concerning the migration of Polish and Russian Jews fleeing Tsarist Russia, see William J. Fishman, *East End Radicals 1875–1914* (Duckworth, London, 1975), chapter two, 'A *Stetl* Called Whitechapel: the Social Milieu', pp.31–60. Fishman interestingly evokes the strength of anarchist and libertarian ideas among immigrant Russian Jews in London in the late nineteenth century; he concludes by suggesting that in the 1960s a 'new generation of altruistic youth, Jew and non-Jew', rescued from 'obscurity the story of East End Anarchism' (p.308).

7. Black, *J.F.S. The History of the Jews' Free School, London since 1732*, p.5.

8. Docker, *1492: The Poetics of Diaspora*, pp.153–4.

9. Docker, *1492: The Poetics of Diaspora*, pp.153–4.

10. Docker, *1492: The Poetics of Diaspora*, p.166.

11. Docker, *1492: The Poetics of Diaspora*, pp.155, 251.

12. Docker, *1492: The Poetics of Diaspora*, p.159.

13. Tony Kushner and Kenneth Lunn (eds), *The Politics of Marginality: Race, the Radical Right and Minorities in Twentieth Century Britain* (Frank Cass, London, 1990), p.x.

14. David Cesarini, 'An Embattled Minority: The Jews in Britain During the First World War', in Kushner and Lunn (eds), *The Politics of Marginality: Race, the Radical Right and Minorities in Twentieth Century Britain*, pp.61–3, 75.

15. Cesarini, 'An Embattled Minority...', pp.62, 66–7.

16. John Docker, 'Troubled reflections on my father', in Ann Curthoys and Joy Damousi (eds), *What Did You Do in the Cold War, Daddy? Personal stories from a troubled time* (NewSouth Books, Sydney, 2014), p.110.

17. Cesarini, 'An Embattled Minority...', pp.65, 67, 72.

18. Docker, *1492: The Poetics of Diaspora*, p.27.

19. Cesarini, 'An Embattled Minority...', p.74.

20. See Richard Mendelsohn, 'The Boer War, The Great War, and the Shaping of South African Jewish Loyalties', and Milton Shain, '"If It Was So Good, Why Was It So Bad?" The Memories and Realities of Antisemitism in South Africa Past and Present', in Milton Shain and Richard Mendelsohn (eds), *Memories*,

East End Jews, Anti-Semitism, Bloomsbury 39

Realities and Dreams: Aspects of the South African Jewish Experience (Jonathan Ball Publishers, Johannesburg and Cape Town, 2002), pp.54–9, 83–4.

21 Cesarini, 'An Embattled Minority...', p.75.
22 Rodinson, *Cult, Ghetto, and State: The Persistence of the Jewish Question*, p.182.
23 Docker, *1492: The Poetics of Diaspora*, pp.158–167.
24 John Docker, 'Are Settler-Colonies Inherently Genocidal? Re-reading Lemkin', in A. Dirk Moses (ed.), *Empire, Colony, Genocide: Conquest, Occupation, and Subaltern Resistance in World History* (Berghahn, New York, 2008), pp.81–101; see also my essay, 'A Plethora of Intentions: genocide, settler colonialism and historical consciousness in Australia and Britain', *The International Journal of Human Rights*, 2014.
25 Hermione Lee, *Virginia Woolf* (Vintage, New York, 1999), pp.336, 347–8.
26 Virginia Woolf, *The Years and Between the Acts* (Wordsworth Classics, London, 2012), pp.193–202.
27 Virginia Woolf, *The Years and Between the Acts*, pp.199–201.
28 Hermione Lee, *Virginia Woolf*, p.336.
29 Cf. John Docker, 'Genealogy and Derangement', in Vanessa Castejon, Anna Cole, Oliver Haag and Karen Hughes (eds), *Ngapartji Ngapartji In turn, in turn: Ego-histoire, Europe and Indigenous Australia* (ANU Press, Canberra, 2014), pp.180–186.

11

'One's inner tears of bitterness'

When I try to look objectively into my own mind, I detect feelings of loyalty to: my family; 'race' (Jews); my country, England in particular, and the British Empire generally; places with which I have been connected, such as Kensington and London (born and bred), counties, Middlesex and Sussex, where I have lived, Ceylon, Greece; school; Trinity and Cambridge.
Leonard Woolf, *Sowing: an autobiography of the years* 1880–1904[1]

My loyalty to Trinity and Cambridge is different from all my other loyalties. It is more intimate, profound, unalloyed. It is compounded of the spiritual, intellectual and physical inextricably mixed – the beauty of the colleges and Backs; the atmosphere of long years of history and great traditions and famous names; a profoundly civilized life; friendship and the [Apostles] society.

Leonard Woolf, *Sowing*[2]

[The narrator, on a visit to an Oxbridge college, signaled to her audience as Cambridge:] It was thus that I found myself walking with extreme rapidity across a grass plot. Instantly a man's figure rose to intercept me. Nor did I at first understand that the gesticulations of a curious-looking object, in a cut-away coat and evening shirt, were aimed at me. His face expressed horror and indignation. Instinct rather than reason came to my

help; he was a Beadle; I was a woman. This was their turf; there was the path. Only the Fellows and Scholars are allowed here; the gravel is the place for me. Such thoughts were the work of a moment... [Then the narrator desires to look something up in Trinity Library, Cambridge:] I was actually at the door which leads into the library itself. I must have opened it, for instantly there issued... a deprecating, silvery, kindly gentleman, who regretted in a low voice as he waved me back that ladies are only admitted to the library if accompanied by a Fellow of the College or furnished with a letter of introduction... Never will I ask for that hospitality again, I vowed as I descended the steps in anger.
Virginia Woolf, *A Room of One's Own*[3]

Here then was I... sitting on the banks of a river a week or two ago in fine October weather, lost in thought... On the further bank the willows wept in perpetual lamentation, their hair about their shoulders.
Virginia Woolf, *A Room of One's Own*[4]

Another thing I remember – but perhaps you've forgotten, or perhaps I dreamed it: when you were about 29, we were going for one of those long, wet Swinbrook walks when the rain seemed like one's inner tears of bitterness because of boredom & general futility of that life... And the certain conviction, in my mind, that one had to get away from that dread place at all costs.
Peter Y Sussman, ed., *Decca: The Letters of Jessica Mitford*, letter to Nancy Mitford[5]

My reading in genocide studies, and thinking how colonialism is imbricated with genocide, inclines me to ask harsh questions of Leonard Woolf. And I don't think the answers, or some of the answers, I work out will be favourable to an intellectual who after his lengthy period of imperial service in pre-First World War

Ceylon would present himself to the world for the rest of his life as a tireless anti-imperialist. Yet I also feel ambivalent because I think he revealed all sorts of ambivalencies. I feel puzzled by him, and can't resolve the puzzles. I'll pursue the harsh questions I have in mind and see what happens. One is prompted by the ideas in Hannah Arendt's 1944 essay, 'The Jew as Pariah: A hidden tradition', that I referred to in my Introduction, that Jews have been driven by opposing desires, on the one hand to be parvenus, hoping to assimilate to and be indistinguishable from their neighbours, impossible as that desire would be to fulfill, for they would always be in danger of being regarded and treated as pariahs; and on the other hand, to belong to a tradition she admires, what she calls conscious pariahs, intellectuals, novelists, poets and comedians like Heinrich Heine, Bernard Lazare, Charlie Chaplin, and Kafka, who chose that identity.[6] In Arendt's terms, was Leonard Woolf parvenu or conscious pariah? Was he a parvenu *and* a conscious pariah? Was he an outsider who wanted to be an insider, who yet knew he would always be perceived as an outsider? What were his opposing desires?

In the 1960s, in my ignorance as a comically intense teenage Leavisite, I assumed that 'Bloomsbury' was a phenomenon of London literary and intellectual life, and that image unthinkingly stayed with me through the decades. I knew nothing about the pre – World War I connection to Cambridge. Now, having read Leonard Woolf's autobiographies I see what an elementary error that was, since it's clear that Cambridge became a foundation of his life, identity, consciousness, along with his career in Ceylon, a career that was only possible because of his time at Cambridge: Cambridge as a systemic part of the functioning of the British empire. His family life, childhood, schooling and experience at Cambridge, and then career in Ceylon are evoked in the first two volumes, *Sowing* covering his early years up to 1904, and *Growing* encompassing Ceylon 1904 to 1911.

To explore Leonard Woolf's Jewishness will inevitably lead to intersecting histories, one of which, the story of Jessica Mitford, will give me great pleasure to talk about, since I have been a Jessica Mitford tragic for many years, and have never before had an opportunity to write about her. Jessica Mitford and Virginia Woolf have in common a lifelong anger concerning women and education.

Another intersecting history concerns Leonard Woolf's fervid admiration for longstanding imperial families like the Stephen and Strachey families, in particular the Stracheys operating in India, functionaries of empire at a time of catastrophe for the Indian people. This history will also twine back to the Irish Famine of the 1840s, and the question of a relationship, sickening as it is intimate, between genocide and the British doctrine of laissez-faire free trade.

Parvenu

What immediately struck me once I started reading *Sowing*, first published in 1960 when Leonard Woolf was 80, was how middle class his family were compared to my East End family. At least on the evidence of *Sowing*, Woolf is not interested in finding out if his family had ever lived in the East End, where most English Jews began their family histories. His family, it would appear from his narrative, launched their English life as somehow already middle class and prosperous. His father's father, he tells us, 'was a Jew, born in London in the year 1808'. (Where in London, I wonder, looking at this vague formulation.) His name was Benjamin Woolf and he was 'by occupation a tailor who had done extremely well in his trade', so that a London directory entry of 1835 finds him successively opening shops in Regent Street, Old Bond Street and Piccadilly. From two 'vast oil paintings' of his paternal grandparents that hung on the dining room wall during his childhood, Woolf could see that his grandfather Benjamin loomed over the family as a 'large, stern, blackhaired, and blackwhiskered, rabbinical Jew in a frock coat, his left hand pompously tucked into his waistcoat', while his wife, born Isabella Phillips, was the exact opposite, 'pretty, round cheeked, mild, and forgiving'. I immediately thought of my grandparents, wondering if such a contrast was characteristic of traditional Jewish families, and characteristic too of all traditional English family life? Leonard's mother's family, the de Jonghs, migrated from Amsterdam, and for generations the family lived in or near Tavistock Square.[7]

Leonard's grandfather had an 'inordinate admiration for education and he educated his sons out of their class'. (What of his daughters, I ask myself, though it doesn't appear to be a question Leonard Woolf considers.) Leonard's father Sidney Woolf is sent by his father to University College School and afterwards either to Kings College, London, or to University College in Gower Street, Leonard is not sure which. Extremely intelligent and with a quick, powerful mind, Sidney Woolf would become a barrister, bringing prosperity to his family (his wife bearing 10 children, nine living), but he suddenly died in 1892, at the age of 47. Facing financial disaster, the mother brings the children westwards to a 'much smaller house in Putney, into which she packed her nine children, a cook, a parlourmaid, and a housemaid', using her capital 'on educating her children' as a way of securing the family's future. Leonard Woolf says his mother's gamble came off because 'four of us got scholarships at St Paul's school and three of us scholarships at Cambridge'.[8] I presume this means that the boys received a very thorough education, and the girls in the family comparatively little education, though Woolf – again, curiously – does not mention his sisters here in relation to education.

At St Paul's School, Woolf negotiates and survives its standard hostility, among the masters as well as fellow students, towards anyone looking too intellectual, and its brutish emphasis on sport, by enjoying being competitive at various games and developing a 'carapace', an outer layer of protective personality. He devotes himself to studying Greek and Latin, and does well enough – they 'had turned me at St Paul's into a pretty good classical scholar' – to 'go up' to Trinity College, Cambridge. (I have to naively admit here, I don't understand the phrase that one 'goes up' to an Oxford or Cambridge college: what does the metaphor mean and why is it needed?) Having gone up to Trinity College, Woolf continues to focus on Greek and Latin.[9] So, it would appear, his education, following a narrowly specialised rather than a rounded liberal mode of learning, was all-male, from St Paul's to Trinity College, and Woolf does not stop to speculate if this was a good or bad thing for a person; indeed, he reveals every sign of believing it was an excellent thing for him to receive an all-male education, especially in a Cambridge college where he develops life-long friendships, both with the neighbouring young men in their rooms around him, most notably Lytton Strachey as well as Virginia Woolf's brother Thoby, and fellow members of the Apostles society, which included the philosopher G E Moore.

In terms of his own delight with his new friendships, we can say, in Hannah Arendt's terms in characterising the Jew as parvenu, that Leonard Woolf moulded his university sensibility so as to be indistinguishable from his neighbours. He became a Cambridge man, a Trinity man, expected to encourage and support each other (though Thoby died young from illness) in later life and, after a few short years as an undergraduate, make a brilliant contribution to British letters and intellectual life or go on to become a government minister, judge or bishop.[10] Yet what of brilliant women? Were women perceived to be a threat to the Cambridge male society?

Given my extremely low opinion of my own gender, I can think of few things more boring than sitting around in a male-only group (though, I have to confess, I was in the early 1970s in London part of a men-against-sexism group, as I record in a later chapter).

Virginia Woolf on Cambridge

I mentioned just before that it was curious that Leonard Woolf does not discuss his sisters' education or lack thereof, because of course he had been famously married to Virginia Stephen who, in *A Room of One's Own* (1929), releases her fury that upper-class women were either denied a formal education altogether, as was the case with Virginia and her sister Vanessa, or educated at poorly funded women's colleges at Cambridge such as Newnham and Girton, which she collectively refers to as Fernham. Having read *A Room Of One's Own* not long after reading *Sowing*, what strikes me is that *Sowing* – written as recollections and reflections in an apparently quiet, steady, matter-of-fact impartial judicial way eschewing passion – is a reply to *A Room of One's Own* in all sorts of insistent, unpleasant and even psychotic ways. I hope I can support this perhaps wild assertion. I'm haunted by knowing that Virginia Woolf has been so exhaustively written about that there's nothing new to say, or that I'll say things that others have already said and, being a novice reader just starting to explore her work, I should have known this. Anyway, I'll try to bring the two texts into a kind of joshing encounter in my own way, with my own concerns and concepts. The two texts could not be more different.

Let's speedily reprise *A Room of One's Own* in relation to Cambridge and gender. But first a thought about form and genre. As I read *A Room of One's Own* with delight at its playfulness, I thought maybe we can think of it as an ego histoire, decades before Pierre Nora conceived of ego histoire as a way of writing contemporary history. In my Introduction I referred to how for Pierre Nora in his 2001 essay 'L'ego-histoire est-elle possible?' ego histoire is characterised by intensity and passion; it wrestles with time as fragments; it moves sideways; it plays with genre; it is highly self-reflexive; it asks fundamental questions of the society the ego historian nominally belongs to. Surely, then, I will here exclaim, we can think of *A Room of One's Own* as an ego histoire!

Anyway, indulge me.

Nora's notions of ego histoire belong, I think, to a European modernist tradition whereby we can explore ideas and intellectual personalities through sensibility, embodied in cultural types or figures. We can see this tradition scintillatingly at work in Walter Benjamin, in essays such as 'Karl Kraus' published in 1931,[11] and it's also scintillatingly at work in *A Room of One's Own*, published only a couple of years before, in 1929, based on talks Virginia Woolf had given in 1928 at Newnham and Girton. These are interesting dates, if we recall that in the late 1920s Walter Benjamin and Mikhail Bakhtin published two of the twentieth century's most challenging, brilliant, speculative works, *The Origin of German Tragic Drama* and *Problems of Dostoevsky's Poetics*. Challenging, brilliant and speculative are terms of praise that might easily, I think we would all agree, apply to *A Room of One's Own*, in a period of intensified European-wide engaging in adventurous new thinking about literary form. In her biography, Hermione Lee refers to a letter of 1922 (to Janet Case) where Virginia Woolf, defining herself as a Georgian, dismisses the Edwardians, that older generation of British writers and thinkers such as Shaw, Wells, Galsworthy, the Webbs and Arnold Bennett, who dominated from 1895 to 1914: 'There's not a single living writer (English) I respect; so you see, I have to read the Russians... Orphans is what I say we are...'[12] To adapt the title of Dipesh Chakrabarty's well-known book *Provincialising Europe*, Virginia Woolf wished to provincialise England.

In *A Room of One's Own*, addressing the question of women and fiction, the narrator quickly, playfully, positions herself as an orphan in not being English, as if visiting English male colleges such as those in Cambridge from another world. As in an ego histoire, the narrator foregrounds the process of writing: 'I am going to develop in your presence as fully and freely as I can the train of thought which led me to this', this being her overall view that 'a woman must have money and a room of her own if she is to write fiction'. At every moment she will tell her audience how she comes to know what she knows: 'I give you my thoughts as they came to me'. The narrator confides that the 'I' who is speaking is 'only a convenient term for somebody who has no real being', and her audience can call her 'Mary Beton, Mary Seton, Mary Carmichael or by any name you please'.[13] A quick turning up of the endnote by editor Michèle Barrett tells us that the narrator is alerting her audience to a counter-history, the names of the three Marys alluding to the 'Ballad of Mary Hamilton', where in Scottish history Mary Beton, Mary Seton and Mary Carmichael were known to be, along with Mary Hamilton, companions to Mary Queen of Scots (1542–1587). The narrator of *A Room of One's Own* could also be reminding her listeners of the youthful Jane Austen's *The History of England*, written when Austen was 16 (and illustrated by her sister Cassandra, a curious foreshadowing of Virginia and Vanessa, writer and artist); Austen calling for a rewriting of usual English history that celebrates the Tudors and expressing outrage at Elizabeth I for the execution of her cousin, Mary Queen of Scots.

I recall that Ann and I had some years ago heard a very interesting and entertaining talk at the State Library of New South Wales by our friend, Mary Spongberg, the feminist historian and historiographer, on Mary Queen of Scots and Jane Austen's 1791 *The History of England*. Also, in our *Is History Fiction?*, Ann and I refer to Mary Spongberg's argument, which we very much agree with, in her *Writing Women's History since the Renaissance* (2002), that women's historical writing has kept alive a Herodotean stream of historical writing which evokes a plethora of histories – of the everyday, genealogy and family history, the history of those marginal to power, personal histories, scandalous history.[14] In *Is History Fiction?* and in a more recent essay, Ann and I suggest that there are two major streams of Western historical writing descending from antiquity, the Herodotean and the Thucydidean. The Herodotean indicates for us, as it does for Mary Spongberg, historical writing that is open and capacious, exploring truth through the narration of many stories, fables and parables, and engaging with histories that are social, cultural, religious, gendered, sexual and erotic, as well as diplomatic, political, and military. By contrast, Thucydidean historical writing homes in on the diplomatic, political and military, to states and the interaction of states, a focus whereby women rarely figure; it offers a single authoritative account in a magisterial tone.[15] I place *A Room of One's Own* in the Herodotean stream, and Leonard Woolf's *Sowing*, as well as his other autobiographical volumes, in the Thucydidean.

I only recently read Jane Austen's history, when after Ann's father died soon after Christmas 2014, we had the melancholy task of cleaning out the family house in beachside Manly in Sydney, and came across what was evidently Ann's mother Barbara's copy of *The History of England* in a lovely facsimile edition. I'll quote from an inspired passage on Elizabeth, who has just been referred to as 'that disgrace to humanity, that pest of society'.[16]

> It was the peculiar Misfortune of this Woman [Elizabeth] to have bad Ministers – Since wicked as she herself was, she could not have committed such extensive mischief, had not these vile & abandoned Men connived at, & encouraged her in her Crimes. I know that it has by many people been asserted & believed that Lord Burleigh, Sir Francis Walsingham, & the rest of those who filled the chief Offices of State were deserving, experienced, & able Ministers. But oh! How blinded such Writers & Readers must be to true Merit, to Merit despised, neglected & defamed, if they can persist in such opinions when they reflect that these Men, these boasted Men were such Scandals to their Country & their Sex as to allow & assist their Queen in confining for the space

of nineteen years, a *Woman* who if the claims of Relationship & Merit were of no avail, yet as a Queen & as one who condescended to place confidence in her, had every reason to expect assistance & protection; and at length in allowing Elizabeth to bring this amiable Woman to an untimely, unmerited, and scandalous Death… She was executed in the Great Hall at Fotheringay Castle (sacred Place!) on Wednesday the 8th of February – 1585 – to the everlasting Reproach of Elizabeth, her Ministers, and of England in general.[17]

Like Jane Austen in *The History of England*, the narrator of *A Room of One's Own*, to be identified as Scottish is to be free to cast a witheringly irreverent gaze over English institutions like Cambridge where the sons in middle – and upper-class families have for many generations been sent, scandalously deploying family resources that could have been used to also send their daughters to such institutions. The narrator thinks of the rivers of gold that for centuries have flowed into the male colleges; she creates a sumptuous scene, a luncheon party that lasts for hours on a tranquil October day, before them sole in cream, partridges, sauces and salads, succulent sprouts, a roast, a cake, and white and red wine, to be enjoyed at the male Cambridge college she has been invited to. Such leisured repast would, she surmises, enable the exercise of 'rational intercourse' and enjoyment of 'friendships' for the male scholars who are usually in attendance there. The narrator, however, suddenly notices an outsider at the scene, an outsider she perhaps wistfully relates to, 'a cat without a tail', a Manx, 'truncated' and a 'little absurd', padding softly across the college quadrangle. Later in the afternoon, she contrasts the wealth of the male college with the poverty and meagre fare of the female college she makes her way to for dinner, which consists of a 'plain gravy soup', beef with greens and potatoes, followed by prunes and custard, biscuits and cheese, accompanied not by wine but water from a jug. 'One cannot', she reflects, 'think well, sleep well, if one has not dined well.'[18]

Implicitly, *A Room of One's Own* is being highly critical of an England which is 'under the rule of a patriarchy', to which Virginia Woolf's father Leslie Stephen the well-known Victorian biographer belonged, that enforces on upper-class families a centuries-long tradition discriminating against daughters, however intelligent and talented. 'Let us suppose', writes the narrator, 'that a father from the highest motives did not wish his daughter to leave home and become writer, painter or scholar'.[19] I was struck by this sharp-edged sentence, so clearly referring to the situation of the Stephen sisters, kept without formal education at home while their brothers, first Thoby and then Adrian, were sent to Trinity college.

Perhaps the narrator was alluding as well to the family situation of Jane Austen, about how Jane and Cassandra were kept at home while their brother James was given a university education. At any rate, *A Room of One's Own* often refers warmly to Jane Austen and her novels, not least *Pride and Prejudice*.[20]

A Note on Jessica Mitford

A Room of One's Own invokes an ongoing contemporary experience for upper-class women, resonating with the plight of the Mitford sisters, not only Jessica but Nancy, Diana, Unity and Debo. The intelligent and talented, if politically divergent, Mitford sisters never received any schooling, in contrast to their brother Tom, the only son. Virginia Woolf must also have spent time thinking about the Mitfords, in any case, in the opening paragraph of *A Room of One's Own* the narrator hopes she can produce 'some witticisms if possible about Miss Mitford', presumably a glance towards Nancy Mitford's novels.[21]

In the opening chapter of Jessica Mitford's *Hons and Rebels*, first published in 1960, the same year *Sowing* came out, we read:

'If the fight for equal education for women raged somewhere as a part of the twentieth-century struggle for equal rights, no hint of these controversies reached us at Swinbrook. Tom, of course, had been sent away to school at the age of eight, and thence to Eton; but my mother felt that school for girls was unnecessary, probably harmful, and certainly too expensive'.[22] Jessica saying that her mother thought educating her girls was 'too expensive' reminds us of the bitter reproach in *A Room of One's Own* that the boys in upper-class families were financed to the deprivation of daughters.[23] Heroically, at the age of 19, Jessica ran away from female imprisonment in the family home of Swinbrook with her cousin Esmond Romilly, Churchill's nephew, staying in France near the Spanish border in order to try and assist in any way they could the republicans in the Spanish Civil War, returning to London where their baby died, and then travelling to the United States where they led a picaresque life and moved in liberal intellectual circles.

Through all her witty, self-parodying, often hilarious stories told in *Hons and Rebels* and in its sequel *A Fine Old Conflict* (1977), Jessica revealed a lifelong anger and anguish concerning education. In *A Fine Old Conflict*, in a chapter 'Intermission: Happy Families', Jessica talks of the visit her mother, known to her daughters as Muv, made to Oakland to stay with Jessica and her family after World War II. In the car from the airport, in the awkward silence of meeting again after so many years, Jessica's daughter Dinky suddenly speaks up, 'Granny Muv, when are you going to scold Decca for running away?' They all laughed, and the visit was a great success, with Jessica becoming fond of her mother: 'It was during this visit that she began to exhibit that impartial loyalty to all her children that was to become a salient characteristic of her old age'. In this chapter, Jessica recalls a time in 1971 when she exchanged letters with Nancy reflecting on their respective relationships with their mother, including one letter where Jessica had written about 'my unsuccessful attempt to get

Muv to let me attend' grammar school science courses.[24]

In *Decca: The Letters of Jessica Mitford* (2006) Jessica, in a letter to Nancy, in referring to this episode reveals far more anger than she admits to in *A Fine Old Conflict*:

> The thing that absolutely burned into my soul was the business of not being allowed to go to school. So much so that when she came here when Dinky was 7, the subject came up and I found myself literally fighting back tears of rage. Do admit it was maddening. One thing I specially remember: when I was about 11, I wanted to be a scientist… because I had just read The Stars in Their Courses by Sir James Jeans. So, noting I should have to go to college in that case, I biked to Burford and rather shudderingly went to see the headmaster of the Grammar School. He said I could be admitted to the grammar school (which had a scientific laboratory, that's why I wanted to go) if I could pass a fairly easy exam., which I cld. learn to do by reading a list of books he gave me. I was v. excited over this, rushed home to ask Muv if I could get the books, take the exam., and bike to school each day. A cold NO was the only answer, no reason given. After that lessons with the [governess] seemed totally pointless, although I admit I could have learned far more than I did.[25]

It's of interest to note of this letter that Jessica was born in 1917, with the traumatic refusal by her mother of this opportunity for education occurring when she was 11, that is, 1928 or 1929, at the time Virginia Woolf was addressing, joking with, teasing, challenging, revealing anger and anguish to, the young students of Newnham and Girton, and then transforming her talks into *A Room of One's Own*. (Hermione Lee in her biography records that in 1930 Virginia Woolf was reading with some fascination James Jeans' *The Universe Around Us*.)[26]

A Room of One's Own versus *Sowing*: Virginia contra Leonard

In the contestation I'm creating, there are, I think, multiplying contrasts. Leonard Woolf's text is uniformly celebratory of Cambridge as we can see from my second epigraph, his 'unalloyed' loyalty insisting on the historical achievements of its male traditions, which are beyond questioning and criticism. Woolf's writing thereby denies itself irreverence and parody and self-parody, qualities, one might venture, alien to the parvenu in history, mired in an anxiety to belong. Unsurprisingly, it is dour. Leonard Woolf's vision of the world in this as in the other volumes of his autobiography is so to say Thucydidean, offering a single authoritative account in a magisterial tone.[27]

By immediate contrast with Leonard Woolf's (apparently) straightforward writing, lifeless on the page, Virginia Woolf's writing, as we all know, increases its fame decade by decade by its liveliness, especially gained, I rather perversely think, by its exuberant deployment of the semi-colon; by quick use the narrator in the one sentence can write in a syncopated way (here calling to mind an interest of Edward Said), changing direction, reversing perspective, expressing a sudden new thought; and so, maybe, the narrator's enjoyment of the semi-colon draws on a deep well of carnivalesque, of turning perceptions inside out and upside down; as in *kunstchaos*, the art of chaos as philosophical technique.[28] (Feeling uneasy at this sentence, I have just googled Virginia Woolf and use of the semi-colon, and quickly realise that I'm very much a Johnny-come-lately in this much noticed and much parodied aspect of her writing. So, my apologies.)

In *A Room of One's Own* the narrator calls for the rewriting of history as the reverse of the Thucydidean, where men are the key actors. Nevertheless, the narrator reflects that while on a visit to the Reading Room of the British Museum she was surprised to observe that male historians not only busy themselves talking about war, politics and diplomacy, in the Thucydidean mode.

They also produce a large literature pointing out and attempting to explain at length the apparent inferiority of the female sex, revealing a strange 'anger' while doing so. 'How to explain', she idly muses, 'the anger of the professors?', even if it is an 'anger disguised and complex, not anger simple and open'. Why, she ponders, if 'England is under the rule of a patriarchy', if men enjoy so much power, hold so many positions and offices, do they feel it necessary to stress so repetitively women's inferiority? Why are they so agitated? Then the narrator turns over a new thought, that the male professor is 'concerned not with their inferiority, but with his own superiority'; the professor is protecting 'a jewel to him of the rarest price', the 'self-confidence' that flows from his 'innate superiority'. The possible quizzical gaze of women threatens 'his power to believe in himself'.[29]

At this point in *A Room of One's Own* the narrator mischievously notes that these speculations are her 'contributions to the dangerous and fascinating subject of the psychology of the other sex'.[30] Yet her subtle phrase about male 'anger disguised and complex, not anger simple and open' in relation to women, is uncannily prescient. In my view, it anticipates the narrative strategy of Leonard Woolf's *Sowing*, which defends, yet indirectly, as in allegory, Cambridge men's 'innate superiority' and 'self-confidence' (to use again to the narrator's words in *A Room of One's Own*) against female irreverence, especially its free-wheeling carnivalesque mocking of the power and importance that men arrogate to themselves. However, the anger of the writer of *Sowing* is not so indirect that the reader can't register his almost Beadle-like 'horror and indignation' at women for trespassing against the male desire to be superior.

In *Sowing* there are two such moments of what I'll call textual violence that stand out from the supposedly smooth surface of its rational presentation. One is a moment of horror and indignation, the other a more muted but nonetheless palpable flash of anger. Both moments involve images associating women with animals. The first occurs not long after Leonard Woolf begins the section of the book on Cambridge, when 'I went up to' Trinity College in October 1899. Woolf describes how Henry James' late novels like *The Sacred Fount*, *The Wings of the Dove* and *The Golden Bowl* in their elusiveness and nuance entranced and almost hypnotised him and his fellow Trinity friends Lytton Strachey and Saxon Sydney-Turner. He then says that the 'tremendous effect of Henry James's later novels upon us at Cambridge' is shown by a conversation between G, H and F, three Fellows of Trinity with whom he and Saxon were acquainted; they played cricket with them with a walking-stick and tennis ball in their rooms. Woolf tells us that during these years he used sometimes to 'write down', immediately after they had occurred, 'conversations or scraps of conversation which had seemed to me significant or amusing'. Woolf entitles the record of the conversation between the three Fellows 'The Cat, the Worms, and the Rats', which at first concerns their cat which is ill, then moves on to an allegorical story of extreme misogyny.[31]

With great relish, transmuted into a kind of faux-apologetic ruefulness at what they are witnessing, F relates a story about biking in France with a friend in the Rhone valley during vacation time and coming across 'the most repulsive sight' they had ever seen. At a fair in a small village they watch 'Madame Boug, the champion rat catcher', 'a tall, big woman and stark naked except for a tightly fitting red pair of drawers', catching rats in a pit with her teeth.

> ... when there were only three left, she worked them up into a corner and as she was killing one another seized her ear, and I saw another leap up from under her breast right over her neck. I daresay they bit her in the breast too, but it was really so repulsive, you know, that we made off feeling quite sick.[32]

F the Cambridge man concludes his story by observing that the rat catcher was a 'big-mouthed woman, quite repulsive, you know'. Woolf tells his readers – surely, given this anecdote, assumed by him to be male – that only recently he had found this transcribed story of a female monster in an old notebook.[33] Why does Leonard Woolf place this story – this aggressive textual act – near the beginning of the Cambridge section of *Sowing*, a story which in its immense crudity has nothing whatsoever in it of the late manner Henry James that Woolf says he and his friends so breathlessly admired? The invocation here of the late James is more like a feint. Perhaps any adequate explanation would have to refer Woolf to psychoanalysis; it reminds me of a scene in *Fawlty Towers* where a psychologist, staying at the hotel and noticing the John Cleese character in a bizarrely contorted pose, drily comments that a whole conference could be held to try and explain him.

The rat catcher anecdote serves, I think, as a frame story for the Cambridge section of *Sowing*, suggesting that in their essence women are degraded and animalistic, foreign to mind and reason.

The second moment of textual violence is famous, when towards the end of the Cambridge section Woolf comments on a visit by the Stephen sisters to Trinity in 1901 to visit their brother Thoby, a visit which makes Woolf nervous and uneasy. It was the first time he had encountered the sisters: Vanessa was then 21 or 22, while Virginia was 18 or 19. Woolf finds them 'just as formidable and alarming' as their father Leslie Stephen, who he'd already met. The two young women 'in white dresses and large hats, with parasols in their hands' are accompanied by their cousin, Miss Katherine Stephen, the Principal of Newnham, there in a kind of supervisory role, 'for in 1901 a respectable female sister was not allowed to see her male brother in his rooms in a male college except in the presence of a chaperone'. Woolf regards Katherine Stephen as 'distinguished, formidable, and rather alarming'.[34]

With women present in his college, Woolf suddenly senses

some kind of danger. Sitting there in Thoby's 'rooms', Vanessa and Virginia were 'silent' and appeared 'demure'. He finds himself thinking of a horse, apparently placid, who turns out to be the reverse, for the 'eye of this quiet beast' has a 'look which warns you to be very, very careful'. So too, says Woolf, at the 'back of the two Miss Stephen's eyes' could be detected a look which would have 'warned him to be cautious, a look which belied the demureness, a look of great intelligence, hypercritical, sarcastic, satirical'.[35] Leonard Woolf, however, after this remarkable invocation of the dangers of riding a deceptively 'quiet beast', doesn't tell the reader what the two young women's eyes, as they sat in the Trinity college rooms, were being skeptical towards, except it be Cambridge itself, for Woolf would have known that 'a look of great intelligence, hypercritical, sarcastic, satirical' is a very good characterisation of the gaze the narrator of *A Room of One's Own* cast over Cambridge some decades before. (He would have had to have known it, since *A Room of One's Own* was published by their Hogarth Press.)

Indeed, much of the Cambridge section of *Sowing* is I think an anxious repudiation of many of the observations of Cambridge, and the wider male intellectual world it sustains, in *A Room of One's Own*. For example, there is a silent tussle between the two texts concerning Virginia and Vanessa's father Sir Leslie Stephen (1832–1904). In *A Room of One's Own*, the narrator has that jagged shard of a sentence, thinking about a father from the 'highest motives' who does not wish his daughters to leave home to pursue art, writing, education, where the reference to 'highest motives' must be ironic, for what does Sir Leslie Stephen's action suggest except that he did not want to be seen to break with the inherited gender patterns of the English upper middle class and aristocracy. Conformity to class overrode his responsibility to his daughters' intelligence and creativity (just as Jessica Mitford's parents also could not break with such conformity in relation to their daughters). Further on in *A Room of One's Own*, the narrator is also surely pointedly criticising her father as a biographer, without naming him, when she writes that usual biographies are 'too much about great men'.[36] In *Sowing*, however, Leonard Woolf openly chides Virginia and Vanessa who in his view, in their exasperation with their father, 'exaggerated his exactingness and sentimentality and, in memory, were habitually rather unfair to him owing to a complicated variety of the Oedipus complex'.[37] Reference to an arcane corner of the Oedipus complex looks like another feint, a diversion for the unwary reader: *A Room of One's Own* had made it utterly clear why daughters of the upper class could be angry with their fathers for denying them school and university and professional careers. For the parvenu, however, looking upwards, upper-class fathers were to be regarded with the highest respect.

The parvenu has an exaggerated admiration for high positions and imperial honours, in Leonard Woolf's case especially for ex-Cambridge men who in later life have been knighted (like Sir Leslie Stephen, who had been at Trinity), or for a knight who has become a lord. In *Sowing* Leonard Woolf defends Sir Leslie Stephen against his daughters with glowing praise for him. On meeting Sir Leslie, some three years before he died in 1904, on a visit to see his son Thoby, Woolf gushes: 'He was one of those bearded and beautiful Victorian old gentlemen of exquisite gentility and physical and mental distinction on whose face the sorrows of all the world had traced the indelible lines of suffering nobility'. He emphasises that Sir Leslie Stephen was 'immensely distinguished' as a 'historian of ideas, literary critic, biographer, and the first editor of the *Dictionary of National Biography*', and that Stephen had been praised by 'Mr Noel Annan, Provost of King's College, Cambridge'.[38]

Throughout *Sowing*, Leonard Woolf the parvenu reveres titled *men* he has known. Mentioning a name, he will almost inevitably add what title the *man* had. At his school before Cambridge he was elected to a small debating society, which he is fairly sure, he adds in a footnote, included 'S. P. Vivian, who eventually became a distinguished civil servant, Registrar-General, with a knighthood.' He remembers in another footnote the 'late Sydney Waterlow', a 'brilliant classical scholar' at Trinity, who was 'later in the Diplomatic Service', his last post as Minister in Athens. He mentions that at the turn of the century three Cambridge philosophers, A N Whitehead, Bertrand Russell and G E Moore were each 'awarded the highest and rarest of official honours, the Order of Merit'. And so it goes embarrassingly on. In other helpful footnotes we learn of friends and followers of G E Moore such as Sir Ralph Wedgwood, a contemporary of Moore's at Trinity, who became Chief General Manager of London and North-Eastern Railway from 1923 to 1939, in 1924 being 'created Baronet'; or Sir Edward Marsh, also at Trinity with Moore, who was for many years Private Secretary to Winston Churchill. There was also a friend at Cambridge, a Scottish aristocrat called Leopold Colin Henry Douglas Campbell, who later became Lord Blythswood.[39]

A Stephen in Sydney

Given Leonard Woolf's admiration for the Stephen family, it's of interest to recall that a Sir Alfred Stephen, related to Vanessa and Virginia, makes an unsavoury appearance in a moment of Australian colonial history; Australian, yet also relating to the ceaseless circulation of people across the British empire and intersecting with the worldwide life of seafarers, ships' cooks and café chefs.

The year is 1879, the scene is Sydney and the NSW country town of Mudgee, and Sir Alfred Stephen is the main judicial actor, as attorney general and also Lieutenant-Governor of the colony of New South Wales, the representative of Queen Victoria in one of her antipodean dominions, thieved from its Indigenous peoples.

For months, there had been large demonstrations against the sentence of hanging for rapes committed in Sydney by two brothers, the Sodwalls, young white men, and in Mudgee by a young Aboriginal man, Alfred. During this time, Sir Alfred Stephen was the target of much public anger, which intensified as the date for the hangings, June 1879, neared.

Among those who protested were members of the Sheba Club, which I knew of because Ann in conversation said she had heard a reference to it at a history seminar and was trying to find out more because it sounded so interesting. An article, 'The Condemned Criminals', in the *Sydney Morning Herald* of Tuesday 10 June 1879, noted that resolutions at protest meetings at the Domain in Sydney, as well as other resolutions from the coastal city of Newcastle and inland towns such as Yass, Richmond, Forbes and Hill End, and as well a petition from the Sheba Club, were presented to Sir Alfred Stephen as Lieutenant-Governor and hence in a position to commute sentences held to be too severe. However, deputations asking for a reprieve or at least delay of the death sentences were, in the view of those protesting, met with highhandedness and cold reproof; they felt, said the *Herald*, grossly insulted.

The *Newcastle Morning Herald and Miners' Advocate*, in an article headed 'The Condemned Criminals – Meeting of Coloured Men', on Wednesday 11 June 1879, reported on a meeting of the Sheba Club in connection with the 'proposed execution' of Alfred, that was to be carried out on the following Tuesday. The meeting, the newspaper told its readers, well attended at short notice, was held on the previous Saturday night at the Sheba Club's rooms, on the corner of George and Park Streets in central Sydney. (A corner I have passed many times in my Sydney life!) Present were 'men of colour from every clime, tall, stalwart, intelligent fellows, quiet and respectful in demeanour, but evidently keenly feeling some great trouble'. The proceedings began with 'one of the most touching and earnest prayers that ever rose from the heart of man', in the hope that God would 'soften the heart of the Lieutenant-Governor'.

A Mr Flowers proposed that a petition be drawn up by the meeting to present to the Lieutenant-Governor, for it was the fitting duty of the Sheba Club to attempt to save the lives of the three condemned youths; of Alfred he said that he was an 'ignorant young man, who certainly had not the advantage of a mother or a schoolmaster to instruct him in the right'. A Mr A White seconded the proposal to draw up a petition; he urged that the 'brightest jewel in the Crown of England was mercy' and there was 'no more merciful woman in the world than the Queen of England'; by showing mercy, Sir Alfred Stephen could add lustre to Queen Victoria's reputation in this regard. A Mr Burrowes moved the next resolution, to the effect that members of the Sheba Club and 'all the coloured men of the city wait as a deputation on the Governor to present to him the petition of mercy'; he pointed out that the 'law was not nearly so stringent in England as in this colony, and far worse cases than those of the white youths and the aboriginal had obtained a reprieve from the Queen'. A Mr Jones said that 'though men of colour, they lacked not patriotism', indeed they were the 'readiest, as was recently proved, to take up the sword and defend the flag and dominion of Great Britain'. (I'm not sure, but the speaker here could be referring to the Second Anglo-Afghan War begun in 1878 when British troops invaded Afghanistan.) It should, Mr Jones continued, be remembered that 'if Victoria was Queen of the whites, she was Empress of the blacks, the ruler over a vast colored people rapidly advancing in the arts and sciences'; he suggested that 'Sir Alfred ought to strive to imitate his noble Queen, from whom mercy flowed like a river'.

The Newcastle Advocate closed its report by reproducing the words of the petition that the Sheba Club would present to Sir

Alfred on the Monday, hoping to stay the proposed execution:

> His Excellency Sir Alfred Stephen, C.B., K.C.M.G., &c, &c, Lieutenant-Governor of the colony of New South Wales.
>
> May it please your Excellency, – We, the coloured citizens of Sydney, humbly approach your Excellency, petitioning for a commutation of the sentence of death passed upon Alfred, one of the aboriginals of this colony. We beseech your Excellency to grant a reprieve for one week, if for no more, in order that the case may be reconsidered, and that if your Excellency decides to commute the sentences of the boys in Bathurst Gaol, the same clemency may be extended to our black fellow countryman. We desire to respectfully remind your Executive that our gracious Sovereign, who is the fountain of mercy, is Empress of many millions of dark men, to whom she has ever extended her protection, and to whom she has meted out equal justice. We do not wish to say a word in mitigation of the crime of which the aboriginal was guilty, but we urge his gross ignorance of the laws of God and man, and his drunkenness, produced by the machinations of others, as fair grounds for your Excellency to temper justice with mercy – even to a coloured man. And your petitioners will ever pray.

During 1879 the daily *Evening News* was prominent in protesting the proposed hangings. One of its journalists was John Haynes, who in 1880 with Jules François Archibald launched the *Bulletin*, soon to achieve lasting fame for its wit and irreverence.

A quarter of a century later, in 1905, Haynes wrote a whimsical, chatty essay, 'Early "Bulletin" Memoirs', for another publication, where he recalled the anti-hanging protests of 1879, which included deputations to see Sir Alfred Stephen to ask for mercy for the prisoners, and also a petition from the Sheba Club, which consisted in memory of 'males and females, town cooks and ships' cooks and stewards, etc'. Haynes attended one of the protest meetings at the Club. He also recalls the large demonstration held the 'night before the executions, all three of which were fixed for the same day'. At the demonstration, torches were held and big coffins carried, 'lit up from the inside and bearing appropriate mottoes, such as "Mercy", "Spare the Youths", and "White Man, be Merciful to the Black Man"'. With the Sheba Club as part of the demonstration, he jokes that on that evening 'there was not a restaurant that did not miss its black cook, and not a galley on Sydney Harbour but was stuck up with cold meats'. Haynes, as a journalist working for the *Evening News*, was permitted to accompany the Sheba Club representatives when they met with Sir Alfred Stephen in order to present their petition; also there, waiting on Stephen, was a white deputation. As Hayne remembers it, employing some long-ago argot, 'Sir Alfred Stephen listened to the white deputation all right, but when the black cloud appeared (one of them being his own cook) he spasmed some'. Stephen accepted the petition from the Sheba Club deputation and then dismissed them from his sight as quickly as he could.

The next day the two white men were saved from the gallows, but the black man was hanged.

From 1880, with Haynes and Archibald in charge, the *Bulletin* took up and gave focus to the increasing dislike in the colony for what the magazine satirically referred to as 'Botany Bay Justice', especially the brutality and cruelty of hanging that the British had instituted in Australia from its inception in 1788, and which was still, in their view scandalously, being carried out a century later.

In my 1991 book, *The Nervous Nineties: Australian Cultural Life in the 1890s*, I had enjoyed myself evoking the *Bulletin*'s insouciance towards Hanging Judges like Sir Alfred Stephens, notorious for being despotic and tyrannical; a judge who in their view actively sought to hang human beings whenever the opportunity arose.[40]

The Stracheys in India

In *Sowing* it is Lytton Strachey's family who 'stand out' in Leonard Woolf's memory as the 'most remarkable family I have ever known', for they, with the Stephen family, were part of the 'intellectual aristocracy' who in the nineteenth century formed a 'powerful section of the ruling class in Britain'. The Strachey 'male members of the British aristocracy of intellect' became 'generals, admirals, editors, judges', retiring with a 'K.C.S.I. or K.C.M.G. after distinguished careers in the Indian or Colonial Civil Services'. Lytton's father was 'Lieutenant-General Sir Richard Strachey, who, like his two brothers had had an extraordinarily brilliant career in India'. Lytton's mother, we learn, came like his father from a 'distinguished Anglo-Indian family'. For three years running, Leonard, besotted, stays with the Strachey family in country houses they've leased for the summer.[41]

What, I think, does this mean, that in 1960 the aged anti-imperialist Leonard Woolf writes with fervent admiration of 'distinguished careers in the Indian or Colonial Civil Services' including Lytton's father Lieutenant-General Sir Richard Strachey, who like his two brothers, Lytton's uncles, had 'an extraordinarily brilliant career in India'? In whose eyes, I think to myself, were the Stracheys in India held to be distinguished and brilliant?

Again, I sense that in *Sowing* Leonard Woolf is fashioning an indirect riposte to *A Room of One's Own*, where the narrator reflects that men – she is talking about white British men – can exercise their desire for self-confidence by 'feeling that one has some innate superiority' over other people: 'Hence the enormous importance to a patriarch who has to conquer, who has to rule, of feeling that great numbers of people, half the human race indeed, are by nature inferior to himself.'[42]

Such irreverent thinking about the psychopathology of a British imperial desire to rule is also present in the gaze

– extremely intelligent, hypercritical, sarcastic, satirical – that the American Marxist historian Mike Davis turns on the British in India in his 2001 book *Late Victorian Holocausts: El Niño Famines and the Making of the Third World*, a striking intervention in the field of world history. In our 2010 edition of *Is History Fiction?* Ann and I welcome Janet Abu-Lughod's idea that idiosyncrasy, meaning the personal voice of the historian, is important in the writing of world history; idiosyncrasy, she feels, is a major source of new vision, for it is people at the edge of a discipline who have inspired 'many of the major transformations in how we think about the world'.[43] As a Marxist in the US, Mike Davis saw the world from a marginal position; as an American, he observed what the British historically did in India with a kind of caustic wonder. *Late Victorian Holocausts* reminds us what Indian commentators and historians, as well as English critical voices, in the late nineteenth century well knew, that through catastrophic economic and political mismanagement the British wrought upon India famines in which millions of Indians died.[44] These were disasters of mass death in which the Strachey brothers were directly implicated, part of the ruling elite associated with the egregious Lord Lytton, viceroy of India between 1876 and 1880. Let's see what Davis's book says about this crew, both in the written text and in displaying photos taken and drawings made at the time, which, Davis says, he intends as 'accusations not illustrations'.[45]

In *Late Victorian Holocausts*, Lord Lytton emerges as a clown of history, afflicted with what the narrator in *A Room of One's Own* diagnoses as male psychosis, the white patriarch exercising his desire for self-confidence by 'feeling that one has some innate superiority' to be exhibited through conquest and rule over great numbers of colonised people, stressing to them their inferiority to himself. Lord Lytton was, in this sense, a needy white patriarch. Ominously, as Davis tells us, he was Queen Victoria's favourite poet, though his verses were denounced for plagiarism by both

Swinburne and his own father, Bulwer-Lytton.[46] (In *Sowing* Woolf makes what he himself refers to as an embarrassing admission, given the disdain of later generations, that he and his early twentieth-century Cambridge circle, of Lytton Strachey, Saxon Sydney-Turner, Thoby Stephen, Clive Bell and himself, very much admired Swinburne and would chant his verses in the cloisters of their beloved Trinity.)[47] Lytton also admitted to Disraeli that prior to his appointment as viceroy he was completely ignorant of every fact and question concerning India.[48] As viceroy, Lytton, this utterly ignorant imperial ruler armed only with the calculus of free trade, would prove ridiculous in the excess of his determined display of superiority, in dress, decorations, pomp, theatricality and hunger for a vanity war to make his name stand out in history, with the omnipresent Stracheys always there to assist plots and plans.

Early in the book, in the opening chapter 'Victoria's Ghosts', Davis has placed two wildly contrasting visual presentations, the one absurd, the other distressing. The first is a photo, with the satirical caption 'The Poet as Viceroy: Lytton in Calcutta, 1877'. At its centre of vision, we see Lord Lytton sprawled on a large chair crowded with regal insignia as if a throne, one shoe on a footrest, legs apart, a long thin penis-surrogate stick extending from the footrest to near his groin as his sceptre of rule, in full regalia extravagant with decorations, a crown near his head, behind him three Indian attendants, two of them holding upright phallus-like ornamental cudgels. Several pages on, Davis has placed a drawing, 'A Family in the Deccan, 1877', of an Indian family, so starved that they are in a skeletal condition, indeed, the page before, Davis had observed that in 1877, apart from the millions who had already died, millions more had reached the 'stage of acute malnutrition, characterized by hunger edema and anemia, that modern health workers call skeletonization'. In the paperback edition of *Late Victorian Holocausts* I am reading, the photo and the drawing are juxtaposed on the cover, with the figures of the starving famine victims resonating with the book's title.[49]

Clowns of history can prove violently destructive on a massive scale. In future generations, Davis tells us, Lord Lytton would be remembered in India as its Nero. While millions of people in southern and central India were dying from hunger, starvation, plague and disease, a singularly uncaring Lord Lytton was absorbed in organising a huge Imperial Assemblage in Delhi to acclaim his poetry promoter Queen Victoria, from 1877 the Empress of India. The climax of the event was a week-long feast for 68,000 officials and maharajas, held to be the largest and most expensive meal in history. It has been estimated, Davis says, that during Lytton's spectacular *durbar*, 100,000 Indian people starved to death in Madras and Mysore. Lytton next turned his attention to the prospect and spectacle of war, hoping to distinguish himself in a great conquest by, as Davis phrases it, 'fomenting war with the blameless Sher Ali, the Emir of Afghanistan'. Here a Strachey comes into view: 'Lytton's warrant, as he was constantly reminded by his chief budgetary adviser, Sir John Strachey, was to ensure that Indian, not English, taxpayers paid the costs of what Radical critics later denounced as a "war of deliberately planned aggression"'.[50]

Sir John Strachey as minister of finance was always there for Lytton to assist in forcing onto Indian society free trade practices, which the British regarded as sacrosanct, as they had, Davis reflects, in Ireland during the potato famine 30 years before.[51] More on Ireland in just a moment. Davis sees laissez faire as ruinous in its effects in a time of drought and famine, indeed, laissez faire directly intensified the famines that killed millions of people. In the eighteenth century, the Moguls had provide relief in times of distress; villages and households, part of intricate webs of mutual obligation, would store grain against the threat of drought; but the peasants could not continue this traditional practice under the British free-trade rule of domination by the market in the latter part of the nineteenth century. As Davis notes, the imposition of modern markets based on the cash nexus 'accelerated rather than relieved the famine', because as grain during times of drought became ever scarcer, prices for grain soared out of the reach of the Indian poor, who consequently began starving to death in harrowing scenes that left many observers appalled and angry, but which left Lord Lytton, 'the laissez faire fanatic', and one presumes his diligent assistants the Strachey brothers, unmoved and indifferent, their only concern to try to wring taxes out of the dying peasants in order, they hoped secretly, to pay for a war in Afghanistan. Lytton, Davis writes, issued strict orders that regulation of the price of grain during the famine years should not be attempted, for such would be an unwarrantable interference in the free play of the market. Furthermore, surplus rice and wheat production, available in non-drought-stricken areas of the sub-continent such as Bengal and Burma, were still being exported to England. 'Londoners', Davis observes, 'were in effect eating India's bread'.[52]

Mike Davis rightly pursues the comparison of the British in India with the British in Ireland, especially in terms of the free trade dogma, which had been strictly applied by the British authorities during the Irish Famine.

Davis now raises the question of genocide, implied by his title concerning holocausts, arguing that the work camps the British did set up were so unsanitary that they became 'extermination camps'.[53]

By 1877, Davis writes, the gathering horror of the famine, despite official attempts to suppress knowledge of it, was becoming known, and belatedly the British in India began to institute a miserly program of relief works, under draconian and punishing conditions; famine relief was an expense the British were very disinclined to fund, and to minimise the payment of relief, British officials made 'relief as repugnant and ineffective as possible' as a way of deterring the starving from seeking it. British officials, for example, 'turned away anyone who was too starved to undertake hard coolie labor'.[54]

Davis compares what Lytton's administration was doing so harshly in India with the actions of Charles Edward Trevelyan the permanent secretary to the Treasury during Ireland's Great Hunger, Trevelyan deploying free market economics as a 'mask for colonial genocide'. Davis points out that just as Trevelyan during the Irish famine had argued that the problem with the Irish was not hunger but their being a selfish, perverse and turbulent people, so British officials, such as Sir Richard Temple, another of Lord Lytton's crew, also blamed the victims of the Indian famines for their plight, that the dying Indians were known for their idleness and their unreasonable dread of marching on command any distance from home in order to reach work camps.[55]

In reference to forced marches the British insisted on in India, I'm reminded of my previous discussion of Tim Pat Coogan's 2012 *The Famine Plot: England's Role in Ireland's Greatest Tragedy*. Coogan refers, for example, to the death march in 1849, known as the Doolough Lake incident, where a large group of starving Irish in County Mayo were refused tickets of relief and food, and forced to walk through cold, hail and snowstorm, hundreds perishing on the way.[56] Trevelyan, Coogan points out, dismissing humanitarian objections, deployed the 'teachings of Adam Smith' to insist on non-intervention, in particular, to deny to the Irish situation price control to ensure the provision of cheap food as a way of relieving starvation. Coogan sees Trevelyan as the 'architect and executor' in Ireland of British government policy, 'a policy that sheltered behind the economic dogma that the laws of business were the laws of God', which it would be sacrilegious to interfere with. Coogan judges the British policies and actions to be genocide.[57] So does Davis for India. In the Famine of 1876–78 Lord

Lytton applied the lessons of the Irish Famine, disavowing any moral responsibility since the drought was a natural event and the market, which represented the sacred workings of Providence, could not be tampered with.

A stray thought occurred to me while pondering what Coogan and Davis say about British claims that laissez faire is Providence in action: here is imperial power, based on the sword, entwined with a risible and highly self-interested Christian fantasy, being imposed on India with its remarkable variety of peoples, religions, and worldviews, Hindu, Muslim, Sikh, Parsee, Jain, Syriac Christian.

Nonetheless, there were those in Late Victorian times who saw Lytton and his crew as indeed responsible for a historical disaster, that they were the architects and executors of mass death. The calumnies that were occurring, Davis tells us, 'inflamed Indians of all classes'. In particular, the 'famished peasants in relief camps throughout the Bombay Deccan' organised 'massive, Gandhi-like protests against the rice reduction and distance test', in what came to be called the 'relief strike'. The movement began in January 1877, with families on village relief refusing orders to 'march to the new, militarized work camps where men were separated from their wives and children'; thousands more joined the protests, leaving the work camps 'in protest at the starvation wage and mistreatment by overseers'. The British were appalled at behaviour they referred to as 'passive resistance'. For their part, a moderate Indian nationalist group, the Sarvajanik Sabha (Civic Association) in Poona embraced the protest movement, warning of the 'human catastrophe that British churlishness was ensuring', and in particular focusing public attention 'on the group most ignored by district officers: the children of famine villages'. With the support of the Sabha, the relief strike 'kindled the broadest demonstration of Indian anger since the Mutiny'.[58]

The Indian press, Davis writes, were also stirred into vocal protest by the disaster, relaying to the English public shocking accounts of 'rebellion and starvation within the relief camps'. Outspoken journalists such as William Digby in Madras 'stirred troubling memories of the Irish famine as well as the Sepoy Mutiny', while in England a 'group of old India hands and Radical reformers', which included names like William Wedderburn, Sir Arthur Cotton, John Bright, Henry Hyndman and Florence Nightingale, 'kept *The Times*'s letters column full of complaints' about Lytton's 'callous policies'.[59] In their eyes, were Lytton and his close associates in India the Stracheys perceived as, in Leonard Woolf's breathless terms, distinguished and brilliant?

In *Late Victorian Holocausts* there are further unedifying glimpses of the Stracheys, especially concerning the establishment of a Famine Commission, convened in early 1878. Davis mordantly observes that the presidency of the commission was 'safely entrusted to Lt. General Sir Richard Strachey, who as a member of the India Council and brother to Lytton's finance chief was unlikely to find fault with himself or his sibling'. When the report was finally submitted in June 1880, it turned out, predictably, to be a whitewash, a political exercise to produce a favourable report absolving the British administration in India of any 'responsibility for the horrific mortality'; furthermore, 'General Strachey protected his brother's policies'.[60]

In the early years of the new century, pretty well at the same time as Leonard Woolf was spending summers admiring the brilliance of the Stracheys' careers in India, there appeared coruscating critiques of the British in India and their self-serving rhetoric about free trade. Journalist William Digby published his harsh criticisms of Lytton's disastrous administration in his two-volume *The Famine Campaign in Southern India: 1876–1878* in 1900. In more general terms the moderate nationalists Dadabhai Naoroji and Romesh Chunder Dutt published damning critiques of the British in India. In 1901 Naoroji's *Poverty and Un-British Rule in India* appeared, while Dutt published *Famines in India*

(1900) and his two-volume *Economic History of British India* in 1902 and 1904. Furthermore, Davis draws attention to a further devastating 'holocaust' that occurred in India between 1896 and 1902, evoked in his harrowing chapter 'Skeletons at the Feast', when another drought turned into another famine. There continued to be massive exports from the wheat belt of northern India to England, the doctrine of free trade still reigned causing sharp increases in food prices, while a 'significant portion' of the much vaunted Famine Fund, a recommendation of Sir Richard Strachey's commission of inquiry, 'had been diverted against the protests of Indians to pay for yet another vicious Afghan war'. Critics argued that malnutrition had reached 'epic levels unprecedented in Indian history'. It was a famine that also affected the northern tip of Ceylon.[61]

Increasingly, Davis comments, international attention was drawn to Britain's crimes against humanity in India during this latest catastrophe, with American observers, horrified by conditions inside the poorhouses that the British introduced in 1896–7, accusing the government of deceiving world opinion about conditions in the Indian countryside. Furthermore, such accusations were made all the more effective by the 'shocking photographs of the famine conditions' reprinted in newspapers around the world, the advent of the 'cheap, handheld Kodak Number One camera' in 1888 having turned 'virtually every missionary in India into a documentary photographer'. In London in 1897, Irish leader Michael Davitt spoke alongside Naoroji and Eleanor Marx at protest meetings against British rule in India, organised by Hyndman's Social Democratic Federation.[62]

(Intrigued by the reference to Eleanor Marx, I looked up the 2014 biography by Rachel Holmes, where there is mention of the 'appalling famine in India' in 1897, which Eleanor Marx and Hyndman believed was caused by 'colonial capitalism that unbalanced the world economies'. Also, for her 'lecture series of 1897

Eleanor chose most frequently the subjects of imperialism and colonialism in India and South Africa, often giving variations on her lecture ironically entitled "Our Glorious Empire".)[63]

In 1900 plague and cholera swept over the whole of India, 'massacring city dwellers and peasantry alike'. Some villagers, Davis reports, knowing the hunger of the Christian missionaries for converts, 'resorted to selling their young children for a few days' supply of food'. 'Outcastes and tribals' were cut down. In 1901 *The Lancet* suggested that a 'conservative estimate of excess mortality in India' in the previous decade was '19 million'.[64]

During the Boer War years, the British diverted money from famine relief in India to help pay for British war expenses in the Transvaal.[65]

But Leonard Woolf at Cambridge from 1899 to 1904 heard nothing, saw nothing, presumably read nothing of the late nineteenth – and early twentieth-century famine disasters in India where so many millions needlessly died.

In the first years of the twentieth century Leonard Woolf, the aspiring parvenu, a student at Trinity College, Cambridge, intensely admired Sir Leslie Stephen the patriarch of the Stephen family, as well as the Strachey family with whom he spent three summer holidays. In the terms posed by Maxime Rodinson, was Leonard Woolf as Jew at Cambridge a victim or executioner? Clearly, he was not a victim.

A late thought about Leonard Woolf's admiration in *Sowing* for Lytton Strachey's father, Lieutenant-General Sir Richard Strachey, as a soldier in India. While reading Sir Walter Scott's *The Antiquary* (1816), I came across an exchange between a character, old Edie the mendicant, telling another, Lord Glenallan, that he had once been a soldier in Britain's overseas wars. Lord Glenallan, clearly given to a far from optimistic view of history, exclaims: 'A soldier! Then you have slain and burnt, and sacked and spoiled?'[66]

1. Leonard Woolf, *Sowing: an autobiography of the years 1880–1904* (1960; Hogarth, London, 1970), p.195.
2. Leonard Woolf, *Sowing*, pp.196–7.
3. Virginia Woolf, *A Room of One's Own* (1929), edited with an introduction and notes by Michèle Barrett (Penguin Classics, London, 2011), pp.5–7.
4. Virginia Woolf, *A Room of One's Own*, pp.4–5.
5. Peter Y. Sussman (ed.), *Decca: The Letters of Jessica Mitford* (Weidenfeld and Nicolson, London, 2006), p.435, letter to Nancy Mitford, 13 October 1971.
6. 'The Jew as Pariah: A hidden tradition', in Hannah Arendt, *The Jewish Writings*, edited by Jerome Kohn and Ron H. Feldman (Schocken, New York, 2007), pp.295–97). I talk about Arendt's essay in my chapter 'Troubled reflections on my father' in Ann Curthoys and Joy Damousi (eds), *What Did You Do in the Cold War, Daddy? Personal stories from a troubled time* (NewSouth, Sydney, 2014), pp.106–7.
7. Leonard Woolf, *Sowing: An Autobiography of the Years 1880–1904* (1960; Hogarth Press, London, 1970), pp.13–16.
8. Leonard Woolf, *Sowing*, pp.14, 25, 34–5.
9. Leonard Woolf, *Sowing*, pp.71–2, 95.
10. Leonard Woolf, *Sowing*, p.198.
11. See Howard Eiland and Michael W. Jennings, *Walter Benjamin: A Critical Life* (The Belknap Press of Harvard University Press, Cambridge, Mass., 2014), p.351.
12. Hermione Lee, *Virginia Woolf* (Vintage Books, New York, 1999), pp.343–344; also p.352.
13. Virginia Woolf, *A Room of One's Own*, pp.3–6.
14. Ann Curthoys and John Docker, *Is History Fiction?* (UNSW Press, Sydney, 2010), pp.156–7.
15. Ann Curthoys and John Docker, 'The Boundaries of History and Fiction', in Nancy Partner and Sarah Foot (eds), *The Sage Handbook of Historical Theory* (Sage, London, 2013), p.203.
16. Jane Austen, *The History of England* (The Folio Society, London, 1993), p.xxi.
17. Austen, *The History of England*, pp.xxi-xxii.
18. Virginia Woolf, *A Room of One's Own*, pp.10–12, 15–16.
19. Virginia Woolf, *A Room of One's Own*, pp.30, 45, 49.
20. Virginia Woolf, *A Room of One's Own*, pp.3, 59–63, 68, 70. Cf. Hermione Lee, *Virginia Woolf*, p.494, letter from Virginia to Vita Sackville-West, 1926, concerning her upbringing: 'No school, mooning about alone among my father's books…'
21. Virginia Woolf, *A Room of One's Own*, p.3.
22. Jessica Mitford, *Hons and Rebels* (1960; Phoenix, London, 2007), p.17.

23 Hermione Lee, *Virginia Woolf*, p.548, quotes Virginia saying she is uneducated 'because my brothers used all the family funds which is the fact' (letter to Ethel Smyth).
24 Jessica Mitford, *A Fine Old Conflict*, pp.151, 154–155.
25 Peter Y. Sussman (ed.), *Decca: The Letters of Jessica Mitford*, p.435.
26 Hermione Lee, *Virginia Woolf*, pp.611–612.
27 See Curthoys and Docker, 'The Boundaries of History and Fiction', p.203.
28 For 'kunstchaos', see John Docker, 'Sheer Folly and derangement: How the Crusades Disoriented Enlightenment Historiography', in Alexander Cook, Ned Curthoys and Shino Konishi (eds), *Representing Humanity in the Age of Enlightenment* (Pickering and Chatto, London, 2013), p.44.
29 Virginia Woolf, *A Room of One's Own*, pp.24–32.
30 Virginia Woolf, *A Room of One's Own*, p.33.
31 Leonard Woolf, *Sowing*, pp.103–9.
32 Leonard Woolf, *Sowing*, p.113.
33 Leonard Woolf, *Sowing*, pp.110, 112–13.
34 Leonard Woolf, *Sowing*, pp.182–4.
35 Leonard Woolf, *Sowing*, p.184.
36 Virginia Woolf, *A Room of One's Own*, pp.46, 98.
37 Leonard Woolf, *Sowing*, p.182.
38 Leonard Woolf, *Sowing*, pp.180–1.
39 Leonard Woolf, *Sowing*, pp.91 n.1, 107 n.1, 133, 142 n.1 and 2, 177.
40 John Docker, *The Nervous Nineties: Australian Cultural Life in the 1890s* (OUP, Melbourne, 1991), pp.44–5.
41 Leonard Woolf, *Sowing*, pp.186–7.
42 Virginia Woolf, *A Room of One's Own*, p.32.
43 Ann Curthoys and John Docker, *Is History Fiction?* p.249.
44 Mike Davis, *Late Victorian Holocausts: El Niño Famines and the Making of the Third World* (Verso, London, 2001), Part I, The Great Drought, 1876–1878, and Part II, El Niño and the New Imperialism, 1888–1902.
45 Davis, *Late Victorian Holocausts*, p.22.
46 Davis, *Late Victorian Holocausts*, pp.28, 30.
47 Leonard Woolf, *Sowing*, p.167.
48 Davis, *Late Victorian Holocausts*, p.43.
49 Davis, *Late Victorian Holocausts*, pp.30, 34.
50 Davis, *Late Victorian Holocausts*, pp.28, 36.
51 Davis, *Late Victorian Holocausts*, p.32.

52 Davis, *Late Victorian Holocausts*, pp.26–7, 31, 33. 44, 175.
53 Davis, *Late Victorian Holocausts*, p.40.
54 Davis, *Late Victorian Holocausts*, pp.32–6.
55 Davis, *Late Victorian Holocausts*, pp.36–7, 40–41.
56 Tim Pat Coogan, *The Famine Plot: England's Role in Ireland's Greatest Tragedy* (Palgrave Macmillan, New York, 2012), pp.91–92.
57 Coogan, *The Famine Plot*, pp.229–31.
58 Davis, *Late Victorian Holocausts*, pp.41–3.
59 Davis, *Late Victorian Holocausts*, p.43.
60 Davis, *Late Victorian Holocausts*, pp.57–8.
61 Davis, *Late Victorian Holocausts*, pp.55–56, 140–146, 401 note 1.
62 Davis, *Late Victorian Holocausts*, pp.147–148, 163.
63 Rachel Holmes, *Eleanor Marx: A Life* (Bloomsbury, London, 2014), p.409.
64 Davis, *Late Victorian Holocausts*, pp.167, 170–71, 175.
65 Davis, *Late Victorian Holocausts*, pp.164–165.
66 Sir Walter Scott, *The Antiquary* (1816; Oxford World's Classics, Oxford, 2009), p.279.

12

A Parvenu in Ceylon: Leonard Woolf as Executioner, with thoughts on Periclean Athens and the Enlightenment

… the first English statesman who repeatedly stressed his belief in races and race superiority was [Benjamin Disraeli]… he laid one of the foundation stones for a fundamental change in British rule in India…. The policy introduced by Disraeli signified the establishment of an exclusive caste in a foreign country whose only function was rule and not colonization. For the realization of this conception… racism would indeed be an indispensable tool.

Hannah Arendt, *The Origins of Totalitarianism*, section on Imperialism[1]

The Woolfs and the Nicolsons had a weekend at Long Barn [home of Vita Sackville-West and Harold Nicolson] in July [1927], with Raymond Mortimer…. In a political discussion about the empire, Harold the diplomat argued for the benefits of colonial rule: 'our English genius is for government'. Raymond opposed him: 'The governed don't seem to enjoy it.' Virginia supported Raymond, and made a modernist argument for decolonization and anti-nationalism…

Hermione Lee, *Virginia Woolf*[2]

There is a highly curious, even, perhaps disingenuous, aspect to the end of *Sowing* that intrigues me. In the final pages, Leonard Woolf tells us that he 'stayed up for five years' at Cambridge, expecting 'as a scholar of Trinity to be high enough up in the examination to get a place in the Home Civil Service'. However, his results were disappointing. While he read 'voraciously both in Greek and Latin and in English and French', he chose not to go to lectures and stuff his head, as he put it, with reading that would merely gain him a high place in an examination. Given his results, he 'decided to take an appointment in the Colonial Service, then called Eastern Cadetships'. One possibility, a little mystifyingly, was ruled out: 'I was over age for India' (this I don't understand, since he was still in his early twenties). However, he applies to go to Ceylon [renamed Sri Lanka in 1972], which was the 'senior Crown Colony', and he scores high enough in the examination list 'to get what I asked for'. In 1904 he joins the Ceylon Civil Service.[3]

The volume closes with Woolf going through the practicalities necessary for his new role. He buys 'tropical suits and a topi at the Army and Navy Stores' and he takes 'riding lessons in the Knightsbridge Barracks'. He partakes of a round of farewells, including, in Bloomsbury, 'dinner with Thoby Stephen and his sisters Vanessa and Virginia in Gordon Square', and also goes to see G E Moore in Edinburgh, where the revered philosopher was now located. He packs 'ninety large volumes of the beautiful eighteenth century edition of Voltaire printed in the Baskerville type', and also arranges to take along a dog, a fox-terrier. In October 1904 he boards the P and O *Syria* at Tilbury Docks for the journey to Ceylon.[4]

The Parvenu's Curse

What intrigues me is that earlier in *Sowing* Leonard Woolf tells us that he is 'naturally of an introspective nature'. Given the reference to visiting G E Moore in Edinburgh, along with his natural capacity for introspection, I expected Leonard Woolf in the final few pages to practise what he insists is the defining feature of his Cambridge group, that in the years 1901 to 1904 they were united in practising Moore's injunction to *question everything*, for, in their eyes, Moore's mind was supremely Socratic. Throughout his evocation of the (male) wonders of Cambridge in *Sowing*, the highest praise is reserved for Moore, a Fellow of Trinity who intellectually dominated the Apostles, 'refertilizing and revivifying its spirit and tradition'. In Woolf's estimation, 'Moore was a great man, the only great man whom I have ever met or known in the world of ordinary, real life'. Moore influenced Woolf and his friends to be 'sceptics in search of truth and ethical truth': 'He and we were fascinated by questions of what was right and wrong, what one *ought* to do.'[5]

I therefore expected Woolf in the final pages of *Sowing* to offer reflections, insightful and substantial, on colonialism and empire: to consider how empires have conducted themselves in history; to wonder if it be a wise, an ethically wise, thing to do, for an intellectual to become one of those who exercises imperial power over subjugated peoples. I thought he might ask the question, *ought* he go as an imperial functionary to Ceylon? But there is no such closing introspective meditation. I'm therefore tempted to ask, did Leonard Woolf practise any kind of Moore-like skepticism towards periods of history that necessarily involve thinking about empires: the time of the ancient Athenians and the statesman Pericles; and the eighteenth-century Enlightenment signified by Voltaire. His weighing down the P and O *Syria* with 90 volumes of Voltaire was presumably to ensure that he could sustain in Ceylon the memory of his time in Trinity as a 'civilized life both intellectually and emotionally'.[6] We must surely smile over the 90 volumes of Voltaire: only the parvenu, we might think, would go over the top in such an absurd way, excessively affirming how he wishes to maintain his metropolitan identity, even if secretly, the 90 volumes hopefully unseen by any philistine gaze, in the British-occupied island he is heading towards.

Soon, we read at the end of *Sowing*, Woolf the youthful parvenu would be riding a horse in a tropical suit and a topi: no self-ironic smile by Woolf at such pompous posturing, we notice. Ceylon might not quite be Anglo-India, where his friend Lytton Strachey's father and other Strachey relatives, in Woolf's eyes, so distinguished themselves as soldiers and administrators.[7] If Ceylon was not India, it still was Britain's 'senior Crown Colony'. In the Strachey and Stephen tradition of imperial service, Leonard Woolf could establish his family as an Anglo-Ceylon family, and indeed, in a way, in association with his sister Bella, he did, as we shall see.

A signal feature of the parvenu in history is to try to scale the heights of a society. Tirelessly. With relentless will. With extraordinary determination.

What I'll suggest now is that Leonard Woolf's parvenu desire, in Hannah Arendt's terms in the Imperialism section of *The Origins of Totalitarianism*, to become part of an 'exclusive caste in a foreign country whose only function was to rule and not colonization', their English race superiority shown by their genius for government, overrode any misgivings a critical intellectual might have had about empires and colonisation. And Woolf certainly regarded himself, in the spirit of Moore and his Cambridge friends, as a critical intellectual. Didn't they belong to a scandalous generation of young men, who would later help form Bloomsbury, along with Vanessa Stephen and Virginia Stephen?[8]

Pericles and the Athenian Empire

I can't, however, detect anywhere in *Sowing* any example of skeptical questioning of Pericles and Periclean Athens, certainly not the irreverence revealed in *A Room of One's Own*. Recall that the narrator there writes that female authors in the nineteenth century felt they had to cloak themselves in anonymity, taking names such as Currer Bell, George Eliot and George Sand, because of a prevailing view that publicity in women is detestable, a misogynist not to say authoritarian injunction coming down from antiquity: 'the chief glory of a woman is not to be talked of, said Pericles, himself a much-talked-of man'.[9] In *Sowing* Leonard Woolf tells us that part of his identity is rooted in 'the Greece of Herodotus, Thucydides, Aristophanes, and Pericles'.[10] I thereby felt confident that, at the end of *Sowing*, with his many years of immersion in Greek and Latin in school and university, Woolf would ponder skepticism towards empire and its associated imperial consciousness in Herodotus' *The Histories* and Thucydides' *History of the Peloponnesian War*.

As Ann Curthoys and I note in *Is History Fiction?* in *The Histories* the wars in the fifth century BCE between Persia and Greece, with associated multiple narratives, are evoked in what would now be called a cosmopolitan international mode of world history, anti-nationalist and anti-ethnocentric, often sharply critical of the Greek city-states, not sparing even democratic Athens from stories of prejudice, ignorance, cruelty, treachery and betrayal. Herodotus as narrator positions himself as a kind of outsider figure in relation to any settled ethnic or national identity (as Virginia Woolf would do in *A Room of One's Own*). The narrator comments ironically on the immediate onset of an imperial consciousness, arrogant and predatory, in the Greeks once the Persians had been defeated in a decisive sea-battle and had fled towards the Hellespont. The Greeks, in this case the Athenians, immediately laid siege to their fellow Greeks on nearby islands, demanding large sums which were given to them out of fear. The Athenian commander Themistocles distinguished himself in these postwar rapacious actions, becoming a war profiteer and willing to betray his fellow Greeks for his safety and gain if the occasion required. So critical on many occasions are the stories of *The Histories* against the Greeks that Plutarch in his 'On the Malice of Herodotus' complained that Herodotus was philobarbaros, malicious towards his fellow Greeks.[11]

Like Herodotus, Thucydides in his *History of the Peloponnesian War*, written in exile from Athens, positions himself as a kind of detached outsider figure in relation to the nearly 30 years war between democratic Athens and its empire, and monarchical Sparta and its league of allies, free to be critical, or admiring, of either. The Peloponnesian war broke out in 431 and was fought intermittently until 404, when Athens surrendered and lost the empire it had acquired, especially to the east of Ionia after the defeat of the Persian invasion and which had provided it with wealth and prosperity and a conviction of historical greatness. Thucydides' *History* is highly skeptical towards Pericles, who as orator and statesman had convinced Athens to proceed to war against Sparta. In his Funeral Oration held for those men first to die in the war, Pericles tells the assembly that Athens shows its greatness by participating in its empire with a 'free liberality', doing kindness to others out of friendship and not out of calculations of profit or loss. For Pericles in this speech, then, Athens, with its moral or honourable empire, is history's ideal society.[12]

The military strategy that the Athenians adopted on Pericles' urging involved the Athenians in the countryside abandoning their land, homes and temples and coming to reside within Athens itself. However, there is not enough space in Athens, so that many have to crowd together between the fortified Long Walls that lead down to the port of Piraeus, and in Piraeus itself. A plague devastates Athens, a catastrophe made worse by the overcrowding that was a consequence of Pericles' military strategy; the first cases occurred in Piraeus and then spread to Athens, whose miseries Thucydides, who himself suffered from the disease, records with anguish. Athens' citizens become angry at Pericles for persuading them to go to war. Pericles then makes another speech to the assembly, in his own defence. He accepts no blame for what has happened, and reveals what those opposed to Athens in the war, as well as Athens' own allies and subject states, regard as Athenian imperial arrogance. Pericles urges his fellow Athenians to remember their 'superiority', the courage and 'intelligence that makes one able to look down on one's opponent'. He reminds them that the 'imperial dignity of Athens' depends on holding on to its empire, even though, he admits in this speech, there is the 'hatred which we incurred in administering it'. Pericles adds that the Athenian empire is 'now like a tyranny: it may have been wrong to take it; it is certainly dangerous to let it go'. The Athenians, unappeased, fine Pericles.[13]

Pericles died two and a half years after the outbreak of the war. Yet, in the *History*, Pericles' urging that the Athenians must continue their empire for the sake of their superiority and imperial dignity, lives on as a shaping force in Athenian public consciousness. Such is revealed in a famous episode that features in the *History*, the Mytilenian Debate, concerning Mytilene, the chief city on the island of Lesbos, which had chosen to revolt from Athens' empire in 428. The Mytilenians felt that, since the end of the Persian war, Athens' imperial arrogance was becoming increasingly insufferable, as indeed did many in the empire, with revolts and attempts to secede becoming common. The revolt, however, disastrously fails, with the Mytilenians having to surrender to Athenian forces after a siege. Back in Athens, its citizens decide to put to death 'the entire male population of Mytilene, and to make slaves of the women and children'. Accordingly, they send a trireme to Paches, the Athenian general now in control of Mytilene, 'with orders to put the Mytilenians to death immediately'.[14]

The next day, however, Thucydides tells us, the Athenians began to think how cruel and unprecedented it would be to destroy not only the guilty but the entire population of a state.

At the suggestion of representatives of Mytilene who are present in Athens, a new assembly is hastily called to discuss what to do. The demagogue Cleon argues that, in the interest of maintaining imperial power, any pity or compassion shown by the Athenians will be read as a sign of weakness not only by the Mytilenians but by the other allies who compose the empire. He concludes his speech by affirming that the Mytilenian revolt has to be punished by mass death as an 'example' to the other allies who, in observing the inevitable consequences, will be warned never to rebel. Cleon's position is opposed by Diodotus, who nonetheless like Cleon puts concern for empire above concern for the Mytilenians themselves, or any other subject peoples. 'Do not be swayed by pity or by ordinary decent emotions', Diodotus tells the Athenians. 'I, no more than Cleon, wish you to be influenced by such emotions.' Diodotus advises that 'good administration' of an empire should work by moderation, for then if a state rebels, it will know that there is a possibility of repentance and the chance of 'atoning as quickly as they can for what they did'. By such calculated moderation will the empire be preserved, for 'those who make wise decisions are more formidable to their enemies that those who rush madly into strong action'. As it happens, when put to the assembly Diodotus' motion of a more moderate course just defeats Cleon's motion in the show of hands, and a second ship is sent which fortunately catches up to the first in time to prevent 'the massacre': 'So narrow had been the escape of Mytilene.'[15] What in modern terms we would call a genocidal massacre was just averted.

The Mytilenian Debate is a chilling revelation of the self-interested morality and imperatives of empire, something, one might have thought, given his thorough training in the classics, about which Leonard Woolf would have reflected upon before he set sail, especially in relation to his declared admiration of Pericles. When Diodotus argues that in the wise administration of its empire Athens should not consider its subject peoples with pity and compassion and that moderation is to be used for strategic purposes of empire management, he is surely echoing the speech where Pericles says that what matters to Athens is its empire, whatever feelings of resentment and hatred might be present from those subject to the empire.[16] Hannah Arendt writes in *The Origins of Totalitarianism* that India had formerly been governed with the 'usual ruthlessness of conquerors': think of Cleon. Then, Arendt continues, Disraeli influenced the British to establish a 'permanent government by administrative measures': think of Diodotus. And we can also ponder that Diodotus's motion just won in the assembly; Cleon's advocacy of the ruthlessness of conquerors just lost, and could always re-emerge as an alternative option of empire management.

We could call it the Parable of Cleon and Diodotus: empire as Janus-faced, as Cleon/Diodatus, empire as ruthless and brutal when need be; empire as moderate and as if in the interests of a subject people. In either disposition, the empire is always working in its own interests.

It may well be that at school and university Woolf diligently learned Greek and Latin in a prescribed pro-imperial way, the Athenian and Roman empires presaging the self-acclaimed greatness of Britain's empire; yet, where had *question everything* gone?

Was it trumped by the self-interest and ambition of the parvenu? I think yes, I think the parvenu had plans, long-range plans, and Ceylon was central to those plans.

Leonard's Voltaire, Horse Riding and Dog

At the end of *Sowing*, Leonard Woolf offers no reflections why he felt it was so important to bring along 90 volumes of Voltaire; the reader is left to assume by his silence that he believed that the Enlightenment revealed no critical thinking about empire and imperial behaviour which might have troubled his decision to go to Ceylon. Again, this is surely disingenuous on Woolf's part. The Enlightenment was a theatrical scene of intellectual contradictoriness, of conflicting interpretations, of controversy and contestations. One important strand was identified by Sankar Muthu in his 2003 book *Enlightenment Against Empire*, that many Enlightenment intellectuals challenged 'the idea that Europeans had any right to subjugate, colonize, and "civilize" the rest of the world'. Sankar mentions Kant, Diderot, Herder, Bentham, Condorcet, Adam Smith, Edmund Burke.[17]

In an essay on Enlightenment attitudes to the Crusades, I point out that David Hume, William Robertson and Edward Gibbon in their histories scorn the Crusades as a singular monument to human folly. Instead of Europe attempting to invade and control the Orient through the Crusades, Europe could have increased its industry and wealth by trade, at the same time as, in Gibbon's words, being 'enriched and enlightened by a pure and friendly correspondence with the climates of the East'.[18]

If Leonard Woolf had read Diderot, as he surely must, given how voraciously he said he was reading in French in the final stages of his time at Cambridge – well, who could be more anti-colonialist and anti-imperial than Diderot![19] Here is one of the final passionate passages of the conclusion of *A History of the Two Indies*:

> Since the bold expeditions of Columbus and da Gama, Europe has witnessed the rise of a previously unknown obsession, the desire for discoveries. People have explored, and continue to explore every part of the world, from one Pole to the other, in search of continents to invade, islands to ravage, peoples to rob, to subjugate and to massacre. If someone could succeed in putting a stop to this mania, he would indeed deserve to be counted among the benefactors of the human race.[20]

That hero of humanity would not be one Leonard Woolf, who

curiously, disingenuously, presents himself to the reader at the end of *Sowing*, about to embark for Ceylon, as a tabula rasa, as if he never thought about colonisation and empire in his life.

As a Jew, Woolf certainly revealed no interest in the German Jewish Enlightenment or *Haskalah* in the late eighteenth century, which was intensely critical of European colonialism, including its religious aspects. In *The Legacy of Liberal Judaism* (2013) my son Ned Curthoys points out that the philosopher Moses Mendelssohn, the renowned major figure of the *Haskalah*, inaugurated a liberal Jewish ethos and intellectual tradition that in the nineteenth century extended to the poet Heinrich Heine and in the twentieth century the philosopher Ernst Cassirer and critical thinker Hannah Arendt. Ned evokes a tradition of liberal cosmopolitanism and public intellectual interventions that continues to this day.[21]

In his opening chapter, Ned writes that Mendelssohn was highly critical of the claims to universality of revealed religions such as Christianity and the colonial institutions they established to spread their teachings.[22] Ned quotes a remarkable passage from *Jerusalem or on Religious Power and Judaism*, published in 1783, one of his most famous works, where Mendelssohn challenges the Christian notion that peoples around the world are in a bereft and benighted state, in desperate need of the Christian Revelation to be brought to them by missionaries who are at the same time colonisers. Here is the passage from *Jerusalem*, which, as Ned points out, alludes to Diderot's *A History of the Two Indies*:

> If therefore, mankind must be corrupt and miserable without revelation, why has the far greater part of mankind lived without true revelation from time immemorial? Why must the two Indies wait until it pleases the Europeans to send them a few comforters to bring them a message without which they can, according to this opinion, live neither virtuously nor happily… According

to the concepts of true Judaism, all the inhabitants of the earth are destined to felicity; and the means of attaining it are as widespread as mankind itself...[23]

Ned points to a similar questioning spirit in Heinrich Heine, who felt that the great task facing humanity was the emancipation of the world from colonial oppression, including the Irish and West Indian Blacks.[24]

Ned wrote an essay a few years earlier, 'Diasporic Visions: Al-Andalus in the German-Jewish Imaginary', about the intense interest in medieval Muslim Spain in Mendelssohn and the German-Jewish Enlightenment. Here Ned suggests that in *Jerusalem* Mendelssohn anticipates twentieth-century postcolonial theory critical of European colonisation. Mendelssohn, Ned writes, 'fiercely disputed the arrogance and *amour propre* of Christianity', and the tendency of German Christians, including Kant, to denigrate Jews in Orientalist terms as Eastern and backward. Mendelssohn also defended the right of the indigenous peoples of eighteenth-century Greenland to pursue their lives free of colonisation by Christian missionaries, especially the German Moravians intent on converting the Greenlanders. As Ned points out, Mendelssohn constructs a scene where the Greenlanders ask the missionaries, why, in our beautiful land of ice and snow, do we need to convert to your Christianity?[25]

Coincidentally, I've recently been reading a book, *The Missionary, the Catechist and the Hunter* (2014), by a Danish friend of ours, Christina Petterson. Like Mendelssohn, Christina is passionately critical of what Protestant missionaries were doing in eighteenth-century Greenland, entwining Christianity with colonialism. In an early footnote, Christina gives some historical background and theological detail concerning the Moravian Brethren, whose presence in eighteenth-century Europe was 'barely tolerated because they were regarded as a threat to the social order'. Moravian theology was characterised by an 'individual conversion experience, a heavy emphasis on emotions, and a strong personal relation to Jesus Christ'; also, the 'physical blood and wounds of Christ were very central to Moravian theology'. The Moravian Brethren, Christina says, arrived in Greenland in 1733 and left in 1900–01, and proved 'significant competitors for the souls of Greenlanders'.[26]

Christina focusses on the Lutheran missionaries sent from Denmark in 1721 as part of the early eighteenth-century Danish colonisation of Greenland, who were in competition with the German Moravians. The Lutheran strategy, Christina says, was to create a new elite by hiring and training catechists from the indigenous population to assist the Danish ministers in teaching the truths of the Christian faith. The indigenous catechists were to help the ministers in their attempt to inculcate a new social morality and new consciousness, a new subjectivity, in a long effort to dissociate those they conceived as pagans from their previous life ways, which were to be denigrated as inferior. The Lutheran missionary was to be the model of reason, masculine reason, by which the elite of indigenous catechists would refashion their personalities, family life and intimate ways of relating to each other, leading to the wider transformation of Greenlandic society. In the new Greenlandic family life, the man as head of the family was to be the undisputed master in a strict hierarchy, and women, held to be perennially irrational and superstitious, were to submit to the husband's total authority. Christina relates, however, that there were outbreaks of dissidence centred on female shamans who, interpreting Christianity in their own way in terms of visions, directly challenged the authoritarian rule of the Lutheran missions and the imposition of the Danish 'patriarchal social order', as in the 'Habakuk heresy' in the late eighteenth century, which, Christina says, became the 'archetype of all Greenlandic charismatic movements'.[27]

In brief, Christina's portrait of the Lutheran missions and missionaries is scathing, in the spirit of Moses Mendelssohn.

I don't think that Woolf, about to leave for Ceylon, was harbouring passionate thoughts critical of European colonisers of non-European peoples, or any desire whatsoever about emancipating any colonial people from the British empire, certainly not the people of Ceylon; nor did he entertain any critical thoughts about the British missionaries in Ceylon he encounters. I'll come back to these missionaries soon.

In a previous chapter I pondered an oddity, that Leonard Woolf does not reveal any knowledge of contemporary events involving the British empire he was about to serve, whose empire, like all empires – like the Athenian empire – frequently faced rebellion, dissidence, dislike and turmoil. After all, only a few years before he embarked on the *Syria* in 1904, the British during the South African War had distinguished themselves by a Cleon-like scorched earth policy against the Boers and the setting up of concentration camps, a feature of imperial rule that, in Hannah Arendt's terms, would be reproduced in twentieth-century totalitarianism: 'Not even concentration camps are an invention of totalitarian movements. They emerge for the first time during the Boer War, at the beginning of the century…'[28] I referred to Mike Davis's comment on imperial perfidy, in *Late Victorian Holocausts*, that during the Boer War years the British diverted money from famine relief in India to help pay for British war expenses in the Transvaal.[29]

Did Leonard Woolf at Cambridge, and at summer holidays with the Strachey family, or during contact with the Stephen family, hear no news at all of the South African War, not a word, not a reference, not one conversation, not one casual mention, not one newspaper article?

Leonard Woolf would have a sort of friendship with a Boer in Ceylon, which we will talk about in a moment.

The strangely unreal quality of the final pages of *Sowing* is also revealed in Leonard Woolf's casual reference to taking horse-riding lessons. What, he could have idly mused, was the horse to empires? In *Guns, Germs and Steel* Jared Diamond notes that the 'transformation of warfare by horses began with their domestication around 4000 B.C., in the steppes north of the Black Sea', a military weapon that was important for conquerors until the early twentieth century; it was not until the World War I that the military dominance of cavalry finally came to an end.[30] Ceylon had long been occupied by the British, but riding a horse could still be important as signifying to the local population power and authority, white men looking down on them from above, having to look up to the superior white man in a tropical suit and topi; with resentment, as Woolf would find.

In the penultimate sentence of *Sowing*, Woolf says he picked up 'a wire-haired fox-terrier' to take to Ceylon, whose name, we learn in *Growing: An Autobiography of the Years 1904–1911* (1961), was Charles.[31] It is well known that Leonard Woolf enjoyed a lifelong love of animals, but he could have reflected here, if only for a moment, that taking an animal from Europe to a colonial possession elsewhere, without requesting any sort of permission from the local population or thinking about environmental consequences, was part of what we would now call ecocide; dogs, like other European domestic animals, were possible transmitters of diseases which devastated colonised populations.[32]

Of course, Leonard Woolf loved his little dog and brought him along for company. But he could have spared at least one introspective Socratic skeptical Moorean thought for the entwined history of European colonisation and European animals.

A Parvenu 'Innocent Imperialist' in Ceylon

Coming back to Maxime Rodinson's leitmotif of world history, was Leonard Woolf as Jew victim or executioner in Ceylon in the years 1904 to 1911? Looking back from old age when writing *Growing*, Woolf, who after returning to England from Ceylon became for the rest of his life a prominent anti-imperialist, professed himself baffled that in the first couple of years in Ceylon he was 'an innocent imperialist':

> I had entered Ceylon as an imperialist, one of the white rulers of our Asiatic Empire. The curious thing is that I was not really aware of this. The horrible urgency of politics after the 1914 war, which forced every intelligent person to be passionately interested in them, was unknown to my generation at Cambridge. Except for the Dreyfus case and one or two other questions, we were not deeply concerned with politics. That was why I could take a post in the Ceylon Civil Service without any thought about its political aspect. Travelling to Jaffna in January 1905, I was a very innocent, unconscious imperialist.[33]

In *Growing*, we see Leonard Woolf, fresh from Cambridge with no more than an undergraduate degree, young and callow ('At the age of 24, I was an arrogant, conceited, and quick-tempered young man'), with no worldly experience, reveling in being a 'very innocent, unconscious imperialist', with an 'imperialist soul'.[34]

As a 'very innocent, unconscious imperialist', he was much advantaged by being a Cambridge graduate, which immediately placed him as a civil servant at the apex of the white hierarchy in Ceylon; also, having been at an all-male college would have eased the transition to the all-male professional world of the British colonial officials in Ceylon. Early on, Woolf tells us that the British were 'divided into four well-defined classes', civil servants, army officers, planters and businessmen. The civil servant like Woolf was 'socially in many ways top dog'; he was 'highly paid', exercised 'considerable' power, and in the eyes of the 'Sinhalese and Tamils enjoyed much greater prestige than the other classes'.

True, the army officers enjoyed high social status, but Woolf observes here and elsewhere in *Growing* that there was hardly any British military presence in Ceylon, and that in his six or so years in various parts of the island he as a white man, perhaps alone in a district, could always rule, almost miraculously, without any opposition; his word was law. (One may comment that if the young civil servant Leonard Woolf had no notion of what force an empire could use against its subjects, those the British had colonised in Ceylon may have had a quite vivid idea of the retribution that would lay in store for those who opposed imperial rule.) Civil servants could perform roles like the Government Agent of a Province, or Office Assistant to the Government Agent, or the Archaeological Commissioner, or District Judge or Police Magistrate or Provincial Engineer, and their social position was much higher, Woolf observes, than the 'hundreds of British planters' who lived 'on their dreary tea estates', even if they belonged to the 'same clubs, played tennis together, and occasionally intermarried' with the civil servants. Businessmen, especially those in 'subordinate posts in banks and commercial firms', were 'socially inferior'.[35]

The civil servants talked only 'shop, sport, or gossip', and considered themselves 'rather grand': 'We were grand because we were a ruling caste in a strange Asiatic country', Woolf says, though he 'did not realize this at the time'. What he did quickly realise after he had arrived in Jaffna in 1905 was that, for the 'purpose of accommodating myself to this society', he had to be a *good fellow* and a *gentleman*; to conceal beneath a carapace that he was intelligent and an intellectual; and to devote himself to playing tennis at the end of every day with the white elite. Woolf observes that in the Ceylon of that time 'among the white people the evening tennis was a serious business, a ritual, almost a sacrament'. In Jaffna, after tennis was over, the players and non-players, including 'the two lady missionaries, Miss Case and Miss

Beeching', and a loudly racist ex-army captain, a 'short, choleric, dictatorial, foul-mouthed old gentleman', sat around in a circle, 'drank whisky and soda', and engaged in the 'ritual of British conversation'. Woolf, somewhat to my surprise, confides that their conversation 'fascinated me and, in a curious way, I never got tired of its humdrum melancholy and monotony', revealing the 'strange quality of our imperialist isolation'.[36]

Indeed, Woolf reveals in *Growing* that in Jaffna he felt a great deal of sympathy, when he was an 'innocent imperialist', towards the white elite of Ceylon; he experienced a kind of pity and compassion for them in their 'isolation' and 'melancholy'.[37] Furthermore, in the 1960s as he writes *Growing*, he admits to still feeling pity and compassion for them and for himself as he then was. Dear reader, please judge for yourself, but I find what Woolf writes here, in the early 1960s, that the white elite deserved sympathy as displaced persons, incomprehensible in its massive insensitivity. Let me quote:

> Like all Anglo-Indians and imperialists who were colonial government servants, we were, of course, 'displaced persons'. After two world wars and Hitler we all understand today the phenomenon and psychology of the displaced person. But that was not the case in 1905. Yet we ourselves on the Jaffna tennis court, though we did not know the name, were in fact the phenomenon and had the psychology of people whose lives had suddenly been torn up by the roots, and, in a foreign country, had therefore become unreal, artificial, temporary, and alien.[38]

I'm not going to rehearse here except in barest outline the situation of displaced persons after World War II in Europe, a good number of them survivors of Nazi occupation and the death camps where millions had perished, much of Europe in ruins, in the most freezing of winters, in desperate circumstances and extreme uncertainty, not knowing where they could go, not knowing in what continent they might end up in, not knowing if any country would take them, often without identity papers. In the years 1944–46, some Jews tried to return to their homes in Eastern Europe, and were met with anti-Jewish violence, the most notorious example being the Kielce Pogrom in Poland on 4 July 1946. Jan T Gross, the historian who wrote *Neighbours: The Destruction of the Jewish Community in Jedwabne, Poland* (2001), published in 2006 *Fear: Anti-Semitism in Poland After Auschwitz*, detailing the brutalities against Jews attempting to go back to their pre-war homes. Gross stresses in *Fear* that these postwar brutalities were committed by those who considered themselves ordinary Polish Christians, just as in 1941 the Jews of Jedwabne were murdered, mutilated and burned not by the newly occupying Nazi German army but by their Christian neighbours. Those Jews in Poland and Eastern Europe who survived the postwar pogroms and other violence became refugees and displaced persons.

I'm so astonished by Leonard Woolf invoking here the 'phenomenon and psychology of the displaced person' in relation to the white colonial elite of Ceylon – 'we ourselves on the Jaffna tennis court' followed by whisky and soda and banal conversation – that I'm beginning to wonder about his vaunted intelligence.

Rather than displaced persons a more accurate and appropriate term for the white colonial elite in their 'imperialist isolation' would be the famous phrase formulated by Hannah Arendt only a couple of years later than *Growing*, in a series of articles in *The New Yorker* in 1963, which became one of the twentieth century's most famous and controversial works. *Eichmann in Jerusalem: A Report on the Banality of Evil* argues that it was ordinary people who could commit the evil of the Holocaust, with the further implication that it is ordinary people who can commit evil acts, anywhere, at any time. In these terms, it was ordinary British people who could commit the evils of empire. In *Growing* Woolf stresses that the white colonial elite at tennis and drinking whisky and soda and discussing trivia as if they were in suburban Britain, always steering away from anything that might provoke disagreement, was composed of ordinary members of the English middle class. As he noted early on in *Growing*, in Ceylon as in India during the first decade of the twentieth century the 'social structure and relations between Europeans rested on the same kind of snobbery, pretentiousness, and false pretensions as they did in Putney or Peckham'. Their conversation after tennis 'consisted almost entirely of platitudes, chaff, or gossip'.[39]

Surely only a driven parvenu like Woolf could bear to live for years with such mind – numbing conversational banality.

Unlike the refugees of the world who were the displaced persons after the Holocaust, the white colonial elite certainly had somewhere to go: they could go back to Britain, where in any case they still had family and had sent their children for education. However temporarily dislocated they might feel, they still could return to Britain at any moment of their own choosing, even if it meant resigning from the colonial civil service, as Woolf eventually did in 1911. In Ceylon the British men could learn administrative skills and professional expertise which could assist their re-entry into metropolitan life, along perhaps with many small rewards for being faithful functionaries of empire. They could also perhaps return with as much local art as they could transport, the kind of art, furniture and jewellery that turns up as old imperial loot in BBC programs like *The Antiques Road Show*, practising in a small private way the kind of egregious large-scale looting of the rest of the world's heritage on display in the British Museum in London, which we should more properly refer to as Loot Central.

Let's explore Hannah Arendt's insight that the British in India, and by extension Ceylon, wished to establish themselves as an 'exclusive caste in a foreign country whose only function was to rule and not colonization', a project where 'racism would be… an indispensable tool'. We can say that being an exclusive caste for the British involved not only monotony and melancholy after tennis every evening, as Woolf mourned on their and his behalf, but many pleasures, not least what Arendt drew attention to, exercising 'race superiority'.[40] It was by racism and a kind of absolute social distance that the British would constitute themselves in Ceylon as the *herrenvolk*, Pierre van den Berghe's evocative term for colonisers.[41]

What is clear in *Growing* is that what Woolf refers to as the 'imperialist isolation' of the colonial elite was self-chosen. The primary rule they lived by was no social mixing with non-whites: 'the complete social exclusion from our social suburbia of all Sinhalese and Tamils'. In those days, 'of course, no "natives" were members of the Jaffna tennis club', the only Tamils being admitted were the 'podyans, the small boys who picked up the tennis balls and handed them to us when we were serving'. Also admitted was the 'great Sinnatamby', a 'big stoutish Tamil' in a 'towering maroon turban', who was the keeper of the courts and also 'served us the drinks'. Sometimes, says Woolf, 'I caught in his eye a gleam' of contempt, but we get no sense that Woolf ever conversed with him as equals. He couldn't of course: that would simply not be allowed in the Senior Crown Colony of Ceylon, for it was the social distance from the colonised that was a key source of their prestige, power and authority; which stressed to the colonised at every moment their inferiority in terms of status and influence. In August 1906 Woolf spent a month as the acting Assistant Government Agent in the Mannar District, finding himself the 'only white man' in its 400 square miles, and here 'for the first time I learnt the profound happiness of complete solitude': 'I never spoke to anyone except clerks, headmen, Tamil villagers, and my own Tamil servants'. So, solitude for whites meant no other whites, though he was interacting daily with Tamil people.

He enjoys what he calls 'this kind of complete solitude'.⁴²

Again, I'm reminded of the narrator in *A Room of One's Own* reflecting that white British men can exercise their desire for self-confidence by 'feeling that one has some innate superiority' over other people: 'Hence the enormous importance to a patriarch who has to conquer, who has to rule, of feeling that great numbers of people, half the human race indeed, are by nature inferior to himself.'⁴³ In Ceylon, it's clear, Leonard Woolf was now such a one.

In 1907 he travelled from Jaffna to take up a new appointment in Kandy. Here a hard day at the office doing administrative work was followed by tennis and then going to the Kandy Club, where 'only white men were members'; it had an air, in addition to 'slight depression' and much drunkenness, of 'exclusiveness, superiority, isolation'. His last posting, beginning in 1908, was in the District of Hambantota, in the extreme south of Ceylon, where he again enjoys a 'life of intense solitude': 'It was a social solitude – I had no social life', for the Sinhalese he talks to during the day for his work 'did not come to my house nor did I go to theirs'.⁴⁴

In *Growing*, though he still remembers the name of his dog, Leonard Woolf rarely provides names for his servants, and indeed still refers to them in 1961 using terms he and the other colonisers must have deployed without hesitation before World War I. He does call Sinnatamby by name, and when Woolf contracts typhoid, he is fortunately treated by an American doctor and then nursed 'patiently and efficiently' by his Tamil servant Appukutty. But it is more usual for Woolf to refer to his servants as 'boy' or 'boys', though they are clearly adults (they would have to be adults, useful for their strength and experience). On the way to Jaffna early in 1905 he has dinner at the Residency of the Government Agent in Anuradhapura; after the dinner, he returns to the 'Anuradhapura Rest House where I was to sleep the night and where I had left my dog, Charles, tied up and with instructions to my boy on no account to let him loose'. The next day he heads towards Jaffna 'with Charles and my boy'. On one occasion in Jaffna he refers to the Tamil orderlies of the Kachcheri administrative office as 'the peons'. In the Kandy section of *Growing*, Woolf records visiting an estate; he climbs up a rocky track to the top of a mountain, 'a coolie carrying my bag and bicycle'. In the Hambantota section Woolf tells us that he was in charge of the Government Game Sanctuary, which attracted 'sportsmen from all over the world' who came for 'big game shooting', of 'elephant, buffalo, and deer'. On one occasion he decides to inspect whether some work decreed by the British authorities had been done on the northern boundary of the Game Sanctuary. He sets out on foot early in the morning with a party which included Engelbrecht the Boer, 'three coolies, and my dog-boy', the 'coolies' carrying his camp bed and the food.[45]

I'll repeat that phrase: 'three coolies, and my dog-boy'. What did Diderot say about Europeans in search of islands to ravage, peoples to subjugate... The pleasures of subjugating the colonised were not ones that Woolf refused to himself, even when his views on Britain's imperial colonising began to change, if silently, even only as murmuring to himself.

Leonard Woolf turns Anti-Imperialist

In *Growing*, Woolf is not beyond self-admiration in telling his readers that he was in full possession of the much trumpeted English genius for administration, that he soon became in Ceylon an 'extremely competent civil servant' who every day worked very long hours.[46] Everywhere in Ceylon where he was in charge he instituted administrative efficiencies and innovations in work practices which he felt sure improved the lot of the local population. But then, as the parvenu does, he pushed too hard, unrelentingly.

In 1906, he had learnt from another civil servant a golden rule that he applied both in Ceylon and when he returned to Britain: 'both in business and in private life, 99 out of every 100 letters received by you, which require an answer, should be answered on the day on which you receive them'. Woolf says that such a rule is 'one of the foundations of office efficiency and one of the great discoveries for saving time and worry'.[47] At first when I read this I was rather impressed and thought, hmmm, yes, maybe that is what one should do (now with emails, letters receding as an historical form); then I thought no, sometimes what one should do is slow things down, not reply immediately, leave it for a day or two, and avert the anxiety that might occur if one thinks one has replied too quickly and therefore said the wrong thing, struck the wrong note.

When, however, Woolf demanded in Jaffna that his office staff observe the rule of answering a letter on the day of its receipt, and even though this was the right thing to do and vastly increased office efficiency, he became 'extremely unpopular and I got the reputation among the Tamils, and later among the Sinhalese, of being a strict and ruthless civil servant'. His 'unpopularity in Jaffna,' Woolf reflects, 'was not undeserved', for though he 'meant well by the people of Jaffna' and what he enforced was 'right', his 'methods were too ruthless'. Nonetheless, something life changing now happened to his inner life: the 'difficulties and frictions' his ruthlessness and severity as a superior caused made him 'for the first time dimly perceive the problems of the imperialist', which set him on the road to becoming 'fully conscious of my position as a ruler of subject peoples': 'my first doubts whether I wanted to rule other people, to be an imperialist and proconsul'.[48]

One incident in particular, involving a horse, sets him on this belated path to awareness. Mr Harry Sanderasekara, a well-known lawyer, complained to the Governor that while driving his trap in the main street of Jaffna, Mr Woolf, riding towards him from the opposite direction, had deliberately hit him in the face with his riding whip. Leonard Woolf puzzled over this complaint because he knew he had done no such thing; but the more he thought about it, the more he realised what it uncomfortably meant:

> ... perhaps for the first time I felt a twinge of doubt in my imperialist soul, a doubt whether we were not in the wrong, and the Jaffna Tamil Association and Mr Sanderasekara in the right, not right in believing that I would and had hit him in the face, but right in feeling that my sitting on a horse arrogantly in the main street of their town was as good as a slap in the face.[49]

Nevertheless, Woolf chooses to keep concealed both from his fellow white civil servants and from the Tamil and Sinhalese 'subject peoples' that he had become critical of the imperialism he was assisting so efficiently to function. He feels that he became 'more and more ambivalent, politically schizophrenic', an 'anti-imperialist' who 'knew from the inside how evil the system was beneath the surface for ordinary men and women'. Yet, he confesses, all through his time in Ceylon he 'enjoyed' being considered, especially by those living in the 'feudal society' of the hill villages, as 'one of the super-Chiefs, the Princes, or the Boyars', as when he rode up to a village in the mountains of Kandy. Arriving there, each member of the crowd welcoming him 'came and prostrated himself, touching the ground with his forehead'. In Ceylon he appreciated the 'flattery of being the great man and the father of the people'.[50] He relished being part of the *herrenvolk*, only revealing his quietly nurtured anti-imperialism after he returned to London, and even then only after he resigned.

The British Empire in Ceylon

Throughout *Growing* Leonard Woolf shows no interest in reflecting on the colonisation in Ceylon he was there to help administer. Almost in passing, Woolf mentions, as we saw before, that in

'Kandy and the mountains, hundreds of British planters lived on their dreary tea estates', though they also 'enjoyed superficially complete social equality with the civil servants'.[51]

Woolf reveals no interest how the British empire facilitated the presence of the hundreds of tea planters whose plantations must have meant uprooting many thousands of Ceylon people from their ancestral lands. Woolf tells us that while in Kandy in 1907 he found it 'boring' continually having to 'deal with the planters and their estates and labour'; also, there was 'much business connected with the sale and settlement of Crown Land'.[52] Woolf might have reflected that the British were establishing in the hill plantations a kind of settler colonisation that they also established in parts of Africa, and which involved, in terms of genocide theory, what Lemkin in 1944 referred to as a two-stage process, the removal of a people or part of a people and replacement by incoming colonisers. Woolf of course in pre-war Ceylon didn't have to hand Lemkin's definition of genocide formulated in the midst of the Holocaust in 1944.[53] But surely a little sensitivity, an interest in the viewpoint of the colonised, could have prompted him to reflect on the plight of those in Ceylon dispossessed of their land and now having to labour on the estates of the invaders, which had been their land. He could also have reflected that by declaring that Ceylon was a Crown Colony the British deprived the people of Ceylon of their sovereignty.

It's a truism of British empire history that the empire, for its own convenience, used colonial possessions for a variety of reasons. Islands could be especially valuable for the banishment of political prisoners, from either Britain itself, or transferred from other, perhaps distant, places across the empire. Like Engelbrecht the Boer, talked about by Woolf in the Hambantota section of the book, its final section. Woolf explains that a 'considerable number of Boers who fought and were captured in the Boer War' were sent to Ceylon and 'interned in camps up country'. He doesn't reflect whether it was ethically right that Britain should establish an archipelago of internment camps in Ceylon, composed of anti-African racists; he doesn't ask a kind of G E Moore question, is this something that the empire *ought* to do? When the war was over, the Boer prisoners of war were repatriated to South Africa as long as they took an oath of allegiance to the king and his successors. One of the Boer prisoners, Engelbrecht, refused to sign, so the British administration sent him to Woolf's district with 'a miserable allowance to live in a disused prison', hoping that he would find life there so miserable he would want to sign the oath and go back to Orange Free State where he came from. Woolf tells us that Engelbrecht, obstinate and stupid, still refused to sign, despite living in poverty and squalor. The British decided that Engelbrecht was to be 'appointed Game Sanctuary Ranger on a small salary', even though he was so racist, behaving 'to the Sinhalese as the Boers behave to the negroes in Africa', and was hated by the local population.[54]

Woolf does not make the obvious comment that in the interests of maintaining the superiority of whiteness the empire decided that a white man should not be seen to be living in poverty and squalor. Engelbrecht the egregiously racist Boer was to be recognised as part of the *herrenvolk* and given an official position. When Engelbrecht comes to court charged with neglect of a Singalese woman whose child he fathered, Woolf as magistrate shows his English genius for fairness and impartiality by finding against Engelbrecht and for the Singalese mother. Yet we quickly learn that Woolf and Engelbrecht are hunting companions, and they go out hunting, or shall we rather say murdering, leopards together, even though Woolf recognised their 'magnificent beauty'.[55] Furthermore, Woolf tells us that the Hambantota people were very aware that he and Engelbrecht were hunting companions and that such knowledge would hardly endear him to them.[56] Woolf, as he himself was aware, was socially including the uber-racist Boer within the white colonial elite, within the full gaze of the people he ruled.

Woolf makes very little comment on the extent of institutionalised official violence that the British government practised in Ceylon, in which Woolf himself directly participated or supervised with his parvenu's hyper-efficiency. In February 1906 in Jaffna, Woolf was asked to take up a special appointment as an Assistant Koddu Superintendent at the Ceylon Pearl Fishery in the Northern Province waters, an activity going back to ancient times; the British administration had now involved itself, with civil servants and white police officers in attendance. The fishing was 'actually done by Arab or Tamil divers', the Arab divers in their thousands travelling from the Persian Gulf in dhows. When in the evening the Arab divers returned in their boats, each boat's load of oysters was divided into three equal heaps: 'The Koddu Superintendent, of whom I was one, then went round and chose two out of the three heaps as the Government's share'.[57]

We are reminded again of Diderot's scathing assessment of Europeans in search of 'islands to ravage, peoples to rob'. The British, who did no diving themselves, robbed the divers of two thirds of their catch.

Woolf makes no critical comment on such British colonial practices of looting, but does go on to complain in a letter to (it would appear) Lytton Strachey that it was like 'coolie work' to keep order among the Arab divers when they got back to shore after a long day's diving and he had to make sure the colonial Government took the largest share of the oysters. Nonetheless, order he kept. Woolf quotes from his letter to Strachey: 'the Arabs will do anything if you hit them hard enough with a walking stick, an occupation in which I have been engaged for the most part of the last 3 days and nights'.[58] If Edward Said required more evidence – which he didn't – for the abundance of essentialising imagery in Orientalist discourse when he wrote *Orientalism*

(1978), Woolf would have been useful here. Woolf insists that he very much admired the Arab divers for their dignity, eloquence, and egalitarianism, observing that they were 'vastly amused' by his use of a walking stick on them.[59]

In Ceylon, Woolf also participated in a supervisory role in British Government prisons in Jaffna and Kandy. This was the 'most unpleasant work' Woolf had to do in Ceylon, one of his duties being 'present in a prison when anyone was hanged or flogged and to certify that the sentence had been duly carried out'. He recounts that the 'flogging of a man with a cat-o'-nine-tails is the most disgusting and barbarous thing I have ever seen', even worse, he feels, than a hanging. The prisoner's back is 'literally flayed by the lashes and every ten lashes he is examined by the Medical Officer' who will stop the flogging 'if in his opinion the man is not in a condition to stand any more punishment'.[60]

In Kandy, Woolf reports, executions occurred in the Bogambra Prison in the early morning. Everyone present waited for Woolf, who stood in front of the gallows 'to give the signal to the executioner for the "drop" which would hang the man'. In two out of the six or seven hangings which Woolf had to certify, 'something went wrong', and Woolf gives the 'repulsive details' of what occurred. Like everyone else present at the executions, he found them a 'horrifying experience', which nevertheless he as a civil servant would carry out, whenever he was called upon to act as a magistrate or judge, 'without fear or favour, impartially, justly, objectively, strictly, even sternly', because the law should be 'strictly maintained'. Later in his life Woolf would, he tells us, come to oppose capital punishment; but in Ceylon in the early 1900s, he efficiently performed his imperial duty.[61]

In the grotesque theatre of the execution scene, Woolf the zealous colonial functionary, with everyone in the prison waiting for him to give the signal for the hanging to begin, was a central figure in its repulsive drama.

Let's remind ourselves of Maxime Rodinson's observation that in world history 'all peoples count among their number both victims and executioners'.[62] In this imperial history, Leonard Woolf as Jew was not victim but executioner.

Leonard Woolf's sister Bella comes to Ceylon

Leonard Woolf's older sister Bella was also not a victim of history. Bella Woolf visits Ceylon to be with her brother, and there prospers, through marriage and being a colonial author. Woolf welcomes his sister's company, for while he was given to solitude and silence, Bella enjoyed conversation. With his pleasure in recording titles, early on Woolf tells us that when he arrived in Jaffna, he was met by the 'Office Assistant, Wilfred Thomas Southorn, who eventually became Sir W. T. Southorn, Governor of Gambia, and who married my sister Bella'. In 1907 Woolf, then aged 27, travels from Jaffna to Kandy to take up a new appointment. Bella came out at the end of 1907 to stay with him, and, being an 'extremely sociable person', she made a 'great difference' to his life there. Bella also tried to steer her brother towards romance and a possible marriage. Leonard had become acquainted with a young 10-year-old woman, who he calls Rachel, daughter of a tea planter family near Kandy, and they go riding together. Bella, who had stayed with Rachel's family for a few days on their estate, tells Leonard that she thinks Rachel's parents would like him as a son-in-law. Leonard enjoys a 'real affection' for Rachel 'without ever at all falling in love with her'. At the moment he might have proposed, and he felt Rachel was waiting for him to propose, he found he couldn't.[63] I'll reflect on this episode in my conclusion.

When Woolf leaves Ceylon for England, Bella, 'now married to the Assistant Director of the Peradeniya Gardens', sails with him.[64]

In her biography of Leonard Woolf, Victoria Glendinning offers an interesting detail about Bella in Ceylon, that while there she wrote a guidebook, *How to See Ceylon*, published in 1914, with later editions in 1922 and 1924.[65]

Leonard Woolf and Bella Woolf were doing very well out of the British empire.

We might say that, sociologically and historically, Leonard Woolf and Bella Woolf belonged to a layer of middle-class Jews who found the empire congenial, offering all sorts of positions that advantaged themselves and their families.

Racism and Orientalism

In his years in Ceylon it is clear that Woolf succumbed to the Parvenu's Curse, he took being an efficient administrator to an almost theatrical extreme as a parvenu would. Woolf realised that in Ceylon, especially as the years went on, he became too severe. He still felt he was always doing the right thing by the people of Ceylon under his charge, for his only concern, he says repeatedly, was their welfare. He 'loved the subject peoples and their way of life'. He especially grew increasingly fond of the Sinhalese: 'everything to do with the Sinhalese seemed to me enchanting'. The Sinhalese are a 'humorous people and they have the same kind of sense of humour as the European'. Even in a 'remote village I felt that I could make a joke which would be appreciated'. His greatest wish was to make their lives 'prosperous'.[66]

He especially took to heart the Sinhalese people of his final district, Hambantota, where, in his two and three quarter years there,

> I worked all day from the moment I got up in the morning until the moment I went to bed at night, for I rarely thought of anything except the District and the people, to increase their prosperity, diminish the poverty and disease, start irrigation works, open schools… But I was ruthless – too ruthless… both to them and to myself.[67]

Sadly for Woolf, his professed love for the Sinhalese and desire to bring prosperity and happiness to their lives, conflicted with his parvenu's anxiety to become socially indistinguishable from the colonial elite and his severity as an administrator.

By the end of his stay he came to realise that while he loved the people he was ruling over, they didn't love him. As if in a climactic moment of a drama, Woolf experiences a traumatic moment of distress and dejection while doing everything he can to deal with an outbreak of rinderpest among the cattle and buffalo in his beloved Hambantota. He spends days shooting infected animals belonging to the villagers, and 'warning owners wherever I found stray cattle that I should have to destroy them if I found them straying again'. One evening, driving through a village, he comes upon 'two cows straying, one already showing symptoms of disease'. He sends for their owner, and realises that in this same village earlier in the day he had warned the villager not to let his cows stray. Woolf feels he must 'make an example' as a warning to the village, takes his rifle from his trap, and shoots the two cows. He knows that it is 'not a pleasant business to ride and drive through villages and shoot the cattle and buffaloes of the villagers whom one knows and likes'. An unpleasant situation develops. The 'whole village' stands on the road looking at the bodies of the cows. Woolf explains to them that the owner had been warned and that the infected cow had to die otherwise it would help 'spread the disease to other people's cattle all over the country'. Woolf registers a 'hostile murmur' among the villagers. As he walks to his trap, they 'followed me and, as I drove away, I still heard the dull hostile murmur of their voices'. He senses that, 'though they were the nicest of people and I was very fond of them', they would have 'thrown stones at me or shot me in the back as I walked to the trap, had they dared'.[68]

Woolf finds himself 'profoundly depressed' by this 'communal hostility', realising that the villagers 'did not believe' what he said to them about why he had to kill the cows: 'to them I was part of the white man's machine, which they did not understand'. Why, he asks himself, can't the villagers understand that his attitude to them was 'entirely benevolent and altruistic', that he was 'merely trying to save from destruction some of the most valuable of their few possessions'? Then he has a moment of insight into what he considers to be the villagers' and general Sinhalese consciousness, which explains why they cannot understand him. That night, after this disturbing encounter, Woolf by arrangement meets the Muhandiram or chief headman of the area: 'The Muhandiram was a very intelligent Sinhalese, English educated.' (The Muhandiram arrives after Woolf has eaten his dinner, perhaps observing the coloniser convention that whites and non-whites could not eat together.) Woolf likes him and he talks quite freely to him as 'I would have to a white man'. But then occurs a discussion that depressed Woolf 'even more profoundly than the Sinhalese villagers'. They stroll out to a headland, and look at Halley's comet, visible just then. Woolf asks the Muhandiram what he thought about the comet and planets and stars, and is extremely disconcerted by his answer, which revealed that the Muhandiram 'believed quite seriously' in 'astrological nonsense', that at the moment of our birth our lives and characters were determined by the position of the constellations.[69]

These two incidents, the angry villagers and the fantastical ideas of the Muhandiram, convince Woolf of the futility of imperialism: 'the absurdity of a people of one civilization and mode of life trying to impose its rule upon an entirely different civilization and mode of life'. When one scratches the mind of even the most sophisticated of the Singalese, such as the Muhandiram, 'so quick-witted, so intelligent, so anglicized and Europeanized', one finds that his mind is ruled by vulgar superstition, by a fundamental lack of reason; and it was this same lack of reason that meant that the villagers simply could not understand Woolf's rational actions, performed for their sake, in trying to manage the rinderpest outbreak. Here a dog again enters the narrative: 'they had less understanding of my ways, my intentions, my affection for them than the half-bred bitch walking at my heels'.[70]

That was the moment of realisation for Woolf that was traumatic: Western civilisation, founded on reason (in an arc from Socrates to G E Moore), could never successfully impose itself on Asiatic societies, which were foundationally and eternally irrational. That is why, he decides, imperialism could not last. And for Woolf personally, this realisation was utterly depressing, because he loved the people he ruled over who were now irrationally rejecting him. He was, he knew, too ruthless, but his ruthlessness exhibited a use of reason of which these Asiatics, he now recognised, were incapable. He could now satisfactorily explain to himself what had happened during the rinderpest incident, in an essentialising mode we, after Edward Said, easily recognise as banally Orientalist.

Nonetheless, in *Growing* Woolf reflects that in his time in Ceylon it was a kind of privilege to experience 'the slow-pulsing life of this most ancient type of civilization', the 'ancient rhythms and ways of primitive life'.[71]

One final reflection here, recalling Moses Mendelssohn suggesting in the late eighteenth century that Christian missionaries were also colonisers.[72] No such thought occurs to Leonard Woolf. In the Jaffna section of *Growing*, he recounts how grateful he is to the 'two Church Missionary Society lady missionaries, Miss Beeching and Miss Case', for saving his dog Charles, who had become lost. Returning by train from a visit to Colombo, they see what was 'obviously a pukka English dog' trotting wearily along looking for its master. They 'got a porter to run after him' and return him to Leonard Woolf. He then gives a description of the ladies:

> The missionary ladies were aged about 26 or 27... Miss Beeching had a curious face rather like that of a good-looking male Red Indian; Miss Case was of the broad-beamed, good-humoured, freckled type.[73]

How curious, given Virginia Woolf's passionate feminism, that Woolf could be so banally sexist. I mentioned this episode in *Growing* to Ann on one of our morning walks, and she thought that in the twentieth century perhaps many men, for generations, had feminist wives and yet thought feminism had nothing to do with them. I suggested that perhaps that did not change till the impact of Women's Liberation in the late 1960s and 1970s. Ann said that maybe that aspect of the impact of Women's Liberation on men was kind of looking back to John Stuart Mill and Harriet Taylor Mill's notions of companionate marriage in the nineteenth century.

Woolf records that in Jaffna there were 'perhaps ten missionaries', which must have meant they were many more elsewhere, invading the whole island.[74] But their presence stimulates no reflection by Woolf on what they were doing there, which was clearly to attempt to destroy the inherited religions of Ceylon, including the Buddhist religion which Woolf in *Growing* says he so much admires,[75] and replace it with a Christian faith that would be held out in a supersessionist way as superior. (In my *The Origins of Violence*, I regard supersessionism as one of the most destructive beliefs in world history, meaning here the view that some religions can be erased or removed or superseded by another religion, seen as history and humanity's only true religion.)[76]

Let's ponder again for a moment the narrator's musing in *A Room of One's Own* on the imperial male, where she irreverently reflects that white English men can exercise in the theatre of empire their desire for self-confidence by 'feeling that one has some innate superiority' over other people.[77] Leonard Woolf to his own satisfaction had demonstrated his superiority over the people in Ceylon, in his rationality as against their superstition, and his superiority in his 'English' capacity for administration.

Concluding Speculations

By the end of his time in Ceylon in 1911, Woolf must have considered that he and Bella had established themselves as an imperial Anglo-Ceylon family of rising importance and consequence. For Leonard Woolf the parvenu, I think, that was exactly what he wished to achieve. That was the plan. That was the whole point of his decision to go to Ceylon and stay there for over six years, however obfuscated by his murmuring at the end of *Sowing* that he was leaving England for Ceylon completely ignorant of anything to do with imperialism and its history. Now he could return, in a kind of triumph, for if he scaled the heights of white colonial society in Anglo-Ceylon, couldn't he now also scale the heights of Anglo-Indian society in England, such as could be found in the Strachey and Stephen families? Wouldn't he now be accepted by them as worthy of joining their ranks? Wasn't he now worthy of marriage into such a circle?

Back in England in June 2011, Leonard had a year's leave before him. While he had felt in Ceylon that the white colonial elite of which he was part were displaced persons, melancholy because uprooted from all they had known, it turned out that he was received by his old Cambridge friends, now living in or about Bloomsbury, 'as one of themselves'. He slipped without much difficulty 'into the kind of place which I had occupied in 1904 when I sailed for Ceylon'. He meets again 'Lytton Strachey, Saxon Sydney-Turner, Virginia and Adrian Stephen, Vanessa and Clive Bell, Duncan Grant, Maynard Keynes'. He could, he tells us in his Epilogue, have returned to Ceylon and 'become a successful civil servant in Colombo and end eventually with a governorship and K.C.M.G.' But he realised that he was 'falling in love with

Virginia', and if she accepted him he would 'resign from Ceylon and try to earn my living by writing'.[78]

Earlier in *Growing*, Woolf confesses that at the back of his mind, 'in its depths, I wanted to be a writer', though, while his interests were 'passionately of the mind', he was never, like Lytton Strachey and others of his friends, 'exclusively intellectual'.[79] I'm puzzled by this: if he wanted to be a writer like his Cambridge friends also wanted to be, why did he go to Ceylon as a civil servant and spend many years there? Why, in 1904, after Cambridge, didn't he come down to London (having previously gone up to Cambridge) and live the life of a freelance writer, for example, earning money by doing reviewing, as Virginia Stephen did both before marrying Leonard and for decades afterwards?[80]

My speculation is harsh and suspicious here, following the logic of the parvenu. Leonard Woolf tells us that he fell in love with Virginia and no doubt he did; their marriage was long lasting and represented a famously productive relationship and partnership.

Yet my suspicion is that Woolf, now established as an Anglo-Ceylon identity (he could have been a Governor if he stayed, his sister had married into the empire's elite of peripatetic officials), was all along driven by a parvenu desire to scale the heights of a chosen area of society. Woolf the bedazzled parvenu desired marriage into one of England's famous imperial families, that he had come to know while at Cambridge. In Ceylon there were some young women, he tells us, who he met and might have married. But, in my suspicious view, they were not high enough for Woolf's parvenu ambition. That is why he could not propose to 'Rachel' in that awkward moment in Ceylon, even though he felt she wished him to propose, leaving him embarrassed and her forlorn. 'Rachel' was a tea planter's daughter. Woolf wanted to marry much higher, and for that ambition to be realised London was the place to be, not Ceylon.

Back in London, Woolf, Glendinning's biography suggests, is attracted to both the Stephen sisters. Not surprisingly, wishing to be a writer, with a store of possible stories from his time in Britain's Senior Crown Colony, he falls in love with the younger sister.[81]

In her biography, Hermione Lee quotes from a letter to Leonard from Virginia Stephen of 6 May 1912 before their marriage in August: 'I sometimes think that if I married you, I could have everything – and then – is it the sexual side of it that comes between us? As I told you brutally the other day, I feel no physical attraction to you. There are moments – when you kissed me the other day was one – when I feel no more than a rock. And yet your caring for me as you do almost overwhelms me. It is so real, and so strange. Why should you?'[82]

Why indeed? That's also what I've been trying to work out, in reflecting on Leonard as parvenu.

A closing puzzle. In *Sowing*, Woolf, we've noticed earlier, said that Moore and he and his friends at Cambridge 'were fascinated by questions of what was right and wrong, what one *ought* to do'.[83] In the Kandy section of *Growing*, Woolf admits to himself, in 1907, his 'growing awareness of the problem of imperialism'.[84] In terms of moral philosophy, I ask: *ought* Leonard Woolf have resigned once he knew that he was now an anti-imperialist who recognised 'from the inside', as he says in *Growing*, 'how evil the system was'?[85] Why, then, didn't he resign in 1907, rather than continuing to be a functionary of empire till 1911? What are the ethics here? What, dear reader, are we to think?

Yet, as we shall see in the next chapter, in Arendt's terms, even while as parvenu Woolf would become an insider and scale the heights of British society in the political-intellectual sphere and in arts and letters through the Hogarth Press he established with Virginia Woolf in 1917, he was still, because of English anti-Semitism, regarded as a pariah; and he also chose, also in Arendt's terms, to be a conscious pariah.

It's time to consider the full force of twentieth century English anti-Semitism.

1   Hannah Arendt, *The Origins of Totalitarianism* (Harvest/Harcourt, New York, 1994), pp.182–3.
2   Hermione Lee, *Virginia Woolf* (Vintage/Random, New York, 1999), p.503. Lee notes that in February 1931 Oswald Mosley formed his New Party; Harold Nicolson joined and edited Mosley's magazine, *Action* (p.608).
3   Leonard Woolf, *Sowing: An Autobiography of the Years 1880–1904* (1960; Hogarth Press, London, 1970), pp.192–4.
4   Leonard Woolf, *Sowing*, p.202.
5   Leonard Woolf, *Sowing*, pp.72, 130–2, 136, 147–9.
6   Leonard Woolf, *Sowing*, p.194.
7   Hermione Lee, *Virginia Woolf*, pp.60–3.
8   See Virginia Woolf, *Moments of Being: Unpublished Autobiographical Writings*, edited by Jeanne Schulkind (The University Press, Sussex, 1976), 'Old Bloomsbury', pp.159–179.
9   Virginia Woolf, *A Room of One's Own*, p.46.
10 Leonard Woolf, *Sowing*, p.13.
11 Ann Curthoys and John Docker, *Is History Fiction?* (UNSW Press, Sydney, 2010), pp.12–17.
12 Curthoys and Docker, *Is History Fiction?*, pp.42–3.
13 Curthoys and Docker, *Is History Fiction?*, pp.42–4.
14 Curthoys and Docker, *Is History Fiction?*, p.39.
15 Curthoys and Docker, *Is History Fiction?*, pp.39–41.
16 Curthoys and Docker, *Is History Fiction?*, p.44.
17 Sankar Muthu, *Enlightenment Against Empire* (Princeton University Press, Princeton NJ, 2003), pp.1–4. See also John Docker, 'Sheer Folly and Derangement: How the Crusades Disoriented Enlightenment Historiography', in Alexander Cook, Ned Curthoys and Shino Konishi (eds), *Representing Humanity in the Age of Enlightenment* (Pickering and Chatto, London, 2013), pp.45 and 194 note 25.

18 John Docker, 'Sheer Folly and Derangement: How the Crusades Disoriented Enlightenment Historiography', p.41, and Gibbon, *The History of the Decline and Fall of the Roman Empire*, ed. D.Womersley (1776–8; Penguin Classics, London, 1995), vol.3, p.728.

19 See Peter Jimack (ed.), *A History of the Two Indies* (Ashgate, London, 2006), Introduction, pp.xxiii-xxiv.

20 *A History of the Two Indies*, p.277.

21 Ned Curthoys, *The Legacy of Liberal Judaism: Ernst Cassirer and Hannah Arendt's Hidden Conversation* (Berghahn, New York and Oxford, 2013).

22 Ned Curthoys, *The Legacy of Liberal Judaism*, p.32.

23 Ned Curthoys, *The Legacy of Liberal Judaism*, p.33.

24 Ned Curthoys, *The Legacy of Liberal Judaism*, p.55, also 213.

25 Ned Curthoys, 'Diasporic Visions: Al-Andalus in the German-Jewish Imaginary', in Christopher Wise and Paul James (eds), *Being Arab: Arabism and the Politics of Recognition* (Arena Publications, Melbourne, 2010), pp.120-4.

26 Christina Petterson, *The Missionary, the Catechist and the Hunter: Foucault, Protestantism and Colonialism* (Brill, Leiden and Boston, 2014), pp.2, 16 n.23.

27 Christina Petterson, *The Missionary, the Catechist and the Hunter*, pp.1–4, 8, 12–15, 18, 21, 23–6, 35, 38, 66, 73, 77.

28 Hannah Arendt, *The Origins of Totalitarianism* (Harvest/Harcourt, New York, 1994), p.440. Another claimant for the signal dishonour of instituting the first concentration camps were the Spanish in Cuba in 1898.

29 Mike Davis, *Late Victorian Holocausts: El Niño Famines and the Making of the Modern World* (2001; Verso, London and New York, 2012), pp.164–5.

30 Jared Diamond, *Guns, Germs and Steel* (Vintage, New York, 1998), pp.76–7.

31 Leonard Woolf, *Growing: An Autobiography of the Years 1904–1911* (Hogarth Press, London, 1961), p.25.

32 See Diamond, *Guns, Germs and Steel*, p.207, concerning dogs and disease, though he is not specifically talking of colonial situations here.

33 Leonard Woolf, *Growing*, p.25.

34 Leonard Woolf, *Growing*, pp.56, 113.

35 Leonard Woolf, *Growing*, pp.16–17, 24, 44.

36 Leonard Woolf, *Growing*, pp.24, 36–7, 44–5.

37 Leonard Woolf, *Growing*, p.44.

38 Leonard Woolf, *Growing*, pp.46–7.

39 Leonard Woolf, *Growing*, pp.17, 46.

40 Hannah Arendt, *The Origins of Totalitarianism*, pp.182–3.

41 Pierre van den Berghe, *Race and Racism* (Wiley, Sydney, 1967).

42 Leonard Woolf, *Growing*, pp.18, 45, 119–120.

43　Virginia Woolf, *A Room of One's Own*, p.32.
44　Leonard Woolf, *Growing*, pp.132, 135, 172, 175–8.
45　Leonard Woolf, *Growing*, pp.24–6, 82, 99, 103, 111, 121, 149, 175–76, 207, 218, 228.
46　Leonard Woolf, *Growing*, pp.70, 106.
47　Leonard Woolf, *Growing*, p.107.
48　Leonard Woolf, *Growing*, pp.109, 111.
49　Leonard Woolf, *Growing*, p.114.
50　Leonard Woolf, *Growing*, pp.157–9.
51　Leonard Woolf, *Growing*, pp.16–17, 47, 84–5.
52　Leonard Woolf, *Growing*, p.156.
53　See Ann Curthoys and John Docker, 'Defining Genocide', in Dan Stone (ed.), *The Historiography of Genocide* (Palgrave Macmillan, London, 2010), p.11.
54　Leonard Woolf, *Growing*, pp.200–202.
55　Leonard Woolf, *Growing*, pp.196, 202–208.
56　Leonard Woolf, *Growing*, p.203.
57　Leonard Woolf, *Growing*, pp.86–92.
58　Leonard Woolf, *Growing*, pp.90–1.
59　Leonard Woolf, *Growing*, pp.94–5.
60　Leonard Woolf, *Growing*, p.166.
61　Leonard Woolf, *Growing*, pp.166–9.
62　Maxime Rodinson, *Cult, Ghetto, and State: The Persistence of the Jewish Question*, trans. Jon Rothschild (Al Saqi Books, London, 1983), p.182.
63　Leonard Woolf, *Growing*, pp.34, 134, 137, 155.
64　Leonard Woolf, *Growing*, p.245.
65　Victoria Glendinning, *Leonard Woolf: A Biography* (Counterpoint, Berkeley, 2008), pp.93 and 446–7 note 36.
66　Leonard Woolf, *Growing*, pp.33, 156, 159, 242, 247.
67　Leonard Woolf, *Growing*, p.180.
68　Leonard Woolf, *Growing*, pp.190–1, 193.
69　Leonard Woolf, *Growing*, pp.191–3.
70　Leonard Woolf, *Growing*, pp.193–4.
71　Leonard Woolf, *Growing*, p.32; also 54 and 79.
72　See also Christina Petterson, *The Missionary, the Catechist and the Hunter: Foucault, Protestantism and Colonialism* (Brill, Leiden and Boston, 2014), which presents a similar argument, that Danish colonisation in eighteenth-century Greenland was conducted by Lutheran missions, seeking a combined religious and social transformation of Greenlandic life.

73 Leonard Woolf, *Growing*, p.26.
74 Leonard Woolf, *Growing*, p.36.
75 Leonard Woolf, *Growing*, p.159.
76 John Docker, *The Origins of Violence: Religion, History and Genocide* (Pluto Press, London, 2008), p.6.
77 Virginia Woolf, *A Room of One's Own*, p.32.
78 Leonard Woolf, *Growing*, pp.172, 246–7.
79 Leonard Woolf, *Growing*, p.172.
80 Hermione Lee, *Virginia Woolf*, pp.210–15.
81 Glendinning, *Leonard Woolf*, pp.120, 125. On p.125, Glendinning writes: 'Leonard revered Vanessa, and still felt her attraction.'
82 Hermione Lee, *Virginia Woolf*, pp pp.305–6.
83 Leonard Woolf, *Sowing*, pp.148–9.
84 Leonard Woolf, *Growing*, p.157.
85 Leonard Woolf, *Growing*, p.159.

13

Conscious Pariahs

In this chapter, I will be more favourable to Leonard Woolf.

I'll do this by pursuing further the implications of Hannah Arendt's 1944 essay, 'The Jew as Pariah: A hidden tradition' I talk about in my Introduction, where Arendt admires a tradition of what she calls conscious pariahs, intellectuals, novelists, poets and comedians like Heinrich Heine, Bernard Lazare, Charlie Chaplin, and Kafka, who chose that public identity.[1] For Arendt the conscious pariah encompasses cultural figures who were able to 'evolve the concept of the pariah as a human type – a concept of supreme importance for the evaluation of mankind in our day', one which has exerted a powerful influence on 'the gentile world'.[2]

In Arendt's terms, I've so far been tracing Leonard Woolf's parvenu desire to become indistinguishable within his Cambridge cohort in the early years of the twentieth century, and, from 1904 to 1911, the British imperial elite in Ceylon.

Now I ask, can we see Leonard Woolf also in Arendt's terms as torn, a parvenu yet also coming out, announcing himself, as a conscious pariah? Here I will try to tease out meanings in Leonard Woolf's story 'Three Jews', part of *Two Stories* along with Virginia Woolf's 'The Mark on the Wall', the publication that launched the Hogarth Press, in 1917, in an edition of 150 copies, Virginia Woolf and Leonard Woolf just beginning to learn their craft as printers; a signal event in the history of high literary modernism.

In *Hannah Arendt: For Love of the World*, Elisabeth Young-Bruehl argues that Walter Benjamin was also a conscious pariah, like Hannah Arendt herself.[3] We can, then, add to Arendt's list. The conscious pariahs would now be: Heinrich Heine, Bernard Lazare, Charlie Chaplin, Kafka, Benjamin, and Arendt.

I also wish to add Leonard Woolf.

I'll also ask: can we see Virginia Woolf as a conscious pariah in Arendt's terms?

Virginia Woolf née Stephen was not of Jewish descent, and she has a relationship to anti-Semitism I'll soon talk about. I'm going to propose nonetheless that she be added to Arendt's list, which would now be: Heinrich Heine, Bernard Lazare, Charlie Chaplin, Franz Kafka, Walter Benjamin, Hannah Arendt, Leonard Woolf, Virginia Woolf.

And, bear with me: I'm also going to propose that we add Jessica Mitford.

Arendt considered that the Jewish parvenu's desire to blend in would be impossible to accomplish, for the parvenu is always in danger of being regarded and treated as a pariah. In the case of Leonard Woolf, that impossibility was surely because of the historical force of anti-Semitism, a prominent strand within the modernist movement of the early twentieth century, not least within Bloomsbury itself.

Another preliminary thought here: coming so late to reading about and into Bloomsbury, I'm surprised by their anti-Semitic culture, I thought they would be more sophisticated, more cosmopolitan, less vulgar, less provincial; more dissociated, as a bohemia, from their class of origin and some of its worst and most common attitudes; and beyond their class of origin, the wider society, from which as a cultural elite they so much wished to differ.

English Anti-Semitism: The Complexities of Virginia Woolf
I've referred before to the work of Tony Kushner and David

Cesarini in highlighting English anti-Semitism in the late nineteenth century and early twentieth century; anti-Semitism that continued after the First World War and impacted on working class Jews generally, as revealed in the reminiscences of my uncles and my mother of growing up in the East End. During these decades, anti-Semitism was ever present in the English middle and upper class. Leonard Woolf, we've noted, says in *Growing* that when he returned to London on leave in 1911, he decided to put off thinking about whether or not to return to Ceylon and 'enjoy myself': 'I did enjoy myself. I found my Cambridge friends living in or about Bloomsbury: Lytton Strachey, Saxon Sydney-Turner, Virginia and Adrian Stephen, Vanessa and Clive Bell, Duncan Grant, Maynard Keynes... I saw a great deal of them all and went to the Russian Ballet and the *Ring* with them, and dined with Vanessa and Clive and with Virginia and Adrian, and stayed with Virginia in a house which she rented in Firle near Lewes.'[4] In *Beginning Again: An Autobiography of the Years 1911–1918* (1964), Leonard Woolf defines Bloomsbury as constituted in friendship: 'We were and always remained primarily and fundamentally a group of friends'.[5] Perhaps there is friendship and friendship. What kind of friends were they?

The biographies, with their access to letters and diaries, reveal another narrative, underlying or perhaps not so underlying, in any case belying the note of easy acceptance on his return that Leonard Woolf appears to be so sure of. In the years following his return in 1911 he must have been aware of less pleasant resonances, and, in the case of Virginia Stephen, certain ambivalences that posed problems for their relationship when they married on 10 August 1912.

As much as Leonard the parvenu had for many years wished to blend in at Cambridge and in Ceylon, he was not necessarily accepted as fully English. In her biography Hermione Lee quotes from the letter to Leonard from Virginia Stephen I've referred to before, of 6 May 1912, where she is agonising over whether or not to marry him, and refers to her sexual feelings: 'I feel angry sometimes at the strength of your desire. Possibly, your being a Jew comes in also at this point. You seem so foreign.'[6] Here I think a strand of centuries-old erotic Orientalism perhaps intersects with Virginia's thoughts, that Leonard as Jewish was to be regarded as Oriental, and the Oriental male had been perceived in literary and visual representation for so long as an ardent, sensual, passionate lover, in contrast in particular to the more measured sensibilities of the English.

While Leonard the parvenu hoped to see himself, and be seen, as English, as an insider, Virginia saw him as foreign and strange, and was especially disturbed by what she felt was his Oriental sexuality. Yet, I have always thought, outsiders are so often drawn to other outsiders, something I tried to explore in my *1492: The Poetics of Diaspora*.[7] The narrator of *A Room of One's Own* positions herself as an outsider, saying she was Scottish not English; elsewhere, in a letter to a friend Virginia Woolf declared she was an orphan in feeling so alienated from older English writing as in Arnold Bennett and Galsworthy, and that is why she was so drawn to reading the Russians, as she whimsically put it. As Hermione Lee notes, Virginia was always devoted to particular English places, Sussex and the countryside around Lewes and the river Ouse, as well as London, very much London.[8] Virginia also became increasingly international in her interests. Leonard, too, having (finally) declared himself to be opposed to British imperialism, became increasingly international in his interests, an internationalism they shared and encouraged in publications by the Hogarth Press from 1917 onwards.

Hermione Lee writes that the Hogarth Press published Russian translations in collaboration with the émigré intellectual S S Koteliansky, always known as Kot, which included Gorky's *Reminiscences of Tolstoi* (1920) and Tchekhov's *Notebooks* (1921).[9]

Victoria Glendinning in her biography tells us that Leonard had become increasingly involved with the Webbs and the Labour Party, Sidney Webb recommending him to be on the Party's Advisory Committee on International and Imperial Questions, and Leonard would become its secretary; at a Labour Party conference in 1917, Leonard met and became friends with Kot, described by Glendinning as 'a Jew from the Ukraine working in London as a translator'.[10]

In *Beginning Again: An Autobiography of the Years 1911–1918* Woolf refers very warmly to his and Virginia's association with Kot, who in 1919 – the same year that they rejected publishing anything from Joyce's *Ulysses*, I'll return to this! – came to see Virginia and Leonard, saying that Gorky had sent him a copy of the *Reminiscences of Tolstoi* which had just been published in Moscow, and had given him the English translation rights. So began, Leonard writes, 'a collaboration between Kot and Virginia and me in translating Russian books', the Gorky translation having instantly been a great success.[11]

Leonard writes entertainingly of their collaborations. Kot would do the first translation in handwriting, and 'we then turned his extremely queer version into English', and to help with this he and Virginia started to learn Russian.[12]

> Kot's English, which I had to turn into my English [where's Virginia gone?], was usually very strange, but it was also so vivid and individual that I was often tempted to leave it untouched. For instance, he wrote: 'She came into the room carrying in her arms a peeled-off little dog', and on another occasion: 'she wore a haggish look'. If he was in doubt about a word, he sometimes looked it up in a dictionary and put all the variants into his translation, occasionally with curious results, e.g. 'he looked in the glass at his mug, dial, face'.[13]

Virginia and Leonard's friendship with Kot was longlasting, and he admired Virginia very much. He reminds Leonard, in his 'passionate and painful intensity', of the ancient Jewish prophets like Elijah, Isaiah, and Jeremiah. For Kot, Leonard reflects, the universe was always 'dark and hostile'. Most of his family in the Ukraine had been wiped out after 1914 by crisscrossing armies of Austrians, Russians, White Guards, the Red Army. 'One brother', however, 'did escape and soon after the war managed to reach Antwerp, and thence London and Canada'. Kot himself had come to London a few years before 1914 on a scholarship, and he became friends with D H Lawrence and Katherine Mansfield.[14]

In a subsequent volume *Downhill All the Way: An Autobiography of the years 1919 to 1939* (1967) Leonard Woolf tells us that Hogarth published three more Russian books, with either Virginia or himself collaborating with Kot in translating them, in 1922. Two of these had just been published in Russia and, again, came to Kot through Gorky: *Stavrogin's Confession* which contained unpublished chapters of Dostoevsky's novel *The Possessed*, and *The Autobiography of Countess Sophie Tolstoi*, written in 1913. Leonard is proud to think how beautifully he and Virginia had printed and designed them.[15]

Virginia Woolf was married to one Jewish intellectual and was a friend of and co-translator with another; perhaps she found particularly interesting, as part of her modernism, that Kot, passionate and painfully intense, regarded the universe as dark and hostile. Yet Virginia Woolf also shared in the anti-Semitic vulgarities of the English upper class and of Bloomsbury. Just as her father could not transcend upper-class attitudes about not educating daughters, Virginia Woolf found it very difficult to free herself from the pull of upper-class anti-Semitism, with its repertoire of jeers, jokes and insults. For Bloomsbury, anti-Semitism seems to have been a kind of sport, an occasion for cleverness, wit, mirth, laughter, highly pleasurable to engage in and share among themselves, as their letters crossed London or sped to and from Sussex. We have to think that Virginia's Bloomsbury circle, those whom Leonard thought had so smoothly accepted him back into their lives on his return in 1911, were far from comfortable in accepting Virginia Stephen marrying Leonard Woolf, who in their eyes was to be regarded first and foremost as Jewish, a reluctantly accepted outsider. Vanessa wrote to Leonard in 1913: 'I think I owe you a letter and I'm afraid of getting into trouble if I don't pay what I owe to the Jews'. How droll. Hermione Lee reports that Clive Bell jested to Mary Hutchinson in 1915: 'I wonder why the Jews instituted the rite of circumscision [sic]. Was there money in it, d'you think, as there is in lambs' tails? Did the Levites traffick in *prepuces*?'[16] (Hhhmmm, I think, reading this, my Jewish family name is Levy, I could be descended from the Levites being so sneered at by Mr Clive Bell, Bloomsbury luminary – fuck you, you fucking racist creep.)

There was, says Hermione Lee, a tinge of anti-Semitism in Maynard Keynes's personal attitude to Leonard, though they got on well enough professionally.[17] In his biography *Universal Man: The Seven Lives of John Maynard Keynes* (2015), Richard Davenport-Hines refers to Keynes's 'thoughtless' participation in the 'endemic anti-Jewish feeling of Edwardian England'. Keynes continued to take pleasure in 'anti-Jewish feeling' in subsequent decades, and it appears to have intensified upon marriage to the ballerina Lydia Lopokova, who he admired in London in the early 1920s, when she danced for Diaghilev's Russian Ballet.

> His marriage to a Russian, in whom the bigotry of the Tsarist regime had been ingrained in girlhood, perpetuated this blight on his character. Their banter together included automatic jibes about the Jews: he considered Judaism as a subject for harsh, superior humour. 'I *smelt* it', he told Lopokova in 1924 after hearing that the Gluckstein family, which owned Lyons Corner

House, had bought the Café Royal where his Tuesday Club held its monthly dinners.[18]

What certainly leaves a rank smell is that from late Victorian times to the Edwardian period, through World War I and beyond into the 1920s, Virginia was fairly surrounded by racism and anti-Semitism. Hermione Lee reports that the pre-war Neo-Pagans, its main figure Rupert Brooke, were even 'more racist and anti-Semitic' than Bloomsbury; after Virginia married Leonard, Rupert Brooke referred to the couple as 'the Jew and his wife'. The painter Jacques Raverat, who would become a friend of Virginia's, told Rupert Brooke that he hated Jews 'because they crucified Christ daily'.[19] (This reminds me of my mother's still bitter memory of growing up in the East End, telling me that 'they used to say we drank the blood of little children'.)

Virginia also partook of the fun of being anti-Semitic. Hermione Lee notes that Virginia would refer to Leonard as 'my Jew', and at meals would say, 'Give the Jew his food'. Lee reports that Virginia was taken aback by what she saw as the extravagant Jewishness of Leonard's family gatherings, talking incessantly, over-dressed, giving terrible presents and requiring 'demonstrations of affection in return'. In letters to Vanessa, Vita, and Ethel Smyth, Virginia joked that the family seemed to have multiplied in numbers every time she saw them, that they 'pullulate' and 'copulate' and 'amass', and was particularly appalled by Leonard's mother as a caricaturable Jewish mother-in-law.[20] Victoria Glendinning adds more details in her biography of Leonard, that to her intimates Virginia would freely express her distaste for his family: 'their accents and voices, their clothes and food, their physical characteristics'.[21] Virginia's distaste for Jewish food reminds me, as I note in my earlier chapter 'East End Jews, Anti-Semitism, Bloomsbury', of David Cesarini writing that during World War I there were letters to the press complaining that Jews on trains would talk in an animated fashion and eat fried fish, the kind of fried fish that my grandmother Rose in London would cook for her family.

Virginia's brother Adrian, Glendinning tells us, was held to be especially good at 'imitating Jews'.[22] Does this mean that Adrian, to Virginia's delight, could have imitated someone like my grandmother or my mother, frying fish, talking animatedly?

Yet, Hermione Lee observes, by the 1930s Virginia Woof had become highly critical of her complicity in the 'prejudices of her class and time', analysing and criticising her own anti-Semitism as part of a critical reading of British culture.[23] Richard Davenport-Hines tells us that 'Keynes's callous flippancies disappeared with the advent of Hitler', and that 'Nazi racial hatreds revolted him from the first'; and in 1933, Keynes wrote that Einstein, who had been forced into exile, had become for 'our generation' a 'double symbol – a symbol of the mind… and a symbol of the brave and generous outcast'.[24] In a following chapter, in thinking about T S Eliot and W B Yeats, we will return to 1933, for Keynes was sadly wrong to think his 'generation' of writers and intellectuals was unified around horror at the advent of Hitler. Some were pleased.

A Conscious Pariah: Leonard Woolf's 'Three Jews'

When I first read in the biographies that Leonard's part in launching the Hogarth Press in July 1917 was the story 'Three Jews', I thought it would be easy to get hold of, Bloomsbury being so famous. Not so, as it turned out, though Sydney University's hardworking interlibrary loan service managed after some time to secure a copy for me online, taken from the *Virginia Woolf Bulletin* of the Virginia Woolf Society of Great Britain, Issue No.5, September 2000. The story goes from pages 4 to 11. On p. 12, editor Stuart N Clarke notes that whereas Virginia Woolf's 'The Mark on the Wall' has been 'frequently reprinted (revised)', this was the first appearance of 'Three Jews' since 1917. I printed it off and read it through, highlighting here and there, and then felt a little baffled how to interpret it. On our morning walk I said to Ann, I don't know what to think, it seems very roughly written, beyond that no ideas are coming to me. I often feel short stories are so cryptic that they are baffling to read anyway. I waited a few days, wrote other parts of this chapter, then decided to adopt what the narrator early on says will be her method of writing in *A Room of One's Own*: 'I give you my thoughts as they came to me.'[25] Fortunately, a few half-ideas made an appearance, and I hastily scribbled some notes about them, before they went away.

My first thought concerned the title, that here is Leonard Woolf the parvenu now coming out as a conscious pariah, a Jew openly and defiantly telling the world in the Hogarth Press's opening salvo that he will not be cowed either by the intense anti-Semitism of the recent war, nor by the self-admiring anti-Semitic raillery of the Bloomsbury circle he had helped to establish. Hermione Lee indicates something of the shock, even repugnance, that 'Three Jews' occasioned in England's intellectual life, quoting a certain Fredegond Shove, a childhood friend of Virginia's, writing to Vanessa when it appeared in 1917: '*Three Jews* – is not that rather too much of a good thing?'[26] The title 'Three Jews', I think, was a tricksterish act, boldly saying the unsayable, or at least the not easy to publicly say, in a highly stressful time for British Jews. Leonard Woolf was suddenly making himself into a stranger in terms of Georg Simmel's 1908 essay, he who comes today and stays tomorrow, disturbing those inside the society who take its values, here English anti-Semitism, for granted.[27] 'Three Jews', while so short a story, anticipates features of Leopold Bloom in *Ulysses* published only a few years later; this I will talk about in a moment.

My second thought about 'Three Jews' concerned the number three, which I cherish as a sacred number. 'Three Jews' has three unnamed narrators, and it sort of moves sideways, as in *The*

Thousand and One Nights, so popular in the eighteenth-century Enlightenment, where there are stories within stories leading to other stories.[28] I also recalled an essay Ann had written in 1991, with its striking title, 'The Three Body Problem: Feminism and Chaos Theory', Ann pondering the possible implications for feminism of a theory prominent at that time in debates about science. How, Ann asked, can we specify the relationship between the separate dimensions of gender, race and class? Ann suggested, thinking about Chaos Theory, that the relationship can never be exactly specified, for interactions between three dimensions are inherently unstable and inconclusive; order breaks into disorder, which might break into order again, then disorder.[29] So I idly wondered: will a story concerning 'Three Jews' also suggest narratives and relationships that can't be easily ordered and resolved into a clear structure of meanings. The sacred number three tantalizes, baffles, perplexes: good, I thought.

Another preliminary thought: this a London story.

I roughly plot out how to proceed. I will talk about the first two narrators and what I take their conversation to imply, then relate some anguished stories by Virginia Woolf and Ann Curthoys about a dress and rejection and betrayal; then go on to the third narrator.

The first narrator tells the reader that, it being Sunday and the first day of spring, he feels 'restless'. Spring inspires him to reflect on colour, of flowers and clothes and sky, contrasting England and the tropics in relation to notions of Englishness and Jewishness. He thinks about pale colours as against strong colours. He looks out of his window, and sees the 'black trees breaking into bud', where even London cannot rob the tulips and hyacinths of their 'reds and blues and yellows'; he notices the 'delicate spring sunshine' and the 'pale blue sky that the chimney pots broke into'. Damn it, he says to himself, feeling trapped. He decides to take the train to the Kew gardens, to get away from flowers and leaves soiled by London's soot; he wants to see and smell the earth, to gaze at the horizon rather than endless houses and chimneys, to find 'where earth and sky meet', to see tropical flowers.

What predominantly he finds at Kew, however, is the 'English spring' with 'its pale blue sky' and its 'delicate green of grass', *delicate* a word that keeps occurring to him in relation to Englishness. The narrator sighs as he observes how 'the quiet orderly English spring… embraced and sobered even the florid luxuriance of great flowers bursting in white cascades over strange tropical trees'. He looks at the 'quiet orderly English people' who have also come to enjoy the gardens at Kew in spring:

> It had stirred them to come out in couples, in family parties, in tight matronly black dresses, in drab coats and trousers, in dowdy skirts and hats. It had stirred some to come in elegant costumes and morning suits and spats. They looked at the flaunting tropical trees, and made jokes, and chaffed one another, and laughed not very loud. They were happy in their quiet orderly English way, happy in the warmth of the sunshine, happy to be among quiet trees, and to feel the soft grass under their feet. They did not run about or shout, they walked slowly, quietly, taking care to keep off the edges of the grass because the notices told them to do so.

The English, he reflects, are not interested in, will never be interested in, the extravagant colours of the 'flaunting tropical trees'. He wanders out through the big gates and finds a tea-house, its garden crowded with people, English people: 'I sat down at the only vacant table, and watched them eating plum-cake and drinking tea quietly, soberly, under the gentle apple-blossom'. Feeling tired, defeated, he feels resigned to being an outsider.

He is joined by another man, also Jewish, who he doesn't know, looking for somewhere to sit. They immediately register a bond;

he looks at his new acquaintance, and regards him as, he is sure, the English people there would regard him, almost simian, his arms hanging 'so loosely and limply by his sides'; he notices a 'bustle and roll and energy in his walk', and his 'dark fat face and the sensual mouth, the great curve of the upper lip and the hanging lower one'; he has a 'clever face, dark and inscrutable', with 'large mysterious eyes' and 'heavy lids'. They begin talking, sharing doubts and puzzles about belonging, or not-belonging:

> I saw the delicate apple-blossom and the pale blue sky behind his large dark head. I smiled. He saw the smile, flushed, and then smiled himself.
> 'You are amused,' he said, still smiling, 'I believe I know why.'
> 'Yes,' I said, 'you knew me at once and I knew you. We show up, don't we, under the apple-blossom and this sky. It doesn't belong to us, do you wish it did?'
> 'Ah,' he said seriously, 'that's the question. Or rather we don't belong to it. We belong to Palestine still, but I'm not sure that it doesn't belong to us for all that.'

Then the narrator asks of his fellow Jew, 'do you wish *you* belonged to *it*?'

Hhhhmmm, I thought, the syntax here seems to slide, so that 'it' might refer both to England and Englishness, figured repetitively in the apple-blossom and pale blue sky, and also to Palestine. We Jews, the narrator ponders, will never be accepted as belonging to Englishness, and he asks, do we wish to belong to Englishness anyway? The second Jewish man agrees that they don't belong to England, then says, 'We belong to Palestine still', then immediately wonders if that be so. The narrator then asks, as he had in relation to Englishness, do you want to belong to Palestine, Palestine signifying a continuing connection to Jewishness? The second Jewish man doesn't answer, but instead asks the narrator if he ever goes to the synagogue. The narrator says no, he doesn't. His new friend says that neither does he, though he does go once a year, on Yom Kippur, out of 'pure habit': 'I don't believe in it, of course; I believe in nothing – you believe in nothing – we're all sceptics. And yet we belong to Palestine still.'

The two Jews' musings here suggest for me a relationship to Spinoza, where the seventeenth-century philosopher created for Jews an enduring historical space for skepticism, irreverence and heresy; for the notion of the non-Jewish Jew, the secular Jew where there is still some connection to Jewishness, though not to institutional Judaism, the synagogue, or hardly so. In talking about Leopold Bloom as a non-Jewish Jew, an admirer of Spinoza, in my *1492: The Poetics of Diaspora*, I home in on the 'Cyclops' episode in *Ulysses*, in Barney Kiernan's pub, where Bloom has gone to meet someone on a business matter, though he clearly doesn't like Irish pubs, and at first stays outside. Bloom's presence angers the men in the bar, especially the 'citizen', a loudly self-proclaimed nationalist; they make scathing references to Jews and to Bloom's darkness of cast; the citizen declares that 'things' like Bloom shouldn't be allowed to contaminate Irish shores. Another Irish citizen sarcastically asks Bloom if he knows what a nation is, and then derides Bloom's answer, that a nation is constituted in the people who live there, implying a society that can be multicultural, multi-religious, multi-ethnic. Whereas Bloom's notions of identity are pluralist and inclusive, the men in the bar insist in a nationalist way on a single identity, a national type, a presumed ethnic essence. The mood turns ugly and threatening. When Judeophobic curses are thrown at him, Bloom becomes enraged, reminding the citizen and other denizens of the pub of great Jews of the past like Jesus, Spinoza and Marx.[30]

I note in *1492: The Poetics of Diaspora*, that Bloom in 'Cyclops' identifies the Jewish tradition he admires, that of the emancipated Enlightenment Jewry that Spinoza did so much to inspire into existence; Spinoza who when a young man had been excommunicated from the Sephardi community in Holland for heresy, who was regarded in Europe as a notorious atheist, who devoted his life to secular reason while always being nonetheless identified as of Hebrew extraction. Bloom knows that in admiring Spinoza he is marking himself off as a particular kind of modern Jew, a non-Jewish Jew, atheistic, secularist and skeptical; a connoisseur of ambiguity and ambivalence, such connoisseurship being one of the great Spinoza's legacies for modernity. In the 'Hades' episode Bloom ponders whether or not he is Jewish with a dazzling play of uncertainty: 'He thought that he thought that he was a jew whereas he knew that he knew that he knew that he was not.'[31]

'Three Jews' looks forward not only Bloom in *Ulysses* but also to Isaac Deutscher's essay of that name, 'The Non-Jewish Jew', which became the title of his book published in 1968.[32]

I'm reminded here that in my preface to *1492: The Poetics of Diaspora*, I recall a conversation in the early 1990s with my friend Marsha Rosengarten at Mama Maria's, a coffee shop, since gone, then near the Sydney Powerhouse Museum. Marsha observed that she thought of me 'as neither Jewish nor non-Jewish',[33] a phrase I treasure, a wonderful double negative which I think is relevant to the conversation in 'Three Jews' about identity and belonging, or not-belonging, the two Jews as neither Jewish nor non-Jewish, neither English nor non-English.

There is another anticipation in 'Three Jews' of Bloom in *Ulysses*, in relation to Zionism. 'Three Jews' was published, according to Stuart N Clarke, the editor of the *Virginia Woolf Bulletin*, in July 1917. There had been sustained lobbying for many years before 1917 of the British government by prominent English Zionists for a Jewish homeland to be established in Palestine; the lobbying bore fruit on 2 November 1917 with the fateful Balfour Declaration, to be put into operation if and when Palestine could be conquered by the British during the World War I, such occurring with the entry into Jerusalem by General Allenby on 11 December 1917. The initial two narrators in 'Three Jews' skeptically refer to *Palestine*, wondering if they do belong to it or wish to belong to it, just as they wonder if they do belong to England or wish to belong to it; they suggest, that is, a distance from Zionism as a nationalist project.

In my chapter 'Nation, race and identity in Joyce's *Ulysses*' in *1492: The Poetics of Diaspora*, I follow Mr Bloom, early on 16 June 1904, as he sets out from his home in 7 Eccles Street, Dublin, to buy from the pork-butcher Dlugacz his favourite parts of meat to cook for breakfast; inside on the counter Bloom sees on a newspaper with a reference to Moses Montefiore, an English philanthropist who was encouraging Jewish colonisation of Palestine. He also picks up there a leaflet advertising a Zionist plan to buy Palestine from the Turkish government. Thinking about it, Bloom rejects this plan, with its suggestion of English colonial practices. Bloom, the stranger, wonders if he belongs to Ireland; or to Zion in a restored Israel, an idea of some attraction given the hostility he experiences in Dublin at Barney Kiernan's pub; or anywhere and nowhere. In 'Ithaca', back home, we see Bloom setting alight to the leaflet advertising the Zionist plan for a colony in Palestine; he submits the leaflet, with the aid of candle flame, to 'total combustion'.[34]

The language of *Ulysses*, we can see, is rich in nuance, humour and density of references, while 'Three Jews' is short, stark and bare boned. Yet it still, I think, can be recognised as resonating with *Ulysses*, the great twentieth-century novel featuring a Jewish character.

The publication of 'Three Jews' in 1917 also resonates with me in another way, a haunting year for my family history, when my father's brother Henry Docker, wounded in action in Belgium, died there on 4 October 1917.

Clothes

Further thoughts occurred to me concerning the first narrator's reflections in 'Three Jews' on the quiet orderly lives of the English, and their quiet clothes, including their 'dowdy skirts'. The narrator contrasts weak colours favoured by the English middle class to the strong tropical colours on display in the Kew gardens. But I also wonder if it occurred to Leonard Woolf, when on his return in 1911 he went with his Bloomsbury circle to see the Ballets Russes, to compare in his mind's eye the spectacular colours on stage in London to the tropical colours of Ceylon which he had so recently left?

This got me thinking of an essay I read and wrote about some time ago, by the cultural theorist Peter Wollen, discussing different kinds of early twentieth-century modernism, that modernism was not only to be defined as stressing functionality as in modernist architecture, or sharp angles as in Cubist painting. Wollen argues that a particular kind of what he refers to as 'decorative modernism' was developing before 1914, in figures like Paul Poiret the decorator and dressmaker, Leon Bakst of Diaghilev's Ballet Russes, and in the art of Matisse, especially in the bold colours of his odalisques. In the years immediately after 1910 Wollen points out, such figures were far more widely known than Picasso and the Cubists. In 1911 Poiret staged a wildly sumptuous phantasmagoric Thousand and Second Night party to celebrate his new Oriental fashions, Orientalism in France having been stimulated anew by fresh translations of *The Thousand and One Nights* by J C Mardrus, a friend of Poiret. From then on, Wollen suggests, the Oriental look became part of the fashion world and the decorative arts, a prominence assisted by the success of the Ballet Russe, especially with Nijinsky in Diaghilev's *Schéhérazade* in 1910, and Bakst's spectacular décor and costume, with its unexpected combinations of massed colours, of emerald green, deep blue and orange red. In Wollen's argument, in the history of modernism the various kinds of modernism, including decorative, swirl contradictorily about, intersecting and interacting.³⁵

As it turns out, while reading Susan Squier's *Virginia Woolf and London*, I was arrested by a page where Squier suggests that in her life and writing, Virginia became increasingly interested in the idea of a Society of Outsiders, a term used in the late work *Three Guineas* (1938). (The sacred number three again!) Squier notes that for Virginia so 'simple an act as choosing an unusual fabric for one's dress may be a form of insurrection' worthy of such a Society, and that in her fifties Virginia 'still remembered with anguish George Duckworth's criticism' of a dress she had wished to wear 'as a young girl'.³⁶ I immediately looked up *Moments of Being* to read the passage, which occurs in some late autobiographical notes, 'A Sketch of the Past', that Virginia Woolf began in 1939 and revised in 1940 in a 70-page typescript.

I quote from *Moments of Being* edited by Jeanne Schulkind, introduced and revised by Hermione Lee.³⁷ Virginia is commenting on the 'rules of the game of Victorian society' she and Vanessa were trained in, which included the clothes they were required to conform to in attending evening gatherings. The sisters had to 'enter the drawing room at eight with bare arms, low neck, in evening dress', to appear 'not only tidy but presentable'.³⁸

> On an allowance of fifty pounds it was difficult, even for the skilful, and I had no skill, to be well dressed of an evening. A home dress, made by Jane Bride, could be had for a pound or two; but a party dress, made by Mrs Young, cost fifteen guineas. The home dress therefore might be, as on one night that comes back to mind, made cheaply but eccentrically, of a green fabric, bought at Story's, the furniture shop. It was not velvet; nor plush; something betwixt and between; and for chairs, presumably, not dresses. Down I came one winter's evening about 1900 in my green dress; apprehensive, yet, for a new dress excites even the

unskilled, elated. All the lights were turned up in the drawing room; and by the blazing fire George sat, in dinner jacket and black tie, cuddling the dachshund, Schuster, on his knee. He at once fixed on me that extraordinarily observant scrutiny with which he always inspected our clothes. He looked me up and down for a moment as if I were a horse brought into the show ring. Then the sullen look came into his eyes; the look which expressed not simply aesthetic disapproval; but something that went deeper. It was the look of moral, of social, disapproval, as if he scented some kind of insurrection, of defiance of his accepted social standards. I knew myself condemned from more points of view than I could then analyse. As I stood there I was conscious of fear; of shame; of something like anguish – a feeling, like so many, out of all proportion to its surface cause. He said at last: 'Go and tear it up.' He spoke in a curiously tart, rasping, peevish voice; the voice of the enraged male; the voice which expressed his serious displeasure at this infringement of a code that meant more to him than he could admit.[39]

As with Leonard Woolf, I wonder what Virginia Stephen, sitting watching the Ballet Russe in 1911, thought of its splash of colours, her encounter with the loathsome George Duckworth, still and always a painful memory? Did she think the bold colours and spectacular choreography were a challenge to Edwardian England and more widely to the Englishness from which she increasingly wished to estrange herself? Did an interest in the daring and adventurousness of the Ballets Russes chime in with her gathering interest in Russian writers?

I've been reading *Mrs Dalloway*, published in 1925, as my night-time reading, continuing my education in Bloomsbury, and I notice a passage where Clarissa Dalloway goes to her cupboard to choose an evening dress for the party she is hosting that night: 'Clarissa, plunging her hand into the softness, gently detached the green dress and carried it to the window. She had torn it. Some one had trod on the skirt.'[40]

I told Ann about what was in the passage in 'A Sketch in the Past', showing her the relevant pages; she immediately became thoughtful, and said she had an experience where a dress was associated with rejection and betrayal. Naturally, on our next morning walk I urged (nagged) her to write the story in an email and send it to me, which she did:

> Hearing and then reading Virginia Woolf's account of her half-brother's scorning of her colourful dress, I instantly responded that I had a dress story too. Anyway, here's mine.
>
> When I was about twenty I shared a flat for two years with a friend I'll call Pat. During the second of the two years, Pat became engaged to a much older man, Raymond. Plans began for the wedding, and I was invited. What to wear? I had a dress my mother had given me when I left home three years before, made of a beautiful soft brown, red, and gold coloured dress material. I loved the material but by this time the dress was old fashioned, and I decided to remake it to wear to Pat's wedding. I bought a pattern and cut it out from the material of my dated and very full-skirted dress. It was all pinned up ready to sew when I learnt that I had been disinvited from the wedding, on Raymond's insistence. He had to make space, he said, for his (more important) guests. Pat had to tell me this, I'm not sure exactly how she worded it now; I remember only that I was truly shocked. I put away the cut-up dress, and for years carried the pieces around from one rented house to another, the paper pattern parts still pinned to the material. Finally, about ten years later, I acknowledged to myself that I would never make this dress, it had such unpleasant associations, and I discarded it. The sad thing is that although I remember hardly anything about the clothes I've worn in the past, I remember with great clarity this cut-up dress, with its

beautiful soft filmy brown, red, and yellow material. Just as I had cut up my dress, never to remake it, Pat had cut up our friendship, and it never recovered.

Ann also wrote in this email:

Maybe every woman has a dress story.

Families expel, disown

About the third narrator in 'Three Jews', the final portion of the story is taken up by the second Jewish man relating that each year on the anniversary of 'my first wife, Rebecca', he visits her grave, on cold November days, at a cemetery in London. He strikes up a conversation with the cemetery-keeper, an old Jewish man, who on subsequent visits relates the sad music of his life, his wife dying, leaving him with two boys to bring up. But then further family disaster strikes. Asked how the boys were faring, the cemetery-keeper, with sudden anger, replies:

> 'Boys? I've only one boy.'
> 'Ah, I'm sorry, very sorry to – '
> 'No, no, it's not what you think… That eldest boy of mine, he's no longer my son – I have done with him; I have only one son now.'

The cemetery-keeper says that, behind his back, the older son had married a Christian servant-girl who had worked in the family home.

> If he had come to me and said: 'Dad, I want to marry a girl' – a really nice girl – 'but she's not one of us: will you give me your permission and blessing?' Well I don't believe in it. Our women are as good, better than Christian women. Aren't they as beautiful, as clever, as good wives? I know my poor mother, God rest her

soul, used to say: 'My son,' she said, 'if you come to me and say you want to marry a good girl, a Jewess, I don't care whether she hasn't a chemise to her back, I'll welcome her – but if you marry a Christian, if she's as rich as Solomon, I've done with you – don't you ever dare to come into my house again.' Vell, I don't go as far as that, even though she was a Goy. But a servant girl who washed my dishes! I couldn't do it. One must have some dignity.

That's how 'Three Jews' ends, with the second narrator saying that he left the cemetery-keeper standing there, 'upright, stern, noble', 'brooding over his son and his graves'.

Who Was Q D Leavis?

Again, I felt baffled by 'Three Jews': how to interpret this story of Jewish religion, class, generations, marrying out, and rejection from the family circle? But then I thought, the story is a kind of reprise of what happened to Spinoza when he as a young man and was expelled from his Jewish community in Holland, part of a long history of expulsions from communities and families in Jewish history, and religious history generally.

I thought of something I only learned in June 2014 in England (26 June, I've just looked up the date in my 2014 diary), when visiting with our London friend Charles Ross two old friends, Bill Browning and Vicki Browning, all of us having been in the same Sydney University circles in the late 1960s. At Sydney University in the English department, Charles had been a tutor in medieval literature, and Bill had been doing a doctoral thesis on Victorian literature, having been trained as a critic at Cambridge; in 1969 I was tutoring in the department; and in 1970 Bill and I had both contributed to a Socialist Scholars conference, to a session that a group of us including Bill organised on new approaches in literary theory, that I'll evoke in some detail in the final section of this ego histoire. On returning to England, Bill and Vicki taught for many years in the King's School, he in literature, she in mathematics, in a kind of old castle that Bill had showed us around on a previous visit; Bill had also published interesting and enjoyable children's novels; now in retirement, they live in a tiny village in Kent.

In 1970 Bill's talk had been on Q D Leavis's 1932 book *Fiction and the Reading Public*, which became a cornerstone of the Leavisite movement from the early 1930s onwards, an investigation of popular reading in the early twentieth century. *Fiction and the Reading Public* held that modern popular literature was destroying the sensibility of the mass of people in Britain, though its ruinous allure was resisted by a discerning minority trained to read literature with discrimination and critical intelligence (talismanic terms), that is to say, by the Leavisites. In this view, which brooked no argument, modern society was in a state of disastrous decline from a culturally richer pre-industrial past, where both popular reading, as with Bunyan, or high literature, as with Shakespeare and metaphysical poets like John Donne who the Leavisites so much admired, were in a state of mutual nourishment.

Over lunch Bill suddenly said, 'John, did you know Q D Leavis was Jewish, that she was Queenie Roth before she married Leavis?' I was startled, had never heard that before, tell me more. Bill said it's in the biography of Leavis by Ian MacKillop; I hastily scribbled the name down in my diary. I said this is so strange, I never knew. I mentioned that for my 1994 book *Postmodernism and Popular Culture* I had written a rather acidly critical chapter on *Fiction and the Reading Public*, and then we talked about Bill's long ago paper on *Fiction and the Reading Public* for the 1970 Socialist Scholars conference in Sydney, where he also had been very critical. We belonged to a kind of diaspora of survivors of the Leavisite critical enterprise.

When at the beginning of July 2015 Ann and I returned to Sydney, I read Ian MacKillop's biography with great interest.

You can quickly tell it is biography as hagiography, for Frank Raymond Leavis (1895–1978), the seer of a new kind of criticism, exacted obedience from his followers, as seers, sages, messiahs and prophets do, even if usually and often disappointed.

F R Leavis, I'm sure, however, would not have been disappointed with MacKillop's *F. R. Leavis: A Life in Criticism* (1995). A puzzle here: why did literary critics before the 1960s use their initials when publishing an article or book? I remember when I first went to Sydney University in 1963 and did English, seeing on the doors of lecturers various names beginning with their initials, at least for the male lecturers; for the women, it seemed more common that their first name was used, though this wasn't the case at Cambridge with Q D Leavis. If initials were supposed to add gravitas to a lecturer's name, why did they? Why couldn't F R Leavis simply sign his name Frank Leavis, author of such and such a book or article? In any case, if I ever did as a young tutor or lecturer present myself as J Docker, I soon stopped. I thought it looked absurdly pompous. I don't think such an odd practice survived the new informality increasingly practised in and from the 1960s. I just asked Ann, who also started at Sydney University in 1963, and she said that in her career she never put 'A Curthoys' on a university office door.

However, after writing the above, I suddenly thought I should check my long-ago BA honours thesis, written in 1966. I reached up to the top shelf of a nearby bookcase, recognised the old black folder, brought it down, looked at the title, 'The Wasteland and The Dunciad', and saw how I had typed out my name: 'J. Docker'. I had to admit to Ann that my high moral ground had just collapsed.

What I eagerly looked for in MacKillop's hagiography was where it broached questions of ethnic ancestry. MacKillop tells us that while Leavis always claimed to be of Huguenot descent, 'his Jewish wife was disowned by her family for having "married out"'. MacKillop relates that Leavis, tutoring at Girton College in the autumn of 1927 met a student there, at a tea-party, Queenie Dorothy Roth, who had arrived in Cambridge in 1925. In her final year at Girton, they fell in love, two people with very different upbringings. Queenie Roth came from London, where her 'great-aunt Augusta... sold peanuts in Petticoat Lane'. Leavis, brought up in the town of Cambridge, introduced her to English provincial life, with its traditional chapel culture and its love of John Bunyan. To her London eyes, MacKillop writes, Leavis 'must have still seemed a country person'. While she knew a 'good deal of England, from the London end', with Leavis she now made contact with the 'provincially rural in Cambridge, and the factor of "Englishness" that later meant so much to both partners'.[41]

In February 1929 Queenie Dorothy Roth and Frank Raymond Leavis became engaged to be married. Now a difficulty presented itself that could not be overcome, opposition to the marriage from her Orthodox Jewish family in London; her parents Morris and Jenny Roth, were shocked by their daughter marrying out, causing a lifelong breach, especially with her mother. MacKillop mentions that there is a story that the family sat *shiva* for Queenie, 'that is, underwent strict household bereavement observances at the betrayal of their religion'. MacKillop doesn't believe the *shiva* story is true, but contact did cease between Queenie and her parents, except occasionally with her father. Leavis himself suffered a 'breakdown, deeply involved as he was in Q. D. R's alienation from her family'. Given the 'drastic break', it appears that Queenie Roth-now-Leavis, made a decision thenceforth to abandon being Jewish altogether. MacKillop writes that there was over many years 'hardly any consciousness of Jewish heritage in the Leavis family', their daughter Kate, who was born in September 1939, later reminiscing that she had no idea that she was 'half Jewish' until her first year at Oxford, when she was told by a contemporary.[42]

Queenie Dorothy Leavis (1906 – 1981), often known as Q D L

would over the years make scathing comments about Bloomsbury and Virginia Woolf, but not at first, when she was still Queenie Roth, student at Girton college. MacKillop tells us that she was a 'member of the exclusive Girton "secret society" called ODTAA ("One Damn Thing After Another")', to which Virginia Woolf delivered a version of *A Room of One's Own*, 'after which she promised to send Queenie Roth some pamphlets'. MacKillop says no more of this conversation, though it may have indicated she was attracted to Virginia's feminism and wished to know more. However, Queenie Leavis, now married, joins with F R Leavis and their particular circle in Cambridge in repudiating Bloomsbury as a contemptible self-congratulatory coterie.[43] Q D L and F R in the rural provincial town of Cambridge, became hostile to the bohemianism associated with the Bloomsbury group, Queenie Leavis here turning her back on London's cosmopolitan life, the metropolis she had grown up in.

In the early 1930s the nascent Leavisite movement, jostling for its position in the critical world, would, MacKillop tells us, define itself against Bloomsbury.[44] Hopefully, Bloomsbury would be destroyed by astringent critical commentary, not least directed at Virginia Woolf; if Virginia Woolf's reputation as writer and critic were to be destroyed, then Bloomsbury as a whole would be fatally wounded. The attacks on Bloomsbury and Virginia seem to have been launched from the very beginning of the Leavis organ *Scrutiny*, which ran from 1932 to 1953, with Virginia, so Hermione Lee tells us, becoming aware that a Miss B (the future professor and Mistress of Girton, Muriel Bradbrook) had referred to her in *Scrutiny* as a 'very bad writer'. Virginia also heard that a 'Cambridge don – called "something like Leaven?" – had a wife who was criticising her in the same publication'.[45]

MacKillop writes, in strangely violent language, that in the late 1930s 'Q D L attempted to deliver a stake through the heart of Bloomsbury in an attack on Virginia Woolf called 'Caterpillars of the Commonwealth Unite!" (A stake through the heart: isn't this how, in Gothic imagination, how a vampire is to be killed? Was Virginia pictured as a vampire in the eyes of the Leavisites? Isn't 'stake' a curiously phallic image for MacKillop to deploy?) Published in *Scrutiny* in September 1938 Q D L's 'Caterpillars of the Commonwealth Unite!' was a 'fierce review of Virginia Woolf's non-fictional work *Three Guineas*', MacKillop explaining that Q D L took exception to Virginia Woolf arguing in both *Three Guineas* and in *A Room of One's Own* before it, that women were being victimised because they were condemned to use up their energies on males and family. Q D L. responded by asserting the superiority of her and her family's way of life at Chesterton Hall Crescent in Cambridge, where she and Leavis lived with their children. The house was light and airy, and there were frequent visitors. Demanding children and difficult careers were successfully combined with running *Scrutiny*, and family life was infused with a great deal of jollity, especially in 'high tea readings of Damon Runyon'.[46] (So, not all modern popular literature was to be scornfully excoriated.)

Hermione Lee tells us that Virginia regarded Queenie Leavis's review of *Three Guineas* as 'all personal'.[47] Michèle Barrett reports that Virginia was 'not profoundly affected' by the 'vitriolic attack', for she had 'always regarded the entire Leavis/*Scrutiny* enterprise as priggish', to be treated with 'a certain contempt'.[48]

Despite Queenie Leavis's *ad hominem* argument against Virginia, the evocation of her life in MacKillop's book makes depressing reading. MacKillop notes that while *Scrutiny* quickly became a success when launched in late 1932, 'a price was paid by Q.D.L.', for once the journal got going, she said she 'did much of the editorial business'. Indeed, she became its 'main office-worker, aiding male contributors, who rarely did the necessary typing'; as she typed, she corrected their spelling mistakes. The strain of looking after *Scrutiny* and believing, with Leavis, that Cambridge was always hostile to their endeavours told on her, so that she was threatened with a nervous disorder. By the early 1950s, MacKillop tells us, Q D L was becoming gravely ill; she was 'down to six stone in weight, though she was working hard, reading, writing, aiding *Scrutiny* and looking after the children'. By now, she was tired of 'drudging for my husband and *Scrutiny*', and sought the 'time in future for my own purposes'.[49]

However hollow Queenie's personal attack on Virginia Woolf's feminism seems now, given these revelations. And perhaps, in providing such insights into Queenie Leavis drudging for decades for the men of *Scrutiny*, MacKillop, his book published in 1995, was himself influenced by the post-1960s feminist movement that had found, and continues to find, Virginia Woolf's writing so inspiring.

Leonard Woolf, in 'Three Jews' in 1917, sent out a challenge to English anti-Semitism by affirming his Jewishness. In contrast, Queenie Roth's life seems to have been a series of negations: of metropolitan London, feminism and Jewishness. She despised Virginia Woolf, yet whereas Virginia Stephen took on a Jewish name, Queenie Roth exchanged her Jewish name – which she still possessed when she briefly met Virginia Woolf at Girton in the late 1920s – for an Anglo name, and then set about extinguishing her Jewishness so thoroughly that her children knew nothing about it. Now I think, what an advantage for her it would have been to continue a connection to Jewishness, in Isaac Deutscher's terms, when he writes in his 1958 essay 'The Non-Jewish Jew', of revolutionaries in thought and action he admires like Spinoza, Heine, Marx, Rosa Luxemburg, Trotsky and Freud, that 'as Jews they dwelt on the borderlines of various civilizations, religions, and national cultures'; they strove 'for the universal, as against the particularist, and for the internationalist, as against the nationalist'; and living 'on the borderlines of various civilizations' they could 'comprehend more clearly the great movement and the great contradictoriness of nature and society'.[50] I agree with Ned Curthoys' view that in this great essay 'Isaac Deutscher's characterization of the non-Jewish Jew as a liminal figure'... encapsulates a liberal Jewish enthusiasm for 'the worldly Jewish outsider figure or pariah'.[51] With F R Leavis, Queenie Leavis devoted herself to a messianic project of recovering the civilisational virtues of Englishness, to be found in the high and popular culture of pre-industrial England, and once recovered by the Leavisites as an enlightened minority, re-fertilising modern English life through criticism and teaching. Yet such a project of recovery and national salvation was always in acute danger of idealizing English history: this became my primary critique of it, when I disengaged as it were, however clumsily and comically, from being a Leavisite in the late 1960s.

As a non-Jewish Jew, Queenie Leavis could in my view have enriched her critical sensibility with perspectives that could perceive British history as contradictory, riven, and multiple in its meanings. She could create a conversation between valuing Englishness in the pre-industrial past, yet taking account of its long history of anti-Semitism. Here she could consider that in medieval times Jews were subject to cruelty and massacre, and then expelled altogether from England in 1290; that their long expulsion only came to an end in the mid-seventeenth century; and that after being re-admitted, they nonetheless often encountered exclusion from many areas of social and political life, along with derision, discrimination, suspicion, contempt and, as we have seen in the First World War, violence. To be a non-Jewish Jew could have enabled Queenie Roth become Leavis to explore – let's say at an angle to F R Leavis – a more profound historical consciousness, history as encompassing persecution and cruelty in pre-industrial as much as in industrial times.

And perhaps too as a non-Jewish Jew, Queenie Leavis could have reflected on the British empire and settler colonialism, since the pre-industrial Englishness she and Frank Leavis cherished encompassed far more than England itself. Here too there are resources in Jewish tradition that she could have called on. I've noted before Ned Curthoys drawing attention to Moses Mendelssohn in the eighteenth-century German Enlightenment sharply critiquing European colonialism in the spirit of Diderot.[52] With such knowledge, she could have investigated, for example, a wider range than usual of texts by John Donne, bringing into the one conversation Donne's metaphysical poems along with a sermon, as the intellectual historian Sarah Irving tells us, he delivered before the Virginia Company (published in 1622) sanctifying conquest and colonisation in the Americas; Donne argued that if the indigenous of a land produce an abundance yet don't share this abundance with others, then under the European-derived law of nations force is justified in remedying this situation.[53] Within the Leavisite project, Q D Leavis had an independent status as extending literary analysis into anthropology and ethnography, as in *Fiction and the Reading Public*. In this spirit, she could have explored a wide range of texts, literary and non-literary, bearing on questions of sensibility and Englishness, such as Donne's chilling justification of imperial violence.

Deutscher reflected that the non-Jewish Jews he admired were 'each in society and yet not in it, of it and yet not of it', enabling them to 'rise in thought above their societies, above their nations, above their times and generations, and to strike out mentally into wide horizons and far into the future'.[54] Perhaps Queenie Leavis could, with such wider perspectives, have been in and yet not in the Leavisite project, of it yet not of it. If she had done so, perhaps Leavisism may have had a more enduring historical presence.

Reflections

Here I return to Hannah Arendt's 1944 essay, 'The Jew as Pariah: A hidden tradition'. I think that in Arendt's terms Leonard Woolf always remained a torn figure, between parvenu and conscious pariah. In publishing 'Three Jews' in 1917, I feel he did become a conscious pariah, the cultural figure who challenges foundational values, provokes anger and hostility, goes out there, unsettles, irritates. In his autobiographies, Leonard Woolf makes it clear that he admired universalist notions of Jewishness, as in his comparing in *Beginning Again* his and Virginia's friend Koteliansky to the prophets Elijah, Isaiah, or Jeremiah: 'For if you knew Kot well, you knew what a major Hebrew prophet must have been like 3,000 years ago.' Leonard regarded Kot's austerely passionate nature as Semitic: 'There are some Jews who, though their ancestors have lived for centuries in European ghettoes, are born with certain characteristics which the sun and sand of the desert beat into the bodies and minds of Semites.'[55] And he believes that such Semitic qualities of sensibility are shared between Jews and Arabs: 'I have felt the same qualities of steely, repressed, purged passion, burnt into a Semite by sun and sand, in an ordinary Arab pearl diver from the Persian Gulf', who had given a funeral speech for a drowned friend:

> [The pearl diver] stood on the shore in Ceylon looking down on his dead comrade – he had died when diving for pearls at the Ceylon pearl fishery – and he made a long speech to the dead man's brother. It was in Arabic and I did not understand a word, and yet I understood every word. It was Isaiah and Jeremiah and Job – and Kot.[56]

In *Growing* Leonard had expressed his admiration for the Arab pearl diver, and the memory clearly stayed with him, the idea of a shared Semitic identity in a kind of deep historical layer between Jew and Arab.[57]

We can recognise an affinity in Leonard Woolf's admiration for the Prophets with what Ned Curthoys in *The Legacy of Liberal*

Judaism refers to, in the German Jewish Enlightenment and post-Enlightenment tradition, as Prophetic Judaism; a tradition where, as in the philosopher Hermann Cohen (1842–1918), what is important is an 'ethics of social love and compassion for the poor man and the stranger'. Cohen valued the 'radical social criticism and interpretive freedom of the Jewish Prophets'.[58] What Leonard Woolf admired as the universalism of the Prophets relates, I think, to his post-Ceylon political activity, or political-intellectual activity, as an anti-imperialist and internationalist.

Yet, I'm going to hazard, certain features of imperial rule, given his time as a colonial functionary of the Empire in Ceylon for more than six years, still influenced and shaped by Woolf's life when he returned to London in 1911, especially the importance to him of belonging to an elite, and seeking to become part of, to stay inside, a hierarchical structure. He was impatient with those he imagined were his inferiors (such as those who helped with the Hogarth Press as it became increasingly busy, as he acknowledged himself), and too beholden to those he regarded as his superiors or more powerful. Virginia Woolf, Victoria Glendinning tells us, disliked Leonard's involvement with the Webbs,[59] which I interpret to mean that in Virginia's view he permitted himself to be too much within their world, the net of obligations they cast; he lost independence, which she prized above all, the writer's trickster freedom.

In similar spirit, I interpret the way Leonard worked so tirelessly for the British Labour Party, in garnering information on international affairs, was to stay inside a structure, for it is clear in the autobiographies that he always knew that his policy suggestions, once Labour was in government, would be ignored, betrayed, by its opportunist and anti-intellectual leaders like Ramsay MacDonald.[60]

In my view, the intellectual should never be part of any political party, for it places that party beyond critique, dissidence, irreverence, contempt, ridicule or parody; beyond the play of uncertainty; beyond the connoisseurship of ambivalence and ambiguity; all necessary qualities, I feel, for the conscious pariah.

As I foreshadowed at the beginning of this chapter, I nominate Virginia Woolf for the honour roll of Hannah Arendt's conscious pariahs, in her choosing to take a Jewish name, both as a married name and a *nom de plume*. She could have published under a writer's name, as had, she points out in *A Room of One's Own*, George Eliot or Currer Bell or George Sand.[61] Given the omnipresent anti-Semitism of England and her own milieu, given her own anti-Semitism, Virginia Woolf, in my view, went out there, forging a reputation as an author with a Jewish name at the heart of early twentieth century literary modernism, a name which resonates to this day as proudly Jewish.

Yet in terms of the conscious pariah going out there, one incident dismays me, their uninterest in Hogarth Press publishing anything from Joyce's *Ulysses*, a decision that, Hermione Lee records, has become notorious.[62] The story involves T S Eliot who, as Hermione Lee points out, admired Joyce and *Ulysses* for being at the forefront of new and experimental modernist literary creation.[63] In *Beginning Again* Leonard Woolf recalls that he and Virginia learned from Eliot 'at the end of 1917 or the beginning of 1918 that Miss Harriet Weaver of *The Egoist*, which had published his *Prufrock*, was much concerned about a MS. by James Joyce which she had'. Harriet Weaver and Eliot were worried that because it might be held to be 'indecent' there would be grave doubts whether it was publishable in England.[64]

As it turned out, Eliot and Harriet Weaver were right to be worried. In April 1918 Harriet Weaver visited Hogarth House (Virginia and Leonard's house in Richmond, Surrey, in Paradise Road) with a brown paper parcel, containing, Lee tells us, the opening episodes of *Ulysses* (presumably the Telemachiad, those concerned with Stephen Dedalus, before Bloom enters the novel). Both Virginia and Leonard were unimpressed by Harriet Weaver's demure appearance, which seemed to predispose them against the novel. They decided to turn down her proposal, in part for practical reasons, because they could not have printed the whole novel themselves on their handpress, and then Leonard found there was no printer prepared to be found liable in case of an obscenity charge. In terms of the quality of writing, Virginia found it merely boring and smutty.[65]

How disappointing I find this lost opportunity to be. The practical reason doesn't hold up for one thing. It's not clear from Lee's account that Harriet Weaver was asking them to print the whole of *Ulysses*, which in any case, as Leonard himself notes in *Beginning Again*, was not yet finished, Joyce was still writing it.[66] Virginia and Leonard could, it seems to me, have published an episode, as Lee records happened around the same time with another journal, the *Little Review*.[67] The *Little Review* was American, and published episodes from March 1918 through to December 1921, when its editors Margaret Caroline Anderson and Jane Heap were tried and convicted for obscenity. In his biography of Joyce Richard Ellmann tells us that the January 1920 issue of *Little Review* published the 'Cyclops' episode, set in Barney Kiernan's pub, from where Bloom is expelled and in effect excommunicated by the Irish nationalist men for being not truly Irish.[68]

The decision by Virginia and Leonard is even more disappointing if we think – as generations of readers since I'm sure have thought – that the stream of consciousness method of *Ulysses*, with all the events in the novel occurring on a single day, Bloomsday, 16 June 1904, would surely have interested the future author of *Mrs Dalloway*, where all occurs also on a single day, 13 June 1923. Hermione Lee records that Virginia herself took careful notes on *Ulysses*, as episodes appeared in the *Little Review* in 1918, reflecting on the importance of stream of consciousness to new fictional forms.[69]

By the end of November 1918, Hermione Lee tells us, they

had agreed the Hogarth Press would publish Eliot's *Poems*, which appeared in May 1919.[70] Here, I think, questions of Jewishness come to the fore for both Virginia and Leonard at least, so I'll speculate. Given the egregious anti-Semitism of certain images in *Poems*, about which I promise to become very agitated in a later chapter, was it beyond Leonard Woolf to think that the Hogarth Press could create in the formative period of high literary modernism a drama of difference for readers to contemplate, between Eliot's anti-Semitism especially in 'Gerontion', 'Burbank with a Baedeker: Bleistein with a Cigar' and 'Sweeney Among the Nightingales', and the philosemitism of *Ulysses* in the creation of Leopold Bloom, the great and beloved Jewish character of twentieth-century literature? After publishing 'Three Jews' in 1917, I feel that not publishing from *Ulysses*, as Harriet Weaver hoped a new small independent modernist English press might well do, it's hard not to think that Leonard Woolf was retreating into the safety of being the parvenu, cautious, afraid, drawing back from the daring and adventurousness of the conscious pariah.

As for Virginia Woolf's rejecting publication of *Ulysses*, was there another reason apart from a priggish distaste? Was there another reason, connected with Bloom's Jewishness? There's a curious sentence in Hermione Lee's biography where Lee writes that Virginia was troubled by T S Eliot's 'passion for *Ulysses*', as if Eliot embodied for her 'the male post-war version of modernism, with its egotistic anti-hero adrift in the modern world: Prufrock, Rupert Birkin, Mauberly, Stephen Dedalus'.[71] I'm puzzled by the mention of Stephen Dedalus here, since the bulk of the novel is concerned with the consciousness of Leopold Bloom.

Did Virginia Woolf reject *Ulysses* because it was devoted to the exploration of Jewishness? In Bloom's admiration for Spinoza that he declares in Barney Kiernan's pub, we can say that his intellectual ancestry looks back to Spinoza in the Early Enlightenment of the seventeenth century. Furthermore, the story of Spinoza resumes a complex history of the Sephardi Jews resident in Moorish Spain for many centuries, expelled in 1492 by the Christian conquerors, with many Sephardim, including Spinoza's ancestors, making their way into inquisitional Portugal. It is a history that touches on cultural figures like the Marrano, the non-Jewish Jew, the stranger, which had and still have a resonance in modernity.[72] Indeed, we can say, have constitutive affinities with Arendt's conception of the conscious pariah.

Was all this too difficult, too foreign, too strange, for Virginia Woolf, the English writer who yet in her formative period as an experimental avant-garde modernist had declared herself an orphan to Englishness and was attracted to and helped translate Russian writing, in association with Kot, for the Hogarth Press? Bloom after all had been made into an orphan in the 'Cyclops' episode by the Irish nationalists in Barney Kiernan's pub when they expelled him from the circle of belonging. In Isaac Deutscher's terms, Bloom was in Ireland yet not in it, of it yet not of it. I think again of Eleanor at a dinner in *The Years*, drawn to someone she is introduced to, Nicholas, a 'foreigner' she thinks, 'clearly not English', perhaps Russian or Polish or Jewish; when another character at the dinner says that Nicholas is an American, he says no, 'I am a Pole'. Eleanor and Nicholas talk, probing ultimate questions of humanity and the future. Eleanor asks Nicholas if he believes that humanity can improve, that there can be a new world. Nicholas hesitantly ventures that 'the soul – the whole being' does wish 'to expand; to adventure; to form – new combinations'. Eleanor realises how much she likes him; he walks with her to the bus stop, and sees her on to her bus. Eleanor looks back, he is still standing on the pavement: 'He looked tall, impressive and solitary standing there alone, while the searchlights wheeled across the sky.'[73]

Why could Virginia, in 1918, not have chosen to be more like her character Eleanor, who in 1937 is receptive to the stranger?

Jessica Mitford

If Virginia Woolf, in anti-Semitic English culture, in marrying a Jewish man and adopting a Jewish name, announced herself as a conscious pariah, so too, a generation later, did Jessica Mitford, by far the most radical and iconoclastic of the famous Mitford sisters. Jessica escaped the desolation of the family home to elope with Churchill's nephew Esmond Romilly in the late 1930s; in 1939 they moved to the US, where she lived for the rest of her life, apart from some travel back to the UK. In her life Jessica suffered many tragedies, the death of two of her children, Esmond dying early in World War II in 1941 flying over the North Sea. Later in the war Jessica met and married a Jewish civil rights lawyer, Bob Treuhaft; they moved to Oakland, California, both joining the American Communist Party, which had a very large African-American membership. Jessica worked for the Civil Rights Congress, which in 1951 presented to the United Nations a petition, *We Charge Genocide*, which was signed by Jessica along with Paul Robeson, Dashiell Hammett, Josephine Baker and Lena Horne, Robeson presenting it to the UN Secretariat in New York. The petition charged the US with genocide under the 1948 UN Convention on Genocide, arguing that the lynching and other forms of assault on the lives and livelihood of African Americans from 1945 to 1951, especially the frenzied attacks on returning Black American veterans, amounted to genocide. Ann and I discuss this petition in an essay for a collection on genocide.[74]

In 1955 Jessica Mitford and Bob Treuhaft, along with their teenage daughter Dinky and Dinky's African-American friend Nebby Lou Crawford (daughter of Matt Crawford, 'an old friend who in the thirties had accompanied Paul [Robeson] on an all-black delegation to Russia'), evaded the FBI, which was in the habit of confiscating passports, including of their friend Paul Robeson; they travelled to Britain, and also to Budapest in Hungary, from where Bob Treuhaft's family had emigrated.[75]

Jessica realised that her racist and anti-Semitic father, notoriously splenetic, would be the reverse of civil if he met her Jewish husband, and she never saw her father again.

Bob Treuhaft's family journeying from Budapest to the US makes me think of Leopold Bloom in *Ulysses*, reminiscing in 'Ithaca' about his father Rudolph Bloom's long diasporic journeys, taking in 'Szombathely, Vienna, Budapest, Milan, London and Dublin'.[76]

Jessica, witty, funny, irreverent, daring and courageous, with an acute sense of the absurdity of the world, a trickster, a wanderer, an exile, stood out against the racism and anti-Semitism of her class the English aristocracy; stood out against the acceptance and promotion of Nazism by many in the English aristocracy, including by her own sisters Unity and Diana, the wife of Mosely the British fascist leader. Like Virginia Stephen, Jessica married a Jewish man and took a Jewish married name, Treuhaft, though she kept the Mitford name as her nom de plume.

I'm going now to conclude my thoughts on Hannah Arendt's 1944 essay 'The Jew as Pariah: A hidden tradition', where she admires conscious pariahs like Heinrich Heine, Bernard Lazare, Charlie Chaplin and Kafka.

In my extended list, the conscious pariahs are Heine, Lazare, Chaplin, Kafka, Benjamin, Arendt, Leonard Woolf, Virginia Woolf and Jessica Mitford.

Further Thoughts

I have a half-thought concerning Septimus in *Mrs Dalloway* and F R Leavis and post-World War I trauma effects. I was reading the harrowing pages on Septimus the ex-soldier as he sat on a seat in Regent's Park in London, his mind deteriorating, tormented, talking to himself, paranoid, feeling mocked, in despair, seeing visions of a dead friend killed in the war, declaring to his frightened wife Reza that they will kill themselves, then announcing that somehow he was king of the world, 'he, Septimus, the lord of men', and that he 'knew the meaning of the world'; he was a messiah, a saviour of humanity, a prophet, 'called forth in advance of the mass of men to hear the truth', the 'supreme secret', the 'profound truths', 'this astonishing revelation', by which the world would be entirely changed for ever.[77]

There are eerie similarities with Leavis. In his biography MacKillop writes of Leavis as a young man being badly affected by the war. In 1915, after completing his first year at Emmanuel College in Cambridge, with conscription looming, Leavis volunteered at a Quaker centre in York, and was assigned to serve in a non-military capacity, as a medical orderly. In France he arrived at the Friends' base camp two weeks after the Somme offensive had begun, and he spent the war on one of the Friends' ambulance trains. By 1916 he knew that all his friends who had gone to war had died. The crews on the ambulance trains dealt with 'constantly changing patients, rarely seeing cures, and often only death'. In 1916 'nearly 400 Australians were set down in the lying ward' of a casualty station. In 1918 'the train carried civilians who were ill with gas'; he 'encountered many Australians wounded in the defence of Amiens'. The train was bombed from the air.[78]

After the war Leavis returned to Cambridge in a 'stunned condition', subject to digestive problems, insomnia and a general speech defect, and rarely able to talk about his war experience.[79]

We may have here some explanation for characteristics of Leavis as a critical personality: his paranoia, sense of being persecuted, intellectual irritability, anger, truculence, delusions of grandeur as the century's great critic, messianic certainty that his mode of criticism was the key to all criticism, and readiness to cry betrayal.

I also have a sad fancy, that when Leavis encountered many wounded Australians, one may have been my uncle, Henry Docker, himself a medical orderly, who was dying.

I entertain another fancy, concerning *Mrs Dalloway* being published in 1925. My mother Elsie Levy, born in 1912, her family leaving England for Australia in 1926, was still living in London, if not the area of London evoked by Clarissa Dalloway's journey on 13 June 1923, in Westminster hearing Big Ben striking, making her way along Victoria Street, Piccadilly, Bond Street, to get to Mulberry's the florists. Now I wonder, perhaps in the East End my mother saw men like Septimus as described in *Mrs Dalloway*: 'Septimus Warren Smith, aged about thirty, pale-faced, beak-nosed, wearing brown shoes and a shabby overcoat, with hazel eyes which had that look of apprehension in them which makes complete strangers apprehensive too.'[80] Perhaps my mother and her brothers saw ex-soldiers in a state of trauma, tormented, talking to themselves; ex-soldiers who may have included Jewish men, or men of whatever religion who may have been teachers at her school. If she did see them, was my mother as a young girl enduringly haunted by such figures, such images?

I nearly said 'gong-tormented', a term I still remember from *Byzantium*, one of the few Yeats poems I recall being taught in my undergraduate Leavisite courses. I just looked up *Byzantium*: it's in the final line, 'That dolphin-torn, that gong-tormented sea.' Gong-tormented, a term, somewhere between an image and a sound, that whenever I engage in a solitary walk keeps coming back to me, back to me.

Conscious Pariahs 161

1 'The Jew as Pariah: A hidden tradition', in Hannah Arendt, *The Jewish Writings*, edited by Jerome Kohn and Ron H. Feldman (Schocken, New York, 1944), pp.295–7.
2 'The Jew as Pariah: A hidden tradition', p.276.
3 Elisabeth Young-Bruehl, *Hannah Arendt: For Love of the World* (Yale University Press, New Haven and London, 2004), p.168.
4 Leonard Woolf, *Growing* (Hogarth Press, London, 1961), pp.246–7.
5 Leonard Woolf, *Beginning Again: An Autobiography of the Years 1911 to 1918* (Hogarth Press, London, 1964), p.23.
6 Hermione Lee, *Virginia Woolf* (Vintage, New York, 1999), pp.305–6.
7 See also Natania Rosenfeld, *Outsiders Together: Virginia and Leonard Woolf* (Princeton University Press, Princeton, New Jersey, 2000), which argues that Virginia was an outsider to Englishness because of her gender, and Leonard because of his Jewishness. However, I try to complicate the notion of Leonard being an outsider by interpreting him through the prism of Arendt's distinctions between parvenu, pariah, and conscious pariah, and Maxime Rodinson's reflections on victims and executioners.
8 Hermione Lee, *Virginia Woolf*, pp.310–13.
9 Hermione Lee, *Virginia Woolf*, pp.366–7.
10 Victoria Glendinning, *Leonard Woolf* (Counterpoint, Berkeley, 2008), pp.190–91.
11 Leonard Woolf, *Beginning Again: An Autobiography of the Years 1911–1918* (Hogarth Press, London, 1964), pp.246–8.
12 Leonard Woolf, *Beginning Again: An Autobiography of the Years 1911–1918*, p.247.
13 Leonard Woolf, *Beginning Again: An Autobiography of the Years 1911–1918*, p.248.
14 Leonard Woolf, *Beginning Again: An Autobiography of the Years 1911–1918*, pp.249–53.
15 Leonard Woolf, *Downhill All the Way: An Autobiography of the years 1919 to 1939* (Harcourt Brace Jovanovich, New York and London, 1967), p.74.
16 Hermione Lee, *Virginia Woolf*, p.308.
17 Hermione Lee, *Virginia Woolf*, p.267.
18 Richard Davenport-Hines, *Universal Man: The Seven Lives of John Maynard Keynes* (William Collins, London, 2015), pp.4, 308. The Tuesday Club was a 'dining-club of officials, City men and financial journalists which met to discuss monetary economics and business' (p.135).
19 Hermione Lee, *Virginia Woolf*, p.289.
20 Hermione Lee, *Virginia Woolf*, pp.308–9.
21 Victoria Glendinning, *Leonard Woolf*, p.142.
22 Victoria Glendinning, *Leonard Woolf*, p.142.
23 Hermione Lee, *Virginia Woolf*, p.310.

24 Richard Davenport-Hines, *Universal Man: The Seven Lives of John Maynard Keynes*, p.309.

25 Virginia Woolf, *A Room of One's Own and Three Guineas*, edited and introduced by Michèle Barrett (Penguin Classics, London, 2011), p.6.

26 Hermione Lee, *Virginia Woolf*, p.308.

27 John Docker, *1492: The Poetics of Diaspora* (Continuum, London and New York, 2001), pp.86-7.

28 Cf. John Docker, 'The Enlightenment and Genocide', *JNT: Journal of Narrative Theory*, Vol.33, no.3, 2003, pp.292-314.

29 Ann Curthoys, 'The Three Body Problem: Feminism and Chaos Theory', *Hecate*, vol.17, no.1, 1991, pp.14-21, and Ann Curthoys and John Docker, *Is History Fiction?* (UNSW Press, Sydney, 2010), p.175, chapter on 'The Feminist Challenge'. See also Anna Cole, 'Twenty Years On: feminism's 'three body problem'', *Women's History Review*, Vol.22, no.4, 2013, pp.559-75.

30 John Docker, *1492: The Poetics of Diaspora*, pp.68-70.

31 John Docker, *1492: The Poetics of Diaspora*, pp.86, 88, 102. In this discussion of Spinoza, I gratefully draw on Yirmiyahu Yovel, *Spinoza and Other Heretics*, vol.I: *The Marrano of Reason* (Princeton University Press, Princeton NJ, 1989).

32 Isaac Deutscher, *The Non-Jewish Jew* (1968; Merlin Press, London, 1981); see also Ned Curthoys, *The Legacy of Liberal Judaism: Ernst Cassirer and Hannah Arendt's Hidden Conversation* (Berghahn, New York and Oxford, 2013), pp.212-14.

33 John Docker, *1492: The Poetics of Diaspora*, p.xi. Jordana Silverstein, *Anxious Histories: Narrating the Holocaust in Jewish Communities at the Beginning of the Twenty-First Century* (Berghahn, New York and Oxford, 2015), p.17, is intrigued not to say amused by Marsha Rosengarten's phrase.

34 John Docker, *1492: The Poetics of Diaspora*, pp.67-8.

35 John Docker, 'Feminism, Modernism and Orientalism in *The Home* in the 1920s', in Ann Curthoys and Julianne Schultz (eds), *Journalism: Print, Politics and Popular Culture* (University of Queensland Press, St. Lucia, 1999), p.121, and Peter Wollen, 'Fashion/orientalism/the body', *New Formations*, no.1, 1987, pp.5-33.

36 Susan Merrill Squier, *Virginia Woolf and London: The Sexual Politics of the City* (The University of North Carolina Press, Chapel Hill and London, 1985), p.152.

37 Virginia Woolf, *Moments of Being*, New Edition, edited by Jeanne Schulkind (Pimlico, London, 2002), Introduction by Hermione Lee; Appendix B, 'Preface to the Second Edition', p.162.

38 Virginia Woolf, *Moments of Being*, p.152.

39 Virginia Woolf, *Moments of Being*, pp.152-3.

40 Virginia Woolf, *Mrs Dalloway*, introduced by Elaine Showalter (Penguin Classics, London, 2000), pp.40-41.

41 Ian MacKillop, *F.R. Leavis: A Life in Criticism* (Allen Lane, London, 1995), pp.28, 100, 101.

Conscious Pariahs 163

42 MacKillop, *F.R. Leavis: A Life in Criticism*, pp.87, 101, 104–5.
43 MacKillop, *F.R. Leavis: A Life in Criticism*, pp.87, 97–8, 169.
44 MacKillop, *F.R. Leavis: A Life in Criticism*, p.228.
45 Hermione Lee, *Virginia Woolf*, pp.14, 613.
46 MacKillop, *F.R. Leavis: A Life in Criticism*, pp.224, 228–9.
47 Hermione Lee, *Virginia Woolf*, p.681.
48 Virginia Woolf, *A Room of One's Own and Three Guineas*, p.xxxviii.
49 MacKillop, *F.R. Leavis: A Life in Criticism*, pp.147–8, 195–6, 266.
50 Isaac Deutscher, *The Non-Jewish Jew*, pp.26–7, 33–5.
51 See Ned Curthoys, *The Legacy of Liberal Judaism: Ernst Cassirer and Hannah Arendt's Hidden Conversation* (Berghahn, New York and Oxford, 2013), pp.213–4.
52 See Ned Curthoys, *The Legacy of Liberal Judaism: Ernst Cassirer and Hannah Arendt's Hidden Conversation*, pp.32–3.
53 See John Docker, *The Origins of Violence: Religion, History and Genocide* (UNSW Press, Sydney, 2008), p.173, and also Sarah Irving, '"In a Pure Soil": Colonial Anxieties in the Work of Francis Bacon', *History of European Ideas*, Vol.32 (2006), pp.250–3, 257.
54 Isaac Deutscher, *The Non-Jewish Jew*, p.27.
55 Leonard Woolf, *Beginning Again: An Autobiography of the Years 1911–1918*, p.249.
56 Leonard Woolf, *Beginning Again*, pp.249–50.
57 Leonard Woolf, *Growing: An Autobiography of the Years 1904–1911*, pp.95–6.
58 Ned Curthoys, *The Legacy of Liberal Judaism*, pp.92, 95.
59 Victoria Glendinning, *Leonard Woolf*, p.173.
60 Leonard Woolf, *Beginning Again*, 217–226; *Downhill All the Way: An Autobiography of the Years 1919 to 1939*, pp.83–5.
61 Virginia Woolf, *A Room of One's Own*, p.46.
62 Hermione Lee, *Virginia Woolf*, p.361.
63 Hermione Lee, *Virginia Woolf*, pp.433–5.
64 Leonard Woolf, *Beginning Again*, pp.245–6.
65 Hermione Lee, *Virginia Woolf*, pp.360, 384–5.
66 Leonard Woolf, *Beginning Again*, p.246.
67 Hermione Lee, *Virginia Woolf*, pp.385–6.
68 Richard Ellmann, *James Joyce* (OUP, New York, 1982), p.502, also, 421–2, 441–2, 497, 502–4; Docker, *1492: The Poetics of Diaspora*, p.69.
69 Hermione Lee, *Virginia Woolf*, p.386.
70 Hermione Lee, *Virginia Woolf*, p.434.
71 Hermione Lee, *Virginia Woolf*, p.433.

72 Docker, *1492: The Poetics of Diaspora*, pp.99–106; Yirmiyahu Yovel, *Spinoza and Other Heretics*, vol.I: *The Marrano of Reason* (Princeton University Press, Princeton NJ, 1989).

73 Virginia Woolf, *The Years and Between the Acts* (Wordsworth Classics, London, 2012), pp.193, 195, 198, 205, 207.

74 Ann Curthoys and John Docker, 'Defining Genocide', in Dan Stone (ed.), *The Historiography of Genocide* (Palgrave Macmillan, London, 2010), p.16.

75 See Jessica Mitford, *A Fine Old Conflict* (1977; Vintage, New York, 1978), ch.10, 'Going Home Again', pp.222–3, 240–1; concerning denial of a passport for Paul Robeson, see pp.237–8.

76 Docker, *1492: The Poetics of Diaspora*, pp.104–5; James Joyce, *Ulysses* (1922), introduction and notes by Declan Kiberd (Penguin, London, 1992), pp.797–8.

77 Virginia Woolf, *Mrs Dalloway*, pp.71–7; 153–165.

78 MacKillop, *F.R. Leavis: A Life in Criticism*, pp.38–44.

79 MacKillop, *F.R. Leavis: A Life in Criticism*, pp.44–7, 105.

80 Virginia Woolf, *Mrs Dalloway*, p.15.

14

Cultural Genocide: T S Eliot, vicious Anti-Semite

> My house is a decayed house,
> And the jew squats on the window sill, the owner,
> Spawned in some estaminet of Antwerp,
> Blistered in Brussels, patched and peeled in London.
> T S Eliot, 'Gerontion', 1920[1]

> The rats are underneath the piles.
> The jew is underneath the lot.
> 'Burbank with a Baedeker: Bleistein with a Cigar', 1920[2]

> Rachel *née* Rabinovitch
> Tears at the grapes with murderous paws
> 'Sweeney Among the Nightingales', 1920[3]

Here and in subsequent chapters of this section of my ego histoire devoted to T S Eliot, I wish to explore how anti-Semitism entwines itself in the poetry of Thomas Stearns Eliot, a longtime friend or at least good acquaintance of Virginia Woolf and Leonard Woolf, though their remarks in their diaries and letters on Tom Eliot, as he was familiarly known to his contemporaries, make entertaining reading. I'll focus on the early Eliot, coincident with World War I and up to the early 1920s. In relation to attitudes towards Jews and Jewishness, the high literary modernism of the early twentieth century was divided and contradictory, torn between what we can call the philosemitism of Joyce's *Ulysses* (1922) in its affectionate portrait of Leopold Bloom, and the Judeophobia of Eliot and his friend Ezra Pound. I'll leave till later chapters Eliot's *After Strange Gods: A Primer of Modern Heresy* (1933/1934), which has a notoriously anti-Semitic sentence that stands out from the page; I'll also talk there about Yeats in the 1930s, concerning his attraction to Nazism.

Eliot's poems and critical essays of the late teens and early 1920s were, in memory, favourites of those members of staff who were Leavisites in the department of English at the University of Sydney in the middle 1960s, under whose spell I fell. Beginning my degree in 1963, looking forward to studying English literature pretty well to the exclusion of anything else, I must have soon purchased at the university bookshop Eliot's *Selected Poems*, published in 1961 by Faber and Faber, along with Grover Smith's *T.S. Eliot's Poetry and Plays: A Study in Sources and Meaning* (1956), considered indispensable for the student in understanding references and allusions. I also early on bought Eliot's *Selected Essays*, a large hardback in a blue cover. Looking at *Selected Essays* now, I see it was published in 1961, and it contains essays such as 'Tradition and the Individual Talent' (1917) and 'The Metaphysical Poets' (1921) that were crucial to the Leavisite project, in its search for a literary tradition that could be proclaimed the canon of English literature, thence to be zealously taught, both in Britain and for export around the world.

Thus equipped, I was ready to read and learn, and hopefully have opinions of my own. Yet, when it came to the anti-Semitic passages of the Eliot poems like those I've just quoted from in my epigraphs, I didn't have an opinion of my own. I didn't have any opinion.

Burlesque and music hall come into this story, as does Bosie, Oscar Wilde's old lover Lord Alfred Douglas, in the early 1920s, for Bosie was also a poet of sorts who wrote a sonnet with multiple affinities to Eliot's own early verse.

What I obtusely didn't realise in the 1960s, and what I perceive now, is how intensely and violently ethnicised and racialised Eliot's early verse is. Towards the end of this chapter, and thinking about my involvement in genocide studies, I'll suggest that these verses, taken together, form a genocidal narrative.

After such knowledge, what forgiveness?

There's a kind of agony in writing this chapter, a history which doesn't reflect well on the young person who was me in the 1960s, the teenage Leavisite doing English at the University of Sydney 1963–1966. It especially concerns 'Gerontion', which I first read – and read many times – in *Selected Poems*, where 'Gerontion' is placed first in the section entitled 'Poems 1920', followed by *The Waste Land*. I read *Selected Poems* intensely, especially 'The Love Song of J. Alfred Prufrock' in the opening section as well as 'Gerontion' in the 'Poems 1920' section. In 'Gerontion' I was particularly taken with the rhetorical question 'After such knowledge, what forgiveness?' situated half way through the poem, and have deployed it here and there in my writings, and now call on it again. I have to turn the question back on to myself, or the self in the early 1960s who was intently reading 'Gerontion'. I cannot remember responding to the lines I've quoted as an epigraph in any way, certainly not objecting to them, certainly not with anger, certainly not by thinking these derisory references to Jews could apply to my mother in our Bondi flat and my grandmother and grandfather living in poverty not far away in Bondi; my mother who had told me so many stories about their life in London before 1926. I can't remember feeling anything at all about these lines, or even noticing them.

Now, in writing this ego histoire, especially in this section on my mother, my feelings about Eliot are becoming increasingly suffused with anger and scorn mixed with anguish. I have to try and understand why I liked him so much in the first place. Why hadn't I reacted to these lines in 'Gerontion'? Why why why? Why, if it comes to that, hadn't I asked a nervous question of my Leavisite tutors to see what they felt about them and how they would explain their presence in poems they quite evidently valued so highly and taught as what modern English poetry should look like? What does ignoring those images – and other such images in 'Burbank with a Baedeker: Bleistein with a Cigar' and 'Sweeney Among the Nightingales', both also in the 'Poems 1920' section of *Selected Poems* – say about my critical consciousness as a Leavisite student in the middle 1960s? What does the ignoring of such lines say about the critical consciousness of my Leavisite teachers?

I'm not sure I can explain why I didn't notice these blatant Judeophobic images. I'm not sure I can forgive myself.

My honours year supervisor: introducing doubt, encouraging detachment

Some years ago, on a visit to London, on the suggestion of our friend Charles Ross, Ann and I bought in the bookshop of the British Library a music disk entitled on the cover 'Historic recordings from the British Library Sound Archive – The Spoken Word, Poets'; the sleeve notes tucked inside tell us that all the featured poets were born before 1900. The poets include Eliot intoning 'Prufrock' (the recording made by an elderly Eliot in 1948) in that studied, careful, slow-motion voice, pitched somewhere between faux-English and mid-Atlantic. I did register a slight irritation listening, while also thinking what a pleasure it was to hear the poem I had read so many times as a student and later spoken. (A thought: why did Eliot in 1948 choose to intone 'Prufrock', why not 'Gerontion' or 'Burbank with a Baedeker: Bleistein with a Cigar' or 'Sweeney Among the Nightingales'?)

Nonetheless, I don't know if I ever wholly admired Eliot. As I noted in the previous chapter when talking about how pompous males insist on having initials before their surnames, a certain 'J. Docker' wrote his University of Sydney BA honours thesis in 1966, my fourth and final year, on '*The Wasteland* and *The Dunciad*', encased within a shiny black cover. I have a distant memory of going to see my fourth-year supervisor, A L French, at the beginning of the academic year and confessing that I couldn't think of a topic for my thesis. I recall that he suggested I compare, as long poems about London, Pope's eighteenth-century *The Dunciad* with Eliot's *The Waste Land*. I must have murmured OK, and he gave me an off-print of an article he'd just published, very critical of Ezra Pound. 'You might be interested in this,' he said. After the honours year, leaving my Bondi parental flat (forever, as it turned out), I ventured south to the University of Melbourne, in 1967-8, to do further work on Eliot. I've just this moment got down from the shelf an MA thesis, its cover post office red, the author a certain 'J. Docker', entitled 'T.S. Eliot – Four Quartets', submitted, I see, to the University of Melbourne in October 1969. (I'd returned to live in Sydney in late 1968, and kept working on the thesis there in a corner house, previously a shop, that Ann Curthoys and I lived in in Balmain.)

A L French himself must have left the Sydney English department in 1967 or thereabouts, as part of the southward exodus of Leavisite or Leavisite-leaning staff, and had evidently gone to the English department at La Trobe University in suburban Melbourne; I vaguely recall a dinner at the Melbourne University's staff club where young J Docker with big black-rimmed glasses sat silently while S L Goldberg, the head of department, and his two lieutenants Jock Tomlinson and Maggie Tomlinson talked to A L French, who was visiting from La Trobe (perhaps Mr French, as I would still have known him, asked that I be invited to be there, his ex-student; I don't know). I never met him again. Oddly, I can't remember who was my MA supervisor at Melbourne. (I've just checked my MA thesis, and it has no acknowledgements at the beginning: what was I thinking?!)

I'll discuss these theses in the black and red covers when I come to the 1960s, to see how that stranger, J Docker, might have managed in writing them to emerge from his teenage Leavisite chrysalis, wings shaking, perhaps J Docker offering qualifications or criticisms as he began to disengage from the Leavisite world. And I still have A L French's offprint of his Ezra Pound essay. I suspect it may have influenced young J Docker a lot in such disengaging. I'm now thinking that A L French stood at a critical angle to the Leavisite project with its granting of exalted status to modernist poets like Pound and Eliot (and Yeats), that he was a kind of Leavisite dissident.[4]

I must also discuss a puzzling question involving Eliot and Bloomsbury: what did Leonard Woolf think of the anti-Semitic images in Eliot's early poetry, which he and Virginia published for their Hogarth Press? Given how introspective Woolf considered himself to be, I wonder why he didn't pause over these blatant anti-Semitic lines in the early poems as he and Virginia set them to type in the basement of their house in November 1918, ready for publication in May 1919.[5] When reading for this ego-histoire Leonard Woolf's autobiographies and the biographies of Virginia and Leonard, I was on the look-out to see what Leonard thought of T S Eliot in relation to anti-Semitism, an issue not unimportant in the century of the Holocaust. But I came up empty handed as it were. Victoria Glendinning reports that in the 1960s Woolf fielded enquiries from scholars concerning the question of Eliot and anti-Semitism. 'He always answered in the same way: he did not know why Eliot was anti-Semitic, and he had never shown any sign of it in his presence. He could not remember whether they had ever even discussed it.'[6] So that's that then. Eliot was never anti-Semitic to Leonard Woolf in person – why would he be when he had so much to gain from the association with the Hogarth

Press? – so Leonard Woolf had no further interest in the question.

Leonard Woolf also had much to gain from an association with the young American poet, whose startling convention-breaking verse could assist the Hogarth Press in its desire to be avant garde, to be at the cutting edge of modernism. Woolf went out of his way to assist Eliot in his transition from young American at large in Europe to life as influential man of letters in England. In *Sowing* Leonard remembers with satisfaction: 'I helped him to become an Englishman by becoming one of his statutory sponsors, and I am, I think legitimately, proud that I not only printed and published *The Waste Land* but had a hand in converting its author from an American to an English poet.'[7] In *Beginning Again* Woolf records how pleased he was to publish the early poems like 'Sweeney among the Nightingales', adding that 'I never tired and still do not tire of those lines which were a new note in poetry and came from the heart of the Eliot of those days'. As illustration, Woolf quotes the final two stanzas about the death of Agamemnon, but doesn't refer to the 'Rachel *née* Rabinovitch' stanza.[8]

In the 1960s then, Leonard Woolf, an old man reflecting on a long life, and J Docker, just starting on a life of criticism, were in strange agreement. In terms of the anti-Semitism of Eliot's early poems, they had nothing to say.

What I think now about these poems

As if we are sitting around in a tutorial class, where you always have the text before you, the tutor saying what do you think of this phrase, that image, I'll now quote the lines from 'Gerontion' again, and do some 'practical criticism' on them, the method of detailed analysis, usually shortened to 'prac crit', that became synonymous with Leavisite teaching as I absorbed it; a method I retained while discarding so much else of the Leavisite approach to literature and history, in my as it were post-Leavisite period. The following jumble of thoughts, at least in some rudimentary form, are perhaps what *should* have occurred to J Docker the teenage Leavisite at the University of Sydney in the middle 1960s; and, speculatively, what *could* have occurred to Leonard Woolf several decades before then.

> My house is a decayed house,
> And the jew squats on the window sill, the owner,
> Spawned in some estaminet of Antwerp,
> Blistered in Brussels, patched and peeled in London.
> T S Eliot, 'Gerontion', 1920

'Gerontion' in this sleazy insinuating passage suggests that the Jews of Europe were now swarming over London, owning it, bringing squalor and degradation ('My house is a decayed house'): England and its inherited culture are being destroyed and consumed, and the agents of that destruction are European Jews, animal-like, sitting there like monkeys on a window sill, squatting like a sub-human species. The images of blisters, patched and peeling, suggest the Jewish owner is diseased, perhaps marked by plague, bringing sickness and pestilence to London, so that, spreading, enveloping, it would become a city of the ailing and dying and dead, a necropolis.

These images converse, I now think, with much other cultural and political history of the early twentieth century, before and after 'Gerontion', in the *fin de siècle* and teens and early 1920s.

We can think, for example, of *Nosferatu*, that famous silent-era German film, directed by F W Murnau, made in 1921, released in 1922, drawing on Bram Stoker's *Dracula* but adding new elements, especially the sequence where the king-vampire, Count Orlok, transfers coffins from his castle in the Carpathian mountains in Transylvania to a schooner, which will journey to the fictional city of Wisborg in Germany, where the Count, in drinking blood as vampires are wont to do, can make the living into the undead.

One of the coffins is filled with rats, which are accidently opened by the sailors on board, who then sicken and die, the Count and his rats bringing pestilence and plague westward to Germany and Europe. As remarkable as Murnau's Expressionist film is in the history of cinema, it has existed ever since under suspicion of anti-Semitism, the bent figure of the Count suggesting a conventional Judeophobic history of representation of the Jew, the rats signifying Jews overrunning Europe, a sinister and fateful iconography.

My mind goes back to what I referred to in an earlier chapter, the essay by David Cesarini entitled 'An Embattled Minority: The Jews in Britain During the First World War'. Recall that Cesarini argues that the position of Jews experienced a 'serious deterioration' during the war and afterwards, always in danger of being suspected by the wider society of disloyalty in being too sympathetic towards foreign-born Jews resident in Britain, especially the Russian Jews who had come to escape persecution in Tsarist Russia. As the war wore on, 'jingoism and xenophobia' increased, a consequence being that 'physical violence occurred in several towns and cities in 1914 and 1915'; in 1917 there were 'major anti-Jewish riots in Leeds… and Bethnal Green'.[9]

Cesarini concludes that the war years revealed in acute form an 'unwillingness' on the part of the English majority to 'comprehend and accept the differences of minorities within society', an unwillingness to recognise that England's population comprised 'varied peoples'.[10]

In terms of Cesarini's passionate reflections, we could say that Gerontion, the I of the poem, constitutes himself as representing the English people in their supposed ethnic purity, who during and after the war were quick to reveal xenophobia and violence – for aren't these lines in 'Gerontion' violent in their extreme derision of those perceived as foreign? Couldn't these lines be seen as possibly inciting violence? In Cesarini's terms 'Gerontion' reveals an 'unwillingness' to recognise 'minorities' and 'different peoples' within England, including minorities and peoples who historically have led, as Cesarini observes of English Jews, 'supra-national' lives, imbued with a necessarily cosmopolitan consciousness.

We could at this point apply some Isaiah Berlin to Thomas Stearns Eliot, that the anti-Semitism of 'Gerontion' was not as it were determined by the age or the surrounding society. In our *Is History Fiction?* Ann Curthoys and I point out that in his 1954 book *Historical Inevitability*, Berlin argues firmly that free choice and individual responsibility always exist in history; we should recognise that individuals in the past could have chosen to act otherwise than how they did; they could have avoided acting in the ways they did act.[11]

In these terms, we can recall Lord Acton's cosmopolitan and pluralist attitude to minorities in the late nineteenth century as a choice that he, Acton, made, and is a choice that Eliot could have made for 'Gerontion' not that long afterwards in the early twentieth century. I'm thinking of Lord Acton's declaration in 'The History of Freedom in Antiquity', an address given in 1877: 'The most certain test by which we judge whether a country is really free is the amount of security enjoyed by minorities.'[12] It's a view that looks forward to Cesarini; it posits a 'test' by which 'Gerontion' fails.

I'll explore this thought more, that Eliot could have chosen to be cosmopolitan in the way Lord Acton had chosen.

In our discussion of Lord Acton in *Is History Fiction?* Ann and I refer to Owen Chadwick's 1998 biography *Acton and History*, which points out that Acton in the nineteenth century, in his upbringing, schooling and adult life, belonged as much to Europe, especially France, Germany and Italy, as to England. Acton was a prominent Catholic intellectual. As part of a Catholic minority, he experienced discrimination. Born in 1834, his mother was German.

He could not be educated at Cambridge or Oxford, because both demanded fealty to the Church of England. Acton hoped for some kind of exemption from a Cambridge college, but the three he applied to could not accept a student who broke college rules by not worshipping in the college chapel. It was decided he should go to Munich University where nearby a German branch of the family lived. Later he became friends with Cardinal Newman, and a member of parliament. As a well-known liberal Catholic, he opposed the secrecy and repressive censorship practised by the Rome Congregation of the Index. He insisted on the right of free research, including into the follies and horrors committed by the church in former times, though he considered that the church at its best was a force for toleration and freedom. He was increasingly suspected in Catholic circles of being rebellious towards papal authority, and was threatened with excommunication. He became an intellectual agnostic and expressed admiration for solitaries and rebels. He believed in the existence of the good atheist, and admired George Eliot as a fellow solitary. In 1895 he was appointed regius professor of history at Cambridge by the Liberal Party prime minister Lord Rosebery; it was now possible to appoint a Roman Catholic for the first time because liberal governments had slowly opened offices to members of every denomination.

Acton, in his 1895 'Inaugural Lecture on the Study of History', its audience including young women from Newnham College, their principal Miss Gladstone, was highly critical of the Crusades, relating that in their 'first fervour' the 'men who took the Cross, after receiving communion, heartily devoted the day to the extermination of the Jews'.[13]

'Gerontion' most decidedly does not speak to Lord Acton's cosmopolitan and pluralist principle that a country is free when its minorities are respected and enjoy security.

I'll now ventriloquise thoughts that Leonard Woolf and J Docker *could* have voiced in thinking about their own Jewish families as they read 'Gerontion'. They could, for example, have registered feelings about that line of derision and contempt for Jews, 'Spawned in some estaminet of Antwerp', as if there is something loathsome in itself in not being born in England, in being born in Europe. Leonard Woolf tells us in *Sowing*: 'My mother was born in Holland of Jewish parents in Amsterdam.'[14] While Antwerp is in Belgium, it is not that far from Amsterdam: he could have taken Eliot's lines as an insulting reference to his own family. J Docker in the 1960s could have thought of his mother relating a family story that the family believed they came from Holland in the eighteenth century.

Leonard could also have thought of his and Virginia's Eastern European Jewish friend Kot, S S Koteliansky, their collaborator in Russian translations of Gorky, Tchekov, Dostoevsky, Leo Tolstoy and Sophie Tolstoy. As I relate in my chapter 'Conscious Pariahs', Leonard had first met Kot in 1917, and learned that while most of his family in Ukraine had been wiped out by invading armies, one of Kot's brothers did escape and soon after World War I managed to 'reach Antwerp, and thence London and Canada'.[15] So, Kot's brother, fleeing a history of persecution and destruction of Jewish life in Eastern Europe, managed to reach safety in Antwerp, and then, moving on, as refugees do in seeking stability and a new life somewhere, came to London and thence travelled to Canada, reaching a continent as far as possible from an older world of Eastern European Jewish life never free of fear, threat and sudden extreme violence.

Leonard Woolf could also, I now think, have instantly recognised the lines from 'Gerontion' as part of a long and continuing anti-Semitism in the literary and intellectual life that surrounded him from boyhood. In *Sowing*, talking of his time at St Paul's School, Leonard Woolf recalls that in his final year he joined a 'small debating society' which met on Saturday afternoons. G K Chesterton, who had been at St Paul's and was six years his senior, had helped found it, and after Chesterton left school he continued the society, with two or three boys still at the school being elected to it: 'How they came to elect me I cannot remember, but I know that I was both surprised and flattered.' G K Chesterton's brother Cecil, a contemporary of Leonard at the school, was also a member, and Leonard reflects that it is 'amusing, in view of the subsequent violent anti-semitism of the Chestertons, to note that three out of the four boys still at school whom they elected to this very exclusive society were Jews'.[16]

George Orwell, in his well-known 1945 essay 'Antisemitism in Britain', refers to 'Chesterton's endless tirades against Jews, which he thrust into stories and essays upon the flimsiest pretexts'.[17]

Leonard Woolf could have also thought of the anti-Semitism of the supposedly sophisticated and cosmopolitan Bloomsbury people, his friends, his wife, his wife's sister: why, he could have exclaimed at least to himself, why did 'Gerontion' not attempt to challenge such English anti-cosmopolitanism – as his own 1917 story 'Three Jews' had so challenged – rather than extending it into the realm of avant-garde modernist literature?

When he and Virginia assisted Eliot's poetic career in his conquest of England by seeking him out and publishing his poems, did they have any misgivings? Leonard confesses to not one. What of Virginia? In Hermione Lee's biography I notice that Virginia Woolf confided to her diary (on 3 December 1918) that the early Eliot poems that they published in May 1919, while 'formally brilliant', bristled with 'obscure sinister violence and disdainful irony'.[18] The Leavisites had a term for insight, aperçu, that they were fond of; I'll now explore Virginia's aperçu. What were the objects of the early poems' 'obscure sinister violence and disdainful irony'?

A Plethora of Intersections: music hall, postcards, Bosie

What strikes me now is how crude the language of 'Gerontion' is in these lines, a kind of demotic doggerel, how much they reveal a coarse-grained sensibility that speaks to the coarse-grained sensibility of the anti-Semitism of the British society of its time, both popular and upper-class: does not challenge it or transcend it or seek distance from it (I call here on Virginia Woolf style semi-colons); revels in it; desires to be in concert with it; serves it; courts it; is inspired by it; savours it.

'Gerontion' was published in the section Poems 1920 of *Selected Poems* and can now be seen as part of British anti-Semitism as a vortex, a tentacular web. The early twentieth century, as Orwell observes in 'Anti-Semitism in Britain', was a time when anti-Semitism was an acceptable and widely enjoyed activity of British society, with Chesterton being 'one of the most generally respected figures in English literary life'. Orwell points to the popularity, at least until the advent and impact of Hitler in the early 1930s, of 'the Jew joke' across a range of cultural media: 'After 1934 the Jew joke disappeared as though by magic from postcards, periodicals and the music-hall stage.' Following Orwell, we can say that British anti-Semitism formed a kind of cultural archive, where jokes, images, motifs, tropes, circulated and were instantly recognisable.

Robert Crawford in his 2015 biography *Young Eliot: From St Louis to The Waste Land* tells us that the young American student Tom Eliot, becoming acquainted with Europe in 1910–11, developed a longstanding interest in burlesque and music hall. While a student in Paris, Eliot must, says Crawford, have known about the public scandal occurring when in 1911 the Théâtre du Châtelet was staging the five-hour extravaganza, *Le Martyre de Saint Sébastien*, with a script by Gabriele d'Annunzio – whose works had just been proscribed by the Pope – along with specially composed music by Debussy and costumes by Leon Bakst. It starred the luminous Russian Jewish ballerina Ida Rubinstein, who had played Cleopatra in a Ballets Russes production the year before, and was admired by Cocteau. In *Le Martyre de Saint Sébastien*, Crawford writes, Ida Rubinstein cross-dressed as Saint Sebastian, 'dancing ecstatically over burning coals, her ultimate fate to be bound to a tree and martyred by being shot full of arrows'. The archbishop of Paris, Crawford adds, denounced the play, threatening to excommunicate any Catholics who chose to see it.[19]

In 1910–11 young Eliot visits London, and, among other sights, perhaps prompted by the Baedeker tourist guide that he was using, found his way to the East End to observe its inhabitants, then writing, Crawford tells us, to his cousin Eleanor Hinkley: 'Whitechapel (note: Jews)'.[20] How remarkable for the American student from St Louis via Harvard in Boston: Jews in the East End; he might have observed my mother's family there. Perhaps they noticed the tourist, lurking in a doorway, come to Whitechapel to furtively gawk at the Jews.

Crawford tells us that London offered for Eliot 'music hall treats', including 'Marie Lloyd at the Pavilion'.[21] In London, once living there from 1915, he continued to admire Marie Lloyd. As London correspondent for the New York magazine *The Dial*, Eliot published in December 1922 a 'London Letter' mourning her death, recalling that she was not only the greatest music-hall artist in England, she was also the most popular, for she 'represented and expressed that part of the English nation which has perhaps the greatest vitality and interest', 'Cockney London, who had crowded to see her for thirty years'. Eliot observes that he himself had seen another music hall comedian, Nellie Wallace, 'interrupted by jeering or hostile comment from a boxful of East-Enders', but Marie Lloyd was never in his experience confronted by this kind of hostility (*The Dial*, December 1922, online).

So, we infer, and as is well known, London music-hall audiences could be rowdy and noisy. In terms of Orwell's comment in 'Antisemitism in Britain' that 'the Jew joke' featured in the 1920s in 'postcards, periodicals and the music-hall stage', questions occur. When Eliot in London visited music halls and when one of the comedians came on stage specialising in ethnic and racial jokes – where anti-Jewish jokes would be part of a standard repertoire that probably also included anti-Irish jokes, which themselves were commonly fused with anti-African jokes – did Eliot, sitting stiffly there, like the 'eternal Footman' in 'Prufrock', 'snicker'? Did Eliot collect postcards with anti-Jewish jokes? Did he enjoy reading periodicals where anti-Jewish jokes and sentiment found a ready home?

In 1920 there appeared one such periodical, the crazed anti-Semitic *Plain English*, founded by Lord Alfred Douglas. Alex Ross, the music critic for *The New Yorker*, in a commentary entitled 'Strange Fruit' in 2000, writes that Douglas emerged after the war as a prominent advocate of 'The Protocols of the Elders of Zion', and was undeterred when in August 1921 *The Times* exposed them as a forgery. Ross quotes particularly egregious examples of racism and anti-Semitism in *Plain English*: 'The negroes in the United States are being organized by the Jew Seligman'; 'There are more Kikes – 'Kike' being the American for Jew – in New York than there are in Warsaw'. There was a loud headline: 'HUMAN SACRIFICE AMONG THE JEWS'. *Plain English* also expressed, says Ross, support for the Ku Klux Klan, and even, in 1921, when Hitler was unknown outside his home town of Munich, a reference to 'Herr Hitler' as the 'spirited' leader of a political party.[22]

Alex Ross tells us that in 1924 Douglas produced his sequence 'In Excelsis', with the following particularly Judeophobic sonnet (wherein 'The Protocols of the Elders of Zion' is alluded to as if *The Times*'s exposure of the forgery in 1921 had never appeared):

> The leprous spawn of scattered Israel
> Spreads its contagion in your English blood;
> Teeming corruption rises like a flood
> Whose fountain swelters in the womb of hell.

> Your Jew-kept politicians buy and sell
> In markets redolent of Jewish mud,
> And while the 'Learned Elders' chew the cud
> Of liquidation's fruits, they weave their spell.
> They weave the spell that binds the heart's desire
> To gold and gluttony and sweating lust:
> In hidden holds they stew the mandrake mess
> That kills the soul and turns the blood to fire,
> They weave the spell that turns desire to dust
> And postulates the abyss of nothingness.

Perhaps, I now think, these images were to some degree inspired by Eliot's *Poems 1920*, even if Douglas's verse is in a tiresomely conventional Victorian rhyming mode, rather than inflected by Eliot's poem's modernist jagged edges; inspired, even if unconsciously, because of the commonality of imagery. The Judeophobic phrasing of the lines in 'Gerontion' emphasising Jews as diseased, as blistered, patched and peeling, and the image of the Jew as 'Spawned', might have prompted images in the opening lines of Douglas's sonnet concerning 'leprous spawn' and 'contagion' in 'English blood'. And perhaps the final image, 'the abyss of nothingness', continuing the shared thread of terms and vision, was inspired by the final line of 'Gerontion', 'Thoughts of a dry brain in a dry season'.

I'm also struck by the strand of images in Douglas's sonnet of Jews inhabiting and spreading a kind of insidious unstoppable deadly miasma. 'English blood' finds itself overwhelmed by corruption as a rising 'flood', which seeks and finds a rhyme in 'Jewish mud'; there is a 'fountain' that swelters; 'English blood' is also being poisoned by a witch's 'mandrake mess' that Jews 'stew'. Such liquid images in 'In Excelsis' could, I fancy, have harvested and re-presented like images in Eliot's 'Burbank with a Baedeker: Bleistein with a Cigar', where, in its succession of burlesque scenes, Venice, the great Renaissance city, is being despoiled by modern-day Jewish businessmen and prostitutes in the figures of Bleistein and Princess Volupine. Eliot's poem is infused with images of water, slime, the simian and disease. The poem opens with Burbank crossing a bridge; we register that he is under threat of destruction by the prostitute Princess Volupine, who meets him at a small hotel, where they are together, and 'he fell': as if slain in battle by the Jewish prostitute, the seductress as succubus. There are more watery images, of 'music under sea', and the prostitute's 'shuttered barge' (degrading the legendary image of Cleopatra) burning on 'the water all the day'; later we see Princess Volupine extending a skeletal 'meagre, blue-nailed, phthisic hand', wasted perhaps from sexual disease, which she is spreading throughout the fabled European city, destroying it. Then Bleistein the Jewish businessman with a cigar is introduced, ape-like, with a 'sagging bending of the knees' and elbows 'with the palms turned out', the Jew as wandering foreigner, 'Chicago Semite Viennese', with his 'lustreless protrusive eye' looking out from the 'protozoic slime' he inhabits, that geological eon just before the coming of complex life on earth; this Jew, without any trace of human culture and cultivation and knowledge, dares to invade Italy, the land of 'Caneletto', of high European art, of everything non-Jews hold dear and essential to European civilisation, now left in ruins by an alien and pre-human life form: 'The rats are underneath the piles./The jew is underneath the lot.' As in at least some readings of Murnau's *Nosferatu*, Eliot's 'Burbank with a Baedeker: Bleistein with a Cigar' associates Jews with 'rats'.

'Burbank with a Baedeker: Bleistein with a Cigar' suggests a mood that will help prepare European historical consciousness for the Holocaust: Jews are to be destroyed, before Jews destroy us, the gentiles, as if gentiles are the victims; a feature, we might think, of much genocidal thinking in modernity, from the Holocaust to Rwanda, the perpetrator who regards himself as an imminent victim who must commit genocide as a kind of preemptive act.

Eliot's anti-Semitic poems as Cultural Genocide

Eliot's anti-Semitic poems present a negation of Jews' right to be human, to exist in England and presumably Europe and the world – to be anywhere – and to be co-creators of modernism and modernity.

In our work on genocide, focusing on Raphael Lemkin's conception of genocide in his 1944 book *Axis Rule in Occupied Europe*, Ann and I argue that Lemkin saw genocide as wide-ranging, that the desired destruction of the foundations of life of a group could include intellectual, cultural and spiritual dimensions.[23] I'll hazard a thought here: Eliot's early anti-Semitic poems present in Lemkin's terms a kind of poetics of genocide, an attempt in verse to sequester modernism for anti-Semitism at the same time as seeking to eliminate Jews from humanity, that their very presence, sub-human and animalistic, desecrates not only the English but humanity itself.

Lord Alfred Douglas's sonnet 'In Excelsis' invokes sexuality when it refers to 'scattered Israel' weaving a spell that binds 'the heart's desire' to 'gold and gluttony and sweating lust', sexuality as prostitution, as physicality for hire, mixed with animal desires like gluttony. This thread of images could, I feel, have been inspired by a similar thread in 'Sweeney Among the Nightingales', with its burlesque scenes set in what one presumes to be a bordello, scenes that remind us, as 'Burbank with a Baedeker: Bleistein with a Cigar' has reminded us, of Virginia Woolf sensing in Eliot's poems 'obscure sinister violence and disdainful irony'. Predictably, 'Sweeney Among the Nightingales' features those to be excoriated as foreign to Englishness, opening with a simian image of 'Apeneck Sweeney', the stage Irishman whose 'arms hang down to laugh'. Assuming the nightingales are prostitutes, there are two prostitutes, both suggesting foreignness, the first being the 'person in the Spanish cape', who is suspected of being 'in league' with the other prostitute, Rachel née Rabinovitch, sketched in as subhuman, monkey-like, a 'silent vertebrate in brown', who is diverted by a waiter bringing in fruit including 'hothouse grapes':

> The silent vertebrate in brown
> Contracts and concentrates, withdraws:
> Rachel *née* Rabinovitch
> Tears at the grapes with murderous paws.

Why, in such images that are the reverse of subtle, is the Jewish prostitute Rachel née Rabinovitch given a name that would signify to the poem's readers that she is to be regarded as Russian Jewish? Here 'Sweeney Among the Nightingales', we might think, speaks to a context David Cesarini evokes in his essay 'An Embattled Minority: The Jews in Britain During the First World War', the xenophobia in wartime British society directed towards foreign-born Jews, especially the Russian Jewish refugees escaping persecution in Tsarist Russia.

In the quick derisive portrait of 'Rachel *née* Rabinovitch' we can see Eliot's early poems as influenced by the fevered world of misogyny in literature and painting discussed by Bam Dijkstra in his *Idols of Perversity: Fantasies of Feminine Evil in Fin-de-Siècle Culture* (1986). Dijkstra himself makes the connection to Eliot, referring to mermaid and siren imagery in 'Prufrock', and vampire imagery in *The Waste Land*, that link to misogynistic images in the *fin de siècle*, the time of Eliot's upbringing, Eliot being born in 1888. Dijkstra refers to the final lines of 'Prufrock' ('the mermaids singing, each to each'), that suggest that the 'siren's physical allure spelled death to man's transcendent soul'. He argues that by 1900 the vampire had come to 'represent woman as the personification of everything negative that linked sex, ownership, and money', the eternal prostitute lusting for the gold which signified 'man's essence'. Dijkstra refers to a painting of around 1914 by Manuel Rosé (1887–1961), 'Interior of a Café', exhibited in San Francisco at the Panama-Pacific Exposition of 1915, where we see a female figure 'cloaked in darkness' beckoning man to his death.[24]

Eliot's early poems add to such *fin de siècle* elements by drawing on music hall and burlesque, not to say the broad strokes of slapstick. 'Sweeney Among the Nightingales' theatricalises xenophobia, relishes it as, in Virginia Woolf's phrase, disdainful irony, as in the 'person in the Spanish cape', who, trying to 'sit on Sweeney's knees', slips and 'pulls the table cloth'; 'reorganized upon the floor/ She yawns and draws a stocking up'. Yet the mocking contempt directed at the woman in the Spanish cape is nothing compared to the belittling of the Russian Jewish woman as sub-human.

Wondering Conclusion

Let's return to Leonard Woolf, when in *Beginning Again* he records how pleased and proud he was to publish the early poems like 'Sweeney among the Nightingales' which introduced a 'new note in poetry and came from the heart of the Eliot of those days'. Woolf says nothing about the 'Rachel *née* Rabinovitch' lines. Instead he quotes with admiration the final two stanzas:

> The host with someone indistinct
> Converses at the door apart,
> The nightingales are singing near
> The Convent of the Sacred Heart,
>
> And sang within the bloody wood
> When Agamemnon cried aloud,
> And let their liquid siftings fall
> To stain the stiff dishonoured shroud.[25]

Contra Leonard W, I see nothing admirable about these stanzas, the first strikes me as intensely anti-Semitic, the second as intensely misogynist.

In my reading, the stanzas suggest that the nightingales, the sinister Jewish prostitutes like 'Rachel *née* Rabinovitch', defile the sacred space of the Christian convent; there is a more general implication, that there should be no place for Jewish women, for Jews, in a Christian land. In a coarse-grained image, we are to understand that the nightingales direct their desecratory droppings, their 'liquid siftings', to fall on the 'stiff dishonoured shroud' of Agamemnon, recalling for the reader that Agamemnon had been killed by his wife Clytemnestra after his return from vanquishing Troy, his murder accompanied by the triumphant singing of the nightingales: woman as eternal murderer of heroic man. For me, Leonard's lifelong cherishing of these stanzas, apparently expressing 'the heart of Eliot in those days', recall his extravagant moment of misogyny in *Sowing*, when two Cambridge acquaintances tell the story of the female rat catcher they claim to have observed in a French village: woman as monstrous, 'quite repulsive you know'.[26]

The final stanza suggests disgust at Clytemnestra as monstrous female murderer, yet other elements of the mythological story suggest different and conflicting perspectives, so well known we have to wonder at Leonard Woolf's blankness in not thinking of them. They vastly complicate the story of Clytemnestra's act of bloody revenge. As we know, Agamemnon, his fleet becalmed, sacrifices his daughter Iphigenia in order that favourable winds will come so that the army can reach Troy. When he returns from the war, he brings with him the prophetess Cassandra as a prize, the gift of his army. Yet he betrays no consciousness that while he returns with the daughter of a foreign king as concubine (and issues a brusque command to Clytemnestra to treat her well), he had put to death his and Clytemnestra's daughter 10 years before;

he appears to have forgotten that her death had ever occurred.[27]

The scene of the murder of Iphigenia is evoked in Aeschylus' *Agamemnon* (lines 187–257), when Calchas the priest tells Agamemnon that he must choose between discontinuing with the plan to attack Troy, or 'slaughter my own child, my home's delight/ In her young innocence, and stain my hand/With blasphemous unnatural cruelty,/ Bathed in the blood I fathered!' Agamemnon makes his choice, to side with the desire of his army and fellow military leaders: 'Rough hands tear at her girdle, cast/Her saffron silks to earth.' Iphigenia's 'eyes/ Search for her slaughterers; and each,/Seeing her beauty, that surpassed/A painter's vision, yet denies/The pity her dumb looks beseech'. Dear reader, I will leave you with the scene of her death as Aeschylus's play relates it:

> Heedless of her tears,
> Her cries of 'Father!' and her maiden years,
> Her judges valued more
> Their glory and their war.
> A prayer was said. Her father gave the word.
> Limp in her flowing dress
> The priest's attendants held her high
> Above the altar, as men hold a kid.
> Her father spoke again, to bid
> One bring a gag, and press
> Her sweet mouth tightly with a cord,
> Lest Atreus' house be cursed by some ill-omened cry.[28]

In killing Iphigenia, Agamemnon had already, before the war began, dishonoured himself.

How strange that Leonard Woolf could not entertain the complexity of the myth, adopting, as does the Eliot stanzas he quotes so warmly, a single male-centred perspective.

One final note here. I've always wondered over the years,

if in a kind of near-dormant way, why *Gerontion* associated its Judeophobic derision with Antwerp, where 'the jew' had been 'Spawned'. Why Antwerp? In the latter part of 2016 I thought again of Antwerp in relation to *Gerontion*. On Saturday 29–30 September, in Toronto, Ann and I attended the Global Confederation Conference at York University on the 1867 creation of the Canadian Confederation; in cosmopolitan spirit, scholars of histories of many places around the world had been invited to talk about how the 1867 Confederation act had been talked about at the time, in Latin America, the US, India, Spain, the Hapsburg Empire, France, Belgium, Ireland, Britain, New Zealand and so on; Ann gave a paper on how the announcement of the Confederation was discussed in the Australian colonies at the time. While listening to the Belgian scholar relating that in the late nineteenth and early twentieth century Antwerp was a major port city for emigration for those in Europe and Russia who wished to journey to the New World including Canada, I thought again of *Gerontion* sneering at Antwerp.[29] Later I googled and registered that Antwerp was a major transit port for Eastern European and Russian Jews, among many other peoples, aiming to reach the New World. Perhaps the narrator of *Gerontion* featured Antwerp because it was a port city, where many peoples and nationalities mixed and jostled together.

My mother spent her childhood in that port city London, and once said to me she couldn't really understand why the family had to leave it. I grew up in the port city of Sydney, have left it to live elsewhere more than once, but still treasure it.

It very much looks like the narrator of *Gerontion* doesn't like port cities like Antwerp, with their cosmopolitan mixing of peoples.

Cultural Genocide: T S Eliot, vicious Anti-Semite 189

1. T.S. Eliot, *Selected Poems* (Faber and Faber, London, 1961), p.31.
2. T.S. Eliot, *Selected Poems*, pp.34–5.
3. T.S. Eliot, *Selected Poems*, p.47.
4. A.L. French, '"Olympian Apathein": Pound's *Hugh Selwyn Mauberley* and Modern Poetry', *Essays in Criticism*, Vol.VX, No.4, October 1965, pp.428–45.
5. Hermione Lee, *Virginia Woolf* (Vintage, New York, 1999), p.434.
6. Victoria Glendinning, *Leonard Woolf* (Counterpoint, Berkeley, 2008), p.236.
7. Leonard Woolf, *Sowing* (Hogarth Press, London, 1960), p.52.
8. Leonard Woolf, *Beginning Again* (Hogarth Press, London, 1964), pp.242–3.
9. David Cesarini, 'An Embattled Minority: The Jews in Britain during the First World War', in Tony Kushner and Kenneth Lunn (eds), *The Politics of Marginality: Race, the Radical Right and Minorities in Twentieth Century Britain* (Frank Cass, London, 1990), pp.61–2, 65–7, 71–2.
10. David Cesarini, 'An Embattled Minority: The Jews in Britain during the First World War', pp.75–6.
11. Isaiah Berlin, *Historical Inevitability* (1954; Oxford University Press, London, 1955), pp.15 note 1, 16–17, 20, 25, 32–34, 50–53, 57, 71, 75; Ann Curthoys and John Docker, *Is History Fiction?* Second Edition (University of Michigan Press, Ann Arbor, 2010), p.118.
12. Lord Acton, 'The History of Freedom in Antiquity' (1877), on website at acton.org of the Acton Institute for the Study of Religion and Liberty.
13. Ann Curthoys and John Docker, *Is History Fiction?* pp.76–82.
14. Leonard Woolf, *Sowing* (Hogarth Press, London, 1960), p.16.
15. Leonard Woolf, *Beginning Again: An Autobiography of the years 1911–1918* (Hogarth, London, 1964), pp.249–53.
16. Leonard Woolf, *Sowing*, pp.91–2.
17. George Orwell, 'Antisemitism in Britain', *Contemporary Jewish Record*, April 1945.
18. Hermione Lee, *Virginia Woolf* (Vintage, New York, 1999), p.434.
19. Robert Crawford, *Young Eliot: From St Louis to The Waste Land* (Jonathan Cape, London, 2015), pp.149–50.
20. Crawford, *Young Eliot: From St Louis to The Waste Land*, p.158
21. Crawford, *Young Eliot: From St Louis to The Waste Land*, p.158.
22. Alex Ross, 'Strange Fruit', review of Douglas Murray, *Bosie: A Biography of Lord Alfred Douglas* (2000), *The New Yorker*, July 24, 2000, online.
23. Ann Curthoys and John Docker, 'Defining Genocide', in Dan Stone (ed.), *The Historiography of Genocide* (Palgrave Macmillan, London, 2010), p.11.
24. Bram Dijkstra, *Idols of Perversity: Fantasies of Feminine Evil in Fin-de-Siècle Culture* (Oxford University Press, New York and Oxford, 1988), pp.266, 351.

25 Leonard Woolf, *Beginning Again*, p.243; Eliot, *Selected Poems*, p.47.
26 Leonard Woolf, *Sowing*, p.113.
27 John Docker, *The Origins of Violence: Religion, History and Genocide* (Pluto Press, London, 2008), p.67.
28 Aeschylus, *The Oresteian Trilogy: Agamemnon, The Choephori, The Eumenidies*. Translated by Philip Vellacott (Penguin, London, 1959), pp.49–51.
29 A selection of essays came out of this conference, see Jacqueline D. Krikorian, Marcel Martel, and Adrian Schubert (eds), *Globalizing Confederation: Canada and the World in 1867* (University of Toronto Press, Toronto, 2017).

15

T S Eliot, an Architect of the Holocaust: Reflections on *After Strange Gods*

> ... I think that the chances for the re-establishment of a native culture [of white Americans] are perhaps better here [in Virginia, in the US South]... You are farther away from New York; you have been less industrialised and less invaded by foreign races...
> T S Eliot, *After Strange Gods: A Primer of Modern Heresy*, 1934[1]

> The population should be homogeneous... What is still more important is unity of religious background; and reasons of race and religion combine to make any large number of free-thinking Jews undesirable.
> T S Eliot, *After Strange Gods*[2]

In 1934 T S Eliot published *After Strange Gods: A Primer of Modern Heresy*, where he presents himself as the arbiter, the Law-Giver, the Messiah, of historical consciousness for his generation; he would reshape Anglo-American civilisation by centring it in his own interests, the urgent concerns suggested to him by his religious turn in and from the middle 1920s towards high Anglicanism.

In *After Strange Gods* a literary, cultural and political policeman, with a totalitarian vision, is at work, roughly putting together in neo-brutalist mode the architecture of a Christian Utopia.

After Strange Gods hails those like in spirit who belong to the future, the future that should be; not surprisingly though for a totalitarian, for the most part the text spends its time excoriating, excluding, inquisitionally excommunicating, more or less viciously, mostly more, those to be judged enemies of the future. On ideological grounds, old friends will be discarded, new friends embraced. Reading *After Strange Gods* brings to mind Ned Curthoys's discussion of Arendt, Lessing and Moses Mendelssohn in his *The Legacy of Liberal Judaism*, where he calls attention to Hannah Arendt saying, in the spirit of Lessing, that we should never put ideology over friendship.[3] That, however, is precisely what Eliot the would-be ruthless Messiah does in this ill-making work.

After Strange Gods, published in February 1934, became notorious for one particular sentence, that I quote for my second epigraph; but I believe it should be infamous for much else, as well as for the racial and ethnic contexts and circumstances in which it took place.

After Strange Gods was based on lectures Eliot had given the year before; did the particular racial and ethnic character of that audience encourage him to strike out, embolden him into fevered gestures of utopianism and dystopianism?

Perhaps, too, there is another frame-story to be found in religious history by which to understand the violence of *After Strange Gods*. In the early Enlightenment, Spinoza in *Tractatus Theologico-Politicus* considered that hatred of those considered enemies of God is the 'bitterest and most persistent of all kinds of hatred'. Later in the Enlightenment, David Hume, in his *The Natural History of Religion*, came to a like conclusion in writing about the dangers of monotheism, that its insistence on one sole object of devotion leads to sectarianism fuelled by sacred zeal and rancour, the most furious and implacable of hatreds.[4]

Enlightenment philosophers disliked institutional Christianity, saw its influence on society and history as pernicious. Eliot had come to identify with institutional Christianity, or at least one particular variant of it, which he regarded as its only true manifestation; all else was heresy, including kinds of Christianity he loftily disdained. In Spinoza and Hume's terms, qualities of hatred, bitterness, rancour, of implacable insistence on a single truth in the name of the sacred, course in abundance through *After Strange Gods*.

I had known for a long time from references to it that there was an ugly anti-Semitic sentence in *After Strange Gods*, though I had never looked it up: not until now. Certainly, none of the Leavisite staff in the Sydney English department in the middle 1960s had in my experience ever discussed *After Strange Gods*, let alone drawn attention to this sentence.

I really wish my Leavisite teachers had directed their students to read *After Strange Gods* and encouraged detailed textual analysis in tutorial discussion of it, because reading a wide range of texts could have initiated thinking about how some of Eliot's early poems, with their sinister anti-Semitism, might look in terms of the later concerns of *After Strange Gods*. The Leavisite staff could have said to their young students, look, in his 1917 essay 'Tradition and the Individual Talent' – study it well – Mr Eliot writes that

> what happens when a new work of art is created is something that happens simultaneously to all the works of art which preceded it. The existing monuments form an ideal order among themselves, which is modified by the introduction of the new (the really new) work of art among them. The existing order is complete before the new work arrives; for order to persist after the supervention of novelty, the whole existing order must be, if ever so slightly, altered; and so the relations, proportions, values of each work

of art toward the whole are readjusted... [we] will not find it preposterous that the past should be altered by the present as much as the present is directed by the past.[5]

Now, the Leavisite staff could have gone on, let's turn this passage back on Eliot himself and see what happens. Let's take *After Strange Gods* as just such a new work of art, a new text that might make us look differently at Mr Eliot's earlier texts, his poems up to and including *The Waste Land*. Any questions?

Sadly, that pedagogical scenario didn't at least in my experience happen.

Perhaps I can make up for that now.

In these reflections, I'll ponder affinities between Eliot and his friend W B Yeats in relation to the 1930s and the Holocaust.

Mr Thomas Stearns Eliot pays homage to the US South

> It is a pleasure to me to think that these lectures were delivered at one of the older, smaller and most gracious of American educational institutions, one of those in which some vestiges of a traditional education seem to survive.
>
> T S Eliot, *After Strange Gods*, Preface, London, January 1934[6]

I've borrowed *After Strange Gods* from Sydney University's Fisher Library. It's only a short book, 68 pages, three lectures he gave at the University of Virginia in 1933; the copy I took off the shelves is a little worn, its cover peeling off a cardboard underlay, and it's held together by adhesive tape; opening up its yellowing pages, one sees that the margins are inscribed, sometimes in pencil, sometimes in biro, with all sorts of comments, exclamation marks and furious underlinings that have accumulated over the decades. I immediately looked up the sentence about the undesirability of a 'large number of free-thinking Jews'. My feeling is that those who do critically discuss *After Strange Gods* home in on this sentence, and, quite properly enraged at such anti-Semitic blatancy, talk about very little else in the book. I've decided, on the contrary, to read and consider the whole book, where textual details intersect with all sorts of histories. I will analyse *After Strange Gods* by deploying a method of analysis inspired by a near contemporary of Eliot's, Walter Benjamin, – if Eliot doesn't mind me calling on a 'free-thinking Jew' – who arrestingly suggested, in the 'Epistemo-Critical Prologue' to his 1928 *The Origin of German Tragic Drama* that what might be most valuable to investigate in a text is the most singular, eccentric and extreme of examples, the most unusual or isolated; examples to be found even in the merest fragment, the minutest thing.[7]

In the fateful as it were 'Holocaust year' of 1933 – the year of Hitler coming to power; of Heidegger joining the Nazi Party on 1 May 10 days before being elected Rector of the University of Freiberg as German universities were dismissing Jewish academics, an activity in which he participated; of book burnings on 10 May by Nazi students and storm troopers in universities across Germany – T S Eliot the acclaimed poet, critic and editor travels from Harvard where he has been lecturing during 1932 and 1933 and makes his way south, quite deep south, to deliver the Page-Barbour Lectures at the University of Virginia on 10–12 May 1933 in Charlottesville, a city known for its university and Jefferson's home Monticello. He had been invited on 3 December 1932 to talk there. I'm presuming that as he journeyed through Charlottesville he caught sight of Confederate flags; perhaps, as he arrived on campus, he saw Confederate flags flying on university buildings, reminding those who looked up at them that Virginia should proudly keep in mind that it was part of the Confederacy during the Civil War defending slavery; since the Civil War, Virginia had been diligently applying Jim Crow laws as part of the post-Reconstruction New South. Historically, the University of Virginia had ties to slavery and the slave trade, along with other universities like Brown, Columbia and Harvard, as well as the Jesuit-run Georgetown University, the leading Catholic institution of higher learning at the time (which in 1838 sold to Deep South plantations 272 of their own slaves, largely from their plantations in Maryland, to assist in university finances).[8]

Let's pause for a moment and consider: Eliot mounted the podium to speak at UVA to give his opening lecture on 10 May, while on the other side of the Atlantic, Nazi students and storm troopers burnt books considered unGerman.

What might have been the racial and ethnic composition of the audience facing him as he spoke? Would he have considered it his ideal audience, almost as if in a utopian vision?

We can be sure there were no black students there, since the University of Virginia was not desegregated before the 1950s, with the university like other southern colleges continuing to resist full integration until well into the 1960s. From googling around various websites, one gathers the unsavoury history of the University of Virginia's racial inclusions and exclusions before and after 1933, and it was not a history that went unnoticed by contemporaries, especially black intellectuals. The university first admitted women to graduate studies in the late 1890s and to certain undergraduate programs such as nursing and education in the 1920s and 1930s. The first African American to apply to UVA was Alice Carlotta Jackson, then aged 22, in August 1935; she wished to join the UVA graduate school to study for an MA in French studies; her application, however, was denied by UVA on the basis of the state's Jim Crow educational policies.

Alice Carlotta Jackson's application to UVA was part of a broader social movement at the time, coordinated by W E B Du Bois's NAACP, that sought to put pressure on Southern states to provide equal access to public higher education for black students. There were protests at her exclusion, by the National Students League, a small but vocal Communist student organisation; and there was coverage of the protests in national newspapers such as the *New York Times*. The university's defence in excluding her and maintaining UVA as an all-white institution was to raise the spectre of the 'mixing of the races'. As it happened, Alice Carlotta Jackson would attend Columbia University in New York, graduating with an MA in English in 1937; she taught at a college in Florida for 45 years, and then for some time at Howard University.

Could the University of Virginia have acted differently early in the twentieth century in relation to admitting African-American students? Were African-American students present in other American universities in the first part of the twentieth century?

It's worth quickly recalling the educational careers of Paul Robeson (1898–1976) and Eslanda Robeson (1895–1965). In his biography Martin Duberman records that Paul attended Rutgers College during 1915 to 1918, and attended Columbia Law School in New York from 1919. He continued the stellar football career he'd begun at Rutgers; on one occasion he was badly injured, taken to New York City's Presbyterian Hospital for an operation, and while convalescing was introduced to his future wife Eslanda Cardozo Goode, always known as Essie, who was working as a pathology technician in the surgery lab; Essie had caught sight of Paul Robeson from frequenting the same Harlem parties. Eslanda, Duberman tells us, was descended from a distinguished lineage of mixed racial stock, her great-grandfather Isaac Nuñez Cardozo, part of a Spanish-Jewish family of considerable wealth that had emigrated to America in the late eighteenth century.[9] In her biography of Eslanda, Barbara Ransby writes that Essie spent her childhood in New York City; in 1912, she and her mother moved to Chicago, where Essie finished high school and enrolled in the University of Illinois on scholarship. During her third year, she transferred to Columbia University's Teachers College back in New York City, completing her degree in 1920.[10]

If we keep in mind Isaiah Berlin's axiom in *Historical*

Inevitability (1954) that individuals in the past could have chosen to act otherwise than how they did,[11] then, in relation to black students, the individuals who controlled the University of Virginia could have avoided acting in the ways they did act.

I wonder: was there a Jewish presence in the University of Virginia in the early 1930s that might have contributed a strand in the audience for Eliot's lectures? Jews settled in Charlottesville from early in the nineteenth century and by the turn of the twentieth century had become essential to the mercantile, civic, educational and cultural life of the city; in the latter part of the nineteenth century, German Jewish families arrived, and in the 1890s Yiddish-speaking Russian Jewish families also settled there. One Russian immigrant in Charlottesville was Hillel (later Ellis) Mopsik, who was born in 1886 in Minsk, left Russia at the age of 10 and passed through London, Philadelphia and New York before moving South; by 1908 he had established a ladies' tailoring shop in Charlottesville, which ran for over 50 years; he married his Russian-born wife Bessie Golin in Richmond, had two children, Harold and Elizabeth, and both went to UVA to study education. A typical pattern appears to be that the grandchildren of the turn-of-the-century Russian Jews entered UVA in the 1930s and 1940s, then moved into the professions of law, medicine and engineering.

The earliest known Jewish student at UVA was Gratz Cohen of Savannah, from 1862 to 1864, after a stint in the Confederate army; he was elected president of the Jefferson Society. There were Jewish students in small numbers in the latter nineteenth century and into the twentieth; they found themselves excluded from the existing fraternities, so in 1915 they organised their own; from the late 1920s, UVA, concerned by the growing number of Jewish students, set limits on their numbers. New York Jews in particular were to be discouraged. In terms of faculty, the first Jewish academic staff were hired in the 1920s, there being two:

Linwood Lehman, professor of Latin 1920–1953; and Ben-Zion Linfield, professor of mathematics, who joined in 1927.

If Jews as faculty and students were in attendance at Eliot's 1933 lectures, when they heard him say that a 'large number of free-thinking Jews [is] undesirable', they most likely smiled grimly to themselves, thinking that UVA was already imposing quotas and restrictions on Jewish students. Given how widespread in the between-wars period quotas for Jews were being applied in American universities, including at elite universities such as Harvard, it would be surprising if Eliot didn't know that quotas and restrictions were present at UVA as elsewhere. Perhaps when he said his infamous line, he smiled to himself, pleased: pleased that in the US such quotas were in place; and pleased to think the white audience facing him, overwhelmingly non-Jewish, would be pleased that the anti-Jewish restrictions were in place.

New York figures as a site of dystopian revulsion for Eliot in *After Strange Gods*, the city personifying a kind of anti-Christ, a demiurge, satanic; mixing, not pure. Yet, we shall soon see, when talking about a remarkable Mark Twain essay on lynching, New York could figure in an entirely different dystopia.

While some Eastern European and Russian Jews, who had fled persecution and pogroms, were in the US moving South, many African Americans, escaping persecution and lynching in the South, were moving north, to New York and Chicago, one of modern history's Great Migrations.

When the white audience at UVA listened to Eliot pronouncing that in the ideal Christian society, his cherished Utopia, the 'population should be homogeneous', one assumes that they immediately thought of Virginia and the South's anti-miscegenation Jim Crow laws forbidding mixing of the white and black races. Yet in Britain and Europe between the two world wars a call for homogeneity of a population would have quite different meanings.

Lynching, a Southern obsession

We must also think that the audience at Eliot's lectures were quite aware of lynchings as a salient even defining aspect of life in the South, including in Virginia; the Ku Klux Klan was an active presence, in Charlottesville as elsewhere. Again, it's impossible not to think that Eliot, who had already been in the US from the previous year on a long stay, was not aware that lynching was integral to the South he was visiting, even if there were differences in frequency between the southern states.

W Fitzhugh Brundage, in his *Lynching in the New South: Georgia and Virginia, 1880–1930* (1993), illuminates a terrible history for us. In an international context, we can see, Brundage argues, that in terms of white-black relations the US was part of a worldwide history in the late nineteenth and early twentieth century, from French West Africa and the Belgian Congo to the American South, of establishing elaborate and ruthless systems of coercion harnessing the labour of blacks; yet when viewed in this comparative perspective, it's clear that lynching remained a peculiarly American phenomenon. It was also, Brundage suggests, a peculiarly southern obsession: 'Lynching, like slavery and segregation, was not unique to the South, but it assumed proportions and a significance there that were without parallel elsewhere. Lynching came to define southern distinctiveness.'[12]

We might interpolate a thought about Foucault here, the famous Foucault Thesis, as in *Discipline and Punish*, that in the passage from premodernity to modernity, punishment was directed at the body; public spectacles of punishment as in hanging, drawing and quartering were staged in order to intimidate populations. Such spectacles became displaced in modernity, Foucault felt, by more hidden yet pervasive kinds of punishment where it was not the body or not only the body but the mind and soul also that were being invaded, controlled and harmed through surveillance, supervision and intellectual disciplines like psychology and cognate fields such as psychiatry claiming scientific expertise in diagnosis and treatment.[13]

Brundage's analysis both supports the Foucault Thesis yet also undermines it. Brundage observes that the intensifying of lynchings in the South in the 1880–1930 period, with their festive crowds composed of men, women and children, souveniring of remains, pleasure in observing torture, mutilation and burning, seemed to be a 'throwback to the brutal rituals of executions at Tyburn in eighteenth-century London': in Foucault's terms, premodern punishment as admonitory spectacle. The Foucault Thesis, however, requires us to believe that in modernity such public spectacles became gruesome phenomena of the past. In contrast, Brundage points out that extreme violence in the South was omnipresent and persistent: with each succeeding decade, the 'proportion of lynchings that occurred in the South rose, increasing from 82 percent of all lynching in the nation during the 1880s to more than 95 percent during the 1920s'. There were an 'estimated 723 whites and 3,220 blacks lynched in the South between 1880 and 1930'.[14]

The 'overwhelming majority' of victims 'were black', and Brundage adds that mob violence remained a lingering threat to blacks for decades after 1930. Brundage refers us to the famous statement of W E B Du Bois in 1903, that 'the problem of the twentieth century is the problem of the color line', involving extreme and open violence by whites against blacks.[15] The Foucault Thesis, of a line from the premodern to the modern, turns out to be too linear, Europe-centred, not thinking of what Europeans did elsewhere in the world to non-Europeans.[16] Contra Foucault, both kinds of punishment, public and hidden from public view, co-exist in modern history.

Brundage is concerned to point out regional variations in mob violence across the overwhelmingly rural South, especially distinguishing between Georgia as representing the Deep South,

Virginia the Upper South. He writes that Georgia, along with Mississippi, were the largest centres of white mob violence, while Virginia was the southern state with the fewest lynchings. But this does not mean lynching in Virginia was negligible; Virginia had many less than Georgia, nevertheless 83 lynchings still occurred between 1870 and 1930. Brundage suggests a number of explanations why lynchings were less likely to occur in Virginia than in Georgia. Virginia's agriculture was diversified, shielding Virginians from the harshest poverty that bore down on staple-crop farmers elsewhere in the South. At the same time, Virginia's future was increasingly directed northward by railroads, trade and outlook. White Virginians also came increasingly to believe racial boundaries could be legally maintained without the need to resort to extra-legal violence. By early in the twentieth century, lynching had become rare.[17]

Brundage writes that there was opposition to lynching in the early twentieth century. In the century's second decade the NAACP established a presence in Virginia. In 1928 an anti-lynching law was passed in the state, in part inspired by the anti-lynching and anti-extralegal violence journalism of Louis J Jaffé.[18] Nonetheless, Brundage's conclusion concerning race relations in Virginia was hardly reassuring for what we might call its moral history:

> On balance, then, the virtual demise of lynching in the state by 1904 did not mark a new era of racial harmony and tolerance. After all, the criminal justice system continued to punish blacks harshly, executing them with frightful regularity. Blacks, moreover, continued to bear the burdens of disenfranchisement, segregation, poverty and pervasive racism Yet, the demise of lynching in Virginia lifted one of the most onerous badges of black oppression.[19]

From Missouri to New York: Mark Twain's Dystopian Vision of Lynching

At the beginning of his introduction to *Lynching in the New South*, Brundage quotes a quip from Mark Twain, that so commonplace were lynchings that we should rename the country the United States of Lyncherdom.[20] I was so intrigued by this reference, and remembering that I had discussed with *A Connecticut Yankee in King Arthur's Court* in my long-ago doctoral thesis 'Literature and Social Thought: Australia in an International Context, 1890–1925', that I did some snooping on the Net. In 1901 Twain wrote a vitriolic essay 'The United States of Lyncherdom'; however, it was not published in his lifetime, Twain dying in 1910; the essay then suffered an unfortunate publishing history. In 1923 it was published in a volume of Twain essays, *Europe and Elsewhere*, with an introduction by its editor Albert Bigelow Paine. In succeeding decades it was taken on trust that the essay Paine edited for publication was what Twain actually penned in 1901, and as such was frequently anthologised and much discussed by scholars as an important statement on the US and race by the great American satirist.

However, as Terry L Oggel points out in 2000 in an essay 'Speaking Out About Race: "The United States of Lyncherdom" Clemens Really Wrote', Paine had committed a grave disservice to Twain's memory and the integrity of American letters. In his essay Oggel details how Paine in his interfering editing diluted Twain's anti-racism and internationalism, altered words, excised sentences and whole paragraphs, and blithely contributed words of his own. Oggel performed an invaluable service by preparing a new version of the text faithful to what Clemens-Twain in 1901 actually penned though mysteriously never published in his own lifetime.[21]

Oggel evokes the rage that infuses Twain's essay. Twain long had contempt for lynch crowds; he admired the courage of two sheriffs, one in Georgia, the other in Indiana, who had stood up to lynch mobs; and he believed that the rule of law was drastically undermined by extralegal violence whether done by individuals or groups. However, the most immediate events that angered him were two newspaper reports from the *New York Weekly Post* of August 1901 indicating the spreading geographical reach of lynching. One recounted that lynchings were on the increase in the South. The other gave details of two recent lynchings, one in Texas, and to Twain's especial horror, another in his home state, leading to a cry in the essay, 'Oh, Missouri!' The newspaper report detailed a terror spree by whites against blacks in the southwest corner of Missouri, only a few miles from Arkansas. A young white woman had been killed on a Sunday afternoon. A black man named Godley was alleged to have committed the crime; he was lynched, as was his grandfather, then an elderly black man was burned in his house, and the mob drove 30 black families from their homes. The frenzy of violence ended on Tuesday, about the same time that it became known that Godley, the first victim, was innocent of the crime. The newspaper report concluded by wondering what was happening to the United States, when supposedly civilised people across the nation continued to behave with such savagery.[22]

Oggel argues that the newspaper report's conclusion inspired Twain's authorial stance: he would write in the outspoken and polemical spirit of Zola, whose *J'accuse* public letter in relation to the Dreyfus case was aimed at the President of France in 1898. In his own conclusion Oggel writes that Twain's essay, the essay he actually wrote in 1901, remains a 'powerful statement by an outspoken writer of international authority against the atrocity of lynching and the horror of rule by force at the turn of the century and in favor of speaking out'.[23]

Having read Oggel's reinstatement of Twain's text, it struck me as a passionate dystopia that could be counterposed to the dystopian narrative in Eliot's *After Strange Gods*. In relation to the importance of New York in *After Strange Gods* indicated in my second epigraph, 'The United States of Lyncherdom' places New York as the endpoint of Twain's dystopia, though where New York is a victim, not as in *After Strange Gods* a progenitor. In the essay Twain laments that because of lynching the honour, the 'foreign reputation', of the US internationally, 'in the four quarters of the earth', is severely threatened. What is being judged around the world is that because of lynching and its 'barbaric accompaniments', Christianity in the US is mere hypocrisy; he notes that the frenzied lynching which had so recently disfigured Missouri ('And so Missouri has fallen, that great State!') occurred in the southwestern corner of the state near Pierce City, in a city and region of 'churches and schools'; by lynching, these white Christian citizens of Missouri became 'assassins'. Christianity in the US has become barbarism and assassination. Twain satirically calls on all those American missionaries who are fruitlessly trying to convert the Chinese in China ('leave them alone, they are plenty good enough just as they are') to return to try to Christianise the US, especially in the lynching fields. Let the missionaries return to the US in 'this her hour of deep distress': 'Oh kind missionary, oh compassionate missionary, leave China! Come home and convert these Christians!'

In Twain's dystopian vision, lynching is an 'advancing disease', which had reached Colorado, California, Indiana, now Missouri, and its victory over the US will be complete when it reaches the east coast and conquers New York:

> I shall live to see a negro burned in Union Square, New York, with fifty thousand people present, and not a sheriff visible, not a governor, not a constable, not a colonel, not a clergyman, not a law-and-order representative of any sort.

The conquest of America by lynching and its associated extreme violence, lawless yet not resisted by the law, is enabled by the Moral Cowardice of the majority population where 'each man is afraid of his neighbor's disapproval', so that when, in Texas, Colorado, Indiana, there is to be 'a lynching the people hitch up and come miles to see it, bringing their wives and children'. He implores the brave few who might speak out and stand against lynching to speak out now in the spirit of Savonarola, the fifteenth-century Italian preacher, reformer, martyr, who stood up to the Medicis of Florence and introduced a democratic voice and prophecies of civic glory: 'A Savonarola can quell and scatter a mob of lynchers with a mere glance of his eye'. At the end of the essay Twain reiterates, that unless a few brave people and returning American missionaries can succeed in halting the tide of lynching sweeping from the South and covering the nation, 'we shall be known abroad as the United States of Lyncherdom, and be no more respected than a Chamberlain war for South African swag'. The implication is that if Britain is dishonoured among the nations by its imperial wars, the US will be dishonoured by the root cause of lynching, the white desire to keep the nation white.

Eliot loves the Southern Agrarians

> I have been much interested, since the publication a few years ago of a book called *I'll Take My Stand*, in what is sometimes called the agrarian movement in the South, and I look forward to any further statements by the same group of writers.
> T S Eliot, *After Strange Gods*[24]

> I speak as a New Englander.
> T S Eliot, *After Strange Gods*[25]

While Mark Twain's essay appeared in distorted form in 1923, there was enough there of incendiary critique of the South in terms of anti-racism and internationalism to pose a continuing challenge to American historical consciousness – including the historical consciousness of the Southern Agrarians, who, I notice, are enthusiastically embraced by Thomas Stearns Eliot in *After Strange Gods*. Eliot begins his first lecture by reassuring his audience that he does not repudiate what he wrote in his early essay 'Tradition and the Individual Talent', though he would now of course modify certain phrases here and there, a minor matter; his topic will be tradition, how it might endure, what threatens it. We cannot, it appears to Eliot, feel confident that tradition can survive in the US generally, for two reasons: the 'immense pressure towards monotony' exerted by the industrial expansion of the latter part of the nineteenth century and first part of the twentieth; and the horrific prospect of the US becoming anything like New York.[26]

Eliot tells his Southern audience that he speaks 'as a New Englander', presumably so they don't identify him as a New Yorker (though, strangely, in 'Tradition and the Individual Talent' he gave every appearance of identifying himself as an Englishman). As a New Englander, he feels the South offers humanity hope because it is, as I note in my opening epigraphs, 'less industrialised' and therefore still largely rural in its traditions; it is 'farther away from New York' and so more racially pure, 'less invaded by foreign races'. He doesn't specify which foreign races, but he presumably means Eastern European and Russian Jews who had found haven in New York. However, the South now has those who he calls the neo-agrarians to speak for it, 'the views of Mr Allen Tate and his friends as evinced in *I'll Take My Stand*'.[27]

What, I wondered, was it about the 1930 book *I'll Take My Stand: The South and the Agrarian Tradition*, that so enchanted Eliot about the Southern Agrarians?[28] I went online and quickly located 'I'll Take My Stand', the introductory statement of principles of the 'Twelve Southerners' who contributed to the volume. In many ways, 'I'll Take My Stand' is a stock manifesto of 'high' modernism, familiar in the twentieth century from the Leavisites in literary criticism, Yeats in poetry, Heidegger in philosophy, as a riposte to modernity, the modernity of industrialism and worship of technology – and their political correlatives of liberalism and democracy – that is rendering European civilisation spiritually empty, hollowed out into uniformity and ennui. We can even glimpse in the rhetoric of 'I'll Take My Stand' the possible influence of the early Marx, that human species being is threatened by the fetishising of commodities in industrial capitalism. In such an era of apocalyptic danger, only a creative minority, informed by pre-industrial rural-derived values, can keep spiritual vitality alive for humanity. That minority is small and always threatened, not only by industrialism but by other modern phenomena such as advertising and 'personal salesmanship'.[29]

The authors of 'I'll Take My Stand', so they tell the world, are 'a single group of men' of 'similar tastes': they 'are Southerners', which means 'all tend to support a Southern way of life against what may be called the American or prevailing way', an opposition that they characterise as 'Agrarian versus Industrial'. These men of similar tastes (apparently never suffering from the monotony and uniformity of agreement) quickly get into their argumentative stride. In industrialising America the South is now a 'minority'; it has hitherto been 'jealous of its minority right to live its own kind of life'. Even in the South, however, some are wavering towards the 'industrial gospel', especially younger Southerners, and they 'must come back to the support of the Southern tradition'. Southerners, while their 'cause is precarious', should seek alliances with likeminded communities outside the South as 'members of a national agrarian movement'.[30]

The traditional 'happiness' of Southern 'labor' is not possible under the advancing 'industrial regime', for under industrialism labour becomes 'mercenary and servile' and 'brutalizing'; in the South, however, labour was 'one of the happy functions of human life', it didn't need any material rewards as under industrialism. (Here, we might think, the manifesto is mimicking the language of William Morris and the craft movement in England.) Under industrialism, which attempts to dominate nature and convert it into 'commodities' rather than recognise its mystery, religion suffers. The arts are also threatened, as is sensibility in general, for art depends, 'like religion, on a right attitude to nature', in particular on a 'free and disinterested observation of nature that occurs only in leisure'.[31]

> The amenities of life also suffer under the curse of a strictly-business or industrial civilization. They consist in such practices as manners, conversation, hospitality, sympathy, family life, romantic love – in the social exchanges which reveal and develop sensibility in human affairs. If religion and the arts are founded on right relations of man to nature, these are founded on right relations of man-to-man.[32]

The 'genuine humanism' admired by the Southern Agrarians – 'our native humanism', which includes 'festivals, laws, marriage customs' – is 'rooted in the agrarian life of the older South'.[33]

How can these Southern men – women don't seem to figure in these androcentric 'man-to-man' effusions – 'defend the traditional Southern life'? The authors do not deny the importance of industries, professional vocations, scholars, artists, the life of cities. Nonetheless, in an agrarian society 'agriculture is the leading vocation', a form of 'labor that is pursued with intelligence and leisure': the 'theory of agrarianism is that the culture of the soil is the best and most sensitive of vocations'. The manifesto ends with a stirring call that when 'a community, or a section, or a race, or an age, is groaning under industrialism', it 'must find the way to throw it off'. The South, in combatting industrialism, this 'evil dispensation', must never lose its 'political genius'.[34]

When modernism is extended to the American South, the results are curious indeed. If we think of British modernism, its frequent idealisation of pre-industrial rural life, so glaring in the Leavisites, is bizarre enough; but it is much much more bizarre when applied to the Deep South, even if such a transference is applauded by T S Eliot, identifying the tradition of 'Tradition and the Individual Talent' with the tradition admired by the Southern Agrarians.

Let's pause for a quick moment over the passage in 'I'll Take My Stand' where the 12 Southerners praise 'the agrarian life of the older South', which was 'deeply founded' in ways of life such as 'festivals, laws, marriage customs'.[35] The questions are obvious: did festivals in the South include what Mark Twain commented on, families gathering at lynchings to celebrate the torture and burning of black bodies? Did the 'laws' the Southern Agrarians admire include Jim Crow laws? Did the 'marriage customs' they revere include black-white marriages, given Jim Crow laws against miscegenation?

When the Southern Agrarians say that the 'culture of the soil is the best and most sensitive of vocations', one could ask: is this a 'sensitive' description of the history of Deep South slavery and the murderous era of lynching that followed the Civil War? When the Southern Agrarians write that industrialism 'has enslaved our human energies to a degree now clearly felt to be burdensome', do we think the reference to 'enslaved' is a 'sensitive' deployment of language?[36] When the Southern Agrarians praise Deep South agriculture as labour 'pursued with intelligence and leisure', are they suggesting that African-American slaves enjoyed 'leisure' as a dimension of their labour? When the Southern Agrarians praise the art of the Deep South because art could rely there on a 'free and disinterested observation of nature that occurs only in leisure', are they suggesting that African-American slaves were 'free' to observe nature in this way? How much creation of art was lost to the African slaves, how much art denied, how many languages were destroyed? Weren't the African slaves subject to relentless processes of cultural genocide?[37]

When the manifesto admires the 'native humanism' of their (white) 'race', was any thought given by the 12 authors to the Native Americans whose genocidal dispossession made replacement by white settler colonisers possible? Looking at this blithe reference to the new 'native' 'race' of the South calls to mind the supersessionism that I discuss in my *The Origins of Violence*, the view that some peoples can be erased or removed or superseded by other peoples and groups, who see themselves as history's true heirs.[38]

Reading 'I'll Take My Stand', surely T S Eliot should have possessed the sensitivity to reflect, given the history of Deep South slavery, lynching, Jim Crow laws, the Klu Klux Klan, exploitation, brutality and mob violence, that this manifesto is quite fantastical. But Eliot didn't think it was fantastical, he applauded, he confided to his University of Virginia audience that he wanted to read more of these Southern Agrarian authors. He regarded them as salvational for the world, as redeemers, as apostles, and he published *After Strange Gods* early in 1934 in London so that the British public could share his admiration for these wonderful Deep South agrarians.

If the Southern Agrarians are the only hope for the defence of tradition in the USA, who or what offers hope in the United Kingdom, and who are the enemies of hope? One thing is clear: while Eliot admires the Southern Agrarians, their language is quite staid when compared to Eliot's own rhetoric in *After Strange Gods*, which is far more lurid, violent and ideologically extreme in its advocacy of uniformity, homogeneity, blood kinship, religious orthodoxy, theocracy, intolerance and censorship.

Growing Up Communist and Jewish in Bondi

1. T.S. Eliot, *After Strange Gods: A Primer of Modern Heresy* (Faber and Faber, London, 1934), p.16.
2. Eliot, *After Strange Gods*, pp.19–20.
3. Ned Curthoys, *The Legacy of Liberal Judaism: Ernst Cassirer and Hannah Arendt's Hidden Conversation* (Berghahn, New York and Oxford, 2013), p.177.
4. John Docker, *The Origins of Violence: Religion, History and Genocide* (Pluto, London, 2008), p.209.
5. T.S. Eliot, *Selected Essays* (Faber and Faber, London, 1961), p.15. See also John Docker, 'The Flâneur under Water, the Flâneur as Dancing Star: creating a conversation between Walter Benjamin, T.S. Eliot, and Hannah Arendt – a meditation', *Westerly* Special Issue, Day of Ideas, 2016.
6. T.S. Eliot, *After Strange Gods*, p.14.
7. Walter Benjamin, *The Origin of German Tragic Drama*, trans. John Osborne (Verso, London, 1996), pp.28–35, 41, 44–7; Ann Curthoys and John Docker, 'Time, Eternity, Truth, and Death: History as Allegory', *Humanities Research* 1, 1999, p.11.
8. See Rachel L. Swarns, '272 Slaves Were Sold to Save Georgetown. What Does It Owe Their Descendants?', *The New York Times*, 16 April 2016, accessed online.
9. Martin Duberman, *Paul Robson* (1989; The New Press, New York and London, 2005), pp.19, 34–5.
10. Barbara Ransby, *Eslanda: The Large and Unconventional Life of Mrs Paul Robeson* (Yale University Press, New Haven and London, 2013), pp.3, 22–5.
11. Ann Curthoys and John Docker, *Is History Fiction?* (University of Michigan Press, Ann Arbor, 2010), p.118.
12. W. Fitzhugh Brundage, *Lynching in the New South: Georgia and Virginia, 1880–1930* (University of Illinois Press, Urbana and Chicago, 1993), pp.1–3.
13. Curthoys and Docker, *Is History Fiction?*, pp.197–8.
14. Brundage, *Lynching in the South*, pp.3, 7–8.
15. Brundage, *Lynching in the South*, pp.2, 8, 14.
16. Curthoys and Docker, *Is History Fiction?*, p.197.
17. Brundage, *Lynching in the South*, pp.10, 15, 140–3, 190.
18. Brundage, *Lynching in the South*, pp.162–3, 189.
19. Brundage, *Lynching in the South*, p.190.
20. Brundage, *Lynching in the South*, p.1.
21. L. Terry Oggel, 'Speaking Out about Race: "The United States of Lyncherdom" Clemens Really Wrote', *Prospects: An Annual of American Cultural Studies 25*, edited by Jack Salzman (Cambridge University Press, 2000), pp.122–7.
22. L. Terry Oggel, 'Speaking Out about Race: "The United States of Lyncherdom" Clemens Really Wrote', pp.117–120.

23 L. Terry Oggel, 'Speaking Out about Race: "The United States of Lyncherdom" Clemens Really Wrote', pp.121, 129.
24 T.S. Eliot, *After Strange Gods*, p.15.
25 T.S. Eliot, *After Strange Gods*, p.16.
26 Eliot, *After Strange Gods*, p.16.
27 Eliot, *After Strange Gods*, pp.16–17, 21 note 1.
28 The Twelve Southerners, 'I'll Take My Stand', Introduction: A Statement of Principles, 1930 http://xroads.virginia.edu/~ma01/white/anthology/agrarian.html
29 'I'll Take My Stand', p.5.
30 'I'll Take My Stand', pp.1–2.
31 'I'll Take My Stand', pp.2–3.
32 'I'll Take My Stand', p.4.
33 'I'll Take My Stand', p.4.
34 'I'll Take My Stand', pp.5–6.
35 'I'll Take My Stand', p.4.
36 'I'll Take My Stand', p.2,
37 Thomas A. Underwood, *Allen Tate: Orphan of the South* (Princeton University Press, Princeton and Oxford, 2000), p.169, refers to a critical review, 'So Did King Canute', of *I'll Take My Stand* by Henry Hazlitt in *Nation* 132 (14 January 1931, pp.48–9), who wrote that reading the essays 'one almost forgets that such culture as the old South had rested on slavery' and was 'confined to a small privileged upper class'.
38 John Docker, *The Origins of Violence: Religion, History and Genocide*, p.6.

16

T S Eliot, an Architect of the Holocaust: Further reflections on *After Strange Gods*

> From the moment of Hitler's accession [in 1933], distinguished exiles from the Reich began to arrive in Britain, Denmark, France, the Soviet Union, Switzerland and the United States. Their names are well known, including Hannah Arendt, Bertolt Brecht, Marlene Dietrich, Thomas Mann, Stefan George, Ernst Toller, Bruno Walter and hundreds of other, scarcely lesser, names.
> W J McCormack, *Blood Kindred: W. B. Yeats, The Life, The Death, The Politics*, 2005[1]

Walter Benjamin said: look in a text for tiny particulars, these might reveal much.

Early in *After Strange Gods* Eliot, defining tradition, directs his audience's attention to a sentence in Joyce's *Ulysses*. Eliot intones that tradition – here echoing one of the more sinister discourses of European race thinking, going back at least to the Spanish Inquisition – involves 'the blood kinship of "the same people living in the same place".'[2] Something odd and rather shifty is going on here. Eliot doesn't tell his UVA audience what would have taken only a moment, that the phrase 'the same people living in the same place' is uttered in *Ulysses*, in the 'Cyclops' episode, set in Barney Kiernan's pub, by a distressed Leopold Bloom.[3] Why not, I think. *Ulysses* had been banned for obscenity in the US but that ban had been lifted in 1933 by a legal opinion of a judge in New York. What is remarkable here is that Eliot sneakily misconstrues what Bloom is saying and the context for his saying it. Eliot suggests to his audience that Bloom means by 'the same people living in the same place' a kind of nationalism, and even more than nationalism, an ethnocentric and racial 'blood kinship'. Yet the reverse is the case.

Actually, I write this with some feeling, since I evoke Bloom's thinking here and the reason for his declaration in my *1492: The Poetics of Diaspora* when discussing the episode in relation to Irish nationalism.[4] Recall that in 'Cyclops', around 5pm on 16 June, 1904, as Bloom is approaching Barney Kiernan's pub, some of the good men of Dublin are drinking there, including a loudly self-proclaimed Irish nationalist, the 'citizen'. They talk about Bloom. A question hangs over their conversation: is Leopold Bloom a true Irishman? When Bloom comes into the bar, the citizen scowls, 'We want no more strangers in our house'. Bloom's presence stirs the men to discuss national identity. They mockingly ask Bloom if he knows what a nation means, Bloom replying, yes, a 'nation is the same people living in the same place', a definition the others find laughably inadequate. The citizen asks Bloom what, then, is his nationality, and when Bloom replies that it is Irish, for here he was born, the citizen spits. The mood in the bar turns menacing. When Martin Cunningham comes in (Bloom has gone to meet him at Kiernan's to help arrange an insurance matter), he immediately proclaims that Bloom is a 'perverted jew... from a place in Hungary'. The narrator declares that it would be an act of God to throw someone like Bloom into the sea. The citizen growls that we shouldn't allow 'things' like Bloom to 'contaminate' Irish shores.[5]

In *1492: The Poetics of Diaspora*, I suggest that the men in the bar unite behind the loud-voiced citizen in his nationalist insistence on a single true identity, a national type, a presumed ethnic essence, whereby Bloom is excoriated as a Jew; his family having migrated to Ireland from Hungary in Eastern Europe, Bloom in their eyes is not and never can be truly Irish. Bloom's reply, that a 'nation is the same people living in the same place', is the reverse of nationalist: it expresses his pluralist, multicultural, Enlightenment stance that a nation includes everyone living in that nation at any one time, whoever they racially or ethnically are, whatever their religion, wherever they have come from. By contrast to the Irish patriarchs in the pub, Bloom figures Enlightenment values of reason and debate, of internationalism and cosmopolitanism.

The Irish nationalists, while decrying their persecution under the English, reveal no sympathy at all for their fellow persecuted in the world. When Bloom says, 'I belong to a race… that is hated and persecuted' at this 'very moment', the Irish men are singularly uninterested; they keep deriding and insulting him in a kind of mob verbal assault.[6]

Recall as well that later, in 'Circe', Bloom eloquently makes clear his belief in internationalism and cosmopolitanism, and his opposition to nationalism.

> BLOOM: I stand for the reform of municipal morals and the plain ten commandments. New worlds for old. Union of all, jew, moslem and gentile… General amnesty, weekly carnival, with masked licence, bonuses for all, Esperanto the universal brotherhood. No more patriotism of bar spongers and dropsical imposters. Free money, free love and a free lay church in a free lay state… Mixed races and mixed marriage.[7]

How curious, perhaps disingenuous, it is that Eliot, who always professed his admiration for *Ulysses* and unsuccessfully urged its publication on that, as it were, mixed-race couple Virginia and Leonard Woolf, the owners of Hogarth Press, doesn't mention or discuss Bloom's vision of a cosmopolitan utopia with his UVA audience.

We might also read Bloom's thoughts here concerning a union of Jews, Muslims and Gentiles in the light of Hannah Arendt talking of Lessing (I'm following Ned Curthoys here) in her opening essay, 'On Humanity in Dark Times: Thoughts about Lessing', in *Men in Dark Times*. There Arendt, discussing friendship as an Enlightenment ideal, writes: 'No insight into the nature of Islam or of Judaism or of Christianity could have kept [Lessing] from entering into a friendship and the discourse of friendship with a convinced Mohammedan or a pious Jew or a believing Christian.'[8]

In referring to the 'patriotism of bar spongers and dropsical imposters', Bloom, remembering their insults, clearly has in mind the citizens in Barney Kiernan's pub in 'Cyclops', the one-eyed monsters of nationalism and ethnic exclusion. In praising 'Mixed races and mixed marriage' he could also be thinking of his own marriage to Molly Bloom née Marion Tweedy, for all its evident difficulties, as exemplary, as a civilisational ideal.

Bloom's cosmopolitan desire to see a union of all is the very opposite of what Eliot declares is his ideal in *After Strange Gods*, where he urges on his UVA audience that a 'population should be homogeneous'.[9] He also deplores a 'spirit of excessive tolerance', the tolerance, one might think, that Bloom enthusiastically embraces in his utopia.

Don't mention cosmopolitanism! The UVA audience would have quickly registered that Thomas Stearns Eliot despises cosmopolitanism, the opposite of homogeneity, and despises as well the bearers of cosmopolitanism, even if they are or were his friends. Hannah Arendt wrote that Lessing held that no doctrine is 'worth the sacrifice of so much as a single friendship between two men'.[10] Eliot in *After Strange Gods* believed that opposing cosmopolitanism was certainly worth the (at least temporary) sacrifice of his friendship with Ezra Pound, his old mentor, adviser, editor and promoter, he to whom *The Waste Land* (which Pound helped edit for posterity) is dedicated: 'For Ezra Pound *il miglior fabbro*'. In Eliot's view Pound was the better verse technician.

It puzzles me why Eliot, given the anti-Semitic imagery in earlier poems such as 'Burbank with a Baedeker: Bleistein with a Cigar', hadn't included any anti-Semitic imagery in *The Waste Land*. Nothing had restrained him before. The short answer is that when Pound excised huge amounts from the bloated manuscript version of *The Waste Land*, one verse that was cut was 'Dirge', with its images that directly recall 'Burbank with a Baedeker: Bleistein with a Cigar'. Here's a continuity to ponder. 'Dirge' had begun in the following way:

> Full fathom five your Bleistein lies
> Under the flatfish and the squids.
> Graves' disease in a dead Jew's eyes!
> Where the crabs have eat the lids

Fortunately for the future reputation of *The Waste Land*, Pound successfully persuaded Eliot to omit 'Dirge', perhaps on technical grounds rather than any objection to its anti-Semitism. Pound must have gruffly pointed out that it was clumsily rhymed doggerel, embarrassing to read, irresistibly risible. Readers, Pound might have roared, will be reminded of that witticism of Oscar Wilde's about Little Nell; they'll laugh at the crudity of 'Where the crabs have eat the lids'; it has to go. After all, Pound was anti-Semitic himself, from before the First World War till near the end of his life. We learn from Robert Crawford's biography *Young Eliot*[11] that when Eliot had earlier sent Pound 'Gerontion' for comment, he had apparently expressed no objections to its notorious lines concerning 'the jew' squatting simian-like on the window sill. In John Tytell's biography, *Ezra Pound: The Solitary Volcano*, we read that in 1922 Pound attacked Harriet Monroe, the editor of *Poetry* (which on Pound's suggestion, published 'Prufrock' in June 1915) for the 'damned remnants in you of Jew religion, that bitch Moses and the rest of the tribal barbarians'.[12]

I wonder if, despite Pound's advice, Eliot had insisted that 'Dirge' be included in the finished version of *The Waste Land*, would Virginia Woolf and Leonard Woolf have baulked in publishing *The Waste Land*, given its anti-Semitic blatancy? Perhaps not, given they'd already published the earlier Judeophobic poems without a qualm. Subsequent readers, through the generations – even perhaps the Leavisites in the English department at the University of Sydney in the 1960s – could have reflected on 'Dirge' as a visible thread between the anti-Semitic earlier poems, *The Waste Land*, and then *After Strange Gods*.

Perhaps in the 1960s play could then have been made with the passage in Eliot's essay 'Tradition and the Individual Talent' I referred to in the previous chapter, so it could now be transcribed thus:

> The existing sections of *The Waste Land* form an ideal order among themselves, which is modified by the introduction of the new (the really new) section called 'Dirge'. The existing order is complete before the new section arrives; for order to persist after the supervention of such novelty, the whole existing order must be altered; and so the relations, proportions, values of each section toward the whole poem are readjusted...

I have always been a little surprised that section IV, 'Death by Water', is so short compared to the other sections. Perhaps, I now think, 'Dirge' was supposed to be interpolated between section IV and section V, 'What the Thunder Said'. Readers from 1922 onwards could then ponder the tender evocation of Phlebas the Phoenician, 'handsome and tall', alongside the smirking enjoyment of the death of Bleistein in 'Dirge', also now under water, his Jewish body excoriated as diseased, that so-conventional trope coming down from the late nineteenth century, reminding us of 'the jew' in 'Gerontion' who is blistered, patched, peeled. Where Phlebas' bones are picked by a current under sea in gentle almost reverential whispers, Graves' disease (usually recognised as an autoimmune condition affecting the thyroid gland)[13] has infected Bleistein's eyes, and crabs are eating his eye lids (which rhymes with 'squids'). How coarse-grained is this! What an infinitely crude comparison readers would have been offered, between the Phlebas evoked as Nordic, and Bleistein over whose death we are to gloat.

Perhaps, if 'Dirge' had stayed in, instead of *The Waste Land* being forever after so warmly celebrated, it might have had to sustain a great deal of searching critical attention in the century of the Holocaust.

Nonetheless, in *After Strange Gods*, Eliot's former patron Ezra Pound is brutally discarded for committing the sin of 'cosmopolitanism'. Certainly, reading Eliot's hostile remarks on Pound here you would never know that they had been such close friends and collaborators in advancing the cause of modernism. The excoriation of Pound follows on from the excoriation of one of Eliot's teachers at Harvard, Irving Babbitt, for 'whose memory' Eliot has the 'highest respect and admiration', yet whose Francophilia and wide cosmopolitan learning are now associated in Eliot's mind with the sins of individualism and eclecticism, that is, Babbitt turning his back on the tradition of institutional Christianity. Babbitt does not therefore reveal what Eliot believes is essential for civilization, an 'orthodoxy of sensibility'. Eliot then says that the 'name of Irving Babbitt instantly suggests that of Ezra Pound', his 'peer in cosmopolitanism'. Granted, Pound is extremely 'quick-witted and very learned', but his attraction to the Middle Ages, for example, completely misses out on 'that which gives them their significance'. Pound wrongly values in the Middle Ages a spirit of heresy and skepticism, and so he ignores a medieval religious aspect that we should enshrine and install as a universal value for modernity: the 'idea of Original Sin'. For Eliot in *After Strange Gods*, human beings are only 'real' when they believe in Original Sin and 'moral and spiritual struggle depending upon spiritual sanctions'. Eliot's judgement on his old friend falls like a hammer: 'Mr Pound, like Babbitt, is an individualist, and still more a libertarian.'[14] Pound has been excommunicated, his onetime friend is now his Inquisitor and Betrayer.

I won't say more about Eliot's rejection of Pound, except to think of Arendt's invocation of Lessing. As is well known, Pound wrote a year's worth of enraged reviews of *After Strange Gods* in 1934 in *New English Weekly*.

Another tiny particular: the image of 'the axe', which introduces us to the violence of language in *After Strange Gods*. Tradition, the tradition that involves 'blood kinship', Eliot assures his audience, is like a tree in autumn, when the wind begins to blow and the leaves blow off it. The leaves are no longer 'vital' to the tree. But we shouldn't worry about that:

> Energy may be wasted at that point in a frantic endeavour to collect the leaves as they fall and gum them onto the branches: but the sound tree will put forth new leaves, and the dry tree should be put to the axe.

By wielding 'the axe' on the 'dry tree', we can separate 'the vital' and 'the real' from the 'unessential' and the 'sentimental'.[15]

Given the violence suggested in the image of 'the axe', the UVA audience would not have been surprised to hear their esteemed lecturer admire violence in the conduct of human affairs as an ideal. We must, he tells them, deprecate 'a spirit of excessive tolerance', indeed human beings will become 'vaporous' if they accord too much respect to 'tolerance, benevolence, inoffensiveness', which presumably means that in the pursuit of Christian truth one should not hesitate to be intolerant and offensive. We should also not hesitate to restrict, to stop people doing and saying things, Eliot admiring taboos.[16]

In *After Strange Gods* Eliot decides to be intolerant and offensive to those of his fellow writers and their near kin who have earned his ideological disapproval, not least D H Lawrence and Lawrence's mother; they are dead trees, to whom the axe should be taken. His attack on Lawrence's mother is startling in its viciousness. What did Lawrence do, what did she do, to earn such violent opprobrium?

Lawrence's writing (at least as sampled in a short story, 'The Shadow in the Rose Garden', which Eliot tells his audience he has lately been reading in Harvard) reveals an 'alarming strain of cruelty' present elsewhere as well in modern literature. In the way Lawrence creates relations of men and women, there is an 'absence of any moral or social sense'; his characters 'betray no respect for, or even awareness of, moral obligations, and seem to be unfurnished with even the most commonplace kind of conscience'. Lawrence's 'insensibility to ordinary social morality' is 'so alien' to Eliot's mind that he is 'completely baffled by it as a monstrosity'. Lawrence, therefore, is for Mr Thomas Stearns Eliot – he who was delivering his lectures at UVA in 1933, the year of the ascension of Hitler, and could pronounce that 'reasons of race and religion combine to make any large number of free-thinking Jews undesirable' – an 'almost perfect example of the heretic'.[17]

How did Lawrence become a heretic? How did he contemptibly become a 'restless seeker for myths'? How did he become 'decadent'? Why does his writing reveal an aspect of Evil, a 'sexual morbidity'? Why was he 'spiritually sick'? For the author of *Lady Chatterley's Lover* was a 'very sick man indeed'.[18]

The fault, Eliot informs his UVA audience, lay with his mother. Or more exactly, Lawrence and his mother are a kind of endpoint of an unfortunate historical process, the 'decay of Protestantism'. Writers in modernity have rejected Christianity, that is, Protestant Christianity, and we can understand what has happened to writers today – we can classify them – by thinking of 'the type of Protestantism which surrounded their infancy, and the precise state of decay which it had reached'. Such is what occurred with Lawrence's lamentable mother: 'nothing could be much drearier (so far as one can judge from his own account) than the vague hymn-singing pietism which seems to have consoled the miseries of Lawrence's mother, and which does not seem to have provided her with any firm principles by which to scrutinize the conduct of her sons'. Because of his mother, Lawrence started life 'wholly free from any restriction of tradition or institution'. Not surprisingly, then, his religious upbringing at the hands of his mother 'gave Lawrence his lust for intellectual independence'.[19]

How gallant is Mr Thomas Stearns Eliot!

The trouble with so many modern writers, Eliot concludes his lectures, is that they will not abide by 'tradition', a tradition which 'must be perpetually criticized and brought up to date under the supervision' of what Eliot recommends, 'orthodoxy'. Such supervision has no room for the kind of Christianity that isn't Eliot's kind of Christianity, or for sympathetic historical understanding at any time. The axe must be wielded, mercilessly. Errant writers, and their mothers, must be brought to heel. Exposed for what they are and fail to be. Damned.

I wonder if the violence of Christian religious history so zealously espoused by Eliot the convert to that particular monotheism can be related to the violence of monotheism as such. I'm thinking of the Egyptologist Jan Assmann's reflections in his 1997 book

Moses the Egyptian, a commentary on Freud's last and wonderfully idiosyncratic book *Moses and Monotheism*, published not long before he died on 23 September 1939, after his escape from Vienna to London just before World War II. I've talked about the long historical conflict of monotheism and polytheism in an essay, 'The Challenge of Polytheism: Moses, Spinoza, and Freud', where I come out rather strongly in favour of polytheism.[20] Assmann, quite rightly in my view, questions Freud's supersessionist narrative, that because of its supposed intellectual and spiritual superiority monotheism rightly superseded polytheism in world history. Assmann points to the fateful consequences for the future when Akhenaten introduced monotheism into ancient Egypt, in particular, the monotheistic presumption of true and false religion. Such a 'murderous distinction', Assmann feels, worked its destructive way forward in terms of ever more distinctions and subdistinctions, between Jews and Gentiles, Old and New Testaments, Christians and pagans, Catholics and Protestants, Calvinists and Lutherans. Monotheism also introduced the notion of certain texts as canonical and others as heresy.[21]

By contrast, in Assmann's view, a great cultural and historical achievement of ancient Egyptian and Mesopotamian polytheism were their practices and modes of cosmopolitanism and translatability. Assmann refers to the international character of the polytheistic religions of the ancient Near East, a common semantic universe where the names of gods could be translated from one society to another. Such internationality and translatability were, he suggests, historically visible in Greco-Roman Isis-religion. He also refers to the 'kind of cosmopolitanism and its belief in the translatability of religious ideas and denominations which flourished in the Roman Empire'. Assmann, in utopian spirit, suggests humanity could recognise cosmopolitanism and translatability as gifts of the ancient polytheistic world to modernity.[22]

Eliot, it is clear, has no such generous view of polytheism. In

After Strange Gods, Eliot makes a swiping reference to 'the dark gods of Mexico', without naming Lawrence, though I think his listeners, as I have, would have instantly recognised that he was making a scornful reference to Lawrence's interest in polytheism.[23]

While overall Freud's *Moses and Monotheism* creates a narrative where monotheism, from Akhenaten through Moses to the Hebrews to Christianity to the present, triumphs over polytheism, this exceedingly interesting and eccentric text (Freud refers to it as an historical novel) does have its contradictory moments. Freud himself mentions that the coming of monotheism brought with it some lasting historical characteristics of an unpleasant kind. Indeed, Freud evokes the new monotheism as a religion of prohibition and enforcement, brought to its new adherents from the top down. Monotheism, says Freud in occasional asides, is 'grandiosely rigid'; it 'severely condemns' any kind of myth, magic or sorcery; it 'bluntly' forbids the image of any living or visionary being; and it was not only 'strict' but with its appearance in the world, the belief in one God gave birth to 'religious intolerance, which was foreign to antiquity long before this and long after'. It strove for 'consistency' and 'harshness'. The quality of 'exclusiveness', its 'negative side, the knowledge of what it repudiates', was vital for its being: such was evident from the very beginning, for Akhenaten effaced the word *god* whenever it was used in the plural, prohibited the names of the gods he didn't like, and indeed everywhere in the Egyptian Empire the polytheistic temples were closed, services were forbidden, and ecclesiastical property seized. From the beginning, Freud concedes, monotheism was a kind of reaction-formation, defining itself against that which it abjured or forbade or prohibited or abhorred.[24]

Eliot's audience, as they listened to the the lectures, may well have applied to what they were hearing terms like grandiosely rigid, severely condemning, bluntly forbidding, strict, intolerant, harsh, exclusive; that Eliot's Christianity was indeed a reaction-formation, continuously defining itself not in positive terms but insistently, from beginning to end, against that which it wished could be abjured and prohibited.

There are, however, some touches and moments in *After Strange Gods* when Eliot approves of something. Eliot very much believes in a medieval tradition which should be recreated and enforced in modernity: we should all live in a Christian theocracy, where there is no distinction between Church and State. The unity of Church and State requires homogeneity of race and religion; by such unity of values, we should be able to clearly distinguish between 'Good and Evil'.[25]

When Eliot writes in *After Strange Gods* that there should be an identity of 'the morals of the State' with the morals 'of the Church',[26] I started to think about Spinoza: what would Spinoza say? I wonder: when Eliot told his UVA audience (which probably included some Jewish staff and students) that 'reasons of race and religion combine to make any large number of free-thinking Jews undesirable' (did Eliot slyly glance at the Jewish people present when he said this, did he smirk just a little?), did he have in mind Spinoza, the great Jewish philosopher of early Enlightenment free thought? That Eliot was familiar with Spinoza we know from his doctoral thesis, written at Oxford during his stay there from October 1911 until June 1914, and eventually published as a book in 1964 under the title *Knowledge and Experience in the Philosophy of F. H. Bradley*. As a student during the middle 1960s I must have bought a copy of it, and have carried it about with me, through all the successive moves Ann and I have made through the decades, keeping it yet never reading it; I've glanced at it now, and it certainly shows a knowing familiarity in side-glances towards 'the *Theologico-politicus*'.[27]

Leopold Bloom first led me to Spinoza in *Ulysses*, during his travails in Barney Kiernan's pub. When Bloom is expelled by the nationalist citizens, he shouts defiantly: remember the great Jews of the past like Jesus, Spinoza, Marx.[28] Why Spinoza, I thought. So, I decided to explore Spinoza in relation to Bloom.

In my chapter 'Strangers amongst the nations: Mr Bloom and Spinoza' in my *1492: The Poetics of Diaspora*, I think about Spinoza as a non-Jewish Jew, a Marrano, a harbinger of modernity in his fragmented consciousness. Spinoza's Spanish and Portuguese ancestry is important for my story. When the Jews of Spain were expelled early in 1492 by the Christian monarchs Isabella and Ferdinand, the majority journeyed into a welcoming Ottoman Empire, while some moved into Europe, usually initially to Portugal. In Portugal, however, the Spanish Jews were within a few years forcibly mass-baptised, becoming part of the conversos or New Christians, who were frequently also Marranos or secret Jews. Further, the Inquisition was instituted in Portugal in 1536, and pursued even more enthusiastically there than in Spain. For the next few generations the crypto-Judaic practices of the Portuguese Marranos had to be ever more subterranean; and as in Spain, there were distinctions based on supposed blood lines between Old and New Christians; it was the visible success of the New Christians as part of the new Iberian urban bourgeoisie that inspired the Statutes of the Purity of Blood which could be used to bar New Christians from public and ecclesiastical offices and honours. Over the centuries the New Christians entered Western European countries as Portuguese merchants and physicians, medicine being one of the few professions in Portugal not barred by the blood purity regulations.[29]

(Yes, blood lines and blood purity, Statutes of the Purity of Blood, *limpieza de sangre* – a crimson thread in *After Strange Gods*; recall Eliot's acclamation of the importance of 'blood kinship' to his conception of a unified race and religion; he also feels that 'tradition' is 'of the blood, so to speak, rather than of the brain'.)[30]

What distinguished the conversos and Marranos who went

north in the succeeding centuries was that they now knew very little of their former religion. As they moved into Europe and tried to return to Judaism, they often revealed a skepticism towards both Judaism and Christianity, skepticism which especially found voice in the greater religious freedom of Holland in the seventeenth century. Benedict (Baruch) Spinoza (1632–77) was among the Sephardic sceptics of Portuguese descent who set the elders of the Amsterdam Jewish community on edge. Born of Marrano parents in Amsterdam, he was educated within the Portuguese Jewish community there. For Spinoza, many traditional Jewish tenets appeared to conflict with reason and the laws of nature, and he must have made his doubts known, for in 1656, when only 23, Spinoza was excommunicated, though excommunication was not uncommon in Spinoza's day, among the Dutch Calvinists as well as the Sephardim. What was unusual was that Spinoza chose to remain outside the Jewish community after the *herem* (ban), in a world where the unattached and unaffiliated were not yet a common phenomenon. It would appear that the expulsion and exiling of a young man in his twenty-fourth year from his family's community lent a bitter edge to Spinoza's subsequent reflections on the proper relations in history between theology (Jewish and Christian), philosophy and good government.[31]

(It's not clear why Spinoza was banned, but it could be for some or all of the following: he did not believe in the special election of Israel; he did not believe in miracles, which he considered merely absurd; he did not believe in an anthropomorphic God, but rather identified God with Nature; the words of the Bible are not the Word of God; the first five books of the Bible – the Torah – were not written by Moses, but long after Moses; Moses as a political leader infantilised the Israelites by asking them to follow and obey rather than doubt, discuss and debate; Jesus was preferable to Moses, for Jesus's parables concerning right behavior were admirable and stimulated thought.)

Spinoza changed his name to Benedict (latinsing the Hebrew Baruch), and became part of a European-wide circle of philosophers. Spinoza felt the clarifying of the relationship between religion and the state was so historically important and urgent that he interrupted the writing of his most famous philosophical work the *Ethics* to write the *Tractatus Theologico-Politicus*, which was published in late 1669 or 1670. The *Tractatus* argues for the complete separation of both the state and philosophy from theology. The ideal state is a democracy where freedom of judgement is fully granted to the individual citizen and where nothing is esteemed dearer and more precious than freedom. Sovereignty is vested in all citizens, and laws are sanctioned by common consent. The citizen is thereby a subject, not a slave. The good commonwealth, then, grants to everyone the freedom to philosophise. Furthermore, such freedom is of the first importance in fostering the sciences and the arts.[32] We can see why Spinoza's ideas concerning the separation of spheres, religious, political, philosophical, are recognised as so influential as the conceptual foundation of the modern, secular, democratic state.

Spinoza insists on the differentiation of philosophy from theology as separate spheres. Theology does not have to be subordinated to reason nor does reason have to be subordinated to theology, for each has its own domain; the domain of reason is truth and wisdom, that of theology is piety and obedience. The freedom of reason does not derive from 'authority and tradition', which, says Spinoza, are mere shadows; nor does reason 'demand belief in historical narratives of any kind whatsoever', and certainly not the biblical historical narratives.[33]

Spinoza writes in the spirit of a modern skeptical historical consciousness when he turns his attention to the Bible. There is a revealed Word of God, and such is a simple conception of the divine mind as revealed to the ancient prophets (here I think of Ned Curthoys writing of the importance of prophetic ethics in the German Jewish intellectual tradition in his *The Legacy of Liberal Judaism*). He who is blessed abounds in charity, joy, peace, patience, kindness, goodness, faithfulness, gentleness and self-control; one should love one's neighbour as oneself; and the moral value of a man's creed should be judged only from his deeds. Beyond practising such fundamental principles of practical faith, everyone should be allowed the freedom and right to interpret the basic tenets of faith as he thinks fit; the supreme authority to explain religion and to make judgement concerning it is vested in each individual; religion does not pertain to the sphere of public law and authority, but to the sphere of individual right.[34]

In *Tractatus Theologico-Politicus* Spinoza, in urging the separation of spheres and domains between the state, religion and philosophy, was historically fighting for a public space for philosophy and knowledge to work and breathe in. His plea for recognition of individual thought and judgement anticipates Voltaire and the wisdom of the Enlightenment in attempting to establish a public sphere of debate and discussion, a historically sanctioned space for the freedom of intellectuals and the liberty of ideas.[35]

Yirmiyahu Yovel, in his insightful work *The Marrano of Reason*, remarks that the Marranos prefigured modernity in many ways. The inner consciousness of the Marranos was multicontradictory, was confused, dissonant, ambivalent, paradoxical, incomplete, doubting, self-doubting, and potentially or actually heretical. Marranos tended to become this-worldly, believing in neither Christian nor Jewish eschatologies of transcendence, and impatient with any religious establishment. Marrano lives could be marked by sharply different phases, for example, as New Christian in Portugal, New Jew in Amsterdam, so that there is constant rupture with their past, their present, their future. In always having to regard themselves as New, the Marranos, Yovel feels, were proto-modernist outsider figures, both inside and outside of any cultural context.[36]

Spinoza as Marrano iconically embodied a new notion of Jewishness in European and world history: a secular Jew, a non-Jewish Jew; both Baruch Spinoza and Benedict Spinoza; never quite placeable; and a connoisseur of ambiguity.

Spinoza is one of history's great heretics.

Spinoza's conception of the state, religion and philosophy (knowledge, intellectual life, the adventure of ideas) as separate spheres and domains is the reverse of what Eliot attempts to prescribe as normative for intellectuals in *After Strange Gods*. This is an urgent matter for Eliot: intellectuals, writers, artists are to obey the morals of the Church, which are also the morals of the State; they should have no separate spheres of their own, because that means individualism which necessarily defies and undermines tradition and orthodoxy, the tradition and orthodoxy laid down by Church and State and their public ideologues; 'a living and central tradition'.[37]

The obeisance of intellectuals, writers, artists has to be supervised as in past eras of Christian supremacy over all things, over all minds. This proper course of history has been stupidly interrupted by modern doctrines of individualism, personality, cosmopolitanism, democracy, liberalism and industrialism, all of which, along with heresy and heterodoxy, constitute the 'Forces of Evil'. For the 'separation from tradition and orthodoxy' leads straight to the '*diabolic*' (Eliot's slightly hysterical italics).[38]

Now, who can do this supervising of intellectuals, writers, artists? Looking around, Eliot can only see himself. It will be Mr Eliot who will reprove, surveille, superintend, assume the position of panopticon, of Cyclops the giant with one huge eye on his forehead, since he's the only truly traditional, orthodox Christian in this terrible era.

Of course, it's too late for Eliot's benighted contemporaries and their mothers, but Eliot, the Great Leader, the Grand Inquisitor, the Prophet, the Messiah who God has sent down to dwell among us, will school all new intellectuals, writers and artists in what the Church, the State and Mr Eliot require of them.

And here's a problem, a stumbling block for Eliot: what can we do with the 'large number of free-thinking Jews' who live by the image of Spinoza? – they're intractable, stubborn, see things differently, search out new perspectives, are unimpressed by Christian tradition and orthodoxy for obscure reasons, are of impure blood, inhabit the halls of heterodoxy, and let their minds drift sideways towards heresy.

The only thing to do is for the Church and the State to keep their numbers down. But how? Yes, Jewish students and staff can be minimized by quotas, as at American universities, that's a start, that's good. But what of 'free-thinking Jews' who are not in universities, who are freely participating in the world as intellectuals, writers, artists?

The answer, for Eliot, delivering his lectures in the 'Holocaust year' of 1933, publishing them in 1934 in *After Strange Gods*, lay clearly – if unspoken – in the application of force as suggested by these dates. He had, along with the rest of the world, observed such force in action: in 1933, Hitler and his brownshirts and their bookburning had compelled into exile from Germany many writers and intellectuals, many of them Jewish; Jewish academics were dismissed from German universities, Jewish intellectuals and writers were denied employment and income generally. Hitler knew what to do when it came to securing a desired homogeneity of population and race.

Clearly, Eliot during 1933 had registered no horror at what Hitler and Nazism were doing in relation to Jews in Germany: otherwise, he would have not included the egregious sentence 'reasons of race and religion combine to make any large number of free-thinking Jews undesirable'; he would not have rushed out *After Strange Gods* by Faber and Faber as soon as practicable, in February of 1934.

Publishing *After Strange Gods* must have been deeply satisfying for him; he was bringing forth the luminous 'truth'.[39] He had shown the way; all Britain, Western Europe and the US had to do was follow him, in his Hubris and Megalomania; with, as Hermione Lee records Virginia Woolf observing in 1921, his 'wildly glittering eyes' that disturbingly revealed his will for power. Hermione Lee reports that one evening in April 1934, there was a gathering of Bloomsbury people at Tavistock Square (including, then, Virginia Woolf and Leonard Woolf; as well as Maynard Keynes, Julian Bell and Elizabeth Bowen), along with Eliot, 'talking about Eliot's new book *After Strange Gods*, and about religion and morality'. Disappointingly, while Hermione Lee reports on their comments on morality and religion, she provides no information of what they specifically said about *After Strange Gods*: did they notice at all the violently anti-Semitic sentence? Did they challenge Eliot on it? Did Leonard Woolf as usual affect not to notice? Later, Virginia Woolf confided to her diary that Eliot looked more than ever 'like a great toad with jewelled eyes'.[40]

In publishing *After Strange Gods* in early 1934, as Nazism tightened its grip on Germany and intellectuals were escaping into a long exile, Eliot must have felt he was speaking to a European context which he felt historically favoured him. History was on his side.

At this point, we can recall the theory of genocide created by the free-thinking Polish Jewish intellectual Raphaël Lemkin in his 1944 book *Axis Rule in Occupied Europe*. Lemkin had attempted a definition of genocide-like phenomena before, though without coining the term genocide as he did in *Axis Rule*. As Ann Curthoys and I note in our essay 'Defining Genocide' in the collection *The Historiography of Genocide* (2010), in 1933 Lemkin, then a public prosecutor in Warsaw, sent a paper to a League of Nations conference in Madrid on the Unification of Penal Law. He proposed that the crimes of barbarity and vandalism be considered as new offences against the law of nations. Acts of barbarism, ranging from massacres and pogroms to the ruining of a group's economic existence, undermine the fundamental basis of an ethnic, religious or social collectivity. Acts of vandalism concern the destruction of the cultural heritage of a collectivity as revealed in the fields of science, arts and literature. Lemkin always regretted that the 1933 conference did not enact his proposals in international law. He felt that if they had been ratified by the 37 countries represented at Madrid, the new laws could have inhibited the rise of Nazism by declaring that attacks upon national, religious and ethnic groups were international crimes and that the perpetrators of such crimes could be indicted whenever they appeared on the territory of one of the signatory nations.[41]

In another essay, 'Genocide: definitions, questions, settler-colonies', Ann and I note that Lemkin included as part of his definition intellectual and spiritual genocide, when elements of the nation or group such as the intelligentsia and the clergy that provide spiritual leadership are killed or removed. In Poland and Slovenia during Nazi occupation, Lemkin observes, the intelligentsia and the clergy were in great part separated from the rest of the population and deported for forced labour in Germany.[42]

In *Axis Rule in Occupied Europe*, Lemkin included deportation as a recurring feature of historical genocides.[43]

In contemporary genocide theory Donald Bloxham highlights the wider contexts of Nazism in modern Europe, from the late nineteenth century to World War II, in the demands for homogeneity of exclusive nationalisms in eastern and south-eastern Europe. The desire for homogeneity, he argues, was frequently manifested in genocidal destruction of minority communities, including through the forced removal and deportation of unwanted populations, and such practices of destruction of minority communities through removal and deportation became a preparation for the Holocaust.[44]

Now we can see how 'reasons of race and religion combine to make any large number of free-thinking Jews undesirable' relates to genocide, to the Holocaust.

In *After Strange Gods*, Eliot slyly doesn't specify how to reduce in number 'free-thinking Jews'. Yet the book addresses a context where every day Hitler and Nazism were deploying specific ways to persecute and destroy the German Jewish community. It was Hitler and Nazism that filled in for readers the silent dots that came after Eliot's sentence.

In the Anglophone world, *After Strange Gods* became, we could argue, a prescription for homogeneity of a population to be achieved by deportation enacted through an array of means, including detention and concentrations camps.

In *After Strange Gods*, Eliot became an architect of the Holocaust: an influential architect, because of his fame and standing in international letters.

Eliot and Yeats: concluding reflections on Rough Beasts

In the 1930s T S Eliot shared with his friend W B Yeats affinities of which I was unaware when a teenage Leavisite, and have only recently become conscious of, in the writing of this ego-histoire.

From memory, we teenage Leavisites were directed not to Yeats's early poems, held to be vague and sentimental in their Celtic Twilight mythologising, but to a small body of late poems, to be admired for their tautness and directness: 'Easter 1916' and 'The Second Coming' from *Michael Robartes and the Dancer* (1921), 'Sailing to Byzantium' from *The Tower* (1928), and 'Byzantium' from *The Winding Stair and other poems* (1933).

I've always liked 'The Second Coming', whose final two lines – 'And what rough beast, its hour come round at last,/Slouches towards Bethlehem to be born?' – inspired the title of a collection of essays Ann and I were involved with in the early 1980s, *What Rough Beast? The State and Social Order in Australian History*, produced by the Sydney Labour History Group.⁴⁵ But very recently I learned of something I never knew before, Yeats's affectionate embrace of Nazi Germany in the 1930s. I've been reading W J McCormack's scathing revisionist history *Blood Kindred: W. B. Yeats, The Life, The Death, The Politics*, which I've drawn on for my epigraph.

Reading McCormack's biography of Yeats (1865–1939), we can immediately register similarities with Eliot in the 1930s, and indeed McCormack draws a thread, as I have been doing, from the anti-Semitism of 'Gerontion' to the notorious sentence in *After Strange Gods*.⁴⁶ Yeats, McCormack writes, entertained a mystical yet sinister vision of 'Blood Kindred'. He was drawn to Mussolini's *fascisti*, to L'Action française in the mid-1920s, and after 1933 to Hitler's Germany. In June 1934, he accepted a Nazi literary prize, a Goethe-Plakette. He was attracted to a language and imagery of violence. He was fond of the notion of a Unity of Culture, a notion which, McCormack points out, he shared with Eliot (and Heidegger).⁴⁷

McCormack is not sure that Yeats was an anti-Semite, but he does record that the poet was attracted to the idiom of anti-Semitism, rather glaring in a letter Yeats sent to Maud Gonne on Christmas Day 1933, concerning an event at the PEN Club in London:

> Blood pressure was very high & as a result I was very cross. I looked around, saw several Indian authors & a lot of refugees from Germany, got the impression every woman there was a Britannia and was suckling a little Polish Jew.⁴⁸

McCormack suggests that one difference from Eliot was that Yeats tended to conceal his views, or, as McCormack puts it, Yeats 'characteristically held back from an open endorsement of his inner needs and desires'. In the 1930s, McCormack attests, no commentary on the plight of the Jews under Hitler can be found in his writings, private or public.⁴⁹

Now I wonder: did Yeats' involvements with Nazi Germany, and his friendship with Maud Gonne and her daughter Iseult, both vulgarly anti-Semitic and energetically pro-Nazi,⁵⁰ also help prepare the affective and conceptual foundations of the Holocaust? Was there a profound complicity here with *After Strange Gods*?

I'll take my leave of Eliot now, though will return to him when revisiting my middle 1960s Leavisite misadventure. Thinking of the vile bile of this strand of modernism, we can perhaps make play with some lines of 'The Second Coming':

> ... what rough beasts, their hour come round at last,
> Slouch towards Bethlehem to be born?
> All around them reel the indignant desert birds.

We can by contrast contemplate the joyous utopian vision of that free-thinking Spinozan non-Jewish Jew, Mr Leopold Paula Bloom:

> BLOOM: I stand for... New worlds for old. Union of all, jew, moslem and gentile... General amnesty, weekly carnival, with masked licence, bonuses for all, Esperanto the universal brotherhood... Free money, free love and a free lay church in a free lay state... Mixed races and mixed marriage.

1. W.J. McCormack, *Blood Kindred: W.B. Yeats, The Life, The Death, the Politics* (Pimlico, London, 2005), p.57.
2. Eliot, *After Strange Gods*, p.18.
3. James Joyce, *Ulysses* (1922), introd. and notes by Declan Kiberd (Penguin, London, 1992), p.430.
4. John Docker, *1492: The Poetics of Diaspora* (Continuum, London and New York, 2001), pp.68–71.
5. Joyce, *Ulysses*, pp.430–445.
6. Joyce, *Ulysses*, pp.431–2.
7. Joyce, *Ulysses*, pp.610–11.
8. Hannah Arendt, *Men in Dark Times* (Harvest, New York and London, 1995), p.29.
9. Eliot, *After Strange Gods*, p.19.
10. Arendt, *Men in Dark Times*, p.29.
11. Robert Crawford, *Young Eliot: From St Louis to* The Waste Land (Jonathan Cape, London, 2015), p.315.
12. John Tytell, *Ezra Pound: The Solitary Volcano* (1987; Ivan R. Dee, Chicago, 2004), p.243. It's worth noting that Pound also shared Eliot's antipathy to New York City, Tytell observing of a 1909 visit there that Pound 'deplores the racial characteristics of the city, its horde of new Slavic and Jewish immigrants, who were producing, he asserted, a mongrel nation' (p.62).
13. Cf. Warwick Anderson and Ian R. Mackay, *Intolerant Bodies: A Short History of Autoimmunity* (Johns Hopkins University Press, Baltimore, 2014).
14. Eliot, *After Strange Gods*, pp.26, 39–42.
15. Eliot, *After Strange Gods*, p.18.
16. Eliot, *After Strange Gods*, pp.18, 20, 42.
17. Eliot, *After Strange Gods*, pp.20, 35–8, 59.
18. Eliot, *After Strange Gods*, pp.44, 46, 58, 60–1.
19. Eliot, *After Strange Gods*, pp.38–9, 58–9.
20. John Docker, 'The Challenge of Polytheism: Moses, Spinoza, and Freud', in Jane Bennett and Michael J. Shapiro (eds), *The Politics of Moralizing* (Routledge, New York and London, 2002), pp.201–222. See also Docker, 'In Praise of Polytheism', *Semeia* 88, 2001, special issue edited by Roland Boer on A Vanishing Mediator? The Presence/Absence of the Bible in Postcolonialism, pp.149–172.
21. Jan Assmann, *Moses the Egyptian: The Memory of Egypt in Western Monotheism* (Harvard University Press, Cambridge, Mass., 1997), pp.1, 3, 6–8, 12, 168–170, 211; Docker, 'The Challenge of Polytheism', pp.202, 216.
22. Assmann, *Moses the Egyptian*, pp.20, 45–54, 136, 168, 193, 209, 217; Docker, 'The Challenge of Polytheism', p.217.
23. Eliot, *After Strange Gods*, p.41.

24 Sigmund Freud, *Moses and Monotheism*, translated Katherine Jones (Vintage Books, New York, 1967), pp.18, 20–21, 24–29, 31, 35, 41, 57, 82; Docker, 'The Challenge of Polytheism', pp.215–216.

25 Eliot, *After Strange Gods*, pp.46, 53, 58.

26 Eliot, *After Strange Gods*, p.52.

27 T.S. Eliot, *Knowledge and Experience in the Philosophy of F. H. Bradley* (Faber and Faber, London, 1964), p.178.

28 Docker, *1492: The Poetics of Diaspora*, p.70; Joyce, *Ulysses*, pp.444–5.

29 Docker, *1492: The Poetics of Diaspora*, pp.88, 100.

30 Eliot, *After Strange Gods*, pp.18. 20, 30.

31 Docker, *1492: The Poetics of Diaspora*, p.89.

32 Docker, *1492: The Poetics of Diaspora*, pp.91–2.

33 Docker, *1492: The Poetics of Diaspora*, p.92.

34 Docker, *1492: The Poetics of Diaspora*, pp.92–3.

35 Docker, *1492: The Poetics of Diaspora*, pp.98–9.

36 Docker, *1492: The Poetics of Diaspora*, pp.99–102; Yirmiyahu Yovel, *The Marrano of Reason* (Princeton University Press, Princeton NJ, 1989), pp.ix, 7, 15–17, 23–6, 29–30, 54, 63, 91, 96, 108, 111, 136, 189.

37 Eliot, *After Strange Gods*, p.49.

38 Eliot, *After Strange Gods*, pp.53, 56.

39 Eliot, *After Strange Gods*, p.25.

40 Hermione Lee, *Virginia Woolf*, pp.433, 631.

41 Ann Curthoys and John Docker, 'Defining Genocide', in Dan Stone (ed.), *The Historiography of Genocide* (Palgrave Macmillan, London and New York, 2010), p.10.

42 Ann Curthoys and John Docker, 'Introduction – Genocide: definitions, questions, settler-colonies', *Aboriginal History* Vol.25, 2001, pp.1–15, introduction to special section on "Genocide'? Australian Aboriginal history in international perspective'; Raphaël Lemkin, *Axis Rule in Occupied Europe: Laws of Occupation, Analysis of Government, Proposals for Redress* (Columbia University Press, New York, 1944), pp.xi, 83, 89.

43 Curthoys and Docker, 'Defining Genocide', p.12.

44 Donald Bloxham, *The Final Solution: A Genocide* (Oxford University Press, Oxford, 2009), and 'Response – Discussing Genocide: Two Moralities and Some Obstacles', *Journal of Genocide Research* 13, no.1, 2011, pp.135–52; John Docker, 'Instrumentalising the Holocaust: Israel, Settler-Colonialism, Genocide (Creating a Conversation between Raphaël Lemkin and Ilan Pappé)', *Holy Land Studies*, Vol.11, no.1, pp.1–32, 2012, here pp.4–5.

45 Sydney Labour History Group, *What Rough Beast? The State and Social Order in Australian History* (George Allen and Unwin, Sydney, 1982), pp.69–70.

46 McCormack, *Blood Kindred*, pp.100–102.
47 McCormack, *Blood Kindred*, pp.3, 4, 6, 9, 12–13, 18–19, 20, 29, 59, 65, 115, 139–140, 152.
48 McCormack, *Blood Kindred*, p.105.
49 McCormack, *Blood Kindred*, pp.10, 102, 111, 162.
50 McCormack, *Blood Kindred*, pp.21, 29, 56, 106, 197.

17

Jewish Culture as co-creator of Modernism and Modernity: A Journey from London to Odessa

In this chapter I counter the attempted cultural genocide of Eliot's poems' anti-Semitism against Eastern European and Russian Jews with an opposing narrative, a literary, cultural and intellectual journey from London – where my family lived in the East End during the same time as Eliot's anti-Semitic verses were appearing – across Europe to the port city of Odessa on the Black Sea – from where, my uncle Jock Levy once told me, my aunts Anne and Jeannette's family histories originated. Eliot's early poems contrast with other kinds of modernism and modern thought in the early twentieth century: the art of Marc Chagall and surrealism that I discuss with the help of the insights of Isaac Deutscher; the legendary Ida Rubinstein in dance and theatre; the writings of Elias Canetti and Veza Canetti, representatives of a remarkable Spanish Jewish diaspora in Eastern and Central Europe; and, assisting in the final stage of the journey to Odessa, the Russian Jewish writer Isaac Babel.

In this journey I feel personally involved, if only because all her life my mother kept a book of stories by Sholom Aleichem.

Marc Chagall
I'll launch my journey eastwards with the help of an essay by

Isaac Deutscher, 'Marc Chagall and the Jewish Imagination' in his collection *The Non-Jewish Jew*, an essay I read many years ago and found historically illuminating.

'Marc Chagall and the Jewish Imagination' was, a footnote tells us, first given as a talk on the BBC Third Programme, 12 August 1965. Deutscher begins by referring to his 'adolescent fascination with Chagall in the early 1920s'. Now near the end of his life (he died in 1967) Deutscher wishes to explain why in his view Chagall, the Russian Jewish artist, his roots in a traditional *Shtetl* in Eastern Europe and Russia, rose to become so important a figure in modernist art. Deutscher records that even in his youthful works, before 1910, Chagall can be recognised as a forerunner of surrealism, hailed as such by André Breton, while German art historians describe him as the originator of Expressionism. Yet, Deutscher reflects, to become an artist at all, Chagall had to stage a revolt against his Jewish inheritance, for 'Judaism's hostility towards the visual arts is notorious', and when Chagall was growing up it was still rigorously enforced by the biblical command, 'Thou shalt not make any graven image'. Deutscher believes that 'rabbinical orthodoxy stunted the growth of the visual arts far more cruelly than even Calvinism did'. While the *Shtetl*, the little town within the Jewish Pale of Settlement in Eastern Europe and Russia, had its 'superb cantors and musicians, its bards, poets, and composers of folk tales', the walls of the Synagogue were 'bare and grim, even though sublime liturgical poetry and song resounded under its roof'.[1]

Chagall, 'just before the close of the nineteenth century', was one of the first generation of Russian and Polish Jews who, Deutscher feels, began to paint in 'defiance of tradition, outside the Synagogue, in opposition to it', as part of a wider revolt, an 'act of emancipation', that was 'directed against Jewish clerical obscurantism as well as against Russian oppression'; directed as well against the 'realistic and naturalistic conventionalities that still dominated Russian painting'. Through the 'breath-taking originality and courage' of Chagall, so evident in his early paintings like *The Musicians, The Wedding, The Couple, The Holy Family, Circumcision* and *La Kermesse*, the 'long suppressed visual imagination of the Jew burst like a volcano exploding in rainbows'. Yet, Deutscher argues, Chagall remained 'the painter of his native *Shtetl* Vitebsk' throughout his life, wherever he lived, in Berlin, Paris, New York. In Paris, even while he absorbed the 'influence of Cezanne, Van Gogh, and Gauguin', and borrowed some formal devices from Picasso and the Cubists, Vitebsk provided his vision, his lifelong motifs: 'The multi-coloured apparitions which people Chagall's surrealistic world are beggars and butchers, cattle-dealers and soldiers, petty shop-keepers, itinerant preachers, and homeless fiddlers'. In the world he created, fantasies of unexpected miracles collide with the 'nightmares of the Jewish existence'. Hope is always attended by disillusion, dream by nightmare, to be met with 'Jewish humour and self-irony'.[2]

Deutscher compares Chagall's painting to Sholem Aleichem, who 'created in his Menakhem Mendel the Jewish Quixote of Eastern Europe, a figure as sublime and grotesque as the old Knight Errant', but where Sancho Panza was included 'within his character'.[3]

The pattern of hope and disillusion recurred throughout his life. Chagall responded to the Russian Revolution for its 'early heroic appeal', followed by 'subsequent disillusionment and moral depression'. The revolution 'suddenly opened undreamt-of horizons before Chagall'; he was appointed Commissar of Art for the Vitebsk Province; and supported by Lunarcharsky, 'Lenin's great Commissar of Education', Chagall opened his Academy of Art which carried 'daring avant garde art' to the children of 'illiterate Byelorussian *muzhiks* and Jewish toilers' who flocked to it. In the days of the Tsars, Deutscher observes, Moscow, 'the Holy of Holies of Greek Orthodoxy, was practically out of bounds for

Jews'. After the revolution, in this 'great and inspiring time', the Yiddish State Theatre was opened in Moscow, and Chagall began his 'great work for that theatre', producing murals and stage designs for the plays of Gogol, Chekhov and Sholem Aleichem. Nonetheless, in the early 1920s Chagall, who conceived of art as representational, found himself hemmed in between the 'hostile doctrinaires of abstract art' and party officials who were already insisting on socialist realism. Discouraged, Chagall left Moscow and Russia in 1922.[4]

Deutscher reflects that Chagall was not by temperament a 'tragic artist'; during the years of his return to Western Europe after Moscow, in the period between 1923 and 1933, Chagall enjoyed a period of 'respite, enjoyment, and triumph'. Yet, throughout his life, tragedy was 'thrust upon him'; and the 'ordeal of European Jewry comes to fill his canvases'. Such, says Deutscher, can be particularly seen in the long series of *Crucifixions*, for Chagall's Christ is not Christian, he is the 'epitome of the Jewish martyrdom', always wrapped in the Jewish prayer shawl; in the world below him are the crowds of terror-stricken and fleeing Jews, their synagogues and sacred scrolls enveloped in 'fire and smoke'. Furthermore, while in Christian representations, 'all suffering is concentrated in Christ' and is overcome by His sacrifices, in 'Chagall's Crucifixions Christ does not vanquish suffering'; Christ is not divine, he is a man who is eternally burned by the fire of the world yet remains indestructible.[5]

I think here of Ned Curthoys evoking in his *The Legacy of Liberal Judaism: Ernst Cassirer and Hannah Arendt's Hidden Conversation* (2013) what he refers to as counter-history in nineteenth-century thinkers such as Heine, Geiger and Cohen, concerning the figure of Christ in the post-Enlightenment German Jewish intellectual tradition; in various ways, they resisted the conventional Christian notion that Jesus was divine, and sought to reclaim Jesus as a Jew, meanwhile demolishing Christian theological assertions that Jesus was not a Jew. Heine, for example, Ned points out, did accept Christ's divinity, yet ironically and provocatively, noting that if Jesus was divine, then so was his 'cousin' Spinoza, who was still reviled in Christian Europe as a notorious atheist.[6]

In this wonderful essay, Deutscher suggests that Chagall when young rebelled against the severe restrictions of Jewish tradition forbidding the visual and representational, to enter and contribute to and help shape the universal world of modernist art; yet Chagall remained deeply passionate about Jewish history, and would always mourn what the Russian Revolution doomed, traditional Russian Jewish life: 'Chagall was to be the last painter of the *Shtetl*'.[7]

I find Deutscher's final sentence about Chagall and the Holocaust in relation to his post-World War II paintings very moving: 'Over the ashes of Majdanek and Auschwitz he weeps his *Kaddish*, the great prayer for the dead.'[8]

Modernism and Dance: Ida Rubinstein

Even though Isaac Deutscher does not discuss her in 'Marc Chagall and the Jewish Imagination', we can extend his historical argument to Chagall's contemporary and friend Ida Rubinstein (1885–1960). Like Chagall, she was a Russian Jew who burst into and helped create modernism with *éclat* and brilliance, paving the way as well for what would soon also occur, the enthusiastic participation of Jews in visuality everywhere, not least in film including Hollywood.

I've garnered the following biographical information with the invaluable assistance of Vicki Woolf's 2000 book *Dancing in the Vortex: The Story of Ida Rubinstein*, though I couldn't resist adding comments and asides.[9]

Ida Rubinstein was born on 5 October 1885. In 1887 and 1888 her father and mother, Ernestine and Lvov Rubinstein, died in a typhus epidemic; she and her older sister Irene grew up in St Petersburg with their aunt, Madame Horwitz, part of a network of wealthy Jewish families who dealt in international finance and the construction of railways. They adopted a lifestyle which made them indistinguishable from the Russian aristocracy of the time (here I think of Hannah Arendt's portrait of the Jewish parvenu); they were accepted as part of the elite of Russian society and so were cushioned against the anti-Semitism rife during the reigns of Alexander III and Nicholas II. If Chagall grew up in poverty in Vitebsk, within the Pale of Settlement, Ida Rubinstein lived in almost unimaginable luxury in her aunt's house on the Angliskaya, the 'most fashionable street' in St Petersburg. Ida had a French governess and a Russian teacher. She was taught and became fluent in English, French, German and Italian. When she became interested in ancient Greece, a classical scholar was employed to instruct her in the Greek languages, ancient and modern. She had a passion for French, Russian, German and English literature; in later years, she would outrage her friends by arguing that Dostoevsky was a greater genius than Shakespeare.[10]

As she grew up, Madame Horwitz took Ida to all the best theatres in St Petersburg, unknowingly preparing Ida for her later career; her aunt also arranged for Ida to have dancing, singing and drama lessons with teachers attached to the Imperial Theatres such as the Maryinsky Theatre. Ida, tall and willowy, was beginning to secretly harbour an ambition to be on the stage, but could not do so openly, since 'it was most definitely not acceptable to become a member of the theatrical profession itself'. Ida, however, was determined to rebel against her class. In 1905 she visited the studio of Léon Bakst (also Jewish), already renowned for his book illustrations and interior decoration; when in 1906 he opened a school of art in Serquiewskaia Street, Chagall and Countess Tolstoy were among his pupils; and he designed for the Maryinsky Theatre, where Nijinsky was trained and from which he graduated in 1908. Bakst had met Serge Diaghilev through his friend Alexandre Benois and all three worked on the magazine *The World of Art*, which Diaghilev had founded in 1898. Bakst was destined arguably to become the greatest stage designer of the twentieth century. His designs and choice of colours, especially his mingling of 'oranges and crimsons' in Ballets Russes productions, influenced fashions and interior design far beyond ballet itself: 'Almost single handedly Bakst changed the taste of European society.' In their spectacular, sensational and scandalous 1909 and 1910 Paris seasons, Bakst and Diaghilev demonstrated that 'ballet could stand on its own, for the first time in European history, as a great theatrical art, rivalling opera and drama'. Diaghilev was to use Ida in these 1909 and 1910 seasons in Paris and took her to the 'zenith of her success on the stage'. Bakst's working relationship with Ida Rubinstein would last until his death in December 1924.[11]

Yet it was not an easy journey for Ida to break free of her class, the confinements of gender and respectability, and the evil history of medical interventions into people's freedom exhibited in psychiatry, psychology and cognate so-called sciences of the mind. In Paris in 1908, Ida prepared to stage a ballet based on Oscar Wilde's poetic drama *Salomé*, with Bakst again keen to design the sets and costumes, at the same time taking private lessons in dance from the renowned Russian dancer and choreographer Mikhail Fokine, who recalled in his reminiscences: 'I felt it would be possible to do something unusual with her in the style of Botticelli. She was tall, thin and beautiful and was interesting material from which I had hopes of molding a unique scenic image'. Ida was to play the role of Salomé and perform the Dance of the Seven Veils. However, her sister Irene and other relatives living in Paris, hearing of the project, were horrified at the idea of Ida becoming a professional stage performer and appearing as Salomé. Irene and her husband the 'celebrated Docteur

Professeur Lewinsohn' had seen Bakst's costume designs for Ida and realised 'the obvious fact of Ida's nudity' at the end of the Seven Veils. Lewinsohn coldly informed Ida that he had no option but to protect her against herself, that he intended to use his medical standing to shield not only her reputation but preserve the social standing of the entire Rubinstein and Horwitz families. He then carried out his threat, committing Ida to the asylum at St Cloud. (It's worth recording, for those of us who think about the torn fabric of kinship in history, that Ida would later make a complete break from her sister and brother-in-law.)[12]

Here we must think of the late nineteent and early twentieth-century psychiatric attack on women. Recall Charlotte Perkins Gilman's 1892 story 'The Yellow Wallpaper', where the narrator, diagnosed as suffering from hysteria, finds herself in effect gaoled in a colonial mansion by John, her physician husband ('I am a doctor, dear, and I know'); she is forbidden to work or write, though she does so surreptitiously, the story we read. Dr John her husband also threatens to send her to a prominent Philadelphia neurologist, Dr S Weir Mitchell, who, advertising himself as a specialist in women's nervous disorders, propounded the virtues of his rest cure, near total inactivity and isolation. Charlotte Perkins Gilman herself, suffering from depression, was fortunate to survive Dr S Weir Mitchell's rest cure. We are reminded of the severity of the rest cure prescribed by English medical specialists for Virginia Woolf.[13]

News of Ida's confinement in the asylum in Paris soon reached Madame Horwitz, who arranged for Ida to be freed and to return to St Petersburg. Ida decided that she would be more independent as a married woman, and in 1908 she married a cousin madly in love with her, Vladimir Horwitz. The marriage was never consummated, and, now Mme Ida Rubinstein, she felt free to continue her nascent career, independent and wealthy in her own right. However, when she tried to stage *Salomé* in St Petersburg, it was stopped by the censor. Ida returned to Paris. In 1909 Diaghilev prepared *Cléopâtre* for his first Ballets Russes season in Paris, with Ida Rubinstein cast in the title role; Fokine had recommended Ida to Diaghilev for her 'strangely androgynous beauty'. It would also feature Nijinsky as her slave; Cleopatra was to disrobe accompanied by the 'beautiful and haunting music of *Mlada* by Rimsky-Korsakov'; Bakst created spectacular Egyptian sets, producing a 'powerfully sensuous impression on an unprepared Paris'; the performance 'launched a new age of exoticism'.[14]

In the audience Jean Cocteau took notes and described in bedazzled Orientalist terms the moment when Ida as queen of the Nile was unveiled 12 times: 'There she stood, unswathed, eyes vacant, cheeks pale, lips parted, shoulders hunched, as she confronted the stunned audience. She was too beautiful, like a too-potent oriental fragrance.' Another observer added that, on her first entrance, the audience could register Nijinsky, her slave Amune (the Egyptian god of the air), crouching at her feet like a panther ready to pounce if danger threatened, snarling and baring his teeth. The climax of *Cléopâtre* was the bacchanale, where the audience sees Nijinsky as Amune sensuously making love to the Egyptian Queen, though Cleopatra had set a particular condition, that he then take poison and die; after their coupling dance, Cleopatra glides slowly towards him with poison as he whimpers and begs her to stop. Amune dies, as his true love appears, played by Pavlova, who weeps heart-rending tears over the corpse.[15]

Cléopâtre made Ida Rubinsein the female star of the Ballets Russes in that legendary 1909 season, when Diaghilev and Nijinsky also became household names. Now notorious, admired and revered, Ida settled into Paris life, replacing the family she felt had betrayed her with a circle of close and loyal friends, including Sarah Bernhardt and Gabriele d'Annunzio. For their 1910 season in Paris, the Ballets Russes staged *Schéhérazade*, which was an even greater triumph for the now famous company than *Cléopâtre*. The production starred Ida Rubinstein as Zobeida and Nijinsky as her Golden Slave, with Fokine as choreographer, Bakst as designer of sets of 'vibrant colours', and music by Rimsky-Korsakov. Rubinstein's 'unique physical appearance gave her a sensuality and omnipotence that was both wanton and regal'. The ballet was 'wild, demonic and erotic', staging an 'orgy in the harem followed by violent death'. *Schéhérazade* opened on the night of 4 June 1910, and was 'a sensation', shocking, titillating, dazzling, the 'performers sensually caressing and petting as they stimulated sexual intercourse', with Nijinsky in a costume of 'baggy gold pants' and gold bracelets on his arms, fingers, ankles and toes. The ballet opens with the Shah and his brother suspecting that their wives are being unfaithful, and they pretend to go off on a hunt; as soon as they leave, the wives and concubines in the harem bribe the Chief Eunuch to release the slaves, Nijinsky the Golden Slave winding himself around Zobeida's body. The Shah returns and orders his soldiers to kill everyone. When the Golden Slave is mortally stabbed, Nijinsky in his final death throes shoots his legs upward, stands on his head and rotates his lifeless body. The Shah shudders at the thought of ordering the Queen's death but then commands it; Zobeida, however, seizes a dagger and stabs herself.[16]

Bakst's designs for *Schéhérazade* 'immediately revolutionized fashion' in dress, turbans, cushions and materials: 'The strange combinations of brilliant vibrant colours, blues and greens, oranges, reds, vermillion and gold were to set trends throughout Europe and beyond,' banishing the 'sweetpea simpering colours so beloved of the Edwardians', replacing them with 'screaming scarlets, magentas and purples'; orange colour, tempered with jade greens, turquoise and violets, became a signature of the Ballets Russes.[17] (We think here of Virginia Woolf's humiliation by her odious older half-brother George Duckworth in her choice of vivid colour for an evening dress.)

Ida is painted, sculpted and photographed many times over the decades. In 1909 P Phillipe sculpts two bronze figures of her. In 1910 she is painted nude by Serov. Jacques-Emile Blanche paints her as Zobeida in *Schéhérazade*. She sits for the fashionable photographer Bert, and Leon Bakst draws hundreds of sketches of her 'both as herself and for his designs for her various roles'.[18]

Ida falls in love with and has a three-year relationship with the American painter Romaine Brooks, whose life in Paris was largely shared with her companion of 40 years, the American poet Natalie Barney. Brooks was well known for her interior decorations and portraits deploying colours influenced by Whistler, a palette of black, white and grey. Ida figures in Brooks' paintings many times. Ida is the main model for Brooks' painting *Azalée Blanche*, which she started in 1911 and took many years to complete. In *The Passing*, first exhibited in 1925, a 'stark naked Ida' is depicted 'lying on a suspended white slab shaped like a lily surrounded by dark space'. In 1911 Brooks paints Ida as St Sebastian, *The Masked Archer*, sub-title *The Persecuted Woman*. Ida is sought after as well by other artists, including *Portrait of Ida Rubinstein*, by Antonio de La Gandara, where Ida appears 'mysterious and threatening'. In these portraits, Ida transcends the confining image of the *femme fatale* in the *fin de siècle*: 'She is mysterious and threatening but, above all, it is the overt sensuality that envelops you like the embrace of a razor.' Brooks commented that Ida fascinated her because was 'very Russian, very Dostoyevskian', and because she was 'Jewish… the perfect incarnation of her race', reporting that Ida had once told her that 'her mother was a Gypsy and her father Jewish'. As Vicki Woolf suggests, Ida kept re-inventing herself; she took possession of femme-fatale imagery, incorporating it into a constant play of metamorphosis and transformation.[19]

I'll try to speed up now and present Ida's biography almost in note form. Reluctantly, I'll skip over the remainder of Vicki Woolf's very interesting book, and plunder the Chronology at the end (actually, I've already drawn on it for details here and there). In 1909, after the end of the Ballets Russes season, Ida performs Cleopatra-type dances at the Olympia in Paris and then the London Coliseum; she sails to New York to appear at the Metropolitan Opera House; and in music halls in France and Italy, she performs *The Dying Swan*. Druet photographs her. In 1910 Ida Rubinstein meets Walter Guinness, later Lord Moyne, and they continue a love relationship until his death in 1944. During 1913 Ida reveals herself, like her friend Lord Moyne, to be an enthusiastic traveler. In July 1914 Ida finances and sets up her own hospital for war wounded in the Carlton Hotel, 'where she works as hard at nursing the soldiers as any of the medical staff'; her nurse's uniform is designed for her by Bakst. Ida continues to be 'involved with L'Association Genérale des Combattants et Mutilés for many years after the war'.[20]

In 1917 Ida buys a 'private aeroplane and a yacht larger than the British royal yacht'. Ida gives poetry recitals, 'several performances of which are cancelled because of the German bombardment of Paris' (I didn't know of this bombardment of Paris). In 1918 Romaine Brooks 'paints Ida in her nurse's uniform', which bedazzles Cocteau. In 1920 Ida and Sarah Bernhardt appear at a grand gala at the Opera in aid of Russian refugees in France. In 1920 and 1921 Ida makes two films, *La Nave* and *San Giorgio*. In 1922, Ida appears in a 'charity performance for a monument to those who fell at the Battle of the Somme'. Also in 1922 Sarah Bernhardt 'schools Ida in *La Dame aux Camélias*', in the part she herself had made famous. In March 1923 Sarah Bernhardt dies, and in November Ida fulfills a promise to Sarah with a gala performance of *La Dame aux Camélias* 'for soldiers wounded in the war'; 'Ida goes on to give fifty performances'. In December 1924 Léon Bakst dies in Paris.[21]

In 1925 Ida 'appears at the Théâtre de Vaudeville as Natasha Filippovna Barashkov in *The Idiot* by Dostoievsky', the play running for the whole of April. In June 1926 Ida appears in a performance of *La Dame aux Camélias* in aid of her favourite cause, the 'war wounded soldiers of the Association des Ecrivains'. In June 1931 Ida's company *Les Ballets Ida Rubinstein* begins its London season at the Covent Garden Opera House, its artistic director and choreographer Bronislava Nijinska, the younger sister of Nijinsky. Ravel and Stravinsky are involved: 'For the performances of his *Boléro* and *La Valse*, Ravel conducts the orchestra, as does Stravinsky for the premiere of his new ballet *Le Baiser de la Fée*'. Ida performs *Le Martyre de St Sébastien* 'in aid of the French hospital in London'. On 21 July 1934 Ida is appointed to the Légion d'Honneur. On 27 March 1935 Ida appears as Clytemnestra in a performance of Aeschylus' *The Choephori*, The Libation Bearers. In 1936 Ida converts to Catholicism, and soon after becomes one of the Dominican Order's tertiary sisters, 'a lay person committed to an altruistic life of charity'. In May 1938 Ida plays Joan of Arc in the premiere of the concert-oratorio *Jeanne d'Arc au Bûcher*.[22]

In May 1939 Ida is awarded the grand cross of an Officer of the Légion d'Honneur. After the outbreak of war with Germany, Ida 'sets up a hospital in a wing of Etioles, close to Corbeil, where she nurses wounded French soldiers'; she also gives 'several money-raising charity and morale-boosting performances of *Jeanne d'Arc au Bûcher* in France and abroad'. In February 1940 'Ida as *Jeanne d'Arc au Bûcher* is broadcast on Radio Paris as a live performance'. In 1941 Ida has to 'flee to the south of France, where she and her secretary, Madeleine Koll, cross the Mediterranean to Algeria'. Lord Moyne, Secretary of State for the Colonies, arranges for Ida and Madeleine to get from Algeria to Casablanca, then onto a plane to Lisbon, then to England. In June, Ida arrives in London 'with no financial resources whatsoever'; Lord Moyne installs Ida 'in a suite at the Ritz and totally finances her throughout the war years'. Ida assists in the 'nursing of the

Free French Forces in England' in the sanatorium at the British Legion headquarters in East Grinstead; she eventually acquires her own hospital in Camberley; and she 'adopts an air squadron'. In November 1944, Lord Moyne, now Minister-Resident in the Middle East, along with his driver, is 'gunned down in the streets of Cairo by the Stern Gang', both dying.[23]

With the European war at an end on 8 May 1945, Ida returns to Paris, where, Vicki Woolf writes in her chapter on World War II, she found that 'her magnificent house on the Place des Etats-Unis' had been razed to the ground; built up over three decades, her wonderful library of 'first editions of Russian, French, English and Italian literature', and 'her collection of manuscripts of all the works she had personally commissioned', had all disappeared. Ida leaves Paris for Biarritz. In 1950 Ida 'moves to Vence in the south of France and becomes a virtual recluse'. Also in 1950, Nijinsky dies in a 'hotel in London, in the arms of his wife Romola'; in 1953, the 'ashes of Nijinsky are taken to Paris and buried in the Montmartre Cemetery'. For one month every year, until her death, 'Ida retreats to the medieval Abbey of Hautecombe, near Chambéry, to pray and meditate'.[24]

In her penultimate chapter, Vicki Woolf writes of the final years of Ida's life in Vence, a 'small picturesque town on a hillside in the Maritime Alps, twenty two kilometres above Nice', among 'mimosas and lemon trees'. Ida 'died quite suddenly at her home, alone, on 20 September 1960, of a heart attack'. On 29 September, 'Ida Rubinstein was buried in a corner of the cemetery at Vence', in the 'very far end, in the most uncared-for part, where the truly religious are laid to rest'. Here all the 'stones are quite plain and set into the earth; all ostentation is left to those in the main part of the graveyard'.[25]

In Paris, when they heard of her death, the Free French Pilots 'organized and arranged a special plaque, in honour of Ida, to be put on her gravestone'.[26]

I salute Vicki Woolf for so wonderfully and movingly re-presenting for us Ida Rubinstein's remarkable life. Some reflections:

Let's return to the insights of Hannah Arendt and Isaac Deutscher. I think we can see Ida Rubinstein as a 'conscious pariah' in terms of Hannah Arendt's wartime essay 'The Jew as Pariah: A Hidden Tradition', where she focusses on 'Jewish poets, writers, and artists' such as Heine, Lazare, Charlie Chaplin, and Kafka. Arendt, we recall, begins this 1944 essay by recording with some bitterness that historically the Jewish people have given 'short shrift and perfunctory recognition' to those who 'really did most for the spiritual dignity of their people, who were great enough to transcend the bounds of nationality and to weave the strands of their Jewish genius into the general texture of European life'. Rather than regarding the historic emancipation of the Jews as 'a permit to ape the gentiles or an opportunity to play the parvenu', those who were 'conscious pariahs' made of emancipation that which it 'really should have been – an admission of Jews *as Jews* to the ranks of humanity'.[27] Ida Rubinstein broke from the parvenu culture of the Jewish elite in St Petersburg, who wished to be indistinguishable from surrounding upper-class Russian life. Yet she never forsook her Jewish name (nor her single name when married), neither in the Ballets Russes in 1909 and 1910, nor later when she created her own companies. Her exuberant performances, extravagant public personality, and sponsorship of creative production in dance and theatre across Europe, in London and in the US, certainly, in Arendt's terms, transcended the 'bounds of nationality', indeed, we can say, she became a figure of what Raphaël Lemkin referred to as world culture.[28]

I think we can also see Ida Rubinstein as a 'non-Jewish Jew' in Isaac Deutscher's terms, joining those he celebrates in that 1958 essay, Spinoza, Heine, Marx, Rosa Luxemburg, Trotsky and Freud, as Jews who 'dwelt on the borderlines of various civilizations, religions, and national cultures': 'They were born and brought up on the borderlines of various epochs. Their mind matured where the most diverse cultural influences crossed and fertilized each other'.[29] Ida Rubinstein lived and created on many borderlines: between Russia and Europe; between Europe and a fabled Orient; between 'high' and 'popular' culture'; between (like Heine) Jewry and Christianity; and in terms of gender and sexuality. She enacted an international and cosmopolitan life as an adventure of identity, to recall for duty a phrase I've always liked.[30]

Yet there is a difficulty in applying Deutscher's essay to Ida Rubinstein I must wrestle with. Deutscher writes that their being on the 'margins' and 'borderlines' enabled the non-Jewish Jews he talks about to rise 'above their times and generations, and to strike out mentally into wide new horizons and far into the future'.[31] In her final chapter, Vicki Woolf reflects that in her total devotion to the theatre Ida left a legacy that we still enjoy today: 'The vast number of dancers and musicians, artists, designers, poets and actors who are beholden to her include virtually anyone who was touched by the theatre, in any of its forms, especially ballet'. Yet, Vicki Woolf sadly concludes her book, Ida Rubinstein is now 'almost forgotten'.[32] The future, however, will always have its surprises. Vicki Woolf's book reinstates Ida Rubinstein in the cultural history of modernity, from the *fin de siècle* and Art Nouveau onwards into the aesthetic adventures of modernism, and that her name should always, when we celebrate in cultural memory the continuing importance of the Ballets Russes, be alongside Diaghilev and Bakst.

Here is another possible thought: we can envisage Ida Rubinstein on the borderlines of modernism and postmodernism. Reading about, and trying to visualise, the Ballets Russes in their 1909 and 1910 Paris seasons with Ida Rubinstein starring makes me think of what in my book *Postmodernism and Popular Culture: A Cultural History* I refer to as a late twentieth-century postmodern aesthetic of flamboyance, extravagance, excess, parody, self-parody, similar to carnival and carnivalesque in suggesting a kind of chaos of values.[33] Now I see a postmodern aesthetic of excess as a reprise of the Ballets Russes and their wonderful enduring contribution to a strand of modernism that was distinct from and always in tension with the kind of modernism of (say) *The Waste Land*, with its absolutist vision of modernity as emptiness and desolation.

Perhaps we can also sketch a borderline between early twentieth-century anarchism and twentyfirst-century anarchism. When in 1910 Ida was painted by Serov, many were shocked because she 'posed nude for it in a chapel that was once part of a monastery', revealing her 'joy in being provocative and shocking'[34] – perhaps, we might think now, as a protest against the Catholic Church's historic doctrines of male supremacy. We might, for the same reason, think of Pussy Riot's protest dance in Moscow's main cathedral, Pussy Riot reprising the *mise en scène* of Ida Rubinstein's early twentieth-century iconoclastic daring. Perhaps both Ida and Pussy Riot reveal an anarchism that is in conversation with Gabriele d'Annunzio, when after World War II, with a small army, he quixotically captured the town of Fiume from Yugoslavia in order to give it to Italy, creating in 1919 and 1920 the Free State of Fiume as an anarchist utopia. Vicki Woolf writes that Ida visited d'Annunzio just before the expedition set out, and he excitedly tells her of his secret plan to capture the town.[35]

Ida Rubinstein, conscious pariah, non-Jewish Jew: I salute you!

Sephardim in Europe: Elias Canetti, Mathilde Canetti, Veza Canetti

The Sephardim, the Spanish Jews expelled by the Christian monarchs Ferdinand and Isabella in 1492, have become a life fascination for me. My 2001 book *1492: The Poetics of Diaspora* was designed as an adventure of uncertain identity, inspired by remembering something that my mother would occasionally suggest, that the family's Jewish ancestry was possibly of

Portuguese descent; look at the olive skin of your uncle Lew, she would say; my uncle Jock once said to me that he thought the family came to England from Holland in the eighteenth century. *1492: The Poetics of Diaspora* became in the writing a kind of whimsical romance, hoping genealogy would reveal that my East End family was of Sephardi origin and so could connect me back through the centuries to pre-1492 Moorish Spain, and beyond Moorish Spain the medieval pre-1492 Judeo-Islamic trading and social world of plurality and *convivencia* that stretched from Moorish Spain through North Africa and the Levant to India and China.

It was of course a failed romance, the family history is almost wholly Ashkenazi (as

I always knew in my heart of hearts it would be). Yet the journey in *1492: The Poetics of Diaspora* into the lost world of pre-1492 Moorish Spain – readers might think here of Maria Rosa Menocal's wonderful book *Ornament of the World: How Muslims, Jews, and Christians Created a Culture of Tolerance in Medieval Spain* (2002) – continues always to attract me, the idea of Moorish Spain as a historic example to the world, an alternative to the modern nation state that seeks ethnic, religious and cultural homogeneity; its creation of a society as a tapestry of religions, its intellectual brilliance in poetry and philosophy, in medicine and science, in art and architecture; its adventurousness in the creation of cities and urban life, in state craft, in travel and travel literature.

I was delighted to read in Ned Curthoys' *The Legacy of Liberal Judaism* the long interest in German Jewish thinkers, from Moses Mendelssohn onwards, in Moorish Spain and the medieval Judeo-Arab world; present also, as Ned points out, in Lessing's play *Nathan the Wise*, Lessing and Mendelssohn being close friends.[36] Ned evokes Heine's mid-nineteenth century poetic interest in Moorish Spain and discusses his 1851 poem 'The Moorish King' (*Der Mohrenkönig*) which evokes the sadness of Boabdil, last ruler of Muslim Granada, its fall signifying final victory over Andalusia by the Christian monarchs. Yet, the poem's narrator is sure, the memory of Boabdil and Granada will never fade, the idea of Andalusia will never be defeated:

> His fame will never die away,
> Not before the last string
> From the last Andalusian guitar
> Will jarringly break and spring.

Ned writes: 'Heine's Sephardic poetics of memory, his profound sympathy towards Judaism's succour in Arab lands and the experience of both Moors and Jews at the hands of the Catholic Inquisition, scandalously celebrates the hybridity of *Mestizo* cultures.'[37] As we shall see, Heine keeps figuring in these histories.

When hundreds of thousands of Sephardi Jews were expelled from Spain in 1492, a minority, still a considerable number, sought refuge elsewhere in Europe, some in Italy, others in Portugal, others in the Americas. In Portugal they came under the watchful eye of the Inquisition, compelled to become New Christians (conversos) and Marranos (New Christians still secretly treasuring elements of Jewish consciousness), and by the seventeenth century some of these Marranos made their way from Portugal to Holland, their most famous representative Spinoza (who as a young man they excommunicated). The majority of the expelled Sephardi Jews, however, went southwards and eastwards. In an essay I very much admire, 'Staging the Quincentenary: the Middle East and the Americas', which I talk about in *1492: The Poetics of Diaspora*, Ella Shohat, an American cultural theorist of Iraqi-Jewish descent, observes that in 1492 the *Reconquista* of Moorish Spain by the Spanish Catholics – begun in the eleventh century with the fall of Toledo and completed in the surrender of Granada in January 1492 – coincided with the

Conquista, the invasion of the New World. Columbus's leaving for what he thought was India in order to convert its inhabitants to Christianity occurred almost at the same moment as the final defeat in Spain of the 3 million Muslims and Spain's expulsion of 300,000 Sephardi Jews. Columbus's voyages themselves were largely financed, Shohat points out, by wealth taken from the defeated Muslims and confiscated from Jews through the Inquisition. When, Shohat writes, the Sephardi Jews were expelled by decree of King Ferdinand and Queen Isabella, they were welcomed to the Ottoman Empire, with Sultan Beyazid II ordering his governors to receive Jews cordially. The Sephardi Jews settled in Morocco, Tunisia, Egypt, Turkey and the Ottoman Balkans. Over 70 per cent, Shohat says, found refuge in Ottoman Empire regions while the remainder went to Western Europe and the Americas.[38]

In *1492: The Poetics of Diaspora*, I was aware that some of the expelled Sephardim had gone to Turkey, and also to Salonika, where for centuries Sephardi Jews formed the largest community, continuing to speak Ladino (Judeo-Spanish). Salonika was a thriving port city in the northern Aegean that was for a very long time part of the Ottoman Empire, until captured by nationalist Greek forces in 1912; early in 1943, in Nazi-occupied Greece, almost the whole of Salonika's Sephardi Jewish population, some 46,000 people, were deported to Auschwitz; the community, once known as Malkah Israel, Queen of Israel, was destroyed.[39]

Yet, I confess, I knew nothing of the history and presence of Ladino-speaking Sephardi Jewish communities who had settled and thrived in the Balkans, and not only the Balkans, in the heart of central Europe, in Vienna. It was only a few years ago, in early 2013, that I came across the name of Elias Canetti (1905–1994), saw that he was winner of the 1981 Nobel Prize for Literature, and, what really caught my attention, that he was of Sephardi descent. I sent away to Gleebooks for his three autobiographies, written in German and translated as *The Tongue Set Free* (1979), *The Torch in My Ear* (1982), and *The Play of the Eyes* (1986). The autobiographies feature two powerful Sephardi women, his mother Mathilde Canetti née Arditti (of Italian Sephardi descent, from Livorno),[40] and Veza Calderon, a close friend of his Vienna years in the 1920s who he would later marry. Elias and Veza moved to London in 1938. I read the autobiographies carefully, and will now prac crit style explore them textually.

17 August 2015: as I write this section of this chapter, I realise, from looking up Veza Canetti's name on the Net, that in Austria in the 1990s considerable controversy broke out concerning their relationship, feminist critics arguing that while Elias treated her as his muse and literary assistant, he concealed from public view her independent interests as an intellectual and writer, charges that Elias denied, saying that he always admired and encouraged her; the controversy was renewed with the publication in 2007 of a book I knew nothing about, Julian Preece's *Rediscovered Writings of Veza Canetti: Out of the Shadows of a Husband*. I've asked Sydney University's Fisher Library to get the book for me on interlibrary loan, and will read it with great interest when it arrives. What I have learnt from the Net is that Veza Canetti was a playwright, novelist and short story writer: none of this information is, as far as I can recall, present in Elias's autobiographies, though there is a passing mention in *The Torch in My Ear* of Veza as a translator from English into German.[41]

Nonetheless – perhaps this sounds too defensive of Elias – the autobiographies do create Veza as a fascinating intellectual figure with powerful ideas about literature and culture that I will discuss soon, ideas that relate to modern, and postmodern, cultural theory. They are the kind of ideas that, in terms of method, influenced how Ann and I wrote *Is History Fiction?* – though not then knowing of Veza Canetti! I have much to catch up on then. Nevertheless I will now continue my prac crit of Elias's autobiographies, particularly drawing out threads as they concern the two powerful women in his life (at least until his and Veza's exile after 1938 in Britain). Such will also be a journey into the kinds of modernism that were being created in the 1920s and 1930s and explored in the autobiographies, in Vienna but also in Berlin. The names of Karl Kraus and Brecht will be important here. And Heine, Heine as point of difference.

In the autobiographies there are also resonances with my years as a teenage Leavisite that I wish to ponder. As he records in his opening volume *The Tongue Set Free*, in his youth Elias Canetti became, as I had in relation to F R Leavis, 'a devoted slave to Karl Kraus'.[42] How did he become free?

Elias Canetti and his mother Mathilde Canetti née Arditti

Biographically, what I gleaned from Elias Canetti's autobiographies is that Elias and Veza were multilingual and cosmopolitan, as were all the Sephardi communities in the Balkans and Central Europe; they were at ease visiting or living in various European cities or in Britain. Veza, born in 1897 of mixed Sephardic-Hungarian heritage, was some eight years older than Elias, and was already a notable presence in Vienna, where she had lived for many years, its avant garde intellectual life dominated by the satirist Karl Kraus, in terms of his writing and public performances. Veza made visits to family and friends in Britain and could speak and read English, a treasured language she could share with her new friend Elias when he came to live and study in Vienna (in order to please his mother, he came to study chemistry, though he had no intention of taking it up as a career; chemistry: shades of Primo Levy). Elias grew up in a Ladino-speaking community in Bulgaria, and lived in England when still a child from 1911 to 1913 with his mother and father in Manchester, where his father carried out family business interests connected to trade with the Balkans; tragically his father, who had wished when young to follow a career in the theatre yet succumbed, unwillingly, to the family desire that he be a businessman, died in Manchester from a sudden heart attack when 'he wasn't even thirty one'.[43] Elias's stricken mother then left Manchester with its deeply unhappy memory to return to Europe, there to dedicate herself to bringing up their three sons, Elias the eldest. Later Elias would go to school in Switzerland and university in Vienna, and would choose German as his writing language (an interesting reprise of the Sephardim in Moorish Spain like Maimonides, who wrote in Arabic).

In the opening volume, *The Tongue Set Free*, Elias Canetti recalls growing up in a Balkan Sephardi community which, he came to feel, was so preoccupied with business that it had historically deteriorated intellectually and culturally, betraying its cultivated heritage in Moorish Spain. They had lost touch with the values of their ancestors 'in Spain, four or five hundred years earlier', who were 'people to be proud of, physicians, poets, and philosophers'.[44] It was a heritage with which Elias himself would later attempt to connect, especially as he pondered the meaning for history of the mass expulsion of 1492. At least, this is how I interpret his intellectual journey in the autobiographies.

In 'Part One: Ruschuk, 1905–1911' Elias Canetti is a small child growing up in Ruschuk on the lower Danube in Bulgaria, a town that inherited the heterogeneous texture of Ottoman empire life, composed of people of varied backgrounds, Bulgarians mixing with Turks, Greeks, Albanians, Armenians, Gypsies, Rumanians and Russians, with many languages spoken around one; his family's neighbourhood was where the Sephardim lived, many of them well-to-do merchants like his own family. The Ruschuk Sephardim always knew several languages, including French, which they learnt at the school of the Alliance Française. They were 'pious Jews', but considered themselves a 'special brand of Jews' because of their Spanish background; through the centuries since their expulsion from Spain, the Spanish they spoke with one another had changed little; the first children's songs Elias knew were Spanish, he heard only Spanish romances; above all, he had to learn 'a Spanish attitude', for with 'naïve arrogance, the Sephardim looked down on other Jews'; and it would have been unthinkable to marry a *Todesca*, a Jewish woman who was a German or Ashkenazi Jew. 'I wasn't even six years old', Elias recalls, 'when my grandfather warned me against such a misalliance in the future.' Within the Sephardim, there was also a haughtiness – visible in his own mother – about coming from one of the old and rich Sephardi families: 'The proudest words one could hear about a person were: "*Es de buena famiglia* – he's from a good family".' From an early age, Elias records, he could not understand how, 'schooled in the great works of world literature', his mother could so stubbornly retain this inherited Sephardi sense of superiority. He objected to such 'arrogance of background' and set himself life-long against it: 'I cannot take people seriously if they have any sort of caste pride.' The Sephardim lived a life that was intensely, fiercely, theatrical.[45]

Not surprisingly, knowing what we know of traditional grandfathers who always believed they had a right to dominate families, dramatic conflict occurred when Elias's father disobeyed his father by deciding, with Mathilde, Elias's mother, to move to England where one of her brothers had started a business in Manchester. They had found Ruschuk 'too confining and too Oriental' (by Oriental Elias seems to mean the Orientalist trope of indolence, or static being), and they wished to escape the even more confining 'tyranny of the grandfather', a 'ruthless patriarch'. The grandfather opposes them going, blames Mathilde for the desire to emigrate, and then becomes increasingly angry with his son: 'a few days before the departure, he cursed his son solemnly in the courtyard, in front of the relatives who were present and who listened in horror… Nothing, they said, was more dreadful than a father cursing his son'. As a child in Manchester during 1911–13, Elias was very close to his father, who insisted the children now speak at home not Ladino but English. Elias realised his father loved England, because in England 'people were free', people are 'honest'; his father also loved England being an 'island'. There was a difference between the parents here, Elias realising that his mother 'doted on Vienna' where she had grown up and been educated, and had met and fallen in love with his father.[46]

A few months after Elias started school, his father brought home a book, *The Arabian Nights*, in an English edition for children, to assist his learning to read; it was a 'solemn and exciting' event that 'determined my entire life after that'. In the same series for children, his father introduced Elias to Grimm's fairy tales, *Robinson Crusoe*, *Gulliver's Travels*, *Tales from Shakespeare*, *Don Quixote*, *William Tell*. In the evening, after his father came home from work, Elias would tell him what he had read (it had to be in English), then his father would bring home a new book. His lifelong interest in 'characters', he feels, as in the characters in these stories which always haunted him, began then, in the 'seventh year of my life'; the only character missing was Odysseus, who would become a key figure for Elias in his youth (and later, he feels, influenced the writing of his novel *Auto-da-Fé*).[47]

Sometimes on a Sunday, Elias and his father strolled near the 'little Mersey River' that flowed not far from where they lived. Elias notes that the 'Sephardic colony in Manchester' had grown quickly, settling 'not far from one another in the outlying residential districts of West Didsbury and Withington. Exporting cotton goods from Lancashire to the Balkans was a profitable business.' It was alongside the Mersey that a fateful conversation occurred. One Sunday his father spoke tenderly yet 'very urgently' to Elias: 'You will be what you want to be... You don't have to become a businessman like me and the uncles. You will go to the university and you will be what you want most.' Elias says that he always regarded that conversation as his father's 'last wish' that would guide him through life, especially when later he was put under extreme pressure by his strong-willed mother to bend to what she wanted his life to be. In May 1913 the family, the mother and her three sons, leave Manchester for Vienna. On the way they stay for a few months in Switzerland, in Lausanne, where his mother in a very demanding not to say fairly brutal way teaches Elias, now eight years old, German, in preparation for attending school in Vienna; German, he had observed, was special to his mother, as the language of her intimacy with his father, 'their loving conversations', so dreadfully ended with his death when she was only 27. He also hears something by a relative that intrigues him, said in relation to Mathilde's sense of belonging in Vienna: 'the idea that a city can love a human being, and I liked the idea'.[48]

The family lived in Vienna between 1913 and 1916. Here Elias could observe his mother's detached attitude to Jewish religion. There were quite a few Sephardim in Vienna, with a temple on Zirkusgasse. On Sunday mornings Elias was sent, at the insistence of a male relative who was staying at a hotel in Praterstrasse, to the Talmud-Torah School at 27 Novaragasse, to learn Hebrew. Elias recalls the school in terms that are familiar from the childhood reminiscences of my uncles in London and Isaac Deutscher in Poland. The school was a 'woeful place', the teacher appeared 'ridiculous, a poor, groaning man who looked as though he were standing on one leg and freezing'; he had 'no control over the pupils, who did whatever they pleased'; as it turned out, they did learn how to read Hebrew, yet were never 'told any Bible stories'. Elias complained to his mother how stupid the instruction in the school was; she agreed, explaining she only let him go there so that he could properly learn to say 'the kaddish (the prayer for the dead) for Father': 'In the entire religion, that was the most important thing, she said, nothing else mattered except perhaps the Day of Atonement'. In any case, his mother had 'already escaped her religious community by attending school in Vienna as a child'; as a 'woman, having to sit off to the side, she didn't much care for the worship in temple', and she considered religious education a 'male issue'.⁴⁹

In relation to religion, Elias' mother, we can reflect, possessed what Ned Curthoys identifies in the German Enlightenment as a kind of Sephardic mystique which treasured the memory of multi-religious Moorish Spain; a mystique that recognised the importance of Spinoza's pluralism that refuses any distinction between true and false religions, and memorably explored such pluralism in Lessing's *Nathan the Wise*.⁵⁰

Elias perceives his mother's attitude towards religion in similar terms: 'Mother wasn't religious, and didn't distinguish between the various religions. A performance of Lessing's *Nathan the Wise* at the *Burgtheater* had determined her attitude in these matters once and for all.' Elias recalls of his early life in Manchester that his mother blithely chose to disregard the Jewish prohibition against eating pork, to Elias's astonishment and dismay, for he had been told in graphic terms, as part of early religious instruction, that Jews were not permitted to eat pork including bacon like Christians did. His irreverent mother, however, ate pork in front of him: 'I started feeling nauseated, I went out and vomited'. He would come to realise that his mother 'felt one had to find what was common' to all religions: 'She distrusted anything leading to the acute and bloody fight of religions against one another', and the fact that people still fought wars was an 'irrefutable proof of how greatly all religions had failed'. Elias also came to realise how important the *Burgtheater* was to her life, that she had conceived an ardour for it in Vienna as a child; a passion she had shared with Elias's father, woven into their love for each other. Now, in Vienna, Elias is impressed by his mother's passion 'when she spoke about the great heroines of the *Burgtheater*'.⁵¹

What, from the age of 10, became the substance of Elias's life were the evening readings and conversations about literature and drama with his mother, for whom he felt a 'blind trust'.[52]

Elias admires his mother for her powerful intellect and intense interest in literature, and even decades later as he thinks about her, he is 'amazed' at her strength of mind working out her opinions and attitudes. Indeed, from Elias Canetti's evocation she calls to mind certain affinities with Virginia Woolf, Leonard Woolf, Walter Benjamin, Hannah Arendt. She was independent in her literary opinions; she loved Dickens, introducing Elias to *Oliver Twist*, *Nicholas Nickleby* and her favourite, *David Copperfield*, which 'she regarded as his literary best'. In terms of literary forms, she found poetry too limited: 'She was bothered by the smallness of the form in poems, they ended too quickly for her'; because she 'set great store by passion, she found it plausible only in drama', supremely so in Shakespeare. She was fiercely anti-war, and kept a special collection of anti-war books, Latzko's *People in War*, Leonhard Frank's *Man is Good*, Barbusse's *Fire*. She did not see history as a story of progress: 'she didn't believe the structure of the world was good… She never got over her shock at the war. It passed into the experiences of her sanatorium period, she knew people there who were virtually dying before her eyes.' (Here I'm reminded of *Mrs Dalloway*.) She was anti-racist and internationalist; after they had returned to Vienna from England, with Germany at war with Russia, Elias then still a child picked up an anti-Russian slogan 'Crush the Russians!' at his elementary school and repeated it at home; his mother upbraided him for saying such ugly things: 'A Russian is a human being like you or me. My best friend in Ruschuk was Russian. You no longer remember Olga.' (Here I'm reminded of Leonard Woolf's post-Ceylon internationalism.) Her political views were always her own: 'she was a loner and never joined any pacifist group'. (Here she reminds me of Benjamin.) She felt, in any case, that participation in 'any public activities' was of no use, 'because no one would listen to a woman in this male world of war'. (Here she reminds me of the feminism of *A Room of One's Own*.) In terms of her feminism and anti-war stance, she would say that it would be 'better if women were conscripted too, then they could fight against it seriously'.⁵³

Elias' mother had a sharp eye for what she felt was superficiality and meretriciousness: 'I recall the scornful way she came down on Stefan Zweig's *Jeremiah*: "Paper! Empty straw! You can tell he hasn't experienced anything himself. He ought to read Barbusse instead of writing this nonsense!"'⁵⁴ Here I'm reminded of Hannah Arendt's coruscating review in 1943 of Stefan Zweig's *The World of Yesterday: An Autobiography*, which revealed values Arendt regarded as repugnant: Zweig's boasting of how unpolitical he was in his native Austria, confident that he could live in peace with the social and political standards of his time; his relentless pursuit of literary fame and success with its attendant comic vanity, to the extent that he could not recognise the greatest writers of the postwar period, Kafka and Brecht, who were not successful in conventional terms; his comfortable certainty and delusion that he belonged to an international literary elite of the famous and renowned, which would always protect him from the anti-Semitism increasingly directed from the late nineteenth century at his fellow Jews, with whose affairs and fate he had never concerned himself; and when, in the era of Nazism, he became a victim of anti-Semitism, he 'felt so disgraced that he could bear his life no longer'.⁵⁵ Zweig suicided in 1942 in Brazil just after completing *The World of Yesterday*.

Yet the autobiographies also chart how Elias' relationship with his mother would break down, would go disastrously wrong. As his teenage years went on and he began increasingly to think for himself, Elias felt that his mother had changed, she was reverting to the narrow utilitarian attitudes of the mainstream Sephardic community. Increasingly, he came to believe, she was insisting that he give up any idea of being a writer and should devote himself to acquiring a professional career. In effect, his mother went from the person after his father's cataclysmic death he was most close to and willingly dominated by, to his formidable enemy: 'War had broken out between us and it got more horrible from week to week'.[56]

Nonetheless, as an 'admirer of Odysseus', with an interest in metamorphosis and transformation, he liked 'invented stories in which someone turned into someone else and concealed himself'.[57] He would for the while appear to obey his mother. He would go to Vienna to become qualified for a career in science.

Veza Canetti née Calderon

> And the Raven, never flitting, still is sitting, *still* is sitting
> On the pallid bust of Pallas just above my chamber door;
> And his eyes have all the seeming of a demon's that is dreaming,
> And the lamp-light o'er him streaming throws his shadow on the floor;
> And my soul from out that shadow that lies floating on the floor
> Shall be lifted – nevermore!
>
> Edgar Allan Poe, *The Raven*

I'll cavalierly skip over the remainder of volume one *The Tongue Set Free* and much of volume two *The Torch in My Ear*, to arrow in on how Elias met Veza, at the same time as he became a devoted follower of Karl Kraus. In *The Torch in My Ear* we can pick up Elias, from the age of 19, in Vienna during 1924 and 1925, studying chemistry at the university. In the chapter called 'Karl Kraus and Veza' Elias tells us that on Saturday afternoons he visits some friends, Alice Asriel and her son Hans, in their home on Heinestrasse near the Prater Star. They would excitedly tell him about Karl Kraus: 'He was, I heard, the strictest and greatest man living in Vienna today. No one found grace in his eyes. His lectures attacked everything that was bad and corrupt.' So also did his magazine, *Die Fackel (The Torch)*. Kraus hated war, and during the Great War had printed anti-war pieces in *Die Fackel*, despite the censors. He exposes corruption, denounces graft. He has written an 800-page play, *The Last Days of Mankind*, containing everything that had happened in the war, and would read aloud from it, his audience spellbound. He is a whole theatre by himself.[58]

Furthermore, if Elias went as he should, as he must, he would see Veza. Both mother and son cried together: 'What about Veza! Do you know Veza? Have you ever heard of Veza?' Elias likes the sound of her name, it 'reminded me of one of my stars, Vega in the constellation of Lyra'. 'We know her,' exclaim mother and son. 'She lives on Ferdinandstrasse with her mother... A beautiful woman with a Spanish face... She's read more than all of us put together. She knows the longest English poems by heart, plus half of Shakespeare. And Molière and Flaubert and Tolstoy.' They said that the 'longest English poem that she knew by heart' was Poe's *The Raven*, and she 'looked like a raven herself, a raven magically transformed into a Spanish woman'. She's 27, they say, and at every lecture she sits in the front row while Karl Kraus performs.[59]

(Intrigued by Elias's reference to 'Vega in the constellation of Lyra', I look up the EarthSky website, which tells us that the blue-white star Vega is known as the Harp Star in Greek mythology, part of Lyra, said to be the harp played by the legendary musician Orpheus; when Orpheus played this harp, neither god nor mortal could turn away.)

Elias is skeptical of his friends' claims that Kraus and Veza could be so special, but, fatefully, on 17 April 1924, he attends 'the three-hundredth lecture of Karl Kraus', Alice Asriel having given up her ticket at the Great Concert Hall for him so he could attend with Hans. And he does indeed see Veza with her 'raven hair' enter and sit in the front row. Then Kraus comes out on stage and is greeted with thunderous applause; Elias sees that the audience laughs at his every satirical allusion almost before he's said it; his voice changes all the time; everyone is spellbound. At intermission, Hans introduces Elias to Veza, and they explore their connection to the Sephardim: 'I knew her mother was a Sephardi, née Calderon'; she recognises his name as being Ladino. Veza asks, from his accent, if he is Swiss, and Elias replies that he would like to be Swiss because of his having lived there. In turn Veza says: 'I'd love to be British'. Veza says she would like to hear about his childhood in England, and invites him to drop in on her soon.[60]

After that lecture, Elias becomes a devotee of Kraus, and would hear at least a further 100 lectures.[61]

After another year goes by, Elias summons up the will and determination to visit Veza in the apartment she shares with her mother, and an old step-father, another of the business-obsessed Sephardi patriarchs, against whom Veza insists on her right to her own life, as Elias's mother had with her father-in-law.

Since we are talking about Vienna, I will venture now some obvious psychoanalysis, though I should add here that in the autobiographies Elias Canetti doesn't like Freud, he believes that Freud, with his focus on the individual, will be no help at all in what became for Elias a life project, to understand the crowd in history, finally publishing his book on the subject, *Crowds and Power*, in 1960. Elias displaces his mother, who had been his childhood authority in knowledge, with a new intellectual authority figure, Kraus (just as, to continue in this vein, I had as a teenage student at the University of Sydney in the 1960s displaced my father's desire that I become a revolutionary, with the intellectual authority of F R Leavis).[62] He displaces his mother (27 when his father died in Manchester) with Veza (who is presently 28), Veza with whom he will be able passionately to discuss ideas, but now as an equal, with Veza always supportive of his desire to be a writer. Therein is the difference between Kraus and Veza: whereas Kraus as surrogate father appears to demand total agreement from his devotees such as Elias had now become, Veza as surrogate mother seeks a relationship where there can be a large margin for disagreement and disputation, for differences. Kraus imprisons; Veza, as we shall see, helps to set Elias free by showing how she set herself free from Kraus's mesmeric personality.

Sociologically, we can say that Elias and Veza were part of a new generation of Balkan and Central European Sephardim who rebelled against the business obsession of the older Sephardi generations, entering the world of ideas and the freedom and experimentation of modernism; where ideas and literature became life itself.

21 August 2015: the interlibrary loan copy of Julian Preece's *Rediscovered Writings of Veza Canetti: Out of the Shadows of a Husband* has just arrived at Sydney University's Fisher Library. I've picked it up and see that it has to be returned by 11 September. Feeling a little panicky about time, I decide to read it now.[63] Preece suggests that the Austrian feminist critics of the 1990s delivered too harsh a judgement on Elias, though they rightly drew attention to the power and interest of Veza Canetti's largely forgotten writings, which were published from the early 1930s onwards, and how much Veza influenced Elias. Preece argues for a nuanced approach, based on his access to diaries, papers and letters. He enthusiastically agrees that Veza should be appreciated and recognised as an important literary and intellectual figure in her own right. How admirable her fiction is, he notes, has become especially clear with the publication in 1999 of *The Tortoises*, which Veza began writing in 1939, the novel recounting Nazi persecution in Vienna before World War II, Veza and Elias having fled to London in the wake of the Kristallnacht in November 1938. Preece regards *The Tortoises* (which I have sent away for) as a great novel; he also draws attention to Veza's fascinating correspondence from the 1930s with Elias' younger brother Georg, a doctor, living in Paris, who for many years, Preece says, was the lover of Roland Barthes.[64]

Preece argues that in the beginning, in the 1920s, the much

younger Elias had a great deal to learn from Veza's friendship; later, their relationship was more equal, and they formed, he believes, like Sartre and Simone de Beauvoir, a great literary and intellectual partnership, involving intense discussion of literary differences (especially concerning what she perceived as the misogyny of *Auto-da-Fé*), exchange of ideas, and mutual influencing. Preece admires their 'multilingual internationalism, which was reflected in their selection of favorite authors', always opposed to 'chauvinistic nationalism'. In Vienna and later in exile in London, Preece writes, Ladino was their language of everyday communication, even in the presence of others, suggesting the closeness of their relationship.[65] (Perhaps, too, I think, reading this about their speaking Ladino, Elias and Veza wished to treasure their Sephardi descent and history, to keep it alive in Britain, where they were outsiders, and still wrote largely in German.)

If Preece feels that the Austrian feminists during the 1990s are too critical of Elias Canetti, he also expresses his distaste for the biographers of Iris Murdoch, with whom Elias had an affair, for their dismissals of Canetti as 'an unpleasant individual'.[66]

Reading Preece's book I was struck by his admiration for Elias' autobiographies, which I also find admirable. I found particularly interesting his comparing Elias and Veza's creative partnership to Sartre and Beauvoir, which surely makes us think how important in literary and intellectual history such partnerships are.

I like this sentence in his penultimate paragraph: 'I hope to have shown in this book that their literary relationship was dynamic and that influence was mutual because each inhabited the imagination of the other.'[67]

I bring the book back to Fisher Library on the set date, in the late afternoon, absurdly fearing I might be scolded even though I hadn't been late in returning it. The librarian looks at it, says 'that's OK', and I turn and walk towards the library's exit doors, just a little nervous that I might be called back, as if a wayward student. Why, at my age, am I still afraid of librarians?

Let's return to the autobiographies and the developing relationship of Elias and Veza. The autobiographies are largely composed of portraits of particular people, shaped as characters, chronological, yet like fragments that compose a mosaic, reflecting on each other. I think they are great literature.

Young Elias, entering his twenties, and the older young woman Veza quickly become friends, but friends in a jousting way, eagerly discussing books and ideas, often disagreeing. In the section of *The Torch in My Ear* concerning Vienna 1924–25, in the fragment 'Patriarchs', Elias observes that everyone in Vienna 'found Veza exotic', by her presence introducing a very different history to modern Europe, as if an 'Andalusian who had never been in Seville, but spoke about it as though she had grown up there'; she was a figure recognisable from *The Arabian Nights*, or Persian miniatures. At Kraus's lectures, 'she drew attention, the most exotic creature' in the audience. Her 'beauty was breathtaking', with her 'conspicuously parted, blue-black hair'. On the occasion of his first visit to her home, he feels like 'an inexperienced creature, barely out of boyhood, clumsy, unpolished… awkward, insecure, gross'.[68]

On this first visit he sees Veza's room, which she has furnished to 'her own taste, in colors she liked, with books and paintings, unsettled and yet serious'. Here occurs their first disagreement, over the character of Lear, for both had 'recently heard *King Lear*, one of Karl Kraus's grandest readings'. Naively, Elias asks Veza 'why Lear has to die in the end'. He feels that 'Lear, who had grown so old, ought to grow even older', that Lear deserves at the last 'to have peace and quiet'. So, Veza replies, you would like 'people as old as the Biblical patriarchs?' When Veza goes on to say she does not necessarily want old men to keep living, he realises that he has blundered into a deep area of pain for her. Veza tells him about her frightening step-father, Mento Altaras, who 'lives two doors away' in the apartment, an old man, 'almost ninety', a former businessman in the Baltic Sephardi mould, 'one of the richest men in Sarajevo and Bosnia', who daily made life near insufferable for her and her mother Rachel Calderon, constantly demanding meat and wine. Veza, when she was 18, had fought back against the 'sinister' old man, banging his cane, spouting 'dreadful Ladino curses and threats', insanely paranoid that people wished to steal his money, a 'figure from hell', shouting in the house '*Mi arrobaron las paras* – They've stolen my money!' Veza, nonetheless, had made her room inviolable, the space of her intellectual life in opposition to domineering Sephardi patriarchs, attempting to the very end of their lives to control their families by fear.[69]

The highlight for me of the three autobiographies, or at least of the Sephardi thread I'm following, occurs in the third section of *The Torch in My Ear*, concerning the years in Vienna 1926–28, in two fragments, 'The Asylum' and 'The School of Hearing'. 'The Asylum', Elias says, refers to how in her room Veza 'had won her freedom', with remarkable 'strength and resolution', against her 'enemy', the hideous old man who 'cared only about himself': the very opposite of Veza. Now, says Elias, the 'asylum that Veza had created for herself became my asylum, too'. Conversation with Veza is like an 'alchemical process', purifying and clearing his mind, for in talking with her 'everything was different from anything I had ever known before'. His past feels 'dissolved': 'I had no history'. They love talking intensely about literature, ideas, and, inevitably, Karl Kraus. They recite poetry to each other. When Veza asks him to read out Goethe's *Prometheus*, he is delighted that she so much likes his reading. Veza, hoping to arouse his liking for the Edgar Allan Poe poem, recites *The Raven* and he realises how obsessed she is with it, and that she 'wasn't put off by my astonishment at how obsessed she was'. After an initial resistance, Elias finds himself 'caught' by the poem: 'The bird flew into my nerves; I began to twitch to the rhythm of the poem.'[70]

The conversation soon turns to Karl Kraus, and here Elias the young devotee is alarmed and stunned by what Veza reveals of her attitude to him, a critical distance, an irreverence. Veza says she has 'utmost veneration' for Kraus, but 'she wouldn't let him prescribe what one could or couldn't read'. As an example, Veza shows Elias a copy of Heine's *French Conditions*, 'one of the most intelligent and most entertaining books she'd ever read'. Elias is frightened and appalled: 'I refused to take hold of the volume. There was no one Karl Kraus so utterly disapproved of as Heine.' (Canetti doesn't say why.) 'I didn't believe her: I thought she was playing a joke on me, and I was even terrified about the joke.' But Veza 'insisted on showing her independence', teases him by holding the title under his nose, leafs through the pages in front of him. Still Elias refuses to believe she could be interested in Heine. Veza replies that in her bookcase, which contains the heart of her library, the books she cannot live without, is a complete edition of Heine. After this 'blow, which she enjoyed dealing me', Veza shows him her library of works and novels and authors he had expected to see: Goethe, Shakespeare, Molière, Byron's *Don Juan*, Victor Hugo's *Les Misérables*, *Tom Jones*, *Vanity Fair*, *Anna Karenina*, *Madame Bovary*, *The Idiot* and *The Brothers Karamazov*. Again, however, Veza 'proved her independence from Karl Kraus', pointing out Kraus's narrowness, that he is not interested in novels or paintings, in anything that could weaken his wrath at the world.[71]

Elias is 'shocked' that Veza could sit in the front row at Karl Kraus's readings, 'sparkling and full of expectation', even though she enjoyed reading Heine's *French Conditions*: 'How did she dare sit in front of Kraus.' Elias contrasts his own veneration: 'He was my conviction. He was my strength.' He represented justice, indeed 'he *was* justice'. Every sentence uttered by Kraus was 'a demand' for agreement, and Elias willingly accepted that demand: 'I was filled with him as with a Bible.' Elias tells Veza that Kraus would only have to frown and 'I would have thrown myself into fire for him', 'I would have broken off with my best friend'. Later he realises that he was blurting out to Veza his 'secret slave emotions', that he had been treating Kraus as his 'god'. Veza, 'though not really religious', dislikes Kraus's ambition to replace God with himself, since in her view 'no human being' has the right to become God. Elias learns that the Bible is the book she reads most frequently, that she 'loved the stories, the psalms, the proverbs, the prophets', and more than anything else the Song of Songs.[72]

Elias realises the importance to Veza of the characters created in the books she read. He knows that since boyhood he too had been interested in characters from literature and myth, that he felt as if 'I consisted of many characters', yet his interest was still 'vague'. In Veza he finds he has 'met a person who had found characters in great literature and inserted them for her own multiplicity': 'She had implanted them in herself, they thrived in her. And whenever she wanted them, they were available.' For Elias it was an 'exciting spectacle' watching Veza 'slowly move among her characters'. And he comes to recognise how important for her independence is her awareness of various characters: 'They were her support against Karl Kraus. He could never have touched them; they were her freedom. *She* was never his slave.'[73]

In the fragment 'The School of Hearing' in the Vienna 1926–28 section Elias reports on further jousting conversations with Veza when he visits her in her sanctuary. Again Veza confronts him with her independence of mind and her distinctive literary judgements; she sharply questions what she takes to be his characteristic misogyny. Their exchanges could almost be on the stage, they are a theatre of disagreement, challenging each other, but above all, it is Veza who challenges her young friend, as he desperately tries to defend his views. Elias 'soon noticed that she felt something like a chauvinism for everything that was female', and that she 'gave in unresistingly to glorifiers of women'. Elias finds this glorification of women 'ridiculous and I made no bones about my feelings', as a way of staking off his 'territory against her; otherwise, I would have gradually surrendered to her rich literary background'. They dispute the merit of various writers: 'she loved Flaubert, I Stendahl'.[74]

Their sharpest disagreement is over the relative merits of Tolstoy and Gogol. Veza 'would hit me over the head with Tolstoy': 'Anna Karenina was her favorite female character', and in regard to her 'Veza could get so violent that she actually declared war against Gogol, *my* great Russian'. Elias finds Anna Karenina 'boring', though for a hidden reason ('because she had absolutely nothing in common with Veza'), and resists her judgment. Veza then 'reached for her torture instruments and raked Gogol over the coals instead of me'; she pounces on Gogol's 'weaknesses', even attacking *Dead Souls*, and then expressing contempt for Gogol's Russian years after his return home, when 'he tried to prove at any cost how pious and how devoted to the government he was'. She tells Elias that 'she knew of nothing more horrible in world literature than those final years of Gogol's', yet he was 'only forty three when he died'.

> And what did I think – in comparison with that – of the later development of Tolstoy, who had grown twice as old, and written *Anna Karenina*, which I absolutely didn't understand at all (said Veza), and had then produced various works that even I, an inveterate misogynist, would have to respect? But until the very last hours of his life, he had demonstrated an unparalleled stubbornness, courage, even magnanimity – what the English call 'spirit'. She just couldn't take a person seriously if he had a higher regard for Gogol than for Tolstoy.

Elias refuses to yield: 'I was destroyed, but I didn't give in, even if I *was* destroyed.' He attacks the late 'Tolstoy, the count': 'Had he ever left his manor? Had he ever been exiled?' Veza immediately replies: '*The woman* was what happened to him, she said, and he *had* left his "manor" and died in exile.'[75]

Elias observes that their 'bitter, drawn-out feud' came to a sort of compromise over 'Gorky's jottings about the old Tolstoy', which Elias had given Veza to read, and which they both equally admire: 'Veza was deeply moved by this picture of old Tolstoy. She called it the most beautiful present I had ever given her.' Elias says that at this moment the 'worst was over', Veza saying something that deeply 'tore' his heart: 'That's the thing I wish for most in the world: that you write like this someday.' They continued to argue over literary questions for years, Elias says; there were 'battles, but there was never a victor'. Veza applied a 'secret caution, a tender concern', that the battles never became too bitter: 'It was impossible for her to wound me deliberately. I would never have hurt her for anything in the world.' Elias considers that this period was a quiet 'apprenticeship' for him, learning 'intimacy with a thinking person'.[76]

Thinking back now to that time in the latter 1920s, Elias contrasts Veza's confident possession of her own critical values with Karl Kraus's authoritarianism, for Kraus, he would come to realize, 'crushed everyone'. In following Klaus so completely, Elias feels now that he gave in to a 'proclivity for intolerance', he became part of 'the tremendous resonance known as a crowd'.[77]

Nonetheless, during these jousting conversations in Vienna in 1926–28 with Veza, Elias could not yet discard the 'legacy of intolerance' that he absorbed from Kraus. He still idolised him.[78] It took a painful yet liberating visit to Berlin in 1928 to effect a separation from Kraus as his intellectual father.

Berlin: destroyed by Brecht, disillusion at last with Kraus, meeting Isaac Babel

In 1928 Elias was invited to Berlin by Ibby Gordon, a Hungarian poet who had been living in Vienna for about a year; they would meet in a coffeehouse, and he appreciated how witty and funny she was; Ibby asks Elias to help translate her poems into German; then, armed with Elias's translations, she moves to Berlin, where her poems are well received in avant garde circles; she gets to know and hang out with writers and artists like Brecht and George Grosz; she writes to Elias urging him to come to Berlin for his summer vacation, she has a friend who would hire him as a translator between English and German. On 15 July 1928 Elias leaves for Berlin. Ibby's friend turned out to be Wieland Herzfelde of the Malik publishing house, well known for publishing Georg Grosz's satirical drawings; it was also well known for its interest in established Russian writers such as Tolstoy and Gorky, and new writers such as Isaac Babel – from Odessa; more on Babel soon. Malik also publishes translations of the American writer Upton Sinclair, who was then greatly respected in Europe; Sinclair was part of the America fad, rampant in Berlin, with Brecht and George Grosz succumbing to it; Elias was hired to help Herzfelde who was planning a biography of Sinclair.[79]

Wieland knows everyone and introduces Elias to everyone right away. Elias is conscious of only being 23 and unpublished, yet finds that Berlin's radical literary scene is welcoming and receptive to anyone who is new to the city: 'it was astonishing how people treated me: not with scorn, but with curiosity, and above all, never with condemnation'. Nonetheless, Elias, still under Karl Kraus's influence, finds himself judging Berlin in the harsh spirit of Kraus in Vienna condemning with 'contempt' any sign of 'greed, selfishness, or frivolity'. Later he would realise that in Vienna all 'objects to condemn were prescribed by Kraus': 'You were not even allowed to look at them; he had already taken care of that for you and made the decision. It was a *sterilized* intellectual life that we led in Vienna, a special kind of hygiene prohibiting any intermingling whatsoever.' (Reader, I know, this was Leavisism for me in Sydney in the 1960s.) Now Elias finds that Berlin is the 'very opposite' of Kraus's Vienna, a kind of energetic, turbulent, not to say frenzied, sociability where 'contacts of any sort, incessant, were part of the very substance of living'.[80]

Unfortunately, being a Krausian devotee leads Elias into fractious encounters with Brecht. He is taken by Ibby and Herzfelde to the café Schlichter, where 'intellectual Berlin hung out'. Elias is struck by the appearance of one of its habitués, distinguished by his 'proletarian disguise', 'very emaciated', even though he was 'only thirty', looking as if he has always been old. Brecht. They sit in a circle. Brecht let on how much he despises lofty convictions, he only prizes whatever is useful. Elias spouts Kraus, intoning that a writer should 'write out of conviction and never for money'. This annoyed Brecht, who was so 'driven by his goal that it made no difference whatsoever he got money for it or not'. From then on, Brecht showers the young visitor from Vienna with 'scorn' at whatever Elias says. No sooner does Brecht come out with 'a cynical sentence' than Elias replies with a 'severe and highly moral sentence'.[81]

In full Krausian flight Elias says that a 'true writer' has to isolate himself in order to accomplish anything; Brecht replies that 'his telephone was always on his desk, and he could write only if it rang often'. Elias rails against the 'advertisements contaminating Berlin'. Brecht replies that on the contrary, 'advertisements had their good points: he had written a poem about Steyr Automobiles and been given a car for it'. Elias is repelled, these are 'words from the devil's own mouth'. Brecht was so proud of his Steyr car that he drove it into the ground; however, after an accident, 'he managed to wrangle a new one by means of an advertising trick'. There was, Elias feels, 'something Anglo-Saxon' about Brecht, 'in its American variety', Berlin at the time emulating New York 'with neon lights and cars'; there was 'nothing Brecht felt so tender about as his car'.[82]

Then, almost bafflingly, Kraus himself, he whom Elias 'venerated more than anyone else in the world', turns up in Berlin, not long before the premiere of *The Threepenny Opera*. Elias is dismayed to see that Kraus his 'god' is friendly with Brecht, indeed 'he treated Brecht with love, as though Brecht were his son, the young genius – his *chosen* son'. Elias observes that Kraus's demeanor in the circle of Berlin writers is quiet, cordial, unassertive to the point of being tentative and non-judgmental. Not only is Elias profoundly shocked, he is sure that Brecht senses his dismay, is perhaps secretly amused.[83]

There is another calamitous surprise for Elias in Brecht's Berlin. Even during what he refers to as their almost daily 'collisions', Elias was reading Brecht's *Manual of Piety*, and found himself 'enchanted by these poems', poems such as 'The Legend of the Dead Soldier', 'Against Seduction', 'Memory of Marie A.', 'Poor B.B.'.[84] Elias's sense of himself as a writer is turned inside out: 'My own writings crumbled into dust'; 'they simply no longer existed; nothing was left of them, not even shame'. He thinks back on Veza praising his poems, encouraging him to keep writing. Now, 'everything had been shattered at one blow. I had no pity for all my stuff. I swept it away with no regret: garbage and rubbish.' He continues to be repulsed by Brecht's 'compulsive disguise' and 'wooden speech': 'But I admired, I loved, his poems'.[85]

(Reader, later I will tell of a similar calamitous realisation about my teenage poetry in the Sixties.)[86]

Berlin also annihilates his Krausian contempt for Heine. He gets to know Ludwig Hardt, who gave performances reciting literary works, and was very much respected by the avant garde, including Brecht. Elias knew that Hardt and Kraus had had a falling out. Hardt and Elias both attend a party, where Hardt climbs on tables and recites. They get talking, Hardt pokes fun at Elias's disdain of Heine, then recites several Heine poems, and suddenly Elias feels his dislike of Heine crumbling, scattering: Hardt 'had struck an irreparable breach in me for Heine'. His faith in Kraus is jolted, a double blow after seeing Kraus meekly sitting next to Brecht 'who had written an advertising poem for cars'. Years later, in Vienna, Elias and Hardt become friends.[87]

Meeting Isaac Babel in Berlin also assisted in Elias's break from being a Krausian/Leavisite-like disciple. In the fragment 'Isaac Babel' Elias tells us that the two books that had made Babel famous, *Red Cavalry* and *The Odessa Tales*, had both been published in German by the Malik publishing house; Babel had come to Berlin from Paris, where he had visited his wife, a painter; even though he was returning to Russia via Berlin, Babel loved Paris and French literature, especially Maupassant as his 'true master' in the short-story form; Gorky had 'discovered Babel and watched over him'. Babel felt an outsider to Berlin, with its frenetic social life centred around the 'lives of celebrities', whose 'peacock ways' did not interest him 'more than other lives, perhaps even less'. Babel is drawn to Elias, who also feels an outsider to Berlin in the same way; Babel was 'very curious', as a writer he wanted to see and study all kinds of people, 'not those who hung out in the artists' restaurants' like the Schlichter. Babel's favourite place was Aschinger's restaurant, and there Elias and he would go, standing side by side 'eating a pea soup'. At Aschinger's Babel looked around at everyone with a kind of calm intensity: 'He rejected nothing when seeing, for he felt equally serious about everything'.[88]

They talk about literature. Babel likes Stendahl as well as Maupassant, and he prefers Maupassant to Chekhov; also, to Elias's delight, Babel admires Gogol, who Elias 'loved more than anything'. Babel says that French literature lacks a Gogol; then he reflects for a moment, and adds that on the other hand the Russians don't have a Stendahl. Elias feels that Babel came to mean more to him than anyone else he met in Berlin.[89]

In the final Berlin fragment 'Escape' Elias reflects on his three months stay. He confesses that he felt tempted to stay in Berlin, but increasingly he feels repelled: 'You moved in a chaos, but it seemed immeasurable'; there was a frenetic desire for whatever was new. The reigning aesthetic philosophy, which succeeded the 'long and drawn-out shrieks of Expressionism', was the *Neue Sachlichkeit* ('New Thingness'): 'Things floated like corpses in the chaos, and human beings became things'.[90]

During his last two weeks in Berlin, Elias sees Babel every day, learning from the older writer (Babel was 11 years his senior) to study humanity in all its variety, without judging, without condemning, without claiming a superior morality. He realises how much Babel's gaze on the world is preferable to how he had been taught by Kraus: 'I learned how wretched judging and condemning are as ends in themselves'. He now knows that his 'lengthy apprenticeship' as a disciple of Kraus is over.[91]

5 October 2015: a strange thing occurred last night when Ann and I were watching an episode on DVD of the Italian crime series, *Inspector Soneri: Fog and Crimes 3*, set not in Ferrara like the earlier two series, but in Turin. There is an enigmatic exchange involving Kraus in the episode entitled *The Secret Room* (*La Stanza Segreta*). Soneri's ex-partner Angela has been framed for the murder of a rather unsavoury character, Rino Pellizzi, who had used a modelling agency he co-owns to blackmail people. Soneri interviews the other owner, Signora Santapaola, who presents herself as a respectable businesswoman. At one point in the interview – to be precise, at 31 minutes, 56 seconds – Signora Santapaola, talking of how she is coping with the death of her business partner, quotes a saying, 'keeping busy eases pain'. Soneri asks, 'who said that, Tiziano Ferro'? No, says the Signora, it was 'Karl Kraus'. Soneri looks doubtful, implying it was a banal proverb that could have been said or sung by a popular singer like Ferro, not the savage satirist Kraus. Soneri (rightly) doubts her façade of respectability, wonders if she was complicit in Pellizzi's blackmailing sideline,

involving a secret room where he videos respectable men with teenage prostitutes, unmasking respectability being a motif deep in the detective and crime genre.

Ann and I look at each other, wondering if Signora Santapaola had really said 'Karl Kraus'. After watching the episode, wizard Ann tracks back and finds the exchange, which we watch again in slow motion, while I take notes.

I'll now move on to Isaac Babel.

Isaac Babel's Odessa, and a Green Dress

Beside their shared detachment as outsiders to Berlin, Elias Canetti is drawn to Babel for another reason, one that involves his Balkan upbringing. Thinking about the 'colorfulness, wildness, and energy' of Babel's Odessa stories reminds him that he 'had heard about Odessa as a child'; they bring back childhood memories of the Black Sea.[92]

I'm keen to read Babel's Odessa stories, and purchase from Gleebooks *The Collected Stories of Isaac Babel* (2002), edited by his daughter Nathalie Babel, translated by Peter Constantine, introduced by the American critic and writer Cynthia Ozick.[93]

The back cover tells us he was born in Odessa in 1894 and was killed by Stalin's secret police in 1940. In her introduction Cynthia Ozick ranks Babel with Kafka, each inventing a distinctive type of literary modernism. Ozick provides biographical background information. Babel's family was poor, and he was brought up in Odessa in the district of Moldavanka; as a child he knew Yiddish and Hebrew, but also fell in love with French, his first stories being 'composed in fluent literary French'. He welcomed the Revolution and 'zealously attached himself to the Bolshevik cause'. In 1920, as a war correspondent, he rode with the Red Calvary in their invasion of Poland, hoping to bring Communist salvation; however, he wrote in his diary, the men looted and murdered prisoners, despite he and the military commander begging them not to. Six years later, Babel's *Red Cavalry* stories made him instantly famous. However, with Stalin's rise to power in 1924, the literary and artistic ferment of the immediate post – revolutionary years had begun to ebb; Babel's wife Evgenia, who he had married in 1919, emigrated to Paris, where their daughter Nathalie was born in 1929. In Paris in 1935 he attended a Communist-sponsored International Congress of Writers for the Defense of Culture and Peace; this was to be the last occasion he met with his wife and daughter.[94]

In her Preface, Nathalie Babel adds more biographical details concerning his arrest and death. Babel was detained in Moscow on 15 May 1939; his lodgings were searched and his correspondence, drafts and manuscripts were confiscated; none of it has ever resurfaced. His trial took place on 26 January 1940, in one of Lavrenti Beria's private chambers. He was shot the next day and his body thrown into a communal grave. In 1954 Babel was rehabilitated. Much of this information came to light only in the 1990s when access to the KGB's archive on Babel became possible.[95]

Concerning Babel's rehabilitation in the early 1950s, we learn from the chronology at the end of the volume that Stalin died on 5 March 1953; on 23 December 1954, Babel was officially exonerated; in 1956, Nikita Krushchev denounced Stalin at the 20th Party Congress in February 1956.[96] In these terms, Babel's rehabilitation was part of a post-Stalin thaw that culminated in Krushchev's denunciation of Stalin.

I've read the Odessa stories now. I'm delighted by them, I agree with Elias Canetti about their 'colorfulness, wildness, and energy.'[97] A curious initial thought occurs to me about my uncle Jock once saying to me that in Odessa there were Jewish gangsters; now I wonder if his knowledge came through reading Babel's stories, indeed, if everyone's knowledge of the Jewish gangsters of Odessa came through reading Babel. And that is no bad thing!

What follows are a few idiosyncratic observations of what

interests me in the stories. After reading them through, I see there is a play with time, the stories are not in chronological order, they compose themselves into a sort of mosaic of past and present, reminding me of Quentin Tarantino's brilliant 1990s surrealist film *Pulp Fiction*. In terms of time, then, the stories reveal no interest in realism (which I always find boring); the stories remind me of carnival in early modern Europe, relishing a kind of poetics of the grotesque body which Russian critic Mikhail Bakhtin, also writing from the 1920s, evokes in his *Rabelais and His World* (which I copiously drew on for my book *Postmodernism and Popular Culture*), bodies broken, misshapen, shattered; bodies creating, destroying; and as in the art and festivity of early modern Europe, relations are turned Upside Down and inside out, creating a chaos of values.

Indeed, thankfully, I can't detect realism anywhere. In the story 'Lyubka the Cossack', nickname for the formidable Jewish innkeeper Lyubka Shneiweis, we can enjoy some of Babel's remarkable painterly prose, an evocation of midday heat:

> The sun hung from the sky like the pink tongue of a thirsty dog, the immense sea rolled far away to Peresip, and the masts of distant ships swayed on the emerald water of Odessa Bay. The day sat in an ornate boat...[98]

The final surreal image here of the ornate boat reminds me of Paul Klee's famous 1923 painting 'Sindbad the Sailor'. If Klee was variously influenced by Expressionism, Cubism and Surrealism, so too, we might think, was Babel's highly visual literary language. In the story 'Sunset', I was struck by another such surreal image: 'The sun soared up into the sky and spun like a red bowl on the tip of a spear.'[99]

Elias Canetti finds Babel's Odessa interesting because as a port city 'it was open to the world', the kind of city where Elias himself feels at ease.[100] I like this, I feel at ease in port cities like Sydney, or my as it were diaspora city of origin, London. I quickly pick up on a strand of images and references in the stories which evokes Odessa as very much open to the world. Contraband from afar is abundant: 'The black cook from the *Plutarch*, which had pulled in three days before from Port Said, had smuggled in big-bellied bottles of Jamaican rum, oily Madeira, cigars from the plantations of Pierpont Morgan, and oranges from the groves of Jerusalem. This is what the foamy waves of the Odessan Sea throw onto the shore…'[101]

In 'Lyubka the Cossack', Mr Trottyburn, chief engineer of the *Plutarch*, accompanied by two sailors, one an Englishman, the other a Malay, come to Lyubka's courtyard, lugging contraband they had brought from Port Said. Mr Trottyburn unwraps his merchandise: 'cigars and delicate silks, cocaine and metal jiggers, uncut tobacco from the state of Virginia, and black wine bought on the Island of Chios'. In 'The End of the Almshouse' Odessa is referred to as 'Russia's Marseille', built on the 'site of Khadzhibei' (a footnote tells us that 'Khadzhibei was the small settlement where in 1794 Czarina Catherine II decided to build a powerful Black Sea harbour, which she then renamed Odessa').[102]

Something else interests me, a carnivalesque motif of World Upside Down shaping the stories, the inversion and reversal of usual power and status relations in festivities in early modern Europe. As in carnival, there are powerful female figures. 'Lyubka the Cossack' begins by telling us that in Lyubka Shneiweis's establishment in the Moldavanka, there is a wine cellar, an inn and an oat store; there is a dovecote for a 'hundred Kryukov and Niklayev doves', owned by Yevzel, a retired soldier with a medal, who on Sundays goes to Okhotnitskaya Square where he sells doves to 'officials from town and to the boys of the neighborhood'; also living in Lyubka's courtyard are 'Pesya-Mindl, cook and procuress, and Zudechkis the manager, a small Jew with a build and beard' like Moldavanka's Rabbi. Lyubka has a baby, Davidka, and we see the procuress Pesya-Mindl rocking its cradle, while she reads a Hasidic book, *The Miracles and Heart of Baal-Shem*. Lyubka is a shrewd businesswoman, loud, a rogue, enjoys her life, laughs at her drunken crazy customers like Mr Trottyburn and his sidekicks.[103]

Benja Krik is a figure of carnival, of reversal of power. Benya Krik is known as Benya the King, the king of Odessa's Jewish gangsters, a title which, we see in 'The King', annoys the new chief of the Czarist police who has come to Odessa and wishes to assert his authority; he tells his men that Benya Krik and his fellow gangsters must be destroyed, since 'when you have His Majesty the Czar, you can't have a King too'. The police decide to raid the wedding feast for Benya the King's sister Dvoira: more on Dvoira in a moment. However, King Benya, hearing of the police plot, decides to upstage the police chief, forestalling the raid by burning down the police station. In the Odessa of Babel's stories Benya is lord of misrule and his gangsters are carnival royalty, the 'Moldavanka aristocrats', who at the wedding were 'jammed into crimson vests, their shoulders encased in chestnut-colored jackets, and their fleshy legs bulged in sky-blue leather boots'. In 'How Things Were Done in Odessa', King Benya, dressed as both royalty and trickster, is 'wearing a chocolate jacket, cream pants, and raspberry-red half boots'. In 'The Father' every day at sunset, Benya's men, 'the kings of the Moldavanka', drive in procession to Ioska Samuelson's brothel: 'They rode in lacquered carriages and were dressed up in colorful jackets, like hummingbirds'.[104]

How did Benya become King of the gangsters? How did his sister Dvoira, desperate to marry, leave the family home so she could wed? Just as in the life of Veza Calderon, the patriarch's claim to absolute power over his family has to be bitterly contested. In 'Sunset', the family dictator Papa Krik brutally controls the lives of his two sons, Benya and Lyovka, and his daughter Dvoira, and here, I was rather astonished to see, we come to another story of a green dress, reminding us of Virginia Woolf's humiliation by her half-brother George Duckworth when she tried to wear a green dress in the evening (I talked about this in my earlier chapter 'Conscious Pariahs'). In 'Sunset' Dvoira, no longer young and suffering from 'goiter', fears she will never be married; then she hears of an elderly widower who might marry her, and she rushes off 'to wash her green dress' and hangs it in the yard to dry. Papa Krik, however, doesn't like widowers, takes the green dress and hides it in his cart, then goes to work. 'Dvoira heated up the flat iron so that she could press her dress, but the dress was nowhere to be found, and Dvoira threw herself on the ground and had a fit.'[105]

The brothers Benya and Lyovka so resent their father's tyranny that they decide to kill him, but are wary of his violence and strength. They say to their sister: 'This evening, if you see the old man has killed us, then go right up to him and smash his head in with your iron colander.' Dvoira joyfully agrees, and as it turns out, the father during the fight does get the upper hand and brutally bashes his sons, until she smashes 'her father's head with the heavy iron colander'. The old patriarch is defeated, and some months later Benya, now free to exercise his considerable leadership skills, becomes King of the gangsters.[106]

What happened to the Odessa world of gangsters and the whole traditional Jewish life in the city? The coming of centralised military and bureaucratic control from far-away Moscow is what happened. The stories date the destruction from 1919. 'Froim Grach' charts what occurs when Benya Krik contests the authority of the new Soviet order, perhaps hoping to preserve their independence. As explained in a footnote, the 'counterrevolutionary army (the Whites)' fought the Bolshevik forces in southern Russia and Ukraine from 1918 to 1920. 'Froim Grach' begins by relating that in 1919 Benya Krik's men ambush the rear guard of the

White Army, 'slit all the officers' throats, and captured part of their supply unit'. As a reward, they demand that the 'Odessa soviet allow them three days of "peaceful insurrection"'. I'm not sure what that means but in any case the local soviet does not give them permission; in reply, Benya's men loot all the stores 'lining the Alexandrovsky Boulevard'. The soviet effects its own reply: 'Within a month Benya Krik's men were being lined up and shot.' The Odessa branch of the Cheka, later to become the KGB, have got to work.[107]

Froim Gach, a 'one-eyed' old carter known to be a leading gangster with Benya Krik, perhaps even more important than Benya, goes to see the Cheka and asks them not to kill any more of the gang. Old Froim assumes that the Cheka can be bought off as the former Czarist functionaries could be. He says to the Cheka leader Vladislav Simen, 'who had come from Moscow': 'Let my boys go, boss! Just name your price!' He is taken outside and shot with 10 bullets by Red Army men. Borovoi, one of the local Cheka men, is upset, telling Simen: 'you're not an Odessan, you can't understand what the old man represented.' Simen reminds Borovoi that 'now we are the power, the state power! You must remember that!' In any case, Simen continues, people like Froim Gach would have been of no use 'to the society we are building'. Borovoi will continue to work for the Cheka, but knows that the death of the old rogue represents the death of a whole way of life. The following story, 'The End of the Almshouse', also evokes the ruthlessness of the new order, where some in the city are advantaged, while others, 'the retired cantors, wedding jesters, circumcision-feast cooks, and washed-up sales clerks', are rendered surplus to requirements.[108]

Fragments

I'm pondering what Elias Canetti tells us in *The Torch in My Ear* of the importance to Veza of the characters created in the books she read, that in Veza he 'met a person who had found characters in great literature and inserted them for her own multiplicity': 'She had implanted them in herself, they thrived in her. And whenever she wanted them, they were available.' For Elias it was an 'exciting spectacle' watching Veza 'slowly move among her characters'.[109] I realise now how widespread in modern thought attempting to understand the world through characters has been and continues to be, that characters have a kind of philosophical or epistemological or hermeneutic resonance; and by characters we can understand not only so-called realist characters, but all sorts of cultural, mythological and fantasy figures. After all, I think, Ann and I shape our *Is History Fiction?* around particular historians conceived as characters; in our Introduction we say how much we agree with Edward Said in *Orientalism* telling his readers that, in contrast to Foucault, he focusses on the contribution to the making of ideas and discourses of particular intellectual personalities; this, we said, will also be our working method, where particular historians become something like characters in a historical novel, or figures in a tapestry. We added that we could think of such intellectual personalities in the way that the philosophers Deleuze and Guattari in *What is Philosophy?* have considered philosophers in history as 'conceptual personae' or 'thought figures', or the ways Hannah Arendt in *Men in Dark Times* discussed thinkers in terms of biography, anecdote, vignette and social genealogy. And in a footnote we acknowledged that Ned Curthoys had got us thinking about conceptual personae in terms of Deleuze and Guattari, and Hannah Arendt.[110]

Thinking about the world through characters occurs often in Walter Benjamin and Hannah Arendt's writings. Benjamin was certainly interested in such a working method, his essay 'Karl Kraus' analysing the Viennese satirist in terms of figures such as Cosmic Man, Demon, and Monster.[111] Arendt in turn analysed her friend Walter Benjamin in terms of characters. In her beautiful introductory essay to Benjamin's *Illuminations* Arendt suggests that it might be helpful to try and understand his enigmatic sensibility through the folk figure of the Hunchback who always brings misfortune; the *flâneur* to whom things reveal their secret meaning as he aimlessly strolls through the crowds in a big city, and Benjamin's *flâneur*, she feels, is transfigured as Klee's 'Angelus Novus' (which Benjamin owned), the angel of history; Brecht as friend, with whom he could practise 'crude thinking' (*das plumpe Denken*), perhaps Brecht as down-to-earth Sancho Panza and Benjamin as highflown theorist; Kafka as an exemplary failure in life and letters; and more: the collector; the pearl diver.[112] And Elias Canetti's three autobiographical volumes are largely structured as stories of characters conceived as intellectual personalities.

In his fragment in *The Torch in My Ear* detailing his unfortunate collisions with Brecht in Berlin, Canetti pauses for a moment to give his overall opinion of Brecht's achievements. Elias feels that Brecht's view of the world was 'somewhat monotonous', and it was 'this view that increasingly determined the character of his plays'; in his poems he 'started out far more vividly than anyone else in his day'; later, 'with the help of the Chinese', Brecht 'found his way to something like wisdom'.[113]

In his *Understanding Brecht* Benjamin gives an example of such Chinese-inspired Brechtian wisdom in his 1939 commentary on Brecht's poem 'Legend of the Origin of the Book Tao Te Ching on Lao Tzu's Way into Exile'. Benjamin writes that the quality of friendliness played a special role in Brecht's imagination. In the 'Legend' the teacher Lao Tzu, now 70 and frail, poor and with no possessions, has decided to journey, through valley and across mountain, away from where he has lived, where kindness no longer prevails and malice is once again on the increase. He and the boy who leads the ox on which the sage sits encounter a friendly customs official, and Lao Tsu writes down for him, over seven days, 81 maxims. Benjamin comments that the wise man's wisdom would never have been extracted from him if it had not been for the factor of friendliness, that friendliness does not consist in doing small things casually, but in doing the very greatest things as though they were the smallest, and that what we also learn about friendliness is that it 'does not abolish the distance between human beings but brings that distance to life'.[114]

Elias Canetti's mother Mathilde Canetti coming from a Livorno family reminds me of a passage in Yotam Ottolenghi and Sami Tamimi's *Jerusalem: A Cookbook* (2012), when they talk of a Libyan-Jewish dish in Tripoli of fish cooked in a spicy tomato sauce:

> Claudia Roden tells of the Jews of Livorno, Italy, and a similar traditional dish of a whole fish cooked in sweet tomato sauce. The Marranos, Jews from Portugal and Spain who arrived in Italy in the seventeenth century, were among the first to introduce tomatoes to Italy and, as many of the Livornese Jewish merchants maintained a presence throughout the Mediterranean, Tripoli included, it is likely that these culinary traditions traveled with them.[115]

In *The Book of Jewish Food: An Odyssey from Samarkand and Vilna to the Present Day* (1997), Claudia Roden tells us that in the sixteenth and seventeenth centuries, Jewish merchants, many of whom were Sephardim and Marranos from Spain and Portugal, pursued maritime commerce in Italian cities such as Ancona, Ferrara, Livorno and Venice, trading with their relatives and coreligionists around the Mediterranean: 'Through these contacts they introduced New World food products such as tomatoes, pumpkin, potatoes, corn and haricot beans, the seeds and plants brought back to Spain and Portugal from South America by the Conquistadors'. The 'most glorious community was that of

Livorno'. There was also a 'curious gastronomic link' between Livorno and nineteenth-century London, a cookbook entitled *The Jewish Manual*, published in 1846, its author assumed to be Lady Judith Montefiore, including 'many recipes very similar to those cooked in Livorno today'. The family of Lady Judith's husband, Sir Moses Montefiore, came from Livorno. Claudia Roden adds that London Jewish high society at the time was 'dominated by families of Marrano and Sephardi origin', and 'Italian, Spanish and Portuguese dishes were much in evidence on the grander tables'.[116]

Near the end of Canetti's third volume, *The Play of the Eyes*, concerning the years 1931 to 1937, in the fragment 'The Spanish Civil War', Elias reports on conversations during this stressful time in world history with an older friend of his, the somewhat enigmatic Dr Sonne, who has a profound knowledge of the 'centuries-long war between Christianity and Islam, of the Moorish period and the Reconquista', and is acquainted with the three key languages of Spanish, Arabic and Hebrew. Sonne urges his young friend to recover and embrace medieval Moorish Spain as fully part of his cultural heritage. Elias realises that his very upbringing in a Ladino-speaking community had held him back from such knowledge; he thinks of the 'arrogance of my family' who claimed a right to all things Spanish only as a way of asserting their caste pride, so they could 'feel superior to other Jews'. He realises that his mother, who shared this caste pride, while she was 'well read in all the literatures of Europe', had shown no interest in introducing him to Spanish literature; indeed, she 'knew next to nothing of Spanish literature', even though she had 'seen plays by Calderón at the Burgtheater'. His mother regarded Spanish as the inherited spoken language of the Sephardi community, which is how, he ponders, he was brought up, in the Ladino 'songs and sayings of my childhood'. Now, at the age of 30, influenced by Dr Sonne who translates medieval Sephardi/Hebrew and Moorish poetry for him, he views Ladino culture 'with respect'; he now feels entrenched in his Spanish past, and is determined never to lose its language; when he (with Veza) 'had to leave Vienna shortly thereafter', he takes Spanish with him into exile.[117]

A note here on the death of Ida Rubinstein's friend Lord Moyne: Walter Edward Guinness, 1st Lord Moyne, was born 29 March 1880 into a wealthy Anglo-Irish family. Lord Moyne's name suggests interesting intersecting histories, including Diana Mitford in one direction, Zionism and Israel in another.

A businessman and politician close to power, friend of Winston Churchill, Lord Moyne in 1939, from the outbreak of war, sought the internment of Diana Mosley, an elder sister of Jessica Mitford. Diana was his former daughter-in-law, who had left his son Bryan in 1932; in Berlin in 1936 she remarried, her new husband the British fascist leader Sir Oswald Mosley, with Hitler and Goebbels as witnesses. Winston Churchill became prime minister on 10 May 1940. Under pressure from Lord Moyne, the British government interned Diana Mosley in June 1940.

Lord Moyne served as the British minister of state in the Middle East until 6 November 1944, when he was assassinated in Cairo by Zionist terrorists of the LEHI group (Stern Gang); one of its leaders was Yitzhak Shamir, who plotted the assassinations both of Lord Moyne and, in 1948, Count Folke Bernadotte.[118] In *The Fateful Triangle: The United States, Israel and the Palestinians* (1983), Noam Chomsky writes that the Zionist movement, like other nationalist movements, perpetrated terror in support of its aims; once established, the Israeli state honoured the perpetrators as heroes, including the murderers of Lord Moyne.[119] In 1975 Egypt returned the bodies of the two LEHI assassins, Ben Zuri and Hakim, to Israel in exchange for 20 prisoners from Gaza and Sinai; they were laid in state in the Jerusalem Hall of Heroism, where they were viewed by prominent politicians of the day, including Prime Minister Yitzhak Rabin; Ben Zuri and Hakim were re-interred in the military section of Mount Herzl in a state funeral with full military honours. Britain lodged a formal protest, but Israel replied that Ben Zuri and Hakim were heroic freedom fighters.[120]

In 1936 in Paris Walter Benjamin was enjoying reading Heine, his biographers Howard Eiland and Michael W Jennings report. Benjamin knew that he was distantly related to Heine, and there were parallels between their lives. Heine was banished from Germany after his enthusiastic support for the revolutions of 1830; he then moved to Paris, and from 1832 served as the Paris correspondent for the *Augsburger Allgemeine Zeitung*, then the newspaper with the largest readership in Germany; the series of letters he wrote mixed commentary on the July Monarchy in France with scathing observations on political repression at home; the letters appeared in book form under the title *Französische Zustände* (Conditions in France), and were immediately banned in Prussia and Austria; Benjamin was particularly interested in the ways Heine had raised journalistic commentary to the level of art.[121]

8 October 2015: Gleebooks has just rung to say that Veza Canetti's novel *The Tortoises* has come in. I promise to pick it up in the morning. If it concerns Kristallnacht, it might very well be relevant to what my mother might have been feeling in the latter 1930s.

I've just got it from Gleebooks and brought it home. I see that it was unpublished in her lifetime; it was first published in 2001. All I've had time to read so far is the first short paragraph: 'Eva, going up the hill, kept her head down. She fixed her gaze firmly on the earth, as if she were searching the ground. She was walking very slowly.'[122]

Sunday 10 January 2016 was a beautiful Sydney day. Ann and I attended the 100th birthday party of my uncle Jock Levy at the Montefiore Home in leafy Hunter's Hill; I recall going there to see my grandfather many years before. It was a happy and heartwarming occasion, full of Jock's relatives and old friends, and I was very pleased to meet up again with my cousins Brett and Gregg, Jock's sons, and also have a chance to chat with Norma Disher, at 93 still going strong as she told Ann and me; indeed, she is a remarkable lady, with a lifetime's memory of Sydney radical theatre and film, including knowing Jock after World War II in New Theatre and then launching with Jock and their friend Keith Gow the Waterside Workers Film Unit. She reminded us that she had met Ann and me three or four years before at the Glebe Society, when Ann gave a talk on 'radical Glebe', and we said yes, yes, we remember that well. We enjoyed knowing that she also lived in Glebe, for a very long time, we are fellow Glebeites. I wanted to ask her a particular question: if my mother in the late 1930s help found the Jewish Youth Theatre, and Jock and Lew acted and produced plays and readings for it, what did my mother do? Norma suggested, what we already suspected, that my mother may have helped backstage with the costumes, drawing on her skill in sewing she'd practised in her factory work. We agreed that we must catch up in Glebe; Norma is in the Glebe Society work group that looks after the habitat in Glebe for the blue wren.[123]

It was also a pleasure to chat with my cousin Sandra Levy, daughter of Lew Levy and her mother Anne; Sandra had created and produced *Palace of Dreams*, a TV series inspired by her Russian Jewish family on Anne's side. I said I was writing an autobiography and had written a chapter, the present one, where I reflect on Jock once telling me that my aunts Anne and Jeannette's family histories originated in Odessa. No, no, no, Sandra exclaimed, the family came from Minsk, a history that fascinated her, and she has visited New York where the family had gone and found verifying documents, which she could show me; she had never heard any story about the family having a connection to Odessa. I said of course you must be right, it's Minsk, yet I'm still sure Jock had mentioned Odessa and I particularly remembered the story because he talked about Odessa's Jewish gangsters.

Later, I thought, when we got home, perhaps Jock had told me that the family had passed through Odessa, not that they had originated there. From googling, it appears that generally Russian Jews from the 1880s had moved westward to European port cities like Bremen and Hamburg in order to embark for the United States in particular. Could any have moved southwards to Odessa, I wondered. Sandra graciously said how much family stories can differ.

Sandra since that occasion has shown me documents she has researched across the world showing the Minsk family's journeys from Minsk into diaspora, including a memoir essay, 'My Early Years', written by Charles Bogin in 1974, who had migrated from Minsk to New York. The captivating detail of his childhood memories of growing up in the Jewish quarter of Minsk reminded me of my uncles Jock and Lew's memories of their childhood life in the East End of London in the early twentieth century, before they migrated to Sydney, that I included in my *1492: The Poetics of Diaspora*.

Yet I'm not displeased that Jock's anecdote moved me to create an intellectual and cultural journey from London to Odessa. And there must have been something about Odessa that stirred Jock's interest; as Ann says, family stories, even if wrong, always mean something, and that something can be very interesting.

Jewish Culture as co-creator of Modernism and Modernity 303

1. Isaac Deutscher, *The Non-Jewish Jew and other Essays*, edited and with an Introduction by Tamara Deutscher (Merlin Press, London, 1981), 'Marc Chagall and the Jewish Imagination', pp.153–5.
2. Deutscher, 'Marc Chagall and the Jewish Imagination', pp.155–9, 161.
3. Deutscher, 'Marc Chagall and the Jewish Imagination', p.158.
4. Deutscher, 'Marc Chagall and the Jewish Imagination', pp.159–160.
5. Deutscher, 'Marc Chagall and the Jewish Imagination', pp.161–2.
6. Ned Curthoys, *The Legacy of Liberal Judaism* (Berghahn, New York and Oxford, 2013), pp.54–5.
7. Deutscher, 'Marc Chagall and the Jewish Imagination', pp.160–161.
8. Deutscher, 'Marc Chagall and the Jewish Imagination', p.162.
9. Vicki Woolf, *Dancing in the Vortex: The Story of Ida Rubinstein* (Routledge, New York and London, 2000)
10. Vicki Woolf, *Dancing in the Vortex: The Story of Ida Rubinstein*, pp.3–5, 157.
11. Vicki Woolf, *Dancing in the Vortex: The Story of Ida Rubinstein*, pp.6, 8, 10, 12–14, 159.
12. Vicki Woolf, *Dancing in the Vortex: The Story of Ida Rubinstein*, pp.15–17, 33–4.
13. John Docker, *The Nervous Nineties: Australian Cultural Life in the 1890s* (Oxford University Press, Melbourne, 1991), pp.21–3, 25 note 9.
14. Vicki Woolf, *Dancing in the Vortex: The Story of Ida Rubinstein*, pp.18–19, 23–6, 29.
15. Vicki Woolf, *Dancing in the Vortex: The Story of Ida Rubinstein*, pp.30–1.
16. Vicki Woolf, *Dancing in the Vortex: The Story of Ida Rubinstein*, pp.31, 36, 38–43.
17. Vicki Woolf, *Dancing in the Vortex: The Story of Ida Rubinstein*, p.43.
18. Vicki Woolf, *Dancing in the Vortex: The Story of Ida Rubinstein*, pp.46, 48, 159.
19. Vicki Woolf, *Dancing in the Vortex: The Story of Ida Rubinstein*, pp.44–7, 161.
20. Vicki Woolf, *Dancing in the Vortex: The Story of Ida Rubinstein*, pp.160, 162, 170.
21. Vicki Woolf, *Dancing in the Vortex: The Story of Ida Rubinstein*, pp.163–5.
22. Vicki Woolf, *Dancing in the Vortex: The Story of Ida Rubinstein*, pp.166–9.
23. Vicki Woolf, *Dancing in the Vortex: The Story of Ida Rubinstein*, p.170.
24. Vicki Woolf, *Dancing in the Vortex: The Story of Ida Rubinstein*, pp.143, 171.
25. Vicki Woolf, *Dancing in the Vortex: The Story of Ida Rubinstein*, pp.149, 152.
26. Vicki Woolf, *Dancing in the Vortex: The Story of Ida Rubinstein*, p.153.
27. Hannah Arendt, *The Jewish Writings*, edited by Jerome Kohn and Ron H. Feldman (Schocken, New York, 2007), 'The Jew as Pariah: A Hidden Tradition', p.275.
28. See Ann Curthoys and John Docker, *Is History Fiction?* (UNSW Press, Sydney, 2010), p.112.

29 Isaac Deutscher, 'The non-Jewish Jew', pp.26-9; see also Ned Curthoys, *The Legacy of Liberal Judaism*, pp.213-214, who has a longer quotation of this beautiful passage.

30 See John Docker and Gerhard Fischer (eds), *Adventures of Identity: European Multicultural Experiences and Perspectives* (Stauffenburg Verlag, Tübingen, 2001).

31 Isaac Deutscher, 'The non-Jewish Jew', p.27.

32 Vicki Woolf, *Dancing in the Vortex: The Story of Ida Rubinstein*, pp.156-7.

33 John Docker, *Postmodernism and Popular Culture: A Cultural History* (Cambridge University Press, Melbourne, 1994), p.xviii.

34 Vicki Woolf, *Dancing in the Vortex: The Story of Ida Rubinstein*, pp.48-9.

35 Vicki Woolf, *Dancing in the Vortex: The Story of Ida Rubinstein*, pp.163-4.

36 Ned Curthoys, *The Legacy of Liberal Judaism*, chapter one, '"This Man of Our Destiny": Moses Mendelssohn, *Nathan the Wise* and the Emergence of a Liberal Jewish Ethos', pp.14-43, and chapter two, 'Diasporic Visions: The Emergence of Liberal Judaism', pp.44-65.

37 Ned Curthoys, *The Legacy of Liberal Judaism*, pp.55-6.

38 Ella Shohat, 'Staging the Quincentenary: the Middle East and the Americas', *Third Text*, 21 (1992-93), pp.95-105; *1492: The Poetics of Diaspora*, pp.208-210.

39 Docker, *1492: The Poetics of Diaspora*, pp.213-214, note 57.

40 Elias Canetti, *The Tongue Set Free* (1977; Granta, London, 2011), p.104: 'In a sort of hereditary loyalty to Turkey, where they had always been well treated, most [Balkan] Sephardim had remained Turkish subjects. However, Mother's family, who originally came from Livorno, were under Italian protection and traveled with Italian passports.' In relation to Turkey, Elias recalls (p.230): 'I always felt as if I came from Turkey, Grandfather had grown up there, Father was born there. In my native city, there were many Turks, everyone at home understood and spoke their language… To all this were joined the tales of earliest days: how the Turkish sultan had invited us to live in Turkey when we had to leave Spain, how well the Turks had treated us ever since.'

41 Elias Canetti, *The Torch in My Ear* (1980; Granta, London, 2011), p.81.

42 Elias Canetti, *The Tongue Set Free*, p.107.

43 Elias Canetti, *The Tongue Set Free*, p.57.

44 Elias Canetti, *The Tongue Set Free*, p.204.

45 Elias Canetti, *The Tongue Set Free*, pp.4-6, 53.

46 Elias Canetti, *The Tongue Set Free*, pp.32-3, 41-2, 62, 95-6, 220.

47 Elias Canetti, *The Tongue Set Free*, pp.39-41.

48 Elias Canetti, *The Tongue Set Free*, pp.41-2, 50, 65, 67, 70, 73.

49 Elias Canetti, *The Tongue Set Free*, pp.85-7.

50 Ned Curthoys, *The Legacy of Liberal Judaism*, pp.23-34.

Jewish Culture as co-creator of Modernism and Modernity   305

51 Elias Canetti, *The Tongue Set Free*, pp.94, 201, 216–7.
52 Elias Canetti, *The Tongue Set Free*, p.89.
53 Elias Canetti, *The Tongue Set Free*, pp.90–92, 154–5, 157–8, 260.
54 Elias Canetti, *The Tongue Set Free*, p.158.
55 Hannah Arendt, *The Jewish Writings*, pp.317–328.
56 Elias Canetti, *The Tongue Set Free*, pp.123, 159.
57 Elias Canetti, *The Tongue Set Free*, p.220.
58 Elias Canetti, *The Torch in My Ear* (1980; Granta, London, 2011), pp.57, 65–6.
59 Elias Canetti, *The Torch in My Ear*, pp.67–70.
60 Elias Canetti, *The Torch in My Ear*, pp.68–73.
61 Elias Canetti, *The Torch in My Ear*, p.71.
62 See John Docker, 'A Space for Self-Fashioning: An Antipodean Red-Diaper Baby Goes to University in the Sixties', in Dee Michell, Jacqueline Z. Wilson and Verity Archer (eds), *Bread and Roses: Voices of Australian Academics from the Working Class* (Sense Publishers, Rotterdam/Boston/Taipei, 2015), pp.57–67.
63 Julian Preece, *The Rediscovered Writings of Veza Canetti: Out of the Shadows of a Husband* (Camden House, New York, 2007).
64 Preece, *The Rediscovered Writings of Veza Canetti*, pp.5, 12, 17, 48, 52.
65 Preece, *The Rediscovered Writings of Veza Canetti*, pp.3–5, 7–8, 26–7, 39, 42.
66 Preece, *The Rediscovered Writings of Veza Canetti*, p.52.
67 Preece, *The Rediscovered Writings of Veza Canetti*, p.166.
68 Elias Canetti, *The Torch in My Ear*, pp.124–5, 127.
69 Elias Canetti, *The Torch in My Ear*, pp.127–131, 135–136.
70 Elias Canetti, *The Torch in My Ear*, pp.155, 157–8.
71 Elias Canetti, *The Torch in My Ear*, pp.158–159.
72 Elias Canetti, *The Torch in My Ear*, pp.159–160.
73 Elias Canetti, *The Torch in My Ear*, pp.160–1.
74 Elias Canetti, *The Torch in My Ear*, p.216.
75 Elias Canetti, *The Torch in My Ear*, pp.216–7.
76 Elias Canetti, *The Torch in My Ear*, pp.218–9.
77 Elias Canetti, *The Torch in My Ear*, p.220.
78 Elias Canetti, *The Torch in My Ear*, pp.219, 246.
79 Elias Canetti, *The Torch in My Ear*, pp.261–3, 267–8.
80 Elias Canetti, *The Torch in My Ear*, pp.268–9.
81 Elias Canetti, *The Torch in My Ear*, pp.272–5.
82 Elias Canetti, *The Torch in My Ear*, pp.273–7.

83 Elias Canetti, *The Torch in My Ear*, pp.277-8.

84 See Bertolt Brecht, *Selected Poems*, translated and introduced by H.R. Hays (Harcourt Brace Jovanovich, New York, 1947), *Hauspostille*.

85 Elias Canetti, *The Torch in My Ear*, p.275.

86 Cf. John Docker, 'A Space for Self-Fashioning: An Antipodean Red-Diaper Baby Goes to University in the Sixties', p.64.

87 Elias Canetti, *The Torch in My Ear*, pp.294, 298-9.

88 Elias Canetti, *The Torch in My Ear*, pp.286, 289, 291.

89 Elias Canetti, *The Torch in My Ear*, pp.292-3.

90 Elias Canetti, *The Torch in My Ear*, pp.308-9.

91 Elias Canetti, *The Torch in My Ear*, pp.312-3.

92 Elias Canetti, *The Torch in My Ear*, pp.286-7.

93 Isaac Babel, *The Collected Stories* (W.W. Norton and Company, New York and London, 2002), 'The Odessa Stories', pp.129-195.

94 Isaac Babel, *The Collected Stories*, Introduction by Cynthia Ozick, pp.11-15.

95 Isaac Babel, *The Collected Stories*, Preface by Nathalie Babel, pp.20, 24.

96 Isaac Babel, *The Collected Stories*, 'Isaac Emmanuelovich Babel, a Chronology', by Gregory Freidin, p.500.

97 Elias Canetti, *The Torch in My Ear*, p.286.

98 Isaac Babel, *The Collected Stories*, pp.155, 157.

99 Isaac Babel, *The Collected Stories*, p.189.

100 Elias Canetti, *The Torch in My Ear*, p.287.

101 Isaac Babel, *The Collected Stories*, pp.136-7.

102 Isaac Babel, *The Collected Stories*, pp.158, 183.

103 Isaac Babel, *The Collected Stories*, pp.155, 159.

104 Isaac Babel, *The Collected Stories*, pp.134, 137, 151, 162.

105 Isaac Babel, *The Collected Stories*, p.186.

106 Isaac Babel, *The Collected Stories*, pp.186, 190.

107 Isaac Babel, *The Collected Stories*, pp.170-1. Concerning the Cheka, see Sheila Fitzpatrick, *The Russian Revolution*, new edition (Oxford University Press, Oxford, 2008), pp.76-8.

108 Isaac Babel, *The Collected Stories*, pp.171-5, 184.

109 Elias Canetti, *The Torch in My Ear*, pp.160-1.

110 Ann Curthoys and John Docker, *Is History Fiction?* (University of Michigan Press, Ann Arbor, 2010), Introduction, p.10, and p.239, note 19, referencing Ned Curthoys, 'Hannah Arendt and the Politics of Narrative', *JNT: Journal of Narrative Theory*, vol.32, no.3, 2002, pp.348-70, at 349; Gilles Deleuze and

Felix Guattari, *What is Philosophy?* Translated by Graham Burchell and Hugh Tomlinson (Verso, London, 1999), p.73; Hannah Arendt, *Men in Dark Times* (Jonathan Cape, London, 1970).

111 Walter Benjamin, *Reflections: Essays, Aphorisms, Autobiographical Writings*, edited and introduced by Peter Demetz (Schocken Books, New York, 1978), pp.239–273.

112 Walter Benjamin, *Illuminations*, introduction by Hannah Arendt (1968; Schocken Books, New York, 2007), pp.6–7, 12–13, 15, 45.

113 Elias Canetti, *The Torch in My Ear*, p.274.

114 Walter Benjamin, *Understanding Brecht*, translated by Ann Bostock (Verso, London, 1983), pp.70–74; John Docker and Subhash Jaireth, 'Introduction: Benjamin and Bakhtin – Vision and Visuality', *JNT: Journal of Narrative Theory*, vol.33, no.1, 2003, pp.10–11.

115 Yotam Ottolenghi and Sami Tamimi, *Jerusalem; A Cookbook* (Ten Speed Press, Berkeley, 2012), p.234.

116 Claudia Roden, *The Book of Jewish Food: An Odyssey from Samarkand and Vilna to the Present Day* (Penguin, London and New York, 1997), pp.415–6.

117 Elias Canetti, *The Play of the Eyes* (Granta, London, 1986), pp.292–7.

118 Lawrence Joffe, 'Yitzhak Shamir Obituary', *The Guardian*, 2 July 2012, online.

119 Noam Chomsky, *The Fateful Triangle: The United States, Israel and the Palestinians* (Pluto, London and Sydney, 1983), pp.166, 197–8.

120 *The Times*, 6 and 7 June 1975.

121 Howard Eiland and Michael W. Jennings, *Walter Benjamin: A Critical Life* (Harvard University Press, Cambridge, Massachusetts and London, 2014), p.527.

122 Veza Canetti, *The Tortoises*, translated by Ian Mitchell (New Directions, New York, 2001), p.3.

123 See Lisa Milner, *Fighting Films: A History of the Waterside Workers' Federation Film Unit* (Pluto Press Australia, Melbourne, 2003), pp.41–2.

18

A Radical Jewish Intelligentsia in the 1930s

Theodor Herzl arrived just in time to report the first Dreyfus trial [in 1894] for a Vienna paper. He heard the rabble cry 'Death to the Jews!' and proceeded to write *The Jewish State*... Lazare likewise was an eyewitness of the Dreyfus trial... As he came face to face with the rising hatred of the mob, he realized at once that from now on he was an outcast and accepted the challenge. Alone among the champions of Dreyfus he took his place as a conscious Jew, fighting for justice in general but for the Jewish people in particular.
Hannah Arendt, 'Herzl and Lazare', 1942[1]

'Henceforth I am a pariah.'
Bernard Lazare, quoted in Arendt, 'Herzl and Lazare'[2]

The frame-story I'm drawn to for this chapter is Hannah Arendt's intense interest, developed during World War II, in the notion of 'conscious pariah', a term that she specifically traces to the late nineteenth – and early twentieth-century French Jewish thinker Bernard Lazare (1865–1903). I think the term can help me understand the Jewish youth theatre set up in Sydney during the 1930s by, among others, my uncles Lew and Jock Levy and my mother Elsie Levy; they and their friends were 'conscious pariahs' who constellated together to form an active, energetic, adventurous, out-there radical intelligentsia.

My interest in the 1930s Sydney Jewish youth theatre leads me not only to Arendt's portrait of Bernard Lazare but also to a literary figure the Sydney Jewish youth theatre discussed and performed and hoped other critical intellectuals in Sydney would be interested in and challenged by: the late nineteenth – and early twentieth-century Viennese Jewish writer Arthur Schnitzler. In particular, I talk about two of his texts, his 1900 story *Lieutenant Gustl* and his 1924 novella *Fräulein Else*. *Fräulein Else* in particular got me thinking about the dangerous – and continuing – connections in modernity between so-called sciences of the mind (neurology, psychology, psychoanalysis, psychiatry) and the state in terms of the power to institutionalise and imprison. Foucault is the major theorist of this sinister historical nexus, and I wish here to salute his insight and support it by making my own explorations.

Following Schnitzler's texts leads me to ponder anew Aeschylus' *Agamemnon*, Euripides' *Andromache*, Charlotte Perkins Gilman's 'The Yellow Wallpaper', Virginia Woolf and Leonard Woolf, and *Thelma and Louise*.

Dear Reader, if I reveal a certain degree of irritation and suspicion at the close historical relation between the state and its institutions, and those medically trained who claim absolute knowledge of the human mind, I will explain later in this ego histoire, in relation to a small experience of my own as a child in my early school years, my personal experience of IQ tests.

⚜

I've referred before to Arendt's interest in the notion of 'conscious pariah' in her 1943 and 1944 essays 'We Refugees' and 'The Jew as Pariah: A Hidden Tradition'. More recently I read for the first time her 1942 essay 'Herzl and Lazare', a kind of prequel, where Arendt suggests that Lazare, anarchist (defender of Bakunin), Dreyfusard and for a time part of the early Zionist movement, and Theodor Herzl, the formative Zionist figure, drew different conclusions from the frenzied anti-Semitism that infused and surrounded the Dreyfus trial as a signal *fin de siècle* event. Arendt suggests that both of these intellectuals, who stood apart from the religious tradition of Judaism, realised that 'the Jew had become the pariah of the modern world'. For both, Arendt feels, 'their Jewish origin had a political and national significance'; they could find 'no place for themselves in Jewry unless the Jewish people was a nation'.[3]

Here, however, Arendt writes, the similarity between Herzl and Lazare came to an end, widening into the 'great difference' which ultimately led to a personal breach when they were serving together on the executive committee of the Zionist Organization. Herzl's solution of the Jewish problem, Arendt reflects, was 'escape or deliverance in a homeland'; Herzl concluded that in the light of the Dreyfus case, the whole of the gentile world was hostile; there were 'only Jews and anti-semites'. Indeed, Arendt writes, Herzl preferred to deal with pronounced anti-Semitic gentiles, once exclaiming that 'the more anti-Semitic a man was the more he would appreciate the advantages of a Jewish exodus from Europe!' In these terms, Herzl considered that pogroms could have their value; in a footnote Arendt observes that, in relation to the notorious Kishinev pogroms in the Russian Empire in 1903, Herzl wrote to a correspondent that the Zionist movement could (in Herzl's words) 'derive some measure of advantage from the threatening calamity'.[4]

For Lazare, Arendt points out, the territorial question was secondary, and he objected to Herzl's idea that politics must be conducted from above. On the contrary, what Lazare sought was a 'mobilization' of the Jewish people 'against its foes'. Lazare looked around for 'real comrades-in-arms, whom he hoped to find among all the oppressed groups of contemporary Europe'. He realised that the 'shameful complicity of the powers in the East

European pogroms' indicated something very profound about modernity, 'the threatened collapse of all moral values under the pressure of imperialist politics'. In a footnote, Arendt draws attention to Lazare writing, in his book *The Jews in Rumania* (1902), how compromised was the moral standing of the major powers because of war, conquest and colonialism: in Lazare's scathing assessment, what can we think of 'England, who wiped out the Boers? Russia, who oppressed the Finns and Jews? France, who massacred the Annamites... and is now getting ready to butcher the Moors? Italy, who ravages in Eritrea today and in Tripoli tomorrow? Or Germany the savage executioner of the negroes?'[5] (By Annamites, Lazare is referring to the French seizure of central Vietnam in the 1880s; by Germany as 'savage executioner of the negroes' he appears to be alluding to the Herero genocide pursued by imperial Germany in south-west Africa in the late nineteenth and early twentieth century.)

In Arendt's view, while Herzl engaged in politics from above, in activities like negotiating with the Turkish sultan to try to purchase Palestine, Lazare rejected Herzl's positioning himself among an elite group of saviours. In March of 1899 he had written to Herzl that he felt obliged to resign from the Zionist Organization's executive committee because (in Lazare's words) it 'tries to direct the Jewish masses as if they were an ignorant child... That is a conception radically opposed to all my political and social opinions.' Lazare instead suggested that fighters for human freedom must be internationalists, they should seek their own people's freedom along with the freedom of all other peoples. Lazare, however, Arendt says, finding no supporters in France, chose to retreat into absolute isolation; he was perceived as an utter 'failure' and was passed over in silence by his Jewish contemporaries, only to be recovered for posterity by Catholic writers like his friend Charles Péguy. In Arendt's bitter assessment, the Catholic writers generously recognised, as his own

Jewish people did not, that 'Lazare was a great Jewish patriot as well as a great writer'.[6]

[Lazare's prescient critique of the Zionist Organization's belief – salient in the history of Political Zionism to this day – that it should direct the Jewish masses as if they were an ignorant child recalls a similar critique by Spinoza of Moses as political leader; Spinoza in *The Tractatus Theologico-Politicus* writes that in Exodus Moses infantilises the Hebrews, teaching the Hebrews how to think and act and behave in the same way as parents teach children who have not reached the age of reason.][7]

Arendt always exhibited a tenderness towards those regarded in history as failures, as we know from her introduction to *Illuminations* when she refers to both Kafka and Walter Benjamin as failures in their lives.[8] For Arendt, failures can be the most interesting of people; failures can energise new currents in history, as Lazare would do in terms of his internationalism and notion of conscious pariah: an internationalism of the conscious pariah. Her 1943 and 1944 essays 'We Refugees' and 'The Jew as Pariah: A Hidden Tradition' were inspired by Lazare's notion of the conscious pariah she so treasures in 'Herzl and Lazare', the three essays together doing much to re-establish Lazare as an influential intellectual figure, even if in 'The Jew as Pariah: A Hidden Tradition' Arendt sounds a melancholy note, that 'nothing now remains' of Lazare's heritage: 'Even his memory has faded.'[9] The three essays certainly illuminate for me the Jewish youth theatre set up in Sydney during the 1930s as continuing Lazare's defiant internationalism.

'We Refugees' values a thread of Jewish tradition, 'the tradition of Heine, Rahel Varnhagen, Sholom Aleichem, of Bernard Lazare, Franz Kafka, or even Charlie Chaplin', who prefer the status of conscious pariah, adding that all 'vaunted Jewish qualities – the "Jewish heart", humanity, humor, disinterested intelligence – are pariah qualities'.[10] Peering back into history, I would like to think that the Sydney Jewish youth theatre exhibited such élan.

In 'The Jew as Pariah: A Hidden Tradition', Arendt admires these poets, writers and artists as 'bold spirits' who tried to make of the 'emancipation of the Jews that which it really should have been – an admission of Jews *as Jews* to the ranks of humanity'. In section two of the essay, 'Bernard Lazare: The Conscious Pariah', Arendt points out that Lazare particularly objected to what he referred to as the spurious doctrine of 'assimilation', a doctrine which he considered should be actively resisted: the Jew should come out openly as a representative of the pariah, which meant openly becoming a 'rebel', since for Lazare it was the duty of every human being to resist oppression; the Jew's fight for freedom as pariah and rebel joins the fight for freedom of the downtrodden of Europe striving to achieve national and social liberation; the Jew as pariah and rebel must make himself responsible for what society has done to him.[11]

In this essay, Arendt admires those who attempted to 'weave the strands of their Jewish genius into the general texture of European life'.[12] It is in these anti-assimilationist and cosmopolitan terms, I think, we can see the young conscious pariahs and rebels of the Jewish youth theatre intervening, with their diasporic awareness of Jewish cultural and intellectual life around the world, in the general texture of Australian life.

It is their diasporic internationalism I will focus on, especially their interest in the Austrian modernist Schnitzler.

✧

I always knew that my mother Elsie Levy and her two younger brothers Lew and Jock had in the 1930s belonged to a Jewish branch of the Communist Party, and that they were involved in the creation of a Jewish youth theatre, but I couldn't remember the exact name.

Talking it over with Ann, we think there may be gender

differences here concerning Elsie and her brothers, that I'll have to try to think about. Much will have to be surmise and speculation.

In *1492: The Poetics of Diaspora*, in Lew and Jock's 'Childhood memories: reminiscences of my uncles Lew and Jock' that they recorded for me, they talk of their childhood relations with their sister, Lew reflecting: 'One memory which needs to be stressed and underlined is that you will have noted that we haven't made any reference to Elsie. But that is not because of any particular reason except this, that she was several years older than Jock and I and being a woman or rather shall I say being a girl she was more or less put to the back of our minds, because Jock and I specifically sought refuge in our own company.'[13]

My mother's education in London must have been her last formal schooling, before the family's arrival in 1926, when she was 14; she then managed – for the sake of the migrant family, to try and establish itself financially – to get paid work. Lew and Jock, younger than her, attended schools in Sydney while she worked in clothing factories whose harsh working conditions she would sometimes talk about when I was growing up, how you were watched all the time, even going to the toilet was only grudgingly allowed. It doesn't appear that the Clothing Trades Union was much help in fighting for better conditions. In his book *In Women's Hands: A History of Clothing Trades Unionism in Australia*, Bradon Ellem reflects that while the workforce was heavily female, the union for much of its life in the twentieth century was controlled by male officials, and women's skills went largely unrecognised, remaining significantly undervalued.[14]

The lives of Elsie and her two brothers were to some extent divergent; and in this chapter I will try to notice and comment on other possible divergences. For example, who, I wonder, were my mother's friends? Did she, in the latter 1920s and into the 1930s, become friendly with other young women in the clothing factories she worked in? Or in the clothing union she joined? Or in the Communist Party on joining it? How important to her were other women in her world?

One thought: did Elsie Levy read the same books as her younger brothers? From the books she left the family and which I inherited, in or from 1937 she was reading William Zukerman's *The Jew in Revolt* published in that year and she may also have been reading the essays commenting on contemporary issues that Zukerman was contributing to *Harpers Magazine* in the 1930s. Did Lew and Jock share her interest in Zukerman?

I suppose what I'm thinking is that because of age and gender differences, my mother and her brothers – three bright children of an immigrant family, producers rather than consumers, we might say, thinking of Sorel's distinction – contributed in distinctive ways, sometimes together, sometimes differently, to the creation in the 1930s of a radical Jewish intelligentsia, which also included Sydney eastern suburbs figures like Rosine Guiterman, university trained and very active in the Sydney theatrical scene. In Ann and Joy Damousi's collection *What Did You Do in the Cold War, Daddy? Personal Stories from a Troubled Time*, Ron Witton, born in 1944, the son of German Jewish refugees who had arrived in Australia in 1939, reminiscences that his parents were helped by Rosine Guiterman. He recalls that her home was opposite Old South Head cemetery and he remembers visiting it around 1949 when he was five or so years old.[15]

In preparing to write his essay for *What Did You Do in the Cold War, Daddy?* Ron became increasingly interested in Rosine Guiterman and from intensive research wrote a fascinating biographical essay (now online in *Dictionary of Sydney*, 2015).[16] Here Ron tells us that Rosine Lion, born in London in 1886, came to Australia with her family in 1893. Her schooling was interrupted by her family traveling to and from England, but she managed to matriculate and enrolled in Arts at the University of Sydney. She had a great love of Shakespeare's plays, encouraged by her mother when she was still a child. At university, her interest in Shakespeare came to the notice of Mungo MacCallum, the foundation Professor of Modern Languages and Literature, and he inspired her to a lifetime study of Shakespeare. She graduated with a BA degree in 1908; in 1911 she gained her MA in English, and also won the coveted Sydney University Prize for English verse, the first woman to do so; in the same year, Rosine set off for London, and at Colombo met David Guiterman, a businessman, who had boarded the ship there. They became engaged and would later marry in the Great Synagogue, Sydney, 10 September 1913. She became a teacher, taught English, History, French and Latin. She always shared her enthusiasm for the theatre with her students, encouraging them to stage plays.

Throughout her life, Ron records, Rosine made a significant contribution to theatre in Australia. Rosine was active in the left-wing New Theatre in Sydney which was founded in 1932. She was also prominent in more mainstream theatre. Ron notes that the *Sydney Morning Herald* in a preview of 30 April 1936 reported that for the Little Theatre on May 6 and 9, Rosine Guiterman would be producing *Richard III* in modern dress, substituting telephones for page boys and a revolver for a sword. On 21 November 1936 the *Sydney Morning Herald* reported that Rosine Guiterman would that evening be producing, at the Maccabean Hall in Sydney, Gotthold Lessing's play *Nathan the Wise*; a prologue would be spoken by Miss Amelia Lessing, a lineal descendant of Lessing's, and by Arthur Mendelssohn a descendant of Lessing's close friend Moses Mendelssohn, whose character and ideas, the *Herald* notes, are expressed in the play; the proceeds of the play were to benefit the German-Jewish Relief Fund. On 20 August 1937, the *Herald* reports that Rosine Guiterman's production of *King Lear* attracted such large audiences that the organisers decided to give another performance at Bryant's Playhouse in Forbes Street [near King's Cross].

Ron Witton's drawing attention to *Nathan the Wise* as a notable ceremonial occasion particularly interested me, not least because of Ned Curthoys' writing about *Nathan the Wise* in his *The Legacy of Liberal Judaism*.[17]

On Monday 23 November 1936, two days later, I notice the *Herald* reported on the staging of *Nathan the Wise*. Gotthold Lessing's 'great play of tolerance and dramatic plea for semitic understanding', said the *Herald*, 'was finely produced and played at the Maccabean Hall on Saturday night'. Before the curtain rose, Miss Amalia Lessing showed the audience a special German copy of her ancestor's play. The play was produced by Mrs Rosine Guiterman: 'The costumes and settings were all admirably in keeping with the oriental background, and an almost tangible atmosphere of the East seemed to be created.' Lewis Levy performed one of the leading roles. The production was in aid of the German-Jewish refugee fund as well as the 'Jewish national fund' [an international Zionist body].

On Thursday 26 November 1936, the *Hebrew Standard of Australasia* contributed further details: the cast of *Nathan the Wise* were all Jewish; before the curtain rose, Rosine Guiterman explained that the play was written because of the great appreciation that Lessing, a Christian, had for his Jewish friend Mendelsohn; Mr Arthur Mendelssohn, a descendant of Mendelssohn, was to have spoken but he was called away to Melbourne the previous day; also as an introduction to the play, Mrs H Wolfensohn sang Psalm 30 (I think it's Psalm 30, the print is unclear) in Hebrew; and for the production, Janet Solomon performed an exhibition dance.

In the early decades of the twentieth century, theatre in Australia was a diverse and very active scene, and my uncles eagerly set about contributing to it, but in ways that often stressed a distinctive Jewish contribution in the spirit of Arendt's characterisation of Bernard Lazare, universalist and internationalist.

In an essay that became part of *1492: The Poetics of Diaspora*, Lew reminisces about his life in the 1930s, including how the Jewish youth theatre came about. He relates how the family, having not been met by a fabled brother of his fantasist *Luftmensch* father Phil Levy after the family's arrival in Sydney in 1926, moved into the then working-class Sydney suburb of Paddington. Lew's first school was Paddington Junior Technical School in Oxford Street, where he stayed till sixth class; he then won a scholarship to Sydney Technical High School in Albion Street, Darlinghurst. He remembers interminable playground fights, the reasons for them being twofold, that he looked odd, forced to wear strange clothes fashioned by his mother because of their poverty rather than the regular uniform (Lew helped with the family's finances by delivering newspapers in the mornings around Rushcutters Bay and Darling Point, and after school working in a garage dispensing petrol); and that he was identified as a Jew, even though 'we weren't practicing Jews, whatever our surname implied'.[18]

Lew left school in 1932 during the depths of the Depression. With his mother Rose's support (I've always thought my grandmother's name was beautiful – Rose) he went from one interview to another in search of an apprenticeship, always unsuccessfully. The family had by then moved to Bondi; he and younger brother Jerome (I'm not sure when he became universally known as Jock) would spend the rest of the day surfing at Bondi Beach, a few minutes walk from where they lived. Bondi, Lew writes, changed their lives; it became their university. Here they joined a group of men who sat in deckchairs in the Pavilion 'talking of politics and music and books and Aboriginal rock art and Marx'. Social change was an urgent topic in the group's conversations, an interest accentuated, Lew writes, by the rise of fascism in Italy and Germany, especially Germany. They devoured books that were infused with social critique – John Reed's *Ten Days that Shook the World*, Michael Gold's *Jews Without Money* (Gold being part of *New Masses*), Upton Sinclair's *Oil*, *The Jungle*, and *Boston: The Trial of Sacco and Vanzetti*. Other authors they devoured were Dreiser, Dos Passos, Jack London, Lillian Hellman, Langston Hughes and Liam O'Flaherty.[19]

One of the group of older men, Syd Mostyn, was a bootmaker by trade, a gentle man who made elegant shoes and did shoe repairing; Mostyn had left England when young, and he had clearly read widely and deeply; at Mostyn's flat, Lew and Jock learned to appreciate the riches of music, especially Beethoven, music which sent out 'a challenge, to change the world'. They were introduced to and got to know Mostyn's partner, Bella Weiner, a dynamic speaker, fluent in Polish, Yiddish and English, who had fled Poland because of its anti-Semitism; in Poland, Bella Weiner had been a member of the Bund, but when Lew met her in Sydney in the 1930s she had become a Communist.[20] (When Ann and I lived in London in 1973–74, we took my mother, then visiting, to Hyde Park to hear the speeches; there she saw Bella Weiner and rushed over to talk to her.)

Through the Bondi Pavilion circle, a kind of proletarian intellectual sphere, they were introduced to the world of left-wing drama. A play that deeply impressed Lew with the power of theatre was *Winterset* by Maxwell Anderson, dramatising as a kind of crucifixion the execution (in 1927) of the two immigrant Italians Sacco and Vanzetti. He was also impressed by Irwin Shaw (*Bury the Dead*), John Steinbeck (*Of Mice and Men*), Albert Maltz (*Private Hicks*, *Merry Go-Round*) and Clifford Odets' *Waiting for Lefty*, *Till the Day I Die* and *Awake and Sing*.[21]

In the early 1930s Lew, Elsie and Jock joined the Communist Party. Lew and Elsie also joined the Clothing Trades Union, an 'organization unbelievably conservative'. Elsie had helped Lew get his first job, Elsie working as a machinist in a clothing factory; he went from being a general rouseabout to finally learning the trade of tailor's cutter. He always wanted, however, to become an engineer.[22]

In these reminiscences, Lew Levy tells of how the idea for a Jewish Youth Theatre came about:

> [Syd] Mostyn and [Bella] Weiner were instrumental in forming a Jewish branch of the Communist Party which included my sister Elsie, my brother Jock and the two Hyman brothers, Bizzy and Buzzy, and me. It was from this group that there emerged the idea that we should form a Jewish Youth Theatre.[23]

Lew recalls that a problem was 'the paucity of translated Jewish dramatic literature'; they performed Sholom Aleichem, I L Peretz and Israel Zangwill, but such was not enough to exclusively occupy a theatre group that wished to perform at least four plays every year; they therefore widened their choices and selected plays which could 'inspire an audience to the adoption of a socially critical view'. Their first theatrical space was a rented room in Macquarie Place, where they set about with enthusiasm and ingenuity to build a stage with the help of a resourceful carpenter; to sew curtains, and even, Lew remembers, to make their own spotlights. Bella Weiner conjured up chairs, and this and that trade union allowed them use of a Gestetner and gave them paper for it. Lew couldn't remember how it happened, but he became the producer, his only guides being Stanislavsky's *An Actor Prepares* and Nemirovich-Danchenko's *My Life in Art*. They put on 'Maxim Gorky's *Lower Depths*, Chekhov's *The Cherry Orchard*, Green's *Hymn to the Rising Sun* and a host of interesting and provocative plays'; and Jock Levy quickly began to reveal that he was a brilliant and mesmerising actor: 'He was tall, handsome, he moved easily and his voice was beautifully modulated.'[24]

Lew writes that the Jewish youth theatre years were exciting and stimulating, creating a sizeable audience, Jewish and non-Jewish; there developed close and enduring friendships and many marriages. The theatre, however, could not survive the beginning of the war; in 1940, Lew recalls, 'the men (and I was one) were called up for military service, and the women into essential industries or into military support auxiliaries. The audience dwindled.'[25]

Lew was discharged in 1941 and he and Anne married the following year; he worked extremely hard, as a fitter in an oil refinery by day and studying at night, to qualify as a professional engineer, fulfilling a dream to follow a vocation that he saw as essential and creative in serving humanity.[26]

༺ ༻

From searching Trove on the internet, that wonderful digital resource of Australian newspapers, I can reconstruct a chronology of at least some of the plays and performances that the Jewish youth theatre staged during the 1930s, from 1936 onwards; Trove charts as well the occasions Lew and Jock also participated in 1930s theatre more generally. Here I list what I found.

On Saturday 29 August 1936, the *Sydney Morning Herald* reported that members of the Jewish community have formed a Jewish Youth Theatre League, whose object, says a preliminary announcement put out by the new theatrical group quoted by the *Herald*, is 'to make known to English-speaking people' the 'tremendous amount of Jewish writing over the last century' that 'remains almost unknown', but which is articulated in theatre as 'that art-form in which the specifically Jewish mentality was so lucidly expressed'. The opening program in November 1936 would comprise Marc Arnstein's *The Eternal Song* and Pinero's *The Playgoers*; the producer was Miss Esther Hart.

On Saturday 6 March 1937, the *Sydney Morning Herald* reported that the Jewish Youth Theatre League was inviting the public to a lecture and discussion on Arthur Schnitzler on Sunday, 8 pm, in room 3, floor 4, McIlrath's Buildings, 124 Oxford Street, Darlinghurst; Schnitzler, the *Herald* added, was an important literary figure, and he should inspire an interesting and educational evening.

On Saturday 10 April 1937, the *Herald* reported that the Jewish Youth Theatre League has announced plans to stage, on 22 May, Israel Zangwill's *The Melting Pot*. On Saturday 15 May the *Herald* noted that Mr Lewis Levy would be the producer. There is no further report by the *Herald* of the performance at the Railway Institute, at least no report that I picked up while Troving.

On Saturday 21 August 1937, the *Herald* reported that Mrs Rosine Guiterman's production of *King Lear* at Bryant's Playhouse was excellent; Lewis Levy and Jerome Levy were convincing in their roles.

On Saturday 9 October 1937 the *Herald* reported that the Jewish Youth Theatre League's forthcoming program, to be held on the 3rd floor, 21 Macquarie Place, was to comprise a talk by Miss B Weiner on 'The Conditions of the Jews in Poland'; Polish Jewish folk songs would be recited; and *The Eternal Song* by Marc Arnstein would be performed.

On Monday 14 February 1938 the *Herald* reported that the Jewish Youth Theatre League would hold a debate on the subject 'That Assimilation will not solve the Jewish Problem' at the Jewish Cultural Home, 21 Macquarie Place; the public is invited to attend. By special request, Israel Zangwill's *The Melting Pot* would be revived on 20 February.

On Saturday 26 February 1938 the *Sydney Morning Herald* reported that the Jewish Youth Theatre on 3 March, at the Jewish Cultural Home, 21 Macquarie Place, would be presenting, for the first time in Australia, a complete program of translations from

Yiddish, including *After the Funeral*, by I L Peretz.

On Wednesday 11 May 1938 the *Herald* reported that the Jewish Youth Theatre League had produced the night before, at the St James Hall, *Israel in the Kitchen* by Noah Elstein, a comedy of provincial English working-class Jews, notable for its vivid women characters; the audience, said the *Herald*, derived much entertainment from the play.

On Saturday 23 July 1938 the *Herald* reported that Maxim Gorki's *The Lower Depths* was to be presented that night by the Jewish Youth Theatre at the Railway Institute.

On Saturday 3 September 1938 the *Herald* reported that *Awake and Sing* by the famous American playwright Clifford Odets, will be presented by the Jewish Youth Theatre at St James Hall, Phillip Street, on the following Saturday; the play was being produced by Mr Louis [sic] Levy.

On Monday 27 March 1939 the *Herald* reported that the Jewish Youth Theatre had on Saturday given an excellent performance of R E Sherwood's drama *The Petrified Forest*: 'As Gabby, the sophisticated young woman, and central character in the play, Miss Rae Sanders played a difficult part with success. She was ably supported by Jerome Levy, as Allan Squier, the disillusioned literary man.'

On Saturday 25 November 1939 the *Herald* reported that Mr Lewis Levy, a foundation member of the Jewish Youth Theatre, would be speaking the following evening at the Jewish Cultural Home, 173 Phillip Street, on his experiences in the cultural life of Melbourne, and of his productions there with the Kadimah younger set.

In his essay in *1492: The Poetics of Diaspora* Lew Levy writes of his stay in Melbourne in 1939, where he had gone because he remained unemployed in Sydney and felt himself a burden on the family in the precarious times of the Depression; in Melbourne he made contact with Ralph Gibson, then the Communist Party

State Secretary, who suggested that he work for the Party.

> I had a general brief to raise funds for the Party from Jewish left and liberal supporters, speak at factory gate meetings and, generally, do whatever I could to encourage the Jewish community to participate in the anti-fascist struggle. This latter I did by becoming involved in a Jewish cultural organization, the Kadimah, located in Carlton, liberal-leftist in its political orientation, in which I formed a theatre group. The Kadimah enjoyed a very wide support particularly among those Jews who had not moved from the wrong side of the tracks to St Kilda, the goal of the upwardly mobile. I remember two plays which enjoyed a wide audience, both of which I had been associated with in Sydney, Zangwill's *The Melting Pot* and [Noah Elstein's] *Israel in the Kitchen*.[27]

In Melbourne, Lew also met Rochel Holcer, a talented professional Polish actress who, with her husband, had fled Poland to join relatives in Melbourne; she gave readings, mainly in Yiddish, to enthusiastic audiences at the Kadimah, but she wished to extend her audience by learning and performing in English; Lew was asked to be her English teacher. To Lew's surprise, her first request was to learn Rudyard Kipling's 'Boots', which she transformed into a powerful anti-war statement.[28]

On Saturday 11 November 1939 the *Sydney Morning Herald* reported that the Sydney Jewish Youth Theatre will be holding a play reading the following evening at 173 Phillip Street of Ernst Toller's dramatic masterpiece *Pastor Hall*, a biting indictment of Hitler's fascism.

On Thursday 18 May 1944, under the title 'Rochel Holcer to Visit Sydney Again', the *Hebrew Standard of Australasia* reported, in an article written and signed S.M. [Syd Mostyn?], that he had been the President of the Jewish Youth Theatre, and that Holcer's repertoire was wide and varied, including Jewish and non-Jewish writings, her art nourished by Jewish history and her experiences in Cracow and Warsaw. Such, wrote S.M., was strikingly demonstrated by her rendering of Rudyard Kipling's poem, 'Boots'. S.M. approvingly noted that the *Sydney Morning Herald*, in its review, had written that Holcer transformed Kipling's half-humorous verses, suggesting the Cockney's grumbling at monotony and discomfort on the march, into an agonised cry for freedom, a fiery revolt against war and all its horrors.

༺༻

As someone trained as a Leavisite in the 1960s in 'high' English literature, I feel massively ignorant of these 1930s plays and particular literary figures and cultural histories. Also, there is nothing in the brief reference in the *Sydney Morning Herald* that indicates why in 1937 the Jewish Youth Theatre League wished to focus on Arthur Schnitzler, who gave the lecture on him, what plays and stories the lecture commented on, what was the discussion like of the lecture, and who might have been in the audience. While I cannot supply these details, what I can do, and what personally interests me to do, is to make my own readings of *Lieutenant Gustl* and *Fräulein Else*.

My method will be to explore the authors and plays that interested the Sydney Jewish Youth Theatre, using my literary critical skills.

Naturally I googled and found some preliminary information, and as well I have profited from the foreword by Margret Schaefer to *Desire and Delusion* (2003), her contemporary translations of three of Schnitzler's novellas including *Fräulein Else*.[29]

So, a portrait with broad brush strokes: Schnitzler, 1862–1931, from a medical family, was trained as a physician at the University of Vienna, and was appointed assistant doctor in the psychiatric clinic of Theodore Meynart, where Freud also trained.[30] From the

1890s onwards, Schnitzler wrote innovative plays and novellas. The relationship between Schnitzler and Freud was particularly fraught: more on this soon.

Schnitzler was a member of the avant-garde group Young Vienna (*Jung Wien*). Because of his interest in the psychosexual, he became a controversial figure, especially when his 1897 play *Reigen* or *Merry-Go-Round*, featuring 10 pairs of characters before and after a sexual encounter, was staged in Berlin and Vienna in 1920 and 1921; the play caused an anti-Semitic storm in Germany and Austria, with Schnitzler accused of being a Jewish pornographer. Nonetheless, *Reigen* was translated into French as *La Ronde* and increasingly enjoyed a long film and theatrical career, adapted to varying situations; in 1950 *Reigen* was made into a French language film by the German-born director Max Ophuls as *La Ronde*; Roger Vadim's 1964 film *Circle of Love* and Otto Schenk's 1973 *Der Reigen* are also based on the play; in 1998 David Hare reworked it for the stage as *The Blue Room*.

There is more. Discussing the collaboration of Baz Luhrmann and Nicole Kidman in helping create a camp burlesque cinematic mode in *Australia* and *Moulin Rouge!*, Laleen Jayamanne, in her wonderful book *The Epic Cinema of Kumar Shahani* (2015), a treasure of intellectual adventure, writes, in her chapter 'Shahani and Baz Luhrmann: Directing as Choreographic Act', that Luhrmann saw Kidman in the theatre production of *The Blue Room*, in which she played all the roles.[31]

In 2002 Suzanne Bachner created an adaptation called *Circle* exploring twenty-first-century sexual mores.

In 1929 *Fräulein Else* was made into the German silent film *Fräulein Else* featuring Elisabeth Bergner; in 1946 the novella was made an Argentine film, *The Naked Angel*. Margret Schaefer tells us that a dramatic version of *Fraulein Else* in English was staged in London in 1932 by T Komisarevsky, with Else's stream of consciousness turned into a monologue spoken to the audience.[32]

When I read the notice by the Jewish youth theatre of a lecture and discussion of Schnitzler, I remembered coming across his name in Hannah Arendt's *The Jewish Writings*, where, in her review of Stefan Zweig's autobiography *The World of Yesterday* (1943), Arendt writes dismissively that Zweig, ignoring 'the greatest poets of the postwar period, Franz Kafka and Bertolt Brecht', acclaimed mediocre writers like Arthur Schnitzler.[33] Yet now, I wonder if Hannah Arendt was too harsh.

Let's briefly reprise these two narratives, *Gustl* first, written in comic key.[34]

Lieutenant Gustl opens with Gustl's irritated thoughts at being at a concert in Vienna, a religious-themed oratorio, not listening to a word of the performance; he had been given a spare ticket by his friend and fellow officer Kopetzky; bored, restless, fidgety, the occasion reminds him of the tedium of a Mass; he regrets he'd come, he's desperate that it end, it's interminable. We listen in as he mulls over the recurring events of his life, his days spent running up debts playing cards with fellow officers in tavern or coffeehouse, or spending time with Steffi his favourite prostitute when she's not with a paying client, or seeking duels with anyone who in his opinion momentarily looks at him in the wrong way or voices an opinion that can be construed as attacking his honour as an imperial soldier.

We soon learn that on the next afternoon, at 4 pm, he is to cross sabres with a Doctor who had recently offended him at a party 'at the Mannheimers'. In conversation the Doctor had said something like the army practising maneuvres was just playing at war and then insultingly added that perhaps not all who joined the army did so out of patriotic motives. Gustl, who regards himself as 'usually a courteous person', recalls that he had become furious, had brushed aside an elderly gentleman who wanted things to be settled amicably, and demanded satisfaction for this attack on military honour. Gustl feels he was right to take personally the Doctor's insinuation against the army, the fellow's insolence was unbelievable, though the reader gets the impression from an aside to himself that Gustl had been thrown out of high school and that's why he was placed in a military academy. In any case, he has been assured, the 'the court of honour' sees nothing wrong in the duel with the Doctor taking place.

Gustl's thoughts then wander to the Mannheimers' party and how there were probably Jews there, though you couldn't tell because the Mannheimers were converts and the wife was 'a pretty blonde'; a little later he remembers that he would have liked to have seduced her; he also feels annoyed that so many officers are Jews, and so many in the audience appear to be Jews ('this is amazing, half of the audience are Jews... you can't even enjoy an oratorio in peace any more'). More stray anti-Semitic observations occur to Gustl, a Christian from a farming family, who he frequently calls upon to pay for his gambling debts; he remembers 'Jewish jokes on the march'. Also, maybe there were socialists at the party, maybe this Doctor was a socialist.

Calamity, however, soon occurs for the young lieutenant, not in soldierly activity but in the theatre that night. A cinematic scene unfolds.

The oratorio seems to be going on forever. Gustl looks around, becomes annoyed that a man appears to glance at him, this might have to lead to a duel, he'd settle arrangements in the foyer after the oratorio is over, if it ever is over. He whiles away some of the time being predatory, seeing if there are any young women there that he can pick up after the performance. He espies a young woman who might be by herself, a 'pretty girl' standing by 'the balustrade'; at performance end, he's impatient to get to the cloakroom for his things so he can approach her, but the cloakroom has a long queue; he tries to jump the queue, shouting for his ticket, but his clamour and pushing annoys a 'fat man' in front of him. Incomprehensibly, the large man in front tells Gustl to stop shoving, be patient and quieten down. Enraged at this insult, Gustl tells him, 'Shut up, you!' Annoyed, the large man turns around, revealing that he is a master baker Gustl knows, he goes to the same coffeehouse. The immensely strong baker grabs hold of the hilt of Gustl's sabre, he won't let go, he says to Gustl in a low voice that if Gustl makes the slightest disturbance he'll pull the Lieutenant's sabre out of its scabbard, smash it and send the pieces to his regimental headquarters: 'Do you understand, you fool?' The baker nevertheless continues in more kindly vein: 'But I don't want to ruin your career... So, behave!... There, there, don't be afraid, no one heard anything... everything's all right now... there! And so that no one thinks we had a quarrel, I'll be very friendly to you now! – Good night, Lieutenant, it was a pleasure – good night!'

For the rest of the story, after this humiliation, Gustl wanders about Vienna in an anguished daze, falls asleep in the Prater on a bench, feels he must now suicide because the baker will tell the story to his wife and family and before long it will get back to his regiment and his honour will be in tatters, he'll have to resign in disgrace: 'I'm over and done with... lose honour, lose everything!' In the morning, waking up on the bench, he wanders towards his regular coffeehouse, thinking since he's hungry, he hadn't eaten after the dreadful incident the night before, he might as well have an early breakfast and then he'll kill himself. But, very fortunately, at the coffeehouse, which is just opening, the waiter asks Gustl if he had heard the sad news? The master baker Mr Habetswallner who provides their rolls died from a stroke the night before when he reached his apartment building. Trying not to show it, Gustl feels an overwhelming joy, the baker can't tell anyone now, his honour is saved: 'I think I've never been so happy in my entire life... He's dead – he's dead! No one knows a thing, and nothing has happened!' Gustl enjoys eating the master baker's rolls that accompany his coffee, calls for a 'Trabucco cigar', and looks forward to the afternoon duel when he can run through the Doctor who had so insulted his honour at the Mannheimers' party.

I first read *Lieutenant Gustl* online, and then in print, and increasingly feel it's a brilliant work, a technical triumph of *fin de siècle* experimental art, and a scathing satirical overturning of historical traditions, both Austro-Hungarian and internationally, of masculine notions of honour.

Schnitzler, Margret Schaefer reminds us, is valued in modernist literary history for introducing into European literature interior monologue and stream of consciousness, *Lieutenant Gustl* being published some 20 years before the technique was deployed by Joyce in *Ulysses* and Virginia Woolf in *Mrs Dalloway*.[35]

For this portrait of a fairly despicable officer, Schnitzler was, so Evan Bates tells us in a prefatory note to his edition of *Great German Short Stories*, deprived of his medical officer's rank in the Austrian army.[36]

In her foreword to *Desire and Delusion*, Margret Schaefer tells us that in 1921, in his diaries, Schnitzler confided his intention to write a novella, *Fräulein Else*, in the mode of *Lieutenant Gustl*. Schaefer regards Else as 'one of the great female portraits in literature', comparable to the interior monologues of Molly in *Ulysses* and Mrs Dalloway.[37] Alongside *Lieutenant Gustl*, *Fräulein Else* constitutes I think a triumph of the modernist deployment of *Kunstchaos*, an important tradition in European literature where, in the words of P Lacoue-Labarthe and J-L Nancy in *The Literary Absolute* (1988), chaos is 'produced by art or philosophical technique'.[38]

Else, 19 years old, in the bloom of youth, is staying with her rich aunt Emma at the Hotel Fratazza in San Martino di

Castrozza, a mountain resort for the European bourgeoisie. The novella begins with a tennis scene. Else is playing with her cousin Paul and his lover Frau Cissy, though their love relationship is not admitted in public, a secretiveness that irks Else; Else leaves to walk back to the hotel, and as we listen in to her thoughts, her conversation with herself, her *Selbsdenken*, we register that she is part of the large Viennese Jewish bourgeoisie that wishes to be indistinguishably assimilated ('I'm even a blonde, a strawberry blonde'); she is pleased that she attracts admiring glances from young men; she is a virgin; she entertains daring thoughts ('One should try everything – even hashish'); and she looks forward to a life of romance. Yet she also reflects on the shadows that threaten her wellbeing and future.[39]

Early in the novella, Else looks back to when she was 13 or 14, remembering a dream, that she had been staying with her family on the Riviera: 'Marble steps going down into the sea. I'm lying naked on the marble.' While Else is taking pleasure in this sensuous memory, for the reader of European literature from classical times on there is another suggestion, of death by sacrifice. She knows how restricted her middle-class girl's upbringing has been. Her older brother Rudi was allowed to stay out at night from an early age and is now free to travel by himself wherever he likes, and he is educated for a profession and so can gain work elsewhere in Europe; her cousin Paul is a gynaecologist, trailing a suggestion that while Paul is kind and supportive to Else, he is a man making a medical career out of women's bodies. Else's thoughts keep coming back to all the times she has been refused permission to train for any independent work; her family has stopped her, she remembers with irritation, from training as an actress ('They wouldn't hear of my going into the theatre. They laughed at me.')[40]

The chief shadow over her and her family's life is her father, the patriarch who throughout history can sustain and support a family yet also destroy it; her father, she thinks bitterly, is supposedly a brilliant defence lawyer yet is also an inveterate gambler at baccarat and on the stock exchange, he cannot control his gambling and drains away family money, even purloining trust funds. He's an embezzler, which is why she is dependent on her aunt to be at the resort; the rest of the extended family have declared that they will no longer cover his debts: 'His undoing is his passion for gambling. He can't help it; it's a kind of insanity.'[41]

Ominously, at the resort Else receives a letter by express post from her mama in Vienna – not, she notes, from her father – begging Else to approach Herr von Dorsday, a family friend, an older man, a wealthy art dealer, who had bailed out Else's father once before. The matter, her mama writes, is desperately urgent. Unless a gambling debt is paid in a few days' time to a Dr Fiala in a matter involving trust funds, an arrest warrant will be ordered and her father will almost certainly be sent to gaol and the family will be ruined, especially mother and daughter dependent on the father, for her brother might be able to work in a bank in Holland. Else, her mama implores, must save her father.[42]

Herr von Dorsday has been lurking about already, even before the letter from her mama arrives. He traps Else into an unwelcome conversation on her way back from tennis: 'What a deep bow he's making and how he's eyeing me!' Else suspects Dorsday is attempting to disguise more humble beginnings: 'I don't like him. He's just an artful social climber. A first-class tailor isn't enough, Herr von Dorsday! Dorsday! I'm sure your name used to be something else.' She regales him in her thoughts: 'your stupid monocle and your white flannel suit'. She remembers that when she was 12 or 13, Dorsday 'stroked my cheeks', saying: 'Becoming quite a young lady, aren't we?' Else feels repulsed by Dorsday as an ageing voyeur, roué, 'lecher'.[43] She regards him, in Hannah Arendt's terms, as a parvenu.

Else reads over and over her mama's letter; she bitterly recognises that her father has betrayed her, he wants her to approach the art dealer personally in some kind of compromising way, to 'solicit' a loan that will save him ('Why didn't Papa just board a train and come here?'). Yet Else feels she has to approach Dorsday for the money ('thirty thousand gulden'), that she has no choice: if the debt is not paid in three days the family will be destroyed. In a painful scene Else does ask Dorsday if as a family friend he could forward the money to Dr Fiala by the required date. Else is trembling as she asks, and she realises that Dorsday has sat her down on a bench. He is looking at her in a way that she finds 'indecent'. She becomes aware that he is 'pressing his knee' against hers while standing in front of her. Dorsday says to Else he will repay her father's debt, but only on one condition that she immediately finds deeply degrading, that makes her feel like a prostitute. ('How could you ask this of me, Papa? It wasn't right of you, Papa.')[44]

Dorsday then tells Else of his 'one condition', that Else should come during the night to his hotel room, or to a clearing in the forest, and he will look at her unclothed for 15 minutes.[45] For the remainder of the novella, Else's mind disintegrates in agony and extreme distress. She feels she is being forced to become like a 'slave' to Dorsday.[46]

Yet Else acts, she is an actant in Bruno Latour's terms, she chooses to act, she refuses passivity, she will make of her fate an allegory, a universal fable, out in the open, not hidden, not secretive.[47] She will recreate herself in Hannah Arendt's terms as a conscious pariah. In her thoughts, she says to Dorsday: 'I'm not your slave.'[48] She will stage a theatrical scene, 'a grand performance', she will defy the patriarchal collective of older men, including Dorsday and her own father his accomplice, who support each other in furtive predatory behavior directed at young women and girls. Even her mother, she thinks, is complicit, sending an urgent follow-up telegram saying that Else must now ask Dorsday for 50, not 39, thousand gulden: 'They're all murderers… Mama is a murderess.'[49]

Back in her hotel room, Else chooses her costume for her staging of the event. She wraps herself in her 'big black coat that reaches down to [her] ankles', with no clothes underneath. She asks herself: 'Should I undo my hair? No. Then I'll look like a madwoman. But I don't want you all to think I'm crazy. Only shameless. A prankster.' She doesn't want her performance to be dismissed as that of a mad person; she wants to present herself as an emblem. Now, she feels ready: 'The performance can begin.'[50] She walks downstairs and enters the public part of the hotel where the guests are assembling before dinner: 'If [Dorsday] gets to see me, then everybody should get to see me.' As Else proceeds towards the card room in the hotel where she feels Dorsday would be, she hears Schumann's 'Carnival' being 'beautifully' played in the music room.[51] I take the suggestion here to be that Else's crafting of her theatrical scene, to disrobe before everyone, is the carnivalesque act of a 'prankster', turning the social conventions of the Viennese and European bourgeoisie upside down.

Reading *Fräulein Else* led me to reflect on several literary works that I've written about before.

I think here of my book on postmodernism and popular culture where I talk about Mikhail Bakhtin in his *Rabelais and His World* arguing that in early modern Europe carnival fool figures exercise a licence to expose conventions, to challenge, to defy. Fools, says Bakhtin, assume in the sexual sphere the right to make public what is usually regarded and guarded as private. They have the right to blunt language and to anger, to rip off masks, to rage at others with a primeval, almost cultic rage, at the same time not exempting themselves from parody and mockery.[52] In her thoughts as we read them, Else the 'prankster' exercises that bluntness and rage and scorn at her world, at the same time mocking herself to the point of self-laceration.

As we learn in the novella's final scenes, Else carries out her carnivalesque action: she does not unclothe herself for Dorsday in secret in his room in the hotel or in the woods, but takes off her 'big black coat' in the hotel in the sight of all the guests; she faints and is carried by her cousin Paul to her room, where, drifting in and out of consciousness, she hears her aunt saying she must be admitted 'into an asylum', which appals Else: 'She can go to the devil. I'm not going to let myself be taken to an asylum. I'm not insane.' While her aunt and her cousin whisper about what to do, Else takes the packets of Veronal she has hidden on her night table, her final dying thoughts fragmenting in images of release.[53]

> Don't wake me up. I'm sleeping so well. Tomorrow morning. I'm dreaming and flying. I'm flying… flying… flying… sleeping and dreaming… and flying… don't wake me…tomorrow morning…
> *El…*
> I'm flying… I'm dreaming… I'm sleeping… I'm dream… drea… I'm flying.[54]

I agree with Margret Schaefer's high assessment of *Fräulein Else*, Schnitzler's tragic novella is great literature, answering the anguished cry across the ages of Iphigenia in Aeschylus' *Agamemnon*, when Agamemnon, heedless of her tears and cries of 'Father', sacrifices his daughter for the sake of military glory in the war against Troy; the desire of patriarchal men to arrange the world for themselves even when it destroys those closest to them.

In *Agamemnon* father silences daughter, gags Iphigenia's mouth with a cord. Else, in staging her rebellious scene, is more like Andromache in Euripides's play of that name, a fierce spirited powerful voice even in her enslavement consequent upon Troy's defeat. I've just looked up what I wrote about the play in my *The Origins of Violence*, in a section entitled '*Andromache*: the slave as the stranger who disturbs'. The widow of the Trojan warrior Hector savagely slain by Achilles, Andromache is taken to Greece as a slave and allotted to Achilles' son Neopotemus; she has memorable exchanges with Menelaus the Spartan king, who is created in the play as unworthy and despicable; under threat of death, Andromache in her scornful replies to Menelaus's threats and insults, easily proves the superior in wisdom, insight, perceptiveness and humanity; she accuses Menelaus of cruelty, murderousness, deceit and treachery. In *The Origins of Violence*, in talking of Andromache in relation to Menelaus, woman to man, slave to ruler, Oriental to European, I thought of the long cultural history of World Upside Down, in particular of Natalie Zemon Davis's essay 'Women on Top' about male-female inversions in early modern Europe in carnival, festive practices and pictorial representation.[55]

Fräulein Else makes me think of other possible resonances and connections. Else is appalled at the threat by her aunt Emma that she be committed to an asylum; here I think of my *The Nervous Nineties*, where I write about Feminist Gothic in that troubled historical period, a literature of frightening confinement, of despair at enforced limitation, of fear of inevitable defeat by an unchangeable gender order, itself in alliance with male medical professionals, themselves in alliance with the power of the state. I talk about Charlotte Perkins Gilman, well-known American feminist and author of the famous 1892 short story 'The Yellow Wallpaper'. Gilman did enjoy education and training for a career, studying art for a time at the Rhode Island School of Design, and becoming a lecturer at large, earning her living by designing greeting cards, teaching art and tutoring children. At 24, she marries a local artist; after the birth of their daughter Katherine, however, Charlotte became seriously depressed, and was persuaded by her husband to consult a well-known Philadelphia neurologist, Dr S Weir Mitchell, who advertises himself as a specialist in women's nervous disorders, and goes about propounding the virtues of his rest cure; for Charlotte this meant that she was forbidden to paint or write and her reading was limited to two hours a day. Charlotte just manages to survive the authoritarianism of both her husband, who had insisted on treatment by Dr S Weir Mitchell, and Dr S Weir Mitchell, a villain of history, who like other medical men made a career out of policing women's minds.[56]

Here I also think of my chapter from London to Odessa, gratefully drawing on Vicki Woolf's *Dancing in the Vortex*, her biography of Ida Rubinstein, who did become trained as dancer and actor, though against her family's wishes. Vicki Woolf tells us that when Ida in 1908 was preparing to perform in Paris for the Ballets Russes a work based on Oscar Wilde's *Salomé*, where she was to enact the Dance of the Seven Veils, her sister Irene, hearing of the project, was horrified at the idea of Ida becoming a professional stage performer and appearing as Salomé. Irene's husband Dr Lewinsohn used his medical standing to have her institutionalised.[57]

Vicki Woolf writes movingly of what might then have occurred:

> Dr Lewinsohn did just as he threatened; Ida was committed to the asylum at St Cloud as mentally unstable. There are no details of how she was transported to the asylum against her will. The beautiful, willowy, thin creature could not physically have fought for long. Perhaps she was sedated or, more likely, her supreme belief in herself and her pride allowed her to be taken in the most dignified way possible, dressed in her most sumptuous finery, haughty, walking alone in this tragic turn of fate. How she was treated in the asylum, how she behaved, how she coped, we shall never know. It certainly did not dampen her ardour or curb her resolve.[58]

How did medical men across the world such as Dr Lewinsohn in Paris or Dr S Weir Mitchell in Philadelphia accrue such evil power?

In *Fräulein Else* Else's yearning for the kind of education and training for a career by which her brother Rudi was advantaged and could lead an independent life, reminds me of Virginia and Vanessa Stephen, denied the education that their brother Thoby enjoyed at Cambridge. During Virginia's breakdowns early in her marriage to Leonard Woolf, there was an ever-present threat posed by eminent medical men that she be institutionalised – a threat warded off by Leonard to, I think, his eternal credit. Victoria Glendinning in her biography draws attention to Leonard saying (in *Beginning Again*) that he 'went to see one or two recommended mental hospitals… and found them too awful to contemplate'. Glendinning also draws attention to Virginia's own fear and loathing of those she referred to as 'nerve doctors', a dislike that emerges in the 'depiction of their insensitive approach to the mentally ill Septimus in *Mrs Dalloway*'.[59]

In her biography of Virginia Hermione Lee also points out that Leonard averted 'the horrible prospect of her being incarcerated in a lunatic asylum'. Lee writes scathingly that the authoritarianism of the medical profession at the turn of century, especially towards women, prescribing a combination of entire rest and excessive feeding, had been pioneered by none other than 'the American neurologist Silas Weir Mitchell in the 1870s', he who is satirised, as Lee observes, by Charlotte Perkins Gilman in *The Yellow Wallpaper*.[60]

There's another resonance I'm thinking about for *Fräulein Else*: its final cinematic sequence when Else repeats to herself that she is flying, flying, flying, immediately brings to mind Geena Davis and Susan Sarandon in the final scene of *Thelma and Louise*, when, pursued by a horde of American police, they look at each other and decide not to be incarcerated; they choose not to be classified as mad women and criminal; and as we all know, they choose death by soaring over a cliff, in a great film of female rebellion.

1. Hannah Arendt, 'Herzl and Lazare', in Arendt, *The Jewish Writings*, edited by Jerome Kohn and Ron H. Feldman (Schocken Books, New York, 2007), pp.338–42.
2. Bernard Lazare, *Le Fumier de Job* (Paris, 1928), 'Herzl and Lazare', in Arendt, *The Jewish Writings*, p.341 note 4.
3. Arendt, 'Herzl and Lazare', pp.338–9.
4. Arendt, 'Herzl and Lazare', pp.339, 341 note 10.
5. Arendt, 'Herzl and Lazare', pp.339–40, 342 note 14.
6. Arendt, 'Herzl and Lazare', pp.340, 342 note 19.
7. John Docker, *1492: The Poetics of Diaspora* (Continuum, London, 2001), p.134.
8. See John Docker, 'The Flâneur under Water, the Flâneur as Dancing Star: creating a conversation between Walter Benjamin, T.S. Eliot, and Hannah Arendt', *Westerly*, Special Issue – Day of Ideas, 2016.
9. Arendt, *The Jewish Writings*, 'The Jew as Pariah: A Hidden Tradition', p.286.
10. Arendt, *The Jewish Writings*, 'We Refugees', p.274.
11. Arendt, *The Jewish Writings*, 'The Jew as Pariah: A Hidden Tradition', pp.275, 284.
12. Arendt, *The Jewish Writings*, 'The Jew as Pariah: A Hidden Tradition', p.275.
13. John Docker, *1492: The Poetics of Diaspora* (Continuum, London and New York, 2001), p.158.
14. Bradon Ellem, *In Women' Hands? A History of Clothing Trades Unionism in Australia* (New South Wales University Press, Sydney, 1989. (My thanks to Judith Keene for gifting me this book.)
15. Ron Witton, 'Growing up and living with the Cold War', in Ann Curthoys and Joy Damousi (eds), *What Did You Do in the Cold War, Daddy? Personal stories from a troubled time* (NewSouth, Sydney, 2014), pp.227–228.
16. Ron Witton, 'Guiterman, Rosine', *Dictionary of Sydney*, 2015 http://dictionaryofsydney.org/entry/guiterman_rosine
17. Ned Curthoys, *The Legacy of Liberal Judaism: Ernst Cassirer and Hannah Arendt's Hidden Conversation* (Berghahn, New York, 2016), pp.14–43.
18. Docker, *1492: The Poetics of Diaspora*, p.160.
19. Docker, *1492: The Poetics of Diaspora*, p.162.
20. Docker, *1492: The Poetics of Diaspora*, pp.161, 164–165.
21. Docker, *1492: The Poetics of Diaspora*, pp.161–162.
22. Docker, *1492: The Poetics of Diaspora*, pp.162–165.
23. Docker, *1492: The Poetics of Diaspora*, p.165.
24. Docker, *1492: The Poetics of Diaspora*, p.166.
25. Docker, *1492: The Poetics of Diaspora*, pp.166–167.
26. Docker, *1492: The Poetics of Diaspora*, p.167.

A Radical Jewish Intelligentsia in the 1930s   341

27 Docker, *1492: The Poetics of Diaspora*, p.163.
28 Docker, *1492: The Poetics of Diaspora*, p.164.
29 Arthur Schnitzler, *Desire and Delusion: Three Novellas*, selected and translated by Margret Schaefer (Ivan R. Dee, Chicago, 2003), Foreword, pp.vii-xxi.
30 Margret Schaefer, Foreward to Schnitzler, *Desire and Delusion*, pp.vii-viii.
31 Laleen Jayamanne, *The Epic Cinema of Kumar Shahani* (Indiana University Press, Bloomington and Indianopolis, 2015), p.174.
32 Margret Schaefer, Foreward to Schnitzler, *Desire and Delusion*, p.xix.
33 Arendt, *The Jewish Writings*, 'Stefan Zweig: Jews in the World of Yesterday', p.324.
34 Arthur Schnitzler, 'Lieutenant Gustl', in Evan Bates (ed.), *Great German Short Stories* (Dover Publications, New York, 2003), pp.187–211.
35 Margret Schaefer, Foreward to Schnitzler, *Desire and Delusion*, pp.xiv-xv.
36 Evan Bates, Note to *Great German Short Stories*, p.viii.
37 Margret Schaefer, Foreward to Schnitzler, *Desire and Delusion*, pp.xv, xx.
38 John Docker, 'Sheer Folly and Derangement: How the Crusades Disoriented Enlightenment Historiography', in Alexander Cook, Ned Curthoys and Shino Konishi (eds), *Representing Humanity in the Age of Enlightenment* (Pickering and Chatto, London, 2013), p.44.
39 Arthur Schnitzler, 'Fräulein Else', in Margret Schaefer (ed.), *Desire and Delusion*, pp.196, 199, 203, 241.
40 Schnitzler, 'Fräulein Else', pp.193, 202–205, 208, 230, 262.
41 Schnitzler, 'Fräulein Else', p.225.
42 Schnitzler, 'Fräulein Else', pp.193, 200.
43 Schnitzler, 'Fräulein Else', pp.194–195, 200, 203, 206, 220, 222.
44 Schnitzler, 'Fräulein Else', pp.198, 201, 213–215.
45 Schnitzler, 'Fräulein Else', pp.220–221.
46 Schnitzler, 'Fräulein Else', pp.230.
47 See Bruno Latour, 'Agency at the time of the Anthropocene', *New Literary History*, Vol.45, 2014, pp.1–18.
48 Schnitzler, 'Fräulein Else', p.251.
49 Schnitzler, 'Fräulein Else', pp.218, 221, 237, 244–245, 260.
50 Schnitzler, 'Fräulein Else', pp.241–244.
51 Schnitzler, 'Fräulein Else', pp.238, 241, 247, 249.
52 John Docker, *Postmodernism and Popular Culture: A Cultural History* (Cambridge University Press, Melbourne, 1994), p.199.
53 Schnitzler, 'Fräulein Else', pp.235, 238, 240–241, 253, 256–8.
54 Schnitzler, 'Fräulein Else', pp.263–264.

55　John Docker, *The Origins of Violence: Religion, History and Genocide* (Pluto, London, 2008), pp.74–79.

56　John Docker, *The Nervous Nineties: Australian Cultural Life in the 1890s* (Oxford, Melbourne, 1991), pp.21–22.

57　Vicki Woolf, *Dancing in the Vortex: The Story of Ida Rubinstein* (Routledge, New York and London, 2000), pp.16–17.

58　Vicki Woolf, *Dancing in the Vortex*, p.17.

59　Victoria Glendinning, *Leonard Woolf: A Biography* (Counterpoint, Berkeley, 2008), pp.148, 163.

60　Hermione Lee, *Virginia Woolf* (Vintage, New York, 1999), p.179.

19

Dostoevsky's *Notes from Underground*

'Well, how about it, Papa? What if I just auctioned myself off this evening? To save you from prison?... I'll talk to Herr Dorsday, the Vicomte von Eperjes, and will solicit money from him. I, the high-minded Else, the aristocrat, the marchesa, the beggar maid, the embezzler's daughter.'
   Schnitzler, *Fräulein Else*¹

'Without power and tyranny over someone I cannot survive.'
   Underground Man in Dostoevsky, *Notes from Underground*²

I'm very pleased that the Sydney Jewish Youth Theatre's interest in Arthur Schnitzler, the lecture and discussion on him staged by the group on 7 March 1937 (but what did they talk about? I'm haunted by this), got me thinking about his 1900 story *Lieutenant Gustl* and his 1924 novella *Fräulein Else*. Reading these Schnitzler stories makes me wonder about my own long fascination, from the 1980s, with Russian cultural theorist Mikhail Bakhtin's conception of different kinds of narrators in the history of fiction, that he develops for modernity in terms of a contrast between Tolstoy and Dostoevsky. It's a contrast that became and remains very important to me, one which I have explored and keep exploring in a widening circle of cultural histories. It relates – I think – to a 1960s and 1970s New Left anarchist thread, that in terms of literary criticism and literary theory I would translate into a dislike of authoritarian narrators.

During the 1980s, I found an essay in Bakhtin's *The Dialogic Imagination*, 'Forms of Time and of the Chronotope in the Novel' particularly illuminating, and read it over and over. Here Bakhtin entertains us with his theories of narrative: of how time and space are organised in different genres; of different conceptions of character, for example, those that might be fixed characters, as against those that might change, transform, metamorphose. Then I turned to his *Problems of Dostoevsky's Poetics*, in particular to his notions there of monologic and dialogic texts, and of polyphony and heteroglossia.[3]

Dostoevsky versus Tolstoy

In his *Problems of Dostoevsky's Poetics* Bakhtin develops a contrast between Tolstoy and Dostoevsky which I found helpful in my 1991 *The Nervous Nineties*. Who, Dear Reader, do you prefer: Tolstoy or Dostoevsky? In *Problems of Dostoevsky's Poetics*, Bakhtin makes his preference clear: he is highly critical of Tolstoy's fictional mode. Whatever its greatness, Tolstoy's fiction is, to use one of Bakhtin's favourite terms, monologic. Tolstoy as author dominates his text. The author, all-knowing and all-controlling, constructs his characters, juxtaposes and contrasts them one to another, and then evaluates them. The author does not speak with them but about them. They are not active subjects, but become objects of his fixed authoritative gaze, his all-encompassing field of vision. Characters are denied anything like equal rights with their author. Standing above and outside the narrative, the author gives to his characters a definitive, final meaning.[4]

Recall Tolstoy's almost comical lofty ruminations on Natasha and feminism at the end of *War and Peace*.[5] Section X of the Epilogue considers Natasha's life as it unfolded, its opening sentence: 'Natasha was married in the early spring of 1813, and by 1820 she already had three daughters and one son, whom she had passionately wished for and was now nursing herself.'

Married to Pierre, her life, according to the author, found full satisfaction in 'bearing, giving birth to, and nursing her children'. Her face now 'bore an expression of softness and serenity'; one only saw 'a strong, beautiful, and fruitful female'. Natasha was not interested in a 'French' view according to which 'a girl, once married... should not abandon her talents'. There was discussion early in the nineteenth century, as there was later in the century, says the author, about questions of 'women's rights'. However, 'these questions not only did not interest Natasha', she 'decidedly did not understand them'. Natasha realised that the 'whole significance' of marriage 'consists in the family'. All of Natasha's 'inner forces' were directed at serving her husband and children. She saw it as her duty to respect Pierre's 'intellectual pursuits, of which she understood nothing', and she directed the whole household to be 'on tiptoe when Pierre was busy reading or writing'.

The author is at pains to repeat this latter point in the next section, XI: 'To all that belonged to her husband's intellectual, abstract pursuits, without understanding them, she ascribed enormous importance, and she was in constant fear of being a hindrance to this activity of her husband.'[6]

Here in the Epilogue to *War and Peace*, the author does not allow Natasha the independence to speak her thoughts, to possess any consciousness outside of that which he ascribes to her; he does not permit her the possibility of considering feminist ideas about companionate marriage such that, if they had rights to education as men were granted, she and her husband could together enjoy the stimulation and excitement of 'intellectual, abstract pursuits' and she also could write if she wished to, contributing her own viewpoints and insights to controversies current or longstanding.

In *Problems of Dostoevsky's Poetics* Bakhtin argues by contrast that Dostoevsky's texts are dialogic and polyphonic. Here the author acts as organiser and participant in the dialogues, the clashes of conflicting positions and voices, but without retaining for himself the final word. His characters remain unfinalised and with strong rights as autonomous subjects in the narrative. Indeed, the author tends to recede from view. Bakhtin points out that when people discuss Dostoevsky's novels they keep coming back to various characters – Raskolnikov, Myshkin, Stavrogin, Ivan Karamazov, the Grand Inquisitor – as 'author-thinkers' themselves, taking philosophical positions that we consider in their own right. So independent, individual and unmediated are they are as characters that we tend to forget Dostoevsky himself as their author. Dostoevsky's novels are polyphonic because in them he creates not voiceless slaves but free people, capable of standing alongside their creator, capable of not agreeing with him and even rebelling against him.[7]

Bakhtin evokes *Notes from Underground*

> It [*Notes from Underground*] is constructed as a dialogue (a conversation with an absent interlocutor), saturated with overt and hidden polemic, and contains important elements of the confession... Almost all the themes and ideas of Dostoevsky's subsequent work are outlined here in simplified and stripped-down form.
>
> Bakhtin, Problems of Dostoevsky's Poetics[8]

A little strangely, in my *The Nervous Nineties* I didn't discuss Dostoevsky's famous 1864 novella *Notes from Underground*, which I now realise is a key text for Bakhtin's argument that Dostoevsky resumed a long European cultural history of the carnivalesque that reaches back to antiquity in genres like the symposium and the free-wheeling menippea; works through carnival in early modern Europe; and then is recovered and reshaped by Dostoevsky, who creates for modernity the polyphonic novel.

While reading Schnitzler's *Lieutenant Gustl* and *Fräulein Else*,

I mentioned to Ned Curthoys how interesting I found them as interior monologues, with no author in sight. In response, Ned suggested I read *Notes from Underground*. There may be a line of descent there; he reminded me that Bakhtin in *Problems of Dostoevsky's Poetics* features analysis of *Notes from Underground* as a formative text for the polyphonic novel. I said from distant memory I might once have read *Notes from Underground*, I'm not sure now, I have a hazy image in my mind's eye of the narrator every day walking along a pavement towards an officer, who never gives way, the narrator does, every time he is forced into the gutter, and every day he says to himself, next time I won't give way. I said I would read *Notes from Underground* and see if my memory's right; in any case, I couldn't remember anything else. Ned said I'd love it, it's so wonderfully extreme, for example, the crazed speeches the narrator near the end launches at the young prostitute Liza.

I have now read *Notes from Underground*, and it is indeed an astonishing book, with resonances, especially in Liza, the novel's true hero, with other rebellious female cultural figures I've been thinking about, Virginia Woolf, Ida Rubinstein, Charlotte Perkins Gilman, Fräulein Else and – Dora, in Freud's infamous sinister 1905 *A Case of Hysteria (Dora)*; of which more soon.

The young Dostoevsky, Bakhtin says, a follower of Gogol and admirer of famous texts like 'Notes of a Madman', carried out an as it were 'small-scale Copernican revolution' against his apparent master. In the process, the 'Gogolian hero becomes Dostoevsky's hero': everything in Gogol's stories that are there to provide the so-called 'objective' sociological and historical features and aspects of the hero, what we would usually call social realism, are now transferred by Dostoevsky into the 'agonizing self-awareness' of the hero: 'We see not who he is, but *how* he is conscious of himself.'

> Not only the reality of the hero himself, but even the external

world and the everyday life surrounding him are drawn into the process of self-awareness, are transferred from the author's to the hero's field of vision... they cannot serve as causal or genetic factors determining the hero, they cannot fulfill in the world any explanatory function. Alongside and on the same plane with the self-consciousness of the hero, which has absorbed into itself the entire world of objects, there can only be another consciousness; alongside its field of vision, another field of vision; alongside its point of view on the world, another point of view on the world. *To the all-devouring consciousness of the hero the author can juxtapose only a single objective world – a world of other consciousnesses with rights equal to those of the hero.* (Bakhtin's *italics*.)[9]

[Bakhtin may be unfair to Gogol at least in relation to 'The Diary of a Madman', which I've recently read, Ned having given it to me as a Christmas present; while a vastly simpler story than *Notes from Underground*, 'The Diary of a Madman' reveals only the field of vision of the writer of the diary entries. We peruse over his shoulder a fantasist's interior monologue, wherein the lowly clerk Aksenty Ivanovich believes he hears dogs talking to each other and finally imagines that he is the king of Spain ('There is a king of Spain. He has been found at last. That king is *me*.').][10]

Dear Reader, I'll also let a side-thought tumble out: reading Bakhtin's passage above I think back on Virginia Woolf's early twentieth-century admiration for Dostoevsky, her view that he provided an exciting alternative to the tedious social realism of the generation of British male writers just before hers, the ponderous Arnold Bennett and his ilk; also, Ned has just been urging me to read Virginia W's *The Waves* because of its Dostoevsky-like technique and because people have said that one of the characters, who comically claims to have come from Australia, might be a portrait of the ex-American T S Eliot. I've started reading it now, and, in support of what Ned advised, Bakhtin's passage here provides an explanation of *The Waves*' world of different consciousnesses with equal rights to think and talk. Also, *Problems of Dostoevsky's Poetics* first appeared in 1929, while, so David Bradshaw tells us in his introduction to the Oxford World's Classics edition of *The Waves*, Virginia Woolf first began thinking about it in 1926, the first draft was finished in 1930 and the second and final draft was completed early in 1931.[11] In Bakhtin's terms, she carried out a Copernican revolution against her immediate predecessors, the patriarchal fathers of British literature.

In his Introduction, David Bradshaw writes that '*The Waves* has practically no plot and the precise locations of its action (there is very little) lie mostly undisclosed'.[12] Bakhtin wrote in similar terms that the 'life of the Underground Man is absolutely devoid of any plot'.[13]

Bakhtin tells us in *Problems of Dostoevsky's Poetics* that *Notes from Underground* is a confessional *Ich-Erzählung*, and originally the work was entitled 'A Confession'. However, he points out, as a confession *Notes from Underground* is 'not a personal document but a work of art'.[14]

The hero or anti-hero, the sole narrator, a one-time functionary in the Czarist bureaucracy, the Underground Man, proud of being in his own view more educated, literary and intelligent than anyone he thinks about or encounters, is not a conventional social-realist character but a cultural type, a man without a name: 'he figures not as a person taken from life', Bakhtin observes, 'but rather as the subject of consciousness and dream'. What we register is his 'self-consciousness' and the 'inescapable open-endedness, the vicious circle of that self-consciousness'; every 'psycho-pathological' aspect of his inner consciousness the hero 'knows perfectly well himself'. The Underground Man is not an objectified image but a pure voice: 'we do not see him, we hear him'; always eavesdropping, he is preternaturally aware of every word someone says or might say about him, but he resists and refuses anyone's definition or summation of his personality, he 'seeks at whatever cost to retain for himself' a 'final word about himself'. Underground Man exercises his freedom in admitting to his many pathological failings, only he has the right to confess to them. He wants, then, his own personality to be unfinalised and indeterminate. What he also wants is to domineer and tyrannise over anyone he can, especially those lower than him in the society, but also anyone who he feels is contemptuous of him as a nobody; then some kind of revenge must be sought, obsessively, sedulously, however long it takes.[15]

Bakhtin points out the curiosity of the Underground Man's character: while he restlessly seeks to know at every point what others think of him, his pride cannot bear any critical judgements and especially anyone who might make him ever appear as 'the weak and passive party'. The Underground Man, Bakhtin notes, even 'hates his own face, because in it he senses the power of another person over him, the power of that other's evaluations and opinions. He himself looks on his own face with another's eyes, with the eyes of the other.' As the novella goes on, Underground Man's tone becomes increasingly negative, increasingly spiteful towards all others, including himself, 'sharper and more shrill'. In particular, he cannot stand being 'the one who is understood, accepted, forgiven', as he finds when with Liza (Bakhtin, unfortunately for his intense admirers like myself, does not name Liza but refers to her as 'the girl'). Bakhtin points to the scene where Liza comes to the Underground Man's seedy apartment on his invitation, and he senses that she, a lowly prostitute, understands and accepts and loves him as he is; even though they make delirious love, he feels crushed and humiliated, and enraged that she now has become the heroine in the demented drama of his life, the drama he knows is demented. He brutally insists that she go, he peeks through the room divider to make sure she is getting dressed and is about to leave, for by expelling her from his home he can, he hopes, crush and humiliate her, he can destroy her soul.[16]

He must have destroyed Liza's soul. But has he? I'll return to these final scenes.

I'll mention here one more idea in *Problems of Dostoevsky's Poetics* that I had not come across before, that of the 'loophole', a notion that Bakhtin sees as adding a vital dimension to *Notes from Underground*, and which he believes is very important to Dostoevsky's work as a whole, to aesthetic philosophy more generally, and perhaps to history and humanity. Bakhtin asks:

> What, then, is this loophole of consciousness and of the word?
>
> A loophole is the retention for oneself of the possibility for altering the ultimate, final meaning of one's own words… This potential other meaning, that is, the loophole left open, accompanies the word like a shadow. Judged by its meaning alone, the word with a loophole should be an ultimate word and does present itself as such, but in fact it is only the penultimate word…[17]

As with other Dostoevsky texts, the 'loophole makes the hero ambiguous and elusive even for himself'. Indeed, says Bakhtin, the 'loophole' makes all the self-definitions of Dostoevsky's heroes unstable; the 'word in them has no hard and fast meaning, and at any moment, like a chameleon, it is ready to change its tone and its ultimate meaning'. For the Underground Man, Bakhtin reflects, the loophole means his confession can be self-ironic, self-parodying, unsure of itself, so that, 'chameleon' like, his thoughts and speech dwell in ambiguity; for all his claims to self-knowledge as promised by a confession, he does not know himself, suggesting also that no one else can either know him or know themselves. And perhaps, Bakhtin suggests, Liza understands this doubleness about the Underground Man, his ranting and snarling against others and himself as if completely certain of what he thinks, yet also his self-doubt and uncertainty; it is perhaps one reason why she is drawn to him, why she has fallen in love with him.[18]

As I was reading and busily underlining Bakhtin's sentences about the loophole, especially when I came to his phrase the 'loophole left open', I remembered with a start Derrida's concept of the supplement, his notion that every text has a supplement that undoes its claim to total or complete meaning. Surely, I thought, there is a theoretical similarity here. Discussing Derrida's *Of Grammatology* in my *Postmodernism and Popular Culture: A Cultural History* (1994), I pointed out that for Derrida (he'd been talking about Rousseau's *Confessions*) the supplement is another name for what he admires as the restless play of unconfinable substitutions of meaning.[19]

After I'd written this paragraph, I idly googled, and I see that others have made this connection between Bakhtin's 'loophole' and Derrida's 'supplement', well before me.

I read *Notes from Underground*

> A novel [says Underground Man] needs a hero but here I've *deliberately* gathered together all the features of an anti-hero and the main thing is, all this will produce a most unpleasant impression, since we have all lost touch with real life, we are all cripples, each one of us to a greater or lesser degree.
>
> Dostoevsky, *Notes from Underground*[20]

I start reading *Notes from Underground* in the 2009 Penguin Classics edition (which also includes *The Double*), translation Ronald Wilks, Introduction Robert Louis Jackson. I note with interest in the Chronology at the beginning that when in 1864 *Notes from Underground* was published, so also was the first part of Tolstoy's *War and Peace*.[21] In Bakhtin's terms, here's a conjunction to ponder. If *War and Peace* as we all know features a narrator who assumes he knows all, *Notes from Underground* features that celebrated figure, the Unreliable Narrator.

Underground Man is a writer who enjoys the craft of being a writer and is very proud of his skill at recalling past episodes and conversations and creating dramatic scenes. He is the writer of notes about himself and episodes in his life he wishes to remember or unwillingly remembers, and in writing he thinks of other writing, which he sometimes likes, sometimes opposes; he theatricalises himself, plays out scenes from literature, in ways we would now think of as cinematic. Sometimes, he knows, he sounds bookish in his speeches to others, and Liza in particular finds him bookish and quietly tells him so.

Writing his confession, Underground Man reflects on the genre of the confession. As Bakhtin says, he presents his confession as a kind of anti-confession, a parody of a confession if a confession (especially a male confession) shapes a life from womb to tomb as if always coherent and comprehensible, as if proceeding towards a goal of achievement or redemption and hence an important journey for others to consider for instruction or illumination or emulation in some way, a life to be guided by, a life that offers ideals for us all to strive for, a life that will improve the world. Underground Man feels that Heine revealed a proper skeptical spirit when, commenting on Rousseau's *Confessions*, he had reflected 'that true autobiographies are almost impossible and that a man will most certainly lie about himself', in Rousseau's case, Heine thought, out of 'vanity'.[22]

In his own view (though, we will learn by the end, this is not his only view), Underground Man's life in St Petersburg has no meaning and matters to no one there or anywhere else; the only reason to talk about himself is that it gives him the 'greatest pleasure', including the pleasure of reveling in his own 'bitterness' and 'degradation', along with the pleasure of 'self-mockery', wringing humour, even hilarity, out of the many scenes of his humiliations.

The best thing is to do what he does, belong to the Underground where the rule is 'to do nothing'; to be an historical pessimist and consider all high ideals, any striving for the supposedly sublime and beautiful, an absurd waste of time.[23]

As Bakhtin says, Underground Man does not chart any kind of purpose or goal for his life, rather the 'psycho-pathological' drama of his life remains and whirrs within the 'vicious circle' of his 'self-consciousness'.[24] Only Liza, perhaps, in their failed romance, almost, for a moment, nearly but not quite, draws him beyond that vicious circle, which, even if anguished, he closes again.

Actually, I'm not sure I agree here with Bakhtin concerning Underground Man's not charting any purpose or goal for his life. I think by the end Underground Man does perceive a loophole for himself, a destined role in the world.

I'm enchanted from the unnamed narrator's first words onwards, addressed to unnamed 'gentlemen' who are the readers in his head, – 'I'm a sick man… I'm a spiteful man. I'm an unattractive man'. In his opening sallies, Underground Man relates that he is now 40, he used to be a civil servant, and relished being rude to people who came to his desk with petitions for assistance; he snarls at them, feels 'inexhaustible pleasure whenever I succeed in upsetting anyone', which happened often because they were usually so 'timid'. Often he lies, then quickly tells his (possible, future) gentlemen readers that he has just lied. For example, he lied when he said that he is spiteful, because that would suggest he achieved something definite in life: no, he says, he's never 'managed to become anything: neither spiteful, nor good, neither a scoundrel nor an honest man, neither a hero nor an insect'. Always anxious and fretful, he self-harms, refusing to see the doctors about his ongoing illness, which might be caused by something being wrong with his liver: 'I know better than anyone that by all this I'm harming no one but myself.'[25]

His aim in life, Underground Man says to himself, is to strive for 'conscious inertia', except when he is performing the 'most contemptible actions'.[26] Underground Man confides that more than once he has sought out situations in St Petersburg where he was sure to experience extreme humiliation.

Underground Man's feverish thoughts, then, not only dwell in self-laceration, on his aloneness, loneliness, friendlessness; on his feeling sure that his colleagues despised him when he worked in his office, before he received a modest bequest from a distant relative and left work altogether. His thoughts also spill over with assertiveness and a plethora of spite; his self-admiration in his quoting from literature and imagining he is acting out literary scenes (from Byron, Pushkin, Lermontov); his boastful claim to represent the 'educated man of the nineteenth century' more truly than anyone else; his open admission of his every mean thought and occasional viciousness, especially his desire for revenge against anyone who might humiliate him or has humiliated him, whether in his estimation lower than he is on the social scale, or higher.[27]

I note obsessive references to 'one particular officer' quite early, who apparently irritates Underground Man because he 'simply wouldn't be brought to heel and had a nasty way of rattling his sabre. For eighteen months he and I waged war over that sabre. In the end I triumphed. He stopped the rattling.' I decide to follow this thread, wondering if Underground Man's triumph over the officer occurs only in his own mind. Underground Man relates that one night he was passing 'some wretched tavern' and saw 'some gentlemen standing around a billiard table' and doing battle with their cues, and 'then one of their company was thrown out of the window'. Underground Man feels 'envy' for the ejected gentleman and decides to walk into the billiard room, get into a fight, and be thrown out of the window as well. But he finds that he is incapable of getting into a fight and so being ejected via a window; if this were a literary scene, he reflects, it could have involved a quarrel that might have led to a dramatic and honourable 'duel'. Instead, he was 'confronted by an officer' and experienced a humiliating backdown, he being 'short and emaciated' while the officer was 'about six feet tall'.[28]

This is how, in Underground Man's telling, the incident with the six-foot-tall officer occurs:

> I was standing by the billiard table, inadvertently blocking the way of this officer who wanted to get past. He took me by the shoulders in complete silence and without a word of warning or explanation shifted me from where I was standing to another place and then walked on, as if he hadn't even seen me. I would have forgiven him for beating me, but in no way could I forgive him for moving me from one place to another and completely failing to notice me.[29]

Underground Man feels that the gentlemen in the tavern, including the officer, are treating him 'like a fly', they would never consider a duel with a 'wretched civilian clerk', and as for impressing them with 'literary allusions' they would 'ridicule' him, they 'would simply die laughing'.[30]

With 'bitter feelings' Underground Man withdraws from this scene of humiliation by such ignorant people, so inferior in intelligence to him, determined that one day he would force the officer to take notice of him. His anger and loathing for the officer grows and grows; he must force the man to recognise his presence even if it takes 'several years'. He often sees the officer in the street, and observes him closely: 'Only, I can't say whether *he* recognized *me*.' He stalks him, eventually finds out his name, follows him to his flat and pays the caretaker ten copecks to tell him what he knows. One morning, though he had never before 'engaged in literary activities', he writes a story denouncing the officer, libellously, but it wasn't published because at that time 'there was still no denunciatory literature'. He composes a letter begging the officer to apologise; if the officer doesn't, he warns, he would 'in fairly strong terms' demand a duel; but he doesn't send it. A brilliant idea then occurs to him; every afternoon, he doesn't know why, he is drawn to 'strolling down the sunny side between three and four o'clock' of Nevsky Prospekt, or rather, he admits, he doesn't stroll along the fashionable avenue along with generals, Horse Guards officers or hussars, genteel ladies, a prince, a countess and 'the whole of literature'. In a parody of the Parisian flâneur, Underground Man recalls how he must have looked, 'the wretchedness and vulgarity of my small darting figure'. Again, the image of the fly comes to him: 'I was a fly in the eyes of all those society people, a revolting obscene fly – more intelligent and nobler than anyone else – that goes without saying – but… humiliated by everyone and insulted by everyone.'[31]

He often sees the officer on Nevsky Prospekt, noting that while he would step aside for generals, he would bear right down on nobodies like Underground Man 'as if there were empty space before him and under no circumstances would he give way'. The Underground Man 'bitterly made way for him every time': '*I* was the one who always stepped aside and he didn't even notice that I was giving way.' An 'amazing idea' occurs to Underground Man, so daring it makes him feel 'sheer joy', 'ecstatic'; next time he simply won't step aside; the plan will work. He decides to dress more formally, he asks for his salary in advance, he buys 'black gloves', a 'respectable hat' and a 'beaver' collar for his overcoat to replace his old and inferior 'racoon'. Even so, every time he tries to front up and if necessary collide with the officer, he gives way and the officer walks on without noticing him: 'He calmly walked right through me and I rolled to one side like a ball.'[32]

At night, after these repeated failed attempts, he begins to despair, he becomes delirious, but then 'everything came to the happiest possible conclusion'.

> Suddenly, about three paces from my enemy, I unexpectedly made up my mind, screwed up my eyes – and we collided squarely, shoulder to shoulder! I didn't yield one inch and I passed him – on an absolutely equal footing! He didn't even look around and pretended not to have noticed. But he was only pretending, of that I am certain. To this day I'm quite sure of that! Of course, I came off the worse, as he was the stronger; but that wasn't the point. The point was, I had achieved my purpose, upheld my dignity, hadn't yielded an inch, and had put myself on the same social footing as him in public.[33]

Jubilant, feeling avenged, certain that the officer had noticed him and acknowledged his presence even if he hadn't turned around, Underground Man celebrates his triumph by singing Italian arias, then spends a few months dreaming of being a hero.[34]

(The question belatedly occurs to me: why did I remember at all the incident with the officer, given that I couldn't remember anything else in *Notes from Underground*? I also recall a well-known event in Freud's life story, told in the biographies, when he was 12; as he was walking one day with his father Jacob, an anti-Semite threw his father's hat into the gutter, sneering, 'Jew, get off the pavement'. I talk it over with Ann. What if we all have a fear of precisely this experience in some other context in our lives? What would we do? I also remember the incident my uncles Lew and Jock tell in my *1492: The Poetics of Diaspora*, their memory of playing in the street in London as children, outside their house, and being attacked by anti-Semitic 'louts' yelling 'bloody Jews, Jew bastards' – denying the right of Jews to be in public, to share public space as equals. Ann reminds me that lots of feminist scholars have discussed the fraught history of women and public space.)

The next incident that interests me is when Underground Man, after 'three months on end dreaming', feels once more an 'irresistible need to plunge into society', he's unable to bear his 'solitude any longer', and again he unerringly seeks a situation that invites disdain and contempt. In a sequence that leads to his meeting Liza in the brothel, he decides to make an unannounced visit to 'Siminov, an old school friend of mine', though he's not sure of any remaining friendliness: 'I suspected that he found me extremely repulsive, but as I wasn't really certain of this I still visited him.' Also, he recalls, he still owed Simonov 15 roubles and had never paid him back.[35]

Siminov, clearly disconcerted by Underground Man's turning up uninvited, is talking with two other old school fellows, Ferfichkin and Trudolyubov, who immediately anger Underground Man by ignoring him, treating him as 'some kind of common house-fly'; he remembers that at school 'all of them had hated me there', and now would despise him because of his 'unsuccessful civil service career', his 'scruffy clothes', his evident 'ineptitude and mediocrity'.[36]

He does realise that they are discussing something important to them, which turns out to be that they are taking out for a farewell dinner another old schoolfellow, Zverkov, now an army officer who has been posted to some remote part of the provinces. It's clear they all admire Zverkov, but Underground Man hates him from schooldays for being so cocksure that he would be a success in life. They plan to meet at the Hotel de Paris the next evening, and make it clear to Underground Man that he is not invited, he is not part of Zverkov's intimate circle of friends, though when Underground Man insists, they reluctantly agree. At the Hotel de Paris, Underground Man immediately chokes with anger at what he takes to be Zverkov's patronising manner, he feels welling within him 'an imminent explosion'. He starts yelling out furious denunciations of the assembled company, mainly insulting their lack of intelligence, which in turn infuriates them, seeing their farewell dinner in honour of their officer friend facing ruin. Zverkov, he sees, 'was silently eyeing me as if I were some nasty insect'. The dinner turns disastrous, Underground Man becomes increasingly offensive, he challenges Ferfichkin to a duel, which makes everyone there collapse with laughter.[37] Over and over, it appears to him, his fear that he will be seen as a mere insect, as insectoid shall we say, comes true.

Then occurs a wonderfully cinematic scene of madness and dementia which, even after 40 years, he remembers as the 'nastiest, most ridiculous and ghastliest moments of my whole life'. While Siminov and the others, sitting on a sofa, take no notice of him, Underground Man, for three hours 'walked along the wall on the other side of the room, directly opposite the sofa, back and forth, from table to stove', always keeping to the same line. Only once, he records, did they turn towards him: 'to be exact, just as Zverkov started holding forth about Shakespeare and I suddenly broke into contemptuous laughter. I gave vent to such artificial, revolting snorts that they all broke off their conversation at once and for about two minutes – gravely and without laughing – watched me as I walked along the wall…' When the others say they're going to 'Olympia's', Underground Man suddenly abases himself, asks for their forgiveness, says he wants to come too, and then begs money from Siminov, who, disgusted, throws some at him. They leave without him.[38]

Liza: Medusa, Woman on Top

> 'Apollon', I whispered in a feverish patter… 'run down to the pub right away and bring some tea and ten dry biscuits. If you refuse you'll make me the unhappiest of mortals. You don't know what kind of woman she is… That's the whole point! Perhaps you're thinking things… But you don't know what kind of woman she is…!'

> 'I don't know, to this day I still cannot decide, but then I was of course even less able to understand it than I am now. Without

power and tyranny over someone I cannot survive. But… reasoning won't solve anything, so there's no point in reasoning.'
Notes from Underground[39]

Underground Man has been to Olympia's brothel before, so he knows where they are heading, though he is unsure of his reception there. ('Damn that Olympia! Once she laughed at my face and refused me.') He sees and hires a 'solitary night cabby', his 'coarse peasant greatcoat' covered in snow, in his impatience thumping 'the driver on the neck with my fist'. When he arrives at Olympia's establishment, he's bewildered to find that the others aren't there, it's clear to the reader that he doesn't realise he's been tricked.[40]

Underground Man is introduced by Olympia to Liza, a new prostitute working there, a young Russian woman from Riga. He forgets about his ex-acquaintances, and engages her in long gruelling duelling exchanges about family life, love, marriage, lecturing her on their virtues, until she reveals that she has been brutally ejected from her family home ('it was worse than here'). Liza, just 'twenty', is 'tall, strong and well-built', there is 'something kind and simple-hearted' in her face, yet strangely unnerving. He is drawn to her, though he catches sight of himself in a mirror: 'My agitated face struck me as utterly repulsive: pale, vicious, mean, my hair disheveled.' They lie together: 'All at once I saw right next to me two wide-open eyes surveying me curiously and intently.' Liza's eyes, he finds – the novella here perhaps recalling the mesmerizing eyes of a Medusa – are 'scrutinizing me'; she does not lower her eyes before his, nor does she alter her expression, 'so that finally I was overcome by a kind of eerie feeling'. Annoyed at her composure, which makes him in turn feel sadistic, he tells her that one day she will die a common prostitute, from consumption, carried out from a house of ill fame in a coffin.[41]

Liza answers back Underground Man's interrogation and taunting. When he lectures her on the virtues of fathers, Liza replies that some fathers – here anticipating Else's bitter thoughts on her father in *Fräulein Else* – are 'glad to sell their daughters rather than give them in marriage honestly'. He lectures Liza on marriage as beautiful and sublime, the life, he tells her, she will never have, and Liza gently mocks him for sounding just like a book. In revenge, gripped by angry spite, Underground Man sets out to humiliate her, telling her how much she disgusts him. He launches into a long Hogarth-like 'Harlot's Progress' (recall the sequence of the paintings and engravings: a young woman from the country becomes a prostitute in London, dying in the final image in her early twenties), detailing to Liza how by the age of 22 her life will have descended into ruin and death. Now he is sure he has accomplished what he wished to happen, to comprehensively break her soul, heart, being.[42]

Then his nerve fails him when he sees the effect on Liza:

> No, never, never before had I witnessed such despair! She lay there prone, her face buried in the pillow, clasping it with both hands. Her bosom was heaving. Her whole young body was violently shaking, as if she were having convulsions. Stifled sobs constricted her chest, then they rent it – and suddenly they broke free in wails and shrieks.[43]

Struck by remorse, Underground Man gives her his address and asks her to come and see him.

Now we arrive at the final sequence of Undergound Man's musings, when he recalls that Liza a few days later does indeed take up his invitation to visit his apartment. During this uncertain time before she comes, Underground Man finds himself in a state of dread and confusion, though he's not quite sure why: 'Something was rising, constantly and painfully rising in my soul, and wouldn't calm down'. He feels tormented, distraught. He doesn't want her seeing his 'poverty-stricken' flat, his 'oilskin sofa with the stuffing sticking out'; she'll notice his ragged dressing gown 'with which I can't even cover myself up!' He fears that his servant Apollon, who he dislikes intensely for his calmness and restraint, who he hates beyond anyone else, who he cannot subdue and bend to his will, will look down on her: 'That swine's bound to insult her.' But then he thinks, if she comes, he might be able to take control of the situation, enjoy an adventure; with Liza he could 'shape a human being's entire soul the way I wanted'. He looks forward to 'developing her, educating her'. He entertains an idea from literature of the George Sand variety that he could be 'her saviour': he would marry her, he will say to her: 'you are mine, you are my creation, pure and beautiful… you are my lovely wife'.[44]

To distract himself while anxious that she will come yet dreaming about the malleability of Liza's soul if she does, he picks a particularly vicious fight with Apollon (another in a succession of wonderful cinematic scenes), withholding his wages for no reason except to attempt yet again to prove that he is the master ('à la Napoléon') and Apollon a mere servant, whereas Apollon usually 'treated me with intolerable condescension'. While screaming at Apollon, Liza enters, stopping 'to stare at us in bewilderment'. Then follows the climactic cinematic scenes, a contestation in the romance tradition, an intense struggle between his desire to dominate her, and her power to answer back, with what I'm calling her Medusa eyes ('She sat down… all eyes').[45] Yet this will be a failed romance: a key obstacle cannot be overcome, on his, not her side.

A diversion, a side journey, is needed here. What do I mean by romance?

[R is for romance. In Xiaolu Guo's *A Concise Chinese-English Dictionary for Lovers* (2007), there is an entry for 'romance in fantasy, fiction, legend, novel, story, tale; exaggeration, falsehood, lie; ballad, idyll, song'.[46]]

My minimal definition for romance as a genre: a love relationship with obstacles.

I should explain what I mean by Liza's Medusa eyes. In 1990 Ann and I published an essay 'Popular Romance in the Postmodern Age' in the cultural studies journal *Continuum*.[47] I've just looked at it again and rediscovered what we said. We relate how in the 1980s, when we took to enjoying reading Mills and Boon novels, we were risking derision and contempt from our peers; still, in the cultural studies field, we were already pariahs, having been fairly brutally excommunicated at a cultural studies conference in Sydney several years before, in 1983, at a particular inner city university, when we dared to give a joint paper saying how much we enjoyed the TV serial *Prisoner* (or *Cell Block H*), set in a women's prison; at that time, for a long time, in the aesthetic hierarchy that ruled in cultural theory, popular texts were considered unworthy of any kind of affectionate treatment and especially of detailed textual analysis; they were sub-literature, para-literature, trash, schlock, drek; when we completed our presentation, a prominent cultural-studies practitioner, sitting in the front row, jumped up and began shouting at us; we stared at him, like Siminov and his friends when they gravely and quietly looked at Underground Man as he paced up and down at the Hotel de Paris; it was then time for the coffee break in a nearby large room, where Ann and I found that those we regarded as our colleagues, including some erstwhile friends, ignored us and would not come near us; large spaces opened around us, ones we dared not cross.[48]

We first started reading some Mills and Boon novels for a popular-culture discussion group. When that ended, we continued our reading. Our initial attitude was that any single M and B would be representative of the whole lot. We soon realised how wrong that was. We were struck by the vast range in writing style, narrative strength and gender politics. We were also struck by the exuberance of the genre, how 'mad' and frequently crazy M and Bs are, how much they enjoy their own extreme situations (often drawing on fairytale elements, of Cinderella and foundling stories). After a while, as with any genre, we began to pick out ones we enjoyed and favoured, and knew which not to bother with.

We found ourselves drawn to an older Mills and Boon writer, Sara Seale, with her complicated dialogue, gentle ironies, play of half-suggestions, restrained expression of emotion; the most Jane Austenish of the M and B writers we'd so far encountered, we thought (though this is not quite how I would see Austen now). Yet we also enjoyed more recent M and B contributors, like the heavy-breathing Melinda Cross, with her confident heroines and emotional heroes, her novels set in the US. We began to distinguish M and B 'national schools', for example, the Canadian. The Canadians we like include Sandra Field. Many of her romances set on the east coast, her novels witty and sexually explicit, journeys of social exploration into modern middle-class Canada; and Vanessa Grant, her romances moving about the coast of western Canada, her heroines always individualistic, strong, resisting emotional commitment. We compared these and other writers and hoped no one would ever hear us talk like this. Nor see us up the back in the second-hand sections of bookshops or in book exchanges we began on weekends to spend hours at, going through piles of old M and Bs searching for copies of a Seale, a Field, a Grant, a Cross or other favourites. On vacation, we took to exploring book exchanges in country towns.

For a while, we thought there were no interesting Australian contributors to the genre, until we stumbled on two we particularly liked, Edwina Shore and Emma Darcy – the last playful pseudonym suggesting how self-conscious is the romance genre, how aware of its ancestors it wishes to be, and this sent us back to nineteenth-century romance, to re-read its classics. Indeed, it was precisely because of reading M and Bs that we could now see that Jane Austen favourites like *Pride and Prejudice* and *Persuasion* were obviously, generically, romances. And we thought of the ways contemporary romance continuously draws on different aspects of Austen's novels, or Charlotte Bronte's *Jane Eyre*.

Romance can, we decided, do so much; it can be tragic, or, as with the cosmology of melodrama, offer a happy ending as the overcoming of the harsh fate that decrees separation and failure. Because the obstacles to the relationship can be anything in the characters' own biography and psychology, in differences of attitude and values concerning gender, class, region, ethnicity, subculture, whatever, it can endlessly socially explore. It is not fixed in any ideology, nor is it necessarily tied to heterosexuality in the lovers. For the romance to succeed, hero and heroine must think through for themselves a metamorphosis: think of Mr Darcy and Elizabeth Bennett in *Pride and Prejudice*; romances from Jane Austen onwards are dramas of transformation, involving key characters who learn about themselves in conflict with each other, and much of the pleasure of the genre lies precisely in the agon, the contest, the jousting, between the hero and heroine.

We saw romance in terms of a postmodern aesthetic, a poetics of excess, enjoying extravagance, flamboyance, fantasy and delight in extremes; and maybe that changed to some degree our view of Jane Austen.

In the first decade of the 2000s I returned to thinking about popular romance in an essay, 'The question of Europe: Said and Derrida', in a collection of essays, *Edward Said: The Legacy of a Public Intellectual* (2007), edited by Ned Curthoys and Debjani Ganguly. I set out to explore their differences, or rather, say how much I liked Edward Said as thinker, and how much less and less, as I got older, I liked Derrida.[49] Yet I did wish to disagree with Said on one point. Rather playfully, I found myself chiding Said's well-known disdain for mass culture. I mention in 'The question of Europe: Said and Derrida' that in a book which Ann and I long planned to write, and had written quite a few chapters for, but which we never got round to completing (Ann says I should, maybe I will), entitled at first 'Popular Romance and the

Orient' and then 'Disorienting Europe', we suggest a genealogy for Mr Darcy and Elizabeth Bennett as cultural figures. Via Mario Praz's 1930 book *Romantic Agony*, we note that Byron's Oriental poems *The Giaour* (1813), *The Corsair* (1814) and *Lara* (1814), helped create the Gothic and Romantic Fatal Man as proud, arrogant, devilish, yet tortured, brooding, melancholy; related to Milton's Satan, an angel fallen but still beautiful; and fused with other cultural figures – the bandit hero, the noble ruffian, admired brigand, generous outlaw, sublime criminal. Praz also contends that there is a matching Gothic and Romantic Fatal Woman, whose beautiful eyes bewitch, a gorgon, a Medusa, to whom men are irresistibly drawn even as she tortures, torments and destroys them; desire and pleasure are mixed with terror, pain, suffering and sadness.

Ann and I then go on to propose that in nineteenth century and later popular romance, taking *Pride and Prejudice* (1813) as its primary progenitor – a novel in which romance wittily mixes with other generic elements, of social and psychological realism, stage comedy and pantomime, anti-romance, mystery, suspense and melodrama – the Fatal Man in the haughty personage of Mr Darcy, and the Fatal Woman figured in the lively independence and betwitching eyes of Elizabeth Bennett, are placed within the one text, the one drama of confrontation, there to joust and duel, especially over his assumption of superiority and her issue of challenge to that assumption. The heroine does not succumb: she defies, resists, challenges the power of his gaze, and his hypnotic eyes, with the power of her gaze, her hypnotic eyes. Here is the source, we contend, of much of the attraction and pleasure of the popular female romance tradition that *Pride and Prejudice* did so much to enduringly shape, for in their incessant conflict both hero and heroine reveal themselves to be capable of change, transformation, metamorphosis.[50]

I'll stop pondering the fascination of the romance genre

now, except to mention my latest thought, that perhaps we can compare *Pride and Prejudice* to Plato's so brilliant philosophical novel *The Symposium*. I think now that the mixing and contrasting of various generic elements in *Pride and Prejudice* that I evoked just before, distributed among the various characters, can be thought about as different and contrasting perspectives on love, from the optimistic to the deeply pessimistic, from depressing failure to the farcical. I therefore now want to see *Pride and Prejudice* as a symposium, especially as I wrote about Plato's *Symposium* in my 2008 book *The Origins of Violence*. I relate that Bakhtin in *Problems of Dostoevsky's Poetics* wrote that in Plato texts like *The Symposium*, Socrates is created as but one character among others, he is not necessarily to be taken as the voice as it were of the text, the only character to be taken seriously or to be regarded as central; in antiquity, says Bakhtin, the symposium was a carnival genre, its setting usually a banquet, permitting a right to frank speech, to eccentricity and ambivalence, to a combining of the serious and the comic. Bakhtin notes that the scene of *The Symposium* is one of after-dinner relaxation, urbane and witty, between friends and acquaintances, where the entertainment is the art of conversation itself. While the participants in the banquet dialogue are all male, a major contributor to the conversation is off-stage, Socrates' friend and teacher Diotima, 'a woman from Mantinea'.[51]

As in *Pride and Prejudice* with its kaleidoscope of representations of love, so *The Symposium* explores how multiple representations of love glance off each other, in long speeches by and exchanges between Phaedrus, Pausanias, Eryximachus, Agathon and Aristophanes, whose burlesque fantasy is a highlight of the novel. Socrates' contribution to the discussion, a mystical interpretation of homosexual desire and love, is highly curious in its mode. When asked for his opinion by his companions, Socrates doesn't answer directly but instead recounts a conversation he once had with a female philosopher, Diotima, who taught him, he says, his method of proceeding by question and answer; she was also, he confides, 'my instructress in the art of love'. Socrates then tells his friends about a question-and-answer session with Diotima where she had treated him at times quite roughly for his philosophical ignorance and inadequacy, while leading him to see the sacredness that ideally inheres in the desire for beauty, goodness and truth. What featured in their conversation, as happily reported by Socrates himself, were male-female inversions of knowledge, wisdom and rigour of argumentation.[52] Near the end of the banquet, Alcibiades makes a tipsy appearance, then a crowd of revelers arrive, amid general uproar. Nothing about the nature of love, then, is agreed to and established as true, and the symposium ends in a kind of disorganised and comic chaos of different attitudes and viewpoints.

We might say the same or similar of *Pride and Prejudice*: while the melodrama suspense concerning the disappearance of Lydia is resolved by Mr Darcy's detective-like intervention, and love succeeds after the removal of various obstacles between Mr Darcy and Elizabeth, and Jane Bennett and Mr Bingley, the novel's kaleidoscope of perspectives on love and marriage, unresolved, unresolvable, continues in the reader's mind. *Pride and Prejudice* delights us, but it also haunts and disturbs.

After this speculative outburst, feeling rather pleased with myself, I googled on impulse, and found my bringing *The Symposium* and *Pride and Prejudice* into some kind of relationship is a commonplace of liberal arts courses on the history of conceptions of love from antiquity to the present. I'm just incrementally adding to a tradition of thought.

If, as I'm pondering, the relationship between Underground Man and Liza is somehow part of this romance tradition, with various glaring qualifications such as Underground Man falling considerably short of being a Byronic Fatal Man, what is the key obstacle that so disastrously ends their relationship? Let's turn in our fingers to the final threads of the novel, Underground Man remembering events that occurred many years before, with agony, with regret, yet with a sense he could not do otherwise than what he so appallingly did.

Very briefly: Liza murmurs that 'I want... to get away from that place... altogether...' Hearing this, Underground Man becomes enraged and shouts at her that her plea to be rescued is laughable, 'I'm laughing at you'. Humiliating her is a sport for him; also, he can't forgive her for viewing his apartment in all its shabbiness, for seeing him 'hysterical' and realising that 'I'm a cad, the vilest, most ridiculous, pettiest, stupidest, most jealous of all the worms on earth'. Underground Man delivers this tirade while 'in tears'. But then Underground Man is taken by surprise: 'She understood from all this what a woman will always understand first and foremost if she loves sincerely, namely, that I myself was unhappy.' Liza holds out her arms to Underground Man, suddenly rushes towards him, throws her arms around his neck and bursts into tears, while he also 'sobbed as I had never sobbed before'. He collapses on the sofa, 'face downwards' and 'sobbed really hysterically for a quarter of an hour', while Liza is embracing him, and he feels powerfully drawn to her.[53]

At this point, dear Reader, contemplating this remarkable tableau, we surely think of Natalie Zemon Davis's essay 'Woman on Top'. Underground Man certainly begins to realise the implications of Liza being on top of him as it were: as he lay face down, his face buried in his 'cheap leather cushion', the 'thought entered my overwrought brain that our roles had now been completely reversed', that Liza was 'the heroine and that I was just such a humiliated and crushed creature' as she had appeared to him in Olympia's brothel a few nights before. While Liza is embracing him, rapturously and fervently, he feels powerfuly drawn to her, other and contrary feelings flare up in Underground Man, of hatred and desire for 'mastery and possession'. He now insults her so 'definitively' that he can't tell the story; he is sure that Liza now realises that his 'fit of passion was indeed revenge, a fresh humiliation for her', that he is acting now out of a '*personal, jealous hatred of her*' (*italics* by Underground Man); she understands now he is 'incapable of loving her', that he is 'loathsome'.[54]

Liza prepares to leave and never see him again. Underground Man, frantic in his impatience for her to be gone, constantly goes over to the screens behind which she is dressing, peeping at her 'through the narrow gap between them': 'She was sitting on the floor, leaning her head on the bed and she must have been crying.' He knocks on the screen to remind her to go, and when Liza emerges and gives him 'a pained look', he turns away from 'her stare'. As Liza made her way towards the front door, Underground Man ran after her, unclasped her hand and 'put something into it and then clasped it again': his final humiliation of her, as if all along she was nothing to him but a prostitute to be paid for her services. But, – Liza was not crushed. After she had gone, he notices on a table a 'crumpled, blue five-rouble note, the very one that I had thrust into her hand a moment before'.[55] Her final act was to scorn him completely, to free herself from his defining her being.

Underground Man feels 'utterly miserable'; he recognises that in his cruelty he had been carrying out a bookish scene, what he had done was merely 'cerebral'; perhaps in his heart he did love her; he rushes out into the street, but can't see her: 'Never again did I meet Liza, nor did I hear what became of her.' His memory of Liza ever afterwards would continue to be fused with anguish, uncertainty and shame; he realises that in not forming a relationship with her and returning her love, he has 'missed out on life'. Yet he recognises that precisely because he 'kissed her feet' that day, if they had formed a relationship, he would still torment her with hatred for being (in Natalie Zemon Davis's memorable term) a woman on top in her refusing his money and returning it to him.[56]

At this point, in a traumatised state of dazed contradictory feelings, Underground Man considers ending the writing of his Notes.[57]

In his very final reflections Underground Man suggests perhaps the overriding reason why he had to refuse a love relationship with Liza. He will always be distraught that he may have done the wrong thing. But in the scale of things he has constructed for himself, he does not wish to transform his life and consciousness that living with Liza might lead to. The metamorphosis demanded by romance is that which he comes to reject, for, as he relates in the last couple of pages, he has conceived a higher ambition for himself that requires that his life and personality stay as they are, craving superiority as a writer and pursuing a life of humiliation because of what he refers to as 'my narcissistic, underground spite'; even if that means he will be viewed by any future readers not as a hero but 'an anti-hero'. Liza would prove a distraction from this higher ambition, for women are satisfied with a single ambition, to love: 'for women love comprises their total resurrection, their total salvation from any kind of ruin, their total regeneration and cannot manifest itself in any other kind of way'.[58]

Underground Man explains to himself his ambition, the destiny he dreams of: he believes he can claim representative status for himself in history, he represents humanity in the nineteenth century, he represents modernity itself, he represents the future, because he at least openly admits that 'we are all cripples, each one of us to a greater or lesser extent', living only 'according to books'. Only he, Underground Man, has had the courage to live out a representative life of underground misery and humiliation, yet which also always involves a striving for power over others: 'Without power and tyranny over someone I cannot survive.' He chides his gentlemen readers: 'as far as I'm concerned, I've merely carried to extremes in my life things that you've never had the courage even to take halfway… what's more you've interpreted your cowardice as common sense and found comfort in deceiving yourselves'. So, he declares, 'perhaps I'll prove to be "more alive" than you'.[59]

Uncannily anticipating Yeats' 'Second Coming', Underground Man writes:

> Leave us to our own devices, without our books, and we'll immediately get into a muddle and lose our way – we shan't know what side to take, where to place our allegiance, what to love and what to hate, what to respect and what to despise.[60]

So ends Underground Man's reflections.

Sitting at the café this morning in Perth, where since the middle of 2016 Ann and I have lived, looking sightlessly into the near distance, I thought: maybe Underground Man was right to prophesy that his mode of being, with its desire to dominate and shape the soul of others who come within his power – his masculine power, however much his own claims to masculinity were derided by other men, – in all its banality of evil, in all its derangement and torment, did become the story of the twentieth century and continues now, in the twentieth first: think of fascism and Nazism, think of dictators in the 1930s and later and those to come; think of the British Empire and its genocidal subjugation of so many peoples; think of the idiotic American imperium; yet think of how much peoples of the world, especially those considered lower, have resisted, fought back, against any and all empires of domination, not least the British Empire, which was forced to an end like all empires before it.

Here, I hazard, is the allegory of Liza's final scorning of Underground Man. And, I think, I will return to these thoughts when, in considering the later 1930s on the eve of the Holocaust, I come to Virginia Woolf's *Three Guineas* and its radical questioning of the close historical relation between masculinity and war.

In a final short paragraph appended to *Notes from Underground*, the long-absent author makes a belated appearance, saying that Underground Man couldn't help continuing to write his Notes in a kind of infinite repetition. But, the author feels, 'here we might call a halt'.[61]

I'll press on now to consider Freud's psychoanalytic novella 'Dora', how it looks in the light of Bakhtin's distinction between Dostoevsky and Tolstoy; how it looks in the light of Underground Man's declaration, 'Without power and tyranny over someone I cannot survive'; and especially how it looks in the light of Schnitzler's *Fräulein Else*.

1   Arthur Schnitzler, *Desire and Delusion: Three Novellas*, translated by Margret Schaefer (Ivan R. Dee, Chicago, 2003), p.204.

2   Fyodor Dostoevsky, *Notes from Underground and The Double*, translated by Ronald Wilks, with an Introduction by Robert Louis Jackson (Penguin Classics, London, 2009), p.113.

3   John Docker, *The Nervous Nineties: Australian Cultural Life in the 1890s* (Oxford University Press, Melbourne, 1991), p.x; Mikhail Bakhtin, *The Dialogic Imagination* (University of Texas Press, Austin, 1981), pp.86–110; Mikhail Bakhtin, *Problems of Dostoevsky's Poetics*, edited and translated by Caryl Emerson (Manchester University Press, Manchester, 1984).

4   Docker, *The Nervous Nineties*, pp.116–7; Bakhtin, *Problems of Dostoevsky's Poetics*, pp.5–7, 14–17, 69–73, 111–37.

5   Leo Tolstoy, *War and Peace*, translated, annotated and introduced by Richard Pevear and Larissa Volokhonsky (Vintage Books, London, 2009), pp.1154–8.

6   Tolstoy, *War and Peace*, pp.1157–58.

7   Docker, *The Nervous Nineties*, pp.116–7.

8   Bakhtin, *Problems of Dostoevsky's Poetics*, pp.154–5.

9   Bakhtin, *Problems of Dostoevsky's Poetics*, pp.48–50.

10 Nikolay Gogol, *The Diary of a Madman, The Government Inspector and Selected Stories*, translated by Ronald Wicks (Penguin, London, 2005), pp.176, 181–2, 189.

11 Virginia Woolf, *The Waves*, edited with an Introduction and Notes by David Bradshaw (Oxford World's Classics, Oxford, 2015), pp.xii-xiii.
12 Virginia Woolf, *The Waves*, Introduction, p.xii.
13 Bakhtin, *Problems of Dostoevsky's Poetics*, p.253.
14 Bakhtin, *Problems of Dostoevsky's Poetics*, p.227.
15 Bakhtin, *Problems of Dostoevsky's Poetics*, pp.51-3, 59, 254.
16 Bakhtin, *Problems of Dostoevsky's Poetics*, pp.228-9, 235, 253-4.
17 Bakhtin, *Problems of Dostoevsky's Poetics*, p.233.
18 Bakhtin, *Problems of Dostoevsky's Poetics*, pp.233-7, 253-4.
19 John Docker, *Postmodernism and Popular Culture: A Cultural History* (Cambridge University Press, Melbourne, 1994), p.138.
20 Dostoevsky, *Notes from Underground*, p.117.
21 *Notes from Underground*, p.ix.
22 *Notes from Underground*, p.36.
23 *Notes from Underground*, pp.6-7, 16.
24 *Notes from Underground*, p.51.
25 *Notes from Underground*, pp.3-5.
26 *Notes from Underground*, pp.7, 34.
27 *Notes from Underground*, pp.13-14, 43.
28 *Notes from Underground*, pp.4, 44.
29 *Notes from Underground*, p.44.
30 *Notes from Underground*, p.45.
31 *Notes from Underground*, pp.44-8.
32 *Notes from Underground*, pp.47-9.
33 *Notes from Underground*, pp.49-50.
34 *Notes from Underground*, pp.50-1.
35 *Notes from Underground*, pp.53-4, 59.
36 *Notes from Underground*, p.55.
37 *Notes from Underground*, pp.55, 65, 69-70.
38 *Notes from Underground*, pp.71-3.
39 *Notes from Underground*, pp.107, 112-13.
40 *Notes from Underground*, pp.74-8.
41 *Notes from Underground*, pp.78-81, 84.
42 *Notes from Underground*, pp.86-93.
43 *Notes from Underground*, p.94.

44 *Notes from Underground*, pp.98–101.
45 *Notes from Underground*, pp.101–2, 106–7.
46 Xiaolu Guo, *A Concise Chinese-English Dictionary for Lovers* (Vintage, London, 2007), pp.143–7.
47 Ann Curthoys and John Docker, 'Popular Romance in the Postmodern Age', *Continuum*, Vol.4, no.1, 1990, pp.22–35.
48 Docker, *Postmodernism and Popular Culture: A Cultural History*, pp.159–160. See also John Docker and Ann Curthoys, 'Stuart Hall and Cultural Studies, circa 1983', *Cultural Studies Review*, vol.23, no.2, 2017, pp.162–73. (This is a review essay, reflecting on Stuart Hall, *Cultural Studies 1983: A Theoretical History*. Edited and with an introduction by Jennifer Daryl Stack and Lawrence Grossberg, Duke University Press, Durham, 2016.)
49 John Docker, 'The question of Europe: Said and Derrida', in Ned Curthoys and Debjani Ganguly (eds), *Edward Said: The Legacy of a Public Intellectual* (Melbourne University Press, Melbourne, 2007), pp.263–290.
50 John Docker, 'The question of Europe: Said and Derrida', pp.266–7.
51 John Docker, *The Origins of Violence: Religion, History and Genocide* (Pluto, London, 2008), pp.94–5; Bakhtin, *Problems of Dostoevsky's Poetics*, p.120; Plato, *The Symposium*, translated by Walter Hamilton (Penguin, London, 1987), p.79.
52 Plato, *The Symposium*, pp.79–85.
53 *Notes from Underground*, pp.109, 111–12.
54 *Notes from Underground*, pp.112–13.
55 *Notes from Underground*, pp.113–15.
56 *Notes from Underground*, pp.116–7.
57 *Notes from Underground*, p.117.
58 *Notes from Underground*, pp.114, 117.
59 *Notes from Underground*, pp.113, 1178.
60 *Notes from Underground*, p.118.
61 *Notes from Underground*, p.118.

20

Undutiful Daughters

Dear Dr Schnitzler,
... I have tormented myself with the question why in all these years I have never attempted to make your acquaintance... I think I have avoided you from a kind of reluctance to meet my double... Whenever I get deeply absorbed in your beautiful creations I invariably seem to find beneath their poetic surface the very presuppositions, interests, and conclusions which I know to be my own... So I have formed the impression that you know through intuition – or rather from detached self-observation – everything that I have discovered by laborious work on other people.

Sigmund Freud to Arthur Schnitzler, 14 May 1922[1]

... *Fräulein Else* is a comment... most particularly on Dora, the subject of Freud's 'Fragment of an Analysis of a Case of Hysteria'. But Schnitzler understands Else better than Freud understood Dora.

Margaret Schaefer, Foreword to Schnitzler, *Desire and Delusion*[2]

In this one case history... sexual relationships are discussed frankly, the organs and functions of sexual life are called by their right names, and my account may well give readers with a strong sense of propriety the impression that I did not shrink from discussing such subjects, in such language, with a young woman. Am I supposed to defend myself against that accusation too? I simply claim the rights of the gynaecologist... and say for anyone to consider conversations of that nature a good means of exciting or satisfying sexual desires is the sign of a perverse and strangely prurient mind.

                              Freud, Foreword to *A Case of Hysteria (Dora)*.[3]

At our third sitting, she [Dora] said, as she came in, 'Doctor, you're aware, aren't you, that this is the last time I'm coming to see you?'

                                          Freud, *A Case of Hysteria (Dora)*[4]

Freud's long essay, or short book, or treatise, or novella, written up from his case history notes of 1901, was published in 1905 as 'Fragment of an Analysis of a Case of Hysteria'. He had high hopes of it being recognised as of great importance for psychoanalysis not only as an investigation of female hysteria, a preoccupying topic of the *fin de siècle*, but as an exemplar of a new methodology; a fully objective, detached, scientific reading of the Unconscious, where the Unconscious was to be considered the repository of the truth of the human psyche; now its secret life could be exposed and explored, systematically, exhaustively, infallibly, flawlessly. The essay would be of epochal significance, for psychoanalysis, for knowledge of the mind, and for Freud himself as theorist of what constitutes the essence of humanity.

However, as Freud was acutely aware, from the very beginning of his writing up his notes in narrative form, his hopes for the essay were haunted by the spectre of catastrophic failure. The essay alas had to be presented to the scientific community he was addressing as a 'fragment' because Dora – the name Freud gave to Ida Bauer, born in 1882, a young Jewish middle-class Viennese woman compelled by her father against her will to see Freud – had chosen to leave before the analysis was finished to Freud's scientific satisfaction, so that he could not be certain of it as a proof of his method. This was especially frustrating because Freud was so confident, if circumstances had permitted, that he could have provided a 'full explanation of this case of *petite hystérie*': 'From my experience with other patients, I do not doubt that my analytical methods would have enabled me to do so.'[5] To his discomfort, Freud had to admit to his fellow medical specialist colleagues that, though he was sure he was right because his method was right, he could never be completely sure; and all because of a young woman whose conscious opinions about things that mattered most to her he despised, and who had dared to leave after the third interview.

In the longer term, Freud's essay has had to endure choppy waters for decades now. It has been witheringly critiqued by generations of feminist theorists. And it is now more likely to be taught in a department of literature rather than in psychology courses, according to Ritchie Robertson's coruscating Introduction to Anthea Bell's translation, given the title *A Case of Hysteria (Dora)*, for Oxford World's Classics.[6] I learned a lot from Robertson's reflections on how brutal Freud's interrogations of Dora were in his attempt to cure her; a cure she herself never sought for a pathological condition she never agreed she had; a cure she came quickly to regard as risible, not to say absurd and ridiculous.

Robertson tells us, and I very much agree with him, that *A Case of Hysteria (Dora)* should be read as a work of fiction, a novella, despite Freud's insistence that it is a model of scientific observation, careful interpretation and scrupulous argumentation. We must now, Robertson writes, see Freud as an 'unreliable narrator', and we should 'apply Freudian methods of interpretation to Freud himself'.[7] Turning Freud against himself is what I will also try to do, in my own so to say carnivalesque Bakhtinian way. In these terms, I will explore the inverse relationship between the Unconscious and the Conscious that Freud attempts to impose on Dora. Then I will turn the Unconscious Freud against the Conscious Freud, in the spirit of Phyllis as Woman on Top, as Natalie Zemon Davis tells us in her famous essay, turning Aristotle's claim to intellectual authority inside out and upside down: so too Dora did to Freud when she chose to refuse his fantastical claims, leaving Freud fuming, resentful and vindictive, embarrassingly unable to conceal his chagrin from his colleagues who he so hoped to impress and convince.[8]

We can say that when Dora walked out of Freud's increasingly threatening theatre of analysis – and, I will suggest, planned seduction, – she walked into world literature and world culture, in the company of Liza in *Notes from Underground*, the heroine of Charlotte Perkins Gilman's *The Yellow Wallpaper*, Ida Rubinstein, Virginia Woolf and Fräulein Else. She regained her freedom as an actant. And her upending the totalising pretensions of psychoanalysis presaged Gay Liberation's attack in the 1960s and 1970s on psychology's nefarious institutional powers and as a faux science of the mind.

I think there is a great deal in common between the harsh treatment of Liza by the narrator-persecutor of *Notes from Underground* and the harsh treatment of Dora by Freud the narrator-persecutor of *A Case of Hysteria (Dora)*; Liza and Dora both devastatingly defeat their narrator-persecutors, leaving them profoundly unsettled and unnerved. To borrow Bakhtin's terms concerning Dostoevsky, Liza and Dora rebel against the narrator who would encapsulate and delimit them; they refuse to assent to their narrator-persecutors retaining for themselves the final word. Liza and Dora assert their rights as autonomous subjects in the narrative; in Bakhtin's idiom, they insist on remaining unfinalised and unfinalisable.

Bakhtin's metaphor, of the loophole left open that shadows the word, has me wondering: does Freud's novella, his so-called scientific proof (if unfinished) of the exact characteristics of her supposed pathological condition, possess a loophole that is left open, suggesting meanings he and his text can't control? Does he realise that every word of his own is shadowed by other meanings that chameleon (if I can use chameleon as a verb) his pompous yet brittle and aggrieved self-presentation? Was Freud in his 'Dora' novella capable of self-irony and self-parody, as the Underground Man was so capable? If not, is he inferior to Underground Man in this respect? In other respects, however, I feel, Freud is a match for Underground Man in malice, the pursuit of revenge if thwarted in any way, and desire for power and tyranny over another person, without which, as Underground Man remarked of himself, he could not survive. Freud's own neuropathological condition we will have occasion to explore as well.

In the latter part of the essay, I turn to Foucault's illuminating reflections on the history of psychiatry and psychoanalysis in relation to the notion of hysteria, and Xiaolu Guo's autobiography *Once upon a time in the East*, which invokes a history of sexual abuse that throws a searching light on Freud's 'Dora'.

Freud as Tolstoyan Narrator

I'll begin my journey into *A Case of Hysteria (Dora)* by applying Bakhtin's distinction between Tolstoy and Dostoevsky.

Recall that in *Problems of Dostoevsky's Poetics* Bakhtin says that the Tolstoyan tradition is monologic; the author is all-knowing and all-controlling; his characters are not active subjects, but become objects of his fixed authoritative gaze, his all-encompassing field of vision; characters are denied anything like equal rights with their author; and the author gives to his characters a definitive, final meaning.

Here we can situate Freud as monologic narrator in *A Case of Hysteria (Dora)*, analysing Dora as it were from above (or behind, given that Dora lay on a sofa, Freud eerily sitting on a chair behind her; think of Freud's consulting rooms on display in Vienna and in Hampstead in London), denying her her own consciousness and equal rights as an interlocutor. Yet, when Dora asserted her equality, becoming an active subject and contesting with quiet and dignified bemusement Freud's assertions and then politely ending the sessions, Freud's certainty as Tolstoyan author goes awry. He doesn't know how to proceed. Bakhtin noted that Dostoevsky's *Notes from Underground* comes within the genre of confession, *Ich-Erzählung*. So too does *A Case of Hysteria (Dora)*. For a scientific treatise, and given his own positivist ideals, it is surprisingly personal. Freud uses the I voice in the first sentence of his 'Foreword' and as the first word of his opening chapter 'The Clinical Picture'. After Dora tells him she won't be returning, his I voice begins to quaver with anger; he's hurt; he's bewildered; his imperious confidence falters; and he becomes querulous. The proposed scientific demonstration turns into a narrative of protest against Dora, as if he's now a victim of her cruelty; he verbally abuses her, accuses her of demeaning and humiliating him, of dismissing him as she would a mere governess.

> She had been listening without, as usual, raising objections. She seemed to be moved, said goodbye in the most charming way, wishing me every happiness in the New Year, left – and did not come back… I knew she would not be back. It was an undisputed act of revenge for her to break off the treatment so suddenly, when I had every expectation of bringing the analysis to a happy conclusion, thus dashing all those hopes.[9]

The treatise becomes a novelistic drama of faltering ambition, of anguish, of rage, where what he assumed would be a victory for his method – and for his designs on Dora's body and mind – has turned into ashes and dust. Narrative and narrator disintegrate.

In *Notes from Underground*, Underground Man looked forward to a pleasurable adventure, he would shape a human being's entire soul the way he wanted, Liza would be created anew; so too Freud in *A Case of Hysteria (Dora)* looked forward to the pleasure of reshaping Dora's soul. Now, wretchedly, he has to confess to his peers what happened.

Freud's Splicing Technique: Unconscious/Conscious

Freud's methodology soon becomes apparent, a reversal of Unconscious and Conscious that can be applied to all human beings, or at least those in a pathological state; not to himself, he's a doctor, a gynaecologist, a psychoanalyst, a scientist. He applies this reversal to Dora. In terms of the truth of Dora's psyche, he will favour the evidence of her Unconscious rather than her Conscious, which he dismisses as of no truth value, to the point where he doesn't believe a word she says. Her Conscious, nevertheless, is of great negative importance, for the reverse of whatever Dora says consciously will constitute the truth of her Unconscious; that's how, triumphantly, scientifically, he knows what her Unconscious desires are. His task then is to communicate to Dora – bluntly and brutally, as Robertson says in his Introduction[10] – what the true state of her affections are, who she really loves despite her Conscious insisting otherwise. Enlightened by such knowledge, Dora would then be cured of her false consciousness, she would possess a new consciousness transformed by knowing the truth of her being.

Nonetheless, when Dora first recounts the experiences that she believes have profoundly disturbed and harmed her in her life, that have caused her anxiety and trauma, Freud appears quite sympathetic. Dora has been brought to Freud for treatment for 'hysteria' by her father, accompanied by her father's friend Herr K, a key figure in this history. In a long footnote Freud remarks that he is a little concerned that at least some of her hysteria may be hereditary, for he is aware that before his marriage Dora's father 'had contracted syphilis'; as a 'neuropathologist' Freud recognises that 'a father's syphilis can easily be regarded as the cause of his children's neuropathological constitution'. Freud adds that a *'strikingly large* percentage of the patients I have treated by psychoanalysis are the offspring of fathers who have suffered from *tabes* or paralysis'. He learns that Dora from the age of eight years had suffered from nervous symptoms such as 'complete loss of voice', and the 'many customary treatments tried, including hydrotherapy and localized electric-shock therapy, were unsuccessful'. Now 'eighteen', Freud will treat her by psychoanalysis, confident that its methods will succeed.[11]

Freud at once perceives Dora's intelligence and 'precocious intellectual development'. He realises too that Dora is wary of doctors, in a way that reminds us of Gilman's *The Yellow Wallpaper* and Virginia Woolf. Freud learns that Dora had grown up to become a 'mature girl exercising her own independent judgement', and that she used to 'mock the efforts of the doctors and finally rejected medical assistance'. She did not dislike the family doctor personally, but always resisted having him called in to give advice. Any suggestion of 'consulting another doctor met with opposition from her', and 'only her father's express command brought her to me'. He sees that Dora is a 'girl in the bloom of youth, with intelligent and pleasing features', but her parents were becoming very anxious about her; there was a change in her character, she was in low spirits, she was 'clearly not happy with herself', she experienced weariness and absent-mindedness, she tried to avoid company, she was 'unfriendly to her father', she had suffered 'her first fainting fit', and mother and father were alarmed to find in her desk a note contemplating suicide because 'she couldn't bear her life any more'. However, she continued to occupy 'herself in attending lectures for ladies and pursuing serious studies'.[12]

(Here we could be reading about Virginia Stephen at home studying, while her brother Thoby was at his college in Cambridge, his being there to some degree enabled by money that could have gone to Virginia and could have enabled her to study at university. Dora's brother Otto Bauer certainly enjoyed higher education, at the University of Vienna, and it would be interesting to know if money that should have rightfully gone to Ida for a university education went to her brother instead, perhaps a European-wide gender pattern in upper middle-class families. Otto Bauer, who became a prominent Austrian socialist intellectual, is mentioned at one point in Hannah Arendt's *Origins of Totalitarianism*, suggesting in 1907 that nationality be separated entirely from its territorial status, to be only a kind of personal status.[13] Freud, as Robertson points out, doesn't explain what the 'serious studies' were that Dora was applying herself to, and we don't know if he asked her about them: a pity, because her serious studies may have been associated with critical perspectives that informed her skepticism towards the medical profession in general and psychoanalysis in particular, that was more and more interfering with the lives of Ida and other young women she knew or knew of in Vienna. Formally educated, Ida may have had the confidence to match her brother in intellectual productivity and stature.)[14]

From now on, I will refer to Dora by her actual name, since Freud's essay became known outside the scientific community for which he was writing. It came to the notice of Ida herself, who then realised that Freud, without her permission, had published an analysis of her that included intimate details of her life. Also, on one of our morning walks, Ann said to me as I was repeating myself by saying how nauseating and incredible I found Freud's assertions about Dora, why not say Ida instead, why accept Freud's name for her? Hhhhmmm, I said, maybe. I'll see if switching back and forth works.

Given how well known Freud's 'Dora' novella is, I'll try and briefly summarise the key turning points for Ida that triggered her traumatised state over a long period, at least as far as I can draw these out of Freud's account, which is far from clear however many times one reads it; in particular, as Robertson comments in his Introduction, it's unclear from Freud's text just how old, or rather young, Dora was during the incidents that most distressed her, those that involved close family friend Herr K.[15] (I immediately think of Herr von Dorsday in Schnitzler's *Fräulein Else*.)

In a nod to positivism, Freud tells his scientist colleagues that he had to work out the 'real facts' of Dora's 'case history' from the conflicting stories told him by Ida, and Ida's father, whose 'intelligence' he admires; Ida's father, the patriarch who had forced Ida 'in spite of her resistance' to begin treatment with Freud. (Freud doesn't appear in the least ethically concerned that Ida had not wanted to be the object of his treatment.) Ida's father's story is that he and her mother had become close friends with another couple, Herr K and Frau K, at various places outside Vienna, and Frau K had taken to nursing her father through 'his severe illness' (presumably his syphilis) which Dora's mother had declined to do (Dora's mother was bitter that she had contracted syphilis from her father, and they now had no sexual relations).[16]

Freud learns that Ida was convinced that her father and Frau K had become lovers while she was tenderly nursing him, despite Ida's father's assertion to the contrary: 'When she [Ida] was in an embittered mood, the idea that she had been delivered up to Herr K.'s mercies as a price for his toleration of the relationship between Dora's father and his wife came forcibly into her mind'. (We can marvel at Freud's bizarrely legalistic gloss here: 'Of course, the two men never concluded a formal agreement in which she was an object of barter'.) Ida's father tells Freud that Herr K had 'always been very kind to his daughter Dora' when she was a child, 'going for walks with her… and giving her little presents, but no one', Ida's father continued, 'would have seen anything wrong in that', though even Freud is a little skeptical when the father tells him that for a year Herr K was 'able to send

Dora flowers every day while he was in the same town, use every opportunity to make her expensive presents, and spend all his free time in her company without her parents seeing anything like sexual advances in his conduct'.[17]

On one occasion, it was arranged that Dora would stay in the K household for several weeks while her father was to return to Vienna. However, Dora suddenly said to her father, 'very firmly', that she 'wanted to go back with him, and she got her way'. A few days later, said the father to Freud, Dora gave the reason, 'that Herr K. had made advances to her on a walk after an outing on the lake'. Next time her father met with Herr K, Herr K denied that he had made any such advances, and said that Dora had obviously imagined the incident. Dora's father tells Freud that Dora wanted him to break off all contact with Herr K and also with Frau K, but he could not do so, because he was sure 'Dora's story of the husband's immoral conduct is a fantasy', and in any case he could do nothing to impair the 'genuine friendship' that bound him to Frau K. He reassured Freud on this latter point: 'I am sure that in my state of health I need not assure you that there is nothing wrong in our relationship.'[18]

'Please', Dora's father pleaded with Freud, 'try to bring her round to a better way of thinking.'[19]

Now Freud the disinterested scientist listens to and weighs the truth-value of Ida's version of events. Freud is sure that if her experiences with Herr K actually happened, then such 'would have given rise to the psychological trauma' from which she was suffering. Ida tells Freud of what in her view occurred with Herr K when she was 'fourteen years old' (Robertson tells us that she was actually 13, but that Freud may have written 14 because this was the legal age of consent in Austria at the time), and Freud concedes that if the incident occurred, it would likely 'have the effect of a sexual trauma'.[20] Freud relates the details of the incident:

> Herr K. had arranged with her [Dora] and his wife that the ladies would come to his shop in the main square of B. that afternoon, to watch a church festivity. However, he persuaded his wife to stay at home, told his assistant that she could take time off, and was alone when the girl arrived at the shop. When the church procession was about to begin, he asked her to wait for him at the door to the stairs leading to the floor above, while he let down the roller blinds. He then rejoined her, and instead of going through the open door he suddenly held the girl close and pressed a kiss on her lips.[21]

Freud makes no comment at all on the sordid planned seduction of a 13-year-old girl, suddenly finding herself alone in the gloom of the shop with an older man, which immediately leads one to think that his intended readership would also have found nothing concerning. Indeed, Freud at this point may have been playing to his and their voyeuristic pleasure in the details of the story, the *mise en scène*.

He then learns from Ida of her response, that she was 'overcome by violent revulsion' and 'tore herself away, hurried past the man to the stairs, and from there to the door of the building'. Ida tells Freud that she did not break off all contact, although afterwards 'she did avoid being alone with Herr K'. Ida had kept the secret to herself 'until she confessed it in the course of treatment'.[22]

If Ida told Freud of her secret, of her 'violent revulsion' at Herr K when he tried to seduce her when she was 13, then she must have been hoping that, unlike her father, she would be believed, and Freud could see why she had been distressed and traumatised for so many years of her young life.

It would not be long before Ida realised that, to the contrary, Freud was not going to accept anything as true she had confided to him. Rather, he was going to join with her father in betraying her. First of all, he tells his readers in a footnote, he has gained a very favourable opinion of Herr K: 'I happen to have met Herr K., since it was he who came to see me with the patient's father, and he was a still youthful man of attractive appearance.' Secondly, he cannot believe Ida because the situation in the darkening shop with an older man was, in his considered view, 'likely to give a virginal girl of fourteen a clear sensation of sexual arousal'. That Ida denied being sexually aroused at that moment, instead felt horror and revulsion, demonstrates that the 'fourteen-year-old child's conduct is already entirely and fully hysterical': 'I would without another thought' – obviously – 'consider anyone a hysteric if a cause for sexual arousal evokes overwhelmingly or exclusively feelings of disgust in her'.[23]

If Ida must have had some hope, a thin sliver of hope, that Freud would believe her, she may also have had doubts, given her knowledge of what the patriarchal men of her upper-middle-class stratum considered justifiable behavior towards girls and young women: here are further intersections with *Fräulein Else*, *Fräulein Else* as a riposte to *A Case of Hysteria (Dora)*, with Else's disgust at her father and his in effect selling her to Dorsday in order to cover his gambling debts. In 'Dora' Ida's suspicion, as reported by Freud, is that her father wanted to barter her with Herr K because he wished to continue his relationship with Frau K, hence her intense disgust at her father's betrayal, hence her anger at her father.

Freud posits that when Ida said she felt 'violent revulsion' towards Herr K and anger at her father, such was only her Conscious speaking, and that from her Conscious statements he could now deduce the reverse: the truth of Ida's psyche was that Ida, in her Unconscious, sexually desired both Herr K and her father. For the rest of the novella, Freud tells Ida – increasingly brutally – that she is undeniably in love, sexually in love, with her father and Herr K. He then asks her to tell him about her dreams, and he interprets two of them, with a great deal of self-admiring ingenuity in following chains of association and substitution, as affirming these Unconscious desires. Ida, however, it appears from the text, withdraws within herself, Freud noticing that she becomes quiet and noncommittal as he relentlessly continues with his speculations about her Unconscious.

Nonetheless, at one point, Ida mentions that Herr K had given her a 'valuable jewel-box as a present some time ago', implying that here was another example of his years-long stalking of her. Freud immediately comments to Ida that a 'box of jewels' is a favourite term for 'female genitals'. Ida then famously comments, 'I knew *you* were going to say that', suggesting that she was now anticipating every move the psychoanalyst was making, his interpretations had become tiresome and predictable; especially when, a little later, Freud – charging on – tells her once more that her Unconscious dream life is yielding the 'opposite' of her Conscious: 'You are thus confirming how intense your love for him [Herr K] was.'[24]

Transference Interruptus

The following is my own narrative of what might have occurred in the denouement of the novella; it's time to carnivalise Freud, turn *A Case of Hysteria (Dora)* upside down and inside out.

Ida must have felt profoundly insulted that Freud had dismissed her own conscious assessment of how she had been stalked through much of her young life by an older man who her father wished to appease because he was sleeping with this man's wife; she would have been deeply humiliated that her father and Herr K had both gone together to force her to be treated by Freud, her father and the perpetrator now shamelessly colluding. Then she had to listen to Freud's endless fantasia of dream interpretation and his smug certainties about her Unconscious desires. She'd had enough, more than enough. Next time she came at the appointed time, she would tell him she was terminating her visits.

She would defy her father. She would be an undutiful daughter.

Freud, meanwhile, was, dreamily, considering a delicious thought: that by the ordinary processes of 'transference' which he imagined would manifest itself in the psychoanalytic situation, his patient Dora would necessarily and inevitably transfer her Unconscious sexual desire and love for her father and Herr K to another middle-aged man – himself. It would be a seduction by transference that he wished to prolong as long as possible, so enjoyable would its slow unfolding be; Freud himself tells his readers that 'in many cases of hysteria, I have spent days, weeks, or years on each case'. He told Ida 'that it would take about a year to cure her entirely'. It's clear from a thread in the text that Freud from the very beginning was sexualising the treatment, that he desired her. He had had his eye on her for quite a while: 'I first saw her in the early summer of her sixteenth year, when she was suffering coughing and hoarseness, and even then I suggested psychological treatment.' Opportunity came two years later, when, as Freud relates, Ida's father had 'put her in my hands for psychotherapy'. Freud insisted on treating Ida even though she had said no. When Ida mentioned that when she woke from a dream (the first dream), she always smelled smoke, Freud immediately concluded that her 'dream had a special relationship to me'. Ida, however, 'objected' – reasonably enough – to this 'exclusively personal interpretation', patiently pointing out that 'both Herr K. and her Papa were passionately fond of smoking', and she herself smoked.[25]

Freud was not deterred, the transference must be occurring, it's a psychic law, it will deliver Dora to him, though her Conscious remained a problem. He came to the view 'that one day it occurred to her… to wish that I would kiss her'. This must have been an Unconscious desire, for Ida's pesky Conscious, Freud sourly notes, then intervened, stepped in to disapprove, and he thinks that it was at this moment that her Conscious told 'her mind to break off the treatment'.[26]

Robertson in his Introduction points out that Freud created a sexual scenario unwarranted by what Ida told him had occurred in the darkened shop when she was 13.[27] Ida had said that after the unwanted kiss by Herr K 'she could still feel the pressure of his embrace on her upper body'. Freud then offers his readers, eager for more details, a 'reconstruction' that perhaps owed more to nineteenth-century pornographic texts than the (supposedly) sober annals of science. 'I think', Freud eagerly ventures, 'that in that stormy embrace she felt not only the kiss on her lips, but also Herr K.'s erect penis pressing against her body.'[28] Stormy embrace: where did that come from? Certainly not from Ida's memory that she had related to him.

We can make our own 'reconstruction' here. Freud was sexually excited by Ida's description of the unwanted kiss, he imagines it as a 'stormy embrace' and when he hears, or creatively mis-hears, Ida's description, experiences an 'erect penis', which he began furtively to masturbate. Was there a danger of Ida seeing what was visibly happening with the perfectly disinterested scientist-doctor? No, because Freud always positioned himself behind the sofa on which his patients lay, blowing cigar smoke over them, perhaps darkening the room with toxic fumes. There may have been some awkwardness if his wife Martha Bernays had chanced to come in to provide her husband with more cigars, knowing his neuropathological need for them, unless she was under strict instructions never to make an appearance for any reason.

Freud's notorious cigar smoking, ever present, incessant, which he couldn't give up even though it was a dangerous kind of self-harming (he accused Ida of self-harming at one point as part of her psychopathology),[29] is an important presence in his consulting room as an eroticized theatre of seduction. In his biography *Freud: A Life for Our Time*, Peter Gay tells us that Freud in 1897 told his onetime colleague and confidante Wilhelm Fliess in Berlin that addictions like those to cigarettes and cigars are substitutes for masturbation, in Freud's view the primal addiction.[30] Freud's ever-present cigar, a surrogate penis, ejaculated its acrid smoke over his patients' heads. Undetected, he could point it at the back of Ida's head. The cigar was always erect, like the priapic figurines from Mediterranean antiquity that he positioned prominently around the consulting room, compelling his patients, including his young forced-patient Ida, to look at them. Hopefully, Ida would be sexually excited by them, especially in her Unconscious, Freud's ally in her inevitable seduction.

We might dwell for a playful moment on Freud's obsession with his ancient Mediterranean figurines. Peter Gay writes of Freud's delight in ancient Mediterranean and Near Eastern statuary, from his early days as a researcher in Paris, arriving there in 1885, visiting the Louvre and lingering over the antiquities. Back in Vienna, established at Berggasse 19, Freud's growing collection began to crowd the apartment. Wolf Man is reported as observing that Freud's consulting room reminded him not of a doctor's office but of an archaeologist's study. Gay adds that Freud's 'antique objects gave him sheer visual and tactile pleasure; Freud caressed them with his eyes or fondled them as he sat at his desk.' At times, Gay notes, Freud would take a new acquisition to the dining room to study and handle it there.[31]

The mind rather boggles: given the prominence of priapic figurines in his collection, we are forced to contemplate Freud at the dinner table, the patriarch surrounded by his family, his wife and children staring as he fondled and caressed every new priapic addition to his collection.

All was going well for Freud, seduction was getting closer and closer as he chipped away at Ida's Conscious, revealing to her the truth of her Unconscious: but then occurred disaster, a clear case of Transference Interruptus.

In his bitter Afterword Freud explains how transference ideally works, that it is a 'necessary and requisite part' of psychoanalysis as an 'analytical technique'. Nevertheless, becoming aware of the transference as it begins to take effect is 'by far the most difficult' aspect of his 'work': 'the therapist has to detect transference almost on his own from slight indications, and without being high-handed'. This is vitally important, because, Freud avers, 'only when the transference has been resolved' will the patient fully accept that the therapist is 'right' about her condition; only then will she be cured.[32]

Freud hastens to assure his fellow scientists that the process is completely impersonal and disinterested: 'it is a matter of indifference to him whether he has to overcome a feeling aroused in the patient in connection with his own person or with someone else'.[33] Here of course we must apply Freud's technique of reversal to himself. When Freud says he is completely indifferent to his patient being 'aroused' in 'connection with his own person', this is his Conscious speaking: reverse that, and we know what his Unconscious was desiring, a full transference of Ida's supposed sexual love for Herr K to himself.

If Freud's Conscious was urging him not to be high-handed, his Unconscious must have been urging the opposite. What his Unconscious sought was always about Freud himself, his ego, his egomania, that he was at the centre of the spider web with which he was encircling his patient Ida Bauer, whose seduction he had been contemplating ever since he saw her living in Berggasse 32, the street where he lived.[34] Perhaps, from her childhood, he had been quietly and unobtrusively stalking her. Perhaps as well, Ida may have long sensed a threatening presence in the street. He was there, but when she looked around he wasn't there. Now he was sitting behind her, emitting poisonous hurtful words.

When the transference doesn't fully occur, because Ida famously walks out after 'barely three months',[35] Freud in part blames himself, he should have told her earlier that she was already transferring her Unconscious feelings for Herr K to himself; he delayed too long. Freud believes there must have been something about himself that reminded Ida of the scene with Herr K she falsely regarded as unpleasant. He doesn't know what unnerved her about himself – though perhaps, at least some of the more sensitive of his readers (if there were any) might have thought, it was the scene of seduction itself in his consulting room, with his sinister masturbatory presence behind her, the fog of cigar smoke reminding her of Herr K's darkening the light in his shop. Now Freud unhappily considers the possibility that by walking out she was revenging herself on the psychoanalyst through her Conscious just as she wished to revenge herself on Herr K for the many occasions he had acted objectionably to her. In any case, what she has done to Freud is unconscionable, Ida has exhibited to him 'feelings of cruelty'.[36] He's now a victim of her perfidy.

Mostly in the Afterword, the very ugly Afterword, Freud speculates on the possible reasons why Ida's stubborn Conscious had thwarted the transference, reasons to do with Ida's, in his view, abnormal sexual interests and identity; abnormal in terms of what should be, that Ida and every other young woman were properly destined to a conventional heterosexual marriage and raising children. He believes that Ida has inherited, from a 'perversion in infancy', a 'tendency to bisexuality'. He suspects she may be mired in the immorality of 'homosexuality'.[37]

Freud defiantly insists to his scientist community that just because Ida walked out doesn't mean his methods of analysis are not correct, 'in spite of any admonitions from philosophers' – a spiteful attack on another field of inquiry worthy of Underground Man's abundant store of malice. Freud's Conscious also tells him that while Ida's walking out may have demonstrated his 'helplessness and lack of ability' in treating her, he is, all the same, 'inclined to think that there is considerable therapeutic value even in such a fragmentary treatment as Dora's'.[38] From this Conscious statement we can deduce the reverse: his Unconscious was fearful that the scientific community whose admiration for his analytic methods he was seeking, would see the short three months of treatment as an abject failure, and his reputation, and the reputation of psychoanalysis as a superior kind of psychology, might now falter.

Ida and Feminism in the *Fin de Siècle*

In Ida Bauer, Freud, always a little wary of her intelligence, met a Woman on Top, who overturned the relationship Freud tried to force on her, of passive patient and domineering and tyrannical expert (the role Underground Man tried to assume with Liza). Freud attempted comprehensively to possess Ida's soul: as a 'gynaecologist' with 'rights'[39] to invade her body, insistently asking her about intimate physical symptoms; he worked hard to control her mind by getting her to disbelieve what she consciously knew; and he looked forward to seducing her by transference. Ida came quickly to recognise that her middle-aged inquisitor was just another sexual predator of her father's and Herr K's generation of Viennese upper-middle-class men, possibly syphilitic as most of them were, including her father. She also realised that psychoanalysis was his sly modus operandi: no crude attempts at seduction and rape like Herr K, but rather always suggesting to her that his cure was for her own good, he was rescuing her from hysteria, and he was her saviour. Ida regarded him with silent contempt, only occasionally making a crisp observation about how obvious he was being in his jejune psychoanalytic interpretations.

Ida showed considerable courage in walking out on the treatment. She must have known she risked being institutionalised by Freud. After she told Freud she was leaving, he said: 'You know that you are always free to leave the analysis.'[40] Freud's reassurance here was disingenuous, and in any case, the reverse of this Conscious statement was precisely that his Unconscious did desire to punish her by incarceration. Robertson tells us that in

1897 Freud wrote to Fliess concerning G de B, a female cousin of Fliess who Freud was treating. Freud reported that the treatment was not going well, G de B was vehemently resisting his interpretation of her symptoms that she had performed fellatio on her father when she was a child. Freud kindly lets Fliess know what he has in store for his cousin: 'I have threatened to send her away'.[41] Ida must have been very aware that many young women of her generation had been threatened by psychologists of various kinds with institutionalisation or were institutionalised (we recall Ida Rubinstein early in the twentieth century being incarcerated by her doctor brother-in-law): a nightmare shadow over all their lives. After all, Ida had earlier in her life been forced, presumably at an institution, to undergo hydrotherapy and electric shocks.[42]

Near the end of his Afterword, Freud records for his colleagues that Ida, who he still regards as 'my patient', came to visit him a year and a quarter since she had ended 'her treatment'. Ida, he sourly notes, came on the 'first of April', as if to mock him. Ida relates that for a few weeks after she had left treatment she felt confused, then found herself to be in a state of 'great improvement': 'her attacks of illness came less often, and her spirits lifted'.[43] The further she got away from Freud, she implied, the better for her. There was also a significant development in her life. Ida decided that her treatment lay in her own hands. When Ida heard that one of Herr and Frau K's children, who had always been sickly, died, she paid them a visit to express her condolences. Ida then brought matters out in the open:

> She told Frau K.: I know you are having an affair with Papa. Frau K. did not deny it. She made Herr K. admit that the scene by the lake [when he propositioned her at a resort and she slapped his face], which he had disputed, had been as she said, and took her Papa that news, which vindicated her. She had not been in touch with the family again.[44]

Ida did suffer a set back some time later, when she saw Herr K being knocked down by a vehicle in the street, though he escaped serious injury. She then told Freud that 'she lived for her studies and had no intention of marrying'.⁴⁵

Ida's comment here suggests a strong possibility that her studies, in which Freud had shown no interest, may have included an engagement with *fin de siècle* feminism, a perspective which gave her strength to endure the three months of Freud's treatment where he tried to humiliate and diminish her at the same time trusting in the sexual success of transference. His offensive bluntness and final fury may have been inspired by his own opposition to nineteenth-century feminism and its spokespeople, including John Stuart Mill, Robertson noting in the Introduction that in 1883 Freud wrote to his fiancée deploring the program for the equality of the sexes put forward in *The Subjection of Women* (1869).⁴⁶

Late nineteenth-century feminism may have pointed out what cultural history now takes as given: that the ascription of hysteria to women in the *fin de siècle*, in art and literature as much as in psychoanalysis, revealed the intensity of male hysteria during that period, that threshold period opening onto the twentieth century. Such knowledge may have intensified her wariness of Freud, she may have quickly decided, given his aggression towards her, that he was certainly a male hysteric, though perhaps she could not have known, as a century of biographical research has revealed, the wide range of his neuropathologies. There was his self-harming by obsessive smoking; when Fliess advised Freud to give up smoking cigars on health grounds, he received a frosty reply. Freud not only continued to self-harm but also endangered the health of his colleagues when he insisted they smoke during meetings of his circle of young acolytes, Freud assuming the role of authoritarian and monologic patriarch. Then there was his friendship with Fliess, a friendship in which both were as lunatic as the other. Robertson tells us of Freud's acceptance of Fliess's theory that there was a relation between the nose and the genitals; Freud induced Fliess to operate on the nose of one of his patients, Emma Eckstein, who he regarded as hysterical, the result being a near-fatal haemorrhage which turned out to have been caused by Fliess leaving a half-metre of gauze in her nasal cavity. Freud, Robertson comments, instead of criticising Fliess's egregious incompetence, told his colleague that her nosebleeds were really hysterical in origin, an attempt to obtain her doctor's love.[47]

Then there was Freud's fantasist belief in telepathy, which leads me to think, perhaps a trifle fancifully, that he may have sought through telepathy to establish an intimate relationship between his priapic cigar and the priapic figurines of the ancient Mediterranean world on display around him, that the figurines somehow came alive in the cigars perennially in his mouth, they were engaged in telepathic communication.

I might recall here that in my 1994 book *Postmodernism and Popular Culture: A Cultural History*, when talking about carnival in early modern Europe in terms of Bakhtin's *Rabelais and His World*, I had occasion to refer to Fliess' comment on female masturbation in his 1902 essay 'On the Causal Connection between the Nose and the Sexual Organ': 'Women who masturbate... can only finally be cured through an operation on the nose if they truly give up this bad practice.'[48] I had been struck by this quote while reading Jeffrey Moussaieff Masson's *The Assault on Truth: Freud's Suppression of the Seduction Theory* (1992), in a chapter where he discusses Freud and Fliess's treatment of Emma Eckstein.[49] In an endnote, I write that Rabelais would surely have quizzically pondered the sight of a physician some centuries in the future taking seriously a joke descending from thousands of years of folk humour about the connection of the nose with the sexual organ. The horrifying results of such solemnity for Emma Eckstein has now become part of the general knowledge of one of the great disasters in the history of psychoanalysis. Masson wrote that the length of gauze left behind not only imperilled her life but led to her suffering permanent disfiguration.[50]

Robertson reflects that 'Dora', along with the case histories of Rat Man and Wolf Man, are the three pillars that supposedly constitute the empirical basis of psychoanalysis as a science, and have been studied by generations of psychoanalysts as part of their training. Yet, in Dora, Rat Man and Wolf Man, they do nothing of the kind.[51]

In 'Dora', in her dramatic riposte to Freud, Ida Bauer destroyed one of those foundations, it toppled over and lay in fragments at her feet. She kicked them away in disgust, as an insult to her and every other young woman whose lives, well being and freedom were threatened by the state-supported hubris and fantasies of psychoanalysis.

Robertson notes that the cases of Rat Man and Wolf Man also cannot sustain psychoanalysis as a science.[52] Peter Gay observed that Freud felt that the antiquities in his consulting room could assist his speculations, particularly when most puzzled by a patient; bewildered by Rat Man's thoughts and revelations, Freud asked him to observe and think about the antiquities in the consulting room.[53]

Freud's analysis of Ida dissolved when she became an actant and took charge of her own situation; he could not explain Rat Man; and, as Robertson notes, Wolf Man's dreams were so 'bizarre' that no interpretation could support a claim to a general scientific method.[54]

Foucault on Hysteria

On 13 June 2017 a parcel arrived from Gleebooks in Sydney, a copy of Michel Foucault's *Psychiatric Power: Lectures at the Collège de France 1973–1974*. I'd seen a reference to the book, and thought it might help me when a few chapters hence I try to evoke my

IQ fiasco when I was 11; I know I've mentioned this before, I'm trying to lay down a thread. Opening the book, I glance at the contents page and see that in lecture 12, the final lecture, of 6 February 1974, Foucault talks about the 'battle of hysteria' and the 'irruption of the sexual body'.[55] This immediately caught my attention: what if Foucault's insights here are relevant to Freud's 'Dora'?

And I think they are. Foucault constructs a history that stretches from the latter nineteenth century at the time of Jean-Martin Charcot's famous or infamous psychiatric clinic in Paris; through Freud's psychoanalysis in the early part of the twentieth century; to the 1960s and 1970s when the anti-psychiatry movement developed, developments that Foucault's own writings helped stimulate into being. The psychiatrists of the latter nineteenth century and the psychoanalysts of the twentieth century, Foucault suggests, wished to assert power over those they defined as hysterics, wished to assert power by defining them as hysterics; however, the hysterics, the female hysterics, fought back against male medical power, though their resistance, even temporary victories, would always be countered by new assertions of doctors' power, new strategies of control in altered definitions in the medical field. In turn, in the anti-psychiatry movement, these strategies would once again be challenged. Foucault argues that the way hysterics challenged Charcot anticipated the anti-psychiatry movement a century or so later; there's a genealogy here of considerable interest.

Freud says that from 1850 to 1870, psychiatric power, especially through Charcot, consolidated itself by creating the 'neurological body'. This new field of medicine that Foucault variously refers to as 'neurology' or 'neuropathology' or 'neurological clinical medicine', then became the scene of an 'encounter of the patient body and the doctor-body'. In this encounter, we can see that the doctor's will to power and control can be challenged by the patient's will: 'The doctor will give orders, he will try to impose his will, and the patient… may always feign inability or unwillingness.' In this situation, the doctor has to 'depend on the patient's will.' However, by clinical observation the 'patient can be circumvented and short-circuited'.

> Broadly speaking, the neurologist says: Obey my orders, but keep quiet, and your body will answer for you by giving responses that, because I am a doctor, I alone will be able to decipher and analyze in terms of truth.[56]

It is in these controlling terms, in this new medical field, Foucault says, that the 'hysteric' is created as a category for modernity.[57]

What then occurs, especially with Charcot at Salpêtrière hospital, in 'struggles for control between doctors and hysterics', can only be described, Foucault reflects, in terms of military metaphors of 'battle' and 'confrontation'. In his satirical account Foucault tells his audience that Charcot and his associates sought to reveal in hysterics a stable, consistent, regular set of symptoms and behaviours, legible on a patient whenever the neurological examination took place. The attacks hysterics were liable to, Charcot believed, occurred in a predictable and typical scenario. Charcot decided that the hysterical attack could be codified on the model of epilepsy, proceeding through various phases of illogical, disordered movement enacted in passionate postures, expressing emotions like lustfulness, terror and delirium.[58]

Here, Foucault suggests, Charcot began to lose control, because the hysterics, asked to perform attacks of hysteria and epilepsy, could if they wished provide a kind of mocking surplus, a 'surplus-power' that swung power over to the hysterics. Charcot – the doctor, the neurologist – could not control 'this overabundance of hysterical symptomology'. He found himself 'losing out'. To attempt to regain control, Charcot deployed hypnosis, so that the patient would, he hoped, now produce hysterical symptoms exactly when and how he wished them, to be observed and analysed. From 1878 onwards, Charcot's treatment was defined by the triad of hysteria, epilepsy and hypnosis. Such became the elements of what Foucault ironically refers to as 'Charcot's grand stagecraft'. Hypnotised, with Charcot thereby dictating what symptoms should be put on display, the hysteric became a 'kind of functional mannequin'. The doctor regains 'the upper hand'. Yet, once again, the hysterics assert power, even a 'triumph', by acting out in hypnosis the required directions with profusion and enthusiasm.[59]

A notion of trauma now enters Charcot's scenography, as some kind of past event – 'a violent event, a blow, a fall, a fear, a spectacle' – that, when known by the neurologist, can trigger hypnosis at will. However, once again, the hysterics find a counter-manoeuvre. They enjoy providing as instances of their traumas, detailed stories of their sexual life – an aspect of his clinic that, says Foucault, Charcot 'does not talk about'; stories abundant with a 'lubricity' that overwhelmed his own ordered narratives of the pathological hysteric. Fearing this abundance of stories of sexuality, Charcot retreated into denial. It was an absence in Charcot's mode of analysis of hysterics that Freud noticed when he trained with Charcot in 1885–6. Foucault comments:

> My impression is that this sexual bacchanal should be taken as the counter-maneuver by which the hysterics responded to the ascription of trauma: You want to find the cause of my symptoms, the cause that will enable you to pathologize them and enable you to function as a doctor; you want this trauma, well, you will get all my life, and you won't be able to avoid hearing me recount my life and, at the same time, seeing me mime my life anew and endlessly reactualize it in my attacks![60]

Such, Foucault feels, became the 'hysteric's victory cry': the hysterics had replaced the 'neurological body fabricated by the doctors' with the assertion of their own 'sexual body'.[61]

Nonetheless, the hysterics' victory would, post-Charcot, once more be challenged, in the 'medical, psychiatric, and psychoanalytic take over of sexuality', in the rise of 'a medicine of sexuality'.[62]

So ends lecture 12. In a Course Summary, Foucault adds that after the 'mockery of medical authority' that Charcot endured in his hospital, various attempts were made by neurologists to restore the doctor's power and control. Psychoanalysis, our interest here, attempted such a restoration of the 'doctor's sovereign science' by taking the doctor-patient relationship away from the hospital and into the realm of 'private consultation', promising the patient that all she has to do is say anything that crosses her mind; the couch would become the 'privileged place' for her to speak, while the doctor will withdraw 'entirely into silence and invisibility'. The 'notion of transference' in this process, Foucault adds, becomes 'essential to the cure', whereby the 'doctor's power' is exercised to his satisfaction.[63]

I think Foucault's historical sketch is very illuminating for Freud's 'Dora'. Freud takes neurology out of the hospital or asylum, where the neurologist can be mocked by the patients; he institutes a scenario where he appears to permit Ida Bauer to talk about what matters to her; but to assert his sovereign power he cannot stay silent, he must take command of the situation. Here the notion of the unconscious is necessary for Freud and psychoanalysis as a realm to which he the doctor has privileged access. Freud insistently and relentlessly berates Ida Bauer with supposed revelations of her inner being in terms of sexual desires, desires only he knows exist because they inhabit and agitate her unconscious which he can explain by ingenious interpretation. In what Foucault strikingly calls the scene of neurology as an 'encounter of the patient body and the doctor-body' (I like this phrase!), his body and mind is now in charge, he has demonstrated the scientific power of expert analysis, which then simply has to move to the next stage of transference whereby the patient's complete subjection to his power and will is complete. What could go wrong? Freud chomped contentedly on his cigar. Suddenly Ida Bauer made an unexpected dramatic move, and psychoanalysis' house of cards all came tumbling down, for all the world to see.

Like Foucault in lecture 12 of *Psychiatric Power* talking about a 'sexual bacchanal', contemporary cultural history is also interested the theatre of hysteria created in Charcot's psychiatric clinic at the Saltpêtrière. In her fascinating commentary in *The Epic Cinema of Kumar Shahani* (2015), film theorist Laleen Jayamanne, drawing on the work of Rae Beth Gordon, enriches Foucault's account in drawing out the relationship of Charcot's theatre of hysteria to popular stage performances in the café concert, music hall and cabaret of late-nineteenth-century Paris. Jayamanne observes that many actors, including Sarah Bernhardt, and the public attended Charcot's clinic in order to understand the fascination exerted by the histrionic performances of hysteria combined with epilepsy, including convulsive movement, acrobatic contortion, delirium and hallucination. These performances produced a vast repertoire of histrionic gestures, highly useful for those patients who went on to become performers in popular theatre after they left the clinic. The theatre of excess at Charcot's clinic, Jayamanne suggests, influenced the popular genre of so-called epileptic performers as well as the performances of puppets, acrobats and clowns in cabaret and burlesque, and influenced the emerging new form of cinema.[64]

In the twenty-first century Charcot's theatre of excess at the Saltpêtrière may, we might think, prove far more interesting to think about in terms of enabling possibilities of cultural performance than Freud's destructive psychoanalysis.

Xiaolu Guo: An Undutiful Daughter

A question occurred to me in the morning of 7 April 2017, while sipping coffee in a sea-side café in Perth, overlooking the Indian Ocean, with cargo ships from the far reaches of the world fixed on the horizon like Coleridge's painted ships on a painted ocean. When in the past I have written about young female characters – especially Rebecca the Sephardi traveler in the imagined medieval world of Sir Walter Scott's *Ivanhoe*, who I write about in my *1492: The Poetics of Diaspora* – have I always somehow been thinking about, yes, subliminally, my mother as a young woman, the young woman Elsie Levy I never knew, and have no photos of? The undutiful daughter who became a radical actant in Sydney in the 1930s, a young Jewish conscious pariah who married out?

Which brings me to Xiaolu Guo's *Once upon a time in the East: A story of growing up*, published in London in 2017.

I became interested in Xiaolu Guo when I came across an article she'd written for the UK *Guardian* online, "Is this what the west is really like?' How it felt to leave China for Britain' (10 January 2017); she talked about her books and films, and two books in particular piqued my interest, the novel *A Concise Chinese-English Dictionary for Lovers* (2007), and *Once upon a time in the East* which was just about to be published. I immediately emailed Gleebooks in Sydney, and received them not long after.

There are many aspects of Guo's life as she narrates it in *Once upon a time in the East* that fascinate me: her growing up (eventually) in a Communist family in Wenling, a middle-sized town in the south of China (defined as south of the Yanktze River); her lifelong journey of exile that began by leaving the south and moving to Beijing to study film; her precarious existence when she graduated, working as a scriptwriter to earn money in an authoritarian society she found stifling for creativity because of censorship and self-censorship; the winning of a scholarship to study film in a surreally English village outside of London; her moving to live in the east of London, in Hackney, which she valued for it being so multi-ethnic; her learning English and writing *A Concise Chinese-English Dictionary for Lovers*; her writing more novels and making avant garde films; and her fears now about Brexit making life very uncomfortable for those visibly different, and a recent move to Berlin so that she has two Western cities of possible residence. Guo also values as a kind of ontological necessity a diasporic relationship with China and Chinese history, even if precariously maintained; she no longer has a Chinese passport, it was taken away from her when she acquired a British one.

Before leaving China for Britain in 2002, Guo had written novels in Chinese; she observes that novel writing was not common in Chinese literary history: 'The novel was still a very new format for us Chinese, since the dominant literary forms then were poetry, essays and short stories… The novel… was alien to the Chinese literary tradition.'[65]

Guo chooses to live in lifelong exile. I see her as an outsider, in Georg Simmel's sense of 'The Stranger': recall that for Simmel the stranger is the wanderer who comes today and stays tomorrow; she always remains a potential wanderer, disturbing those who feel they naturally belong to a society by her detached observation of things that they cannot see.[66] If James Joyce was an Irish outsider to the English language he played with as only an outsider can, so too does Guo in her Chinese-English dictionary; her work reminds me of Hannah Arendt referring, in her Introduction to Walter Benjamin's *Illuminations*, to Benjamin and Kafka as unclassifiable.[67]

Guo comes to see herself as one of life's orphans and nomads. 'I was born an orphan', she begins the narrative. 'Not because my parents had died, no, they were both still very much alive. Rather, they gave me away.' As far as she can work it out from stories she was later told, as a newborn baby she was given to a peasant couple, who lived in a mountain village, somewhere in her parents' province, by the East China Sea; but the couple were too poor to feed her anything but mashed yams, and she began to starve; they journey to the seaside and place the tiny baby with her grandmother, in the fishing village of Shitang where her grandmother and grandfather eke out a bare existence; her grandfather was a Hakka fisherman, but he lost his boat, which meant everything to him; Guo stays there looked after by her grandmother, who she loves; almost every day her remote morose bitter grandfather beats her grandmother; and one day he suicides. She stays there for five years, scrawny and ill-fed, always hungry.[68]

Her spirit was sustained by prophecies that later in her life she would become a great traveler. She learns of her ethnic descent marking her as an outsider. When she is six, one of her grandmother's neighbours tells her she was 'Hui, not Han Chinese'. Her grandfather refuses to explain what Hui means; her grandmother says she is illiterate and doesn't know. She goes to see the stationmaster, in charge of the village's long-distance bus service, reputed to be knowledgeable about the world. The stationmaster sketches for her a possible ancestry, romantic and adventurous: the Hui might be descended from the Turks or the Tartars, or the Mongols, who don't grow rice but ride horses; Guo could, he suggests, be a descendant of Genghis Khan and one day she will conquer the world. On one occasion her kindly grandmother, walking with difficulty because of bound feet, takes her to a Taoist temple buried in a bamboo forest, terrifying for a child, full of grotesque half-human, half-monster statues. The Taoist monks are very poor; none of the villagers visit their temple to donate food or money. Guo's grandmother brings along some oranges, and asks an old monk what will happen in life to her granddaughter, what will be her fate? The monk studies Guo's palms, then after a while pronounces her fate: Guo is a peasant warrior, she will cross the sea and travel to the Nine Continents, she will travel the world. The old monk would say no more.[69]

When Guo is seven, her parents come and take her to the provincial town of Wenling, where they live in the Communist compound. Her mother shows her no affection, often beats her, and openly favours her brother; she feels an affinity with her kindly and wise father, a traditional Chinese artist who draws landscapes and seascapes. She realises that it is her mother, harsh, humourless and literal minded, who had insisted she be dumped in a mountain village as a baby. She learns the curious story how her mother and father came to be together: as an artist her father was considered an intellectual, and was therefore arrested and publicly vilified during Mao's Cultural Revolution. Guo's mother, a Red Guard, participates in the Party's campaign to punish people like her father, now considered a class enemy, and she would, while he was on stage (wearing a 'Stinking Number Nine' placard) being humiliated before the people, beat and spit on him ('I went straight to your father, spat on his head and kicked him in the spine'). However, somehow, she took pity on him and fell in love with him, and would visit him in the pig shed in the re-education labour camp where he is confined. Her family were outraged, this endangered their lives, but she persisted and they married. Her mother left the Red Guards and worked in a large silk factory. Guo's learning that her mother had defied her family, that she was an undutiful daughter, was the only thing Guo can respect about her mother, who is relentlessly severe towards her.[70]

After the Cultural Revolution, Guo's father was rehabilitated. In their province he became a well-known and respected artist again, earning fame when for six months he walked along the coastline of southern China sketching. Unlike her mother, her father would always support her later desire to become a film-maker in Beijing and win a scholarship to study in Britain.

One day Guo's father tells her about the origins of the family name. In the old days, he explains, people built two layers of wall around their cities, and 'Guo is the space between them'. Guo means an 'in-between zone'. Guo asks him where the first Guos came from. Her father spent most of his days painting the ocean, and at that moment was sketching a 'troubled sea and a rising moon'.

> 'I don't think anyone has ever known the real origins of the Guo family, Xiaolu', my father sighed. 'Our country has one of the longest continuously recorded histories in the world, but the Cultural Revolution destroyed it. They burnt all the history books and destroyed the museums. But I think we can trace the Guos back to the Yuan Dynasty, the period when the Mongols conquered China. Our ancestors were Hui Muslims, but they might also have been Persian Mongols. They were tribes with their own religion and culture. There's really no such clean-cut thing called *the Chinese*.'

Taking out an old map, Guo's father points to a large area circling the border between Iran and Mongolia: that's where the Guo family came from, from a borderland. Originally they were horsemen, 'nomads', then their ancestors 'moved all the way down to the south of China'. Guo wonders where she could possibly belong in the world: 'We were really a family of orphans, it seemed to me. Orphans of a nomad tribe.'[71]

By the end of *Once upon a time in the East*, Guo comes to decide that 'home' is not necessarily to be defined by place: 'home' is where one writes. 'I was,' Guo reflects, surrounded by boxes in a London flat, 'my own home now.'[72] I mention Guo's definition of home to Ann and we ponder it, and I also emailed my fellow ego histoiriste Anna Cole residing in the Virginia Woolf and Leonard Woolf town of Lewes, urging her to read *Once upon a time in the East*, Anna being a connoisseur of in-betweenness.[73] Home is where one writes. I like it. I think about it, here, in 2017 in Perth, the other side of the continent from Sydney, the other side of the world from London, my diaspora cities.

What interests me now is to follow a particular thread in Guo's autobiography in the light of Freud's breathtaking insensitivity to Ida Bauer, for Guo relates the sexual abuse of her as a young girl that had devastating effects on her throughout her life, even after many years, even when she had journeyed far from where they had occurred in her childhood. Guo writes that for a 'young girl in 1980s China, sex was an ordeal endured at first with terror, then with mute disgust and finally numbness'.

> I was twelve when I was first sexually assaulted by a man. It didn't just happen once. The abuse lasted for about two years. When I left primary school to attend middle school, which was located in another part of town, it stopped, for whatever reason. And since then I have never tried to remember or to forget those sexual acts. 'Remembering' is the wrong word to use here, because those moments are embedded in my brain, on my retina, under my skin, in my loins. They don't need to be *remembered*. I can instantly *see* and *feel* them if I want to. Forgetting them would be like forgetting I have two hands or a mouth.[74]

Guo decides it is time to say openly what the abuser's name was, Hu Wenren, who was never punished for what he did to her: 'Maybe he did it to many other girls, and we were all too scared to fight back.'[75]

Hu Wenren was a young man who worked as a secretary in her father's office; he knew the way Guo took from school back home, and to her father's office. 'He would wait for me.' She felt 'fright and shame in the face of physical invasion': 'no power, no dignity, no hope'. He makes horrible threats against her if she tells anyone. 'I hated him with a burning fury, but I never dared tell anyone.' Even when the sexual abuse ended, Guo felt no sense of relief, instead she felt 'unpredictable danger lurking at every corner like a miasma'.[76]

When Guo goes to the Beijing Film Academy, she immerses herself in film, especially in the European auteur and avant garde tradition of Godard and Truffaut, as well as old Hollywood musicals like *Footlight Parade*, with its famous scene of seemingly free-spirited female bodies forming a human waterfall, the choreography crafted by Busby Berkeley. During the film theory class, discussing 'female presentation in Hollywood cinema', the teacher shows some clips of Rita Hayworth and Marilyn Monroe, then introduces the students to feminist film theorist Laura Mulvey's essay 'Visual Pleasure and Narrative Cinema', with its argument that women are the image and men are the bearer of the look. 'I couldn't help but wonder if Western girls were also subjected to the constant sexual harassment we Chinese girls in the countryside were. We didn't wear miniskirts or sexy dresses, but we were abused nevertheless.'[77]

One of the films the students watched was *La Chinoise*, made by Godard in 1967, the year after the start of the Chinese Cultural Revolution, introducing the students to the 'jump cut' method of editing and his use of montage. One of the other students was Mengmeng, who lived on campus in the same room as Guo, in the girls' dormitory. One night, lying in the dark, Guo tells her room mates about the 'sexual abuse I had suffered as a young girl'. Mengmeng tells the young women that she too had been abused: 'I hated the man who abused me and I still hate him, intensely. He lived next door. He was always coming into our house when my parents were away and groping me. He threatened to cut out my tongue if I told my parents.' Mengmeng was too frightened to tell her parents. Another young woman tells the others that she too was abused and had been too scared to tell anyone. The young women lay in the dark of the dormitory waiting for sleep to come, but 'it didn't. With an unspoken, but almost collective feeling, we girls were dreading these memories would return to us in our dreams. They were monstrous shadows over our

Undutiful Daughters 413

unconscious minds.' Mengmeng tells Guo that she often experiences nightmares.[78]

In her third year at the Beijing Film Academy, out of nowhere Guo was contacted by her childhood abuser, who had left a note for her with the door lady of her dormitory, saying: 'It's me, Hu Wenren. I am in Beijing and I want to see you.' Shaken, Guo tells Mengmeng, who is enraged, and insists on ringing the hotel number Hu Wenren had left with his note. Mengmeng tells Hu Wenren to come to the Yellow Pavilion, a café near the film school. There, in a way that recalls Ida Bauer's telling Freud how she confronted Herr K after she had walked out on Freud's so-called treatment, Guo and Mengmeng confront Hu Wenren. Mengmeng takes charge, saying in a loud voice so that everyone in the café can hear: 'Are you planning to molest some young girls here in Beijing? I thought you only dared abuse local girls.' Everyone looked over at the scene as it unfolded: 'Hu's face was shocked and stupefied. This provocation seemed to hit him like a blunt instrument.' Mengmeng continued: 'We know what you've done. And it's not only you. We know quite a few pathetic men like you and we're going to teach all of you a lesson. Just be aware that the police know where you are now.' Guo and Mengmeng, briskly and dignified, then 'walked out of the café, leaving him there'.[79]

Recall that Robertson in his Introduction had surmised that in 'Dora' Freud had deliberately changed Ida's age from 13 to 14, presumably so that there could be no possibility Herr K's action in attempting to rape a 13 year old in his darkened shop could be brought to the attention of the police.

In Britain, Guo has a failed relationship with a much older man, Daniel, and sadly reflects:

> Yet again, I was facing the question of love and sex, both of which, in my case, had been conditioned by trauma from the past. After Hu Wenren's abuse and Jiang's violence [a fellow student at the

Beijing Film Academic who was so violent that she decided never again to go with a Chinese man], I felt that men always let me down, or hurt me, or sent me to a place which set off alarm bells inside me. Relationships. I didn't understand the concept. Coupling didn't make sense. Intimacy was invariably pierced by the bleakness of my heart, a shell-like thing with pins and hard edges that fiercely prevented any merging with another.[80]

Concluding Fragments

In her autobiography, by being an autobiography, Xiaolu Guo could tell her story of a life profoundly affected by the sexual abuse she had suffered as a child. It was a story that Ida Bauer had tried to tell Freud, but he was not interested, he had other interests, his own. Arthur Schnitzler's pro-feminist attitude was very different: in constructing Else's interior monologue and stream of consciousness in *Fräulein Else*, he created a haunting text whereby Else could tell her story of anger and revulsion at the upper-middle-class men of Vienna, including her father, who were indifferent to how much they harmed young women, including their own daughters.

Let's return to our epigraphs, to the letter Freud wrote to Schnitzler in 1922, claiming that he and Schnitzler were doubles, that they came to very similar 'presuppositions, interests, and conclusions', Freud through psychoanalysis, Schnitzler through literature. Schnitzler probably thought when he got Freud's letter: I hope I don't think like you, and just to make that very clear, I will shape *Else*, the novella I am writing now, to that effect. He could see what Freud was doing: by claiming Schnitzler as his double, he would, as in *ressentiment*, deny and reduce Schnitzler's independence of mind, make him like himself, his double, *son semblable*, with similar viewpoints and conceptions. *Fräulein Else*, published in 1924, was his answer both to 'Dora' and Freud's attempt in the 1922 letter to claim his, Schnitzler's, mind and soul; an answer that proves ever more influential than Freud's despicable 'Dora'. Where Freud chose to attempt to be a Tolstoyan narrator, interpreting Dora to herself, talking over her, Schnitzler looked to a Dostoevskian mode, an author withdrawing from the scene, letting Else think, speak, protest, agonise, act.

In *Once upon a time in the East*, Guo tells us that as a child in Shitang, she would often see her grandmother weeping silently in the back of the kitchen, or in front of a white porcelain statue of Guanyin the Goddess of Mercy that she had hung on the kitchen wall. Every day, rather than praying to Buddha, she would pray to Guanyin, the most popular goddess in that region. Her grandmother tells Guo the legend of Guanyin, her name literally meaning One who listens to the cries of the world. Thousands of years ago, Guanyin resisted and defied the wishes of her father, a cruel king. One day, the king asked her to marry a wealthy but unloving man. She told her father that she would agree to marry, as long as the union would ease the three great misfortunes of humanity: ageing, illness and death; if her marriage could not help with any of these sufferings, she would rather retreat into a life of religion. Her father becomes enraged that she would not marry a man of power and wealth, and punishes her by forcing her into a life of hard labour, giving her little to eat and drink. Still Guanyin would not yield to his demands, and the king agrees to her wish to enter a temple and become a nun; however, he orders the monks to give her the toughest chores in order to break her spirit. But again the king is thwarted, for Guanyin is so kind-hearted that even the animals around the temple want to help her. Her father becomes so frustrated that he burns down the temple so that she would perish in the fire. As she was dying, however, a white tiger saves her and takes her into an underground world. When she wakes up, Guanyin finds herself in the land of the dead; she sees the suffering souls around her and hears their cries; her gaze soothes the crying children and soon they begin to smile and play; the men find peace within themselves; the dried willow trees flush green again; the dead lotus begins once more to blossom. Filled with compassion, Guanyin releases the good karma she has accumulated during her life, and frees all the suffering souls in the underworld back to Earth. From then on, the world worshipped Guanyin, calling her the Goddess of Mercy.[81]

In the early 1960s during the Cultural Revolution, Guo tells us, Mao banned Western symbols like the Virgin Mary or Jesus Christ. Then, as part of Mao's anti-feudal and anti-superstition movement, the government in Beijing declared that anything linked to China's feudal past, such as images of kings and queens, grassroots religious practices, temples, were to be destroyed. (I wonder if Mao the iconoclastic messiah can be compared in history to the ancient Egyptian monotheistic pharaoh Akhenaten, spreading terror in forced obeyance to the one idea?) At anti-feudal public meetings in the village market square, statues of the Goddess of Mercy were smashed. Guo's grandmother hid her precious porcelain figure in her wardrobe until the middle 1970s, when images of Guanyin were finally allowed again: 'my grandmother could regain her faith in an afterlife through prayer – surely the next life would be better than the one she had endured so far'.[82]

Guo's grandmother preserved in memory the legend of the Goddess of Mercy, and passed it on to her granddaughter.

Clearly, we can interpret the lives I've been trying to evoke for chapters now, fictional and non-fictional, of Guo, Liza, Else, Ida Bauer, Ida Rubinstein, the heroine of *The Yellow Paper*, Virginia Woolf, as undutiful daughters in the spirit of the remarkable, anti-patriarchal, legend of the Goddess of Mercy.

Undutiful Daughters   417

1   Ernst L. Freud (ed.), *Letters of Sigmund Freud* (Dover Publications, New York, 1992), Letter 198, pp.339–340.
2   Arthur Schnitzler, *Desire and Delusion*, selected and translated by Margret Schaefer (Ivan R. Dee, Chicago, 2003), Foreword, p.xv.
3   Sigmund Freud, *A Case of Hysteria (Dora)*, translated by Anthea Bell, with an Introduction and Notes by Ritchie Robertson (Oxford World's Classics, Oxford, 2013), p.5.
4   Freud, *A Case of Hysteria (Dora)*, p.89.
5   Freud, *A Case of Hysteria (Dora)*, p.19.
6   Robertson, Introduction to *A Case of Hysteria (Dora)*, p.lv.
7   Robertson, Introduction to *A Case of Hysteria (Dora)*, pp.xxviii–xxix.
8   Natalie Zemon Davis, *Society and Culture in Early Modern France* (Standord University Press, Stanford, 1975), pp.135–136. See also John Docker, *Postmodernism and Popular Culture: A Cultural History* (Cambridge University Press, Melbourne, 1994), pp.194–5.
9   Freud, *A Case of Hysteria (Dora)*, pp.93–4.
10 Robertson, Introduction to *A Case of Hysteria (Dora)*, p,li.
11 Freud, *A Case of Hysteria (Dora)*, pp.15–17.
12 Freud, *A Case of Hysteria (Dora)*, pp.15, 17–8.
13 Hannah Arendt, *The Origins of Totalitarianism* (Harvest/Harcourt, New York, 1994), pp.231–2 note 32.
14 Robertson, Introduction to *A Case of Hysteria (Dora)*, pp.xii–xiii.
15 Robertson, Introduction to *A Case of Hysteria (Dora)*, p.xxxi.
16 Freud, *A Case of Hysteria (Dora)*, pp.18–21.
17 Freud, *A Case of Hysteria (Dora)*, pp.20, 26, 28.
18 Freud, *A Case of Hysteria (Dora)*, pp.20–21.
19 Freud, *A Case of Hysteria (Dora)*, p.21.
20 Freud, *A Case of Hysteria (Dora)*, pp.21–2; Robertson, Introduction to *A Case of Hysteria (Dora)*, p.xxxi note 65.
21 Freud, *A Case of Hysteria (Dora)*, p.22.
22 Freud, *A Case of Hysteria (Dora)*, pp.22–3.
23 Freud, *A Case of Hysteria (Dora)*, pp.22–3 and 23 note 2.
24 Freud, *A Case of Hysteria (Dora)*, pp.58 59.
25 Freud, *A Case of Hysteria (Dora)*, pp.15–19, 62, 103.
26 Freud, *A Case of Hysteria (Dora)*, pp.62–3.
27 Robertson, Introduction to *A Case of Hysteria (Dora)*, p.xxxi.
28 Freud, *A Case of Hysteria (Dora)*, p.24.

29 Freud, *A Case of Hysteria (Dora)*, p.94.

30 Peter Gay, *Freud: A Life for Our Time* (Dent, London, 1988), p.171.

31 Gay, *Freud: A Life for Our Time*, pp.47–8, 170–73, 326, 602.

32 Freud, *A Case of Hysteria (Dora)*, pp.100–1.

33 Freud, *A Case of Hysteria (Dora)*, p.100.

34 Robertson, Introduction to *A Case of Hysteria (Dora)*, p.viii.

35 Freud, *A Case of Hysteria (Dora)*, p.99.

36 Freud, *A Case of Hysteria (Dora)*, p.103.

37 Freud, *A Case of Hysteria (Dora)*, pp.97, 103 note 1.

38 Freud, *A Case of Hysteria (Dora)*, pp.97, 103.

39 Freud, *A Case of Hysteria (Dora)*, p.5.

40 Freud, *A Case of Hysteria (Dora)*, p.90.

41 Robertson, Introduction to *A Case of Hysteria (Dora)*, p.li.

42 Freud, *A Case of Hysteria (Dora)*, p.17.

43 Freud, *A Case of Hysteria (Dora)*, pp.103–4.

44 Freud, *A Case of Hysteria (Dora)*, p.102; also Robertson, Introduction to *A Case of Hysteria (Dora)*, p.xxix.

45 Freud, *A Case of Hysteria (Dora)*, p.104.

46 Robertson, Introduction to *A Case of Hysteria (Dora)*, p.xiii.

47 Robertson, Introduction to *A Case of Hysteria (Dora)*, p.xxxix.

48 John Docker, *Postmodernism and Popular Culture: A Cultural History*, p.168.

49 Jeffrey Moussaieff Masson, *The Assault on Truth: Freud's Suppression of the Seduction Theory* (Harper Perennial, New York, 1992), p.57.

50 Docker, *Postmodernism and Popular Culture: A Cultural History*, p.298, note 12.

51 Robertson, Introduction to *A Case of Hysteria (Dora)*, pp.vii-viii.

52 Robertson, Introduction to *A Case of Hysteria (Dora)*, p.vii.

53 Gay, *Freud: A Life for Our Time*, p.264.

54 Robertson, Introduction to *A Case of Hysteria (Dora)*, p.vii.

55 Michel Foucault, *Psychiatric Power: Lectures at the Collège de France 1973–1974*, edited by Jacques Lagrange, translated by Graham Burchell (2003; Picador, New York, 2006), Lecture of 6 February 1974, pp.298–333.

56 Foucault, *Psychiatric Power*, lecture 12, p.304.

57 Foucault, *Psychiatric Power*, lecture 12, pp.297–8, 303–4.

58 Foucault, *Psychiatric Power*, lecture 12, pp.308–10.

59 Foucault, *Psychiatric Power*, lecture 12, pp.311–316.

60 Foucault, *Psychiatric Power*, lecture 12, p.322.

61 Foucault, *Psychiatric Power*, lecture 12, pp.317-8, 321-3.

62 Foucault, *Psychiatric Power*, lecture 12, p.323.

63 Foucault, *Psychiatric Power*, lecture 12, p.343.

64 See Laleen Jayamanne, *The Epic Cinema of Kumar Shahani* (Indiana University Press, Bloomington and Indianopolis, 2015), pp.174-176 and 264 note 3; Rae Beth Gordon, *Why the French Love Jerry Lewis: From Cabaret to Early Cinema* (Stanford University Press, Stanford, 2001).

65 Xiaolu Guo, *Once upon a time in the East: A Story of Growing Up* (Chatto and Windus, London, 2017), p.201.

66 John Docker, *1492: The Poetics of Diaspora* (Continuum, London and New York, 2001), pp.86-8; Georg Simmel, 'The Stranger', *The Sociology of Georg Simmel*, edited and translated Kurt H. Wolff (The Free Press, Glencoe, Ill., 1950), pp.402-8.

67 Walter Benjamin, *Illuminations*, edited and introduced by Hannah Arendt (Schocken, New York, 2007), Introduction p.3.

68 Guo, *Once upon a time in the East: A Story of Growing Up*, pp.9-10, 19.

69 Guo, *Once upon a time in the East*, pp.25-6, 53-5.

70 Guo, *Once upon a time in the East*, pp.82-5.

71 Guo, *Once upon a time in the East*, pp.96-8.

72 Guo, *Once upon a time in the East*, p.314.

73 Anna Cole, 'Making a debut: myths, memories and mimesis', in Frances Peters-Little, Ann Curthoys and John Docker (eds), *Passionate Histories: Myth, Memory and Indigenous Australia* (ANU E Press, Canberra, 2010), pp.205-218.

74 Guo, *Once upon a time in the East*, p.132.

75 Guo, *Once upon a time in the East*, p.133.

76 Guo, *Once upon a time in the East*, pp.133, 149.

77 Guo, *Once upon a time in the East*, pp.181, 184-188, 219, 248.

78 Guo, *Ocne upon a time in the East*, pp.188-191.

79 Guo, *Once upon a time in the East*, pp.209, 211-2,

80 Guo, *Once upon a time in the East*, pp.256-7, 281.

81 Guo, *Once upon a time in the East*, pp.18, 21-2.

82 Guo, *Once upon a time in the East*, p.22.

21

Israel Zangwill's *The Melting Pot*: An Undutiful Daughter, Marrying Out, a Troubled Utopia

> The procession of the Pogrom [the Odessa massacre of 1905] was led by about ten Catholic (Greek) Sisters with about forty or fifty of their school children. They carried ikons or pictures of Jesus and sang 'God Save the Tsar'. They were followed by a crowd containing hundreds of men and women murderers yelling 'Bey Zhida', which means 'Kill the Jews'. With these words they ran into the yards where there were fifty or a hundred tenants. They rushed in like tigers. Soon they began to throw children out of the windows of the second, third, or fourth stories… But this did not satisfy the stony-hearted murderers. They then rushed up to the child, seized it and broke its little arm and leg bones into three or four pieces, then wrung its neck too. They laughed and yelled, so carried away with pleasure at their successful work.
> *Public Health*, Nurses' Quarterly, Cleveland, Ohio, October 1913, a report quoted by Israel Zangwill in Appendices to *The Melting Pot*[1]

My interest in the 1930s Sydney Jewish Youth Theatre now leads me to the English Jewish author Israel Zangwill (1864–1926), whose most famous play *The Melting Pot* (1908) the Theatre apparently staged on 22 May 1937 (*Sydney Morning Herald*, 15 May 1937). *The Melting Pot* was set in New York, the great port city so despised by T S Eliot in *After Strange Gods*, we might recall, as 'invaded by foreign races', Eliot proclaiming that a 'population should be homogeneous' and that therefore 'reasons of race and religion combine to make any large number of free-thinking Jews undesirable'.[2] Zangwill included the epigraph above, from an eyewitness account of the 1905 Odessa pogrom, as part of the Appendices to the 1914 edition of *The Melting Pot*, suggesting that the extreme desire for a society to be a monoculture can inspire extreme violence, as in the early-twentieth-century pogroms in the Russian Empire, events that inspired the creation of characters and narrative in Zangwill's play.

The Melting Pot was a success in the US in 1909 and 1910, and was reputed to have been approved by former President Theodore Roosevelt when he attended a performance.

Although there was no report of the performance in the theatre notices of the *Sydney Morning Herald*, so no clue to its reception there, the Sydney publication *Workers' Weekly* did track the play in some detail. On Friday 7 May, under the heading 'Jewish Youth Theatre', *Workers' Weekly* informed their readers that Lewis Levy, who is producing the play, reports that the 'progress of the rehearsals is very pleasing'. *The Workers' Weekly* concludes its preview, and this information must have come from their conversation with Lewis Levy:

> This play is as vivid and vital today as when it was written in 1907. The clash of racial antagonisms, the fostering of national and religious enmities is an urgent problem that is demanding solution. Zangwill's conception of this question is most artistically revealed in his work, 'The Melting Pot'.

After the play was staged on Saturday 22 May 1937, the *Workers' Weekly* filed a warm report on the following Tuesday, 25 May.

> A large and enthusiastic audience witnessed a fine presentation of Israel Zangwill's 'The Melting Pot', by the Jewish Youth Theatre League at the Railway and Tramway Institute last night.
>
> America is the melting pot, the crucible into which are pouring the oppressed people of all other lands. In the free atmosphere of the western Continent the wrongs and hates of the Old World are to find no fruitful soil. There, a new humanity is to be created. But Zangwill, while hopeful, sees in America's 'unemployed millionaires' and other evidences of prejudice and oppression, the menace of a transplantation of the evil conditions that existed in Europe, specifically, in Tsarist Russia.
>
> Jerome ('Jock') Levy gave a good characterization of 'David Quixano'. A splendid voice, fine sensitiveness and fervor made his performance, despite some blemishes, an outstanding one… One final word of commendation, this to Lewis Levy. Last night's success can be attributed in no small degree to his work as producer.

The play may also have stimulated discussion of the question of assimilation: on Monday 14 February 1938, the *Sydney Morning Herald* reported that the Jewish Youth Theatre League would hold a debate on the subject, 'That Assimilation will not solve the Jewish Problem', at the Jewish Cultural Home, 21 Macquarie Place, and soon after, according to the *Herald*, Zangwill's *The Melting Pot* was revived on February 20. If those debating on 14 February 1938 did contend that assimilation would 'not solve the Jewish Problem', they may have been anticipating Hannah Arendt telling in her wartime essays 'We Refugees' (1943) and 'The Jew as Pariah: A Hidden Tradition' (1944) of her dislike of Jewish assimilation ('a permit to ape the gentiles or an opportunity to play the parvenu'), and her admiration, by contrast, for conscious pariahs.[3]

The next staging of *The Melting Pot* appears to have occurred in Melbourne in 1939, and here concern at the imminence of world war in the strength and spread of European fascism may have provided a pressing context. Lew Levy in his essay in *1492: The Poetics of Diaspora*, writing of his stay in Melbourne during that year, mentions that in the Jewish cultural organisation Kadimah, liberal-leftist in its political orientation, he formed a theatre group which staged *The Melting Pot*, attracting a 'wide audience'.[4]

Until coming across reference to *The Melting Pot* being staged by the Sydney Jewish Youth Theatre I had barely heard of Israel Zangwill. I don't know how much my uncles and my mother knew about him or what in general they thought of him; he died in 1926, when they as children migrated to Sydney; they may have known of him in their intense intellectual discussions in the 1930s for his international reputation when he was alive as the voice of Anglo-Jewry, and may have been acquainted with a variety of his writings, but it appears from Lew Levy's reminiscences in *1492: The Poetics of Diaspora* that the Sydney Jewish Youth Theatre was primarily or only interested in Zangwill as a dramatist: 'We played and read Sholem Aleichem, Peretz and Israel Zangwill.'[5]

I'll make a preliminary investigation now, before focusing on the play, then in further chapters muse more on Zangwill, my ideas fanning out as it were.

From casting about in various sources, elements of a portrait of Zangwill roughly emerge. On my shelves I locate with my finger *J.F.S. The history of the Jews' Free School, London since 1732*, by Gerry Black, which tells me that the most cherished school prize, open only to boys, was the Commemoration Prize, and it was won by Israel Zangwill twice, in 1877 and 1878. Zangwill, Black writes, later wrote about the East End school in Spitalfields in his 1892 book *Children of the Ghetto*, and was known as one of JFS's best known alumni, described by Black as a 'novelist, dramatist and leading Zionist'.[6] The ascription of Zionist may have to be qualified. It appears he had a troubled relationship with Zionism, sharing its nationalist and settler colonial interest in a Jewish homeland yet also attracted to internationalist and universalist values through his marriage into a remarkable scientific and literary family, the Ayrtons; a family that was both non-Jewish and Jewish, a mosaic. Israel Zangwill married out, which interests me, because *The Melting Pot*'s two central characters marry out and my mother married out. As did Hannah Arendt. And come to think of it, I married out.

Next I read two helpful essays by the Zangwill scholar Meri-Jane Rochelson. In her 1999 essay, 'Israel Zangwill and *Children of the Ghetto*', Rochelson tells us that Israel Zangwill was born on 21 January 1864 in Ebenezer Square in London's East End; his parents were immigrants from Latvia and Poland, his father pious and traditional, his mother more independent-minded; a traveling peddler, his father supported his large family as they moved around southern England, living in Plymouth and Bristol before returning to Whitechapel when he was eight. After attending and becoming a pupil-teacher at the Jews' Free School in Bell Lane, he received his degree with triple honours from the University of London in 1884. Israel Zangwill was a nonobservant Jew, Rochelson reflects, who 'yet insisted professionally and personally on being recognized as Jewish'. He pursued a career as a 'humorist, a journalist, and writer of fiction'. When *Children of the Ghetto* was published in 1892 it created a sensation in both Britain and the US, the first half evoking the life and frequent poverty of the East End, the second half exploring the consciousness of young middle-class Jews. The novel, known as the first Anglo-Jewish bestseller, established its author as the 'preeminent literary voice of Anglo-Jewry'.[7]

In 1903 Israel Zangwill married Edith Ayrton (1874–1945), a novelist and political activist in the suffrage movement. The couple, Rochelson tells us, shared a 'faith in universal concepts of morality that they saw as deriving from, but also transcending, Judaism and Christianity'; a kind of 'universal religion', a 'universalist religious ideology'. At the same time, Rochelson points out, he was an active participant in Jewish world politics. In 1895 he met Theodore Herzl (1860-1904) in London, and became an 'ardent if sometimes critical supporter' of Zionism. In 1905, however, after Herzl's death, Zangwill diverged from Zionism to form the Jewish Territorial Organization, whose goal was to establish a Jewish homeland anywhere that land could be obtained. In 1923, towards the end of his life, Zangwill, in a speech in New York to the American Jewish Congress, committed what was perceived as 'political heresy' by criticising the Zionist organisations, after which his 'reputation among Jews rapidly declined'. Rochelson suggests that, along with the triumph of modernism making his literary work look dated, Zangwill's 'increasingly controversial position in Jewish politics' led to a 'steep decline' in the reputation of *Children of the Ghetto* until it became 'virtually unknown'.[8]

In her 2007 essay 'Edith Ayrton Zangwill and the Anti-Domestic Novel' Rochelson tells us of the extraordinary family Israel Zangwill joined when he married Edith Ayrton in 1903. Her father William Ayrton was a 'physical scientist and electricity pioneer'. Her mother was Matilda Chaplin Ayrton, who along with other young women who desired to be medical students, notably including Sophia Jex-Blake, unsuccessfully sought admission to Edinburgh University in 1870-71. From 1873 to 1879 Matilda and husband William lived in Japan, where Matilda set up a 'school for midwives and where Edith was born'. In 1879 Matilda obtained her medical degree in Paris. However, before Edith's ninth birthday, Matilda died, and in 1885, two years later, her father married Hertha Marks, a 'young Jewish woman who had studied mathematics at Girton College, Cambridge'. Hertha Ayrton contributed to the science of the electric arc and invented the Ayrton Fan, used by British troops in World War I.[9]

Edith Ayrton, then, Rochelson continues, was from an early age brought up by a Jewish stepmother, and like Hertha Ayrton she became a suffragette, both of them active as speakers, demonstrators and financial contributors. She did not, however, become a scientist, but a feminist novelist well known in her own right. Between 1901, two years before she married Israel Zangwill, and 1928, two years after he died, Edith Ayrton Zangwill wrote six novels and many articles and stories; as a suffragette and pacifist, she gave speeches and wrote articles for the Women's Social and Political Union, 'often uniting the causes of peace and women's rights'. Edith became treasurer of the Women's Peace Crusade, was on the executive committee of the Women's International League for Peace and Freedom, and in the early 1930s was chair of the British section of that group's Disarmament Committee, obtaining signatures for its international petition campaign. Edith was a friend and supporter of the British birth-control advocate Marie Stopes, and from 1917 to 1945 they conducted an extensive correspondence.[10]

Israel Zangwill also, Rochelson notes, became 'active in the suffrage and pacifist movements of the early twentieth century', and just as he embraced her 'cause of women's rights and made it his own', so too did Edith, including after his death in 1926, lend 'support to Zionist causes'.[11]

~~~⁂~~~

I'm intrigued by Rochelson saying that after their marriage in 1903, Israel Zangwill and Edith Ayrton, Jewish man and non-Jewish woman, shared a 'faith in universal concepts of morality that they saw as deriving from, but also transcending, Judaism and Christianity'; a kind of 'universal religion', a 'universalist religious ideology'.[12] There is a possible thread of connection here to an aspect of my hero Benedict Spinoza that may relate to the ideas and spirit informing *The Melting Pot*: Spinoza's notion in his controversial *Tractatus Theologicus Politicus* of a universal morality beyond any specific institutional religion.

In my *1492: The Poetics of Diaspora*, I refer to Spinoza in *Tractatus Theologico-Politicus* (published late 1669 or 1670) outlining the fundamental principles of practical faith. There is a revealed Word of God, and such is a simple conception of the divine mind as revealed to the ancient prophets; this is to obey God with all one's heart by practising justice and charity, which are to be held in universal esteem; he who is blessed abounds in charity, joy, peace, patience, kindness, goodness, faithfulness, gentleness and self-control; one should love one's neighbor as oneself. In addition, the moral value of a man's creed should be judged only from his deeds; everyone should be allowed the freedom and right to interpret the basic tenets of faith as he thinks fit; the supreme authority to explain religion and to make judgement concerning it is vested in each individual; and religion does not pertain to the sphere of public law and authority, but to the sphere of individual right.[13]

☙ ❦ ❧

Let's evoke the narrative and key dramatic moments and turning points of *The Melting Pot* and also discuss the very interesting appendices that Zangwill added for the 1914 edition, where he expands on doubts suggested in the play concerning the utopian ideal of an inclusive American melting pot for all its peoples, doubts that particularly concern African Americans. The play and the appendices form a kind of continuous text, utopia shadowed by unresolved dystopian anxieties. Can the centre, the utopian dream of American inclusivity, hold?

I read *The Melting Pot* in the British Library, in the Rare Books and Music Room where we always go and usually sit in the same desk area when Ann and I were making our now annual visit to London, in 2016, and scribbled lots of notes in a cute Marimekko exercise book, with a pencil and pencil sharpener bought at the bookshop on the ground floor, but my memory might now be inexact for certain details I didn't record but probably should have.

The Melting Pot explores ways that history is not necessarily destiny, that histories do not determine identity and consciousness through the generations; in diaspora, far from dangerous histories elsewhere, there may be different ways of being Jewish, and different ways of being Russian, and in America, or rather in New York, these differences might play out in surprising and unpredictable ways. In genre the play is a melodrama foregrounding crises and confrontations, crossed with romance, romance as a possible love relationship with obstacles that may destroy the lovers' hopes; and the obstacles are formidable indeed, creating the play's intense conflicts and suspense. Only transformation and metamorphosis can reduce or remove the obstacles for its two key characters, two young people on the threshold of a new American life, a Russian-Jewish man and a non-Jewish Russian woman.

The play is in four packed lively acts and concerns the far-flung consequences of the early-twentieth-century pogroms carried out against Jews in the Russian empire, usually referred to as the Kishinev pogroms of 19 and 20 April 1903, Kishinev then being the capital of Bessarabia, followed by the Odessa pogrom of 1905, leading to Jewish refugees scattering across the world. The young man is David Quixano, a self-taught violinist who in his previous life had been considered a wonder-child in the Russian Pale; in New York he finds haven, along with remnants of his family who also survived the pogroms, including his uncle Mendel, an elderly music teacher who also plays in a theatre near their apartment to help pay the rent, and his old grandmother (I think grandmother) who only speaks Yiddish, the language of the Pale. There are also comic scenes involving Kathleen, 'a young and pretty Irish maid-of-all-work', presumably the Christian servant needed to work on the Sabbath, an Irish stage character who would have been familiar to American audiences.

(Concerning the need for non-Jewish servants on the Sabbath, we should remember Exodus 35: 2, when God through his messenger Moses commands the Israelites: 'Six days work shall be done, but on the seventh day there shall be to you an holy day, a sabbath of rest to the LORD: whosoever doeth work therein shall be put to death.' Not a warning to be lightly disregarded.)

In Act I we learn of the international spirit of 'the Settlement' David goes to. It welcomes migrants from everywhere, Dutch, Greek, Polish, Norwegian, Welsh, Armenian; David quotes famous lines from the Statue of Liberty on Ellis Island: 'Come unto me all ye that labour and are heavy laden and I will give you rest.' At the Settlement, David meets and is drawn to a young Russian woman, Vera Revendal, who has 'a touch of the exotic in her appearance', and likewise she is drawn to him. An immediate obstacle, however, is her at least initial anti-Semitism. When Vera visits where David lives, she feels insulted when Kathleen the maid speaks to her as if she is Jewish, Vera haughtily replying no, 'I am a Russian'. Vera is curious to know why David's name sounds Spanish, suggesting that she thought he was a Christian, not knowing that he is of Spanish Jewish descent, his Sephardi family, as she and we learn during the play, having made its way after 1492 from Spain via Holland to live in Poland. David is out, Vera is told, he's playing at the 'Crippled Children's Home'; aware now that he is Jewish, Vera decides to 'conquer her prejudice'. On a desk in the apartment, she notices printed music, including a Mendelssohn concerto; there is a book by Nietzsche, but she can't see any Russian books; David's grandmother is a traditionalist, she is sad that for the family to get by in this new land Mendel and David have to work on the Sabbath, which should be the day of rest.

We learn more about Vera, that she plays the piano, she had been trained in St Petersburg; in Russia she had also been arrested as a Revolutionist, but, she says, 'I escaped my gaolers'; Vera tells of her fear of being sent to Siberia. Vera and David share a 'melancholy', both in different ways fated to be exiles, he because of the pogroms, she as a political exile from the Czarist autocracy. David, Vera quickly realises, is 'crazy about America'. He is writing an American symphony, and Vera foresees a bright future for him, that one day 'David will turn out a Rubinstein' (the pre-World War I audiences would have recognised the reference to Anton Rubinstein, 1829–1894, the famous Russian pianist who had performed in America during 1872–3, I hope I've got this right). 'America is God's Crucible', David exclaims to Vera, the 'great Melting-Pot where all the races of Europe are melting and re-forming!' Invoking Nietszche, David is sure that the new American will be the 'fusion of all races', perhaps the 'coming superman'.

There is now a sudden dramatic turn threatening David and Vera's growing friendship, when she tells him that she is from Kishineff. David immediately becomes agitated, crying out that his mother and father had been massacred there, while he had been shot in the shoulder and left for dead: 'the Death-March!... Mother! Father! Ah – cowards, murderers! And you!' It is unclear from this anguished speech that he knows Vera's exact relationship to Kishineff, though he learns that her father lives there.

When Act II opens, it is a month later. Vera and David are learning more about their very different histories in Russia. Vera tells David that her father is a Baron, so Vera too is part of the Russian nobility, with all its prejudices; she was, she confesses, 'brought up to despise your race'. Vera stresses how much she had broken away from the nobility's political traditions, in particular, that she chose not to follow her father's beliefs, she became in effect an undutiful daughter: he is a 'Reactionary, I am a Radical'.

Meanwhile, David's uncle Mendel, who thinks highly of David's musicianship and believes that he should further his studies in Germany, is becoming anxious about his growing affection for Vera. He warns David against marrying out: 'Many countries have gathered us. Holland took us when we were driven from Spain – but we did not become Dutchmen. Turkey took us when Germany oppressed us, but we have not become Turks.' In marrying out, Mendel is suggesting, David will lose his distinctive Jewish identity. Mendel becomes increasingly angry: 'You are mad already – your dreams are mad – the Jew is hated here as everywhere – you are false to your race.' Mendel could be reminding David of another character hovering about in the play, Quincy Davenport, a rich American who is openly anti-Semitic. Davenport, we learn, hopes to marry Vera (I think my memory is right here). David wishes to reject Europe, as he tells Vera, because it is 'sodden with blood, red with bestial massacres', while holding out very high hopes for New World America as an alternative, a new beginning in history.

In Act III, the Old World comes to New York, when Vera's father the Baron, accompanied by his new young wife the Baroness, arrives to see Vera. Will Vera bow to paternal authority, and renounce her new love in the New World? Or will she continue to be an undutiful daughter?

We learn that rich man Quincy Davenport had sailed his yacht to Odessa to transport the Baron and Baroness to New York, trusting that they will steer Vera away from David and towards himself as a more suitable suitor. There follows an interesting confrontational scene between rich white American and the Baron as a Czarist functionary directly involved in what he proudly refers to as the 'Jew-massacres in Kishineff': 'I was on the spot. I had charge of the whole district.' Quincy demurs at such language, chiding the Baron that we in America are a 'bit squeamish' talking about massacres. The Baron retorts: 'Squeamish! Don't you lynch and roast your n——— ?' Quincy reminds the Baron of the notoriety of the Czar's 'Black Hundreds'.

In this heated conversation, the Baron refers to Jews in what we would now recognize as genocidal language, they are sub-human. At Kishineff, he says, 'we stick the swine'; he believes the Jews in Russia overall are 'ten million vermin' overrunning the society: they 'ruin our professional classes by snatching all the prizes and professorships'. When Quincy asks what is Russia 'going to do' with the Jews, the Baron replies that there will be forcible religious conversion, murder and expulsion: 'One-third will be baptized, one-third massacred, the other third emigrated' to the US. The Baron becomes irritated when Quincy says that in the US, 'We're going to stop all alien immigration'.

In the conversation with Quincy, we learn more details about Vera's dissident response to her upbringing. The Baron recalls that since being a schoolgirl, Vera was a rebel against the Czar. The Baron is not of happy to learn from Quincy of David's affection for Vera, he must be a 'Jew-beast', part of the 'Jew-vermin', and, ominously, he packs a pistol in his luggage.

Immediately on meeting up with his daughter in New York, there is open conflict and confrontation. Vera is reminded how egregiously conservative, anti-Semitic, racist and contemptuous of any kind of egalitarianism they are. The Baroness pours scorn on opponents of the Czar: 'Ze Intellectuals and ze Bund, zey all hate my husband because he is faithful to Christ and ze Tsar'. The Baron announces how appalled he is at the very idea that in America a 'gentleman' would sit in a public car 'squeezed between working-men and shop-girls, not to say Jews and Blacks'. Unimpressed and appalled, Vera tells them that in Russia she had 'fought against the autocracy'; in the US she fights against 'poverty'. Fiery exchanges break out about David Quixana, Vera telling them that she admires him, in the long tradition of the Sephardi mystique, as 'a noble Jew': 'In Spain his ancestors were hidalgos, favourites at the Court of Ferdinand and Isabella; but in the great expulsion of 1492 they preferred exile in Poland to baptism.' The Baron declares that David is an 'unbaptized dog'. Vera reminds him that he admired the music of Rubinstein, who was a 'Jewish boy-genius, just like my David'; the Baroness retorts that Rubinstein was 'not a Jew', his parents were 'baptized soon after his birth'; Vera acknowledges that Rubinstein was the 'Court pianist and was decorated by the Czar', it being well known that the family had converted to Russian Orthodoxy, but he was, she insists, still a Jew.

David is now introduced to Vera's father, and recoils in horror. The Baron launches a verbal assault on his daughter's new friend by vigorously defending pogroms: 'The pogrom is a holy crusade. Are we Russians the first people to crush down the Jew...' David angrily replies, relating bondage in biblical Egypt to the extreme anti-Semitic violence of Czarist Russia:

> Yes, it is true. Even Christianity did not invent hatred. But not till the Holy Church arose were we burnt at the stake, and not till Holy Russia arose were our babes torn limb from limb. Oh, it is too much! Delivered from Egypt four thousand years ago, to be slaves to the Russian Pharaoh today.

David remembers the time of the Kishinev pogrom. It was Easter and carried out in the name of Christ, though he didn't know then that 'this Christ, whom holy chants proclaimed re-risen, was born in the form of a brother Jew'. He recalls the terror of the pogrom, conducted by 'the mob' and soldiers led by Vera's merciless father, a 'butcher'.

Vera, the audience would not have been surprised to learn, chooses her love for David over the paternal authority of her father the brutal Czarist Baron; she also reveals no interest in Quincy Davenport as a suitor, preferring, in the romance tradition, love over wealth; she invokes the biblical Ruth, who was not Jewish but a Moabite: 'now, David, I come to you, and I say in the words of Ruth, thy people shall be my people and thy God my God'.

Act IV occurs on 4 July, Independence Day. Kathleen the comic Irish servant reappears; when we first meet her she is rather anti-Semitic, now she has become part of the Jewish family, indeed she now speaks some Yiddish; Mendel's old *Mutter* remains dubious at the turn of events in the coming together of David and Vera, referring to David as 'meshuggah', touched in the head. David proclaims the 'glory of America, where all races and nations come to labour and look forward!' The hatreds of Europe are to be left behind, and there will be a coming together of 'Celt and Latin, Slav and Teuton, Greek and Syrian, – black and yellow'. Vera adds: 'Jew and Gentile'. Vera gives David three kisses: 'I will kiss you as we Russians kiss at Easter – the three kisses of peace', reclaiming Easter away from centuries-old Christian violence against Jews. A light is cast over the scene by the Statue of Liberty, and the play ends.

So there it is, the play staged in the US in 1909 and 1910 as a great success, and then put on in the latter 1930s by the Sydney Jewish Youth Theatre also as a great success, and by Lew Levy in Melbourne in 1939. I ponder what the Sydney audiences might have thought and talked about in the post-performance discussion, and I think yes, there could be many questions that the play stimulates that the audience could have raised, creating a lively conversation. The most urgent is what Lew Levy focusses on that we can read in the preview in *Workers' Weekly* of 7 May 1937, that the play is so alive today, in the latter 1930s, because it highlights an increasingly urgent contemporary situation, the 'clash of racial antagonisms, the fostering of national and religious enmities'. In this aspect, the play is an intense allegory of the rise of fascism and Nazism in societies and regimes in eastern and western Europe between the world wars, the brutality of Mussolini and Hitler, the intensifying persecution of Jews, the deportation of minorities.

Other questions that could have interested the audience concern Jewish identity and historical consciousness: the Jewish characters present many ways of being Jewish, questioning that in modernity there can be a single Jewish identity, from the traditionalism of the grandmother to Mendel sternly warning his nephew that the Jew is hated in the US as everywhere else in the world. Mendel presented for the audience to consider a basic Zionist perspective on modernity that emerged not only from the early-twentieth-century Russian empire pogroms, but also from the anti-Semitism associated with the Dreyfus affair in France: Jews can never be integrated into non-Jewish societies, neither in Eastern Europe and the Russian empire nor in supposedly Enlightened western European societies, only in a separate Zionist homeland could they escape persecution and contempt. Yet Mendel's pro-Zionist perspective is challenged by David, who at one point opposes working 'for a Jewish land… [being] a Zionist'. Instead, he extolls the desirability of life as part of, contributing to, America as a melting pot; that is, that living in diaspora with all its possibilities for the creation of new identities may be preferable to the Zionist vision of the world's Jews being indrawn to a homeland in Palestine.

When David as it were sings the diasporic 'glory of America, where all races and nations come to labour and look forward' and there will be a coming together of 'Jew and Gentile', 'Celt and Latin, Slav and Teuton, Greek and Syrian, – black and yellow', he might have raised an image for the audience of the Jewish Golden Age in medieval Moorish Spain, a *convivencia* of many religions, cultures, ethnicities, Jewish, Muslim, Christian. The audience could have interpreted what David is saying, the coming together of so many different peoples, not necessarily as David did, as heralding a fusion of identities (the 'fusion of all races'), but as consonant with an internationalism and cosmopolitanism that many of them admired and aspired to; a cosmopolitanism at ease with many cultures, many identities, many peoples.

Vera acknowledging that Anton Rubinstein had converted and become the 'Court pianist' who was 'decorated by the Czar' yet nonetheless was still a Jew, perhaps recalled for the audience the intriguing figure of the Marrano in sixteenth-century Catholic Portugal, where Jews after the expulsion from Spain in 1492 had to become New Christians while secretly, in thought and imagination and sensibility, continuing aspects of Jewish identity; there developed in Marranos a doubled consciousness, skeptical and ambivalent, perhaps one reason that Spinoza in Holland in the seventeenth century was expelled from the Sephardi community, in 1656. Spinoza became for modernity the figure of the secular Jew, the non-Jewish Jew, and perhaps such is the identity that David chooses: contra his uncle Mendel's dismay, when David marries out, he nonetheless does adopt a distinctive Jewish identity in the image of the great Spinoza.

David, the audience realises, is not presented as the play's single authoritative voice. His utopian celebration of America as an all-inclusive melting pot that marks it off completely from a discredited Europe is questioned more than once. Quincy Davenport's anti-Semitism reminds the audience of the strength of Judeophobia in the US, how widespread it might be, and it hasn't been left behind in Old World Europe. In his testy conversation with Davenport, the Baron in his exceedingly unpleasant way reminds the audience of the history of extreme violence in the US towards African Americans, of lynching in the present and slavery in the not too distant past. David wishes to reject Europe, as he tells Vera, because 'it is sodden with blood, red with bestial massacres' – yet this contrast between Old World and New World is pertinently challenged by the brutal Baron.

The Baron perhaps unwittingly mentions another similarity

that crosses Old World and New World. In Russia, says the Baron, we see that the Jews are ruining 'our professional classes by snatching all the prizes and professorships'. Sydney audiences in the 1930s for *The Melting Pot* would have been well aware of Nazi practices in Germany in dismissing Jewish staff from universities. Knowledgeable about American history through reading radical writers and playwrights, they would also have known that from the 1920s onward there were restrictive quotas for Jewish students at American universities. Some in the audience might have known that in his 'After Strange Gods' lectures in 1933, T S Eliot implicitly endorsed quotas for Jews in the professions, when he told his audience at the University of Virginia, in Charlottesville, that 'reasons of race and religion combine to make any large number of free-thinking Jews undesirable'.[14]

(As I write these sentences on 29 August 2017, I think of the neo-Nazis in Charlottesville a few weeks ago, 11–12 August, out in garish grotesque force as if swarming out of the Underworld to defend the statue of the Confederate general Robert E Lee, a bronze monument forged in 1924; the night before the larger demonstration, the neo-Nazis entered the campus of the University of Virginia and brutalised protestors gathered around a statue of Jefferson, holding hands in non-violent solidarity. I idly wonder about T S Eliot in 1933 coming to stay in Charlottesville to give his heretic-hunting 'After Strange Gods' lectures, during which he paid homage to the American South because it was so different from New York; I wonder if during his time there his hosts showed him the statue, installed less than a decade before, as they strolled about the town. Did they all stand there admiring it, rubbing a hand over the bronze, holding back tears in a properly manly way, while Mr Eliot felt the occasion demanded that he launch, in his faux-English voice, into a speech proclaiming what great men, great Christians, racially pure, these Confederate generals and their followers were, that's when America was great, and though I don't live here anymore I would rejoice with you if we could return our nation to what it had been, living the true values of the South, at the same time as hopefully we wipe New York off the map.)

I think I'll leave these stray speculations about what the Sydney audiences were inspired by *The Melting Pot* to talk about; maybe more thoughts might occur to me, maybe I've left out something obvious. I've told Ann about the play, and she says maybe it should be called a 'discussion play'. I like that.

One thing more though: that David in the play is Sephardi and so by descent from Spain thence Portugal and Holland may have had a special resonance for my uncles and my mother, given family lore that I heard as a child, that the Levy family were descended from Portuguese-Sephardi Jews who came to Holland and thence to London. A further resonance may have been that both Lew and Jock had met at the Sydney Jewish Youth Theatre two young Russian-Jewish women, cousins who had migrated to Sydney, who they would marry. And for my mother, a further resonance, to think about David and Vera, Jew and Christian, marrying out and perhaps following in their own way the kind of universal practical faith that Spinoza argued for in *Tractatus Theologico-Politicus* and Israel Zangwill and Edith Ayrton advocated in London early in the twentieth century, a kind of universal religion deriving from but also transcending Judaism and Christianity. For unlike her brothers, my mother would marry out.

I'd like to explore something further. The play as a whole, conceived as various characters with various viewpoints contesting each other, what we can think of as polyphonic, a discussion play, casts doubts on David's utopian hope that the 'glory of America' means that 'all races and nations' will come together, including 'black and yellow'. In particular, the Baron reminding Quincy Davenport

– and hence the audience – of lynching as a persisting feature of American society, may have led Israel Zangwill to add appendices for the 2014 edition where he ponders the question, do anti-Semitism and the extreme violence against African Americans mean that Jews and African Americans will always be excluded from the American melting pot, that there are and always will be boundaries against their inclusion and therefore American society will always stay divided and fractured? Is America fated to be a failed society? Or can we be more optimistic?

In the appendices, we read an Afterword by Zangwell where he reflects on *The Melting Pot*. Here Zangwill is far from sure of anything. He says that the play 'sprang directly from the author's concrete experiences as President of the Emigration Regulation Department of the Jewish Territorial Organisation' which will soon have 'fostered the settlement of ten thousand Russian Jews in the West of the United States'. He disavows that the melting pot means assimilation: 'The process of American amalgamation is not assimilation or simple surrender to the dominant type, as is popularly supposed, but an all-round give-and-take by which the final type may be enriched or impoverished'. He is aware of the 'anti-Semitism of American uncivilisation', yet this might change, as might hostility towards African Americans: 'Even the negrophobia is not likely to remain eternally at its present barbarous pitch'. Zangwill notes that 'there are at work forces of attraction as well as of repulsion', adding rather enigmatically that 'even upon the negro the "Melting Pot" of America will not fail to act in a measure as it has acted on the Red Indian, who has found it almost as facile to mate with his white neighbours as with his black'.

In the Afterword, Zangwill plays out his affirmations and doubts and hesitations in relation to African Americans and the melting pot. He very much supports intermarriage between different races, and decries as 'monstrous' the view that 'millions of people in America have the moral right to exclude others', a thought he extends to 'Canada and Australia'. In intermarriage, he reflects, 'philolencosis, or love of the white, is a force of racial uplifting for the black'. Nonetheless, he writes, this is 'not to deny that the prognathous face is an ugly and undesirable type of countenance or that it connotes a lower average of intellect and ethics, or that white and black are as yet too far apart for profitable fusion'. He feels 'privileged to know' 'negroes of genius' like Henry O Tanner, the painter, and Paul Lawrence Dunbar, the poet, who show the 'potentialities of the race' even without white admixture; and as men of this stamp are capable of attracting white wives, the 'fusing process' should begin at the top with 'types like these'. Furthermore, in a two-way process we can see that African-American culture, as in rag-time and the 'sex-dances' that accompany it, has spread to 'white America and thence to the whole white world'.[15]

Zangwill continues to worry at what he sees as the problems posed by his notions of the physical appearance of African Americans, especially in relation to intermarriage of black and white and their children. I'll indent a quote here:

> ... the negroid hair and complexion being, in Mendelian language, 'dominant', these black traits are not easy to eliminate from the hybrid posterity; in view of all the unpleasantness, both immediate and contingent, that attends the blending of colours, only heroic souls on either side should dare the adventure of intermarriage. Blacks of this temper, however, would serve their race better by making Liberia a success or building up an American negro State, as Mr William Archer recommends, or at least asserting their rights as American citizens in that sub-tropical South which without their labour could never have been opened up.

Reader, I don't know quite what to say about this mélange of eugenics and historical speculation. I'll just leave it there for us to contemplate.

On reading the Afterword, I googled the names Zangwill mentions, and came up with the following biographical sketches. Henry Ossowa Tanner, 1859–1937, was the first African-American painter to gain international fame. He frequently depicted biblical scenes, and is best known for his paintings 'Nicodemus Visiting Jesus', 'The Banjo Lesson' and 'The Thankful Poor'. Born in Pittsburgh, Pennsylvania, he studied at the Pennsylvania Academy of the Fine Arts; in 1891 he moved to Paris, where he lived his whole life and was readily accepted in French artistic circles; in 1899 he married a white American singer, Jessie Olssen; in 1923 he was named honorary chevalier of the Legion Honor; he died in Paris.

The African-American writer Paul Lawrence Dunbar (1872–1906) was a poet, novelist and playwright. He was born to parents who had been enslaved in Kentucky before the American Civil War; his father Joshua had escaped from slavery in Kentucky before the war ended; he travelled to Massachusetts and volunteered for the 55th Massachusetts Infantry Regiment, one of the black units to serve in the war: and after being emancipated, his mother Matilda moved to Dayton, Ohio. Dunbar was one of the first African-American writers to establish an international reputation. He wrote in several dialects, including 'the Negro dialect' associated with the antebellum South, and was praised by William Dean Howells. He wrote the lyrics for the musical comedy, *In Dahomey* (1903), the first all-African-American musical produced on Broadway, which also toured in the UK and the US. He also wrote poetry and novels in conventional English.

William Archer (1856–1924) was a Scottish critic and writer. He spent large parts of his boyhood in Norway; later, he was educated at the University of Edinburgh; in the 1870s he spent a year in Australia; he introduced Ibsen to the English public, translating *A Doll's House* in 1889; a friend of George Bernard Shaw, he arranged to have Shaw's plays translated into German. In 1910 he published *Through Afro-America, an English reading of the race problem*, ranging across topics such as African Americans, United States – race relations, Southern States – Cuba, Panama.

Reader, I'll leave *The Melting Pot* here. Because it is open-voiced, undecided, raising interesting questions, I can see why it may have been so attractive for the Sydney Jewish Youth Theatre to stage. It doesn't offer definitive solutions or a program or set values or sure directions where history should go, yet it is passionate about racism and the horrifying racial violence directed against African Americans and Jews.

The first Appendix concerning the 1905 pogrom makes harrowing reading; I only gave a short except in the epigraph to this chapter. The Appendix explains more fully what occurred, as recorded in 1913 in *Public Health*, the Nurses' Quarterly. The writer explains that she was a 'Red Cross nurse on the battlefield'. The chief doctor of the Jewish Hospital of Odessa has sent a telephone message, 'Moldvanko is running in blood; send nurses and doctors'. Doctors and nurses from the Jewish Hospital jump in the ambulance and go to the City Hospital, who send out many nurses; the City Hospital hang silver crosses about their necks, so they would not be recognised as Jewish by the Holiganes (Hooligans).

> Then we went to Molorosiskia Street in the Moldvanko (slums)… The blood was already up to our ankles on the pavement and in the yards. The uproar was deafening but we could hear the Holiganes' fierce cries of 'Hooray, kill the Jews', on all sides… We had no time to think. All our thoughts were to pick up wounded ones, and to try to rescue some uninjured ones. We succeeded in rescuing some uninjured who were in hiding. We put bandages

on them to make it appear that they were wounded. We put them in the ambulance and carried them to the hospital, too. So at the Jewish Hospital we had five thousand injured and seven thousand uninjured to feed and protect for two weeks. Some were left without homes, without clothes, and children were even without parents.

In the excerpt I quote for the epigraph, the Red Cross nurse observes of the perpetrators of the pogrom: 'They laughed and yelled, so carried away with pleasure at their successful work.' This got me thinking of the insights of Holocaust scholar Dan Stone, as I note in my *Origins of Violence*, when he writes of modern genocides and massacres, as in Cambodia and Rwanda, the Rape of Nanjing and My Lai; integral to them, Stone argues, is the enjoyment of violence, including killing and anticipation of killing, and the theatre of violence itself; the perpetrators enjoy the acts of violence to a degree that can be called orgiastic, and in the act of killing they form temporary ecstatic communities, experiencing a heightened sense of belonging to their own group; a collective effervescence in belonging, often involving as it were ordinary people.[16]

If the perpetrators of pogroms against Russian Jews early in the twentieth century formed temporary ecstatic communities, including the 'forty or fifty' school children led by 'ten Catholic (Greek) Sisters' participating in the Odessa massacre, so too we can think that the perpetrators of the vicious lynching of African Americans, with white families and children present in what were regarded as festive occasions, also formed temporary ecstatic communities.

There is a link here, in terms of extreme violence carried out by those who consider themselves ordinary people, between anti-Jewish violence in Europe and the settler colonial societies of the Americas with their long history, post 1492, of slavery and its aftermaths, – in which Sephardi Jews from Holland were involved. Here is a sobering story, as I would find out.

1   Israel Zangwill, *The Melting Pot* (1908; 1914 edition), Appendices.
2   T.S. Eliot, *After Strange Gods*, pp.19-20.
3   Hannah Arendt, *The Jewish Writings*, edited by Jerome Kohn and Ron H. Feldman (Schocken, New York, 2007), pp.274-5, 297.
4   Docker, *1492: The Poetics of Diaspora*, p.163.
5   Docker, *1492: The Poetics of Diaspora*, p.165.
6   Gerry Black, *JFS: A history of the Jews' Free School, London since 1732* (Tymsder Publishing, London, 1998), pp.3-4, 89.
7   Meri-Jane Rochelson, 'Israel Zangwill and Children of the Ghetto', *Judaism: A Quarterly Journal of Jewish Life and Thought*, 48.1, 1999, pp.84-6.
8   Rochelson, 'Israel Zangwill and Children of the Ghetto', pp.85, 87-8, 93.
9   Meri-Jane Rochelson, 'Edith Ayrton Zangwill and the Anti-Domestic Novel', *Women's Studies*, 36, 2007, pp.162-164, 173.
10 Rochelson, 'Edith Ayrton Zangwill and the Anti-Domestic Novel', pp.162-3, 168, 171-2.
11 Rochelson, 'Edith Ayrton Zangwill and the Anti-Domestic Novel', pp.162 note 2, 163.
12 Meri-Jane Rochelson, 'Israel Zangwell and *Children of the Ghetto*', p.87.
13 John Docker, *1492: The Poetics of Diaspora* (Continuum, London and New York, 2001), p.93; Baruch Spinoza, *Tractatus Theologico-Politicus*, trans. Samuel Shirley, into. Brad S. Gregory (E.J. Brill, Leiden, 1989), pp.55, 103, 123, 159, 211, 281.
14 T.S. Eliot, *After Strange Gods: A Primer of Modern Heresy* (Faber and Faber, London 1934), pp.19-20.
15 For reflections on ideas of human betterment through racial mixing in the late nineteenth and well into the twentieth century, see Jane Carey, 'A 'Happy Blending'? Maori Networks, Anthropology and "Native" Policy in New Zealand, the Pacific and Beyond', in Jane Carey and Jane Lydon (eds), *Indigenous Networks: Mobility, Connections and Exchange* (Routledge, New York and London, 2014), pp.184-215.
16 Dan Stone, *History, Memory and Mass Atrocity: Essays on the Holocaust and Genocide* (Vallentine Mitchell, London, 2006), pp.198-9, 206-9; John Docker, *The Origins of Violence: Religion, History and Genocide* (UNSW Press, Sydney, 2008), p.27.

22

Sephardi slave trading and slave plantations in Suriname

In Israel Zangwill's *The Melting Pot*, the Sephardi character David Quixano reflects at one point, 'We Jews are cheerful in gloom, mistrustful in joy. It is our tragic history.' David is suggesting that we Jews are a people of suffering, we have always been victims, never perpetrators.

As I will now investigate, such a view is very far from the case, leading me to think that, from a world history perspective, Jewish history should be sweepingly recast.

In the following reflections I'll begin by evoking Zangwill's interest in Spinoza and Heine, with a particular question in mind: Can we see Israel Zangwill in Hannah Arendt's terms as a conscious pariah; in Isaac Deutscher's terms as a non-Jewish Jew? Arendt admires Heine, Rahel Varnhagen, Sholom Aleichem, Bernard Lazare, Franz Kafka and Charlie Chaplin as conscious pariahs.[1] Can we situate Israel Zangwill alongside these figures? In his famous essay 'The Non-Jewish Jew' Isaac Deutscher admires a tradition of modern thought inaugurated by Spinoza as 'those great revolutionaries' Heine, Marx, Rosa Luxemburg, Trotsky and Freud.[2] Can we situate Israel Zangwill alongside these figures (leaving aside one's reservations about Freud)? I don't think so.

I can certainly see the interest of *The Melting Pot* as a discussion play, but the more I read of Zangwill's other work, the more I found aspects of his thought to be deeply troubling: his aesthetic crudity, his support for worldwide European colonisation, and a kind of Jewish chauvinism, a claim to some kind of racial essence.

I could never have predicted the journey I now embark on, through Zangwill on Spinoza and Heine, thence across the Atlantic to Brazil and Suriname by way of a remarkable essay by one of my favourite historians Natalie Zemon Davis, prompting reflections on Sephardi slave trading and slave plantation colonisation. At every step of the writing, I didn't know where I was going next.

In his 1898 book of stories *Dreamers of the Ghetto* Israel Zangwill included a story about Spinoza, who I intensely admire, often think about as a kind of exemplar of how one should act in the world, and have written about, especially in my *1492: The Poetics of Diaspora*, reflecting on how he inaugurated the philosophical tradition of the secular Jew, the non-Jewish Jew, that Isaac Deutscher wrote so memorably about. So I wonder: why was Zangwill drawn to writing about Baruch Spinoza (1632–77) who in 1656 was excommunicated from the Sephardi community in Holland for heresy and thenceforth changed his first name to a Christian form, Benedict, the name he henceforth wished to be known by? I also wonder: why was Zangwill drawn to writing about Heine, for I could see in the contents page of *Dreamers of the Ghetto* that there was also a story about that witty irreverent iconoclastic figure that I know my son Ned Curthoys delights in in his *The Legacy of Judaism*. I thought – wrongly – that I might be able to see Zangwill as part of a long tradition of what Ned refers to as Liberal Judaism. In *The Legacy of Liberal Judaism* Ned traces the tradition from Moses Mendelssohn in the eighteenth-entury German Enlightenment to critical intellectuals in the twentieth century such as Ernst Cassirer and Hannah Arendt, with attention on the way to the place of Spinoza and Heine in that tradition, which Ned refers to as providing for modernity a 'vital legacy of liberal Jewish advocacy, ethical idealism, and refractory historical consciousness'.[3]

Ned points to Heine's admiration for the Golden Age of Spanish Jewry in medieval Moorish Spain, worldly, sophisticated, intellectually adventurous, multicultural and multi-religious, before it brutally came to an end in 1492 in the Christian Reconquista. In admiring Moorish Spain, Ned writes, Heine was in effect provincialising Europe, his disposition challengingly anti-Eurocentric. Heine, Ned suggests, preferred the brilliant, pluralist history of Moorish Spain as a culture of tolerance, a society superior, as a space of sensuous vitality and aesthetic refinement, to modern Europe, which he critiqued for its colonialism, Christian hubris and national chauvinism. Heine was profoundly sympathetic to the experience of both Moors and Jews at the hands of the Catholic Inquisition; in Moorish Spain he scandalously celebrates the hybridity of *Mestizo* cultures. In terms of Jewish heritage, Heine suggested that Spinoza wrote in the revolutionary and utopian spirit of the Prophets. Heine himself felt that the same Prophetic spirit encouraged him to announce that the great task of his own time in the nineteenth century as being (in Heine's words) 'not only the emancipation of the Irish, the Greeks, the Frankfurt Jews, the West Indian Blacks and other repressed people but the emancipation of the entire world'.[4]

I've evoked Ned's portrait of Heine because I think Heine, along with Spinoza who, Ned says, was admired by Heine as a Marrano, will stand as one pole by which to consider Israel Zangwill, and through Zangwill to contemplate the surprising, and certainly shocking, slave trading and settler-colonial slave-owning activities in the Americas of the seventeenth century ex-converso ex-Portuguese Sephardi Jews of Holland, the very Sephardic community that would in mid-century excommunicate Spinoza for heresy.

Yes, owners of slave plantations, and all that means in terms of dispossessing indigenous Brazilian and Caribbean peoples of their lands – what I regard as genocide – and then enslaving both Indigenous and African peoples; in so doing betraying the pluralist and *Mestizo* culture and ideals shared by the Sephardim in pre-1492 multi-ethnic and multi-religious Moorish Spain, a history I found fascinating to write about in my *1492: The Poetics of Diaspora*; a history where Sephardi Jews along with the Moors reached remarkable intellectual heights that made a signal contribution to what Raphaël Lemkin referred to in his writings on genocide as world thought and world culture.[5]

Let's look at the fictional story Zangwill wrote about Spinoza in *Dreamers of the Ghetto*.[6] At first, as I read 'The Maker of Lenses', which imagines a failed romance between Spinoza the philosopher of European-wide repute, a major figure of the seventeenth-century Radical Enlightenment, and Klaartje, the young daughter of his old Latin teacher Dr van den Ende, I felt positive things about it; yet wariness and uneasiness began to intrude, until I became fairly appalled. I'll talk about the story in the way suggested by Walter Benjamin in the prologue to his *The Origin of German Tragic Drama*, that what might be most valuable to investigate in a text are tiny particulars, the minutest thing.[7]

We read in 'The Maker of Lenses' that in the Hague, where he earns a humble living by grinding lenses, Spinoza stands out from the 'blonde Hollanders by his noble Spanish face with its black eyebrows and long curly locks'. He has become an object of hostility to the Christian populace as the suspected author of the *Tractatus Theologico-Politicus* which denies the existence of an anthropomorphic or transcendental God; he is reviled as a traitor to the State and Church, stones are thrown at him in the street as he walks home. Yet he continues to lead an international life, visited by 'illustrious foreigners' and 'beautiful bluestockings', while receiving letters from Oldenburg the secretary of the Royal Society as well as from Leibniz the great German philosopher, his contemporary in the early Enlightenment.

His landlord, the painter Henri Van der Spijek, tells Spinoza that he had been visited by Dr van den Ende, who had been accompanied by his daughter Klaatje and a young man. The landlord refers to Klaatje as 'beautiful', a 'Greek goddess'. Not finding Spinoza at home, they had returned to where they were staying some distance from his lodgings. Unsettled, Spinoza, now stooped and in his fortieth year and near the end of his life, recalls that, unknown to Klaatje, when he was a young pupil of her father he had felt 'passion' for her, though he was sure he had long ago mastered his feelings. Suddenly, however, these feelings return; he becomes agitated; he remembers a young girl with a 'perfect Greek face'. He thinks to himself, 'How learned she was, how wise, how witty, how beautiful!'

Hhhmmm, I thought hopefully, this textual detail, Klaatje being associated with classical Greece and knowledge and wit might be interesting; perhaps the story will create in Klaatje a kinship with female philosophers of the ancient world, like Diotima in Plato's *Symposium*.[8]

Perhaps, also, I thought, 'The Maker of Lenses' might lead outwards to thinking about the British Spinozan philosopher John Toland who early in the eighteenth century wrote an essay, *Tetradymos*, on Hypatia, head of the flourishing Platonic academy in Alexandria in the fifth century.[9]

I looked forward to seeing how the character of Klaatje would be developed in the rest of the story, and then read on.

Spinoza also remembers that at Klaatje's father's place, when he was young and studying with his fellow pupils, there was in the air a palpable 'flavor of romance', of 'spices', that wafted from their 'talk about the new Colonies in the Indies'. Again, I look up, look out the window. Hmmm, I thought, I must come back to this, the story associating Holland's colonies in the Caribbean with romance and spices.

On impulse, Spinoza decides to hurry to where his old Latin teacher and his daughter and their unknown friend are staying, to propose marriage to Klaatje, who he hasn't seen for many years, though he remembers not only her 'noble form' but also her 'noble soul'. When he arrives at their lodgings, where he notices a 'parrot' from Brazil, he is greeted cordially by her father and learns from him that Klaatje now helps teach their students and that she has read Spinoza's *Tractatus*. Klaatje then comes into the room and he sees before him a 'vision of loveliness and shimmering silk and white pearls'. Suddenly – and here I registered an immediate descent into aesthetic crudity, a coarsening of Spinoza's character – Spinoza, not having seen her for decades, in effect immediately proposes marriage to her. Klaatje is startled, becomes confused, murmurs that 'Women are not philosophers', blurts out an anti-Semitic protest 'But thou art a Jew!' and then indicates that she loves a young man who is her suitor, who also then makes an appearance in this disastrous scene. The young man, Spinoza observes, 'was in the pink of fashion – a mantle of Venetian silk dispersed in graceful folds about his handsome person, his neckcloth of Flanders lace, his knee-breeches of satin, his shoes gold-buckled, his dagger jeweled'.

How clumsy this story becomes: the philosopher suddenly proposing to his old teacher's daughter who he hasn't seen since she was a girl, and she meanwhile revealing herself to be not only an anti-Semite but completely superficial in her sense of the world, signified in her love for an equally superficial dandy, about whose presence in the party Spinoza had made no enquiries at all.

Spinoza, the 'bitterness of death' now 'in his soul', makes his way home, his mind returning to philosophy. The story concludes by the narrator declaring in an authoritative voice (a Tolstoyan omniscient voice) that while Benedict Spinoza considered himself a non-Jew, a citizen of the universal republic of letters, he was 'most of all a Jew in his proclamation of the Unity' of all things. His great breakthrough in philosophy, his pantheism that would so influence the German romantics and modern thought in general, was, in view of this story, really an expression of Spinoza's Jewish essence, a claim that there is a racial Jewish essence, that Spinoza's radical Enlightenment philosophy represented the triumph of a 'continuous racial inspiration'.

Another thought intruded itself: how superficial this story was, associating the 'new Colonies in the Indies' with the 'flavor of romance' and 'spices'.

Zangwill's fictional story about Heine is entitled 'From a Mattress Grave', creating a conversation between a dying Heine and Lucy, an English visitor, a grande dame, a story as it went on I found increasingly wordy and laboured.[10] Heine is admired in familiar terms by Lucy as the 'most mordant wit in Europe'; 'perhaps the greatest lyric poet of his age'; an insightful critic of art, politics and philosophy; fond of Byron, Sterne and Swift, also of Lessing; and the 'greatest of autobiographers', keenly aware of 'humour in the grotesqueries of history', for we should all laugh at 'the gigantic joke of the universe'. Lucy and Heine discuss how contradictory he has been in his life, an admirer of Catholic symbol and ritual, converting to Catholicism, yet affirming that he has 'always' been a Jew, he has never left Judaism, but also noting that the Rabbis excommunicated Spinoza.

In 'From a Mattress Grave', we read that Heine's mind, in its contradictoriness, possesses a kind of racial gift for perceiving 'the All' in otherwise bewildering diversity: 'It was', says the Tolstoyan narrator with knowing certainty, 'the Jewish artist's proclamation of the Unity'.

The story also, rather in the spirit of Pangloss in Voltaire's *Candide* (1758) believing that we live in the best of all possible worlds, creates a Heine who entertains no critique of European worldwide colonialism at all. Cromwell, Heine tells Lucy, helped Judaise the English, so that the English could henceforth 'plant our Palestinian doctrine in the South Seas, or amid the josses and pagodas of the East, and your young [English] men are colonizing unknown continents on the basis of the Decalogue of Moses'.

'From a Mattress Grave' enjoins its contemporary English readers in the late nineteenth century, in a high point of British looting of the wealth of nations, to admire British imperial and colonial activities in the Pacific, in Asia and in any other 'unknown continents' the British set their sights on.

I would contrast here Ned Curthoys's reflections on Heine in *The Legacy of Liberal Judaism*, pointing to Heine's profound and passionate anti-colonialism, Heine writing, as Ned points out, that the great task of humanity should be 'not only the emancipation of the Irish, the Greeks, the Frankfurt Jews, the West Indian Blacks and other repressed people but the emancipation of the entire world'.

❦

Neither 'The Maker of Lenses' nor 'From a Mattress Grave' is shadowed by other and competing perspectives concerning worldwide European colonialism as a history of genocidal dispossession of Indigenous peoples, destruction of their foundations of life and their cosmos, and forced labour and enslavement. Yet these textual particulars, especially in the Spinoza story, in references to a parrot from Brazil and Europe's romantic colonies in the Indies, do lead outwards to intersecting histories, of Portuguese, English, Spanish, French and Dutch slave plantation colonising in Brazil and the Caribbean – cruel practices of slavery that became well known in Europe from the eighteenth century onwards. When I'd finished reading 'The Maker of Lenses', something tinkled in my mind, memories of reading for other purposes and coming across references to the Sephardi slave plantations of Suriname. In the third section of the Concluding Mosaic to my *1492: The Poetics of Diaspora*, I confide that I tried in my book to evoke a utopian desire to recover in story and imagination the medieval pre-1492 Judeo-Islamic trading and social world of plurality and *convivencia* that stretched from Moorish Spain to India and China; a *convivencia* enjoyed by Sephardim, Muslims and Christians, mutually influencing and inspiring each other in literature, philosophy, architecture, design, cuisine and statesmanship to the eternal benefit of humanity.[11]

Yet I also wished to stress that the Sephardi Jews of Moorish Spain whose history fascinated me were not innocent in subsequent world history. I note that Richard Price's *Alabi's World* (1990) observes that in the seventeenth century Sephardim entered the New World as a particular segment of the European colonising project; there is mention of how some 200 Portuguese Sephardi Jews, refugees from religious persecution in Brazil, arrived in the Dutch colony of Suriname, in the northern South American part of the Caribbean, in the 1660s and were granted privileges that encouraged the formation of a relatively closed community, with its own religious, judicial, educational and military institutions, a special caste set firmly within the larger imperial coloniser structure. By the 1680s, Price comments, they owned about one third of the colony's slave plantations. In 1690 there was a revolt by Suriname's African slaves, who killed a plantation owner, a Jewish man name Imanuël Machado. The Jewish plantation owners mounted an expedition which killed many of the slaves. There was also, Price observes, a Jewish militia that for years 'hunted down stray rebels'.[12]

[O reader, if you get a moment in all our busy lives, read this book, which Ann Curthoys and I talk about in our chapter on

'Postmodernism and Poststructuralism' in *Is History Fiction?* as an innovative work of historical anthropology; a study of early eighteenth-century Suriname, which presents its narrative through different voices, each voice with its own typeface: those of the Samarakas, the ex-African slaves; the Dutch colonial officials; and the German Moravian missionaries. Throughout there is moving sympathy and sustained interest in the experiences and viewpoints of the ex-African slaves, weaving in their individual biographies.[13]]

In *Alabi's World*, Price recalls the cruelties that were standard practice in the European slave plantations across Suriname; when a runaway slave was recaptured, there would be removal of the Achilles tendon for a first offence, and amputation of a leg for a second. Price then quotes a passage in Voltaire's *Candide* where a Suriname slave describes how he was a victim of these punishments.[14] Intrigued by the reference to *Candide*, I looked up the relevant chapter, XIX, where the two travellers, Candide and Cacambo, travel to Suriname and happen across an African slave who works for a Mr Vanderdendur, owner of a 'famous sugarworks'. They see that he has 'no left leg and no right hand'. The slave tells them that these were punishments Mr Vanderdendur had meted out to him for transgressions: 'Those of us who work in the factories and happen to catch a finger in the grindstone have a hand chopped off; if we try to escape, they cut off one leg. Both accidents happened to me. That's the price of your eating sugar in Europe.' The slave adds that, 'Dogs, monkeys, and parrots are much less miserable than we are.'[15]

―※―

A further memory fairly begged for attention. In *1492: The Poetics of Diaspora*, in an endnote referencing *Alabi's World* concerning Voltaire's *Candide*, I referred to Natalie Zemon Davis in *Women on the Margins: Three Seventeenth-Century Lives* (1995) writing of

William Blake's engravings of punishments meted out to the slaves of Suriname.[16]

⁓⚜⁓

I decide to find out more about the history of slavery in Suriname. A little googling reveals the publication in 1992 of *Stedman's Surinam: Life in an Eighteenth-Century Slave Society*, An Abridged, Modernized Edition of *Narrative of a Five Years Expedition against the Revolted Negroes of Surinam* by John Gabriel Stedman, edited by Richard Price and Sally Price.[17]

Stedman's *Narrative* was originally published in 1796 and immediately became well known. Richard Price and Sally Price suggest that precisely because Stedman was not an abolitionist, his descriptions of the 'behaviour and attitudes of Suriname's masters and slaves', of 'planter decadence and slave dignity', took on a 'special authority', transcending his stated political views; his *Narrative* is 'one of the richest, most vivid accounts ever written of a flourishing slave society'; soon the *Narrative* was being drawn on to support the 'antislavery cause'.[18]

In their Introduction, Richard Price and Sally Price write that the colony was founded in 1651 by the English, but was ceded 16 years later to the Dutch. By the time of the conversation with the mutilated slave in Voltaire's *Candide* in 1759, Suriname had developed into a thriving plantation colony, earning a 'solid reputation, even amongst such rivals as Jamaica and Saint Domingue, for its heights of planter opulence and slave misery'; Stedman's *Narrative*, they add, makes clear that 'Voltaire's choice of mid-eighteenth century Suriname was chillingly on target'. By the mid-eighteenth century, the Suriname sugar estates were large by comparative standards, the average estate having a 'slave force of 228, more than seventeen times as large as contemporary plantations in Virginia or Maryland'; the slaves had come from West and Central African societies. In the plantation districts, the colony's ratio of Africans to Europeans was also 'extreme – more than 25:1, and as high as 65:1'. The colony, then, was a 'maximally polarized society', where some 'three thousand European whites' lived in 'grotesque luxury off the forced labour of some fifty thousand brutally exploited African slaves'. Many slaves died from 'punitive tortures'.[19]

William Blake was among those asked to provide engravings to illustrate Stedman's *Narrative*. Richard Price and Sally Price write that each of Blake's engravings 'successfully blends his own inner vision with Stedman's', producing moving works that express, in the case of slave tortures, 'extraordinary power and pathos'.[20]

Richard Price and Sally Price stress that there was constant slave resistance and challenge to the planters' world, a perpetual war. 'Marronage', they report, 'plagued the colony from its earliest years' as slaves escaped into the rain forests that grew almost to the edge of the plantations; by the mid-eighteenth century, organised bands of maroons kept planters 'living in constant fear for their lives and in constant risk of losing their investments'. By the 1770s, 'heavy speculation, planter absenteeism, and rapid changes in plantation ownership' posed a serious threat to the colony's viability, its whites sensing that 'their world was coming unglued'.[21]

Two details particularly caught my eye in the Introduction. Richard Price and Sally Price write that in 1760 and 1762, the two largest groups of maroons, the Ndjuka and the Saramaka, settled along the upper Marowijue and Suriname rivers, having 'won their independence by treaty, after a century-long guerilla war against the colonists'.[22]

I ponder this: African slave warfare against the European colony had begun early in its existence in the seventeenth century, at least from the 1660s.

Richard Price and Sally Price at one point refer to 'Amerindian and African slave life'.[23] So, there was enslavement of the

Indigenous people of Suriname, suggesting a historical framework of settler colonialism for the colony, which I'll now pursue in relation to the Sephardim in the seventeenth century. This is becoming quite a journey.

In 2016 *The Cambridge Journal of Postcolonial Literary Inquiry* published a remarkable essay by Natalie Zemon Davis, which as I write this chapter in August and September 2017 I somehow saw mention of, entitled 'Regaining Jerusalem: Eschatology and Slavery in Jewish Colonization in Seventeenth-Century Suriname'.[24]

Davis begins as historians are wont to do with an anecdote, that not long before she was talking to a historian friend about the Portuguese Jewish settlers 'of Suriname, with their sugar and coffee plantations and slaves'. What, her friend asked, did they do at Passover? Davis tells him that she had been asking herself the same question, and that was why 'back in 1995 I had started to study the Jews of Suriname, including the Nassys, who had been among the founding families of the colony'.[25]

Davis evokes the versions of the Passover story, the Haggadah, that were probably used by the slave-owning Jews of Suriname as they established their colony in the seventeenth century. Let us, she says, imagine how the Passover seders were conducted around their dining tables, 'how the Portuguese Jewish families might have visualized the Israelites as slaves in Egypt'. Davis highlights an illustrated Haggadah published in Venice in 1628–29, much reprinted and widely circulated, and perhaps the model for 'subsequent Haggadot'. The accompanying woodcut shows the Israelite slaves in Pharaoh's Egypt, toiling with large sacks on their bent backs, being beaten with clubs. A traditional prayer would be chanted, 'The Egyptians treated us badly, they made us suffer'. God is beseeched: 'Pour out Thy wrath upon the nations that know Thee not, and upon the kingdoms that call not upon Thy name'; the nations that do not call upon God's name, Davis adds, are depicted as composed of both white and black people. At the end of the seder, the family would ritually ask the Lord 'to take pity on thy people and thy city... and on Zion', the city being Jerusalem in Palestine. However, Davis writes, the Portuguese Jewish colonists in Suriname, having established themselves along the Suriname River, felt no inclination to leave what they considered an ideal existence on the land where they clustered, that had come to be known across Suriname as the Savannah of the Jews. Among themselves the Portuguese Jews referred to their community as 'Jerusalem by the riverside', with its synagogue and other buildings constructed by those enslaved Africans who were carpenters and bricklayers.[26]

Davis stresses the huge contribution the slaves made to every facet of the Portuguese Jewish colonists' daily existence, not only in plantation work but domestically, for example, the toil of the 'Africans in those Abrahamic households in seventeenth-century Suriname', who

> cleaned the synagogue for the *shamas*, threw fresh sand on its floor, and lit the candles on the Sabbath; who cleaned the Ets Haim school after the boys and kept the cemetery tidy; who grew the food consumed at the seder table and who... helped search for the *hametz* (the leavened foods that must be disposed of), and stoked the fire for the seder meal.[27]

In Davis's essay there is a visual image that I thought was strangely iconic of this history, almost cinematically so: 'Their slaves could row them to the seaport town of Paramaribo in three to six hours.' I'm following Davis here, for she also obviously regards this image as emblematic; she includes a painting circa 1830, 'The Savanna of the Jews', featuring a boat, with Sephardi slave owners sitting on a raised platform, being rowed by the African slaves.[28] Here, then, was a practice that continued at least from the seventeenth century well into the nineteenth, the Sephardim evidently revealing no desire to desist from slavery.

In the essay the reader comes across a startling reference to 'children born to African women and Portuguese Jewish men' that indicates much about gender relations between slave women and male owners.[29] [Davis could have pursued how common this practice was across the slave archipelago of the Caribbean, prescribing that slave women must make themselves available to slave-owner males, one calculating reason being to produce children in order to increase the slave population.]

⁓✺⁓

Davis reflects that slavery is not a negligible topic in Jewish history, for after all God in Leviticus 25:39–46, after bringing forth the Israelites out of Egypt, instructs their leader Moses that while the Jews were not to buy or sell one another, they could buy and sell those of the nations around them; in effect, God is at ease with the institution of slavery, if not for one's own. The disturbing implication here for the story of Passover, Davis is suggesting, is that having with God's assistance escaped slavery in Egypt the Israelites could now freely enjoy their new liberty by enslaving others. For Davis, this is the perplexing 'Passover conundrum', which she will now wrestle with: how can it be explained?[30]

Davis observes that the 'Passover conundrum' in relation to slavery has often been ignored in classic Jewish historiography, which prefers to focus on the 'gradual move toward Jewish emancipation' in the early modern period rather than reflect on 'Jewish participation with Christians in oppressive colonial regimes'. Davis will challenge this conventional historiography by exploring in the history of Suriname a 'formative moment in the relation between Africans and Jews' through biographical reflections on the 'seventeenth-century ex-*converso* David Nassy and his family'.[31]

Davis feels that in Sephardi historical consciousness the flight of the persecuted Israelites out of Pharaoh's Egypt is replicated in the Sephardi flight from sixteenth-century Inquisitional Portugal to freedom to practise their religion in Holland, and then across the sea in Brazil (for a short while) and Suriname (for a long while).[32]

Throughout the essay, in a kind of anxious refrain, Davis attempts to detect, but cannot find, any 'sign that the Nassys and their fellow Jews' saw a 'contradiction between their struggle for equal status' as a free people and their 'purchase of captive Africans'. How can we, Davis asks, comprehend how 'Portuguese Jews were seeking emancipation at the same time they were enslaving others'.[33] Without any such sign, Davis feels, the Passover conundrum cannot be solved.

But I think I can solve it, by going further and further into my misgivings about her argument.

※

Why does Davis, when she talks about Suriname as a 'formative moment in the relation between Africans and Jews', wish to focus exclusively on the African slaves, so devastatingly important in world history as such slavery was and continues to be and indeed becomes ever more important?[34] Weren't there Indigenous nations in Suriname that might figure in her history of enslavement? Actually, there were. Davis mentions Indigenous slaves, though almost in passing, a census in 1684 recording that

> 742 whites settled in the colony, of whom 232 (31 percent) were Jews, almost all Portuguese plus a few Germans; 3,844 black

slaves, 1,158 (30 percent) of them owned by Jewish planters; and 134 indigenous slaves, twenty-nine (22 percent) of them serving as hunters or fishermen or housemaids on the Jewish plantations.[35]

Davis notes that 'intense wars' in the late 1670s and early 1680s were mounted by coastal Indigenous tribes, the Arawaks, Caribs and Waroes, attempting to 'rid the land of the settlers'; in 1684 Governor Sommelsdyk made peace with the Arawak, Carib and Waroe tribes, promising that 'none of them would henceforth be enslaved (the upland indigenous were not included)'. Samuel Nassy, David Nassy's son, 'served as peacemaker, spending days among the Arawaks and arranging gifts to win them over'.[36] I'll return later to the essay's as it were minimal and tangential relationship to the Indigenous nations of Suriname.

Davis's exploration of the Nassy family in the seventeenth century is certainly illuminating for the remarkable, not to say relentless, enthusiasm of the Sephardi Jews of Holland to engage in the African slave trade and African slavery first in Brazil and then in the Caribbean, as well as slave trading in the west coast of Africa and in Amsterdam itself. Hoping to understand 'how Portuguese Jews were seeking emancipation at the same time that they were enslaving others', her key historical personality is David Nassy, who was born in 1612 in Portugal, where he began life as a *converso*, a Marrano, 'that is, as a descendant of a Portuguese Jewish family seemingly converted to Christianity', like the father of Baruch Spinoza and the 'eminent Amsterdam rabbi Menasseh ben Israel', the 'celebrated rabbi, printer, biblical scholar, and publicist' who would famously correspond with Cromwell. After leaving Portugal and coming to Holland, David Nassy, Davis tells us, acted as a go-between in 'Menasseh ben

Israel's efforts to seek', in his 1655 *Humble Address*, the 'readmission of the Jews into England'.[37]

By 1634, Davis narrates, the young David Nassy and his wife Rebecca Drago, had left Portugal and were living openly as Jews in Amsterdam; encouraged by the Amsterdam rabbis, David was circumcised and was learning Hebrew in order to understand liturgy. Fortunately, Nassy had retained a family memory that he was a Cohen, in the priestly line of men descended from the biblical Aaron. He was probably receiving religious instruction from a rabbi, Isaac Aboab da Fonseca, who had been brought from Portugal to Amsterdam as a boy by his ex-*converso* parents. Aboab da Fonseca was learned in classical texts in Latin and Greek and books of history, geography, political thought and literature in Spanish, Portuguese and French. David Nassy, already fluent in Portuguese and Spanish, would also become learned in such impressive ways.[38]

Now Brazil appears in the story of the Nassy family, a Brazil being fought over by the Portuguese and Dutch empires, jostling for imperial power and slave-based riches. Already in 1635, the ex-*conversos* in Amsterdam were seeking permission to settle in Brazil, and in 1641 Aboab da Fonseca was sent from Amsterdam to serve as a rabbi for the Portuguese Jewish congregations firmly established there; both Aboab da Fonseca and David Nassy and his family joined the Jewish community in Pernambuco, finding a land of 'verdant forests and beautiful mountains'. The Dutch East India Company had wrested the sugar-producing regions of Brazil from the Portuguese, and then appointed Prince Johan Maurits van Nassau in 1636 as governor and military commander of the colony. The prince sent successful expeditions to Africa from 1637 to 1642 to seize from the Portuguese the Gold Coast port of Elmina and the Central African port of Luanda, thus giving the Company the opportunity to enter the slave trade directly.[39]

When the Portuguese Old Christian owners fled Brazil, its sugar mills were snapped up by Dutch Reformed and Portuguese Jewish settlers. Many of the Jews, Davis relates, purchased slaves as the West India Company brought them into the 'Recife slave market, selling them to the plantations on credit for sugar, and shipping the precious product back to the refineries in the Netherlands'. David Nassy 'bought property and got a sugar mill going', and he also helped persuade the New Christians of Pernambuco, now 'free of their Portuguese Catholic masters', to return to the Jewish fold and declare themselves to be Jews. Also in Brazil, David Nassy revealed a 'learned interest in natural history', making contact with the 'physician-naturalists' Governor Johan Maurits 'brought to Brazil to study its peoples, plants, and animals'.[40]

Curiously to my mind here is that Davis makes no comment that Brazil's Indigenous nations, presumably part of its 'peoples, plants, and animals', were included by David Nassy and his fellow scholars as part of 'natural history'. What is important to Davis, it would appear, is wholehearted admiration for Nassy's learning. Nassy, Davis points out, collaborated with Joan Blaeu, the 'celebrated publisher and cartographer' of Amsterdam, and 'mapmaker for the Dutch East and West India Companies'. Nassy prepared with Blaeu and translated into Spanish the first volumes of 'Blaeu's celebrated *Grand Atlas*'. In May 1660, Joan Blaeu sent Philip IV of Spain their *Neuvo Atlas o Teatro del Mundo*. Nassy was responsible for the volumes devoted to Northern Europe, Scotland, China, Russia and eastern Europe.[41] My sour comment would be: was such knowledge purely disinterested? Wasn't European cartography a major means by which imperial power, military conquests, interference in other nations' histories, and settler colonising, were enabled? Isn't there a certain irony in David Nassy, a descendant of the Jews of Spain expelled in 1492, now assisting the king of Spain to carry out imperial plans and ambitions?

In relation to Brazil, Davis reveals an aspect of the life of Menasseh ben Israel I'd never seen mentioned before, that he and his younger brother were keen participants in the African slave trade. Davis records that in Brazil, Ephraim Soeiro, 'brother of the learned Menasseh ben Israel, was among the buyers at the Recife auctions in 1639'; in Pernambuco, Soeiro also purchased African slaves. Meanwhile, Menasseh ben Israel carried on 'the Amsterdam end of the trade'. With the family income so supplemented, Menasseh contentedly wrote: 'with our fortune slightly bettered, I am able to devote myself more freely to divine letters'.[42]

By 1654, however, Davis relates, the Portuguese had recaptured Brazil; most of the Sephardi Jews then left, while those who remained 'had to become New Christians again'. In subsequent years David Nassy and his family sounded out opportunities for slave plantation colonising in the Caribbean areas of northern South America. In 1660, Nassy's 'whole family' and their 'fellow settlers' established themselves on the 'island of Cayenne' under a charter granted by the Dutch West India Company. Nassy was often in the Netherlands 'purchasing more land and slaves for the colony'. Then in 1664 Cayenne fell to the French who would not permit any public practice of religion except Catholic; once more 'Nassy's settlers prepared to leave with their slaves'. Nassy, Davis continues, 'shepherded his people' to neighboring Suriname, then under English control. After the Anglo-Dutch war, Suriname fell to the Dutch. Many English settlers 'left Suriname with their slaves for Jamaica and Antigua'. Nassy's group and some other Portuguese Jews, however, had 'sunk roots' along the Suriname River. In 1671 the Sephardim were granted by the Dutch authorities liberty of conscience in matters of religion. Furthermore, they could form their own 'militia unit', just as the Christians had their militia units.[43]

⚘

I'm intrigued by Davis's mention of a Jewish militia. In 1671 Davis tells us, 'fifty-five Jewish men were sworn' into a militia unit, 'including David Nassy, now in his early sixties, and his five sons, Samuel, Moses, Joseph, Jacob, and Joshua'. In a footnote, Davis adds that a '1701 listing of the Jewish militia gave seventy-eight men, all living on plantations or dwellings on the Suriname River'.[44]

Reading this, I expected Davis to describe for us what this large and expanding militia did, what activities did they engage in. Yet she suddenly reveals a puzzling lack of curiosity, a strange silence. Why?

I thought back to what Richard Price and Sally Price note in their introduction to *Stedman's Surinam: Life in an Eighteenth-Century Slave Society*, that slave resistance and challenge to the European planters' world occurred from the earliest years of the Suriname colony, as slaves escaped into the rain forests plantations.[45] In *Alabi's World* Richard Price reflects that cruel tortures, part of public displays to intimidate the slave populations into passivity and obedience, were standard practice in the European slave plantations across Suriname.[46]

I think again of Richard Price referring to a Jewish militia that for years 'hunted down stray rebels'.[47] There is no suggestion in his commentary in *Alabi's World* that the Jewish militia did not engage in the cruel tortures practised across Suriname by the European planters of which the Jewish colonists formed a not insignificant part.

⚘

I notice in a footnote in Davis's essay that she has written an earlier article, 'Judges, Masters, Diviners: Slaves' Experience of Criminal Justice in Colonial Suriname' (2011). The broad sweep of this monumental essay encompasses the late seventeenth, eighteenth and early nineteenth centuries, much of it concerned to recover, in history-from-below mode, how African people on the plantations practised, away from the whites, criminal justice and policing among themselves according to principles they brought with them from African kingdoms; the practice of secret slave courts occurred across the Caribbean, in Jamaica, Antigua and other places in the British West Indies. On the plantations in Suriname, Davis tells us, there was a variation on inherited African legal practices, in that leading women, the cook, the senior house servants, the midwife, also took part in the slave tribunals' deliberations.[48]

I read this long and fascinating essay with great interest, hoping there might be clues concerning Jewish participation in extreme violence such as slave torture, but again, there is a curious silence.

Suriname, we noted before, was notorious throughout the Caribbean for the extravagant cruelty of its punishments, forms of torture involving mutilation, dismembering, disfiguring, whipping, the rack and hanging including drawing and quartering. Did the Sephardi slave plantations practise these forms of extreme violence, or refuse to practise them? I take Davis's silence on this question in 'Judges, Masters, Diviners…' to indicate that the Sephardi slave owners did routinely practise slave torture as part of a general culture involving the different European denominations.

In the essay Davis does mention exceptions among the European owners. John Gabriel Stedman, she notes, singled out 'Mrs Godefroy, the elderly widow with whom he often dined, as a model of the good proprietor'. Born Elizabeth Danforth of English parents in Suriname in 1714, she had outlived two husbands, who had left her sugar and coffee plantations with hundreds of slaves. Davis suggests Mrs Godefroy had instituted a policy of very limited use of whipping on her plantations, which were not shaken by slave uprisings over the decades. Another example Davis finds was the Fauquemberg sugar plantation on the Commewijne River during the near two decades in the mid-eighteenth century when it was managed by a Dutchman, Anthony Tielenius Kruythoff; during his tenure, the roughly 190 slaves did not organise uprisings or escapes to the Maroons, nor did the Maroons attack the plantation; he blamed the slave rebellions of 1759 on 'masters and managers who overworked and underfed their slaves, threatening to shoot or behead them if they did not complete impossible tasks'.[49]

A substantial part of 'Judges, Masters, Diviners…' is devoted to recounting the practices of the European slave courts in Suriname, conducted by judges who were usually also slave owners, and where slave evidence was inadmissable. (Judges or magistrates being slave owners or prominent landowners, and the inadmissability of slave or Indigenous evidence, were, we might think, features of European settler colonial societies across the world.) Davis suggests that examples of the masters' punitive power over slaves that John Gabriel Stedman recorded of his time in Suriname (1773–1777) as a Dutch-Scottish soldier fighting against the Suriname Maroons, were common practices from the seventeenth century onwards. Davis reports that one of Stedman's first sights in Suriname was of a 'woman who had been given 200 lashes and forced to bear a heavy chain attached to her leg for months as punishment for having simply failed to meet her work quota'. He visits a plantation 'only to come upon a young unclothed woman tied by her wrists to the branch of a tree, her back bleeding from 200 lashes', punishment for refusing to be sexually exploited, which was construed as disobedience. On a plantation near Stedman's military post, the manager departed after 'flogging a slave to death for having let another slave slip out of his hands to the woods'; his successor began his reign by (in Stedman's words) 'one morning flogging all the slaves of the estate, male and female, old and young' for having overslept their time by some 15 minutes. He visits another plantation where 'the Scottish owner John MacNeil, had ordered the hamstringing of a handsome young slave because he had been running away from his work'.[50]

Davis notes that other observers in Suriname from the late seventeenth through the eighteenth century talked of 'extended beatings with whips chosen for their sting, after which the open wounds were rubbed with lime juice and pepper'. In this theatre of violence, there was also deployment of something called the 'Spanish buck', involving extensive whipping whose details I won't repeat here, that, Davis says, was only declared illegal in Suriname in 1828. In 1833, three escaped slaves were ordered by a judge to be burned alive as part of a public spectacle of deterrence.[51]

I'm reminded here of the Holocaust historian Dan Stone's essay 'Genocide as Transgression', which I talked about in the previous chapter when discussing the 1905 Odessa pogrom, drawing attention to an aspect of extreme violence in history: perpetrators can be calculative in the same moment that they enjoy the act of violence, including enjoying the theatre of violence itself, to a degree that can be called orgiastic. Stone wishes to make a strong historical point, that we should make no sharp distinction between extreme violence in modernity and pre-modernity, rather stressing continuity across the centuries.[52]

Certainly Davis in 'Judges, Masters, Diviners…' cannot see any validity in the universal Western claim that its systems of justice are more civilised than African principles and practices of justice, those carried out by the slaves in their secret plantation tribunals. On the contrary, she views the European practices of torture and spectacle as barbaric.

Nowhere, as far as I can detect, in this great essay does Davis distinguish between religious denominations, especially the Protestant and the Jewish, in terms of participation in the punitive violence decreed by courts in Suriname and practised by slave owners, managers and overseers on the plantations.

It would very much appear, then, that in the long history of slavery in Suriname the Sephardi settler colonists (along with a small number of Ashkenazi 'German Jews') participated in a common culture of extreme violence and cruelty. It was bemusing to read, as Davis tells us at one point, that around 1700, Huguenots were among the 700 people of European origin in Suriname: the Huguenots, it would seem, having escaped persecution in Europe, rushed over to Suriname to reclaim their religion and to participate in the enslavement of Africans and genocidal displacement and dispossession of Indigenous peoples.[53]

Nor, it would appear from 'Judges, Masters, Diviners…', did the Sephardic settler colonists ever express any objection to slavery. Davis tells us that in 1795 the 'learned physician David Nassy', part of Suriname's Nassy lineage, argued for the equality of human rights, not least in terms of granting citizenship to Jews in Europe, but made a clear exception of black slaves, for (in Nassy's words) 'until they have arrived at a certain degree of civilization, the idea of liberty and equality catapults them into an intoxication, which passes only after they have destroyed everything'; masters were wrong, however, he added, in their 'horrible punishments'; instead they should give their slaves proper care so as to prolong their lives and to multiply births among them,[54] presumably meaning that a strategy of lessened punishments would prolong their lives as slaves in Suriname and help slavery to continue for the forseeable future. The Dutch abolished slavery in Suriname in 1863, so, I'm feeling, slavery in Suriname lasted till then, with tenacious support and participation by the Sephardi community till the very last day, which would then be followed by the virtual slavery of indenture, longstanding in the Americas since the beginning of the Spanish genocidal invasion centuries before following Queen Isabella's opposition to slavery, becoming known as encomienda.

I looked up another very interesting essay by Natalie Zemon Davis, 'David Nassy's "Furlough" and the Slave Mattheus'.[55] Here Davis offers more details of Nassy's doings in the 1790s, when he was granted a three-year leave of absence, or furlough, by the Sephardi community to travel from Suriname with his daughter Sarah Nassy to stay in Philadelphia, taking along with them two slaves, a mulatto slave, Amina, a young girl about 10 years old, who had been sold to Sarah; and Mattheus, who Nassy had possessed since 1774 'on rental' from another estate. At some stage Nassy purchased Mattheus for what he considered a reasonable price. In the 1780s Mattheus received training as a carpenter, and was 'rented out' by Nassy for building tasks in the town. In 1783 misfortune fell on Mattheus, when his mother was sold among other slaves from an estate. On 21 April 1792 David Nassy and his daughter Sarah along with Mattheus and Amina left Suriname for Philadelphia. However, Davis writes, Pennsylvania's Gradual Emancipation Act of 1780 provided that any personal slave brought into Pennsylvania by a new resident must be freed at the end of six months, but within that six-month period a master could indenture, or reserve for servitude. Nassy chose the maximum periods of indenture, of seven years for Mattheus (then aged about 22) and 18 years for Amina, whose name he had changed to Mina.[56]

Nassy, Davis observes, is known to have had conversations with Philadelphia opponents of slavery, but these left him singularly unmoved, leading him while in the American city to write in his February 1795 statement what we have already quoted, that Black people had not yet reached a certain level of civilization for them to deserve the granting of liberty and equality. Mattheus, nonetheless, Davis feels sure, would have come into contact with black abolitionists, for 'Philadelphia was a hub of black – especially free black – life in the new United States', including the 'Free African Society, a benevolent association founded in 1787 by two remarkable ex-slaves, Absalom Jones and Richard Allen'.[57]

We must widen our contextual net here. It seems clear that Nassy in 1795 very much wished to join his voice to the anti-abolitionist cause, whose major intellectual champion in Britain was David Hume, yes, the great Enlightenment philosopher from slave-owning Scotland who otherwise I admire very much. In a notorious 1754 footnote to his essay 'Of National Characters' Hume asserted that Africans would always be inferior to whites since they were incapable of arts, science and learning. Hume's footnote became foundational for the defence of slavery even in his own lifetime, while also being subject to devastating criticism by abolitionists.[58]

Manisha Sinha, in *The Slave's Cause: A History of Abolition* (2016), evoking the long history of fierce controversy between abolitionists and anti-abolitionists in Britain and the US, tells us of the British emancipist Rev. James Ramsay in the latter eighteenth century, for example, who opposed not just the slave trade but also slavery, and particularly objected to Hume's claims of black inferiority. Ramsay published a pamphlet *An Essay on the Treatment and Conversion of African Slaves in the British Sugar Colonies* in 1784, an eyewitness account of the brutality of West Indian slavery. Sinha points out that British abolitionists perfected the tactics of lobbying, petitioning, publication of antislavery tracts, and boycott of slave-produced goods, particularly sugar; in 1792, some 400 000 people signed abolitionist petitions, many from the booming industrial city of Manchester, revealing the working-class roots of popular abolitionism; there was also the illustrator Isaac Cruikshank's sensational print from 1792 of a slave girl suspended by her ankle on a ship's deck, based on the actual murder of two enslaved African women. Abolitionist sentiment spread through English provincial towns and thence to France.[59]

Sinha also charts the rise in the 1780s of Afro-British abolitionists as an important and influential part of the movement to abolish the slave trade, belying the myth that Anglo-American abolition was an all-white movement; rather, she suggests, black testimony was foundational to the abolitionist cause. Sinha instances

Ottobah Cugoano, who published the first black abolitionist pamphlet, *Thoughts and Sentiments on the Evil and Wicked Traffic of the Slavery and Commerce of the Human Species* in 1787; a French translation was published the following year. He collaborated with the famous black abolitionist Olaudah Equiano and other like-minded blacks in London to form a group known as Sons of Africa; like their counterparts in America, Sinha reflects, free blacks in Britain named their societies and called themselves African as a mark of racial solidarity and of a new composite African identity; they had become African in the Atlantic world. Cugoano scorned the racism of Hume, and reversed the racial argument for slavery, referring to the 'inhuman, barbarous European'; and he drew a parallel between Africans and the enslaved children of Israel as the chosen people of God and warned that Europeans would be subject to judgment.[60]

Sinha evokes the importance of Equiano's autobiography *Interesting Narrative* as the first abolitionist slave narrative, of capture, enslavement, and freedom that became the prototype for the well-known nineteenth-century slave narratives. The autobiography, Sinha tells us, is written from the perspective of enslaved Africans, and is sprinkled with observations on the injustice and absurdity of slavery and racism. It was published in 1789, was reviewed widely, including favourably by Mary Wollstonecraft, was published in nine editions, translated into Dutch, French, German and Russian, and published in the US in 1791.[61]

David Nassy's attempted 1795 refutation of abolitionists' arguments reveals a racism that always subtended, from the seventeenth century onwards, Sephardi colonisation in Brazil and Suriname and their slave trading in Africa and Amsterdam as a slave city in Europe. Such unwavering racism is surely one important key to understanding the Passover conundrum.

※

Let's return to Natalie Zemon Davis' dazzling yet problematic 'Regaining Jerusalem: Eschatology and Slavery in Jewish Colonization in Seventeenth-Century Suriname'.

I find particularly puzzling why Davis does not bring into her analysis the intersecting history of the Indigenous peoples of Suriname; why the sympathy and empathy she so powerfully focuses on the enslaved African people, especially in the final passages of her essay,[62] are not extended to the Sephardi colonisers' Indigenous slaves, whose presence in her narrative appears notional, gestural, slight. Here's an arresting example. Davis tells us of a very interesting episode recorded in David Nassy and Joan Blaeu's 1659 *Grand Atlas*, the 'kidnapping by Europeans of indigenous people (the Kalaallit) of Greenland', when in 1605 and 1606 Danish seamen seized 'twelve men to take back to Copenhagen' to be presented as gifts to King Christian IV. Nassy was appalled at what the Danes had done, exclaiming: 'Oh, tyrannical ambition… Oh, execrable inhumanity… Oh, the insolence of great power', and he evokes the terror felt by someone of free birth taken captive or made a slave and exiled from his own land. Nassy recounts how the abducted Kalaallit longed for their lost homeland, how during the voyage to Copenhagen on the Danish ship they resisted fiercely, one was beaten to death, another threw himself in despair into the sea; they fell into melancholy and often wept; and they tried to escape, revealing, Nassy wrote, 'an ardent love of country, a generous venture to recover lost liberty'. Nassy's empathy here for the indigenous Greenlanders, Davis feels, came from his identifying the 'tyrannical persecution of the Jews by the Spanish and Portuguese with the Danish captivity of the Greenlanders', yet, she points out, he completely ignores his own enslavement of hundreds of Africans; he did not, she sadly notes, apply to his own actions the judgement of 'execrable inhumanity' that he angrily directed at the Danish kidnappers.[63] Davis's point here is well and movingly made, yet what baffles me is that her essay does not take any interest in the question, why did David Nassy, if he empathized so keenly with the indigenous Kalaallit of Greenland who revealed such an ardent love of their lost country, trauma and despair at losing it, and desire to recover their liberty – why did Nassy not think of the Indigenous slaves in the Caribbean areas of the north of South America? Why did he never connect the treatment of the Kalaallit of Greenland to Jewish ownership of Indigenous slaves in Suriname?

Davis throughout her essay refers to the Sephardi plantation owners as 'settlers', without betraying any interest in contemporary theories of settler colonialism which may explain why they enslaved Indigenous Caribbean people, even though, we have seen, she notes the 'intense wars' in the late 1670s and early 1680s waged by coastal Indigenous tribes, the Arawaks, Caribs and Waroes, attempting 'to rid the land of the settlers.'[64] Such resistance by Indigenous nations to the invasion of their sovereign lands by European settlers is a recurring feature of the worldwide history of settler colonialism.

Here contemporary genocide studies illuminates. In our essay 'Defining Genocide' in *The Historiography of Genocide* (2008), Ann Curthoys and I point out that in his 1944 *Axis Rule in Occupied Europe*, Raphaël Lemkin argues that genocide is constituted in a two-fold process of destruction and replacement, a process that entwines genocide and colonisation.[65]

In terms that are uncannily similar to those in David Nassy's account of the Danish abduction of the Kalaallit of Greenland, Indigenous peoples around the world have told of how over many centuries they fiercely defended their land against European colonisers; how they were met with extreme violence, including massacres;[66] of their profound connection to their land; how they experienced terror and anguish as their relationship to their land was threatened or broken; how the foundations of their lifeworld and cosmos were assaulted in every conceivable way; how those who survived settler violence might be driven away and displaced and exiled; how those permitted to remain would, to survive, have to work – perhaps as slaves or in slave-like conditions, as in the post-1492 settler colonising in the Americas – for the very settler colonisers who had usurped their world and were treating them as mere sojourners on their own sacred lands; and how they have never ceased to assert their sovereignty which they never ceded to the invading settlers and will never rest in their attempts to recover their lost liberty.[67]

⁂

In my *The Origins of Violence: Religion, History and Genocide*, I relate that in the latter 1990s, when we were living in Canberra and working in humanities at the Australian National University, Ann Curthoys and I were fortunate to attend a speech given by the central Australian Aboriginal leader, Galarrwuy Yunupingu, to the National Press Club (on 13 February 1997). Yunupingu said he was continually astonished by the way the European colonists of Aboriginal lands always referred to themselves as the settlers while designating his people by contrast as nomads. Such a characterisation, he observed, was historically preposterous. The European colonists and migrants, he pointed out, were the inveterate wanderers on the face of the earth, they were the ones who had traveled from distant places and now constantly roamed within the Australian continent. Meanwhile, the Aboriginal peoples, who stay on their own lands as far as they are permitted by the colonisers to do so, to look after their country and because they belong to it, are always referred to as nomads!

In our *Is History Fiction?* Ann and I related Yunupingu's passionate reflections to Herodotus's *Histories* in our discussion of the hubris of colonisers from agricultural societies in regarding themselves as the settlers wherever they restlessly roam, concluding that it is the supposedly settled and urbanised peoples who are the nomads of world history.[68]

Isn't there a certain insensitivity of language when Davis tells us, without comment on the phrase, that in a few short years Nassy's family and the other Portuguese Jews 'had sunk roots along the Suriname River'?[69] Coming from Holland, they had purchased land in distant Suriname that had been intricately, intimately, lived in by Indigenous nations for millennia, land where its every specific feature was woven into their being through the generations in ceremony, song, art, dance, story, mythology, cosmology, law. Yet, we read in the essay, after a few short years in the latter 1660s the Sephardi settler colonisers, in Yunupingu's terms wandering nomadically about with their Indigenous and African slaves, had 'sunk roots' in Suriname as if they now rightfully belonged there, belonged in a land that they knew had been violently wrested from its Indigenous peoples by European imperial powers in a two-fold process of destruction and replacement, in Lemkin's terms a genocidal process of which the Sephardi settlers were very keen to take every advantage.

The Sephardi settlers from afar 'sunk roots' after a few short years: it might be noted that the Indigenous peoples of Australia have lived on the continent at least for 65 000 years.[70]

Another query. Davis evokes the importance to David Nassy and the Sephardi Jews in the seventeenth century of an eschatological desire, a vision of an ideal future of a lost life restored. In their sugar factories in Brazil and then as settler colonisers in the Caribbean, they would restore the Portuguese Jews, forced in Portugal to be New Christians, to a reclaimed Jewish life, which they felt they were especially managing to achieve in their sugar plantations in Suriname under Dutch imperial power and control. I find this curious, for it seems obvious from Davis's account that the Sephardim in Suriname were establishing an ethnocentric monoculture, not unlike the sixteenth-century Portuguese Christian society that had so oppressed them, thus turning their backs on their own Iberian past: the centuries in Moorish Spain where they achieved remarkable literary and philosophical heights in participating in an inclusive multireligious and multicultural *convivencia*.[71]

Leaving aside slavery – which cannot be left aside – how can we admire the Sephardim in Suriname for establishing a monoculture?

Surely monocultures are a scourge of history.

A further reflection follows. In sixteenth-century Inquisitional Portugal the Sephardi Jews were victims of oppression; following escape to Holland, they became in Suriname occupiers of sovereign Indigenous land and oppressors of Indigenous and African slaves.

I conclude this chapter on Suriname and the Sephardim by returning to its beginning. After this historical journey, we must profoundly disagree with the Sephardi character David Quixano in *The Melting Pot*, that 'We Jews are cheerful in gloom, mistrustful in joy. It is our tragic history.' David is certain that we Jews are a people of suffering, we have always been victims, never perpetrators.

The Sephardi participation in the cruel history of slavery makes me think that, from a world history perspective, Jewish history must be sweepingly recast.

1   Hannah Arendt, *The Jewish Writings*, edited by Jerome Kohn and Ron H. Feldman (Schocken Books, New York, 2007), 'We Refugees', p.274.
2   Isaac Deutscher, *The Non-Jewish Jew and other Essays* (1968; Merlin Press, London, 1981), 'The non-Jewish Jew', p.26.
3   Ned Curthoys, *The Legacy of Liberal Judaism: Ernst Cassirer and Hannah Arendt's Hidden Conversation* (Berghahn, New York and Oxford, 2013), p.1.
4   Ned Curthoys, *The Legacy of Liberal Judaism: Ernst Cassirer and Hannah Arendt's Hidden Conversation*, pp.53–6.
5   Raphael Lemkin, 'Genocide – A Modern Crime', *Free World – A Magazine devoted to the United Nations and Democracy* (April 1945), pp.39–43, quoted in John Docker, 'Are Settler-Colonies Inherently Genocidal?' in A. Dirk Moses (ed.), *Empire, Colony, Genocide: Conquest, Occupation, and Subaltern Resistance in World History* (Berghahn, New York and Oxford, 2008), p.81.
6   Israel Zangwill, *Dreamers of the Ghetto* (Harper and Brothers Publishers, New York and London, 1898), p.186ff.
7   See Ann Curthoys and John Docker, 'Time, Eternity, Truth, and Death: History as Allegory', *Humanities Research* 1, 1999, p.11; John Docker, *1492: The Poetics of Diaspora* (Continuum, London and New York, 2001), 'Concluding Mosaic', p.247.
8   John Docker, *The Origins of Violence: Religion, History and Genocide* (UNSW Press, London, 2008), pp.94–95; Plato, *The Symposium*, translated by Walter Hamilton (Penguin, London, 1951), pp.79–95.
9   John Docker, 'The Enlightenment, genocide, postmodernity', *Journal of Genocide Research*, Vol.5, no.3, 2003, pp.348–9.
10 Zangwill, *Dreamers of the Ghetto*, 'From a Mattress Grave', pp.335–368.
11 John Docker, *1492: The Poetics of Diaspora*, p.249.
12 Docker, *1492: The Poetics of Diaspora*, p.249; Richard Price, *Alabi's World* (Johns Hopkins University Press, 1990), pp.4, 9, 11.

13 Ann Curthoys and John Docker, *Is History Fiction?* (University of Michigan Press, Ann Arbor, 2010), p.204.

14 Richard Price, *Alabi's World* (The Johns Hopkins University Press, Baltimore and London, 1990), p.11.

15 Voltaire, *Candide, or Optimism*, translated by John Butt (1759; Penguin, London, 1947), pp.85–6.

16 Docker, *1492: The Poetics of Diaspora*, p.265 note 4; Natalie Zemon Davis, *Women on the Margins: Three Seventeenth-Century Lives* (Harvard University Press, Cambridge MA, 1995), p.320 note 145.

17 Richard Price and Sally Price (eds), *Stedman's Surinam: Life in an Eighteenth-Century Slave Society* (1988; Johns Hopkins University Press, Baltimore and London, 1992).

18 Price and Price (eds), *Stedman's Surinam: Life in an Eighteenth-Century Slave Society*, p.xiii.

19 Price and Price (eds), *Stedman's Surinam: Life in an Eighteenth-Century Slave Society*, pp.xi-xii, xviii.

20 Price and Price (eds), *Stedman's Surinam: Life in an Eighteenth-Century Slave Society*, p.xxxvi.

21 Price and Price (eds), *Stedman's Surinam: Life in an Eighteenth-Century Slave Society*, p.xii.

22 Price and Price (eds), *Stedman's Surinam: Life in an Eighteenth-Century Slave Society*, p.xix.

23 Price and Price (eds), *Stedman's Surinam: Life in an Eighteenth-Century Slave Society*, p.xiii.

24 Natalie Zemon Davis, 'Regaining Jerusalem: Eschatology and Slavery in Jewish Colonization in Seventeenth-Century Suriname', *The Cambridge Journal of Postcolonial Literary Inquiry*, 3 (1), pp.11–38, 2016.

25 Natalie Zemon Davis, 'Regaining Jerusalem: Eschatology and Slavery in Jewish Colonization in Seventeeth-Century Suriname', pp.11–13.

26 Natalie Zemon Davis, 'Regaining Jerusalem: Eschatology and Slavery in Jewish Colonization in Seventeeth-Century Suriname', pp.34–38.

27 Natalie Zemon Davis, 'Regaining Jerusalem: Eschatology and Slavery in Jewish Colonization in Seventeeth-Century Suriname', p.38.

28 Natalie Zemon Davis, 'Regaining Jerusalem: Eschatology and Slavery in Jewish Colonization in Seventeeth-Century Suriname', pp.25, 34–5.

29 Natalie Zemon Davis, 'Regaining Jerusalem: Eschatology and Slavery in Jewish Colonization in Seventeeth-Century Suriname', pp.29–30.

30 Natalie Zemon Davis, 'Regaining Jerusalem: Eschatology and Slavery in Jewish Colonization in Seventeeth-Century Suriname', p.11.

31 Natalie Zemon Davis, 'Regaining Jerusalem: Eschatology and Slavery in Jewish Colonization in Seventeeth-Century Suriname', pp.12–13.

32 Natalie Zemon Davis, 'Regaining Jerusalem: Eschatology and Slavery in Jewish Colonization in Seventeeth-Century Suriname', p.26.

33 Natalie Zemon Davis, 'Regaining Jerusalem: Eschatology and Slavery in Jewish Colonization in Seventeeth-Century Suriname', pp.12, 26.

34 See Stuart Hall, *Familiar Stranger: A Life Between Two Islands* (Duke University Press, Durham and London, 2017).

35 Natalie Zemon Davis, 'Regaining Jerusalem: Eschatology and Slavery in Jewish Colonization in Seventeeth-Century Suriname', p.25.

36 Natalie Zemon Davis, 'Regaining Jerusalem: Eschatology and Slavery in Jewish Colonization in Seventeeth-Century Suriname', p.25.

37 Natalie Zemon Davis, 'Regaining Jerusalem: Eschatology and Slavery in Jewish Colonization in Seventeeth-Century Suriname', pp.13–15, 18.

38 Natalie Zemon Davis, 'Regaining Jerusalem: Eschatology and Slavery in Jewish Colonization in Seventeeth-Century Suriname', pp.13–14.

39 Natalie Zemon Davis, 'Regaining Jerusalem: Eschatology and Slavery in Jewish Colonization in Seventeeth-Century Suriname', pp.14–15.

40 Natalie Zemon Davis, 'Regaining Jerusalem: Eschatology and Slavery in Jewish Colonization in Seventeeth-Century Suriname', pp.15–17.

41 Natalie Zemon Davis, 'Regaining Jerusalem: Eschatology and Slavery in Jewish Colonization in Seventeeth-Century Suriname', pp.19–20.

42 Natalie Zemon Davis, 'Regaining Jerusalem: Eschatology and Slavery in Jewish Colonization in Seventeeth-Century Suriname', pp.14–15, 18–19.

43 Natalie Zemon Davis, 'Regaining Jerusalem: Eschatology and Slavery in Jewish Colonization in Seventeeth-Century Suriname', pp.17, 19, 22–3 and 23 note 46.

44 Natalie Zemon Davis, 'Regaining Jerusalem: Eschatology and Slavery in Jewish Colonization in Seventeeth-Century Suriname', p.23 and 23 note 46.

45 Richard Price and Sally Price (ed.), *Stedman's Surinam: Life in an Eighteenth-Century Slave Society*, p.xii.

46 Richard Price, *Alabi's World*, pp.4, 9, 11.

47 Richard Price, *Alabi's World*, p.11.

48 Natalie Zemon Davis, 'Judges, Masters, Diviners: Slaves' Experience of Criminal Justice in Colonial Suriname', *Law and History Review*, Vol.29, no.4, 2011, pp.927–8, 946–58.

49 Natalie Zemon Davis, 'Judges, Masters, Diviners…', pp.944–6.

50 Natalie Zemon Davis, 'Judges, Masters, Diviners: Slaves' Experience of Criminal Justice in Colonial Suriname', pp.925–7, 941, 943–94, 977.

51 Natalie Zemon Davis, 'Judges, Masters, Diviners: Slaves' Experience of Criminal Justice in Colonial Suriname', pp.942, 982.

Sephardi slave trading and slave plantations in Suriname 483

52 Docker, *The Origins of Violence: Religion, History and Genocide*, pp.14, 27; Dan Stone, *History, Memory and Mass Atrocity: Essays on the Holocaust and Genocide* (Vallentine Mitchell, London, 2006), pp.196–9, 206–9.

53 'Judges, Masters, Diviners...', pp.929–930.

54 'Judges, Masters, Diviners...', p.976.

55 Natalie Zemon Davis, 'David Nassy's "Furlough" and the Slave Mattheus', first published in Pamela S. Nadell, Jonathan D. Sarna and Lance J. Sussman (eds), *New Essays in American Jewish History: Commemorating the Sixtieth Anniversary of the Founding of the American Jewish Archives* (American Jewish Archives, Cincinnati, 2010), and also online at *Buku – Bibliotheca Surinamica*, where I read it.

56 Davis, 'David Nassy's "Furlough" and the Slave Mattheus', *Buku – Bibliotheca Surinamica*, pp.3–7.

57 Davis, 'David Nassy's "Furlough" and the Slave Mattheus', *Buku – Bibliotheca Surinamica*, pp.7–8.

58 David Hume, *Essays Literary, Moral and Political* (George Routledge and Sons, London, n.d.), p.123; Emma Rothschild, 'David Hume and the Seagods of the Atlantic', in Susan Manning and F.D. Cogliano (eds), *The Atlantic Enlightenment* (Ashgate Publishers, Aldershot, 2008), pp.88–96; John Docker, 'Sheer Folly and Derangement: How the Crusades Disoriented Enlightenment Historiography', in Alexander Cook, Ned Curthoys and Shino Konishi (eds), *Representing Humanity in the Age of Enlightenment* (Pickering and Chatto, London, 2013), p.43.

59 Manisha Sinha, *The Slave's Cause: A History of Abolition* (Yale University Press, New Haven and London, 2016), pp.100–101.

60 Manisha Sinha, *The Slave's Cause: A History of Abolition*, pp.122–6, 129.

61 Manisha Sinha, *The Slave's Cause: A History of Abolition*, pp.126–9.

62 Natalie Zemon Davis, 'Regaining Jerusalem: Eschatology and Slavery in Jewish Colonization in Seventeenth-Century Suriname', pp.37–8.

63 Natalie Zemon Davis, 'Regaining Jerusalem: Eschatology and Slavery in Jewish Colonization in Seventeeth-Century Suriname', pp.20–22.

64 Natalie Zemon Davis, 'Regaining Jerusalem: Eschatology and Slavery in Jewish Colonization in Seventeenth-Century Suriname', p.25.

65 Ann Curthoys and John Docker, 'Defining Genocide', in Dan Stone (ed.), *The Historiography of Genocide* (Palgrave Macmillan, London and New York, 2010), p.11. See also John Docker, 'Are Settler-Colonies Inherently Genocidal? Re-reading Lemkin', in A. Dirk Moses (ed.), *Empire, Colony, Genocide: Conquest, Occupation, and Subaltern Resistance in World History* (Berghahn, New York and Oxford, 2008), pp.81–101, and Docker, 'Raphaël Lemkin's History of Genocide and Colonialism', paper for United States Holocaust Memorial Museum, Center for Advanced Holocaust Studies, Washington DC, 26 February 2004.

66 Concerning Lemkin, settler colonialism, genocide, and massacres, see John Docker, 'The Origins of Massacres', in Philip G. Dwyer and Lyndall Ryan (eds), *Theatres of Violence: Massacre, Mass Killing and Atrocity throughout History*

(Berghahn, New York and Oxford, 2012), pp. 3–16. See also Lyndall Ryan's famous massacre map, published online in 2017, of massacre sites in eastern Australia in the nineteenth century, available at https://c21ch.newcastle.edu.au/colonialmassacres/

67 See Ann Curthoys and Jessie Mitchell, *Taking Liberty: Indigenous Rights and Settler Self Government* (Cambridge University Press, Cambridge, 2018).

68 John Docker, *The Origins of Violence: Religion, History and Genocide*, pp. 34–5; Ann Curthoys and John Docker, *Is History Fiction?* pp. 27–8.

69 Natalie Zemon Davis, 'Regaining Jerusalem: Eschatology and Slavery in Jewish Colonization in Seventeeth-Century Suriname', p. 23.

70 See Billy Griffiths, *Deep Time Dreaming: Uncovering Ancient Australia* (Black Inc., Melbourne, 2018); also 'A World in a Grain of Sand', *Griffith Review* 41, 2013, https://griffithreview.com/articles/a-world-in-a-grain-of-sand/ ; also http://insidestory.org.au/digging-deeper-into-a-65000-year-story/

71 See Jane S. Gerber, *The Jews of Spain: A History of the Sephardic Experience* (The Free Press, New York, 1992), and John Docker, *1492: The Poetics of Diaspora*, ch. 3, 'The collision of two worlds: Sir Walter Scott's *Ivanhoe* and Moorish Spain', pp. 34–61.

23

Complicating world history: Continuities between Sephardi settler colonialism in Suriname, Zangwill's support for Exodus-colonialism, and Zionist Israel

We arc back to Israel Zangwill, reflecting on the Sephardi character David Quixano's suggestion in *The Melting Poet* that Jews are perennially a people of suffering, always victims, never perpetrators. I now explore Zangwill's polemical and exhortatory writings, which suggest the reverse: that half a millennium of Jewish participation in European settler colonisation brought tragedy to, and continues to bring tragedy to, other peoples' histories; a participation motivated and guided by the story of Exodus, that those who have previously suffered persecution and bondage have a moral right to inflict conquest, persecution, suffering, violence, dispossession, trauma and tragedy on other societies and peoples.[1]

❧

Early in the twentieth century, Zangwill was profoundly distressed, as were Jewish people worldwide, by the pogroms in the Russian Empire in 1903 and 1905. Zangwill was among those determined to search for possible homelands where Jewish survivors of the massacres could become settler colonisers. Herzl died on 3 July 1904 and a year later Zangwill formed the Jewish Territorial Organization (ITO), believing that the political Zionist movement as Herzl bequeathed it to his successors was narrowing possibilities for the urgent relief of persecuted Jews in being too orientated on Palestine; Zangwill's ITO would seek out other possible places of settlement for a beleaguered and acutely suffering people as well.

Reading what he wrote in *Speeches, Articles and Letters by Israel Zangwill* (1937),[2] I think it's clear that his passionate pleas, ideas, and visions are shaped by the victimological contours of the Exodus narrative, especially in support for European and more particularly British empire colonialism, which he felt Jews should be very much part of. Here Zangwill sharply differs from the anti-colonialism of Heine and Bernard Lazare. He also aligns himself with what Hannah Arendt characterises of Herzl in her 1942 essay 'Herzl and Lazare', that Herzl succeeded in persuading Jewry that politics must be conducted from above. Such is what Herzl and the leaders of political Zionism and the post-1948 Israeli state have always done and still do, focusing on gaining advantages and protection variously from monarchs, high officials and rulers of powerful states and empires. Zangwill, as we shall see, wished to make his own vigorous contribution in his own way to this as it were top-down approach to history and politics.

In Jewish Territorial Organization Leaflet, No.1, 1905, entitled 'What is the ITO?', Zangwill sets out the organisation's manifesto: 'The Ito aims at obtaining a large tract of territory (preferably within the British Empire) wherein to found a great Jewish Home of Refuge.' The Ito appeals to the 'best and most manly side' of the 'Jewish race'. It puts itself forward as a messianic movement: 'The masses of the Jewish people are now joining the Ito in their tens of thousands.' Furthermore, the Ito has already been successful in its appeals to the influential and powerful: 'Outside Jewry the Ito has attracted the most favourable attention. The Organization (which is open to all creeds and races) has been honoured with the support of members of the English aristocracy, of High Dignatories of the Church, and of distinguished Officers of the Army.'[3]

It would appear that the Jewish Territorial Organization did indeed become a kind of mass messianic movement. In another contribution, 'A Land of Refuge', we read a long speech by Zangwill to a mass meeting at the Manchester Hippodrome on 8 December 1907 where a resolution 'in support of the Ito's programme was carried unanimously'. Zangwell spoke of the 'exodus from Russia in 1906', with Jews also being expelled elsewhere, from Romania and Morocco.[4] The problem faced by the Ito is to procure, for the 'Jewish emigrant', the 'Wandering Jew', a 'territory upon an autonomous basis'. Zangwill assures his audience that he has an answer, a 'scheme of purposive colonization', by which the people can practise 'autonomy' and 'liberty', for, 'Whoever heard of people colonizing except to have liberty, to live after their own fashion?'[5] Here I'm reminded how much for centuries European settler colonisers around the world held out a vision of gaining liberty for themselves while depriving Indigenous peoples of their liberty.[6]

In 'A Land of Refuge' Zangwill thunders against opponents of his ideas who say that land in the world is already all taken up, that there is no 'virgin territory'. We should not listen to such murmuring, for those already in a land can be displaced by colonisation, territory can be made virgin again. Zangwill now declares his support for a 'good idea' that Herzl once had 'for Jewish colonization' somewhere in North Africa like Morocco; perhaps Morocco can be procured? Or another possibility: 'There is even a country south-west of Morocco, as large as England, with a splendid seaboard, yet practically a no-man's-land, inhabited only by some nomadic tribes'. Once installed, he adds, the colonising Jews would have a 'role in civilizing this vast region' of North Africa. But how do we procure such lands? Zangwill cautions his audience that 'this is not a world in which everything can be bought for money', referring here to the 'sort of colonization' carried out by the Jewish Colonization Association which 'disposes of the millions of the late Baron de Hirsch' in the Argentine, colonising there 'on soil redeemed from the wilderness'.

Force, Zangwell feels, may be necessary, the kind of military force normally used by the British in their colonising across the globe:

> It may be that ere a Jewish State arises, whether in North Africa or elsewhere, part of the price will have to be paid in blood. Even British protection could not save us from that. Not one of Britain's colonies, neither New Zealand, nor Canada, neither Natal nor East Africa, has escaped defending itself against the native tribes. To 'procure' may partly mean to procure at the cost of blood.[7]

In Zangwill's view, adapting the victimological narrative of Exodus, Jews who are victims of persecution in one part of the world, especially in Tsarist Russia, can justifiably become perpetrators of a violent colonisation involving conquest and destruction of another people somewhere else; those one feels superior to as mere nomadic tribes, such as those in a country south-west of Morocco.

For Zangwill the history of the 'country south-west of Morocco… practically a no-man's-land, inhabited only by some nomadic tribes' is derisory. Zangwill is referring to the Sahrawis, the nomadic people of Western Sahara. We can bring to mind here Harry Berger Jnr's insightful essay 'The Lie of the Land: The Text beyond Canaan' (1989), where he refers to how in Exodus, the Israelites, having fled oppression in Egypt, placed themselves in bondage to a 'possessive nomadism', the species of wandering nomadic group who wish to invade and take over the land of Canaan, Berger contrasting such 'possessive nomadism' to mobile pastoral nomadism, to customary wanderers who do not wish to lose their diasporic freedom to wander and to think as wanderers.[8] From my reading, aided by the investigations of the anthropologist Alice Wilson, who has conducted ethnographic fieldwork with Sahrawis, the Sahrawis very much appear to be mobile pastoral nomads in terms of Berger's distinction. In her illuminating essay 'Ambivalences of Mobility: Rival state authorities and mobile strategies in a Saharan conflict' (2017), Wilson highlights 'Sahrawis' movements between different spaces in northwest Africa and beyond', including transnational movement between Algeria, Mauritania, Spain and France.[9]

Wilson's focus is on the '40-year old conflict for sovereignty over Western Sahara' involving competing claims of the Moroccan sultanate and the Polisario movement. She notes that the UN had been calling for Western Sahara to be decolonised since 1963; Spain's abandonment of its colony Spanish Sahara [1884–1975] led to the territory's partial annexation in 1975 by Morocco, leading to a war with Polisario and a UN-brokered ceasefire in 1991. She notes that Morocco's and Polisario's competing claims on Western Sahara were assessed by the International Court of Justice, whose advisory opinion in 1975 found that the 'people of Western Sahara should have the right to self-determination'.[10]

Wilson sketches in a history going back centuries. Before European colonialism, the 'mobile inhabitants of the northwest Sahara' spanned 'southern Morocco, southwest Algeria, the disputed Western Sahara, Mauritania, and parts of Mali'. Even after the advent of European colonialism, she observes, Sahrawis continued to deploy mobility to avoid a state, crossing colonial borders to 'escape pursuit by French or Spanish authorities'. The Sahrwaris, she argues, continue to deploy strategies of mobility whereby they can move in and out of Moroccan-annexed areas and Polisario-controlled areas; family members live in cities near and far in order to access resources in regional or globalised markets. Given such strategies, Wilson concludes that, contrary to a common view, 'mobile pastoralism', 'long disliked by both colonial and postcolonial governments', is not 'on the decline in the Middle East, in North Africa, and beyond'.[11]

~~~※~~~

In 1911 another essay, 'Jewish Race', records Zangwill's address delivered to the Race Congress in London in that year.

This appears to be the historic First Universal Races Congress held in July 1911 at the University of London. David Levering Lewis, in his biography *W. E. B. Du Bois: Biography of a Race 1868–1919*, tells us that the great Du Bois came to London to attend it. Before the congress began, he addressed the Anti-Slavery and Aborigines Protection Society as well as 'enlightening the ladies of the highly influential Lyceum Club concerning the true state of American race relations'. At the congress, which began on the morning of Wednesday, 26 July, he presented a paper entitled 'The Negro Race in the United States of America', and he took part in a number of sessions. Du Bois considered that the congress 'would have marked an epoch in the racial history of the world if it had not been for the World War'; he was delighted by how international and cosmopolitan the congress was, with attendees from around the world and the many opportunities for conversation and interaction. A thousand delegates representing 'fifty races' were present.

Lewis evokes some of the ideas put forward by speakers during the four days it met. From South Africa came the Bantu educator J Tengo Jabavu, who argued persuasively for the indigenous African languages and traditions of his land. Finance capital, the parasitic by-product of imperial competition, was devastatingly exposed and denounced by the English economist John A Hobson. Muhammad Bey Sourbour underscored the reality of imperial exploitation by advocating for Egyptians some part 'in the making and execution of laws'. The status of women in the world was systematically reviewed, and the imperative moral and social justification for their liberation was applauded. Also present was a Japanese parliamentarian, another from the Cape Colony (its only black member), a Sioux from the United States, the Liberian head of state, and Mrs Annie Besant of the Theosophical Society, who gave a fiery critique of the British Empire. Du Bois would regret, Lewis tells us, that the global implications of the 'labor question' and the time frame for the independence of India and Egypt had not been addressed, but he felt exhilarated that so many of the planet's great problems had been earmarked for systematic investigation.[12]

Zangwill began his speech to the First Universal Races Congress in the voice of a messiah for all humanity, declaring that the 'soul of the Jewish race is best seen in the Bible, saturated from the first page of the Old Testament to the last page of the New with the aspiration for a righteous social order, and an ultimate unification of mankind of which, in all specifically Jewish literature, the Jewish race is to be the medium and missionary'. Asserting Jewish moral superiority as a kind of racial quality, Zangwill tells the audience that Jewish literature is 'very different from the self-glorification of all other epics'. The Jewish people were 'chosen' by God in order to perform the 'role of service, not dominance'. He explains:

> This extraordinary race arose as a pastoral clan in Mesopotamia, roved to Palestine, thence to Egypt, and after a period of slavery returned to Palestine as conquerors and agriculturists, there

to practise the theocratic code imposed by Moses (perhaps the noblest figure in all history), and to evolve in the course of the ages a poetic and prophetic literature of unparalleled sublimity.

Others in the audience may have pondered the significance of God in Exodus telling the Israelites: 'thou shalt not oppress a stranger: for ye know the heart of a stranger, seeing ye were strangers in the land of Egypt' (Exodus 23:9). If God and the Israelites in Exodus were really interested in what Zangwill refers to as their 'aspiration for a righteous social order, and an ultimate unification of mankind', then why did they so relentlessly oppress the strangers they encountered as they pursued conquest of the land of Canaan, yes, the Canaanites, Amorites, Hittites, Perizzites, Hivites and Jebusites? For that matter, for those who knew something of the history, quite a few given how notorious that history was, they might have thought: shouldn't the Sephardim in seventeenth-century Suriname have extended kindness to the Indigenous and African people on their slave plantations? Didn't they encounter them as strangers? Why then did the Sephardi enslave them? Beat them? Torture them?

Zangwill then tells his audience how desirable settler colonialism would be for Jews seeking refuge from persecution. We need, he tells them, 'the creation of a Jewish State, or at least a Jewish land of refuge upon a basis of local autonomy… Many regions of the New World, whether in America or Australia, would moreover be enriched and consolidated by the accession of a great Jewish colony'. Not a few in the audience must surely have felt very uncomfortable with this declaration. They knew firsthand settler colonial oppression. How it denies to the colonised self-determination and their manifold human rights, and how much they historically have resisted it, and are continuing to struggle to regain their freedom, which is a major reason why they are attending the congress. As for the establishing of Jewish colonies in 'America or Australia', the Sioux attendee might have shuddered at the prospect, perhaps thinking that already great Native American nations like the Sioux have lost much of their vast homelands to the American settler colonisers, now the land we have left is to be taken away from us as well, so that we would inevitably be expelled or subjugated and forced into unfree labour close to slavery.

As for Australia, in the late 1930s and early 1940s there was a plan, put forward by the non-Zionist Russian émigré I N Steinberg, for Jewish colonisation in the Kimberleys in the far north of Western Australia. Steinberg was head of the London-based Freeland League for Jewish Territorial Colonization, which appears to be a successor organisation to Zangwill's ITO and he came to Australia to investigate purchasing land owned by the Durack family, wealthy pastoralists.[13] Leon Gettler in his book *An Unpromised Land* (1993) points out that a 'successful Kimberley settlement' would have further devastated 'Aboriginal culture in the region by displacing black Australians'. He observes that 'the problems facing the Aborigines' in the area Steinberg had marked out for occupation did not rate a mention in his and the Freeland League's planning for their Kimberley project; we might have expected there to be 'empathy that one oppressed culture might feel for the other', but in fact the Freeland League expressed no discernible empathy or concern or interest.[14]

The Exodus narrative resurged in Zangwill's writing concerning the possibility after 1918, with the victorious imperial powers poised to carve up the world in new ways, that Palestine could become the political Zionist dream, the Jewish homeland, to the exclusion of the Palestinian inhabitants, who vastly outnumbered the Jewish.

The Palestinian historian Walid Khalidi, in his Introduction to his famous collection of documents *From Haven to Conquest:*

Readings in Zionism and the Palestine Problem until 1948 (1971), argues that from the beginning, specifically from the constituent congress of the World Zionist Organization meeting in Basel, Switzerland in 1897 the overriding Zionist project and desire, assisted by Britain and the US, was to convert – while unheeding 'the agonized appeals of the Palestinian Arabs' – Palestine from a refuge and haven for Jews fleeing persecution into a land they wished to conquer and did conquer, the success of their aggressive strategy and extreme violence becoming the Palestine tragedy. Khalidi notes that at the time of the Basel Congress, '95% of the population of Palestine was Arab and 99% of its land was Arab-owned'. In 1919, he adds, the 'Jewish community in Palestine (the majority of whom were non-Zionist)', formed only 9.7 percent of the population and owned 2.04 per cent of the land.[15]

In an article 'Before the Peace Conference' (February 1919), Zangwill urgently wrote that the 'Jews must possess Palestine as the Arabs are to possess Arabia or the Poles Poland'. How in 1919 was this to be done? Zangwill offers the sinister solution, redolent of ethnic cleansing and genocide: 'the Arabs would gradually be settled in the new and vast Arabian Kingdom', for only 'thus can Palestine become a "Jewish National Home".' In this vision, the consent of the Indigenous Palestinians was never to be sought, they were not to be regarded as subjects in their own history; on the contrary, the decisively majority Palestinian Arab were to be expelled 'gradually', without somehow their noticing what was happening. (In his Introduction to *From Haven to Conquest* Khalidi writes that the Palestinians from early on realised that a nightmare was looming over their lives: 'Ever since 1917 the Arabs had been saying that the "Jewish National Home" was merely a euphemism for a Jewish state.')[16] Certainly Zangwill did not feel the ethical necessity, as a universal human right, that the Indigenous Palestinians, constituting in 1919 over 90 per cent of Palestine's population, should be informed of his plans for them, depriving them of their moral right to inherit Palestine as, in Khalidi's view, their 'patrimony'.¹⁷

Zangwill hoped the 1919 Paris conference would have immediately handed over Palestine to its tiny Jewish population as their national home, and was extremely disappointed when this did not happen. He wrote a furious letter entitled 'The Fiasco of Political Zionism' to *The Jewish Chronicle*, 12 March 1920:

> Had Palestine been handed over to us, as Lord Rothermere now demands, Jewry, with half a million soldiers among the Allies to draw upon, could have run it as easily as the East India Company ran India.

For Zangwill, the creation of Palestine as Jewish was in reach, but the political Zionists and the British Government had lost their nerve. Yet all it needed was boldness; all the elements for success were in place. There was, he angrily points out, a British-Jewish Colonizing Company that could have been the 'medium for the financing and development of the country'; the 'Mandatory Power' could have given a loan. Furthermore, there was a 'British-Jewish General, Sir John Monash, a man of military genius and noble heart, who would assuredly have answered the Government's call'; a Jewish military occupation could then have been effected, for after all there was in 'Palestine itself the nucleus of a Jewish army, with myriads of Jewish troops throughout the Diaspora'. Instead, nothing of the sort happened, the opportunity for Jewish military control of Palestine was lost, and what we are left with is 'this historic fiasco'.¹⁸

Zangwill's top down pro-imperial approach to history is on full display here; Palestine could be run like the 'East India Company ran India'.

On 12 May 1922 Zangwill wrote a letter, 'The Balfour Declaration' to *The Times*, telling its readers that he has a right to speak on these matters because he was the 'first English citizen to whom the late Dr Herzl, the founder of modern Zionism, appealed for cooperation'. Zangwill makes clear that 'modern Zionism has been nothing if not a political movement'. He offers his interpretation of the Balfour Declaration, that what it means is 'the conversion of Palestine into a Jewish State'. He addresses the Mandate's ill-judged promise that the 'six hundred thousand Arabs' must be allowed to stay in Palestine. He grants that the 'six hundred thousand Arabs' in Palestine had been recklessly disregarded both by British political leaders and the Zionist leaders, but their staying would not provide the needed 'solution of the Jewish problem': only sole Jewish occupation, under their own administration and army, can provide that solution.[19]

On 27 March 1925, a year before he died, Zangwill wrote a dejected letter to *The Jewish Chronicle* recording his disappointment with the Balfour Declaration, since it won't guarantee the expulsion, which he phrases as 'the gradual trek of the majority', that is, the Indigenous Palestinians, 'to a territory large and empty enough for a National Home' of their own. This is the tragedy of what has happened to the hope of Palestine as the Jewish state, the lost opportunity of becoming the sole occupiers. The failure of a Jewish Palestine makes his own Territorial movement of vital importance, for we are in a 'moment of history' of 'vast tragic waves of migration'; his movement can deal with 'competitive offers of land from countries in need of population'.[20]

We can bring these three chapters on Zangwill to a conclusion by making some adjustments to how we usually conceive Jewish world history for the last half millennium, as a response to David Quixano's melancholy suggestion in *The Melting Poet*

that Jews have always been victims, never perpetrators. We can now construct a strand of world history, from early modernity to modernity, that bespeaks the reverse; from the early seventeenth century to the present.

In his scintillating book *Israel: A Colonial-Settler State* (1967), the great Middle Eastern scholar Maxime Rodinson observed that, according to the fantastic reasoning of Europeans in the nineteenth century and well into the twentieth, any territory outside Europe was considered open to European occupation, not because it might lack actual inhabitants, but because of its supposed cultural barrenness; in these terms we can say that from the late nineteenth century, both Zionist as well as non-Zionist colonisation organisations wished to become part of the general European imperial coloniser expansion across the globe: the Zionists in Palestine (though perhaps with an area of Uganda added on if they were to take up an offer from the imperial British), the non-Zionists anywhere in the world.[21]

Maxime Rodinson's insight can be pushed back in time, to colonisation in early modern Europe when European hordes began invading other peoples' territories. When the Portuguese, then the Dutch, then the Portuguese again, invaded Brazil and participated in the buying and selling and mass enslavement of Africans, the Sephardi Jews of seventeenth-century Holland enthusiastically followed them; when the Dutch took control of Suriname, the Sephardi Jews of seventeenth-century Holland again enthusiastically followed them, and perpetrated for centuries a settler colonisation that brought a tragic history upon enslaved Indigenous and African peoples well into the nineteenth century. The enslaving Sephardim practised what I am calling Exodus-colonialism inspired by victimology, and such victimological Exodus-colonialism also inspired, from the latter part of the nineteenth century, the Political Zionist desire to take over Palestine and make it into an exclusive Jewish state.

So, for half a millennium, a strand of Jewish history reveals that the mainly Sephardim in Suriname, and mainly Ashkenazim in Palestine, are perpetrators who disregarded the human rights of Indigenous peoples and enslaved peoples (in Suriname) and the human rights of Indigenous peoples (in Palestine). There is another continuity between Suriname and Palestine, a commonality in terms of the perpetration of extreme violence. We have seen that the Sephardim practised extreme violence including torture against African slaves. Recent historiography, as in the writings of Ilan Pappé and Nur Masalha, is increasingly revealing the extreme violence perpetrated by Zionist military forces and the Israeli state in Palestine. Israel Zangwill need not have felt so dejected in the early 1920s that the opportunity for Palestine becoming a Jewish state was lost; his dream came true in 1948, in the *Nakba*, the tragedy brought upon the Indigenous Palestinian population by Zionist ethnic cleansing and settler colonial genocide. In *The Ethnic Cleansing of Palestine* (2006) Ilan Pappé argues that the ethnic cleansing of Palestine during 1948 was top-down, intentional and bureaucratically detailed.[22] Nur Masalha writes in *The Bible and Zionism* (2007) that the 'mini-holocaust (Palestinian *Nakba*, or catastrophe in Arabic) and the exiling of hundreds of thousands of indigenous people which took place in the creation of the State of Israel in 1948... is one of the great war crimes of the twentieth century.'[23]

I should clarify: the continuity in terms of Jewish settler colonial extreme violence between the Sephardim in Suriname and the political Zionists in Palestine does not necessarily lie in direct knowledge and historical consciousness. Rather, the continuity lies in the ways in this strand of Jewish world history Exodus-colonialism continuously inspires and justifies extreme violence, including genocide.

In closing my Zangwill triptych I'd like to make a plea for the desirability in history of a complex historical consciousness.

In his brilliant 1986 essay 'Michael Walzer's *Exodus and Revoluton*: A Canaanite Reading', which has proven so influential in contemporary critiques of Exodus including my own, Edward Said suggests that the narrative of Exodus, considered as a whole, has an inspiring vision of freedom for one people that is yet premised on defeat and even extermination for another, the Canaanites, those who already inhabit the Promised Land, a land which by divine injunction is to be conquered and occupied. Said sees the displaced and dispossessed Palestinians as the present-day Canaanites of the Middle East, part of a world history where Exodus has unfortunately proven all too exemplary, inspiring Puritans in New England to slay Native Americans or South African Boers to lay claim to African lands.[24]

As Harry Berger Jnr in his wise essay 'The Lie of the Land: The Text beyond Canaan' (1989) reflected, in Exodus the Israelites went from being fugitives to becoming captors and victors themselves.[25]

In these chapters on Zangwill, I have traced how for 500 years Jewish settler colonisers in Suriname and Palestine have dwelled on the first part of Exodus stressing suffering and oppression, while passing over its denouement, where we see that those who have previously suffered persecution and bondage consider they have the moral right to inflict suffering and persecution on other peoples.

How different history might be if we could develop a complex historical consciousness inspired by reflections such as those of Said and Berger that illuminate the double character of the Exodus narrative, of victim becoming perpetrator. A complex historical consciousness acknowledges the acute suffering and persecution of a people while at the same time stressing that such suffering and persecution does not justify, can never justify, inflicting tragedy on the history of other peoples.

1. Edward Said, 'Michael Walzer's Exodus and Revolution: A Canaanite Reading', in Edward Said and Christopher Hitchens (eds), *Blaming the Victims: Spurious Scholarship and the Palestine Question* (Verso, London, 1988), pp.161–78.
2. Maurice Simon (ed.), *Speeches, Articles and Letters of Israel Zangwill*, with a foreword by Edith Ayrton Zangwill (The Sencino Press, London, 1937).
3. Maurice Simon (ed.), *Speeches, Articles and Letters of Israel Zangwill*, pp.231–3.
4. I'm reminded that in James Joyce's *Ulysses* (1922; introduction and notes by Declan Kiberd, Penguin, London, 1992, p.432), Leopold Bloom, derided and threatened by the anti-Semitic nationalist citizens in Barney Kiernan's pub, in Dublin 1904, angrily points out that at this very moment Jews in Morocco are being insulted, persecuted, and plundered, 'sold by auction... like slaves or cattles'.
5. Maurice Simon (ed.), *Speeches, Articles and Letters of Israel Zangwill*, pp.234–39.
6. See Ann Curthoys and Jessie Mitchell, *Taking Liberty: Indigenous Rights and Settler Self-Government* (Cambridge University Press, Cambridge, 2018).
7. Maurice Simon (ed.), *Speeches, Articles and Letters of Israel Zangwill*, pp.243–51.
8. Harry Berger Jnr, 'The Lie of the Land: The Text beyond Canaan', *Representations*, Vol.25 (1989), pp.123, 126–9, 134–6, 138 n.12; John Docker, *The Origins of Violence: Religion, History and Genocide* (Pluto Press, London; UNSW Press, Sydney, 2008), pp.118–9.
9. Alice Wilson, 'Ambivalences of mobility: Rival state authorities and mobile strategies in a Saharan conflict', *American Ethnologist*, Vol.44, No.1, 2017, pp.77–90, here pp.78, 82, 86. See also Alice Wilson, *Sovereignty in Exile* (University of Pennsylvania, 2016). My thanks to Daniel Joyce for telling me about Alice Wilson's writings.
10. Alice Wilson, 'Ambivalences of mobility: Rival state authorities and mobile strategies in a Saharan conflict', p.81.
11. Alice Wilson, 'Ambivalences of mobility: Rival state authorities and mobile strategies in a Saharan conflict', pp.78, 81–2, 88.
12. See David Levering Lewis, *W. E. B. Du Bois: Biography of a Race 1868–1919* (Henry Holt and Company, New York, 1993), pp.438–43. See also Caroline Bressey, 'Geographies of Solidarity and the Black Political Diaspora in London before 1914', in Jane Carey and Jane Lydon (eds), *Indigenous Networks: Mobility, Connections and Exchange* (Routledge, New York and London, 2014), pp.251–6.

13. I. N. Steinberg, *Australia: The Unpromised Land* (Victor Gollancz, London, 1948); John Docker, 'Orientalism and Zionism: Dismantling Leon Uris's Exodus', *Arena Journal*, New Series, No.37/38, 2012, pp.276–7.

14. Leon Gettler, *An Unpromised Land* (Freemantle Arts Centre Press, Perth, 1993), pp.142–4.

15. Walid Khalidi (ed.), *From Haven to Conquest: Readings in Zionism and the Palestine Problem until 1948* (The Institute for Palestine Studies, Beirut, 1971), pp.xxii, xxvii, xxxviii, xxxix, lii, lxviii–lxix. See John Docker, 'Dissident Voices on the History of Palestine-Israel: Martin Buber and the Bi-National Idea, Walid Khalidi's Indigenous Perspective', in Julie Evans, Ann Genovese, Alexander Reilly, and Patrick Wolfe (eds), *Sovereignty: Frontiers of Possibility* (University of Hawai'i Press, Honolulu), pp.103–105.

16. Walid Khalidi, Introduction to *From Haven to Conquest*, p.xli.

17. Walid Khalidi, Introduction to *From Haven to Conquest*, pp.xxii, xxvii, xxxviii, xxxix, lii, lxviii–lxix.

18. Israel Zangwill, 'The Fiasco of Political Zionism', *The Jewish Chronicle*, 12 March 1920, pp.350–1.

19. Israel Zangwill, 'The Balfour Declaration', *The Times*, 12 May, 1922, pp.352–3.

20. Israel Zangwill, 'The British Government and the Mandate', *The Jewish Chronicle*, 27 March 1925, p.357.

21. John Docker, 'Orientalism and Zionism: Dismantling Leon Uris's *Exodus*', *Arena Journal*, New Series, No.37/38. 2012, pp.276–7. (This essay first appeared in *Arena* no.75, 1986.) See Maxime Rodinson, *Israel: A Colonial-Settler State?* (1967; Monad Press, New York, 1973), pp.39–40.

22. Ilan Pappé, *The Ethnic Cleansing of Palestine* (Oneworld Publication, Oxford, 2006), pp.23–28, 248–61.

23. Nur Masalha, *The Bible and Zionism: Invented Traditions, Archaeology and Post-Colonialism in Israel-Palestine* (Zed Books, London, 2007), p.1.

24. John Docker, *The Origins of Violence: Religion, History and Genocide* (Pluto Press, London, and UNSW Press, Sydney, 2008), pp.117–118.

25. Docker, *The Origins of Violence*, p.18.

24

My Mother Elsie Levy in the 1930s: A Diaspora Consciousness encounters William Zukerman[1]

How can you imagine your mother as if she's not your mother, before she became your mother?

In this and succeeding chapters I wish to explore the historical consciousness of a person who in the 1930s certainly didn't know that in 1945 she was to give birth to a baby that she and her husband my father named John Edward Docker.

My mother, I feel, would not have simply folded her consciousness and identity into that of her older and authoritative husband; she would have brought to their relationship her own specific history in the 1930s in the Communist Party as an inheritor of longstanding Jewish radical traditions, with her own international and diasporic consciousness, committed to Jewishness as an ethical universalism, intensely aware of what was happening to Jews all over the world, especially in the 1930s in relation to the rise of fascism, including in her own 'diasporic home' in England, and the consequences of the ascension to power of Hitler in Germany in 1933. And she would, I feel, have been very aware of what we might call the Decade of the Long Appeasement of Hitler, in Australia as well as and as much as in Britain and Europe. Of this context, more soon.

To write about historical consciousness, you need an archive of some sort, in books, pamphlets, documents, letters, photos, memories. In these terms, to write about my mother is a challenge. I do have some reading material of hers, which I wasn't really aware of until, as I began writing this ego-histoire in 2011, I decided to write the chapter I've entitled 'A Revolutionary's Bookshelf' on the collection of Marxist and socialist books and pamphlets I inherited from my father when he died in 1983. I had always thought they had all belonged to my father, but as I inspected them closely it became clear that several must have belonged to my mother. I stared at them, and held them in my hands, with a certain wonder. They consist of three books, a pamphlet and an internal Australian Communist Party document; they span from the 1930s into the 1960s.

The books are: William Zukerman, *The Jew in Revolt* (1937), G E R Gedye, *Fallen Bastions: The Central European Tragedy* (1939), and I Rennap, *Anti-Semitism and the Jewish Question* (1942). The inner Communist Party document, typed and yellowing, is: 'The Jewish Communists – The Vanguard of the Jewish People' (not dated, produced during World War II). The pamphlet is: Herbert Aptheker, *The Fraud of 'Soviet Anti-Semitism'* (1962, reprinted in Sydney in 1963).

I'm especially interested in Walter Benjamin's insight in his essay 'Unpacking my Library: A Talk about Book Collecting', that to a 'true collector the acquisition of an old book is its rebirth'.[2] What I now hope is that my mother's books and pamphlets can live again.

In this chapter I focus on Zukerman's *The Jew in Revolt: The Modern Jew in the World Crisis*, which my mother probably acquired when she was still Elsie Levy living with her parents in Bondi.

My Mother Elsie Levy in the 1930s 505

∽✿∾

[The following paragraph I have playfully tried to shape like a single continuous film shot, in the way of Virginia Woolf's *Mrs Dalloway*, which reminds me of Walter Benjamin's 1936 essay, 'The Work of Art in the Age of Mechanical Reproduction', fragment XIII, which I talk about in my *Postmodernism and Popular Culture: A Cultural History*, Benjamin arguing of film that the camera brings about a general 'deepening of apperception' for film audiences.[3]]

In the 1920s and 30s, when he wasn't travelling for the Party, my father Ted Docker lived at his mother Susan Nash's house in south Coogee, near a little cemetery, not far from the wide expanse of the Pacific Ocean, on the eastern coastal strip of Sydney. A little distance away, northward along several beaches and coves (Coogee, Bronte, Clovelly and Tamarama) in Bondi, in O'Brien Street, in a semi-detached house, which I would later know as my grandparents' home, a half mile or so if you walk along Hall Street away from Bondi beach, O'Brien Street branching off westward from Five Ways, a 25-year-old woman, Elsie Levy, was reading a red-covered book that I now have on my desk, William Zukerman's *The Jew in Revolt*, its subtitle *The Modern Jew in the World Crisis*, published in London in 1937.[4]

∽✿∾

Now I think: why was she reading this book, what did it mean to her? Did she agree with it? Who in Zukerman's view was the Modern Jew? What would she have read in *The Jew in Revolt* concerning the Palestinians? That she had kept it all the subsequent years of her life suggests it was important to her, and that she hoped one day it would be read again in her family.

I'd never heard of William Zukerman, but you can learn a lot, a haphazard lot, very quickly. I wondered if he was mentioned in that indispensable reference book for modern thought, Elizabeth

Young-Bruehl's biography *Hannah Arendt: For Love of the World*, and there indeed was an index entry to a couple of pages, which I immediately turned to. Young-Bruehl tells us that Zukerman was the editor of the *Jewish Newsletter*, which he had begun in 1948 and was an outspoken organ of dissent within the American Jewish community; he was a disciple of Judah Magnes, and he knew that Arendt also admired Magnes as she had made clear in a eulogy for him on his death in 1948. In 1953 Zukerman wrote to Arendt and asked her to comment in the *Jewish Newsletter* on an Israeli attack on an Arab settlement, Kybia, which left 52 Arabs dead and provoked a United Nations resolution of censure. In reply Arendt sent Zukerman a note on 1 November 1953 saying that she didn't feel able to write a commentary for the newsletter, she felt so sickened by what had occurred.[5]

Now I had some bearings. I'd come across Judah Magnes's name before when writing an essay for *Holy Land Studies* about prominent dissident Zionists in Palestine who advocated from early in the twentieth century the idea of a bi-national Arab-Jewish state. In particular, Magnes (1877–1948), a founder and first president of the Hebrew University in Jerusalem, was an associate of the philosopher and theologian Martin Buber. In their view, Zionism was not a political movement but primarily spiritual and cultural. Buber believed that the land of Palestine could and should be shared between its indigenous people and the incoming Jews from Europe; there should be two autonomous Arab and Jewish communities living amicably together and cooperating in the one state. The idea of a bi-national state featured in the platform of the Ichud group, formed in Jerusalem on 11 August 1942, that included Buber and Magnes. In *The Ichud* (September 1942) the group declared in its platform that a 'Union between the Jewish and Arab peoples' is essential for the upbuilding of Palestine and for 'cooperation between the Jewish world and the Arab world in all branches of life – social, economic, cultural, political – thus making for the revival of the whole Semitic world'. The Ichud urged that government in Palestine be based upon 'equal political rights for the two peoples', and that there be a 'Federative Union of Palestine and neighbouring countries' which would guarantee the 'national rights of all peoples within it'.[6]

⁓⁕⁓

What about Zukerman in the 1930s? I needed to know more. From googling I gathered that he was a Russian Jew who had migrated to the US, was a journalist, and throughout the 1930s and beyond was a regular contributor to *Harpers Magazine*, author of essays such as 'The Palestine Boom and the Passing of the Zionist Dream' (volume 166, 1932 Dec.-1933 May); 'Jews at the Crossroads' (volume 170, 1934: Dec.-1935: May), and 'Queen Victoria is Dead: Reflections on the Coming Coronation' (volume 174, 1936: Dec.-1937: May). The irreverent tone of the last essay interests me as a possible indication of critical attitudes my mother might have shared in relation to the English society she had left in 1926. When I was a child or teenager, my mother, reminiscing about her childhood in the East End, would refer to how disgusting Oswald Mosley the English fascist leader was, but would then comment that 'we' in the East End would not let him and his Blackshirts in to destroy our community.

I was always puzzled by the way she would say we in the East End in the 1930s as if she still lived, not in Sydney, but in far-away London. I was, of course, being obtuse. It took me a while to realise that in diaspora consciousness, as I note in the preface to my *1492: The Poetics of Diaspora*, time and space are doubled. Diaspora consciousness inheres in a sense of relating to more than one history, to more than one time and place, more than one past and future.[7]

In 'Queen Victoria is Dead' Zukerman reflects on the

forthcoming Coronation of King George VI, with England poised to 'indulge in one of those orgies of pageantry, sentimentality, and royalty-worship which always so amaze and puzzle the foreigner'. Zukerman writes as a well-travelled, cosmopolitan magazine essayist, as familiar with London and the UK as he is with cities and societies on the Continent. He clearly knows London well, but he is also the detached outsider, his observations and reflections comparative and international, and he is frequently scathing of aspects of English society in relation to class and the monarchy. What is so strange, he feels, about England is the paradoxical disjunction between its being a political democracy yet where 'in no other monarchical country does royalty occupy so large a part in the public and private lives of the people'. Furthermore, in no other Western monarchist society in Europe 'is royalty less democratic, so widely separated from the people, so aloof, so profoundly snobbish socially as in this most democratic of all countries'. Think by comparison of Europe, where kings might greet one in the parks or streets of Stockholm and Copenhagen: 'In England such things are unthinkable.' Zukerman blames the continuing influence of Queen Victoria, this 'energetic, strong-headed, narrowminded little hausfrau who ruled over England for more than sixty long years' with a German 'passion for despotic rule', creating the social, moral and family life of the 'entire middle class' in her image. Zukerman believes, however, that the abdication of Edward VIII has dealt a blow to blind reverence, and he hopes that the 'genuine modesty and reticence of the new King' may help to consolidate a 'new, less glamorous position of the Monarchy', more quiet and unassuming as in countries like Sweden and Denmark.[8]

I will assume that Elsie Levy had acquired Zukerman's red-covered 1937 book because she already knew of Zukerman and was enjoying reading and talking about his articles with other young Jewish Sydney eastern suburbs radicals she was friends with. What she could ponder in *The Jew in Revolt* were the book's very strong likes and dislikes, in relation both to the impact of Hitler and Nazism on Europe, and political Zionism in Germany as well as Palestine.

~~~

Zukerman intensely disliked and was apprehensive about the rise of nationalism in the 1920s and 30s, and nationalism's ways of attaining, or attempting to attain, state power. Here he puts forward what we might call the Zukerman thesis concerning the nexus of nationalism and anti-Semitism so visible in Fascism and Nazism. Their anti-Semitism is not, he believes, a simple continuation of previous outbursts of anti-Semitism in European history, during the Crusades and the Inquisition. Rather there is something historically new and distinctive about the prominence of anti-Semitism in the 1920s and 30s, and we can see this new aspect most clearly in Nazi Germany where it was launched. For all its pathological brutality, there is, he suspects, something artificial about Nazi anti-Semitism, something 'unreal, stagey and manipulative about the anti-Jewish outburst in the Third Reich'.[9]

In my mother's copy there is a line in the margin next to Zukerman's argument that what is historically new is that the Nazis have made anti-Semitism the 'chief tool with which they have hewed their way to power'. Zukerman then contends that such a political use of anti-Semitism has become the 'feature of Nazism that is most widely imitated abroad', not only in countries of Eastern and South-Eastern Europe like Poland and Rumania but in the Western democratic countries of Europe, in France, Belgium and England. In Eastern Europe, Fascist parties that previously had been politically marginal could, following the Nazi example in Germany, now deploy anti-Semitism as an 'instrument for the acquisition of State power'. In Poland, led by the Polish Nationalist Party, this instrumentalising of anti-Semitism was occurring to a grotesque degree, swept by a 'wave of anti-Jewish terrorism and physical pogroms for which no parallel can be found in a modern civilized state'. Jews were being 'pogromed in small villages and in large cities, in universities and in marketplaces', with the political aim of establishing a 'totalitarian Nationalist State'. Rumanian Nationalist parties also followed the 'Nazi formula' in making anti-Semitism the chief plank of their political programs, a strategy to 'capture State power in the best Nazi fashion'. Given its success in Germany, the entire fascist world has now come to accept the Nazi faith in anti-Semitism, including Mussolini, who had before 'never hid his contempt for the crude racialism of Hitler'. Everywhere, reflects Zukerman, the 'technique is the same: a movement is begun by fanning the embers or sparks of anti-Semitism into flames', and when the conflagration is well under way 'the fire is diverted from Jewish to other, wider political issues in the interest of Germany or of local Fascism'.[10]

In France, Belgium and England Fascism and anti-Semitism have become 'indissolubly one', bringing 'Jewish suffering and social danger'. In an analysis that must surely have interested my mother, Zukerman writes that in England 'anti-Semitism has become the chief if not the only programme of British fascists', with 'vile anti-Semitic meetings' and 'anti-Jewish demonstrations in the East End of London and other thickly populated Jewish districts'. Mosley's speeches are 'passionate tirades against the Jews, full of bitterness and hatred as though he had been a pupil of Julius Streicher all his life'; and there is a 'streak of sadism' in these speeches and those of his lieutenants 'which is actually frightening'.[11]

Yet, and here is part of his thesis, Zukerman feels there is a kind of historical hope in the way the Fascists and Nazis have identified themselves so completely with anti-Semitism, for the struggle against Fascism and Nazism by the liberal democratic world must also mean a simultaneous fight against anti-Semitism; if Fascism and Nazism can be defeated, Zukerman predicts, anti-Semitism also will be defeated. Already, Zukerman says, there is evident in societies like Poland and Rumania a growing opposition by non-Jews to Fascist and Nazi anti-Semitism because workers and peasants have realised that the 'new role of anti-Semitism' is as a 'fascist screen' behind which are hidden 'other political purposes' that affect them, the workers and peasants, 'as much as the Jews'. Furthermore, in 'Democratic countries' the fight against anti-Semitism is becoming the 'chief task of anti-fascist forces'. In France the slogan of the Popular Front is Against anti-Semitism and Fascism, while in England, in opposition to Mosley, the 'entire Labour movement, and the Liberal world as well, have rushed to the defence of the Jews'. Zukerman notes that the 'scores of thousands of people' who blocked the streets of the East End so that Mosley's forces could not pass into the Jewish quarter 'were not all Jews – not necessarily even all particular sympathisers with the Jews'. The anti-Mosley demonstrators had come to 'obstruct Fascism' and in doing so 'found they had to demonstrate their opposition to anti-Semitism'.[12]

We are, says Zukerman, in the midst of a battlefield, the 'new Armageddon'. At the moment the Fascist offensive has secured their ascendancy: 'Already German Jewry is crushed. Polish and Rumanian Jews are being exterminated…' However, and here is Zukerman's prophecy, when the 'final battle of Armageddon is over', anti-Semitism is bound to be defeated: 'If democracy is to live, anti-Semitism must perish. Fascism itself has made the destruction of Jew-baiting a condition for the survival of civilization.'[13]

In *The Jew in Revolt*, Zukerman is highly critical of Zionism when it associates itself with nationalism. In the spirit of Martin Buber and Judah Magnes he makes a sharp distinction between political Zionism which enshrines nationalism, and what he holds to be true Zionism, which is cultural and spiritual, emphasising agriculture and productive labour. For Zukerman, true Zionism, all that is 'attractive, sympathetic and great in the movement', was brought to Palestine in the late nineteenth century by Russian Jews escaping both persecution by the state and the Ghetto itself. The 'first Jewish settlers in Palestine' in the 1880s were imbued with the 'great social, moral and idealistic tendencies' which were fermenting in pre-Revolutionary Russian society at that time, an idealism they shared with the general Russian intelligentsia; this was the 'age of Tolstoy' when Russian humanitarians 'sought various escapes from industrial civilisation and its evils'. In the Holy Land the Russian Jewish settlers were primarily interested not in 'political ambitions' but in 'rebuilding their own economic and psychic life' and that of the Jewish people as a whole. The Russian Jewish settlers in Palestine 'heartily disliked urban life'; the city was the 'incarnation of the Ghetto from which they were seeking to escape'; a return to the 'simple dignity of the tiller of the soil' was a 'cleansing process'.[14]

Zukerman regards the Zionism initiated by Theodor Herzl in the 1890s, with its 'political schemes' and 'nationalistic sentiments', as a betrayal of true Zionism. In *The Jew in Revolt* he is astonished by the manifestations of political Zionism in Germany, from 1933 onwards, for it not only shares much with Nazism in terms of ideas but also actively co-operates with the Nazi regime. The Nazi policy is to enforce a 'Jewish exodus', a policy of deportation that has spread from the Third Reich to Poland and Rumania and other East European 'anti-Semitic States', and has in England been taken up by Mosley, the leader of the Blackshirts bombastically declaring that when he gets into power he will deport a part of the English Jewish population and treat others as mere guests. Incredibly, Zukerman observes, the Fascist and Nazi plan of a

'Jewish exodus' has found favour and support in the Zionist movement. 'Extreme Zionist propagandists' have popularised the idea in Geneva, Warsaw, London and New York. Furthermore, and just as incredibly, in Nazi Germany itself the Zionists are co-operating with the Nazis, who have shown a 'remarkable readiness to work together with the Zionists in this particular enterprise'. The Zionist Organisation is the 'only political party' other than the Nazi which is permitted in Germany; Zionist newspapers are not only 'not suppressed, but are flourishing'; Zionist meetings are 'encouraged' while meetings of non-Zionist Jews, even of the 'Jewish ex-soldiers', are 'suppressed'.[15]

One reason, Zukerman feels, for the Nazi support is that the Nazis are 'instinctively attracted to a Nationalist movement, even to a Jewish one'. But the 'chief reason' is that the Zionist movement promotes the emigration of Jews into Palestine, which accords with the Nazi 'policy of a Jewish exodus from Germany'. In their turn, the Zionists are not displeased by the consequences of the 'Nazi persecution of the Jews', for it stimulates a 'greater immigration into Palestine' and hence assists in what should be 'the highest Jewish purpose', the 'building of the National Home' there. For such Zionists, 'even the Jewish tragedy in Germany is not too high a price to pay for the attainment of the national ideal, and even Hitler can be considered a "messenger of God" (as he has been called by some Zionists) sent to help the Jews to re-create their national life'. Zukerman notes, however, that the 'great mass of the Zionist movement', for example in Poland, have 'strongly and vehemently opposed' the exodus plan 'even as an aid to the building up of Palestine'.[16]

The chief Jewish promoters of the scheme of exodus and of 'partnership' with the Nazis, Zukerman writes scornfully, are the 'higher Jewish bourgeoisie in England' who are keen to finance it, and the 'extremist Zionist-Revisionists who represent the nearest organised approach to Fascism made by Jews as a body'. Zukerman is scathing of the behaviour of the Revisionists, led by Vladimir Jabotinsky, in the 1930s in Palestine, where they functioned as a 'fascist party', with 'Brown Shirts, Storm Troops, and all the paraphernalia of Fascism'. The Jabotinsky Revisionists hounded out from the Zionist movement 'every Liberal and Labour leader'. In 1931 they were strong enough to oust Dr Chaim Weizmann as leader of the Zionist movement and nearly captured as well the Zionist Congress, while in 1933 they assassinated the 'able Zionist Labour leader, Dr Chaim Arlosoroff'. The Revisionists spoke openly of 'transferring the several hundred thousand Palestine Arabs' to Arab States and of 'establishing a Jewish State' on both sides of the Jordan. The Revisionists were associated with the influx of middle-class Jewish immigrants who, on coming to Palestine, were uninterested in agricultural work and chose to live purely mercantile lives in the cities.[17]

Nevertheless, Zukerman believes that from 1933 onwards, with the assassination of Dr Arlosoroff, moderate Zionists have turned against the Revisionists: 'Revisionism in all its manifestations is dead in the Zionist world'. By the middle of the 1930s, Zukerman feels, Palestine's Zionists have swung towards the Labour movement and its trade union organisation the Histadruth, and so is returning to true Zionism. Zukerman admires the Histadruth, the Jewish Labour Federation of Palestine, because of its 'remarkable network of economic, social and cultural institutions', which created, for example, 'that beautiful cluster of over two hundred agricultural colonies' that is collectively owned and conducted on a 'Socialist or Communist basis'. The Histadruth also organises consumers' and producers' cooperatives, runs a Labour bank, publishes its own newspaper, and has its own Labour theatre, school system, kindergartens, rest-homes, holiday-centres and training centres.[18]

I can only speculate on what Elsie Levy thought of *The Jew in Revolt*. She would surely have been very interested in Zukerman's ideal of the modern Jew, when in his eloquent conclusion he writes that the modern Jew, for whom Marx is a hero, has 'tended mostly towards the radical political parties' and brought to them 'enthusiasm, genius and devotion'; there is now a Jewish trend towards 'social radicalism', a 'turning leftward' especially by young Jews in Europe and 'even in the United States'. (And even in Australia, she might have thought to herself.) In more general terms, Zukerman reflects, a revolt, moral, spiritual, social and economic, is observable among the mass of Jewish people against the 'economic evils of Capitalism', nourishing a 'Social-Revolutionary movement' that is opposed to 'racial and nationalistic' incitements.[19]

Yet Elsie Levy might also have reflected that Zukerman's book gives ground for fear as well as hope; fear that nationalism might overpower the labour values he admires. For example, Zukerman concedes that the Histadruth has not been free of 'defects and blunders', chiefly 'nationalism with its narrowness, fanaticism, group-selfishness, and illiberality'. Like the 'other bourgeois Zionist parties', the Histadruth has joined in the 'cult of a Jewish majority' in Palestine, putting its faith not in the force of 'international Labour goodwill' but in the Balfour Declaration and the 'force of the British Empire'. Zukerman feels that the Histadruth is torn between two loyalties, of international Labour as against 'nationalistic Jewry', and that nationalism always 'proved the stronger'. The Histadruth's 'greatest error' is its 'dealing with the Arab problem'. The Histadruth, by assisting 'Arab labour', could have 'weakened from within Arab opposition and hatred' and helped prevent the 'fascist influences' sweeping through Arab society.[20]

Zukerman says it is true that the Histadruth made some attempts to 'organize Arabs in Trade Unions' and to co-operate with them in industrial centres like Haifa. But these efforts were 'decidedly not whole-hearted', they were not performed with the 'same enthusiasm and love' they bestowed on Jewish Labour and Socialistic enterprises, because of the countervailing influence of the 'demands of nationalism'. Thus the Histadruth 'barred Arabs' from joining their organisation, decreeing that 'Arab and Jewish workers may not belong to the same Trade Union, although in many cases Arab workers have repeatedly asked for admission'. The Histadruth also opposed the employment of 'Arab labour in Jewish enterprises', Zukerman commenting:

> One cannot preach the brotherhood of all workers, and at the same time conduct strikes against the employment of Arabs in Jewish enterprises. Of what value is the talk of goodwill, co-operation and commonalty of Arab-Jewish Labour interests, if at the same time what practically amounts to a colour-ban exists in the Unions?[21]

Nonetheless, Zukerman remains hopeful. The Histadruth, while it has succumbed to 'middle class' nationalism, is still on the road to 'social health and reconstruction'. A 'greater rapprochement between Jewish and Arab Labour is bound to come', transcending the 'present division on racial lines'.[22]

Did Elsie Levy agree with Zukerman's sanguine hope, or did she think his optimism was deluded?

What might Elsie Levy have thought of the attitudes to Palestinians more generally in *The Jew in Revolt*? Zukerman is critical of the Zionists in Palestine, especially the middle class who chose to put 'its faith primarily in legality and force' and ignored the 'Arabs in Palestine', as well as the Liberal Zionists, who in practice did nothing to gain their goodwill. He writes scornfully that the political Zionists, 'these great moralists, the alleged descendants of the Prophets', did not regard the Arabs as 'human beings like themselves' who could 'actually love the piece of desert ground which they call their home' and have a 'moral right to a country where they and their ancestors have lived for eleven hundred years'. After the 'tragedy of 1929', forced to take notice of the 'Arab problem', the 'middle-class Zionist parties' responded in the usual 'grossly materialist way' characteristic of the 'Imperialist middle-class of all nations' in its 'dealings with the natives', boasting of the 'great blessings' that 'Capitalist civilization' was bestowing upon them. Zukerman also observes that the political Zionists in Palestine refused any 'social and intellectual contact' with the Arabs, based on 'human equality and friendship'.[23]

As the years went on, during the perilous time of World War II and later, my mother could well have pondered the fate of Zukerman's predictions and prophecies. Zukerman's thesis, that the struggle against Fascism and Nazism by the liberal democratic world must also mean a simultaneous fight against anti-Semitism,[24] was supported by Hannah Arendt in her 1944 essay 'New Leaders Arise in Europe'. Here Arendt hails the development of a militant Jewish underground movement against the Nazis, saying that it was only possible because Zukerman was right ('one lonely preacher in the wilderness'), there has been a 'fast disappearance of antisemitism all over the European continent'; were it not for this, she adds, 'a Jewish underground movement, Jewish fighting units, and so forth would never have come into existence'.[25]

However, Elsie Levy must surely have begun to suspect Zukerman's claim that from 1933 onwards, with the assassination of Dr Arlosoroff, Revisionism 'in all its manifestations is dead in the Zionist world'.[26] In her biography, Elisabeth Young-Bruehl reports that in late 1948 Arendt was part of a prominent group of intellectuals, including Albert Einstein, who wrote a letter of protest to the *New York Times*, 4 December 1948, when Menachem Begin came to the US to garner support for the Revisionists of his Herut party; the letter compared the Revisionists to the Nazi and Fascist parties and repudiated the blend of 'ultranationalism, religious mysticism and racial superiority' in their ideology.²⁷ Zukerman's prophecy about the disappearance of Revisionism in Zionism and Israel was proving increasingly wrong.

1   Some of the material in this chapter, especially the analysis of William Zuckerman, was published in abbreviated form in my essay 'Genealogy and Derangement', in Vanessa Castejon, Anna Cole, Oliver Haag and Karen Hughes (eds), *Ngapartji Ngapartji In turn, in turn: Ego-histoire, Europe and Indigenous Australia* (ANU Press, Canberra, 2014), pp.173–188.

2   Walter Benjamin, *Illuminations*, edited and introduced by Hannah Arendt (1968; Schocken Books, New York, 2007), 'Unpacking My Library', pp.61, 66.

3   John Docker, *Postmodernism and Popular Culture: A Cultural History* (Cambridge University Press, Melbourne, 1994), p.47. See 'The Work of Art in the Age of Mechanical Reproduction', fragment XIII, in Walter Benjamin, *Illuminations*, pp.235–7.

4   William Zukerman, *The Jew in Revolt: The Modern Jew in the World Crisis* (Martin Secker and Warburg, London, 1937).

5   Elisabeth Young-Bruehl, *Hannah Arendt: For Love of the World*, second edition (Yale University Press, New Haven, 2004), pp.290–91.

6   See John Docker, 'The Two-State Solution and Partition: World History Perspectives on Palestine and India', *Holy Land Studies*, Vol.9, no.2, 2010, pp.147–168, here at pp.154–6; P.R. Mendes-Flohr, *A Land of Two Peoples* (Oxford University Press, New York, 1983), pp.112, 148–9; Young-Bruehl, *Hannah Arendt: For Love of the World*, pp.225–7. See also John Docker, 'Dissident Voices on the History of Palestine-Israel: Martin Buber and the Bi-national Idea, Walid Khalidi's Indigenous Perspective', in Julie Evans, Ann Genovese, Alexander Reilly, Patrick Wolfe (eds), *Sovereignty: Frontiers of Possibility* (University of Hawai'I Press, Honolulu, 2013), pp.86–116.

7   John Docker, *1492: The Poetics of Diaspora* (Continuum, London and New York, 2001), pp.vii–viii.

8   Zukerman, 'Queen Victoria is Dead: Reflections on the Coming Coronation', *Harpers Magazine*, Volume 174, May 37, pp.561–565, 568.

9   Zukerman, *The Jew in Revolt: The Modern Jew in the World Crisis*, pp.19–22.
10 Zukerman, *The Jew in Revolt*, pp.23–4, 29–31, 34–38.
11 Zukerman, *The Jew in Revolt*, pp.39, 41.
12 Zukerman, *The Jew in Revolt*, pp.42–8.
13 Zukerman, *The Jew in Revolt*, pp.49–51.
14 Zukerman, *The Jew in Revolt*, pp.139–41.
15 Zukerman, *The Jew in Revolt*, pp.110–113, 117, 141.
16 Zukerman, *The Jew in Revolt*, pp.114–5.
17 Zukerman, *The Jew in Revolt*, pp.113, 116, 127, 155, 161, 172–3.
18 Zukerman, *The Jew in Revolt*, pp.174–6, 179, 205.
19 Zukerman, *The Jew in Revolt*, pp.250–54.
20 Zukerman, *The Jew in Revolt*, pp.179–82, 185.
21 Zukerman, *The Jew in Revolt*, pp.183–5.
22 Zukerman, *The Jew in Revolt*, pp.187, 196.
23 Zukerman, *The Jew in Revolt*, pp.160–64.
24 Zukerman, *The Jew in Revolt*, pp.42–45.
25 Hannah Arendt, *The Jewish Writings*, edited by Jerome Kohn and Ron H. Feldman (Schocken Books, New York, 2007), 'New Leaders Arise in Europe' (1944), p.256.
26 Zukerman, *The Jew in Revolt*, p.205.
27 Elisabeth Young-Bruehl, *For the Love of the World*, p.232. The letter is reprinted in Hannah Arendt, *The Jewish Writings*, 'New Palestine Party: Visit of Menachem Begin and Aims of Political Movement Discussed', an open letter to the *New York Times*, December 4, 1948, drafted by Arendt and co-signed by her, Albert Einstein, and Sidney Hook, among others, pp.417–19.

25

1938–9: In the Shadow of the Holocaust: G E R Gedye's *Fallen Bastions*, Veza Canetti's *The Tortoises* and Virginia Woolf's *Three Guineas*

⁓⁕⁓

Once more I try to think about my mother in the 1930s, that young Jewish woman with non-Anglo non-Aryan dark hair, that undutiful daughter whose image I seek to have before me; what did she feel what it might have been like for dark-haired Jewish women to be in Vienna at the time of the Anschluss, when on 12 March 1938 Austria was annexed by Germany? What did Jewish men and women around the world feel what it might have been like to be in Vienna at that moment when Austria dishonoured itself in history, so many of its citizens welcoming the Nazis taking over their country?

What I do know is that my mother left to her family a copy of Gedye's *Fallen Bastions*, a work of observer journalism on an urgent mission, a kind of *J'accuse*, an appeal to the world to act. I know it belonged to my mother because of what is whimsically inscribed on the inside of the front cover, in her handwriting, characteristically economical with punctuation, that I remember from her blue paper aerograms she sent me when Ann and I were living in London in 1973–4:

> Elsie Levy
> 42 O'Brien St Bondi
> Private Property

Here I sit, in our Perth house, in which we have been living since July 2016, with the book in my hand, intrigued. Its red cover is now faded, but still clear are author and title and a declaration: 'Left Book Club Edition Not for Sale to the Public'. A few blank pages in we see the full title and sub-title: *Fallen Bastions: The Central European Tragedy*, and where it was published: London, Victor Gollancz Ltd, 1939. Turning the page, there are two contrasting maps of Central Europe, one concerning 1919, the other 1938; and just before the Contents page, there is a passionate Foreword urging opposition to Hitler before it is too late for Central Europe to retain its independence. The first map shows that before 1919, Austria-Hungary stretched from Germany in the west to the east of Europe, bordering Poland, Rumania and Serbia; after 1919, after World War I and the Paris peace conference, all that remained was a shrunken Austria. The second map, of 1938, shows that the now small country of Austria had become part of the German Reich, its immediate borders to the east now edging Poland, Czecho-Slovakia and Hungary. 'There is still time,' Gedye writes as the final sentence of his Foreword, 'but, I think, only just time. That is why, at whatever cost, I had to write this book – while there is time.'[1]

Once again I'm confounded by male authors' pride in and affection for their initials. From googling I learn that G E R Gedye is George Eric Rowe Gedye, 1890–1970, a British journalist, author and intelligence officer, very much admired by Sir Hugh Greene, a director-general of the BBC, who observed: 'That

Gedye was the greatest British foreign correspondent of the interwar years can hardly be disputed.'

I wonder how much the British Left Book Club was known in Australia. Robin Gollan is very helpful here, telling us in his *Revolutionaries and Reformists: Communism and the Australian Labour Movement 1920–1955*, in his chapter on the popular front, that the Left Book Club was founded in London early in 1936, the brainchild of the radical publisher Victor Gollancz; the Spanish civil war gave it an extra sense of urgency that remained with it throughout the 'dark years of Hitler's triumphs and the appeasers' shame'. The Left Book Club produced books concerned with questions of fascism, the threat of war and poverty; for 12 years, from 1936 to 1948, the club poured out books, 257 in all; there was a monthly choice, selected by Gollancz, John Strachey and Harold Laski, which was distributed to all members. The high point of the club's endeavours was in the years from 1936 to the outbreak of World War II, the club devoting these years trying to prevent a new world war; Gollan notes the appearance of Gedye's *Fallen Bastions* in 1939 as part of this effort. Gollan remarks that rarely has any publishing venture had the same concentration of academic and journalistic talent as was thrown into the publications of the Left Book Club between 1936 and 1939; it was a political movement as well; in 1939 it had 57 000 members in Britain, who met in discussion groups and organised meetings, lecture tours, plays and films. Its contributors were diverse; a rally in London could be addressed by a range of political figures from Harry Pollitt, general secretary of the Communist Party, to Lloyd George, with Paul Robeson as 'the moving voice of the poor and the black'.[2]

Gollan comments that the strongest overseas support for the Left Book Club came from Australia, where membership grew steadily, reaching a maximum of about 4000 shortly after Chamberlain's Munich appeasement performance of 29

September 1938. In November 1938 there were 17 groups in New South Wales and 14 in Victoria, discussing the latest books as they arrived from London and taking part in political activities. In November of 1938 the *Australian Left News* was launched, which carried articles on Australian topics, its driving force, as in the Spanish Relief Committee, the Communist Party. As in Britain, the Left Book Club members in Australia in their discussion groups were part of the popular front, which could include liberal anti-fascist and pacifist standpoints. Gollan feels that the Left Book Club did have a significant impact in Australia in influencing trade union opinion and policy; it provided a meeting ground where communists could make common cause with people seized with the menace of fascism, but were not fully persuaded that the Soviet Union was the exemplar of the good society.[3]

Why did my mother insist the book was her 'Private Property', given that she was a revolutionary socialist? Was it a joke, or rather, both impish and protecting it from being snatched by her brothers or her friends in their intellectually eager leftwing circle? Anyway, it makes me smile.

Why was Elsie Levy so interested in this book?

I see from a note I added on a title page that I started reading it on 27 June 2012, and read the whole book through, pencil in hand. I then put it aside till now as I write this chapter, late 2017, early 2018.

I turn over its pages to see what marginal marks and comments I pencilled in in my 2012 reading, hoping they might somehow indicate how my mother, and perhaps her circle, could have responded to the book's evocation of the Anschluss. What I quickly see is that Gedye is not offering a distant impersonal as it were Thucydidean history, all politics and diplomacy and focus on impending war, but, as well as these, a personal narrative of how his life has become imbricated with the life of Central Europe, to which he is deeply attached. He is struck by 'gloomy anticipations for the little country I had come to love', a world he fears will soon be lost.[4]

Gedye says that in his book he will 'jot down recollections of the last twelve years which I have passed so happily, mainly in recording in Vienna the country's struggles, sorrows and joys'. He had come to Austria as Central European Correspondent of *The Times*, it looks like in 1927. He was immediately impressed by what appeared to be Vienna's charm and easygoing tolerance, but soon had to file stories under headlines such as 'Rioting in Vienna. Fierce Demonstrations against the Jews'; headlines which resonated with the final articles he filed, 12 or so years later, that 'dealt with street excesses against the Jews'.[5]

How did the Nazi Anschluss come about? *Fallen Bastions* charts in detail the dismal triumph from the early 1930s of Austria's home-grown fascist governments, evident in leaders such as Chancellor Dollfuss, 'who proclaimed with enthusiasm the death of liberty in Austria', having suspended the constitution in 1933 and then in 1934 infamously setting about destroying Austria's vibrant socialist and social democratic left. Gedye could see at first hand that the workers of Vienna were 'orderly, class-conscious, peaceable wage-earners'; he was personally acquainted with leading socialist figures such as Oscar Pollak, editor of the *Arbeiter Zeitung*, the 'most popular of all Viennese journalists among the foreign correspondents'. Yet, in the 'horrors of February 1934 and the subsequent years of oppression', Gedye is compelled to witness the brutal military destruction of their houses, communities, trade unions and independent press.[6]

Gedye writes sympathetically of the plight of the Social Democrats, the largest individual party of Austria, its leaders such as Otto Bauer struggling against ever increasing state authoritarianism, as liberal philosophy and parliamentary democracy came to an end. Gedye records that Otto Bauer died in exile in Paris, in July 1938, mourned not only by the 'whole Second (Social-Democratic) International, but even by his life-long opponents, the Austrian Communist Party, who sent a wreath and a deputation'.[7] (We briefly met Otto Bauer some chapters back as the brother of Ida Bauer, Freud's 'Dora'. Ida Bauer escaped Vienna in 1939 for France, from where she sailed to New York; she died in 1945.)

Chancellor Dollfuss became 'Dictator of Austria, and pushed ahead with his plans for establishing a corporate, Roman Catholic State'; during 1934 he was assassinated by Nazis, and then succeeded as Chancellor by Kurt von Schuschnigg, referred to by Gedye as another 'Dictator of Austria'. In 1938 Schuschnigg would be swept aside by Hitler in the Anschluss.[8]

Looking at my scribbled marginal notes now, I wonder if in the later 1930s my mother feared that a home-grown dictatorship could take over Australia, to initiate a wave of persecution and imprisonment. Gedye reveals that he is haunted by the fear that the 'cruel and treacherous beast which is Fascism' might come to pass in 'my own country', in Britain: 'Already it seems to be sharpening stealthily its claws.'[9]

When Austria's fascist governments led by Dollfuss and Schuschnigg were consumed by Hitler's Anschluss, with its invasion and occupation by German troops supported by local Austrian Nazis, the Nazi 'torture and plunder began'. Early on in *Fallen Bastions*, as a kind of prelude for the whole book, Gedye recalls what occurred on Saturday, 9 April 1938, when Hitler in person proclaimed Austria for Nazism and himself as 'the great son of this country'. As Hitler spoke, the assembled '20,000 members of the Nazi formations' shouted their betrayal of 'their country's liberty' to Hitler and Germany: 'In these regimented shouts was all the soul of the Nazi movement – the militarization of enthusiasm, the herd instinct, the mob spirit, the threatening, jubilant fanaticism of men who had surrendered gladly every iota of individuality to idolatrous worship of the man addressing them in terms of such extravagant self-praise'; in this 'mass-mesmerism', they registered no 'sense of the ridiculous'.[10] (I will come back to this last point when discussing Virginia Woolf's *Three Guineas*.)

In Gedye's view ever-present betrayal is a feature of the dark times of the 1930s. He is disgusted at Britain and France for refusing to support the 'cause of real liberty and democracy in Austria', freely permitting Hitler's Anschluss to come about; which did not surprise him, since he notes that Britain and France already in the 1930s had embargoed any arms going to the republican Spanish Government.[11]

It's worth quoting Gedye's passionate denunciation of Britain and France, who were now appeasing Hitler just as not long before they had been appeasing Italy and Japan:

> Hitler, it seems, must on no account be baulked. It is the same line of thought that has for two years employed 'non-intervention' in Spain as a cover for the Italo-German war of aggression against the Spanish people which if successful must result in establishing a new outpost of the Fascist bloc on the flank of France, which acquiesced in the rape by Japan and Italy of Manchuria and Abyssinia.[12]

A theme of *Fallen Bastions* is that when governments stood up to them, Hitler and the Nazis fell back, they desisted with their aggression. That is why he felt there might be hope for Central Europe, why it might not be too late – as it turned out to be, for as he records France and Britain kept appeasing and appeasing. From the vantage point of posterity we now look back on Neville Chamberlain as an egregiously deluded clown of history; for Gedye in 1938 living through this history and not knowing what would happen, the appeasing by leaders such as Chamberlain was almost incomprehensible, except, Gedye rather suspects, something sinister was going on, Chamberlain was actually supporting Nazism and was attracted to being a dictator himself. Gedye scornfully notes that the 'great Western Democracies' could never recognise that their concessions to Hitler only provoked further aggression, yet 'Nazism retreats when its bluff is called'. If the Western leaders could so recognise, there might still be a 'hope that we may be spared the otherwise inevitable war'. But what hope can there be with 'Neville *J'aime Berlin*' in charge?[13]

In 1938 Gedye himself along with other correspondents would be expelled from Anschluss Austria by the 'German secret police', and a year later, as he brings his book to completion, he still struggles to reconcile the 'good-natured tolerance I had discovered in the hearts of the Viennese', with the scenes of degradation and cruelty he had witnessed in the streets of Vienna. I'll quote Gedye at some length here, introducing a particular scene that he repeatedly comes back to throughout *Fallen Bastions*.[14]

> It is not so much all the brutalities of the Austrian Nazis which I have witnessed or verified direct from the victims which blurs the image of the Vienna I thought I knew. It is the heartless, grinning, soberly dressed crowds on the Graven and the Kärntnerstrasse… the fluffy Viennese blondes, fighting one another to get closer to the elevating spectacle of an ashen-faced Jewish surgeon on hands and knees before half a dozen young hooligans with Swastika armlets and dog-whips that sticks in my mind. His delicate fingers, which must have made the swift and confident incisions that had saved the lives of many Viennese, held a scrubbing-brush. A storm-trooper was pouring some acid solution over the brush – and his fingers. Another sluiced the pavement from a bucket,

taking care to drench the surgeon's striped trousers as he did so. And the Viennese – not uniformed Nazis or a raging mob, but the Viennese Little Man and his wife – just grinned approval at the glorious fun.[15]

When Elsie Levy read this book in 1939, perhaps then sharing the reading with her brothers and friends, did she and they feel that such could be their fate as Jews in Australia if it became a dictatorship?

In 1934 Austria's social democratic and radical movements were persecuted and killed by 'the Clerico-Fascists'. Gedye writes that the 'Socialists estimated their dead at 1500 to 2000, including a high proportion of women and children, and their wounded at 5000'. Thousands of 'Socialists were sent to concentration camps without trial', though many managed to escape from Austria and went into exile.[16] Could this occur in Australia? Did Gedye's book inscribe fears that were haunting my mother and her circle?

In Australia in the 1930s there were already Jewish exiles and refugees escaping Germany and Austria and Eastern Europe with whom my mother and her brothers in the Sydney Jewish Youth Theatre circle were interacting, learning from them directly of the extreme danger Jews were facing in Europe. I think of Lew Levy's reminiscences in my *1492: The Poetics of Diaspora* that I referred to in a previous chapter, where he talks of meeting Bella Weiner in the Bondi discussion group when he and Jock Levy were in their late teens; Bella, with her 'great mop of dark brown hair and eyes that pierced you through horn-rimmed glasses', had fled Poland because of that country's anti-Semitism. Lew also recounts that in the latter 1930s while in Melbourne seeking work, he met Rochel Holcer, a talented professional Polish actress who with her husband had fled Poland to join relatives in Melbourne.[17] Ron Witton in his essay in Ann Curthoys and Joy Damousi's collection *What Did You Do in the Cold War, Daddy?* recalls that his parents were

Jewish refugees who reached Sydney in 1939, both aged 19, having endured dreadful anti-Semitic discrimination in Germany; they were helped by Rosine Guiterman, the prominent left-wing activist and educator of Jewish descent who was a guardian angel for many newly arrived refugees; Guiterman arranged pre-natal care for Ron's mother who had arrived pregnant.[18]

Ann reminds me that two of the students on the Freedom Ride of 1965 were of Viennese Jewish descent: Wendy Goldstein's parents had left Vienna after Hitler annexed Austria in 1938 and Judith Rich's parents had left Vienna in 1938 or 1939 and fled as refugees to Australia.[19] Consulting Wikipedia, I learn that the well-known social policy advocate and feminist, Eva Cox, her maiden name Eva Maria Hauser, was born into a Jewish family in Vienna in 1938, less than three weeks before the Anschluss; with her mother Ruth she spent the war years in England; in 1948 they joined her mother's extended family in Sydney.[20]

For my mother and her circle, as well as for the specific diaspora of Central European and Eastern European Jews, Australian government attitudes to Nazi Germany and the Anschluss must have been increasingly disturbing. Christopher Waters, in his *Australia and Appeasement* (2012), tells us that senior ministers in successive Australian governments, figures such as Lyons, Bruce, Menzies and Casey, from the time Hitler came to power in 1933, enthusiastically supported an imperial appeasement policy; indeed these men, both in the secret councils of empire and in the public arena, were well out in front of their colleagues in London in calling for more far-reaching measures of appeasement of the dictators of Germany and Italy. Towards the end of the 1930s, government figures welcomed the prospect of the Anschluss; at the 1937 Imperial Conference, Richard Casey proposed that Germany should be allowed a free hand in Europe, particularly urging that the United Kingdom give a green light to a union between Germany and Austria. The 1937 Imperial Conference also saw the retirement of Stanley Baldwin as prime minister and his replacement by Neville Chamberlain, who was then quickly supported in his appeasement policies, especially in 1938 in relation to the Anschluss of 12 March, by Australian ministers. Within a few weeks, London accepted the disappearance of an independent Austria as a fait accompli; Australian government ministers followed by according *de jure* recognition of Germany's act of absorption, and they then supported Chamberlain's appeasement of Germany over Czechoslovakia.[21]

Stuart Macintyre in *The Reds: The Communist Party of Australia from origins to illegality* (1998) points to the warm hospitality shown by Australian government ministers in the latter 1930s to visiting representatives of Italy and Germany. At the end of 1937, Macintyre notes, the Italian government sent a battle cruiser, the *Remo*, on a goodwill voyage to New Zealand and Australia, attracting protests, including by local Italian anti-fascists, aware of the warship's recent involvement in the blockade of republican Spain and its bombardment of Barcelona. In February 1938, when the *Remo* berthed in Melbourne, its sailors seized a local Italian taxi driver in the mistaken belief that he was the leader of Melbourne's *Gruppo Italiano* against war and fascism; he was then beaten and interrogated on board the *Remo* in the presence of an officer of the Commonwealth Investigation Branch, prompting several thousand people to demonstrate against the warship. There were also protests and pickets against the Nazi representative Count von Luckner, who was another guest of the Australian government in 1938. By contrast, Macintyre points out, the Government showed scant sympathy for the victims of European fascism, maintaining strict controls over the entry into Australia of Jewish refugees, even after Kristallnacht of 9–10 November 1938.[22]

The Jewish exiles and refugees escaping Germany and Austria and Eastern Europe must have felt heartened by the demonstrations against the *Remo* and von Luckner and the strong presence in Australia of trade union and radical protests, yet might also have reflected how brutally and swiftly Hitler in 1933 in Germany, and Dollfuss in Austria in 1934, crushed independent trade unions, a free press, democratic rights to free speech and dissent.

Could socialists and Communists in Australia be driven into exile, sent to concentration camps without trial, die in military assaults?

Nonetheless, in Austria survivors did regroup in creating an underground. Socialists and Communists could read in *Fallen Bastions* how active, resourceful and imaginative the underground from 1934 on was in inciting 'ridicule' of the Dictatorship. My mother and her brothers and friends, with their own experience of theatre, could read how the underground 'managed to perpetrate some first-class hoaxes on the Dictatorship, carried out with real Viennese sardonic humour', including distributing a mock invitation card to a ball during Carnival time, traditional merry-making that the regime was becoming nervous about in any case; the mock invitation card, distributed to every 'diplomat, consular official and prominent Viennese', began: 'Invitation to the Ball of the City of Vienna which will be given on February 7th, 1935, by the leaders of Austrian Fascism, slaughterers and hangmen of world-wide fame.'[23]

In succeeding chapters Gedye charts the downfall of Austria's homegrown brand of clerical fascism. He feels that the Anschluss could have been avoided or at least vigorously resisted if during the 1930s Austria's fascist regimes, instead of destroying the Left, had actively joined in with it in a 'Popular Front for the defence of Austrian liberties'.[24]

At a party a short time before the Anschluss, a young woman

confides to Gedye: 'I wonder where we shall all be in three months' time – how many murdered, how many fugitives, how many in prison and how many just jobless and starving'; he later hears that she had become 'a fugitive abroad'. Again I wonder, what did my mother think when reading of this young woman's fears, or when Gedye notes once more that 'Britain and France would not lift a finger' to save Chancellor Schuschnigg, nor the independence of Austria; he thinks balefully of the consequences of that betrayal, 'the then-unimaginable horrors that followed on the Nazi triumph – the thousands of suicides of entirely unoffending citizens, the ruthless arrests of thousands without even a pretence at a charge, in order to extort from them their last penny and drive them from the country, the brutal torture, the shameful humiliations, the murders, the ruined homes...' Just before the Anschluss occurred, Schuschnigg at last contacted leaders of the working class, the successors of those imprisoned or who had gone into exile. They agreed on a common effort to fight Nazism, but the government would have to agree to cancel all previous punitive measures enacted by the clerico-fascist regime in 1934 and so restore to the working class their right to have rights (in Hannah Arendt's wonderful talismanic phrase from *The Origins of Totalitarianism*), their freedom to organise, conduct political discussions, and run their own press.[25]

It was all too late. With the German invasion imminent, Gedye talks to an Austrian Nazi who lives in the same building, seeing the 'lust of plunder' in his eyes. The Nazi tells him how much he looks forward to taking over Austria: 'Just wait until we get at the Jew... And a lot of other people beside the Jews...'[26]

In the high drama of events, Schuschnigg, Gedye records, arranged for a plebiscite to be voted on by the Austrian populace, answering the question: Are you for an independent Austria? Germany threatened that unless the plebiscite was called off, Austria would be invaded. Schuschnigg cancelled the plebiscite.

His voice racked with sobs Schuschnigg announced on the radio to the people of Austria his resignation as Chancellor. What immediately followed was the Anschluss, 'the outrage of a foreign invasion piled on top of local Nazi terror'. Schuschnigg was placed under house arrest. Meanwhile, on the 'Schwarzenbergplatz huge cheering crowds' were acclaiming the triumph of the Nazi takeover, with Austrian flags being torn down and replaced by Swastika banners.[27]

Together with Himmler, all the heads of the Gestapo flew to Vienna to 'instigate and supervise the coming terror'. Thus began 'Austria's Agony', played out in 'prisons, concentration camps, torture chambers, ghettos and cemeteries'.[28]

In Leopoldstadt, the Jewish quarter, 'the wholesale plundering by armed bands of Nazis of the Jews in their homes had set in'. The Jews, one-sixth of the population of Vienna, were

> made pariahs over-night, deprived of all civil rights, including the right to retain property large or small, the right to be employed or to give employment, to exercise a profession, to enter restaurants, cafés, bathing beaches, baths or public parks, to be faced daily and hourly, without hope of relief, with the foulest insults... to be liable always to be turned overnight out of house and home, and at any hour of every day and every night to arrest without the pretence of a charge or hope of a definite sentence, however heavy – and with all this to find every country in the world selfishly closing its frontiers to you when, after being plundered of your last farthing, you seek to escape.[29]

The cruelty, Gedye comments, is of an order that is scarcely believable, as when 'women whose husbands had been arrested a week before without any charge' receive a 'small parcel from the Viennese postman with the curt intimation – "To pay, 150 Marks, for the cremation of your husband – ashes enclosed from Dachau"'.[30]

In the Anschluss, many Jews suicided, and Gedye observes 'Nazis gloating over the daily suicide lists'. 'Some of the horrors', he writes, 'I saw at very close quarters.'[31]

> Hurrying down the stairs of my flat to hear Hitler make his first speech on his arrival in Vienna, I was delayed by men carrying out the bodies of a young Jewish doctor and his mother, who had lived, quiet, decent and hard-working neighbours for years, two floors below. The man had been dismissed from his hospital overnight without a hope of ever being allowed to earn another penny. Nazis had forced their way into his flat and thrust a great Swastika banner out of his window. Being a doctor, escape was easier for him and his mother than for most; they had found it through a hypodermic syringe. The S.S. guards in the basement premises… stood around grinning their satisfaction as the bodies came out.[32]

Again Gedye features in his narrative the scene that particularly horrifies him, observing from his window the 'favourite amusement of the Nazi mobs during many long weeks of forcing Jewish men and women to go down on hands and knees and scrub the pavements with acid preparations which bit into the skin, obliging them to go straight to hospital for treatment'.[33]

Once more we can think here of the Holocaust scholar Dan Stone commenting on the ecstasy of violence often occurring during genocides and massacres, as in Cambodia and Rwanda, the Rape of Nanjing and My Lai, the perpetrators enjoying the violence and the theatre of violence to a degree that can be called orgiastic.[34] It is interesting to see in *Fallen Bastions* that Gedye is drawn to a similar reflection, when he writes of 'the pleasurable orgasm which immeasurable human misery, suffering and despair provide for its devotees, this regime of barbaric savagery'.[35]

We can consider too Gedye's observation that those Jews

so publicly humiliated were 'generally doctors, lawyers or merchants', for the Nazis 'preferred their victims to belong to the better educated classes'. Gedye records that a Nazi order issued in July announcing the 'dismissal of all Jews from all employment, even Jewish, produced 800 attempted suicides, nearly all successful, within a few days'. The 'sweep of the Nazi scythe', Gedye comments, continued to 'cut down ruthlessly the flower of the intellectual and professional life of Vienna, impatient to destroy the last traces of that cultured civilization which for five years had marked out the distinction between Austria and the barbarous Germany of Adolf Hitler'.[36]

In terms of genocide studies, we can say that in the Anschluss the Nazis deployed modes of genocide, the invasion of a targeted group's homes and the destruction of its intelligentsia, as ways of destroying their foundations of life; in chapter IX 'Genocide' of his 1944 *Axis Rule in Occupied Europe*, Raphaël Lemkin argued that genocide can involve removal from homes, as in regulations that were particularly severely enforced in Nazi-occupied central and eastern Europe. He also reflects that intellectual genocide leads to a weakening of a group's spiritual resources.[37]

In terms of massacre studies, Gedye reports in chapter 29, 'Austria – What Now', that the 'daily massacres by deliberately enforced suicide in Vienna had mounted up by July 1938, to over 7000'.[38]

My mother could also read in this chapter: 'Outside a shop in the Praterstrasse labelled in huge yellow letters JEW stands a young girl. Alternately she kneels and rises to her feet. Around her neck is a placard: "Please do not buy from me – I am a Jewish sow."'[39]

Gedye makes it clear that not all Austrians were involved in the pornography of spectator cruelty, and a post-Anschluss underground continued. A 'politically educated washerwoman of my acquaintance' tells him just before his expulsion: 'don't let anyone persuade you in the years to come that we working-people in Vienna have gone Nazi'.[40]

1938-9: In the Shadow of the Holocaust

The German underground was also active. Gedye records for all the world to read of conditions in Dachau, taken from *Germany Reports*, a carefully compiled monthly publication of the underground German Social-Democratic Party published, Gedye adds, formerly in Prague and now in Paris, in English and German. Dachau housed Jews and non-Jews, but the Jews were particularly brutally treated. Jews were not allowed to buy anything at the prison canteen or to smoke. They were constantly beaten, and 'overwhelmed with abusive epithets such as "Sow Jew", "Filth Jew" and "Stink Jew"'. During the working period the non-Jewish prisoners were issued with one piece of bread for breakfast, the Jews received nothing, however the Jews are always paraded with the others to see the bread ration issued. As punishment for articles appearing abroad describing concentration camp life, the Jews, except for one hour mornings and evenings, were forced to stay day and night in special huts, the windows nailed up and painted over; inside the huts the air was so bad that often prisoners became unconscious; epidemics broke out. Gedye also includes an underground account of the 'new camp at Buchenwald', where many prisoners were killed 'outright or beaten to death or driven to suicide', this report appearing in the *Manchester Guardian* in August 1938.[41]

In chapter 28, 'Abrupt Exit of the Author', Gedye tells of the Gestapo ordering the removal of all foreign correspondents from Vienna, where he had lived for the previous 13 years. Unlike Austrians attempting to flee Vienna, he is permitted to take the train to Prague, there to arrive 'on democratic soil'.[42]

After the invasion of Austria, Hitler, with the active acquiescence of Britain and France, would go on to invade Czechoslovakia on 15 March 1939; a story also pursued in *Fallen Bastions*, where Gedye continues to register his disgust at the so-called Great Democratic Powers.

After 1939, my mother kept this book for the remainder of her life. It must have meant a lot to her, perhaps signifying the menace and horror of history that was never too far away. In an essay 'Genealogy and Derangement' I reflect on the dual legacy for me of my father and mother; both were in the Communist Party, yet their historical consciousness could, I thought, be inflected in different ways. I ventured the following: 'If my father revealed a straightforward optimism about history centred in the Soviet Union, my mother's legacy provided a more divided, ambivalent historical consciousness: history as optimism also in belonging to the Communist Party and fealty to the Soviet Union, and yet history also as shadowed by danger, fear, betrayal, and catastrophe.'[43]

I know I'm being speculative. I know I'm guessing.

In her 1943 essay 'We Refugees', Hannah Arendt reflects on her ambivalence towards optimism. She admits that like so many of her fellow refugees 'I, too, had rather be an optimist', but then, she muses, 'sometimes I imagine that at least nightly we think of our dead or we remember the poems we once loved'. No, she feels, 'there is something wrong with our optimism'. She thinks of 'those odd optimists among us' who, having made optimistic speeches, go home and turn on the gas or make use of a skyscraper… They seem to prove that our proclaimed cheerfulness is based on a dangerous readiness for death'. Then she recalls the Anschluss:

> Since 1938 – since Hitler's invasion of Austria – we have seen how quickly eloquent optimism could change to speechless pessimism. As time went on, we got worse – even more optimistic and even more inclined to suicide. Austrian Jews under Schuschnigg were such a cheerful people – all impartial observers admired them. It was quite wonderful how deeply convinced they were that

nothing could happen to them. But when German troops invaded the country and gentile neighbours started riots at Jewish homes, Austrian Jews began to commit suicide.

She writes of 'this insane optimism which is next door to despair'.[44] It is a striking phrase which, I think, illuminates Veza Canetti's *The Tortoises*, the great European novel of the Anschluss.

I now move on to *The Tortoises*, which so much resonates with Gedye's *Fallen Bastions*. I always wished to read and discuss *The Tortoises* ever since in this ego histoire I was drawn to thinking about Veza Canetti's earlier life in Vienna, a Sephardi princess of the mind in interwar Central Europe. Like *Fallen Bastions*, *The Tortoises* focusses on the Nazi Anschluss of 12 March 1938 and its comprehensive denial to Jews of the right to have rights.

I should explain its publication date, 2001, for *The Tortoises* appeared nearly 60 years after Veza Canetti hoped it would.[45] Veza Canetti and Elias Canetti fled Vienna on 19 November 1938, having survived some eight months of the Anschluss and annexation of Austria into Hitler's Germany. In Paris they stayed for a short period with Georges Canetti, Elias's brother (a doctor and biologist, who in the early 1940s became a friend of Roland Barthes when Barthes was a sanatorium patient), and from there they went into exile in London in January 1939. *Die Schildkröten*, *The Tortoises*, was written in early 1939, was accepted by an English publisher in July of that year, but the outbreak of war prevented publication, and for reasons which are not clear, it remained unpublished until 2001. In exile in Britain Veza experienced difficulty, frustration and melancholy as a writer. The non-publication of *The Tortoises* was one of the great disappointments of her life; she continued to write fiction and plays, but they also went unpublished or unstaged. In 1956, after another novel was rejected, she ceased to write creative works. However, she continued to give English lessons and work as a translator; her admired translation of Graham Greene's *The Power and the Glory* had been published in 1947. Veza died in 1963.

9 November 2017: I was delighted to see that a copy of Veza Canetti's novel *Yellow Street*, translated by Ian Mitchell and published in London in 1990 with an affectionate foreword by Elias Canetti, has landed in our letter box, sent by Gleebooks from Sydney; a note at the end tells us that *Yellow Street* first appeared as stories 'in the highly regarded Austro-Marxist newspaper *Arbeiter Zeitung* in 1932–33', but with the 'rise of Fascism, Veza Canetti's works could no longer be published'.[46] It would appear that what happened to *The Tortoises* in Britain at the beginning of World War II sadly replicated what happened to *Yellow Street* in 1934, a year of crisis for Austria, the clerical-fascist assault on leftwing Vienna.

With the publication of *The Tortoises* in 2001, it has become increasingly clear that Veza Canetti is a great modernist writer, in my view significantly adding to a polyphonic thread that Mikhail Bakhtin sees Dostoevsky inaugurating in *Notes from Underground*, developing for modernity a long cultural tradition reaching back into the history of carnivalesque. I've just glanced again at my earlier chapter 'Dostoevsky's *Notes from Underground*', where I refer to Bakhtin suggesting in his *Problems of Dostoevsky's Poetics* that *Notes from Underground* is a formative text for modernist writing. In contrast to Tolstoy's monologic desire that the author be omniscient and omnipresent, the desire of social realism, in *Notes from Underground* there is no so-called objective authorial description of social and historical features. There is only an array of consciousnesses; alongside any one character's point of view on the world are other characters' points of view on the world.[47] Yes, I think, here is the subtle deft quick cinematic movement of

The Tortoises; we as readers are drawn in as spectators. We can think too of Virginia Woolf's *Mrs Dalloway* and *To the Lighthouse*. Here is Veza Canetti's novelistic family, the family of texts *The Tortoises* should have been in from 1939, leaning towards each other, talking intensely and passionately together.

Terror wears a brown uniform and the swastika. It intensifies itself into a black uniform with death's heads on it. It reaches its apogee in a Führer who has nothing human about him other than his inhumanity.

> The two of them [Eva and Kain] sat on the one bed, the one free space in the room. They sat in the same position, both leaning forward with heads bowed.
>
> *The Tortoises*[48]

Let's explore in *The Tortoises* Arendt's haunting insight in 'We Refugees' concerning 'this insane optimism which is next door to despair' in terms of particular characters emblematic of the Jewish intelligentsia: Eva, warm and kind: her husband Andreas Kain the poet and novelist; and his brother Werner the geologist. Another key figure in the drama is Hilde, the lively, high spirited, warm-hearted teenager, tall and blonde, who lives next door to where Eva and Kain have taken refuge, in a lodging house in a village outside Vienna. Kain thinks fondly of the lodging house: 'This was the house, as if designed for him, a house that irritated the bourgeois and delighted the artist because it was so rambling in its construction, so lavish, with absurd hideaway corners'; every room has a spiral staircase; the 'garden as big as the whole country'; its garden is 'ridiculous', everything 'overgrown and running rampant'. He permits himself some wistful daydreaming, that you could escape from their situation 'upon the back of a bird' (perhaps here alluding to magical images in the *Arabian Nights* involving Sindbad the Sailor and the legendary giant bird the Roc), or 'someone lands an airplane in front of the house and you climb in and fly off, straight to the island of happiness…'[49]

Eva, too, is momentarily drawn to the dream of an airplane, to be able to fly away, to leave behind the mortal fear of the door bell ringing and opening the door to brownshirts.[50]

There is a general fear in *The Tortoises* of the door bell ringing: 'The brown uniform, known as the SA, arrives in broad daylight or at dead of night, and rings the bell. Everyone is terrified of this ringing.' Yet 'this city in Central Europe' was 'once known as the happiest of cities'.[51]

In the Anschluss hair colour, physiognomy and ancestry direct one's fate. Eva is acutely aware of the danger and humiliation posed to her by her 'dark hair' that fell across her face as, in the opening page of the novel, she walks slowly up a hill of the village towards where she and Kain live, keeping 'her head down'. Eva, a spectator could see, was once 'beautiful', but now her face showed 'a new sorrow' that 'cut hard lines across it, cutting through the soft shadows'.[52]

When Eva opens the lodging house gate, she 'flinched violently', for from the balcony there 'hung down, broad and long, a flag… mercilessly spreading out its red color'. She sees a man on the balcony holding the flag, making a 'sinister picture'; Eva trips over it and tumbles to the ground; she looks up at the man on the balcony and notices his 'cruel smile'. She immediately conceives an intense dislike for him, he is smiling the 'way Death smiles'; she tells Kain he is an 'evil omen'. Eva and Kain soon come to know that the man holding the flag calls himself Baldur Pilz, the Mushroom.[53] Walter Benjamin, in his 1932 'A Berlin Chronicle', thinking of Nietzsche saying that certain experiences keep recurring, remarks that in the most diverse periods of one's life one meets the Betrayer (in my writings, I know, I keep coming back to Benjamin's observation here). Pilz, the Mushroom, an Austrian claiming to be a Nazi insider, a swindler, imposter, looter, is a key figure of destruction in the novel, and I'll return to him in a moment.

Eva was returning to the lodging house after learning that she and Kain 'have to leave the country'. She tells Kain what she has learnt, then adds how frightening she finds the presence of a German officer and his 'blonde' wife who have just moved in. Eva becomes annoyed at Kain for saying they can stay aloof, they can rise above it, they can take no notice; she reminds him that every day 'new laws rain down on us, laws against people with black hair'; she rebukes him that he doesn't notice how dire their situation has become because 'your features happen to be Slavic and your eyes light in color. But as for me – people suddenly hate me, so much so I hate myself.' She confesses her fear of going out, 'the children in the street, throwing stones at me, that's what I'm afraid of, stupid as it may sound'.[54]

Defiantly, Kain decides to walk into the village to spend time at its coffeehouse. He and Eva are 'regular customers' there, recognised by the usual waiters, Kain is the 'bespectacled gentleman, doubtless a professor at the university'; but the walk to and from the coffeehouse becomes as if a terrifying journey into the Underworld, a phantasmogria of fear and terror; as he strides downhill towards the village, he reminds himself not to lose his composure; a flag darkening the sky is being hoisted by a cluster of youths in brown shirts, directed by a 'gaunt man with sparse hair and no eyes'; in the street, the brownshirts form a cordon, stopping pedestrians and asking whether they are wearing a cross. The scene reminds Kain of 'witch-burnings, of the plague, of Christians living in catacombs', then he thinks, 'no, those aren't the Christians, they are the Jews'; a stream of people come to see the Jews standing in lines, with a particular brownshirt 'putting on a performance, he raises the curtain, we're playing the Middle Ages here'.⁵⁵

Kain reaches the coffeehouse and opens up 'the English newspaper, huge and broad, drinking in the civilized language'; he feels that he is not in a coffeehouse, but on a ship, gliding smoothly forwards on the sea heading for England, he can see and smell the sea. Suddenly he senses 'cold eyes' fall upon him; a lady, 'finely dressed and heavily powdered', has picked him out even though he has 'fair hair', she may have seen his picture in the paper, he is a well-known writer and lecturer. Kain immediately leaves to return home, when a man wearing a swastika jumps out at him and exclaims, 'I am an ardent admirer of yours, and for that reason I advise you – You must leave! You must flee!' When he arrives at their lodging house, he rushes inside, and there finds his older brother Werner, with his 'blue eyes'. The brothers argue. Werner says that he will defy the new order: 'Let them bring in their racial identity tags, they will pass no laws over my soul'; he cannot 'believe that he has been totally deprived of all rights', that he is now considered 'a foreigner, an *untermensch*'; therefore, even though he 'has a visa', he will stay here in Austria, this is 'my homeland'. Angrily yet wearily, for they have the same argument many times, Kain tells his brother that while they may not get out of Austria alive, if he can leave, he will take Werner with him, he cannot leave if Werner remains behind.⁵⁶

Werner, we learn, 'had been dismissed' from the institute where he had worked for so long on his beloved stones: 'It comforted Werner beyond words to delve deeper under the surface of rocks, into the secrets of the earth, of its millions of years'. His colleagues hold a meeting, they all agree he has to go, he is 'small of stature and his nose was not Roman'; but not one has the courage to tell him to his face, and so 'they had left a letter on his desk and put a stone on top of it'.⁵⁷ The novel is a Cain and Abel story, so I will return to its horrifying denouement after talking about young Hilde and her vision of a plane landing in the garden to rescue her friends Eva and Kain; a story of delusion and betrayal involving naïve Hilde and Pilz, the cunning poisonous Mushroom.

In Hannah Arendt's terms, Hilde, so loveable, so irrepressibly affectionate, who dispels the shadows of despair and transforms any room she is in into joy and happiness,[58] is an unwitting allegorical figure of insane optimism.

The idea of escape by plane, what to Kain and Eva was fanciful daydreaming, has also occurred to Hilde as a way of saving them. She tells her older friends that she has a plan, she can get them 'out of Austria in an airplane', she can learn to fly with the assistance of the man who has put the Nazi flag on their balcony, the man Eva and Kain know as Pilz; she had met this man when she passed him in a nearby avenue stopping anyone not wearing a swastika; when he sees the 'blonde' Hilde, he strikes up a conversation, assuring her that he is 'an SA man of high rank'. The man is dumbfounded, Hilde says, when she explains to him that she is not wearing a swastika because 'she is a Jew'; he notices Hilde's expensive 'string of pearls at her throat', and says her father must be a banker; Hilde says no, Papa is a scholar, and her grandmother, who came from the ghetto, was 'tall and fair'. Hilde sees the pilot's insignia on his uniform, asks if he can help her. The man replies that the best thing would be if she could 'buy herself an airplane', and she is overjoyed at the idea. He can teach her to fly, and will also acquire a plane for her. They agree to meet, with Hilde handing over to him money for the plane.[59]

When Hilde tells Eva and Kain that the plan will work, once the plane is purchased they will be able 'in a few hours' to 'land on the island', Eva exclaims she will not countenance this rendezvous between Hilde and this man, he is Pilz the evil Mushroom, he is dangerous, she will not permit it! Kain is also dismayed, he immediately prophesies 'an unhappy end to this deal', the SA man 'would take her money and then lock her up to prevent her from letting a word of this get out'; Kain exaggerates the last point in order to frighten her out of going ahead. But headstrong Hilde, in an insane spirit of optimism, is not deterred, she continues her quest till it yields the disaster Eva and Kain predict. When Pilz moves into the lodging house and Eva and Kain now have only one room to themselves, he meets Hilde again, who is visiting. Eva pleads with Pilz not to take Hilde seriously, and cautions Hilde not to regard Pilz as some kind of protector; but, 'Hilde laughed conceitedly. How mistaken Eva was again!'[60]

Eva warns Hilde that she hasn't got the money to buy a plane, she would have to ask her parents and they would forbid it, for the National Socialist Party has outlawed the withdrawal of large sums of money, it lays down 'how much of one's capital one may withdraw'. Now Hilde brings ruin upon her Papa and family. To pay Pilz for the plane, she presses on attempting to raise the money. In the meantime, Eva and Kain have been forced out of the lodging house by the Nazis who have moved in and taken it over, as have Pilz and his wife Frau Pilz, of 'ash-blonde hair', like her husband on the lookout for anything valuable to loot. Eva and Kain have joined Werner in his tiny flat, along with another homeless Jewish man the elderly kindly Felberbaum. Suddenly a distraught Hilde bursts in, sobbing that her Papa has been arrested, he has been taken away. She tells the story. Pilz kept demanding more money for the plane. Finally, she goes to her father's desk, takes a key and opens the safe, and knowing the secret password takes out her own bankbook with its sizeable sums, locks the safe again, and the next morning withdraws the money from the bank and then meets Pilz in a coffee house and throws the money down on the table for him.[61]

The next day, her detained Papa protests he has absolutely no idea how it has happened, he has not withdrawn any money without the permission of the authorities; the authorities show her father her signature, and Hilde recalls: 'I'll never forget the long look he gave me'. Kain is sure that the 'scoundrel' Pilz was behind the betrayal of Hilde's father to the authorities, that he had played the informer. Felberbaum remembers that he had also met in another guise this man, claiming to be a painter of hunting scenes. Later, we learn that a servant of Hilde's father had seen 'the old man' being led away, he was 'bleeding from the mouth', the servant had gone up to him and 'wiped the blood off his face', but he was 'pushed away and had to leave his master to his unhappy fate'. Hilde never sees her father again.[62]

Werner dies in Buchenwald. Two brownshirts had come to Werner's flat, and when Werner angrily tells them he will not leave the country, they take him away: 'He was taken away in place of his brother, to prison and then to the concentration camp.' Eva and Kain learn that Werner had been arrested instead of his younger brother just as they receive a letter from the British consulate, their lives are now saved from imminent death, they have the required visa at last. The dreadful news arrives of Werner's death and cremation in Buchenwald, Eva and Kain are devastated, on the point of collapse. Hilde accompanies them to the train that will take them out of Austria, but she slips away to spare them 'a despairing outburst'. As the train approaches the border, a cold-eyed Nazi official comes to the doorway of their compartment, and asks Eva and Kain if they have any valuables in their cases, any currency or gold or silver. Her lips trembling, Eva replies: 'We have one object of value. Yes. The ashes of our brother!'[63]

To the very end, the Nazis kept trying to loot.

And someone else during their journey to the border had come into their compartment, 'a man with lively features and black hair that stuck straight up from his head'. The reader/spectator suspects it is Pilz the poisonous Mushroom in another guise, escaping lest he be found by the Nazi authorities to be an imposter, claiming to be 'one of the very first to be in the National Socialist Party'. On the final page of the novel, as the train nears the bridge at the border town of Kehl the 'cheery' passenger with black hair 'lit a cigarette'.[64]

Betrayers and Betrayal would always be with them. A Betrayer will always be with us, haunting lives, haunting history.

Here *The Tortoises* once more resonates with Gedye's *Fallen Bastions*, when Gedye denounces those he caustically refers to as the Great Democratic Powers, Britain and France. During the 1930s and into World War II they betrayed Austria, and before Austria Spain, Manchuria and Abyssinia. After Austria, they betrayed Czecho-Slovakia. Over and over they betrayed the freedom of peoples, the principles of liberty, humanity's right to have rights.

❦

Three Guineas, a long meditative essay of the kind Virginia Woolf had so famously made her own in *A Room of One's Own*, was published by Hogarth Press on 2 June 1938. I see from a scribbled note on the title page that I started reading it in Sydney, in the second half of January 2017, after I had finished reading *The Waves*. *Three Guineas* focused on intricate entwinings of war, masculinity and empire, and its immediate reception was controversial to the point of hostile. Perhaps needless to say, I like it very much.

The essay – provocative, witty, mischievous, irreverent, mocking of power to the degree that it can be appreciated as a contribution to the long history of carnivalesque, of women turning the world upside down, of Women on Top – is not addressed to the Anschluss, though Virginia Woolf was certainly aware of the Anschluss: Endnote 2 to its second section refers to 'Daily paper, March 12, 1938', headline, 'Nazis now control the whole of Austria'.[65] Like *Fallen Bastions* and *The Tortoises*, *Three Guineas* is written in the ominous shadow of the Holocaust.

I'm not sure how to proceed now, not sure how to talk about *Three Guineas* in relation to what I'm broadly trying to do, to somehow, even if indirectly, very indirectly, recover a sense of my mother's sensibility and consciousness as a young Jewish woman in the latter 1930s. In this ego histoire, I've considered certain similarities between my mother and Virginia Woolf, that Elsie Levy was an undutiful daughter, that in Hannah Arendt's terms she chose to be a conscious pariah.

But now, how to proceed. I'll have to make small tentative steps into this scintillating text, tugging at a possible thread of connection here and there, and see what happens.

My mother was part of a tradition, socialist and Jewish, of cosmopolitanism and internationalism.

In *Three Guineas*, so I observe with great interest, there is high praise for cosmopolitanism and internationalism, and such praise relates to what I take to be a key notion in the essay, its play with the idea of a Society of Outsiders. Let's start here, asking why *Three Guineas* so urgently values cosmopolitanism and internationalism in its proposed Society of Outsiders.

Three Guineas asks its readers, a few months after the Anschluss, to turn around a complacent distinction between Britain as liberal and free, and the dictators on the Continent: 'the creature, Dictator as we call him when he is Italian or German, who believes that he has the right whether given by God, Nature, sex or race is immaterial, to dictate to other human beings how they shall live; what they shall do'. Virginia Woolf quizzes her interlocutors (the text being in the form of letters), aren't women in Britain also living under dictatorship, the 'tyranny' of the 'Patriarchal state'? When men in Britain systematically deny work, wages, professions to women, what is the difference? 'Are they not both the voices of Dictators, whether they speak English or German'?[66]

Three Guineas asks: haven't women for a long time in Britain, haven't the 'daughters of educated men', fought for the 'great principles of Justice and Equality and Liberty' denied to them by the same enemy – 'the tyranny of the patriarchal state' whether in Britain or Fascist states in Europe?[67] And the iniquitous distinctions between the sexes are now being extended:

> Now you are being shut up, because you are Jews, because you are democrats, because of race, because of religion... The whole iniquity of dictatorship, whether in Oxford or Cambridge, in Whitehall or Downing Street, against Jews or against women, in England, or in Germany, in Italy or in Spain is now apparent to you. But now we are fighting together.[68]

Three Guineas sets itself against racism, violence and war, masculinity and empire, whether manifest in Britain or in the dictators in Italy, Germany, and Spain.

Luminous women of the past, *Three Guineas* suggests, faced 'poverty, chastity, derision' and a lack of those rights and privileges assumed and guarded by British professional men. Yet exclusion could also offer a kind of freedom: 'freedom from loyalty to old schools, old colleges, old churches, old ceremonies, old countries'.[69]

British society must be challenged to do what it does not do now, 'help all properly qualified people, of whatever sex, class or colour', to enter the professions. Britain should hold that 'ridicule, obscurity and censure are preferable, for psychological reasons, to fame and praise'. Women should spurn the yearning for honours and insignia of conventional success so obsessively and absurdly treasured by men: 'Directly badges, orders, or degrees are offered you, fling them back in the giver's face.'[70]

(In our *Is History Fiction?*, Ann Curthoys and I point out, in contrast to the nineteenth-century champion of positivism the egregious Leopold von Ranke, that the great and highly controversial Enlightenment thinker Benedict Spinoza felt that the philosopher should not seek honours or earthly rewards.)[71]

Women should choose cosmopolitanism and internationalism: 'you must rid yourself of pride of nationality in the first place; also of religious pride, college pride, school pride, sex pride and those unreal loyalties that spring from them'.[72]

Women will sharply question the 'meaning of patriotism' given how they have been and are excluded from British society and history. If an educated man 'says that he is fighting to protect England from foreign rule, she will reflect that for her there are no "foreigners", since by law she becomes a foreigner if she marries a foreigner'. An English woman will then infer that her sex 'has very little to thank England for in the past; not much to thank England for in the present; while the security of her person in the future is highly dubious'.[73]

If an English woman has been taught, perhaps in childhood from the governess, a 'romantic notion that Englishmen, those fathers and grandfathers whom she sees marching in the picture of history, are "superior" to the men of other countries', she could consult and compare the 'testimony of the ruled – the Indians or the Irish, say – with the claims made by their rulers'.[74]

(I'm reminded here of Lady Constance Markewiecz, who I talked about and so much admired in a previous chapter on Irish radical history, 'The Impossibility of Being Irish: Genealogy, the Great Famine, and Anglo-Irish Protestantism'; a cosmopolitan internationalist, Constance told the Dail assembly in 1921 that she would 'sooner die than give a declaration of fidelity to King George and the British Empire', because 'if we pledge our allegiance... this is treading down the people of Egypt and India'.)

At this point, Virginia Woolf, her anger clear at England's imperial presumption that it has the right to colonise, announces a famous refrain of *Three Guineas*, that English women, having been made outsiders to English society and history, should embrace their outsider status, should declare: 'in fact, as a woman, I have no country. As a woman I want no country. As a woman my country is the whole world'. The woman as Outsider will take no 'share in patriotic demonstrations' nor will she assent to any 'form of national self-praise' nor support any 'claque or audience that encourages war'; she will be indifferent to 'military displays, tournaments, tattoos, prize-givings' and any ceremonies that 'encourage the desire to impose "our" civilization or "our" dominion upon other people'.[75]

(Here we might spare a quick glance at *Gulliver's Travels*; in Part II, 'A Voyage to Brobdingnag', Gulliver is surprised to find himself rebuked by the king his host in this land of giants; the king asks Gulliver to give an exact account of the government of England; Gulliver praises the government and customs 'of my own dear native Country', that 'our Dominions consisted of two Islands... besides our Plantations in *America*', plantations signifying colonies. He is confident that the king, once Britain's customary modes of government are explained to him, will seek to imitate them in his own realm. The king listens carefully, takes notes on particular points, then reveals that he is the reverse of impressed by the portrait Gulliver produces for him, it reveals that English history is constituted as a 'heap of Conspiracies, Rebellions, Murders, Massacres, Revolutions, Banishments, the very worst Effects that Avarice, Faction, Hypocrisy, Perfidiousness, Cruelty, Rage, Madness, Hatred, Envy, Lust, Malice, or Ambition could produce'; he is appalled to hear of England's enthusiasm for war; and he asks 'what Business we had out of our own Islands, unless upon the Score of trade or Treaty, or to defend the Coasts with our Fleet'.[76])

We can say that *Three Guineas* is in a great anti-imperial tradition that includes Swift and Lady Markiewicz; or to put that another way: any tradition that includes *Gulliver's Travels*, Lady Markiewicz, and *Three Guineas*, is a great and honourable tradition.

The English woman as Outsider – indeed, part of the 'society, the anonymous and secret Society of Outsiders' – will reject Empire and its absurd claim to an intimate association with God. The English woman will silently address patriotic English men: 'If you succeed in your professions the words "For God and Empire" will very likely be written, like the address on a dog-collar, round your neck.' Those, however, who embrace being Outsiders will possess a mind and will of their own as they attempt to 'abolish the inhumanity, the beastliness, the horror, the folly of war'.[77]

The Outsider observes the close association of ideals of masculinity with the promotion of honours, and an associated obsession, ridiculous in its solemnity, with dress, insignia and medals. *Three Guineas* includes a photo of a high church official in drag, adorned, bejeweled, grasping an absurd phallic sceptre, with an equally absurd head piece, looking grim, determined, joyless, trailing behind him a group of frightened young boys and a solemn besuited attendant.[78]

Believing in non-violence, the Outsider will regard with 'complete indifference' the male love of war; 'what instinct compels him, what glory, what interest, what manly satisfaction fighting provides for him'.[79]

They, the daughters of educated men, will explore the possibilities of indifference, for example, the 'passive experiment' by which young women are silently withdrawing from Christianity. *Three Guineas* quotes a churchman, Canon F R Barry, vicar of St Mary the Virgin (the University Church), at Oxford in 1933, fretting at this development. In the vicar's view, the task before the church is to make civilisation moral, and such a task could not be carried through by men alone; in previous centuries, women predominated in congregations, but now it is being shunned by young student women who are clearly moving away from the Church of England and the Christian faith, to the great concern of the Church at universities.⁸⁰

For the narrator of *Three Guineas*, such is to be applauded, is 'highly encouraging to us as outsiders', but we must take care to interpret this experiment carefully, and it is not to be equated with mere passivity: 'For it seems to show that to be passive is to be active'. By such means, by making their absence felt, we can see the 'power of outsiders to abolish or modify other institutions of which they disapprove, whether public dinners, public speeches, Lord Mayors' banquets and other obsolete ceremonies'.⁸¹

Virginia Woolf's vision of a Society of Outsiders reminds me of Hannah Arendt's vision, in her World War II essays, of an historical community of conscious pariahs, in cultural figures such as Heine, Kafka, Lazare and Charlie Chaplin. Yet there is a difference, for the narrator of *Three Guineas* stresses here how much her Society of Outsiders practises a kind of creative passivity deploying silence and secrecy ('Secrecy is essential'), in acts of withdrawal and indifference, non-cooperation and non-attendance, that is unnerving and deeply disquieting to patriarchal authority.⁸²

⁓⁕⁓

Nonetheless, Women as Outsiders, the narrator points out, might wish to act in a more public way, to issue open challenges to patriarchal authority. Here the narrator offers an amusing anecdote concerning institutional religion. In 1935 the 'daughters of educated men said that they wished to have the profession of religion opened to them'; the priests of that profession in the Church of England, 'who correspond roughly to the doctors and barristers in the other professions', felt highly threatened, how could they reserve the 'right to practise that profession' for the 'male sex'? They turned to the New Testament for reassurance, but here they ran into a serious difficulty, for the New Testament reveals that the Gospels show that the founder of Christianity regarded men and women alike as possessors of the same spiritual capacities: 'There is neither male nor female for ye are all one in Christ Jesus' (Galatians iii, 28). Furthermore, at the time of the founding of Christianity, the New Testament indicates that there were prophetesses who were certainly allowed to preach, St Paul promising, for example, that women can preach in public though they must remain veiled.[83]

The Church, baffled, frightened, unhinged, appealed to another and contrary declaration by Paul, that a woman had to be barred on the ground of her sex from being an official teacher of the Church since such would involve the exercise of authority over men. The Church, that is, *Three Guineas* points out, decided to ignore the teaching of their own founder, Jesus Christ himself, who regarded men and women alike as members of the same spiritual kingdom, so that the profession of religion should be open, Jesus thought, to anyone who received the gift of prophecy.[84]

Then Virginia Woolf makes play with some ironic psychoanalytic speculations on churchmen and gender, returning the gaze; churchmen cannot, she feels, open their profession to women because of their unconscious infantile fixations, with their own power and their related fear of and contempt for women.[85]

Three Guineas suggests that what terrified the Church in 1935 had direct implications for other professions, since the profession of religion can be taken as the highest profession of all; if the Church profession were made open to the daughters of educated men, then there could be no reason why the professions of 'doctors and barristers' should also not be declared open to either gender.[86]

By such 'farce', by such refusal of rational self-examination, as the churchmen revealed in 1935, the other professions were also saved for male privilege, eternally, they must have hoped.[87]

Three Guineas points out that the profession of religion, in Christ's view open to 'anyone who received the gift of prophecy', corresponds to 'what the profession of literature is now'; the inclusivity of literature makes possible what all the professions could be like.[88]

~~~※~~~

Throughout *Three Guineas* the narrator entertains her interlocutors with the creative possibilities of the Society of Outsiders, including inheriting and continuing anarchist traditions, here looking forward to the relaxed structurelessness of the second wave feminism of the 1960s and 1970s:

> this new society, you will be relieved to learn, would have no honorary treasurer, for it would need no funds. It would have no office, no committee, no secretary; it would call no meetings; it would hold no conferences.[89]

The Society of Outsiders would have no 'leaders or any hierarchy'.[90]

The Society of Outsiders, then, would consist of educated men's daughters working 'by their own methods for liberty, equality and peace', mindful of certain 'duties'.[91]

The Society of Outsiders, we've already noted, would be 'anonymous and secret'; also, 'Elasticity is essential'.[92]

The Outsiders would 'bind themselves to earn their own livings', given the 'superior cogency of an opinion based upon economic independence'. The Outsider 'must make it her business to press for a living wage in all the professions open to her sex', and further she must 'create new professions in which she can earn the right to an independent opinion'.[93]

The Outsider would press 'for a wage to be paid by the State legally to the mothers of educated men'. The State should furthermore pay a wage 'to those whose profession is marriage and motherhood'; a 'real wage, a money wage, so that it became an attractive profession instead of being as it is now an unpaid profession, an unpensioned profession, and therefore a precarious and dishonoured profession'. If such were to occur, men could join in the work of 'bringing up children' so that men need not go to the office 'at nine-thirty and stay there till six': 'Culture would thus be stimulated'; men could 'see the fruit trees flower in spring' and 'share the prime of life' with their children.[94]

※

Virginia Woolf's Society of Outsiders 'will dispense with the dictated, regimented, official pageantry' – here I'm reminded of Mikhail Bakhtin saying that in carnival in early modern Europe official ceremonies, solemn and intimidatory, are opposed by comic unruliness and inversionary dissidence – in which men only participate, as in coronations following on from the death of kings, with their display of 'medals, ribbons, badges, hoods, gowns'. On the contrary, the Society of Outsiders has as one of its aims to 'increase private beauty; the beauty of spring, summer, autumn; the beauty of flowers, silks, clothes'; the 'scattered beauty which needs only to be combined by artists in order to become visible to all'.[95]

In Veza Canetti's *The Tortoises* there is admiration for poets as necessary to human dreaming. In *Three Guineas*, the narrator urges her interlocutors to heed the 'voices of the poets, answering each other', voices that always remind us of the 'capacity of the human spirit to overflow boundaries and make unity out of multiplicity'.[96]

※

Virginia Woolf's reflections in *Three Guineas* on how women in the Society of Outsiders experiment with non-violence invites a conversation with Gandhi and his famous notion of *ahimsa*. I say this as someone who regards himself as a Gandhian, as I made clear in my conclusion 'Can there be an end to violence?' to my

The Origins of Violence: Religion, History and Genocide.

In 2004, my colleague Debjani Ganguly and I organised a conference on 'Gandhi, Nonviolence and Modernity' for the Humanities Research Centre, ANU. One of the papers was given by Leela Gandhi, the great granddaughter of the Mahatma; her grandfather, Devdas Gandhi, was the Mahatma's youngest son. Leela Gandhi's conference paper became the opening chapter of the book of essays that Debjani and I edited that came out of the conference, entitled *Rethinking Gandhi and Nonviolent Relationality: Global Perspectives*, published in 2009. In this brilliant essay, '*Ahimsa* and Other Animals: The Genealogy of an Immature Politics', Leela Gandhi opens with an anecdote, where she pictures Gandhi as a young man newly arrived in London to pursue his legal studies. It is a grey day in October 1888; winter is approaching; he feels homesick for subcontinental food, especially vegetables; in any case, he has been abjured by his community back home not to eat meat while in London (from 1888 to 1891). Fortunately, however, his Anglo-Indian landlady has told him of vegetarian restaurants springing up in the city, and, joyfully, he finds one, the Central at 16 Saint Bride Street.[97]

Gandhi's life and consciousness, Leela Gandhi narrates, now changes utterly. According to his autobiography, he notices a book, Henry Salt's *Plea for Vegetarianism*, for sale under a glass window near the door of the café, and after buying a copy he begins greedily to eat the vegetarian food and read the book. During the three years of his legal studies, he meets Henry Salt at a vegetarian convention; he becomes increasingly involved in vegetarianism and reads everything he can about it; he throws himself into organisational and evangelical activism against kreophagy, or meat eating. Leela Gandhi tells us she will now argue that his enmeshment in late-Victorian radicalism including the culture of *fin de siècle* animal welfare, of which vegetarianism was a component, helped inspire his critique of imperialism and contributed to the complexity of his notions of *ahimsa*, that blossomed into the mature politics that, as Henry Salt would later reflect, became famous throughout the world.[98]

In *fin de siècle* London, Leela Gandhi suggests, Gandhi was quick to recognise that the *zoophilia* of his English friends and allies in the vegetarian movement was allied to *xenophilia*, leading to an 'openness to outsiders, aliens, strangers, foreigners'. An hospitable openness to outsiders, aliens, strangers, foreigners was necessarily anti-imperial, leading to sympathy among English vegetarians for Indian political aspirations. For Gandhi personally, the vegetarian movement he absorbed himself in in London led to a consciousness that was transnational, that was opposed to any identification of the state one was in, and therefore involved a 'readiness for self-estrangement' from a confining, single, Indian identity.[99]

Fin de siècle vegetarian 'openness to outsiders, aliens, strangers, foreigners' also led, Leela Gandhi suggests, to a 'radical cosmopolitanism valorizing and promoting difference', often taking the form of a 'culinary cosmopolitanism', visible, for example, in Annie Besant extolling dal and rice as her favourite cuisine. In 1887 a new vegetarian eating house in Charing Cross in London ecumenically and wittily included on its menu Macaroni and Indian sauce, Home-Rule Potatoes and Japanese bean-curd. Furthermore, in vegetarian discourse, meat eating is identified, and opposed, as a promotion of masculinity deeply entwined with imperial conquest and aggressive contempt for 'the rights of inferior races' in the empire.[100]

In his mature politics, Leela Gandhi writes, Gandhi continued to draw on the world of thought he participated in during the years 1888–91, ideas he shared with Henry Salt and his circle; ideas that were in international conversation with the anti-state thinking of contemporaries such as Edward Carpenter, Leo Tolstoy and Peter Kropotkin (Kropotkin had settled in England in 1886).

Nonetheless, she observes, Gandhi interpreted *fin de siècle* animal welfare in his own idiosyncratic way, where *ahimsa*, non-violence, is variously elaborated as revolutionary obstinacy, a refusal of government, the courage of contradictoriness, passive resistance, boycott, non-cooperation and civil disobedience; *ahimsa* bore the promise of his last, unfulfilled dream of India as an ungoverned society; Gandhi demanded that 'the British quit India and that independent India, in its turn, quit governmentality'.[101]

The final harrowing pages of Hermione Lee's biography evoke the last months of Virginia Woolf's life before her suicide on 28 March 1941. Lee records that from the start of the war, she had been 'strained, apprehensive, depressed and on edge'. The war was marked for her by the 'constant expectation of invasion, the air-raids', the 'bombing of London and of their houses, the withdrawal to Rodmell', her 'return in her memory to the most unhappy period of her childhood'.[102]

I'd like to hazard something that's perhaps absurdly far-fetched. There were intensely personal reasons why Virginia Woolf would commit suicide: in her life she had been given to periods of profound depression, she had attempted suicide before, traumatic events of her childhood may have been recurring (including being sexually molested by her half brothers) and she was deeply disturbed by the war.

I'm thinking that there may also be a resonance with the Anschluss that I don't quite know how to talk about or think through; a context of war and suicide, thinking of the multiple suicides that occurred in Vienna in 1938 during the Anschluss and in later years more generally, reflected on by Hannah Arendt in her 1943 essay 'We Refugees': 'Suicides occur not only among the panic-stricken people in Berlin and Vienna, in Bucharest or Paris, but in New York and Los Angeles, in Buenos Aires and Montevideo.'[103]

1938-9: In the Shadow of the Holocaust

In Veza Canetti's *The Tortoises*, written in London in 1939 at the beginning of her exile, Kain's brother Werner in effect commits suicide when he chooses not to use the visa to leave Austria he possesses and is then taken to Buchenwald where he is killed.

In 1941, Veza Canetti was perhaps still hopeful that, as promised by a publisher, *The Tortoises* would be translated into English and published; it wasn't published in her lifetime.

G E R Gedye's *Fallen Bastions* was urgently written in 1939, Gedye having been expelled during the Anschluss from Vienna to Prague. According to a Wikipedia entry, it appears that he moved from Prague to Poland; after Poland was invaded by the Nazis in September 1939, he spent the remaining war years in the Middle East.

On 3 February 1941 Elsie Levy and Ted Docker (I'm looking at my birth certificate for this) married at Bondi Junction registry office; my father, Edward Docker, a Political Organizer, born in Sydney, is 50 years old; my mother, Elsie Levy, born in London, England, is 33 years old.

Consulting the United States Holocaust Memorial Museum website, we see that the Nazis deported thousands of Jews from Austria to occupied Poland and elsewhere in occupied eastern Europe; systematic mass deportations from Vienna, as elsewhere in Greater Germany, began in October 1941.

1. G.E.R. Gedye, *Fallen Bastions: The Central European Tragedy* (Victor Gollancz, London, 1939), Foreword.
2. Robin Gollan, *Revolutionaries and Reformists: Communism and the Australian Labour Movement 1920–1955* (ANU Press, Canberra, 1975), pp.66–8.
3. Robin Gollan, *Revolutionaries and Reformists*, pp.66, 68–70. See also Stuart Macintyre, *The Reds: The Communist Party of Australia from Origins to Illegality* (Allen and Unwin, Sydney, 1998), p.324.
4. Gedye, *Fallen Bastions*, p.90.
5. Gedye, *Fallen Bastions*, pp.11, 13, 16–17.
6. Gedeye, *Fallen Bastions*, pp.27, 73, 82, 89, 92, 99.
7. Gedye, *Fallen Bastions*, pp.35, 63–4, 73–6, 83, 88–9, 106–9.
8. Gedye, *Fallen Bastions*, pp.90, 144–154.
9. Gedye, *Fallen Bastions*, pp.90, 97, 112.
10. Gedeye, *Fallen Bastions*, pp.9, 91.
11. Gedeye, *Fallen Bastions*, pp.66, 210.
12. Gedye, *Fallen Bastions*, p.379.
13. Gedye, *Fallen Bastions*, p.133.
14. Gedye, *Fallen Bastions*, pp.17–18, 54, 178.
15. Gedye, *Fallen Bastions*, p.18.
16. Gedye, *Fallen Bastions*, pp.123–4, 165–6.
17. John Docker, *1492: The Poetics of Diaspora* (Continuum, London and New York, 2001), pp.164–5.
18. Ron Witton, 'Growing up and living with the cold war', in Ann Curthoys and Joy Damousi, eds, *What Did You Do in the Cold War, Daddy?* (NewSouth, Sydney, 2014), pp.226–8.
19. Ann Curthoys, *Freedom Ride: a freedom rider remembers* (Allen and Unwin, Sydney, 2002), pp.66–7.
20. See also Tim Bonyhady, *Good Living Street: The Fortunes of my Viennese Family* (Allen and Unwin, Sydney, 2011).
21. Christopher Waters, *Australia and Appeasement: Imperial Foreign Policy and the Origins of World War II* (I.B. Tauris, London, 2012), pp.22, 26, 36, 44–7, 243–4, 265–6.
22. Stuart Macintyre, *The Reds: The Communist Party of Australia from Origins to Illegality*, p.310.
23. Gedye, *Fallen Bastions*, pp.174–182.
24. Gedye, *Fallen Bastions*, p.210.
25. Gedye, *Fallen Bastions*, pp.228, 245, 258, 262–7, 278–280; Hannah Arendt, *The Origins of Totalitarianism*, new edition with added prefaces (Harcourt, New York,

1976), chapter nine, 'The Decline of the Nation-State and the End of the Rights of Man', p.296. My thanks to Ned Curthoys for guiding me to 'the right to have rights' in *The Origins of Totalitarianism*.

26 Gedye, *Fallen Bastions*, pp.215–16.
27 Gedye, *Fallen Bastions*, pp.289–294.
28 Gedye, *Fallen Bastions*, pp.296–9.
29 Gedye, *Fallen Bastions*, p.305.
30 Gedye, *Fallen Bastions*, p.306.
31 Gedye, *Fallen Bastions*, pp.306–7.
32 Gedye, *Fallen Bastions*, p.307.
33 Gedye, *Fallen Bastions*, p.307, also 322 and 347.
34 Dan Stone, 'Genocide as Transgression', that I refer to in John Docker, *The Origins of Violence: Religion, History and Genocide* (Pluto Press and UNSW Press, London and Sydney, 2008), p.27.
35 Gedye, *Fallen Bastions*, p.357.
36 Gedye, *Fallen Bastions*, p.313.
37 Räphael Lemkin, *Axis Rule in Occupied Europe: laws of occupation, analysis of government, proposals for redress* (Columbia University Press, New York, 1944), pp.xi, 75, 83, 89. See also Ann Curthoys and John Docker, 'Genocide: definitions, questions, settler-colonies', Introduction to special section of *Aboriginal History*, Vol.25, 2001, pp.7, 9.
38 Gedye, *Fallen Bastions*, p.351.
39 Gedye, *Fallen Bastions*, p.354.
40 Gedye, *Fallen Bastions*, pp.93, 162–3, 174.
41 Gedye, *Fallen Bastions*, pp.341–5.
42 Gedye, *Fallen Bastions*, pp.327–39.
43 John Docker, 'Genealogy and Derangement', in Vanessa Castejon, Anna Cole, Oliver Haag and Karen Hughes (eds), *Ngapartji Ngapartji In Turn, in turn: Ego-histoire, Europe and Indigenous Australia* (ANU Press, Canberra, 2014), p.185.
44 Hannah Arendt, *The Jewish Writings*, edited by Jerome Kohn and Ron H. Feldman (Schocken, New York, 2007), 'We Refugees' (1943), pp.266–8.
45 Veza Canetti, *The Tortoises*, translated by Ian Mitchell, Postscript by Fritz Arnold, Hanser Verlag (New Directions, New York, 2001).
46 Veza Canetti, *Yellow Street: A Novel in Five Scenes*, with a Foreword by Elias Canetti, translated by Ian Mitchell (1990; New Directions, New York, 1991).
47 Mikhail Bakhtin, *Problems of Dostoevsky's Poetics*, edited and translated by Caryl Emerson (Manchester University Press, Manchester, 1984), pp.48–50.
48 Veza Canetti, *The Tortoises*, translated by Ian Mitchell (New Directions, New Directions, New York, 2001), pp.21, 102.

49 Veza Canetti, *The Tortoises*, pp.6-7, 33.
50 Veza Canetti, *The Tortoises*, p.19.
51 Veza Canetti, *The Tortoises*, pp.20-1.
52 Veza Canetti, *The Tortoises*, p.3.
53 Veza Canetti, *The Tortoises*, pp.3-5, 9, 41, 98.
54 Veza Canetti, *The Tortoises*, pp.6-9.
55 Veza Canetti, *The Tortoises*, pp.30-2.
56 Veza Canetti, *The Tortoises*, pp.17-19, 31-5.
57 Veza Canetti, *The Tortoises*, pp.123-4.
58 Veza Canetti, *The Tortoises*, 12.
59 Veza Canetti, *The Tortoises*, pp.13-16.
60 Veza Canetti, *The Tortoises*, pp.16-17, 40-43.
61 Veza Canetti, *The Tortoises*, pp.50-1, 89, 99-100, 103, 109, 143-7, 177-181, 183.
62 Veza Canetti, *The Tortoises*, pp.184-5, 194.
63 Veza Canetti, *The Tortoises*, pp.195-8, 217-19, 225, 231.
64 Veza Canetti, *The Tortoises*, pp.23, 230-32.
65 Virginia Woolf, *A Room of One's Own and Three Guineas*, edited with introduction and notes by Michèle Barrett (Penguin Classics, London, 2011), p.290.
66 *Three Guineas*, pp.175, 227-8.
67 *Three Guineas*, pp.227-8.
68 *Three Guineas*, p.228.
69 *Three Guineas*, p.203.
70 *Three Guineas*, pp.204-205.
71 Ann Curthoys and John Docker, *Is History Fiction?* (University of Michigan Press, Ann Arbor, 2010), pp.53-54.
72 *Three Guineas*, p.205.
73 *Three Guineas*, p.233.
74 *Three Guineas*, p.233.
75 *Three Guineas*, pp.234-5.
76 Jonathan Swift, *Gulliver's Travels*, edited with an Introduction and Notes by Robert Demaria, Jr (Penguin Classics, London, 2003), pp.118-123.
77 *Three Guineas*, pp.194, 208, 235, also 295-6.
78 *Three Guineas*, photo of churchman in drag, facing p.246.
79 *Three Guineas*, p.232.
80 *Three Guineas*, p.243.
81 *Three Guineas*, p.245.

1938-9: In the Shadow of the Holocaust   565

82 *Three Guineas*, p.245.
83 *Three Guineas*, pp.249–50. In Galatians 3:28 King James Version, we read: 'There is neither Jew nor Greek, there is neither bond nor free, there is neither male nor female for ye are all one in Christ Jesus.'
84 *Three Guineas*, pp.250–251.
85 *Three Guineas*, pp.253–258.
86 *Three Guineas*, pp.246, 249.
87 *Three Guineas*, p.246.
88 *Three Guineas*, p.251.
89 *Three Guineas*, pp.231–2.
90 *Three Guineas*, p.240.
91 *Three Guineas*, pp.232, 235, 239.
92 *Three Guineas*, pp.235, 239.
93 *Three Guineas*, pp.235–6.
94 *Three Guineas*, pp.236–7.
95 *Three Guineas*, p.239.
96 *Three Guineas*, p.271.
97 Debjani Ganguly and John Docker (eds), *Rethinking Gandhi and Nonviolent Relationality: Global Perspectives* (Orient BlackSwan, Hyderabad, 2009), pp.21–22.
98 Leela Gandhi, 'Ahimsa and Other Animals: The Genealogy of an Immature Politics', p.22.
99 Leela Gandhi, 'Ahimsa and Other Animals: The Genealogy of an Immature Politics', p.23; also 41.
100 Leela Gandhi, 'Ahimsa and Other Animals: The Genealogy of an Immature Politics', pp.24–5.
101 Leela Gandhi, 'Ahimsa and Other Animals: The Genealogy of an Immature Politics', pp.25, 42–4.
102 Hermione Lee, *Virginia Woolf* (Vintage, New York, 1999), p.739.
103 Hannah Arendt, 'We Refugees', p.267.

26

The Holocaust and Jewish Communists in Australia 1943

In this chapter I reflect on my mother Elsie Levy as a Jewish Communist in relation to the agony of what Jews in Australia hoped they could do for Jews in Nazi-occupied Europe during World War II, how in any way so far away they could help. Among the small number of books that I inherited from her, I found an inner Communist Party document, a crumbling and yellowing typescript, undated but from internal evidence I'm inclined to think some time towards the middle of 1943. I'll explain why soon.

Why my mother kept the document I don't know given that I haven't a diary or letters she might have written at that time, but for me it is a precious inheritance, a window onto her World War II years when, married to Ted Docker a high Party official who was often away on Party matters, she was a young woman living in an apartment in Bondi, having children, and every day visiting her parents, my grandparents, a few streets away. The document was written, it becomes clear, by a Jewish Communist Party member in Melbourne where it was given as a spoken report, then sent to Sydney to be discussed by comrades there.

All along while writing this ego histoire I tucked away an idea, that I would have a chapter on this document as a tiny contribution I could make to Holocaust scholarship, focusing on a Jewish Communist document at a certain moment during World War II;

part of its interest, I thought, is that as an inner Party document it might reveal anxieties and admissions of mistakes and shortcomings that, I should imagine, the Communist Party would not have publicly revealed. For a long while I considered transcribing the whole document, but now I have turned my attention to it, it is immediately clear it is too long to do that, and I need instead to describe and quote selectively and interpret; and necessarily interpret from my own perspectives and historical consciousness in the present, as someone who had been in the New Left in the late 1960s and 1970s with its anarchist and pluralist ideals and actions, its liking for particular actions that don't cohere and may never cohere, its dislike of hierarchical organisation, its fissiparousness, its sort of centrifugal adventures.

What frequently baffles my New Left eyes now as I carefully read the document (I photocopied the original so that I could underline and highlight and scribble comments) is how much the Communist Party treasured the ideal of unity, a kind of metaphysics of unity that resulted in startling contradictions which the Party itself didn't seem to notice or be unduly troubled by. While the document is highly political as we might expect, I came across resonances that reminded me of the Central and Eastern European cultural worlds that I have earlier explored in this ego histoire, especially the Sydney Jewish Youth Theatre in the 1930s where I talk about the tensions between Arthur Schnitzler's fictional portrait of Fräulein Else and Freud's portrait of Ida Bauer as Dora; and also Ida Rubinstein, born in 1883 in St Petersburg, who was part of Diaghilev's Ballets Russes between 1909 and 1911 before breaking away and forming her own dance company.

Writing this chapter has been much more difficult than I had imagined it would be, indeed frequently perplexing to the point of being frankly vertiginous. I came across so many names and places and organisations of the past that I had never heard of, one puzzling example being, as the reader will see, 'Kuibyshev', which I initially thought was the name of a person until it transpired that it was a place somewhere in the Soviet Union. I found that for many references in the document I had to do backfilling in search of basic information, with shameless use of google and Wikipedia (a risk I know); for such backfilling I deployed square brackets, but sometimes found I had to use square brackets within square brackets. When I finished the draft I showed it to Ann, who said all my square bracket interpolations going every which way were making her head spin, and suggested that the best thing to do would be to let the reader in on what you are doing from the very beginning and why you're having to use all these square brackets. (Fancifully I think of an image lodged in my memory when in March-April 1919 Ann and I were in Japan and visited the famous Fushimi Inari-Taisha shrine near Kyota, where you climb a mountain through ever receding vermilion shrine gates.)

The 1943 document was divided into a Melbourne and Sydney part. Having once written *Australian Cultural Elites: Intellectual Traditions in Sydney and Melbourne*, musing on Sydney-Melbourne differences, I wonder about an old truism, that Jewishness in Melbourne with its large Polish Jewish population is much more intense than Jewishness in Sydney; could there be such an inflection here, I ponder; and maybe there is.

The Melbourne part of the document

The Melbourne part of the document consists of a number of sections with underlined titles. The opening section, 'The Jewish Communists: The Vanguard of the Jewish People', is prefaced by an epigraph, a quote from Engels: 'Besides we owe the Jews much, too much. Not to speak of Heine and Marx was of the purest Jewish blood.' The section reminds Party members of the central role of the Communist Party in history, for the Party is the 'vanguard of the working class' as it strives to abolish all class divisions and privileges in order to create an 'equal opportunity for the whole of the people to a prosperous and cultural life'. Similarly, the Jewish Communists are 'the vanguard of the Jewish people'; among 'all Jewish parties only they are capable of grasping the Jewish problem in its true light', by means of their 'scientific, Marxist analysis'; only they can 'show the way of solving this problem – the way of Socialism'.

In this 'deciding historical moment' Jewish Communists must 'work for the very survival of their people'. And it is not only 'physical resistance that matters in this struggle', for ever since their appearance the 'Nazis viciously and untiringly worked to demoralize, disrupt and disunite those peoples and nations against whom they were preparing their blow'; a moral and spiritual attack that 'must be answered by us, by a still stronger campaign for raising the morale of the Jewish people and welding them together into a unity of self confidence and defiance'. We must remind 'our people that for 2000 years we never refrained for one moment from contributing to human culture and progress':

> The mighty protest of the ancient Jewish prophets against injustice, oppression and wars! The philosophy of a Maimonides and Spinoza; a poet and courageous fighter against reaction like Heine; scientists like Hertz and Einstein...

Our people must know that in the past 'we fought and routed the Greek conquerors under the great leadership of the Maccabeans'; for '200 years we never stopped revolting against the Roman oppressors'; and under 'Bar Kochba and Rabbi Akiba' we fought a 'national battle of freedom unsurpassed'. In the present moment a 'million Jews are in the Red and Allied armies', thousands of Jews are 'in guerilla bands in Russia and Jugoslavia', and many thousands of 'Jewish fighters have been decorated for bravery like General Kreisler, Captain Fisanowitch in the Red Army and Ft. Lt. Isaacson and many others in the Allied armies'.

Let us spread among our people the knowledge that we 'have nothing to be ashamed of': 'the fact that it was largely due to the Jews that trade and commerce has survived during the darkest mediaeval centuries'; how under capitalism Jews have contributed to the development of trade and industry; and 'many industries have been introduced by Jews, in Australia for example'. We must keep in mind

> the sons of merchants and traders ameliorating malaria infected swamps in Palestine. Sometimes misguided, these heroic Chalutzim were always ready to sacrifice their lives for their people and have succeeded in constructing, in spite of antagonistic colonial administration of the country, a 500,000 strong Jewish community with all its cultural and other institutions developing in the direction of a Nation.

Merchants and traders of yesterday have been successfully taking part in the 'up-building of socialism in the U.S.S.R. as farmers, workers, scientists and intellectuals'; they have accomplished so much in the building of 'a Jewish Biro-Bidjan'.

[This last reference struck a distant tinkle concerning Soviet-era plans for autonomous regions; googling, it appears that Birobidzan, the Jewish Autonomous Region (oblast) in far eastern Russia, was established near the China-Russian border; conceived in 1928 as a home for the Jews in the Soviet Union, no mass Jewish migration developed, and Russian settlers now (as of 2019) heavily outnumber the remaining Yiddish-speaking Jews. Most of the population live along the two main lines of communication, the Trans-Siberian railroad and the navigable Amur River. I learn that there is a history by the admirable Masha Gessen telling the story of the failed experiment.]

Jewish Communists, the document continues, are the only party capable of reaching out and appealing to the 'whole' of the

Jewish people, for unlike 'all anti-zionists, we fully appreciate the importance of the national settlement in Palestine'; unlike the Zionists, 'we are also fully aware of the problems and worries of the rest of the Jewish community'; unlike the Yiddishists, 'we appreciate the great cultural value and importance of the Hebrew literature'; unlike 'many Hebraists, we are also proud of the young Yiddish literature', and unlike 'some self crowned atheists' we can see the 'progressive content of the Jewish tradition under its religious shell'.

Comrades should remember that Lenin wrote of the 'great progressive and universal characteristics of the Jewish culture, its internationalism'.

In 'Jews and Fascism', the document points out that Hitler's forces have suffered 'terrific losses on the Eastern front', the consequence of the 'heroic resistance of the Red Army and the Soviet peoples'; the oppressed peoples of Europe are organising 'military resistance and sabotage'. Conditions have been created where 'fascism could be defeated'. However, the Jews have been made 'the scapegoat' for these defeats. European Jewry was made to pay the 'penalty for Hitler's criminal policy': 'The cold-blooded extermination of the Jews had begun. Millions lost their lives. Striking at the Jews, Hitler was trying to eradicate all liberal and democratic ideas of the European people. But he made them bitter enemies.'

In 'Jews Fight Back', the document relates that the 'Jews, together with all the oppressed peoples of Europe, with all freedom-loving people the world over', continue to resist: 'In the armies of the U.S.S.R. and in Allied countries, in the battalions of Palestine, in the guerilla bands of the Soviet Union, Poland and Jugoslavia, the Jews are heroically defending their rights to a free life.' The 'heroic resistance of our brothers and sisters in the Warsaw ghetto against superior forces will live long' in the annals of peoples' 'fight for freedom'.

In Australia, too, we Jews are 'wholeheartedly behind the war effort of the Australian people and the Curtin Government': 'Thousands of our boys are in the army and the air force. Thousands are in the war industries producing arms for victory.'

In 'National Unity', the document argues that because fascism 'menaces the very existence of every Jew', the 'creation of national unity is our supreme task'. In the USA, England and Australia, the demand is growing for Jewish National unity. In Melbourne, the Council to combat Fascism and Anti-Semitism has the support of all Jewish organisations.

In 'Jewish Communists in the Forefront for Unity', the document reports that 'thanks to our clear policy and correct tactics, we have helped considerably to bring about National Unity', as shown in 'our co-operation with the Zionists on every available opportunity and with other branches of the Jewish community'. At the 1 May celebration at the Kadimah that we organised, 'we had on the same platform with Comrades J. D. Blake and O'Day, Mrs Wynn, the leader of the women's Zionist organization'.

At this point, I begin to encounter references to people, organisations, and events that are quite unfamiliar. The document admits at this point that there are groups that the Jewish Communists have not been able to or don't wish to include in the National Unity they are helping to create, especially the Bundists. We have only 'partially succeeded in our task, even against the disruptive tactics of the Bund':

> When the Bund took up the matter of Ehrlich-Alter executed in the Soviet Union for conducting an anti-Soviet campaign, aiming at splitting the progressive forces, we exposed their lies in a leaflet and at a public meeting. We have succeeded in isolating this group, but our fight against them and others has not finished. We have to work hard in playing our part to bring about complete unity amongst Melbourne Jewry as well as all Jews in the Commonwealth.

Over afternoon coffee I tell Ann about the document's denunciation of the Bund, about which we know little but understand as an independent Polish socialist movement, and its condemnation of 'Ehrlich-Alter'; we stare at each other, we've never heard of 'Ehrlich-Alter'. Ann googles on her i-pad, and reads out an account from Wikipedia, which relates that Henryk Ehrlich (b. 1882) was an activist of the Bund, member of the Petrograd Soviet, Warsaw City Council and the executive committee of the Second International. His father-in-law was noted Jewish historian Simon Dubnow. Victor Alter (b. 1890) was a Jewish socialist activist and publicist for the Bund.

I have to confess at this point that what happened to Ehrlich and Alter during the war I find especially perplexing. I decide to focus on Henryk Ehrlich, to go more into who he was, and why was he executed in the Soviet Union? This exploration will involve many boxes within boxes. Wikipedia says Henryk Ehrlich was an activist in the social-democratic movement in 1904; during the 1917 Russian Revolution he was a member of the Petrograd Soviet executive committee, and of a delegation to England, France and Italy.

After the outbreak of World War II, Ehrlich [sometimes Erlich] made his way to the part of Poland that had come under Soviet control. This was an accident of history, of the dismembering of Poland between Germany and the Soviet Union: when western Poland was occupied by the Nazis, Ehrlich made his way to eastern Poland, with perilous and fatal consequences. He was arrested by the NKVD on 4 October 1939. On 2 August 1940 he was sentenced to death, but the sentence was later commuted to 10 years in the Gulag. After the June 1941 German invasion of the Soviet Union, he was released as part of an agreement between the Soviet Union and the Polish Government in Exile. However, on 4 December 1941, Ehrlich was once again arrested by the NKVD, as was Victor Alter. At the time they both resided in the Polish embassy, and no reason was given for their arrest. The Soviet imprisonment of two prominent socialist activists and leaders of the Second International caused a wave of protests among socialist circles in the West. Eleanor Roosevelt and Albert Einstein made direct appeals to Stalin for their release. However, Soviet authorities remained quiet throughout 1942, and only after the Soviet victory at Stalingrad, 2 February 1943, announced that Ehrlich and Alter had been executed on Stalin's orders.

While the exact place where they are buried is unknown, a cenotaph was erected at the Jewish cemetery on Okopowa street in Warsaw on 17 April 1988. The inscription reads, 'Leaders of the Bund, Henryk Ehrlich, b.1882, and Wiktor Alter, b.1890. Executed in the Soviet Union.' The monument was opposed by Poland's post-war communist government and was only made possible because of the efforts of Marek Edelman (last surviving participant in the Warsaw Ghetto Uprising and a Bundist) and members of the Polish Solidarity Union. The commemoration ceremony was attended by over 3000 people.

On 8 February 1991 Victor Ehrlich, Henryk Ehrlich's son, was informed that according to a decree passed under Russian president Boris Yeltsin, Henryk Ehrlich and Victor Alter had been 'rehabilitated' and the 'repressions' against them had been declared unlawful.

I then googled Simon Dubnow, a name I had heard of, perhaps in relation to my interest in the philosopher Martin Buber, well known for his advocacy of a binational future for Palestine.[1] I noted the following.

The historian and activist Simon Dubnow (1860 – 1941), was one of the first and major proponents of Jewish Autonomism, a non-Zionist political movement and ideology that emerged in Eastern Europe in the late 19th century and early 20th. Jewish Autonomism is often referred to as 'Dubnovism' or 'folkism'. The Autonomists believed that the future survival of the Jews as a nation depends on their developing 'spiritual nationhood' and the viability of Jewish diaspora, as long as Jewish communities maintain self-rule and reject assimilation. Autonomists often stressed the vitality of modern Yiddish culture. Various concepts of Autonomism were adopted in the platform of the Bund. Autonomism and 'folkism' influenced Martin Buber and his collecting of Hasidic legends and folk tales.

While living in Latvia, in Riga, Dubnow was among 25 000 Jews killed in the Rumbula massacre, carried out by the Einsatzgruppe on 30 November and 8 December 1941. His legendary last words before being shot were: 'If you survive, never forget what is happening here.'

If Henryk Erhlich was married to Simon Dubnow's daughter, who was she, what was her name? (Idly I thought of Sophia Tolstoya.) Again I googled, and was delighted to find an entry for Sophia Dubnow-Erlich in the Encyclopedia of Jewish Women by Carole B Balin, who narrates her life in ways that remind me of powerful female figures generally in European cultural and intellectual history, not least Ida Rubinstein. Balin narrates Sophia's political and cultural life, suffused with tragedy.

Balin writes that although she has been typically cast as either the daughter of the historian Simon Dubnow or the wife of the Bundist leader Henryk Erlich, Sophia Dubnow-Erlich was a poet, political activist, critic, translator and memoirist in her own right. Her literary corpus charts one Eastern European Jewish woman's entry into two very disparate spheres of activity. Over a lifetime spanning 101 years (44 in the US), Sophia Dubnow-Erlich engaged in Jewish socialist party politics on the one hand, and Russian Silver Age poetry on the other.

Balin tells us that Sophia, born 9 March 1885 in Belarus, was the eldest child of Simon and Ida (Friedlin) Dubnow. In 1902 she studied at the Bestuzhev Higher Courses in St Petersburg, a four-year degree program equivalent to that of the university, offered to women with parental permission and an annual tuition of 50 rubles. In 1904 university officials expelled her from her courses for participating in a student protest. Undeterred, she entered the history-philology department of St Petersburg University in 1905 and later studied comparative religion and the history of world literature at the Sorbonne (1910–11).

In 1911, Balin continues, Sophia married Henryk Erlich. In deed and in printed word, Balin observes, the couple worked to promote the ideals of Jewish cultural autonomy and socialist internationalism. Dubnow-Erlich wrote for various Bund journals during World War I and the Russian Revolution. By 1918, the political situation drove Dubnow-Erlich and her husband to relocate to Warsaw, where they remained for over 20 years with their sons, Alexander and Victor. When Warsaw fell to the Nazis in 1939 and the family moved eastwards, Henryk Erlich was arrested by Soviet authorities; Dubnow-Erlich moved her family to Vilna, where they lived until 1941. When she reached the US in 1942 she learned of her husband's death by Stalin and her father's murder by the Nazis. Dubnow-Erlich remained politically active in her new land, advocating for civil rights and protesting against the Vietnam War.

Balin concludes by relating that Sophia Dubnow-Erlich died on 4 May 1986 in New York. Her fascinating life and extensive literary oeuvre of varied genres, which has not yet been translated into English (except for her biography of Simon Dubnow), deserves, Balin feels, the full attention of students of history and literature alike, for the tapestry of her life is woven into the very fabric of Eastern European Jewish history of the twentieth century.

Intrigued by the reference in Balin's moving essay to the Silver Age of Russian Poetry, I once again google. I learn that the Silver Age, so named in the 1960s, is applied to the last decade of the nineteenth century and first two or three decades of the twentieth, a *fin de siècle* period which was exceptionally creative in literature, music and art. An early major figure was Alexander Blok and his collection of Symbolist poems *Verses to the Beautiful Lady* (1904). The Silver Age featured the artistic movements of Russian Symbolism, Acmeism and Russian Futurism, also the Mystical Anarchism tendency within the Symbolist movement. The literary careers of Anna Akhmatova, Boris Pasternak and Osip Mandelshtam were launched during this period, and there were connections with the surrealist art of Marc Chagall.

I come across more references to Henryk Ehrlich and Victor Alter soon, which I struggle to understand.

I return to the document. In 'United Emergency Committee for European Jewry', a committee active in 1943, the document admits that Communist Jews have at times had to catch up to actions initiated by others. The Zionists had called the first meeting of the committee and the Jewish Communists joined in: 'We knew that they want to make political capital out of the plight of European Jewry for their own aims, but we were correct in assuming that, if such a meeting took place, we will be able to broaden its aims, enlarge its objectives'. We have succeeded in our task: 'On the new executive, all political tendencies of Melbourne Jewry are represented.'

In 'Council to Combat Fascism and Anti-Semitism', the document relates that Jewish Communists have established contact with many of the members of the council from its inception; the council has performed a great service to the Jewish community by 'stressing the fascist character of anti-semitism' and bringing before the public the 'facts about Jews in Australia and of the world'.

Next comes another moment of self-criticism. In 'Kuibyshev Appeal' the document admits to a failure of leadership: 'Comrades, we must state frankly that we have failed to give a correct lead to this appeal. We were not vigilant enough against disruptive elements that took the lead.' Although the 'disruptive elements' are not named, this could be an allusion to the Bundists, though if it were the Bundists, why wasn't this spelled out as it was in other places in the document? 'After all, it is one of our main functions to strengthen the bonds of friendship between Australian Jews and the Jews of the Soviet Union. The Kuibyshev Appeal could have performed that task. At the first meeting, delegates from all political parties and organisations were present, but we failed to give a clear lead... [we] have still much to learn to be more vigilant and more bold. The duty of the comrades is to help this appeal.'

Reading this section I wondered what was the Kuibyshev Appeal, and found in a Wikipedia entry that the Appeal featured the 'Jewish Anti-Fascist Committee', in which, it turns out, Henryk Erlich and Victor Alter were prominent early on, though not for long. The Appeal was designed to influence international public opinion and organise political and materiel support, particularly from the West, for the Soviet fight against Nazi Germany.

The Wikipedia entry says that the Jewish Anti-Fascist Committee (JAC) was organised by the Jewish Bund leaders Henryk Erlich and Victor Alter, upon an initiative of Soviet authorities, in the fall of 1941; both were released from prison in connection with their participation. Following their re-arrest in December 1941, the Committee was reformed on Stalin's orders in Kuibyshev in April 1942. It looks like Stalin used Ehrlich and Alter to establish the JAC and the Appeal to the West, and then discarded and executed them. New people were then appointed to convey the Appeal to the West.

Solomon Mikhoels, a popular actor and director of the Moscow State Jewish Theatre, was appointed JAC chairman. The JAC broadcast pro-Soviet propaganda to foreign audiences, assuring them of the absence of antisemitism in the Soviet Union.[2] In mid-1943, Mikhoels and Itzik Feffer, the first official representatives of Soviet Jewry allowed to visit the West, embarked on a seven-month tour to the US, Mexico, Canada and the UK to increase support for the Lend-Lease. Wikipedia notes that the Lend-Lease policy, formally titled An Act to Promote the Defense of the United States, enacted 11 March 1941, was an American program to defeat Germany, Japan and Italy by distributing food, oil and materiel between 1941 and 6 August 1945 (when the US dropped the atom bomb on Hiroshima). The aid went to the UK, China and later the Soviet Union, Free France and other Allied nations. It included warships and warplanes, along with other weaponry. The program was under the direct control of the White House, with Roosevelt paying close attention, assisted by Harry Hopkins, W Averell Harriman and Edward Stettinius Jr. Roosevelt often sent them on special missions to London and Moscow. A total of $50.1 billion, equivalent to $565 billion in 2018, 11% of the total war expenditure of the US, was involved.

In the US Mikhoels and Feffer were welcomed by a National Reception Committee chaired by Albert Einstein and B Z Goldberg, Sholom Aleichem's son-in-law, and the American Jewish Joint Distribution Committee. The largest pro-Soviet rally ever held in the US occurred on 8 July at the Polo Grounds, where 50 000 people listened to Mikhoels, Feffer, Fiorello H LaGuardia, Sholem Ash and Rabbi Stephen Samuel Wise, Chairman of the World Jewish Congress. Among others, they met Chaim Weizmann, Charlie Chaplin, Marc Chagall, Paul Robeson and Lion Feuchtwanger.

In addition to the funds for the Soviet war effort – US$16 million raised in the US, $15 million in England, $1 million in Mexico, $750,000 in Mandatory Palestine – other assistance was also contributed: machinery, medical equipment, medicine, ambulances, clothes. On 16 July *Pravda* reported: 'Mikhoels and Feffer received a message from Chicago that a special conference of the Joint initiated a campaign to finance a thousand ambulances for the needs of the Red Army.'

In 'Kuibyshev Appeal' there is no mention of the large pro-Soviet rally as there surely would have been if the Communist Party in Australia had heard about it; I'm therefore deducing the obvious, that the document was produced before 8 July 1943, that is, between the Soviet victory in Stalingrad of 2 February 1943 and early July 1943, and perhaps not that long before early July 1943.

In 'Our Work in Jewish Cultural Organisations', the document is pleased that Jewish Communists continue to take an active part in the Kadimah cultural centre, where 'our comrades spoke with Zionists and others' on important occasions. However, the Bundists are still a worrying presence: the Kadimah is an 'important rallying center of Melbourne Jewry and our task was to work there for Jewish unity against disrupters like the Bund, who want to use [the] Kadimah platform for anti-Soviet and anti-unity activities'.

In 'Jews and the Party', the document reports on some internal difficulties within the Jewish Communists that are hindering proper work. Let us, says the document, be 'quite candid':

> Many of the Jewish comrades don't like to work among Jews; they believe rightly or wrongly that they can do better in general party work, that they have no special duty to work among Jews. In many cases this may be so, but in most instances, it is an evasion of our duty towards the Jewish people, it is an evasion of our duty as party comrades.

Such comrades are rebuked for failing the Jewish people in their hour of greatest need: 'Comrades, in this historic moment, our main task is to mobilise all our forces for the defeat of fascism. The Jewish people, [whose] very existence depends on the outcome of this struggle, can and should be on the vanguard of this fight against fascism. Conditions exist in Australia for Jewish National unity; therefore it is the duty of every Jewish community to assist in this work.' It is our task to 'mobilise the Jewish people in the fight against fascism. By uniting the Jewish people we communists will perform our duty to the party and to our people.'

[In the course of this reproach to some Party members, the author refers to her or himself as 'me', but I can't see any name or initials at the end of the Melbourne section of the document; presumably the Sydney comrades who received the document knew who the author was.]

In 'Party Recruiting', the document notes that 'many Jews sympathise with our movement', but 'we are still working under the old conceptions – to recruit only 100% communists; comrades, this will not do. Our task is to increase our ranks by bringing in sympathisers, people near the party; and it is up to us to make them good communists.' The document then mentions that the 'on-coming executive will have the task of starting a membership drive'.

In 'Women and Youth', the document confesses: 'We also failed to give any attention to women or youth. We have many capable Jewish women comrades performing good party work, and while our party is bringing forward women to many leading positons, we Jewish communists still persist in old methods, despite the fact that our ranks have been depleted by military call-ups and by our share in war industries.' The document expresses concern that 'work amongst Jewish youth has been entirely neglected', noting that the 'new executive will have the task to build up women and youth organization'.

In 'Our Stand towards Palestine', the document returns to the question of Palestine and attitudes to and relations with Zionism. 'Are we', the document asks, 'justified to overlook Palestine, just because we have certain disagreements with the Zionists? Are all the Jews in Palestine Zionists? Not at all!' The document notes that outside the USSR 'Palestine is one of the most important centres of Jewish life', developing in the direction of 'a Jewish nation with its own territory and language, its own economy and national makeup'. In a short period of 20 years, 'cities grew where sands were before, agricultural settlements sprang up where malaria was taking heavy toll of human life, industry developed that is contributing to the war effort and to defeat of fascism'. Recall, the document continues, that the 'Jews of Palestine were the first to render help and assistance to the Red Army and Soviet peoples', for they 'realized that the Red Army saved Palestine from invasion by its heroic defence of Odessa, Sebastopol and Stalingrad'.

The 'Palestinian community', then, is an 'integral part of the Jewish people', and it is 'our duty to see that the Jews in Palestine are not hindered in their development'; in Palestine, 'we have a community of 600,000 Jews with its own workers, heavy and light industries, its own farmers', an economy that is 'employing tens of thousands of Jewish workers'.

'We are', the document affirms, 'against the White Paper. We demand to open the doors of Palestine so that thousands of Jews can be saved from extermination.' [Wikipedia relates that the White Paper of 1939 was a policy paper issued by the British government under Neville Chamberlain in response to the 1936–39 Arab Revolt. The White Paper called for the establishment of a Jewish national home in an independent Palestinian state within 10 years, while rejecting the idea of partitioning Palestine. It limited Jewish immigration to 75 000 for five years, and ruled that further immigration was to be determined by the Arab majority. Restrictions were put on the rights of Jews to buy land from Arabs. Zionist groups in Palestine immediately rejected the White Paper. In circumstances where Jewish refugees from Europe were fleeing violence and persecution, the White Paper's limits were relaxed and legal immigration was permitted to continue indefinitely at the rate of 18 000 a year.]

The document notes the importance of good relations with the Arabs of Palestine: 'Comrades, we are against the suicidal policy of non co-operation with the Arabs. We are sure that the Arabs and the Jews can co-operate and live happily together', for: 'Co-operation between Arabs and Jews in Palestine is our aim.' [It is not clear here who in the opinion of the document is putting forward or practising 'the suicidal policy of non co-operation with the Arabs'. In an essay of 2013 in the collection of essays *Sovereignty: Frontiers of Possibility*, I refer to Hans Kohn in 1929, in a letter 'Zionism is not Judaism', explaining why he has become so disillusioned with mainstream political Zionism; he reflects that the Zionist goal of establishing a nation in Palestine is leading to 'conflict with the Arabs' and that the Zionist movement has not even once made a serious attempt at seeking through negotiations the consent of the indigenous people to Zionist plans, rather relying exclusively upon Great Britain's military might. Hans Kohn was a friend of Martin Buber, who, a decade later, in a 1938 essay 'Keep Faith!', deplored the rise of Jewish terrorism in the late 1930s and a general sanctioning of violence by the Zionist leadership.][3]

In 'Our Stand towards Zionism', the penultimate section, the document states its opinion of Zionism as a movement and worldview:

> Zionism is a political movement aiming at building a Jewish state in Palestine as the only solution to the Jewish problem. Although the Jewish community in Palestine is only a small fragment of the Jewish people and Palestine cannot absorb all the Jews (and not all want to go there) now or after the war; nevertheless, the Zionists believe that a Jewish state in Palestine can solve the Jewish problem all over the world.[4]

The document argues contrariwise: 'We say to the Jewish people that as long as fascism and capitalism exist, they cannot be free and their problems will always exist. Only a socialist world based on equality and justice can and will solve the Jewish problem.'

Then follows an urgent listing of key points.

> Our demands will be:
> 1. Equal rights for Jews in countries in which they live, whether natural born or 'new' Australians.
> 2. The right to strengthen the Jewish community in Palestine. The right to immigration, freedom of construction and development.
> 3. The right to Jewish emigration to other countries.
>
> The Zionists concentrate all their main activities on Palestine, hoping for an allied victory. We communists believe that Palestine cannot be the only solution of the Jewish problem.
>
> But at the present time, the activities are also devoted towards the war effort, towards saving the Jews from occupied countries, against the White Paper – all progressive aims – we have a basis of common activities with them.

In 'Towards Victory', which completes the Melbourne section, the document declares:

> Comrades, you have heard our report. Great responsibilities rest on our shoulders. We have the task to mobilise all forces for the final defeat of fascism. Together with our non-Jewish comrades, we are fighting for a better world.
>
> In the name of suffering humanity; in the name of millions of killed people: in the name of millions of slaughtered Jews;
>
> We demand that a second front be opened in 1943.
>
> Glory to our brothers and sisters who so heroically resisted the fascist invaders.
>
> Glory to our Jewish fighters in the armies of freedom.
>
> Long live the Red Army.
>
> Long live the Unity of the Allied nations.
>
> Long live Jewish unity!

The Sydney part of the document

The 'Report of the Council of Jewish Communists, Sydney' is shorter, and, it strikes me, is occasionally rather defensive as it attempts to respond to the points made by the Melbourne report.

It begins with 'Work amongst Jewish Youth', stressing, 'We believe this sector of our activities to be of great importance and that Sydney should be in the leadership of this'. Although most of our 'young members are quite new to the party', they have shown a 'certain amount of independence' in their activities and can record 'successes'. Through 'guidance', the 'Jewish youth' are becoming an 'organized, integral part of the Australian Youth movement, through their affiliation with non-Jewish organisations'. The Party encourages their active struggle against anti-Semitism, and working for 'speedy victory in this war as an organized Jewish youth', and by such activities 'to find ways and means of the unity of Jewish youth for the whole of Australia'.

In 'Work Amongst Yiddish Speaking', 'we cannot record many successes here' amongst Yiddish-speaking groups: 'The reasons are manifold and show our weaknesses. We will have to devote more time and energy to it, but the main task will be to have the support of the Yiddish speaking comrades of the executive.'

In 'Support for the Soviet Union', the document notes that its main task in this regard is to 'organise the Jewish population for closer collaboration with the Jewish anti-fascist committee in Kuibyshev (USSR)', whose 'appeals have found a deep response amongst all sections of Jews the world over', and in Sydney there is 'much work to be done in uniting all Jews round this.'

In 'Political Campaigns', the document stresses, as had the Melbourne part, the desirability of working with the Zionists: 'At the recent conference of the Zionists of Australia and New Zealand, we have sent our congratulations, detailing 6 points which we think would form the basis for unity amongst the Jews at present.' (The document does not say what the 6 points are.)

'Educational Work' reports that unfortunately a 'regular class on the National and Jewish problems' was 'discontinued owing to lack of attendance due to overtime, activities in their respective branches and zones, and in different organisations'. Nonetheless, the document believes that the 'question of education and especially a Marxist analysis of the Jewish problem is of great importance at present'.

'Discussion of General Jewish Problems' re-affirms that of 'considerable importance' is the 'clarification of our attitude to present time Zionism'. A number of discussions on this problem have been held, and the Sydney comrades 'have prepared a circular on Zionism': 'We have pointed out that the Jewish settlements in Palestine and Zionism are two separate problems. The Jewish settlement in Palestine we consider as a positive, constructive work of the Jewish people, and the results achieved there, we attribute, not to the Zionists only, but a number of objective developments in the life of the Jewish people as a whole.'

'The Communist Party in Palestine' comments on the implications of a new development, that after the 'dissolution of the Comintern, the Communist Party in Palestine was divided into two National groups, a Jewish and an Arab group. We held discussions about the work of the separate groups.' [The Comintern, which had been founded on 2 March 1919, was dissolved on 15 May 1943.] The task of the 'Arab communists' was to 'work among the Arab people for unity against the Axis' and to 'point out the possible benefits for the Arab population from the Jewish immigration there'. The 'tasks of the Jewish communists will be to strengthen Jewish unity, to break down all prejudices and opposition by the Jews towards the Arab problems there, to keep up the good work of the Jews there for closer unity with the Jews of the Soviet Union'.

In 'General Problems' the document briefly reports, without any comment, that a number of 'quite important' problems were discussed, including 'The Kimberlays'. The document here appears to be referring to a plan for Jewish colonisation in the Kimberleys in north west Australia, its leading figure I N Steinberg, who published in 1948, after the failure of the scheme, *Australia: The Unpromised Land*. Steinberg had suggested the plan in 1939 on behalf of the London-based and non-Zionist Freeland League for Jewish Territorial Colonization. Contemporary historiography has been critical of Steinberg's late 1930s and early 1940s plan, highlighting its settler colonialist aims. In the conclusion to an essay, 'Orientalism and Zionism: Dismantling Leon Uris's *Exodus*', first published in *Arena* no.75 in 1986 and reprinted with added commentary in *Arena Journal* in 2012 (New Series, no.37/38), I suggest, drawing on Maxime Rodinson's *Israel: A Colonial-Settler State?*, that the Zionists in Palestine, and non-Zionists such as Steinberg in north west Australia, like other Europeans from the late nineteenth century through the twentieth and into the twenty first, considered that any territory outside Europe was open to European occupation, not because it might lack actual inhabitants but because it was held to be culturally barren and hence an empty space suitable for colonisation.[5]

Recall that in his Epilogue to *An Unpromised Land*, its sub-title on the front cover asking the question, *Australia's north-west – a new Homeland?* (1993), Leon Gettler suggests that in the area chosen by Steinberg and the Freeland League for Jewish Territorial Colonization, Aboriginal living conditions were 'appalling', and if successful their Kimberleys settlement would have been 'just as likely to further devastate Aboriginal culture in the region by displacing black Australians'. Gettler also notes that the problems facing the Aborigines 'did not rate a mention in the planning of the Kimberley project' and that while the Freeland League regarded the region as ideal because it was viewed as sparsely populated, 'the fact remains that black Australians were there in significant numbers and an area marked "Aboriginal Reserve" lay at the south-eastern border of the proposed land purchase'.⁶

Alexandra Ludewig also explores the settler coloniser implications of Steinberg's Kimberley plans in relation to Indigenous peoples in her essay 'Isaac Steinberg in Australien: Der Traum von einer jüdischen Kolonie in West – und Nordaustralien', *Zeitschrift für Australienstudien*/ 'Isaac Steinberg in Australia: Dreaming of Jewish Colonies in Northern and Western Australia', *Journal of Australian Studies*, no.31, 2017, pp.73-4.

From the single mention of 'The Kimberlays' in the document we don't know what the attitudes of Communist Jews in Australia and the Communist Party in general in the late 1930s and early 1940s were to Steinberg's proposed colonisation in north west Australia, in an area owned by the settler-coloniser Durack family; if Steinberg's plan had been accepted, there would have been a double colonisation. What is well known, however, is that Tom Wright, Federal President of the Sheet Metal Workers' Union and a longstanding member of the Communist Party, published a passionate book *New Deal for the Aborigines* in 1939; it was endorsed by the Labor Council of NSW and published in Sydney. A cross between a Zolaesque *J'accuse* and a manifesto for urgent change, *New Deal for the Aborigines* reviews the disastrous effects of white settlement on Aboriginal society. It calls for the protection of 'full-blood Aborigines' and their culture; the creation of non-missionary tribal reserves; inalienable tribal lands; and the right of Aborigines to control social change and economic development.

In June 1944 Katharine Susannah Prichard, a founding member of the Communist Party of Australia, wrote an equally passionate Foreword for the Second Edition of *New Deal for the Aborigines*. Prichard deploys a 'scientific' Marxist framework of social evolution, that the 'progress of humanity' demands the 'development of this country' rather than it continue to be the 'vast hunting ground of scattered tribes of primitive people'.

Nonetheless, 1944 was also the year that Raphaël Lemkin created the term 'genocide' in his *Axis Rule in Occupied Europe*.[7] Prichard uses terms that anticipate Lemkin's concept. 'Most Australians', her Foreword began, 'are conscious of shame in connection with our treatment of the Aborigines'; alluding to a history of massacres that reminds me of Lyndall Ryan's famous digital Massacre Map which went online on 5 July 2017, Prichard refers to stories of 'atrocities committed by pioneering settlers against the native races', which have 'aroused horror and condemnation', and led to 'the original inhabitants… in their own land' being 'dispossessed'. We must 'atone for disgraceful apathy in the past', and ensure 'practical measures for saving' the 'remnant' of Aborigines who have survived 'extermination' and 'extinction'.

Opposing dispossession, extinction and extermination, a 'stain on the record of Australia as a self-governing State', we must recognise, Prichard writes, the necessity 'not only of reserves for full-blooded Aborigines, but also of a new ideal for people of mixed blood'.[8]

In her Foreword, Prichard quotes Marx to the effect that 'the native races know us chiefly by our crimes'. (I'm not sure where in Marx this wonderful quote, a kind of proverb, comes from. I asked Ann to do some sleuthing, and she has come up with some fascinating clues. The Quaker historian William Howitt, in his *Colonization and Christianity: A Popular History of the Treatment of the Natives by the Europeans in All their Colonies*, published in 1838 at the height of humanitarianism, wrote: 'We talk of the heathen, the savage, and the cruel, and the wily tribes, that fill the rest of the earth; but how is that these tribes know us? Chiefly by the very features that we attribute exclusively to them. They know us chiefly by our crimes and our cruelty.' Howitt's book, Ann says, is quoted approvingly in Marx's *Capital*, Vol.1, chapter 31, Marx commenting that the 'barbarities and desperate outrages of the so-called Christian race, throughout every region of the world, and upon every people they have been able to subdue, are not to be paralleled by those of any other race, however fierce, however untaught, and however reckless of mercy and of shame, in any age of the earth'. In this context, Marx refers to both plantation colonies and settler colonies.)]

In the Sydney part of the document, after the brief mention of 'The Kimberlays' in 'General Problems', there follows a section headed 'Publications', which lists publications by the group in the form of circulars, once more focusing on Zionism:

1. The History of the Zionist movement, with an analysis of its political trends.
2. Report on and evaluation of the last Zionist Conference of Australia and New Zealand.
3. Our attitude towards Zionism.

'The Distribution of Our Literature', the final section of the document, reports rather forlornly that, 'This presents a difficult problem, as the Jews in Sydney are not concentrated in one or more districts and the number of Jewish meetings is very small. We are trying to solve this problem.'

Some General Reflections

As I contemplate this 1943 inner party document now, in May 2019, a number of things stand out.

One aspect I find so curious that I mention it to Ann for its blatant contradictoriness. The document says that as a priority Communist Jews always strive for 'unity', indeed 'complete unity', of the Jewish people. Yet the document repeatedly and angrily scorns Bundists for being anti-Soviet, and therefore being splitters and disrupters who must be 'isolated' by a meeting held against them and a leaflet denouncing them, especially condemning the way the Bundists criticise the Soviet Union for executing Ehrlich and Alter. So, in the view of the document, 'complete unity' of the Jewish people involves excluding the Bundists and unnamed 'others' who are also presumably critical of the Soviet Union.

In terms of the document, then, support for the Soviet Union is an absolute, presumably an absolute since the beginning of the Communist Party of Australia in 1919 (and the establishment in that year of the Comintern as the international link with the Soviet Union.) However, there is a particular wartime context here, that at a certain point in World War II it was only the Soviet Union that was militarily opposing Hitler's forces as in the Battle of Stalingrad; that's why the document calls for a second front to be opened up by allied forces in the west against Germany. Joseph Stalin was held to be universally popular, his genial image appearing on the cover of magazines internationally (the Australian *Women's Weekly* had a cover in 1945, in colour, Stalin's face with pipe, looking avuncular). Nonetheless, in socialist circles there was anger around the world that Stalin had ordered the execution of the Polish Bundists Ehrlich and Alter, including by Eleanor Roosevelt and Einstein. For the Party, however, any criticism of the Soviet Union was to be met with exclusion from the 'unity' that was so valued and sought, the 'unity' where the Communist Party would be at the forefront, the vanguard, leading.

There is also anxiety throughout the document when the Party in certain situations realises that it is not leading.

Over and over the document wrestles with the problem of how to relate to Zionism, evidently becoming increasingly prominent in Jewish life. As Marxist internationalists, the writers of the document, its Melbourne and Sydney sections, are baffled by what they see as Zionism's singleness of purpose, that there is only one historical path for world Jewry to follow, and that is to promote the Jewish settlement in Palestine: 'the Zionists believe that a Jewish state in Palestine can solve the Jewish problem all over the world'. Yet the Jewish Communists find it necessary to support the Zionists, they are eager to cooperate with them in joint endeavours, catch up with them when they take the initiative.

In contrast to the Zionists, the document makes it clear, also repeatedly, that the Jewish Communists could never work with the Bundists. The Bundists were intensely disliked by the Party and always characterised negatively as splitters and disrupters, meaning that the Bund was never recognised as a constructive force in its own terms. Where the Zionists are explained as having ideals and purposes, there is no such acknowledgement for the Bundists.

I find the document's stance on Palestine disturbing. I try to understand it. Why did the document so enthusiastically support the settler-colonial belief that the land of Palestine was barren, was sand and swamp that needed to be made productive by the agricultural skills and establishment of industry of the incoming Jewish settlers? Any kind of admirable productivity by the Palestinian Arabs was invisible to the writers of the document; the document reports that two Communist Party branches, a Jewish branch and an Arab branch, were formed, and what the Arab branch should do was inform the Palestinians of all the things that the Jewish settlers were doing that would improve their lives; there is no acknowledgement or interest in anything the Palestinians could do for the Jewish settlement, nor, apart from the mention of 'Arab problems', is there any interest in Palestinian society except that it would be wise to seek an amicable relationship.

I think again of my essay 'The Two-State Solution and Partition: World History Perspectives on Palestine and India' that I wrote for *Holy Land Studies* in 2010, where I evoke Walid Khalidi in his Introduction to *From Haven to Conquest: Readings in Zionism and the Palestine Problem until 1948* (1971), pointing out that in 1942 Jewish land ownership stood only at 5.9 percent of the total area of Palestine. In the desert area of the Negev, Khalidi notes, the beduins grew most of the barley and much of the wheat produced in the country; if, Khalidi writes, there was any blooming in the desert, this was the work of the wretchedly poor beduins, for the area put by the beduins under cultivation in the Negev was three times the total area cultivated by the entire Jewish community in Palestine. Despite all the talk, Khalidi concludes of Zionist claims, the Jews simply did not make the desert bloom.[9]

One reason why the writers of the document so welcomed what they saw as Jewish success in Palestine relates, I think, to their Marxism, especially to the Marxist notion of history as stadial, going through necessary stages before socialism can be reached; a social evolutionary framework visible in Katharine Susannah Prichard's 1944 Foreword. In Ann and my *Is History Fiction?* we point out that Marx was interested in different modes of history, one of which concerns change over a long duration, coinciding with the evolution and history of humanity itself, expressed most clearly in Marx's preface to *A Contribution to the Critique of Political Economy* (1859). The preface argues that we can see in history a sequence of epochal changes from ancient communal forms to feudalism to capitalism; Marx constructs a linear movement in history, a logic whereby one system, or mode of production, gives way to another and then another leading to capitalism and finally, it could be predicted and hoped, to socialism and communism.[10]

In these terms, we can see the document as perceiving and welcoming in the Jewish settlement in Palestine a linear sequence from its Arab condition, feudal and static, into a dynamic capitalist industrial phase of history, in a sequence and logic that goes from the feudal to the capitalist and then, necessarily or at least hopefully, to the socialist. In this sequence and logic, the Indigenous Palestinians belong to the past, the Jewish proto-nation in Palestine to the present and future.

In the immediate context of the Holocaust in 1943 the document agrees with Jews worldwide that the White Paper restricting immigration must be urgently set aside as emigration from Nazi occupied Europe is desperately necessary. In 'Our stand towards Palestine', the writer urges: 'Palestine gave refuge to nearly a quarter of a million Jews from fascist hell, thousands of children from occupied Europe find new homes and a chance to live once more a normal life... We are against the White paper. We demand to open the doors of Palestine so that thousands of Jews can be saved from extermination.'

1 John Docker, 'The Two-State Solution and Partition: World History Perspectives on Palestine and India', *Holy Land Studies*, Vol.9, no.2, 2010, pp.147–168; 'Dissident Voices on the History of Palestine-Israel: Martin Buber and the Bi-national Idea, Walid Khalidi's Indigenous Perspective', in Julie Evans, Ann Genovese, Alexander Reilly, and Patrick Wolfe (eds), *Sovereignty: Frontiers of Possibility* (University of Hawai'i Press, Honolula, 2013), pp.86–116.

2 On 29 September 2015, I gave a talk entitled 'Australian Jewish communists and the question of Soviet anti-Semitism: some ego-history reflections on my mother, Elsie Docker née Levy', for an International Symposium: Judging the Past in a Post Cold War World, Monday 28 September-Tuesday 29 September 2015, University of Sydney. Here I refer to the Doctors' Plot, an anti-Semitic purge staged by Stalin in 1953 in the last year of his life. Isaac Deutscher wrote in an essay 'The Russian Revolution and the Jewish Problem' in his *The Non-Jewish Jew* (pp.82–83), that the 'whole world was treated to a sordid spectacle' when nine professors of medicine, employed as house doctors in the Kremlin, were suddenly arrested and thrown into jail, accused of 'having poisoned some of their illustrious patients' and having planned 'further assassinations' for various nefarious ends; upon Stalin's death, the first move of the new government of Georgi Malenkov was to declare the Doctors' Plot null and void. In general Deutscher argues that Soviet history witnesses constant swings between nationalism and internationalism. What my mother thought of Stalin's lurid Doctors' Plot I don't know, though among her books and pamphlets I inherited there is a pamphlet by Herbert Aptheker, the prominent American Communist historian of African American history, entitled 'The Fraud of "Soviet Anti-Semitism"', first published in New York in July 1962, republished in Sydney by the Australian Communist Party in 1963.

3   John Docker, 'Dissident Voices on the History of Palestine-Israel: Martin Buber and the Bi-national Idea, Walid Khalidi's Indigenous Perspective', in Julie Evans, Ann Genovese, Alexander Reilly, Patrick Wolfe (eds), *Sovereignty: Frontiers of Possibility*, pp.97, 99.

4   Cf. John Docker, *1492: The Poetics of Diaspora* (Continuum, London and New York, 2001), ch.9, '"Sheer Perversity": Zionism and anti-Zionism in the 1940s', pp.171–88.

5   John Docker, 'Orientalism and Zionism: Dismantling Leon Uris's *Exodus*', *Arena Journal*, New Series, No.37/38, 2012, p.276, in special issue on Stolen Lands, Broken Cultures: The Settler-Colonial Present.

6   Leon Gettler, *An Unpromised Land* (Fremantle Arts Centre Press, South Fremantle WA, 1993), pp.142–3.

7   Cf. Ann Curthoys and John Docker, 'Defining Genocide', in Dan Stone (ed.), *The Historiography of Genocide* (Palgrave Macmillan, London, 2010), pp.9–41.

8   Katharine Susannah Prichard, *Stories, Journalism and Essays*, edited by Delys Bird (University of Queensland Press, St Lucia, 2000), pp.57–8.

9   John Docker, 'The Two-State Solution and Partition: World History Perspectives on Palestine and India', *Holy Land Studies*, pp.158–9.

10 Ann Curthoys and John Docker, *Is History Fiction?* (University of Michigan Press, Ann Arbor, 2005), pp.122–3.

27

The Holocaust in Australia: fallout in 1979 of the Kastner-Eichmann association in Hungary in World War II

> To a Jew this role of the Jewish leaders in the destruction of their own people is undoubtedly the darkest chapter of the whole dark story.
>
> Hannah Arendt, *Eichmann in Jerusalem: A Report on the Banality of Evil*[1]

In this chapter I explore another aspect of the Holocaust in Australia, the fallout in the latter 1970s of programs broadcast on a Melbourne community radio station concerning the World War II activities in Hungary of Dr Rudolf Kastner, vice-president of the Zionist Organization in Budapest and a close associate of Adolf Eichmann, a relationship caustically written about in Hannah Arendt's 1963 *Eichmann in Jerusalem: A Report on the Banality of Evil*.

As well as its famous and ever—challenging argument concerning Eichmann and the banality of evil (a notion I feel that illuminates many contemporary situations across the world), Arendt's wonderful book, in its scathing brilliance, has ensured historical awareness of Kastner's working relationship with Eichmann and the question of the extensive Zionist and more general Jewish leadership's cooperation with Nazism during World War II; an awareness that came to public attention in Australia in 1979 in the radio broadcasts by the Melbourne group JAZA (Jews against Zionism and anti-Semitism) and the controversy these broadcasts occasioned.

I should make it clear that in writing this chapter, which necessarily involves a great deal of reporting of historical documents, my sympathies are very largely with Arendt and JAZA. The Kastner and 3CR controversies in 1979 helped inspire my subsequent and ongoing scholarly interest in the history of Palestine/Israel; I will come back to this in my final reflections.

Because the JAZA documents I will draw on are so extensive, I will frequently indent long quotations. I will also quote liberally from *Eichmann in Jerusalem*.

⁕

I'll begin with the many references to Kastner, Zionism and more general Jewish leadership in what Arendt in *Eichmann in Jerusalem* refers to as the whole of Nazi-occupied and Nazi-allied Europe.[2]

William Zukerman's claim in *The Jew in Revolt* that in the 1930s there was active cooperation and partnership between the Zionists and the Nazis became a theme in Arendt's *Eichmann in Jerusalem*. Arendt points out that in the trial of Eichmann, the prosecution, fearing its case against Eichmann would be weakened, was careful not to bring into the open the 'cooperation' of the Jewish leaders throughout Nazi-occupied Europe in the Final Solution, Eichmann receiving such cooperation 'to a truly extraordinary degree', with 'Jewish help in administrative and police work', including the 'final rounding up of Jews in Berlin' being done 'entirely by Jewish police'. Arendt returns repeatedly to what she refers to as the most 'gruesome' example, the case of Dr Rudolph Kastner in Hungary, who came to an agreement with Eichmann to save 'prominent Jews and members of the Zionist youth organizations'. So close was Kastner to Eichmann and other top Nazi officials that he could 'even travel about Nazi Germany without any identification papers showing he was a Jew'.[3]

Arendt's comment on the whole story of cooperation and betrayal of one's own resonates with pathos and horror.

What my mother thought of the Kastner case, when it was put on trial in Israel in the 1950s, or of Arendt's *Eichmann in Jerusalem*, which caused a worldwide controversy when it came out, I don't know. I feel she would have agreed with Arendt's view that many more Jews died because the recognised Jewish leaders enforced passivity by cooperating with the Nazis.[4]

Arendt observes that at his trial in 1961 in Jerusalem, Eichmann, a member of the SS, was at pains to clarify that, even in 1943 or 1944 when the Final Solution was in full swing, he did not hate Jews and had never made a secret, as he had told Dr Kastner, of his lack of such hatred. Eichmann, Arendt says, claimed to have read Theodor Herzl's Zionist classic *Der Judenstaat* which led him to admire Zionism. He studied the organisational setup of the Zionist movement, which earned him an assignment for the SS as an official spy on the Zionist offices and meetings; his schooling in Jewish affairs, Arendt comments, was thus almost entirely concerned with Zionism; furthermore, his first personal contacts with Jewish functionaries, all of them well-known Zionists of long standing, were in Eichmann's view thoroughly satisfactory. Arendt notes that Eichmann came to admire the Zionists he knew as idealists, and he defined an idealist as a man who lived for an idea and who was prepared to sacrifice for his idea everything and, especially, everybody.[5]

> The greatest 'idealist' Eichmann ever encountered among the Jews was Dr. Rudolf Kastner, with whom he negotiated during the Jewish deportations from Hungary and with whom he came to an agreement that he, Eichmann, would permit the 'illegal'

> departure of a few thousand Jews to Palestine (the trains were in fact guarded by German police) in exchange for 'quiet and order' in the camps from which hundreds of thousands were shipped to Auschwitz. The few thousand saved by the agreement, prominent Jews and members of the Zionist youth organizations, were, in Eichmann's words, 'the best biological material'. Dr. Kastner, as Eichmann understood it, had sacrificed his fellow-Jews to his 'idea', and this was as it should be.[6]

Arendt narrates that Kastner moved to Israel after the war, where he held a high position until a journalist published a story about his collaboration with the SS in Hungary. Kastner sued the journalist for libel, but when the case came before the Jerusalem District Court he had to defend himself for his cooperation with Eichmann and other high-ranking Nazis; Judge Benjamin Halevi, later to be one of the three judges in the Eichmann trial, told Kastner that 'he had sold his soul to the devil'.[7]

In *Eichmann in Jerusalem*, Arendt brings into the open for historical discussion what in her view the prosecution at Eichmann's trial tried to conceal from the eyes of the world, the direct complicity of the Jewish leadership across occupied Europe in how the Final Solution was meticulously administered.[8]

> The Jewish Councils of Elders were informed by Eichmann or his men of how many Jews were needed to fill each train, and they made out the list of deportees. The Jews registered, filled out innumerable forms, answered pages and pages of questionnaires regarding their property so that it could be seized the more easily; they then assembled at the collection points and boarded the trains. The few who tried to hide or to escape were rounded up by a special Jewish police force. As far as Eichmann could see, no one protested, no one refused to cooperate.[9]

The members of the Jewish Councils, Arendt continues, were as a rule the locally recognised Jewish leaders, to whom the Nazis gave enormous powers, until, she adds, they too were deported, to Theresienstadt or Bergen-Belsen if they happened to be from Central or Western Europe, or to Auschwitz if they were from an Eastern European community. In Amsterdam as in Warsaw, in Berlin as in Budapest, Jewish officials were entrusted not only to compile the lists of persons and their property but also to secure money from the deportees to defray the expenses of their deportation and extermination, to keep track of vacated apartments, to supply police forces to help seize Jews and get them on trains, then hand over the assets of the Jewish community in good order for final confiscation as well as distributing the yellow star badges.[10]

Why Arendt focusses so much on Kastner is that in her view he was at the centre of the most 'gruesome' episode of such compliance and cooperation. In Hungary, Kastner 'saved exactly 1,684 people with approximately 476,000 victims'. In order to assure quiet and prevent panic, Kastner kept secret his plans from the mass of Jews whose doom he helped arrange. Even after the end of the war Kastner was proud of his success in saving 'prominent Jews', a category, Arendt writes, officially introduced by the Nazis in 1942, as if in his view it went without saying that a famous Jew had more right to stay alive than an ordinary Jew.[11]

I'll now bring to a halt these notes on the thread I've been following in *Eichmann in Jerusalem*. Eichmann, Arendt reflects, expected more than the compliance of the Jewish leaders and the Jews destined for destruction; he expected, and received to a truly extraordinary degree, their cooperation. Arendt contends that without Jewish help in administrative and police work, there would have been 'either complete chaos or an impossibly severe drain on German manpower'.[12]

Arendt argues that 'if the Jewish people had really been

unorganized and leaderless, there would have been chaos and plenty of misery but the total number of victims would hardly have been between four and a half and six million people'.[13]

It seems hardly necessary to say how controversial a text *Eichmann in Jerusalem* immediately became. For the 2006 Penguin edition of *Eichmann in Jerusalem*, Amos Elon wrote an Introduction he entitled 'The Excommunication of Hannah Arendt', relating that the book, which had first been published as a series of articles in *The New Yorker*, launched a civil war among intellectuals in the US and in Europe, that a kind of excommunication was imposed on the author by the Jewish establishment in America, and that the controversy has never really been settled. Furthermore, Elon writes, Arendt's books are still widely read and close to 300 000 copies of her book on Eichmann alone have so far been sold; the book continues to attract new readers and interpreters in Europe; in Israel, there is growing interest among young people searching for different viewpoints than those of official Zionism, and a new Hebrew translation has been published to considerable acclaim. Elon feels that the book undoubtedly seems less controversial now, in 2006, than when it first appeared as new generations of scholars take a fresh, less partisan look on Arendt's other writings on Jewish history, Israel and Zionism.[14]

There is another point to be made about Arendt's view of the Jewish Councils in *Eichmann in Jerusalem*, that she can be seen as homogenizing the Jewish Councils. Dan Stone, in *Histories of the Holocaust* (2010), tells us that recent historiography emphasises how much there were important differences between the Jewish Councils across Europe in different situations, and that there is now a prevailing consensus that they acted in the best interests of the Jews in their care.[15]

In discussing Kastner, Arendt in *Eichmann in Jerusalem* very decidedly argues that he did not act in the best interests of the mass of Jews of Hungary, a view shared by JAZA in 1979.

It is not in the nature of historiography to come to rest on a single historical view; these historiographical debates on the Holocaust will continue restlessly on.

I turn now to the 1979 radio broadcasts in Melbourne by JAZA. Somehow a supportive group of us in Sydney, I think based at NSWIT (before it became UTS, University of Technology Sydney, in 1988), where from distant memory I was a part time sessional lecturer teaching writing, formed a small Sydney JAZA group and must have contacted Melbourne JAZA, who then sent to us typescripts of their material. When in 2010–11 I was going through Ann and my papers in Mitchell Library in Sydney, I came across these typescripts and took extensive notes. I'll focus on what they refer to as the 'notorious' activities of Dr Kastner because like Hannah Arendt they see his association with Eichmann as an egregiously appalling example of Zionist cooperation with Nazism during the Holocaust.

From distant memory of the 1979 events, I had thought the Melbourne JAZA group was directly inspired by *Eichmann in Jerusalem*. But looking at the notes I took in Mitchell Library of their material, this turned out not to be so; they do warmly reference *Eichmann in Jerusalem* and cite passages that I have quoted especially concerning the Jewish Councils and Dr Kastner, and they take care to quote Arendt: 'To a Jew this role of the Jewish leaders in the destruction of their own people is undoubtedly the darkest chapter of the whole dark story.' But they make it clear that they have also pursued their own extensive research into a wide range of literature, including reading the Hebrew writings of the Orthodox Jewish group Naturei Karta. I will now explore Melbourne JAZA writings at some length. While they focus on Kastner, JAZA also wished to place Zionism as a historical movement under intense scrutiny.

In the document they sent entitled 'Background to JAZA 3 March 1979', the JAZA group explains that since 1974 they have made occasional public statements in the name of 'Jews Against Zionism', including in support of the Palestinian cause; some JAZA members and other anti-Zionists of Jewish background have been associated with the 3CR programs 'Palestine Voice' and 'Arab Liberation News' since their inception. Zionist attacks on 3CR resulted in a number of anti-Zionist Jews contacting the station to offer their assistance; at a meeting on 17 February 1979, they established a formal organisation, 'Jews Against Zionism and Anti-Semitism', whose members do not identify themselves as Jewish in any religious sense, but rather as part of their cultural and family background. Their office bearers are: Chairperson Sol Salby; Secretary Harry Nowicki; Treasurer Julian Teischer; Media Officer Geoff Lazarus. Activities so far have concentrated on broadcasts over radio 3CR and the preparation of submissions to an Australian Broadcasting Tribunal inquiry into 3CR.

The following is the Constitution of Jews Against Zionism and Anti-Semitism which lays out certain principles:

> JAZA opposes political Zionism and other forms of racism including anti-Semitism.
>
> We regard the Zionist State of Israel as a racist regime founded on the denial of national rights to the original inhabitants of Palestine and support the Palestinian demand that it be replaced by a democratic secular state in which Jewish, Arab, and other communities can live at peace.
>
> We believe the Palestinians and other Arabs have the right to engage in armed resistance to Israeli aggression. Likewise we support resistance to Zionism by Israeli Jews.
>
> We consider that wherever anti-Semitism appears, it should be vigorously fought and not run away from.
>
> We are proud of our Jewish background which assists us to

fight against oppression and for principles of internationalism and justice that have been part of the Jewish tradition.

There was a progressive Jewish tradition long before anyone ever heard of Zionism and it will continue after Zionism has been defeated.

Reading the JAZA Constitution, I find myself pausing and demurring at the clause, 'We believe the Palestinians and other Arabs have the right to engage in armed resistance to Israeli aggression'. As a Gandhian, I support the contemporary world movement, led by Palestinian civil organisations, for BDS: Boycott, Divestment, Sanctions, as brilliantly articulated by Omar Barghouti in his 2011 book *BDS: The Global Struggle for Palestinian Rights*. Barghouti writes that the majority of Palestinians, even before being inspired by Gandhi, King and Mandela, have been involved in nonviolent resistance; 'all segments of Palestinians society have always resisted with social, political, cultural, and artistic popular resistance, strikes, demonstrations, tax boycotts, women's and trade union organizing'.[16]

Melbourne JAZA sent to us in Sydney more typescript material, under the heading, 'Australian Broadcasting Tribunal – 3CR Inquiry – Notice of Evidence from Jews Against Zionism and Anti-Semitism'. It includes the following points:

> In our opinion, 3CR performs a valuable service to the whole community, including Jews, and it would be against the public interest for any change to be made to the conditions of its licence.
>
> We submit that there has been an organized campaign to ensure that pro-Zionist views are influential in the mass media and anti-Zionist views are discriminated against.
>
> In our opinion the allegations made by the Victorian Jewish Board of Deputies against 3CR are part of that continuing campaign.

We submit that the Board is not elected to represent all people of Jewish background, and it certainly does not represent us... To our knowledge Zionists have never been genuinely concerned about fighting anti-Semitism but have only been interested in making use of anti-Semitism to promote Zionism.

If the Board of Deputies is recognized as an interested party, we ask that it be recognized as speaking on behalf of the Zionist movement or on behalf of the State of Israel.

We submit that any interference with 3CR's licence could not be to prevent anyone being offended since anyone who does not like 3CR's programs need not listen to them. Nor could such interference be to correct any lack of 'objectivity' or 'balance' since the imbalance in the mass media is overwhelmingly in the pro-Zionist direction. We would regard such deliberate political censorship in response to the Zionist campaign against 3CR as a very serious curtailment of freedom of expression in Australia, which should especially be resisted by Jews who have been among the first victims of reaction and therefore among the first to defend civil liberties.

We would like to present detailed documentary evidence of the long history of Jewish opposition to and struggle against Zionism and explain the background in which Zionism went from being a small and despised minority extremist view before the second world war to the successful takeover of Jewish community institutions that has made it such a strong force today. Our evidence will show that far from being anti-Semitic, anti-Zionist [views] in 3CR broadcasts have been expressed just as forcefully by many prominent Jewish writers and leaders such as Judah Magnes, Martin Buber, Albert Einstein, Elmer Berger and even Australia's first Jewish Governor-General, Sir Isaac Isaacs. Opposition to Zionist Israel has ranged from adherents of strictly Orthodox religious views such as the Naturei Karta who have lived in peace with the Arabs and refuse to recognize the State of Israel, to moderate religious views such as the old American Council for Judaism who wished to be recognized as a religion rather than a nationality, to Communist, Socialist and other anti-Zionist political views. Coming from different ideological schools, a wide range of Jewish opinion agrees with the Palestinians that a Zionist exclusivist State in Palestine cannot bring peace to the region, does not serve the interests of either Jews or Arabs and can only cause more conflict and bloodshed.

We wish to provide evidence that Zionism should be excluded because Zionism is offensive to sections of the public, including Arabs whom Zionists regard as racially inferior; anti-Zionist Jews whom Zionists consider 'traitors' and 'self-haters'; and all supporters of national rights for the Palestinians whom Zionists brand as anti-Semites.

Israel is anti-Semitic both in its racial discrimination against Semitic people (Arabs and Oriental Jews) and in its support for the anti-Semitic theory that Jews cannot and should not live among others.

Israel is racist, not only in its anti-Semitism, but also in its close alliance with other racist forces including the white racist regimes in South Africa and Rhodesia and the anti-Semites in Lebanon and Argentina.

We especially wish to document the offensively racist character of Zionism because that explains why 3CR's guidelines must require its exclusion.

Members of our organization have been associated with some of these programs ['Palestine Speaks', 'Palestine Voice', and 'Arab Liberation News'] since their inception and have been responsible for providing some of the material complained about, especially material showing the connection between Zionists and Nazis and other racists.

Since anti-Zionist Jews can obtain little access to the mass media or to any means of disseminating our views among Jews, we have to rely heavily on 3CR as a means of expression.

Our own broadcasts have and will include material of the kind the Board of Deputies wish to harass: matter which impugns the right of the State of Israel to exist and which questions its legitimacy or refers to it as 'so-called Israel'. We regard the Zionist state as a racist regime founded on the denial of national rights to the original inhabitants of Palestine and support the Palestinian demand that it be replaced by a democratic secular state in which Jews and Arabs can live in peace. Why should such an elementary and reasonable proposal require an automatic right of reply?

Also: matter which documents the collaboration between prominent Zionist leaders and the Nazi exterminators of European Jewry, including details of the notorious Kastner case and the judgments given on it in Israeli courts.

Also: matter which explains and documents the similarities between Zionism and Nazism and racist philosophies, including racist statements by prominent Zionists and comments on these by well-known anti-Zionist Jews, characterizing them as Nazi-like and racist.

Melbourne JAZA also sent to us in Sydney JAZA a very long document entitled 'Nazi-Zionist Collaboration: Proof of evidence for the [Australian Broadcasting Tribunal] Inquiry into Radio 3CR from Jews Against Zionism and Anti-Semitism, June 7, 1979.' [I focus on the section of the Melbourne JAZA document entitled 'The Kastner Case'. Again, I indent.]

✦

Since the 'Kastner Case' is the subject of most of the broadcasts concerning collaboration which have been specifically complained about [by the Victorian Jewish Board of Deputies], we shall go into this in greatest detail, and have put some books in as evidence about it.

The Holocaust in Australia 609

The most notorious case of Nazi-Zionist collaboration is that involving Rudolf Kastner.

Briefly, the accusations against Kastner are as follows.

Dr Rudolf Verba, a Doctor of Science now serving at the British Medical Research Council, was one of the few escapees from Auschwitz. In his memoirs published in February 1961 in the *London Daily Herald*, he wrote:

'I am a Jew. In spite of that – indeed because of that – I accuse certain Jewish leaders of one of the most ghastly deeds of the war.

'While I was prisoner number 44070 at Auschwitz – the number is still on my arm – I compiled careful statistics of the exterminations... I took these terrible statistics with me when I escaped in 1944 and I was able to give Hungarian Zionist leaders three weeks notice that Eichmann planned to send a million of their Jews to his gas chambers... Kastner went to Eichmann and told him, 'I know of your plans; spare some Jews of my choice and I shall keep quiet'.

'Eichmann not only agreed, but dressed Kastner up in S.S. uniform and took him to Belsen to trace some of his friends. Nor did the sordid bargaining end there.

'Kastner paid Eichmann several thousand dollars. With this little fortune, Eichmann was able to buy his way to freedom when Germany collapsed, to set himself up in the Argentine...'

Are these accusations true? According to the Government of Israel, they are a lie. When Michael Greenwald, a strongly pro-Zionist Israeli citizen published these accusations against Kastner, the Israeli Government did rather more than demand that his views should not be broadcast... The Attorney General of the State of Israel prosecuted Greenwald for criminal libel.

Let the verdict of Judge Benjamin Halevi in Israel's District Court of Jerusalem speak for itself...

Here then are excerpts from the verdict of Judge Halevi, who later became one of the panel of three judges that tried Eichmann:

'The masses of Jews from Hungary's ghettos obediently boarded the deportation trains without knowing their fate. They were full of confidence in the false information that they were being transferred to Kenyermeze.

The Nazis could not have misled the masses of Jews so conclusively had they not spread their false information through Jewish channels.

The same Jews who spread in Kluj and Nodvarod the false rumor of Kenyermeze, or confirmed it, the same public leaders who did not warn their own people against the misleading statements, the same Jewish leaders who did not organize any resistance or any sabotage of deportations... These same leaders did not join the people of their community in their ride to Auschwitz, but were all included in the Rescue train.

The Nazi organisers of extermination and the perpetrators of extermination permitted Rudolf Kastner and the members of the Jewish Council in Budapest to save themselves, their relations, and friends.

The Nazi chiefs knew that the Zionists were a most vital element in Jewry and the most trusted by the Jews.

The Nazis' patronage of Kastner, and their agreement to let him save six hundred prominent Jews were part of the plan to exterminate the Jews. Kastner was given a chance to add a few more to that number. The bait attracted him. The opportunity of rescuing prominent people appealed to him greatly. He considered the rescue of the most important Jews as a great personal success and a success for Zionism. It was a success that would justify his conduct – his political negotiations with Nazis and the Nazi patronage of his committee [Kastner was the founder of the Zionist Relief and Rescue Committee.[17]]

When Kastner received this present from the Nazis, Kastner sold his soul to the German Satan.'

Judge Halevi's verdict found Michael Greenwald generally

innocent of libel against Kastner, but fined him one Israeli pound (fifty cents) for the one unproven accusation – that Kastner had actually collected money from his Nazi partners for his aid to their slaughter program.

In fairness to Kastner it should be maintained that as well as having been unpaid, it was never established that he ever wore a SS uniform.

Nevertheless, this verdict, and the evidence on which it was based, completely established the truth of everything said on 3CR about the matter.

Public opinion in Israel was almost unanimous in demanding that Kastner and his associates be put on trial. Remember that up to now it was Kastner's accuser who was on trial.

In the authoritative Jewish newspaper *Haaretz* (14 July 1955), the leading political journalist, Dr Moshe Keren, wrote: 'Kastner must be brought to trial as a Nazi collaborator. And at this trial, Kastner should defend himself as a private citizen, and not be defended by the Israeli Government…'

Haboher (23 June 1955), the general Zionist pro-Government paper stated: 'The public wants to know the real facts about Kastner, and not about him alone. The only way to find out the truth is to put all the Rescue Committee people on trial and give them a chance to offer their defense.'

The problem with bringing Kastner and his associates to trial was that his associates were the Government of Israel. As the evening paper *Yediot Achronot* [Aharonot?] (23 June 1955) said: 'If Kastner is brought to trial the entire government faces a total political and national collapse as a result of what such a trial may disclose.'

Accordingly, the Government of Israel did not put Kastner on trial. Instead it filed an appeal against the acquittal of Greenwald for criminal libel.

At the appeal hearings before the Supreme Court, the Attorney General of Israel, Chaim Cohen, explained clearly why the

Government of Israel was defending Kastner so strongly: 'The man Kastner does not stand here as a private individual. He was a recognized representative, official or non-official, of the Jewish National Institutes in Palestine and of the Zionist Executive; and I come here in this court to defend the representative of our national institutions.'

The truth of this statement cannot be denied. Kastner's collaboration was not that of an individual. It was the collaboration of the Zionist leadership... But the story gets worse.

The Supreme Court... accepted the facts established in the lower Court – that Kastner deliberately concealed the truth about Auschwitz from the majority of Hungarian Jews in exchange for Nazi permission to take a thousand or so to Palestine.

But now the really nasty bit. After unanimously acknowledging these facts, the Supreme Court of Israel, by a majority of three to two, found that Kastner's actions were morally justifiable and convicted Greenwald of criminal libel for calling this 'collaboration'.

Kastner's actions only proved that he was a Nazi collaborator. It is the defence of these actions by the Government and Courts of Israel that prove conclusively that Zionism approved of Nazi collaboration.

The majority of the Supreme Court of Israel as articulated by Supreme Court Judge Shlomo Chesin did not rehabilitate Kastner. They joined him.

The majority judgment approved of Kastner's contempt for the Hungarian Jews and could not allow him to be condemned for doing exactly what many other Zionist leaders and half-leaders did – concealing their knowledge of the Nazi extermination plans so that Jews would board the trains to Auschwitz peacefully while their Zionist 'leaders' boarded a different train for Palestine.

It cannot be said that all top Zionist leaders actively approved of Nazi collaboration in this way. Indeed the most precise answer to this sickening judgment of Judge Chesin is provided in the minority judgment of Supreme Court Judge Moshe Silberg:

'Can a single man, even in co-operation with some of his friends, yield to despair on behalf and without the knowledge of 800,000 other people?

This is, in my opinion, the decisive consideration in the problem facing us. The charge emanating from the testimony of the witnesses against Kastner is that had they known of the Auschwitz secret, then thousands or tens of thousands would have been able to save their lives by local, partial, specific or indirect rescue operations like local revolts, resistance, escapes, hidings, concealment of children with Gentiles, forging of documents, ransom money, bribery, etc... Does he [Kastner] decide instead of God?'

... the Nazis didn't want to have a great revolt – 'Second Warsaw' – nor small revolts, and their passion was to have the extermination machine working smoothly without resistance. This fact was known to Kastner from the best source – from Eichmann himself... Kastner, in order to carry out the rescue plan for the few prominents, fulfilled knowingly and without good faith the said desire of the Nazis, thus expediting the work of exterminating the masses'

Judge Silberg's judgment was that of a minority. The Kastner case is therefore... a continuing controversy in which the top Zionist leadership of Israel stand indicted of *continuing* to publicly defend collaboration with the Nazis in the extermination of Jews.

As for Kastner himself, he will cause no further embarrassment to the Zionist leadership with his undisputed claims that everything he did was approved by the Jewish Agency (World

Zionist Organization) leadership in Palestine... On March 3, 1957, he was shot by Dov Eckstein... a paid undercover agent of the Israeli secret service.

Judge Silberg's judgment 'that had they known of the Auschwitz secret, then thousands or tens of thousands would have been able to save their lives', resonates with Arendt's view in *Eichmann in Jerusalem* that 'if the Jewish people had really been unorganized and leaderless, there would have been chaos and plenty of misery but the total number of victims would hardly have been between four and a half and six million people'.

※

In 1979 there was a considerable fallout in the media of the Melbourne JAZA controversies concerning 3CR.

In my papers I see a letter, handwritten and undated, from Melbourne JAZA member Harry Nowicki addressed to 'Dear John/Norie': 'Everyone in Melbourne is immensely pleased to learn about the proposed formation of a Sydney J.A.Z.A., a great morale boost for us. Enclosed is our initial submission to the Australian Broadcasting Tribunal.

Please write about details of background to your formation, members involved, proposed activities etc. Possibly you could make an independent submission to the Broadcasting Tribunal concerning the distinction between anti-Zionism and anti-Semitism'.

I can't remember now how Sydney JAZA was formed except that our numbers were few, and I can't remember what we might have written back to Harry Nowicki. Nonetheless, controversy did break out in the NSWIT student newspaper *NSWIT* concerning Zionist Israel and pro-Palestinian viewpoints in lively letters to the editor. I will follow this thread. On Tuesday 17 April 1979 a letter appeared, 'Jews Against Zionism and Anti-Semitism', signed by John Docker and Norie Neumark, Lecturers, Faculty of Humanities and Social Science.

Dear Eds, We are writing this letter in response to the excellent articles by Adnan Kahili on the Palestine–Israel debate in recent issues of *NSWIT*. Mr Kahili supported his analysis by referring to the work of Jewish scholars who have argued against [the] Israeli occupation of Palestine and have seen it as an example of a more general European settler-colonialism and racist aggression of [sic] Third World peoples. Such Jewish scholars also explode the equation that anti-Zionism is anti-Semitism.

… Our aim here… is not so much to contribute to the intellectual argument as to provide a moral statement, and in particular, to break through the ruling atmosphere that any criticism of Israeli treatment of the Palestinians, or any questioning of Israeli policies, is anti-Semitic.

… Those of us who know the justice of the Palestinian cause must now declare publicly our moral sympathies and our intellectual and moral position.

Indeed, throughout the world the movement of Jews who are standing up in favour of the Palestinian cause is strengthening – for instance, in the U.S. the well-known scholar Noam Chomsky is one of the many who has been exposing the unsavory history of the takeovers of Palestine by the Zionists. In Australia a group in Melbourne called 'Jews Against Zionism and Anti-Semitism' has already come out publicly in support of 3CR against the allegations made by the Jewish Board of Deputies.

It seems timely, therefore, for Jews like ourselves in Sydney, to join together to form a local chapter of 'Jews Against Zionism and Anti-Semitism'. It is especially appropriate for those interested in the media and in education to oppose Zionist and pro-Zionist censorship of the Palestinian point of view. We would like to hear from other Jews who oppose the Israeli occupation of Palestine, who are worried by the extent of local media and educational censorship of the issues, and who, in the longer view, do not want to see the whole of Judaism identified with and tainted by a particular episode in history.' (In my notes is a photocopy of a handwritten letter of the above, in my handwriting, so perhaps I drafted the *NSWIT* letter.)

In *Nation Review* 6 September 1979 there appeared a letter from 'Ehud Ein-Gil, Israel'; in a corner of the same Letters page is a note: 'Anti-Zionist Israeli Ehud Ein-Gil speech at the Unitarian Church, Grey St., East Melbourne 7.30 pm. Sponsored by Jews Against Zionism and Anti-Semitism.' In this passionate letter, Ehud Ein-Gil attacks a leaflet from the Australian Union of Jewish Students concerning his visit to Australia sponsored by Melbourne JAZA.

I hereby state that:

> The Israeli 'Law of Return' is a racist law...
> The plan for the 'Judaisation of the Galilee' is a colonialist enterprise with a racist flavor that should be opposed in its entirety.
> The 1948 war was no more a 'war of independence' than white Rhodesia's 'struggle' for its 'independence' since 1965...
> Zionism is incompatible with basic democratic considerations. It respects some forms of civil rights only with regard to persons of Jewish origin (and not all of them indeed).'

In *NSWIT* letters page Tuesday 18 September 1979, appeared a letter, 'JAZA Speaks', from Harry Nowicki and Albert Langer.

> Dear Eds, While visiting Sydney our attention was drawn to the articles on 3CR... and related material in *NSWIT*.
> ... Zionists are the worst anti-Semitic 'self-haters' of all. From Herzl's first scheme to convert all Jews to Catholicism, to his second scheme to send them to Palestine, to his third scheme to send them to Uganda ('next year in Kampala') there has been a

common thread of Jewish self-hatred which ultimately led to the collaboration with Nazism.

The *basic theme* of Zionism is that there was something *wrong*, or *contemptible*, something *unnatural* or *demeaning* about the life of Jews as an ethnic minority within the various European nations.

… Just look what happened when the Zionists were confronted with the evidence at the public inquiry they had demanded. 3CR issued a unilateral public declaration (not an 'agreement' or 'understanding') which reaffirmed its determination to exclude any pro-Zionist viewpoint from [its] broadcasting and to continue broadcasting the pro-Palestinian and anti-Zionist programs without inciting racial discrimination – exactly as before. The Victorian Jewish Board of Deputies then withdrew its complaints.

Only Zionists have the incredible *chutzpah* (cheek) to claim to speak for others. Obviously nobody can speak for Australian Jews since Jews have all sorts of different opinions just as people do in any other ethnic or religious group. Zionist controlled Jewish organisations claim to speak as representatives of 'the Jewish community' as though Jews were members of some sort of club. They must imagine they are still living in East European ghettos and not in Australia where individual citizenship and voluntary association prevails. Organisations of Australians of other ethnic origins such as Greeks and Italians do not make the fantastic claim to speak for Australia's so many thousand Greeks or whatever, they just speak for the members of their organization. Why can't Zionists do the same?

In fact a Melbourne survey showed that 30% of Jews didn't know what the Victorian Board of Jewish Deputies is and another 30% didn't know what it does. How can it claim to 'speak on behalf of' the 60% who don't know what it is or does?'

In the same Letters page of *NSWIT*, there is a letter by Ehud

Ein-Gil that refers to the 'colonialist-racist nature of Zionism' and argues against the Zionist claim that Israel is a democracy: 'Democracy is first and foremost a political system that respects all its citizens as having equal human and civil rights. The hard fact is that Israeli law-books discriminate [against] citizens of non-Jewish origin.'

In his Introduction, Amos Elon insightfully wrote that for Arendt *Eichmann in Jerusalem* was 'an intensely personal work'.[18] I think for JAZA too their broadcasts on 3CR and their submissions to the ABT involving extensive research, were intensely personal, that Zionism should be opposed because it attempted to enclose all Jewry in a single, nationalist, exclusivist, settler colonial identity tied to a land, Palestine, which they came to as a haven and set about their unending project of conquering, oppressing and expelling the indigenous Palestinians. Zionism in JAZA's view offers a definition of identity which tries to eliminate the historical, contemporary and continuing range of ways of being Jewish, especially living in diaspora and internationalism, and where being Jewish involves the possibility of being a non-Jewish Jew; at one point they reveal their familiarity with Isaac Deutscher's jewel of a book *The Non-Jewish Jew*.

In my opposition to Zionism, I share that personal intensity.

Coming from a Communist and Jewish family background with internationalist ideals, as far back as I can remember, in relation to settler colonial societies like Australia and Israel, I have thought it was and is completely wrong of a people to come from afar and take away from another people their land and world. The Kastner and 3CR controversies in 1979 helped stimulate my subsequent and ongoing scholarly interest in the history of Palestine/Israel that emerged most strongly in an essay in *Arena* in 1986, clumsily entitled 'Orientalism and Zionism: Images of the Arab', a long critique of Leon Uris's drek novel *Exodus*, my first major foray into the history of Palestine/Israel. The essay was reprinted, with the more felicitous title 'Orientalism and Zionism: Dismantling Leon Uris's *Exodus*', in a special issue Stolen Lands, Broken Cultures: The Settler-Colonial Present, *Arena Journal* 2012 I have referred to before. I've just gone through the footnotes of this essay, and see that books and essays I read for it in 1986 included Maxime Rodinson's *Israel: A Colonial-Settler State?* and *Israel and the Arabs*; Noam Chomsky's *The Fateful Triangle: The United States, Israel and the Palestinians*; Walid Khalidi's collection *From Haven to Conquest: Readings in Zionism and the Palestine Problem until 1948*; articles in the journal *Khamsin* (for which Ehud Ein-Gil wrote an essay, 'Religion, Zionism and Secularism', in 1981); and Rosemary Sayigh, *Palestinians: From Peasants to Revolutionaries*, 1979.

I'll bring these reflections to a close by quoting a poem by the great Palestinian poet Mahmud Darwish addressing the expulsion and exiling of the Palestinians from their beloved Palestine in the 1948 Nakba.

> Give Birth to Me Again That I May Know
> Give birth to me again… Give birth to me again that I may know in which land I will die, in which land I will come to life again.
>
> Greetings to you as you light the morning fire, greetings to you, greetings to you.
>
> Isn't it time for me to give you some presents, to return to you?
>
> Is your hair still longer than our years, longer than the trees of clouds stretching the sky to you so they can live?
>
> Give birth to me again so I can drink the country's milk from you and remain a little boy in your arms, remain a little boy
>
> For ever. I have seen many things, mother, I have seen. Give birth to me again so you hold me in your hands.
>
> When you feel love for me, do you still sing and cry about

nothing? Mother! I have lost my hands
On the waist of a woman of a mirage. I embrace sand, I embrace a shadow. Can I come back to you/to myself?
Your mother has a mother, the fig tree in the garden has clouds. Don't leave me alone, a fugitive. I want your hands
To carry my heart. I long for myself… I long for you.[19]

1 Hannah Arendt, *Eichmann in Jerusalem: A Report on the Banality of Evil* (1963; Penguin, New York, 2006), p.117.
2 Arendt, *Eichmann in Jerusalem: A Report on the Banality of Evil*, p.115.
3 Arendt, *Eichmann in Jerusalem*, pp.42, 116–20, 125, 132, 143, 199.
4 Arendt, *Eichmann in Jerusalem*, p.124.
5 Arendt, *Eichmann in Jerusalem*, pp.30, 32, 40–2.
6 Arendt, *Eichmann in Jerusalem*, p.42.
7 Arendt, *Eichmann in Jerusalem*, p.42.
8 Arendt, *Eichmann in Jerusalem*, pp.119–120, 125.
9 Arendt, *Eichmann in Jerusalem*, p.115.
10 Arendt, *Eichmann in Jerusalem*, pp.117–18.
11 Arendt, *Eichmann in Jerusalem*, pp.118–20, 132.
12 Arendt, *Eichmann in Jerusalem*, p.117.
13 Arendt, *Eichmann in Jerusalem*, p.125.
14 Amos Elon, Introduction, pp.vii–xi.
15 Dan Stone, *Histories of the Holocaust* (Oxford University Press, Oxford, 2010), pp.81–6. (My thanks to Ned Curthoys for this reference.)
16 Omar Baghouti, *BDS: Boycott, Divestment, Sanctions, The Global Struggle for Palestinian Rights* (Haymarket Books, Chicago, 2011), p.174. See Ned Curthoys, John Docker, and Antony Loewenstein, 'Palestine's Gandhi, BDS, and International Humanitarian Law', *Overland* 31 May, 2011.
17 Arendt, *Eichmann in Jerusalem*, pp.197–9.
18 Amos Elon, Introduction, pp.viii–ix.
19 Mahmud Darwish, Samih al-Qasim and Adonis, *Victims of a Map: A Bilingual Anthology of Arabic Poetry* (Al Saqi Books, London, 1984, p.10.

28

How I came to see Zionist Israel as a genocidal settler-colonial perpetrator state

Writing about Zionism and Israel has occupied a passionate strand of my intellectual life since the late 1970s. Here I try to work out how, from early in the twenty-first century, I came to view Zionism and Israel as a continuous historical project of genocidal settler colonialism.

༺❀༻

In 2001, I was invited to participate in the Melbourne Writers Festival, my *1492: The Poetics of Diaspora* had been published in that year, a kind of ego histoire before I ever knew of ego histoire. In a session on Jewishness I was met with prolonged jejune hissing when I suggested that the Australian Jewish Diaspora has to recover its independence, its own being, its soul, rather than subordinating itself to serving Israel's ethnic absolutism, with all the hypocrisy that entails for Jewish official support for multiculturalism in Australia.

༺❀༻

In 2002, as reported in *Arena Magazine* 59, June-July of that year, Ghassan Hage and I co-organised an Australian academic boycott of Israel.[1]

I had seen on emails that were coming around, that in the UK Steven Rose and Hilary Rose had sent an open letter to the *Guardian* calling for a moratorium on all future cultural and research links with Israel at European and national levels. I immediately emailed Steven and Hilary, asking if I could put my name to their call. Steven kindly emailed back saying no, you can't, the call is for European academics only, and you'll have to organise your own. This was excellent advice, because, as I soon realised, the situation in Europe and Australia is quite different; the kind of funding projects that Israel is involved with in terms of the European Economic Community didn't as far as I knew exist in Australia.

Accordingly, I quickly sent an email to Ghassan, suggesting we should put out a call for a boycott, saying there may be an extra effect in that it would be a dual initiative from an Arab – Australian and a Jewish-Australian. Our call went out, and was quickly signed by some 100 of the most interesting humanities academics and intellectuals in Australia. Our call was largely symbolic. But symbolic protests – as the great Gandhi knew well – can be powerful, perhaps in changing in quiet and invisible ways the climate of opinion around an issue.

In our public letter, Ghassan and I stressed how much we saw Israeli control of the West Bank and Gaza as part of a long relentless process of 'colonisation'. I think, though we did not say this in the letter, we were so mindful of Israeli colonisation because of all the critiques – critiques we had engaged in ourselves in our separate writings – of Australia as a settler-colony, a settler-colony like other settler-colonies historically established by the British Empire, including the mandated colony of Palestine.

※

In August-September 2003 *Arena Magazine* 66 published my essay 'New History and the New Catastrophe: Ilan Pappé, the

New History, and the Question of Israeli Genocide', where I draw attention to Pappé's revisionist histories suggesting that Zionism in the latter nineteenth century and into the twentieth can be recognised, in Pappé's words, as a 'typical colonialist movement in a colonialist era'; there is a 'basic contradiction between Zionist national ambitions and their implementation at the expense of the local population in Palestine'; the 1948 war securing the foundation of Israel as a nation-state was a 'human and national tragedy for the Palestinian people'; there was no 'voluntary exodus of Palestinians from Palestine' during the war, rather they had been 'expelled', and even though the United Nations sanctioned the return of the Palestinian refugees, Israel refused, and Israel in any case had deliberately destroyed their villages and homes.

In 'New History and the New Catastrophe', I very much agreed with Pappé's call for the creation in Palestine of a single plural society where citizenship is open to all in that historic land.

However, I respectfully disagreed with Ilan Pappé's view of what constitutes genocide. In an interview in September 2002 at the University of Manchester, 'Ilan Pappé: Israeli Jewish myths and the prospect of American war', Pappé talked of the many 'ways the Israelis have dispossessed and persecuted and are dispossessing and persecuting the Palestinians', which he considered to be reminiscent of the 'pre-extermination' phase in Nazi Germany, as in ethnic cleansing and even putting numbers on the arms of Palestinians. Nonetheless, he said, such is to be distinguished from 'genocide', meaning mass or total extermination as in the Holocaust.

I argued, to the contrary, drawing on Ann Curthoys and my 'Introduction – Genocide: definitions, questions, settler-colonies' to *Aboriginal History* volume 25 2001, that neither Raphaël Lemkin's originating definition in Chapter 9, 'Genocide', of his *Axis Rule in Occupied Europe* nor the 1948 UN Convention on genocide that is based on Lemkin's 1944 formulations, equates to genocide in this way. In *Axis Rule in Occupied Europe* Lemkin offers a wide-ranging definition where genocide signifies a coordinated plan of different actions aimed at the destruction of the essential foundations of the life-world of national groups. I quoted Chapter 9:

> The objectives of such a plan would be the disintegration of the political and social institutions, of culture, language, national feelings, religion, and the economic existence of national groups, and the destruction of personal security, liberty, health, dignity, and even the lives of the individuals belonging to such groups.

Lemkin, I noted, defined genocide as proceeding by two phases, destruction of the national pattern of the oppressed group, and the imposition of the national pattern of the oppressor; a process of destruction and replacement that Lemkin's definition directly associates with colonisation.

In late 2004, I was invited to give a talk to a conference, 'Resisting Israeli Apartheid: Strategies and Principles', at the School of Oriental and African Studies at the University of London, held on Sunday 5 December. A large audience packed the lecture theatre for the all-day event; other speakers included keynote speaker Tom Paulin, Mona Baker, Omar Barghouti, Ilan Pappé, Hilary Rose, Haim Bresheeth and Ben Young. To close proceedings, Ilan Pappé gave a Summary of the Day, recalling that the conference had started by 'acknowledging we were here because of Hilary and Steven Rose, whose moratorium initiative moved us all to action'.

My talk was entitled 'Settler Colonialism as Genocide: Implications for a Strategy of Solidarity with the Palestinians'. From memory, Nur Masalha was the chair. I began by thanking the conference organisers for inviting me to come to London from Australia, that it was an honour to be here, and it was a great pleasure to see again Hilary Rose and Steven Rose, who I had met for the first time in London in May 2004, and Ilan Pappé, who visited Canberra and Sydney in August 2004. It is also a delight to meet in person Nur Masalha and Mona Baker after the exchange of so many friendly emails across the world.

I then went on to say how the Australian boycott of research and academic links with Israel that I co-organised in 2002 with Ghassan Hage came about, and rehearsed the argument of my essay 'New History and the New Catastrophe', that contemporary genocide studies has moved away from how genocide was defined from the 1970s to the 1990s as a devastating episode of mass murder, with the Holocaust as the extreme and most appalling example. Rather, in a rapidly changing international field, an energetic strand of genocide studies is returning to Lemkin's original wide-ranging definition of a two-stage process. I also noted that when Lemkin escaped Nazi Germany and found refuge in the US in 1941, he assembled the research material for his 1944 *Axis Rule in Occupied Europe* and began writing chapters for a second book that remained unpublished when he died in 1959. In a significant thread in the unpublished manuscripts, Lemkin researched the historical relationship between genocide and settler colonialism in the post-1492 colonisation of the Americas, including his new home in North America. In his original definition, and in these unpublished writings, Lemkin constitutively and inherently links genocide with colonisation.

In my closing comment, I said that given Lemkin's definition it is clear that Israel constantly and daily pursues the aim of genocide against every aspect it can of the Palestinian life-world. In his unpublished writings Lemkin worked out a methodology of genocide situations, which included analysis of the genocidist group, dissent within the genocidist group, responses of the victims of genocide, and the responses and actions of other groups.² These categories have salience in discussing Israel, dissenters within Israel, and support from the US. I look forward to discussing these issues further with you.

In 2008 my *The Origins of Violence: Religion, History and Genocide* was published. Chapter 5, 'Victimology and Genocide: The Bible's Exodus, Virgil's *Aeneid*', brought into conversation, for their narrative and ethical similarities, two of world history's most powerful and lastingly influential victimological narratives; by victimology, I mean, following Edward Said's classic essay 'Michael Walzer's *Exodus and Revolution*: A Canaanite Reading' and Richard Waswo's illuminating *The Founding Legend of Western Civilization: From Virgil to Vietnam*, the belief that earlier bondage, persecution and suffering justifies later violence, conquest and destruction. In their operation, reception and eventual imbrication in Western history, these texts represent an ethical disaster, with highly destructive consequences for humanity as a whole, especially for indigenous people and peoples already in a land coveted by others as chosen and promised. I note that Lemkin thought that instances of the formerly persecuted becoming persecutors themselves, victims in the past becoming oppressors in the future, are a recurring feature in the history of genocide.³

From 27 December 2008 to 18 January 2009 the world witnessed one of the most terrifying events of the twenty-first century, Israel's all-out assault on the largely defenceless civilian Palestinian population of Gaza, with massive loss of life including many children, a crime against humanity actively or tacitly supported by the West.⁴

At 3 pm Saturday 7 February 2009, the Australian Greens

convened a forum – Justice for Palestinians – at the Sydney Mechanics School of Arts, 280 Pitt Street, Sydney. Ned Curthoys and John Docker of the Committee to Dismantle Zionism were asked to speak about a two-state solution. Ned and I and the other panellists, including a Greens representative and a Palestinian representative – I'm afraid I can't at this distance remember their names – sat out the front on chairs, in a fairly large room upstairs, the audience keenly listening to each speaker.

When it was my turn to speak, I acknowledged the traditional owners of the land on which we met that day.

I will now try to severely abbreviate what I said about the two-state solution; I've just looked up the document I wrote that my speech was based on.

I'll begin, I said, on a personal note. My family background is important for the objections I have to Zionism as an ideology of nationalism and colonialism, and to Israel as a Jewish state. I come from a left-wing Sydney family. My strong feeling is that when Zionism from the late 1940s succeeded in taking over the leadership of Jewish organisations in Australia and carrying with it the mainstream Jewish community, it helped destroy the internationalist and politically progressive Jewish tradition of which my mother's family was a part.

I have, I continued, been asked to speak about the idea of a two-state solution, an idea that has a long and tragic history. For an understanding of the history of this idea and its consequences, I recommended Ilan Pappé's remarkable book *The Ethnic Cleansing of Palestine*, a meticulous reconstruction of an historical tragedy, based on minute research into state archives, diaries, memoirs and Palestinian oral history. It suggests that the idea of a two-state solution began with Britain in the 1930s, who wanted to partition Palestine in order to manage the increasing conflict between the Zionist settlers and the Indigenous inhabitants. The idea of partition was supported from 1937 by the Zionists, and then taken up after World War II by the UN. The UN Partition plan for historic Palestine that became UN Resolution 181, adopted in November 1947, was egregiously unfair. It treated the one-third Jewish, two-thirds Palestinian populations as if they were equal entities. It gave 56 percent of the land, including the best arable land, to the Jews even though at that time they owned far less than 10 percent of the land, indeed only 5.8 percent in 1947. Furthermore, it was an outrage against all humanitarian notions to declare a partition as international law when the UN committee knew that the whole Palestinian population – the Indigenous majority population of the land – was opposed to it. The Palestinian opposition to partition is not surprising. In the words of the great Palestinian scholar, Walid Khalidi, 'The native people of Palestine, like the native people of every other country in the Arab world, Asia, Africa, America and Europe, refused to divide the land with a settler community'. Why, Khalidi asked, should a part of their traditional lands be given over to a group who from early in the twentieth century had made it increasingly clear it wished to rid the land of its Indigenous peoples, at once to de-Arabize and Judaicise Palestine. The Zionists wanted to carry out a massive population transfer, the ethnic cleansing of Palestine.

Partition, I went on, was not enough for the Zionist leadership. David Ben-Gurion, Israel's first prime minister, and his inner circle wanted to go further and expel all Palestinians from Palestine. When it became clear in 1947 that the UN would declare partition, Zionist leaders ostensibly welcomed it, but secretly put into action the now notorious Plan Dalet, a systematic and comprehensive military plan for the ethnic cleansing of all areas of Palestine. The Plan was aimed at removing Palestinians living not only in the areas designated as Jewish by the UN but also in the areas designated as Palestinian. As Pappé tells us, in this massive crime against humanity, in six months in 1948 more than half of Palestine's Indigenous population, close to 800 000 people, were uprooted and expelled, 531 villages were destroyed, and 11 urban neighbourhoods emptied of their inhabitants.

Far from respecting the UN Partition plan, the leadership of Israel since 1948 have consistently refused all international law. Where the Partition itself decreed they should have 56 percent of Palestine, by brutal force they took 80. They rejected UN Resolution 194 of 11 December 1948, which declares the unconditional right of the Palestinians to return to their homes, a resolution made the day after the adoption of the Universal Declaration of Human Rights.

As we now know, partition was as disastrous in Palestine as it was in India. In both cases the fantasy of partition was that pure ethnic states could be created in geocultural areas such as South Asia or the Middle East where populations were historically composed of many communities, religious and ethnic, living alongside and among each other. What in fact it led to was loss of life, freedom and independence for the Palestinians.

The answer is not a two-state solution, which is yet another form of partition. The answer is a free democratic Israel-Palestine, conceived of not as a Jewish state, but as a multi-ethnic secular state which protects the rights of all its citizens, and which encourages the return of all those Palestinians and their descendants who have been driven out since 1948.

It was a very serious, intense, emotional event. My memory is that at the end, the elderly Palestinian man sat still on his chair out the front, the other speakers had left, and Ned and I sat with him, for quite a long time; in silence, together.

━━✤━━

In *Arena Magazine* 99, February-March 2009, p.17, 'Open Letter to Kevin Rudd', Ned Curthoys and John Docker, Committee for the Dismantling of Zionism, letter dated 11 February 2009, with sub-title 'For the Gazans', addressed a plea to the then prime minister of Australia. I'll quote some passages, beginning with the opening paragraph:

> Dear Prime Minister, We are part of an increasing number of people around the world of Jewish descent who are sickened by the coldly calculated massacre of the Palestinians of Gaza and who utterly repudiate Israel's claim that it acts in the name of Jews the world over. Like an increasing number of people around the world of Jewish and non-Jewish descent, we are also sickened by the indifference of Western governments, including your government, to the death, maiming, terror and trauma inflicted on the Palestinians of Gaza, including a disproportionate number of children, in what now resembles a vast outdoor prison or policed ghetto. The apparent indifference of your government to the humanitarian plight of the Palestinians lends support to Israel's crimes against humanity.

Here is our penultimate paragraph:

> On 13 February 2008, in your historic and moving speech apologising to the Stolen Generations of the Indigenous people of Australia you clasped hands and shared tears: please extend the same sympathy and empathy to the indigenous people of Palestine. Since 1948 the indigenous Palestinians of historical Palestine have had their lives, cities, villages, mosques, fields, olive groves, health, dignity, freedom of movement and rights under international law unlawfully transgressed and stolen from them. Please reach out to them; please extend your sympathy to the beleaguered Palestinian people.

Here is the final sentence:

Prime Minister, we ask that you do everything you can to avert the destruction of the Palestinians.

※

On 27 March 2009 Ned Curthoys and John Docker of the Committee for the Dismantling of Zionism put out a 'Petition of Jews who immediately renounce the 1950 Israeli law of return', its opening sentences: 'We the undersigned submit that the 1950 Israeli Law of Return for Jews, which gives Jews alone the right to migrate to Israel and obtain citizenship, is a racist law and an affront to a just, democratic, and non-ethnically determined concept of citizenship. There is little doubt that the Law of Return was and is a key instrument in the Zionist colonization of what remains of historic Palestine, a law which worked in tandem with the Absentee Law of 1950 which allowed the Jewish state to expropriate the land of those Palestinians declared "absentee" but who were in fact forcibly prevented from returning to their original homes by the Israeli military.'

The signatories were Ned Curthoys (Australia), Mike Cushman (UK), John Docker (Australia), Rick Kuhn (Australia), Steven Rose (UK), Jonathan Rosenhead (UK) and Ron Witton (Australia).

※

In *Arena Magazine* 100, April-June 2009, in the Letters and Debate section, a letter entitled 'On the Jewish State' by a number of Jewish academics, accused Ned Curthoys and my 'Open Letter to Kevin Rudd' in *Arena Magazine* 99, February-March 2009, of a 'moral and ethical indifference to the historical reality of the Nazi Holocaust'. Our reply, 'Responding to our critics' begins: 'We formed the "Committee for the Dismantling of Zionism" during the sickening Gaza Massacre of late 2008/early 2009', an attack 'which is now being investigated for war crimes'. We continued:

> Ignoring the specific context of our letter, our opponents begin their retort by implicitly calling for censorship, suggesting that a 'left-wing magazine' should be supportive of Zionism and of the Jewish character of the state of Israel, rather than critical of it. Yet what could be more obvious than that the Left, that is, people of conscience everywhere who oppose racism in all its forms, would be critical of the occupation and colonisation of Palestinians lands (nowhere mentioned by the authors), appalled by the ongoing plight of millions of stateless Palestinian refugees (nowhere mentioned by the authors), and profoundly uncomfortable with the idea of a state that explicitly recognises the political and cultural hegemony, and immigration rights, of one ethnicity alone?

Ned and I then addressed their major accusation:

> Our opponents baselessly argue that we are morally and ethically indifferent to the Holocaust, a routine Zionist attempt to deflect attention from Israel's apartheid policies in the Occupied Territories and its continual violations of international law and the Geneva Convention. Surely, they advise, we must 'know that those Jews who didn't escape Nazi Germany and find refuge in Palestine were killed in mass slaughter'. This suggests that only Jews who reached Palestine escaped the Holocaust, but clearly many escaped Nazi Germany and Nazi-occupied Europe and fled to other parts of the world. We have only to think of Albert Einstein, Hannah Arendt or the coiner of the term 'genocide', Raphaël Lemkin – Jews who found refuge in the United States and then translated their experience as victims of Nazism into a diasporic Jewish politics focussed on sympathy with oppressed and marginalised peoples.

Finally, our phrase concerning 'Dismantling of Zionism' does not imply a 'collective stereotyping of all Israelis as evil oppressors'. We certainly do not regard Indigenous Palestinian Israelis as oppressors (or are they not truly Israelis?), and we are very well aware of the hundreds of Israeli academics who now support an international economic and academic boycott of Israel. We applaud the courageous Israeli physicians who protest at the complicity of official Israeli medical bodies in state-sanctioned torture, and applaud the Israeli anthropologist and activist Geoff Halper, who protests at the ongoing demolition of Palestinian houses, a form of collective punishment that is illegal under international humanitarian law. We refer constantly in our own work to Israeli intellectuals such as Ilan Pappé, Baruch Kimmerling and the late Tanya Reinhart. Our guiding assumptions are that Jews and Palestinians will ultimately benefit from the possibilities of mutual understanding and creative co-existence afforded by a genuinely democratic state in Israel/Palestine. The aim of our committee is to highlight Zionism as a movement whose political leadership since the 1890s to the present has pursued settler colonial and nationalist aims of removing as many Indigenous Palestinians as possible from their fields, orchards, olive groves, villages and cities, culminating in the horror of the genocide of 1948 and continuing, incrementally, to this day.

We remind our readers of the long history of Jewish opposition to Zionism, both religious (see Yakov M. Rabkin's *A Threat from Within, a Century of Jewish Opposition to Zionism*) and secular, and we suggest along with [Judith] Butler that such criticism has strong roots in Jewish history, of Talmudic disputation, of socialism and humanism, of liberal and radical politics, of a certain longing, difficult to redeem, for an alternative future.

There was a media release of a further 'Petition Against the Right of Return to Israel on Behalf of Australian Jews' on 3 March 2010. Some of the key signatories include world-renowned ethicist Peter Singer, actor Miriam Margolyes, legendary feminist campaigner Eva Cox, La Trobe University's Dennis Altman, Monash University's Andrew Benjamin, Sydney University's David Goodman and John Docker, ANU's Ned Curthoys, legal scholar G J Lindell, best-selling author and journalist Antony Loewenstein, writers Susan Varga and Sara Dowse, and many others.

'We are Jews from Australia, who, like Jewish people throughout the world, have an automatic right to Israeli citizenship under Israel's "law of return". While this law may seem intended to enable a Jewish homeland, we submit that it is in fact a form of racist privilege that abets the colonial oppression of the Palestinians. Today there are more than seven million Palestinian refugees around the world. Israel denies their right to return to their homes and land – a right recognized and undisputed by UN Resolution 194, the Geneva Convention, and the Universal Declaration of Human Rights. Meanwhile, we are invited to live on that same land simply because we are Jewish, thereby potentially taking the place of Palestinians who would dearly love to return to their ancestral lands. We renounce this "right" to "return" offered to us by Israeli law. It is not right that we may "return" to a state that is not ours while Palestinians are excluded and continuously dispossessed.'

In 2010 *Holy Land Studies*, Volume 9, Number 2, published my essay 'The Two-State Solution and Partition: World History Perspectives on Palestine and India', contending that the two-state solution for Palestine-Israel derives its plausibility from the long career of partition, as idea and event, in the twentieth century and into the twenty-first; as well as India and Palestine we can think of Ireland, Germany, Vietnam, Korea and Cyprus. I discuss the ideas of the philosopher and theologian Martin Buber who from the time of the Balfour Declaration of 1917 to his death in 1965, advocated a bi-national vision, that the land of Palestine could and should be shared between the Indigenous people and the incoming Jews from Europe.[5]

I also discuss the Introduction to *From Haven to Conquest: Readings in Zionism and the Palestine Problem until 1948* (1971), wherein Walid Khalidi gives us an impassioned Indigenous perspective on the prospect of partitioning Palestine. Khalidi views Zionism as part of the more general movement in modernity of settler colonialism, arguing that from the constituent congress of the World Zionist Organisation meeting in Basle, Switzerland in 1897, the Zionists worked to convert Palestine from a refuge and haven into a land they wished to conquer and did conquer, and the success of their aggressive strategy and violence became the Palestine tragedy. He rejects the Zionist and Western myth that the Indigenous Palestinians had only been in Palestine for some 1300 years, from the time of the coming of Islam. I'll quote this remarkable passage:

> The Palestinian Arabs in the twentieth century were not merely the descendants of the Moslem Arab conquerors of the seventh century, but the cumulative stock that included all the races that had entered and settled in Palestine since the dawn of history. They 'preceded' both Jew and Moslem Arab, in addition to 'incorporating' them. They were the true Palestinians. Unlike the Jews, they never 'left' to 'return'. They had been Arab in culture since the early centuries of the Christian era, but Jewish and pagan before that since primordial times.

Khalidi also objects to the Zionist assertion of greater Jewish attachment to Palestine, writing of the 'depth and poignancy of Muslim Arab love for Jerusalem', a reverence that includes acknowledgement of the Jewish and Christian love of the city, as can be historically witnessed in Saladin when he conquered Jerusalem from the Crusaders.[6]

~~~※~~~

In the Australian journal *Overland*, 31 May 2011, Ned Curthoys, John Docker and Antony Loewenstein published 'Palestine's Gandhi: Omar Barghouti, BDS, and International Humanitarian Law', where we talk about Barghouti's 2011 book *BDS: Boycott, Divestment, Sanctions – The Global Struggle for Palestinian Rights*, a book we very much admire.[7] Barghouti, we suggest, is in the great tradition of Palestinian intellectuals, historians and poets like Edward Said, Walid Khalidi and Mahmoud Darwish. He is a founding member of both PACBI, the Palestinian Campaign for the Academic and Cultural Boycott of Israel, which made its first call for boycott in April 2004, and the general Palestinian Civil Society Boycott, Divestment and Sanctions (BDS) campaign, which made its call a year later, in 2005. Barghouti points out that the 'BDS movement as such does not adopt any specific political formula', for example it steers away from the 'one-state-versus-two-states debate, focusing instead on universal rights and international law'. He does, however, offer his own vision, that on 'a personal level, not as a representative of the BDS movement', he has for over 25 years consistently supported the one-state solution, 'a secular, democratic state: one person, one vote – regardless of ethnicity, religion, nationality, gender, and so on'. Such a right can 'reconcile our inalienable rights as indigenous Palestinians with the *acquired* rights of Israeli Jews as colonial settlers, once they've shed their colonial character and privileges and accepted justice and international law'.

Barghouti sees BDS as part of the tradition of non-violence whose most famous representatives are Mahatma Gandhi, Martin Luther King and Nelson Mandela, though the majority of Palestinians have engaged in 'non-violent resistance even before the inspiration of Gandhi, King, and Mandela'. Mandela and Archbishop Tutu, he reminds us, liken Israeli occupation practices to apartheid South Africa, and he agrees that the present BDS is 'largely inspired by the anti-apartheid struggle in South Africa'; he does not, however, suggest that the two situations are identical, since 'Israel's system of bestowing rights and privileges according to ethnic and religious identity' fits both the UN definition of apartheid in its Convention on the Suppression and Punishment of the Crime of Apartheid of 1972 and the International Criminal Court's Rome statute of 2002.

Barghouti describes Zionism and the Israeli state as one of settler colonialism. He regards Zionism as a form of racism, referring to the Israeli state as 'ethnocentric, racist, and exclusivist' in the spirit of a striking passage from an article by I F Stone, which he quotes:

> Israel is creating a kind of moral schizophrenia in world Jewry. In the outside world, the welfare of Jewry depends on the maintenance of secular, non-racial, pluralistic societies. In Israel, Jewry finds itself defending a society in which mixed marriages cannot be legalized, in which non-Jews have a lesser status than Jews, and in which the ideal is racist and exclusivist.
> I F Stone, 'Holy War', *New York Review of Books*, 3 August 1967[8]

Barghouti also draws attention to the importance of Ilan Pappé's 2006 book *The Ethnic Cleansing of Palestine*.

Barghouti believes that the BDS movement, appealing to people of conscience everywhere, is necessary 'to avert genocide', by which he means Israel's ongoing assault on the Palestinians as a people, enacted through the annexation of Palestinian land, alienation of Palestinians from their arable lands, restrictions on Palestinian housing and construction permits, attacks on Palestinian olive crops, attacks on Palestinian rights of assembly, cultural expression and schooling, the mass imprisonment of young Palestinian men and boys, removal of Palestinian populations from East Jerusalem and Area C of the West Bank, onerous military curfews, attacks on Palestinian freedom of movement, and crippling undermining of the Palestinian economy.

Barghouti points out that Israel's occupation of Palestinian lands captured in the 1967 war, including the West Bank of which East Jerusalem is a part, is illegal in international law. All Israeli settlements established in the occupied territories are a violation of article 49 of the Fourth Geneva Convention of 1949: 'The occupying power shall not deport or transfer parts of its own civilian population into the territory it occupies'. An example in the academic sphere, Barghouti notes, is the Hebrew University, which has moved Israeli staff and students into illegally confiscated land in East Jerusalem. On 9 July 2004 the International Court of Justice in The Hague declared that Israel's construction of the infamous apartheid wall is illegal because it annexes Palestinian land and separates Palestinians from their lands, as it was surely designed to do.

Barghouti dismisses any accusation that the boycott campaign is anti-Semitic. For one thing, as part of the struggle for 'universal rights', BDS is opposed to 'all forms of racism and racist ideologies, including anti-Semitism'. For another, there is growing support for the Palestinian-led BDS from Jews inside and outside Israel. In Israel, on 27 June 2010, following the Palestinian Queers for BDS initiative, 'an Israeli LGBT call' endorsed BDS; Israeli groups of Palestinians and Jews that have endorsed the BDS call include the Alternative Information Centre, the Israeli Committee Against House Demolition, and Who Profits from the Occupation? which is a project of the Coalition of Women for Peace. There is also the 'courageous Israeli BDS group Boycott from Within'. Jewish intellectuals mentioned by Barghouti who have been prominent worldwide in supporting BDS include Judith Butler, Mike Leigh, Richard Falk, Naomi Klein, Ilan Pappé and Ronnie Kasrils.

We conclude our review by suggesting that BDS is a litmus test for humanity, because it asks the world's citizens to act to uphold universal human rights. If BDS fails, we are all diminished.

The editors of *Arena Journal*, it must have been sometime in 2011 or 2012, contacted me to ask if they could reprint an old essay of mine that first appeared in 1986 in *Arena* no.75, on Leon Uris's novel *Exodus*, for an issue they were planning on Stolen Lands, Broken Cultures: The Settler-Colonial Present, in a section on Palestine: Past and Present. I said yes, though I would have to read it again after all this time to check it's OK; we agreed it would be a good idea to add an introductory note and a postscript situating the essay historically and in contemporary contexts. I also gave it a new title, 'Orientalism and Zionism: Dismantling Leon Uris's *Exodus*'.⁹

In the introductory note, I mention that in the 1986 essay I had occasionally directed some whimsy at the 'cumulative crudity of aesthetic effects that pervade *Exodus*' during what turned out to be 'a long critical analysis of Uris's drek text'.

In the Postscript I note that in my 1986 essay 'it seemed to me quite obvious that Israel, like Australia, was and is a settler-colonial state', and that in both cases, 'as far back as I can recall, I have thought it was and is completely wrong of a people to come from afar and take away from another people their land and world'. While writing the article, I continued, 'I profited greatly from reading a scholar whom I very much admire, Maxime

Rodinson', not least his *Israel: A Colonial-Settler State?* which was first published as a supplementary essay to a special number of Sartre's *Les Temps Modernes* which, just as the 1967 Arab-Israeli war was ending, presented contributions, pro-Arab and pro-Israeli, from leading Arab and Israeli intellectuals. Rodinson's essay was translated into English in 1973 as a short book.[10]

What I'd like to do now is briefly follow a thread that occurred to me while I was re-reading Ned Curthoys and Antony Loewenstein and my review of Omar Barghouti's *Boycott, Divestment, Sanctions*. As I note above, Barghouti refers to and quotes to good effect I F Stone's essay 'Holy War', *New York Review of Books*, 3 August 1967. I stared at the date for a long moment, and recalled Maxime Rodinson's *Israel: A Colonial-Settler State?* Wasn't it published in 1967, is there a connection here? I reached for Rodinson's book and looked at the Introduction, where Peter Buch tells us that I F Stone in 'Holy War' brought to American attention Sartre's collection of contrasting viewpoints, with Stone singling out Rodinson's contribution as 'by far the most brilliant'. Buch adds that in the *Middle East Journal*, Spring 1968, Irene Grendzier, welcoming the special issue of *Les Temps Modernes* as a document of extraordinary value, also characterizes Rodinson's contribution as 'by far the most profound, if not the most controversial, summary of the position that Israel is a colonial fact… the most thorough and historically documented statement' of this position.[11]

I agree with Irene Grendzier and I F Stone: Rodinson's *Israel: A Colonial-Settler State?* was a brilliant and profound intervention, and remains so.

―※―

In *Holy Land Studies*, Volume 11, Number 1, 2012 I published 'Instrumentalising the Holocaust: Israel, Settler-Colonialism, Genocide (Creating a Conversation between Raphaël Lemkin and Ilan Pappé)'. The essay came about because I considered it was time to bring together into the one field of analysis two areas of scholarly investigation which in my view should closely relate to each other but presently are hesitant to do so: genocide studies and studies of the history of Palestine. I wished to do so by a detailed analysis of Ilan Pappé's remarkable work of 2006, *The Ethnic Cleansing of Palestine*. Here I was helped by an essay in *Holy Land Studies* in 2010 by Martin Shaw, 'Palestine in an International Historical Perspective on Genocide', who to my mind convincingly argues that the term 'ethnic cleansing' should not be considered as an alternative to 'genocide' since population expulsions such as Bosnia in the 1990s were clearly designed to destroy ethnic or national communities, and so fell within the ambit of genocide as Lemkin had defined it, as well as within the terms of the 1948 UN Convention on genocide. Following Shaw, I decided to reinterpret as genocide the events and processes to which Ilan Pappé refers as ethnic cleansing.[12]

I explained that my focus in the essay would be on Zionism as a discourse and practice of settler-colonialism, imbricated with nationalism and an instrumentalisation of the Holocaust, noting Idith Zertal's observation that the instrumentalising of the Holocaust, the use of it as a political resource, is longstanding in the history of Zionism and Israel.[13]

In terms of methodology I wished to follow Lemkin's suggestions in his manuscript essays and noted that Ann Curthoys and I read in 2003 in New York in the American Jewish Historical Society and New York Public Library, that throughout history there are recurring features and techniques of genocide. In his Research Index Cards in the American Jewish Historical Society, Subseries 3, Box 9, Folders 1–21, dated 1948–9, Lemkin focusses on aspects of genocide perpetrated by the English, French and post-independence Americans that constitute a comprehensive historical process over a number of centuries: dispossessing indigenous peoples of their land (with or without permission of central authorities), kidnapping, enslavement, removal and deportation often involving forced marches, stealing of children, disease through overcrowding on reservations with inadequate food and medicine, curtailing and deprivation of legal rights, cultural genocide, mass death.[14]

In Folder 11, Box 8, Subseries 2 in the American Jewish Historical Society, there is a diagrammatic entry, 'Revised Outline for Genocide Cases', where Lemkin offers detailed categories by which to analyse historical genocides.[15]

I compare the recurring features of genocide that Lemkin discerned in world history in 'Revised Outline for Genocide Cases', in its section 'Physical Genocide', to Pappé's analysis of the events in Palestine of 1947–9. In 'Revised Outline for Genocide Cases', Lemkin refers to 'Methods and techniques of genocide', listing under 'Physical' features such as: 'massacre and mutilation'; 'deprivation of livelihood (starvation, exposure, etc. – often by deportation)'. Pappé refers to the many massacres that occurred during 1947–9 as techniques, 'a key tactic', to accelerate the 'flight of the population' and 'massive expulsion' that he believes was the aim of Zionist planning even before the final formulation of Plan Dalet, the master plan for systematic and total expulsion. Pappé identifies its leading figure, David Ben-Gurion, as the chief perpetrator, organiser, strategist and planner of what he calls the ethnic cleansing of Palestine and I call its genocide.[16]

Pappé records that on 29 November 1947, the 75 000 Palestinians in the city of Haifa were 'subjected to a campaign of terror'; perpetrator methods included rolling down from above 'barrels full of explosives' and 'huge steel balls' into the Arab residential areas, and pouring 'oil mixed with fuel down the roads' which they then ignited; when the Palestinian residents came running out of their homes to try to extinguish the flames, 'they were sprayed by machine-gun fire'. On 31 December 1947 the Haganah's High Command, part of Ben-Gurion's Consultancy group, ransacked the village of Balad al-Shaykh, massacring many of its inhabitants; the local Haganah commander was ordered to kill the largest possible number of men, but refrain from attacking women and children. At their next meeting, however, the Consultancy decided no such restraint would be necessary, since it complicated operations.[17]

Plan Dalet was adopted on 10 March 1948, and initially targeted the urban centres of Palestine, Pappé writing of such urbicide: 'About 250,000 Palestinians were uprooted in this phase, which was accompanied by several massacres, most notable of which was the Deir Yassin massacre'. Concerning this most infamous of Zionist massacres, Pappé points out that Deir Yassin was a 'pastoral and cordial village' that had reached a non-aggression pact with the Haganah in Jerusalem, but it was doomed because it fell within the areas designated in Plan Dalet to be destroyed. Because of their prior agreement, the Haganah decided to send in the Irgun and Stern Gang troops, who on 9 April 1948 burst into the village, spraying the houses with machine-gun fire and killing many inhabitants; the remaining villagers were gathered in one place and executed, including a row of children lined up against a wall. Pappé writes that Palestinian sources, combined with Israeli military archives, confirm that 31 massacres were perpetrated by Jewish forces from late 1947 to early 1949.[18]

Pappé suggests there were 'numerous cases of rape' of Palestinian women by Jewish soldiers. At Deir Yassin a number of the 'women were raped and then killed'. In July 1948 Zionist 'operations of uprooting, deportation and depopulation' involved 'seeing relatives being executed, and wives and daughters being abused, robbed and in several cases raped'. Survivors of the attack by Jewish and Druze soldiers on Safsaf on 29 October 1948 recall 'how four women and a girl were raped in front of the other villagers'. In a three-page section Pappé refers to many instances of rape across Palestine during 1948 and 1949 gleaned from UN and Red Cross sources. Israeli perpetrators of rape have also talked about incidents decades later. *Ha'aretz* of 29 October 2003 published a story of one such incident based on the testimonies of rapists. Pappé writes of this incident that on 12 August 1949, a platoon of soldiers in the Negev captured a 12-year-old girl and locked her up in their military base: 'For the next few days she became the platoon's sex slave as the soldiers shaved her head, gang-raped her and in the end murdered her'; 22 soldiers took part in the 'barbaric torture and execution of the girl'. Robbery and looting could also be accompanied by molestation of women. Eyewitnesses reported the 'callous and humiliating way' in which women were 'stripped of all their jewellery to the very last item', the women then being 'harassed physically by the soldiers', leading in Tantura to rape.[19]

In a section of the essay entitled 'Forced Removal and Deportation' I note that in 'Nature of Genocide' Lemkin observed that deportations under harsh conditions are a recurring technique of physical genocide, instancing the Spanish treatment of the Moriscos, deported from Spain by being loaded on ships in unbearable sun, thousands dying from sunstroke; he compares this technique of deportation under harsh sun to the deportation and forced march of 1 200 000 Armenians. In relation to the North American history of genocide, Lemkin's cards (Series 3, Subseries 3, Box 9, Folder 14) refer to how during the Creek removal, warrior prisoners chained together were followed by the old and infirm, in intense heat, with infectious diseases rampant, while the sick were transported on overcrowded boats. Pappé writes of the 'inhuman' expulsion of some 50 000 people from the Palestinian cities of Lydda and Ramle, the attacks being ordered by Ben-Gurion on 10 July 1948. During the urbicide of Lydda, Jewish troops 'went on yet another rampage of murder and pillage', 426 men, women and children being killed; many were massacred inside a mosque after surrendering (176 bodies were found in the mosque). Israeli troops barged into houses, dragged out the families, looted their homes, then robbed the refugees and ordered them to march towards the West Bank 'in one of the warmest months of the year, in one of the hottest places in Palestine'. After Ramle was also attacked, the people of both cities were 'forced to march, without food or water, to the West Bank, many of them dying from thirst and hunger on the way'.[20]

In a penultimate section entitled 'Cultural Genocide: Memoricide', I note that in his unfinished autobiography 'Totally Unfinished Man', written shortly before he died in 1959, Lemkin confided that the notion of cultural genocide 'was very dear to me'. His manuscript 'Revised Outline for Genocide Cases', under the heading of cultural methods and techniques, lists: 'Desecration and destruction of cultural symbols (books, objects of art, religious relics, etc)'; 'Loot'; 'Destruction of cultural centers (cities, churches, monasteries, schools, libraries)'; and 'Prohibition of cultural activities or codes of behavior'.

Ilan Pappé does not use the term cultural genocide in *The Ethnic Cleansing of Palestine*, but he does brilliantly deploy the concept of memoricide. For Pappé, memoricide is an aspect of the leitmotif of his book, the execution of the 'master plan of expulsion and destruction' and then replacement, of de-Arabisation and Judaisation. He likens memoricide to a palimpsest: 'the erasure of the history of one people in order to write that of another people's over it'; the continuous imposition of a Zionist layer and national pattern over everything that had been Palestinian. Zionist political and military leaders, recognising that historically Arab Palestine represented a heterogeneous mixing and living together of Muslims, Christians and Jews, strove to turn an 'ethnically mixed area into a pure ethnic space'. Pappé refers, for example, to the Zionist ethnic cleansing of the 'thriving cosmopolitan city' of Haifa. Such settler-colonial and nationalist homogenising was an attack on the cosmopolitanism and internationalising of space that historically characterised the Levant and Middle East.[21]

In the introduction to my *The Origins of Violence* I propose that supersessionism is one of the most destructive beliefs in world history, the view that some peoples can be erased or removed or superseded by other peoples and groups, who see themselves as history's true heirs. Pappé explores in detail instances and policies of what I conceive of as settler-colonial supersessionism, and he conceives as memoricide, in relation to the village scapes of Palestine, especially in the way the Jewish National Fund created national parks on the sites of 'eradicated Palestinian villages', at the same time as attempting to make Israel look European, in particular, by choosing to plant conifers instead of the 'natural fauna indigenous to Palestine': 'Pine trees were planted not only over bulldozed houses, but also over fields and olive groves'. Sometimes traces of almond and fig trees, olive groves or clusters of cactuses can still be found, reminders of the Palestinian villages, but JNF official narratives describe them as part of wild nature. The JNF parks provide parking spaces, picnic areas, playgrounds and access to 'nature', replacing 'Palestinian sites of trauma and memory' with 'spaces of leisure and entertainment for Israelis'. The fruit gardens Palestinian farmers planted around their houses are 'referred to as an inherent part of nature'.[22]

Yet, while the JNF ecologises, as Pappé pithily puts it, the 'crimes of 1948' in an effort to 'conceal the enormity of the Palestinian tragedy', the post-1948 exiled Palestinians themselves, residing in refugee camps and diasporic communities, have not forgotten their villages laying buried beneath Israel's recreational parks, nor have they stopped insisting on their legal Right of Return granted to them by the United Nations in Resolution 194 of 11 December 1948, guaranteeing that those made exiles and refugees have the right to return to their country and property.[23]

In my essay, by way of a conclusion, I reflect that in the conversation arranged between Raphaël Lemkin and Ilan Pappé I regarded my two interlocutors, in the manner of Hannah Arendt in *Men in Dark Times*, as distinctive intellectual personalities who, in their writings and historical situation, share many things. Their work combines knowledge with deep passion and compassion. They share the condition of exile, Lemkin in the late 1930s escaping from Poland to Sweden and thence to the US, while in 2007 Pappé, facing denunciations by the Knesset and calls for him to be sacked from his post at Haifa University, left Israel to live in Britain, where he became a Professor in the Institute for Arab and Islamic Studies at the University of Exeter, a story he tells in his autobiography *Out of the Frame: The Struggle for Academic Freedom in Israel* (2010).[24]

In *Out of the Frame*, Pappé narrates his personal journey, growing up in a typical German Jewish household in Haifa in the late 1950s, his parents having lost their immediate family in the Holocaust. In his childhood he was 'bewitched' by Herzl's utopian visions. Later he became an anti-Zionist historian who, in terms of a German Jewish legacy in Israel, is proud now not of Herzl but of Martin Buber. 'How', he asks himself, 'did Herzl's dream become Palestine's nightmare?'[25]

Pappé now sees the Zionist project as an attack, shaped by the particularism of settler-colonialism and nationalism, on the Judaism he values, an ethical Judaism inspired by universal human values and which, he feels, exists only in the diaspora. For Pappé, Zionism's betrayal of ethical Judaism is most evident in its instrumentalising of the Holocaust. As he writes in *Out of the Frame*, 'Worst of all was the Zionist and later Israeli abuse of the Holocaust memory to justify the dispossession of Palestine that disconcerted and outraged me'.[26]

In *Out of the Frame* Pappé embraces the term 'genocide' to describe contemporary Israel's oppression of the Palestinians, especially in Gaza, where the Israelis have created a 'prison camp'. Pappé now sees Zionism as an 'ideology that endorses ethnic cleansing, occupation and massacres', an ideology enacted in 'the genocide in Gaza' including in the 2009 'massacre' and up to the present. The Israeli state, 'more than any other in the world', is 'destroying and dispossessing an indigenous population', supported by an Israeli population, from the political left to the political right, that makes 'uninhibited calls' for the 'complete elimination' of the Palestinians.[27]

I salute the historiographical achievement of *The Ethnic Cleansing of Palestine*, a work that places Pappé in a pantheon of scholars – we can think of Walid Khalidi, Edward Said, Nur Masalha and Saree Makdisi – who have investigated and analysed the tragedy for the Palestinian people that Zionist settler-colonial genocide has wrought and continues to inflict. In his Acknowledgements Pappé tells us that the book is 'written first and foremost for the Palestinian victims of the 1948 ethnic cleansing'. In his Preface, Pappé writes that it is his 'own *J'Accuse* against the politicians who devised, and the generals who perpetrated, the ethnic cleansing'.[28]

―――

In *Holy Land Studies* in 2014, Haifa Rashed, Damien Short, and John Docker published 'Nakba Memoricide: Genocide Studies and the Zionist/Israeli Genocide of Palestine', an essay which aroused considerable interest.[29]

Rashed, Short and Docker argue that Genocide Studies is haunted by an absence and a fear. The absence is of any sustained continuing discussion of Zionist Israel as a possible example of a nation founded on genocide. The fear is of becoming another victim of Zionist intimidation and retaliatory attacks if there were to be such discussion. In Foucault's terms, we suggest, Genocide Studies is uneasily aware that Zionism, as a worldwide movement with a vigilant scholarly and ideological wing, is a panopticon. Genocide Studies knows it is being watched and can be threatened with vilification at any moment, even in a pre-emptive gratuitous way. To fend off such attacks, it has chosen to be intellectually submissive; that is, to suppress a key (Socratic) foundation of intellectual life, to follow inquiry wherever it may lead. In particular, Genocide Studies is haunted by the fear that the historical analysis of settler colonialism, based on Raphaël Lemkin's definitional linking of settler colonialism with genocide, may lead to recognition of Zionist Israel as a genocidal settler-colonial state.

We investigate the ways Genocide Studies as an institutional academic discipline in its various manifestations, in single-authored books, in collections of essays, and its key journal, *Journal of Genocide Research*, is structured around a mode of silence concerning the manifold ways Zionist Israel perpetrated genocide in the Nakba of 1948 against Palestinian society, and is still perpetrating genocide, incrementally but relentlessly, on the Palestinian people. It is a key position of Nakba Studies that the Nakba of 1948 has never ended.

We note that Ilan Pappé in his 2006 *The Ethnic Cleansing of Palestine* defines 'memoricide' as the continuous imposition of a Zionist layer and national pattern over everything that had been Palestinian. We wish to extend the notion of memoricide to Genocide Studies itself.

If we sample publications of Genocide Studies, we find that year after year Zionist Israel as a possible case study is an egregious absence. In terms of canonical essay collections, monographs and important reviews in the field, we pointed to the absence of substantive discussion in Robert Gellately and Ben Kiernan's 2003 collection *The Spectre of Genocide*; Adam Jones' 2004 collection *Genocide, War Crimes and the West: History and Complicity*; and Kiernan's 2007 book *Blood and Soil*. In A Dirk Moses' collection *Empire, Colony, Genocide* – in which Docker has a chapter entitled

'Are Settler-Colonies Inherently Genocidal? Re-reading Lemkin' – Patrick Wolfe has penetrating comments on Zionism, Israel and the Palestinians in his essay 'Structure and Event: Settler Colonialism, Time, and the Question of Genocide', especially in his extensive notes; however, in the case studies section of the collection, there is no substantive discussion of Zionist Israel. In the case studies section of the collection *The Historiography of Genocide* edited by Dan Stone – in which Ann Curthoys and John Docker have a chapter 'Defining Genocide' – Zionist Israel is an egregious absence, including in a final chapter on genocide of Indigenous peoples that does not mention the Palestinians. There is further absence in Alexander Laban Hinton and Kevin Lewis O'Neill's 2009 collection *Genocide: Truth, Memory, and Representation*, and Donald Bloxham and A Dirk Moses' 2010 collection *The Oxford Handbook of Genocide Studies*. In neither *The Meaning of Genocide* nor *The Rise of the West and the Coming of Genocide*, the two volumes that compose Mark Levene's *Genocide in the Age of the Nation-State* (2005), is there any discussion of Zionism and Israel in relation to the Nakba.

Taken together, these canonical collections and books on genocide in Genocide Studies represent an archive of Nakba memoricide.

In our essay we consider the implications for Genocide Studies of the important review by Mark Levene of Ilan Pappé's *The Ethnic Cleansing of Palestine*, Levene's review appearing in *Journal of Genocide Research* in 2007. Levene writes that the 'Zionist takeover of Arab land' as revealed by Pappé is 'shocking' and 'sickening'. He finds Pappé's book 'convincing and compelling, and absolutely demands the attention of readers and researchers engaged with the subject of genocide and its suboptimal variants'; a little later he adds that Pappé's work is 'an extremely important book for genocide scholars'. He writes:

How I came to see Zionist Israel 651

With at least 5,000 men, women and children slaughtered in the massacres, 531 villages and 11 major towns destroyed and up to 800,000 folk uprooted, mostly into exile, the point of Pappé's effort can only be affirmed. The injustice of the Nakba, all these years on, is of ongoing relevance – just as much as the Armenian genocide…

In our view Levene's review presents Genocide Studies with a signal challenge. Levene refers the Nakba for its 'ongoing relevance' to one of modern history's iconic genocides, the Armenian Genocide. Levene is presenting Genocide Studies with an urgent question: how can it not, after Pappé's book, become fully interested in the Nakba if it is comparable in terms of historical importance to the Armenian Genocide?

Levene's review of *The Ethnic Cleansing of Palestine* refers to the extent, ferocity and horror of the Zionist/Israeli massacres during the Nakba, including the 'infamous massacre' of Dayr Yasin in April 1948. The 'standard operating procedure', Levene writes, of Zionist troops was to surround a village, and even though the villagers might surrender, 'able men and boys were lined up, and sometimes shot', and in the worst cases 'a more general massacre ensued'; a 'particularly appalling case study' of how these operations were extended to towns is revealed in the 'assault on Arab Haifa'.

We are led to ponder the refusal of Massacre Studies to include chapter-length case studies on the Nakba in its essay collections, beginning with *The Massacre in History* edited by Levene and Penny Roberts, which helped launch the contemporary scholarly interest in massacres. In the Introduction, written by Levene, there is mention of the killing by Baruch Goldstein of 'twenty-nine Palestinian Muslim worshippers' in Israeli-occupied Hebron, in February 1994, and some reflections on Dayr Yasin as well as the Sabra-Shatila massacre in Beirut in 1982. The chapters are very interesting, ranging in time from the medieval to modernity. Yet in not including a case-study chapter on a Zionist-Israeli massacre, for example, Dayr Yasin, the collection was, we felt, in danger of setting out a template of exclusion for the future of Massacre Studies.

Exclusion of the Middle East as an area of interest is also evident in *Theatres of Violence: Massacre, Mass Killing and Atrocity throughout History*, published in 2012 and edited by Philip G Dwyer and Lyndall Ryan. Docker has a conceptual chapter 'The Origins of Massacres' at the beginning of the volume. Despite the multiple massacres perpetrated by Zionist forces in the Nakba, detailed by Papp in *The Ethnic Cleansing of Palestine* and mentioned by Levene in his review, in the 20 chapters of *Theatres of Violence* there are no chapters on the Middle East and certainly no case study devoted to the Zionist/Israeli massacres during the Nakba, not only in 1947–49 but continuing as in the 2009 assault on Gaza.

In our view, the expanding field of Massacre Studies needs to be wary of perpetrating Nakba memoricide, even though the existence of multiple massacres in the Nakba is undeniable.

ow In our Conclusion we note that in Genocide Studies – and, we can add, Massacre Studies – international Zionism has achieved one of its most successful scholarly-ideological victories. In its silent refusal to entertain substantive studies of the Nakba, Genocide Studies is on ethically dangerous ground. Because the field fears Zionist intimidation and *ad hominem* attack, it judges that a determined disinclination to pursue critical scrutiny of the Nakba as genocide serves its self-interest as a growing discipline. Genocide Studies is now on the edge of an ethical precipice, a crisis of intellectual bad faith, claiming to be making scholarly choices onl, when those choices are subtended by political considerations.

In 2017 I published in *Holy Land and Palestine Studies* 16:1, 27–45, an essay, 'Reconceptualising Settler-Colonialism and Genocide with Special Reference to Palestine, Sri Lanka and Australia: Reflections on Damien Short's *Redefining Genocide: Settler Colonialism, Social Death and Ecocide*'. I began the essay by reflecting that in 2016 Genocide Studies' degree of intellectual bad faith in relation to Palestine catastrophically accelerated. On 26–29 June the International Network of Genocide Scholars (INoGS), the sponsor of the *Journal of Genocide Research*, chose to hold a conference at the Hebrew University of Jerusalem at its Mt Scopus campus, built on stolen Palestinian land in occupied East Jerusalem. In the months before there were gathering protests at the ethical implications of this location. PACBI, the Palestinian Campaign for the Academic and Cultural Boycott of Israel, urgently called for the conference to be held elsewhere. A statement signed by 275 academics, including this author, called on INoGS to respect the international Palestinian-led academic boycott of Israel, pointing out that the conference is being held at the very time that in wider genocide studies Israel's actions are increasingly being viewed through the lenses of ethnic cleansing and genocide linked to settler-colonialism. The statement quoted a comment of mine: 'Genocide studies is now, it seems clear, actively seeking opportunities to be complicit in Israel's flouting of international law, not least the Fourth Geneva Convention'.

The conference was sponsored by a number of Israeli academic institutions, including the Hebrew University. Omar Barghouti, a founding member of PACBI, in his brilliant 2011 book *BDS*, presents a devastating critique of the Hebrew University's imbrication in Israel's continuing colonisation of Palestinian lands. In 1968, a year after Israel's military occupation of Gaza and the West Bank, which includes East Jerusalem, the Israeli authorities confiscated areas of Palestinian land which were then given to the Hebrew University to expand its campus. Yet numerous UN resolutions, Barghouti points out, have recognised that East Jerusalem is an inseparable part of the occupied Palestinian territories; by moving Israelis, both staff and students, to work and live on occupied Palestinian land, the Hebrew University is violating article 49 of the Fourth Geneva Convention of 1949. Barghouti quotes the relevant sentence: 'The occupying power shall not deport or transfer parts of its civilian population into the territory it occupies.'

In holding its conference in Jerusalem, mainstream Genocide Studies in the form of INoGS dishonoured itself in history. Utterly grotesquely, before the eyes of the world, INoGS has openly collaborated with Israel as a settler-colonial genocidal perpetrator state that seeks international respectability, and in so doing has itself become a perpetrator organisation in the ideological-scholarly realm. Furthermore, INoGS is eagerly supporting Israel's efforts to destroy the non-violent Gandhian BDS movement initiated and sustained by Palestinian civil society, thereby openly showing contempt for the Indigenous Palestinian victims of a genocidal state. It is well to quote one of those Indigenous voices, from an academic colleague, Dr Haidar Eid, a member of PACBI, commenting on INoGS' betrayal:

> I am an academic living in besieged Gaza. I have witnessed three massacres committed by Israel, I almost lost my own life and saw my comrades, colleagues, relatives, and students perish in them. I have read with agony the names of 44 of our students and colleagues who lost their lives and 66 families wiped out by Israeli weapons. INoGS is lending its name to the perpetrators of these crimes in a move that is not unlike holding a conference on racism in apartheid South Africa.

In a just world, Israel would be prosecuted under Article 2 of the

1948 UN Genocide Convention, and INoGS would be prosecuted under Article 3 for 'Complicity in Genocide'.

INoGS's betrayal imperils the future of genocide studies, which in its intense life as both a discursive concept since 1944 and a United Nations legal convention since 1948 has proven to be an extraordinarily fruitful and intellectually challenging field that humanity needs to keep flourishing in order to understand both world history and our present day world.

※

In the same year that INoGS and mainstream Genocide Studies so dishonoured itself, Damien Short's *Redefining Genocide: Settler Colonialism, Social Death and Ecocide* was, I went on to argue, very much to be welcomed.

Damien Short is a noted genocide scholar, sociologist, editor of *International Journal of Human Rights*, director of the Human Rights Consortium and Extreme Energy Initiative in the School of Advanced Study in the University of London, a bold and fearless thinker, unafraid to push human rights, genocide studies, environmental studies, towards new or neglected fields of inquiry. In its innovative reach, his *Redefining Genocide* has implications for genocide studies in the widest sense, not only in the links it draws between genocide and ecocide, but also in the way its analyses of genocide can help us rethink the relationship between genocide and the role of the state.

Drawing throughout on Lemkin's wide-ranging definition of genocide, Damien Short brings together a series of breakthrough essays. His approach is collaborative; the individual case studies focus on Palestine (with Haifa Rashed), Sri Lanka (with Vinay Prakash) and Canada (with Jennifer Huseman).

In relation to Palestine, Rashed and Short describe Israel's genocidal actions as an application of an 'ecocidal method'. On the West Bank, Israel has reserved water for its own use to the severe detriment of Palestinian well-being and human rights; in Gaza, Israeli Defence Forces have deliberately targeted water and sewage infrastructure to a calamitous degree; and fuel and electricity restrictions have periodically paralysed water and waste-water services. A 2012 UN report spells out that around 90 percent of the water in Gaza is currently undrinkable. Israeli firms are encouraged to dump hazardous waste in the Occupied Territories, affecting the population in terms of asthma and related illnesses.

As *Redefining Genocide* unfolds, what becomes clear to readers is that the aspects of the Zionist Israeli genocide of Palestine that Rashed and Short highlight resonate with the genocide in Sri Lanka.

In the chapter on Sri Lanka Damien Short and Vinay Prakash pay particular attention to the continuing Sinhalese genocide of Tamils that is occurring in the wake of the civil war from which in 2009 the Sinhalese military forces emerged victorious. In Lemkinian spirit, they discuss aspects of the Sri Lankan genocide as cultural, physical, economic, biological and environmental, evident in a long history that predates the civil war. The Sinhalese genocide of the Tamils is revealed to be coordinated, comprehensive and convergent.

In terms of cultural genocide, Short and Prakash refer to the realm of national myth, as in the Mahavamsa, one of Sri Lanka's major epics; a substantial section of radical Sinhalese Buddhists and politicians views the 'Mahavamsa as the indisputable truth and as a justification for atrocities against minorities'. The epic is held to explain the 'mythical origins of the Sinhalas as a colonizing people' with the 'arrival of an "Aryan" prince, Vijaya'. In the epic, Prince Vijaya, arriving on the island and as a way of establishing a kingdom, felt compelled to 'follow Vedic and caste customs' and to establish 'matrimonial alliances with the Kshatriyas from southern India', an important caste group from one of India's prominent Tamil kingdoms. The Mahavamsa accordingly suggests, Short and Prakash point out, that there was a mixed heritage in the creation of the Sinhala state, that the Tamils are not only kinfolk but also co-founders. But this bi-national aspect of the Mahavamsa is ignored by Sinhalese nationalists in modern Sri Lanka; in their view, the epic confirms that only the Sinhalese Buddhists constitute the state and nation, all non-Buddhists such as the Tamils regarded as lesser beings.

Physical genocide was combined with cultural and intellectual genocide, as in the anti-Tamil riots of 1981 that saw the 'complete devastation' of the Jaffna public library, which had a repository of 100 000 books, manuscripts and palm-leaf inscriptions from antiquity. The 1981 vandalism and desecration were a prequel to the commencement of the civil war, in the anti-Tamil pogroms and massacre of 1983, carried out by Sinhalese rioters with the direct participation of the military, identifying homes to be attacked by the use of electoral lists. The extreme Sinhalese violence of 1983 led to mass numbers of Tamil homeless and refugees, and migration to India, Western Europe, Canada and Australia, creating a far flung diaspora.

During the last phase of the civil war in 2009, the number of Tamil civilians killed by the military was by some estimates up to 1000 a day; total deaths of civilians could be as high as 40 000; the Sri Lankan military targeted hospitals in the no-fire zones and engaged in extrajudicial killings. The security forces limited humanitarian relief supplies to the war zone, indicating the deliberate use of starvation of the civilian population as a method of warfare. The UN Commission on Human Rights and Human Rights Watch have documented the use of rape and murder, especially targeting Tamil women who complained of sexual abuse by the security forces.

In terms of genocide as economic, Sinhalese settler colonisation, especially in the Eastern Province, was and is encouraged by the government in order to change the demographic balance. Postwar, since 2009, 'settler-colonial-style land grabs' have 'accelerated', usually carried out by the military, who declare former Tamil areas to be 'high security zones'; the government has resettled thousands of Sinhalese soldiers and civilians from the south in Tamil areas with incentives of free housing; there is constant 'Sinhalisation' in changing the names of villages and streets, and there are reports that Buddhist icons and statues have been constructed over destroyed Hindu temples. Tamil fishing is impaired; graves and cemeteries are destroyed; the military raid Tamil farmers' water sources for their own cultivation projects, and also take away water pumps. The government attempts to suppress Tamil mourning and memorialisation of those who died in the civil war.

Reading *Redefining Genocide*'s powerful analyses of the Zionist Israeli genocide of Palestine and the Sri Lankan genocide of Tamil society makes me think that we should re-emphasise the directing role of the state and associated military forces in some cases of settler-colonial genocide.

There are historical situations, as in settler colonies such as Australia in the British Empire in the nineteenth century, where the structural processes of destruction and replacement that Lemkin observed were genocidal for Indigenous peoples even if the imperial state and its representatives in the settler colonies, influenced by humanitarianism, expressed an intention to be beneficent and protective of Indigenous peoples. Yet, at the same time as the settler-colonialism which the imperial state instituted, encouraged and facilitated involved taking the land, and even when the terrible human effects of taking the land became clear, at no stage did government authorities imperial or local, or the settlers – nor, for that matter, humanitarians – ever consider withdrawing from the Australian continent, a continent which they had invaded and was not theirs.

Other histories and situations of genocide may not reveal any intentions to be beneficent and protective, but rather the combined genocidal operations of both settler-colonialism and active state power, bureaucracy, omnipresent planning and constant participation by or in coordination with, the military. Historically and in contemporary times, we can observe situations where settler-colonialism becomes a calculated instrument of what Lemkin in Chapter 9 of *Axis Rule in Occupied Europe* refers to as a synchronised plan of genocide, involving concerted aims, the creation of convergent processes, being relentlessly and unceasingly executed.

Such would explain the remarkable range of similarity of genocidal features between Zionist Israel and Sri Lanka even while they have distinct histories. In these terms, what we see in both Palestine and Sri Lanka are the operations, comprehensive and coordinated, convergent and synchronised, of a perpetrator state and its military arm, taking forms which at times are extremely violent, at other times thought out to the tiniest bureaucratic detail.

⚜

A final reflection on ecocide and international law.

In Damien Short's passionate argument, announced in his early chapter 'The genocide-ecocide nexus', genocide and ecocide are 'inherently linked, institutionally, empirically and theoretically'. However, just as genocide is an international crime recognised in the 1948 UN Convention, humanity, he urges, should consider the proposition that environmental destruction must also be considered an international crime. Short points to his own research in the UN Archives in Geneva where at various times UN committees did consider criminalising ecocide, perhaps by extending the terms of the Genocide Convention. Such, he acknowledges, did not occur, but he calls our attention to the new field of green criminology with which, he believes, genocide studies should keenly engage.

Short argues, for example, that Alberta's tar sands extraction is the 'world's most destructive mining project', with potentially disastrous effects on nearby indigenous communities in Canada, the Indians of Treaty 8 and beyond. In Chapter 6 'Tar sands and the indigenous peoples of northern Alberta', Short and his co-author Jennifer Huseman explain that 'indigenous communities feel that they are in the final stages of a battle for survival that began in North America in the fifteenth century' in the long history of post-1492 European settler-colonialism. The communities have identified their present situation as 'genocide': in Lemkin's terms, destruction by mining projects of their traditional lands, with an enormous impact on their foundational ways of life and cultural and physical health and well-being. Short and Huseman also believe that Alberta's tar sands mining represents a threat to the planet: 'The Alberta tar sands... are so energy intensive to extract that their continued production threatens the very survival of us all'.

Short, then, poses an urgent question for humanity in the Anthropocene. Shouldn't such environmental destruction as exhibited in Alberta tar sands mining – and we can add the horrifying destruction in 2019 of parts of the Amazon rain forest – be regarded as an international crime comparable to genocide and crimes against humanity?

1. Ghassan and my boycott call was widely covered in the press: 'Academics split on Israel sanctions', *The Australian*, May 22, 2002; 'Boycott just the way to rap Israel', Letter to the Editor, signed by Ghassan Hage, John Docker and 90 other Australian academics, *The Australian*, May 22, 2002; 'Storm of protest over petition calling for boycott of Israeli academics', *The Age*, June 6, 2002.

2. See John Docker, 'Are Settler-Colonies Inherently Genocidal? Re-reading Lemkin', in A. Dirk Moses (ed.), *Empire, Colony, Genocide: Conquest, Occupation, and Subaltern Resistance in World History* (Berghahn, New York and Oxford, 2008). See also John Docker, 'Raphael Lemkin's history of genocide and colonialism', the United States Holocaust Museum, Center for Advanced Holocaust Studies, Washington DC, 26 February 2004.

3. John Docker, *The Origins of Violence: Religion, History and Genocide* (Pluto Press, London, 2008), chapter five, 'Victimology and genocide: the Bible's Exodus, Virgil's *Aeneid*', pp.113–144; Edward Said, 'Michael Walzer's *Exodus and Revolution*: A Canaanite Reading', in Edward Said and Christopher Hitchens (eds), *Blaming the Victims: Spurious Scholarship and the Palestinian Question* (Verso, London, 1988), pp.161–178; Richard Waswo, *The Founding Legend of Western Civilization: From Virgil to Vietnam* (Wesleyan University Press, Hanover, 1997); Ann Curthoys, 'Expulsion, exodus and exile in white Australian historical mythology', *Journal of Australian Studies*, Vol.23, 1999, issue 61.

4. See Jeremy Salt, 'The Reckoning', *Arena Magazine* 99, February-March 2009, pp.29–30.

5. John Docker, 'The Two-State Solution and Partition: World History Perspectives on Palestine and India', *Holy Land Studies*, Volume 9, Number 2, 2010, pp.154–7

6. John Docker, 'The Two-State Solution and Partition: World History Perspectives on Palestine and India', pp.157–160. See also John Docker, 'Dissident Voices on the History of Palestine-Israel: Martin Buber and the Bi-national Idea, Walid Khalidi's Indigenous Perspective', in Julie Evans, Ann Genovese, Alexander Reilly, Patrick Wolfe (eds), *Sovereignty: Frontiers of Possibility* (University of Hawai'i Press, Honolulu, 2013), pp.86–116; John Docker, 'Sheer Folly and Derangement: How the Crusades Disoriented Enlightenment Historiography', in Alexander Cook, Ned Curthoys and Shino Konishi (eds), *Representing Humanity in the Age of Enlightenment* (Pickering and Chatto, London, 2013), pp.41–52; Nur Masalha, *Palestine: A Four Thousand Year History* (Zed Books, London, 2018).

7. Omar Barghouti, *BDS: Boycott, Divestment, Sanctions – The Global Struggle for Palestinian Rights* (Haymarket Books, Chicago, 2011).

8. Barghouti, *BDS: Boycott, Divestment, Sanctions – The Global Struggle for Palestinian Rights*, p.78.

9. John Docker, 'Orientalism and Zionism: Dismantling Leon Uris's *Exodus*', *Arena Journal*, New Series, No.37/38, 2012, pp.241–8.

10. Maxime Rodinson, *Israel: A Colonial-Settler State?* (Monad Press, New York, 1973), Introduction by Peter Buch.

11 Rodinson, *Israel: A Colonial-Settler State?*, Introduction by Peter Buch, pp.9–10.

12 John Docker, 'Instrumentalising the Holocaust: Israel, Settler-Colonialism, Genocide (Creating a Conversation between Raphaël Lemkin and Ilan Pappé)', *Holy Land Studies*, Volume 11, Number 1, 2012, pp.1–32, here pp.4–5.

13 Idith Zertal, *Israel's Holocaust and the Politics of Nationhood* (Cambridge University Press, Cambridge, 2011), pp.5, 173.

14 John Docker, 'Instrumentalising the Holocaust: Israel, Settler-Colonialism, Genocide', pp.8–9.

15 I feature 'Revised Outline for Genocide Cases' in Docker, 'Are Settler-Colonies Inherently Genocidal? Re-reading Lemkin', in A. Dirk Moses (ed.), *Empire, Colony, Genocide: Conquest, Occupation, and Subaltern Resistance in World History*, pp.88–90.

16 Docker, 'Instrumentalising the Holocaust: Israel, Settler-Colonialism, Genocide', pp.10–11, 13, 16–22.

17 Docker, 'Instrumentalising the Holocaust: Israel, Settler-Colonialism, Genocide', pp.16–17.

18 Docker, 'Instrumentalising the Holocaust: Israel, Settler-Colonialism, Genocide', pp.17–18.

19 Docker, 'Instrumentalising the Holocaust: Israel, Settler-Colonialism, Genocide', p.20.

20 Docker, 'Instrumentalising the Holocaust: Israel, Settler-Colonialism, Genocide', p.22.

21 Docker, 'Instrumentalising the Holocaust: Israel, Settler-Colonialism, Genocide', p.24.

22 Docker, 'Instrumentalising the Holocaust: Israel, Settler-Colonialism, Genocide', pp.26–7.

23 Docker, 'Instrumentalising the Holocaust: Israel, Settler-Colonialism, Genocide', p.27.

24 Docker, 'Instrumentalising the Holocaust: Israel, Settler-Colonialism, Genocide', p.27.

25 Docker, 'Instrumentalising the Holocaust: Israel, Settler-Colonialism, Genocide', pp.27–8.

26 Docker, 'Instrumentalising the Holocaust: Israel, Settler-Colonialism, Genocide', pp.2, 28.

27 Docker, 'Instrumentalising the Holocaust: Israel, Settler-Colonialism, Genocide', p.28.

28 Docker, 'Instrumentalising the Holocaust: Israel, Settler-Colonialism, Genocide', pp.28–9.

29 Haifa Rashed, Damien Short, John Docker, 'Nakba Memoricide: Genocide Studies and the Zionist/Israeli Genocide of Palestine', *Journal of Holy Land and Palestine Studies*, Volume 13, Number 1, 2014, pp.1–23.